Essential
Check Point™
FireWall-1® NG

Essential
Check Point™
FireWall-1® NG

An Installation,
Configuration, and
Troubleshooting Guide

Dameon D. Welch-Abernathy

✦✦ Addison-Wesley

Boston • San Francisco • New York • Toronto • Montreal
London • Munich • Paris • Madrid
Capetown • Sydney • Tokyo • Singapore • Mexico City

Many of the designations used by manufacturers and sellers to distinguish their products are claimed as trademarks. Where those designations appear in this book, and Addison-Wesley was aware of a trademark claim, the designations have been printed with initial capital letters or in all capitals.

The author and publisher have taken care in the preparation of this book, but make no expressed or implied warranty of any kind and assume no responsibility for errors or omissions. No liability is assumed for incidental or consequential damages in connection with or arising out of the use of the information or programs contained herein.

The publisher offers discounts on this book when ordered in quantity for bulk purchases and special sales. For more information, please contact:

U.S. Corporate and Government Sales
(800) 382-3419
corpsales@pearsontechgroup.com

For sales outside of the U.S., please contact:

International Sales
(317) 581-3793
international@pearsontechgroup.com

Visit Addison-Wesley on the Web: www.awprofessional.com

Library of Congress Cataloging-in-Publication Data

Welch-Abernathy, Dameon D.
    Essential Check Point FireWall-1 NG : an installation, configuration,
and troubleshooting guide / Dameon D. Welch-Abernathy.
        p. cm.
    ISBN 0-321-18061-5 (pbk. : alk. paper)
        1. Computer networks—Security measures—Computer programs.
    2. Computer security—Computer programs. 3. FireWall-1. I. Title.

TK5105.59.W455 2004
005.8—dc22

                                            2003021797

ISBN 0-321-18061-5
Text printed on recycled paper
1 2 3 4 5 6 7 8 9 10—CRS—0807060504
First printing, January 2004

Contents

Frequently Asked Questions   **xxiii**

Preface   **xxxi**

How This Book Came to Be   xxxi

What This Book Is and Is Not   xxxi

Conventions   xxxiii

Acknowledgments   xxxiv

Chapter 1   **Introduction to Firewalls**   **1**

What Is a Firewall?   1

What a Firewall Cannot Do   2

An Overview of Firewall Security Technologies   3

     Packet Filters   3

     Application Layer Gateways   4

     Stateful Inspection   5

     Technology Comparison: Passive FTP   5

     Technology Comparison: Traceroute   6

What Kind of Firewall Is FireWall-1?   8

Do You Really Need FireWall-1?   9

More Information   11

Chapter 2   **Planning Your FireWall-1 Installation**   **13**

Network Topology   13

     A Word about Subnetting and VLANs   15

Developing a Site-Wide Security Policy   15

     Senior Management Buy-In   16

     The What, Who, and How   16

     Implementing Firewalls without a Written
         Security Policy   18

     An Example of a Security Policy   19

Fun with Check Point Licensing   20
    Types of Licenses   21
    Getting Licenses   24
Summary   26

Chapter 3 Installing FireWall-1   27

Selecting an Operating System   27
    Windows NT/2000   28
    SPARC Solaris   29
    AIX   30
    Nokia IP Security Platform (IPSO)   31
    Linux and Secure Platform   32
Installing the Operating System   34
    Preparing for the OS Installation   34
    Guidelines for the OS Installation   35
    Securing the Operating System   37
Beginning the FireWall-1 Installation   39
    Installing an NG FP3 Management Console
      on Windows 2000   40
    Installing an NG FP3 FireWall-1 on an IP350   49
Upgrading from FireWall-1 4.1   52
Summary   53

Chapter 4 Building Your Rulebase   55

The Management GUIs   55
    Introducing SmartDashboard (a.k.a. Policy Editor)   56
    Configuring Management Users via `fwm` or `cpconfig` 58
    Configuring Management Users via Policy Editor   60
    Configuring Which Hosts Can Use Management GUIs   63
    Files Modified by SmartConsole   65
    SmartDashboard/Policy Editor Restrictions   65
    GUI Demonstration Mode   66
The Rulebase Components   66
    Objects   66
    Services   73
    Time   77
    Topology and Anti-Spoofing   80
    Global Properties   82

The Rulebase   85

    The Parts of a Rule   85

    Sample Rules   87

    Order of Operations   88

Making Your First Rulebase   90

    Knowing Your Network   91

    Defining Objects   92

    Defining the Rules   94

    Tweaking the Global Properties   96

    Rules That Should Be in Every Rulebase   99

    Installing the Policy   100

Frequently Asked Questions   101

    4.1: Which Files Make Up My Security Policy?   102

    4.2: How Do I Edit `objects_5_0.C` and
        `rulebases.fws` Manually?   102

    4.3: Does Any Service Really Mean Any Service?   104

    4.4: When Should I Reinstall My Security Policy?   104

    4.5: Which Characters or Words Cannot Be Used
        When Naming Objects?   104

    4.6: Are the Global Properties per Firewall or Global?   106

    4.7: How Do I Enable DNS Verification When
        I Use the Rulebase Property to Allow
        DNS Queries?   106

    4.8: Are the GUI Clients Backward Compatible?   106

    4.9: How Do I Enable Specific Rules on Specific
        Interfaces?   106

Troubleshooting   107

    4.10: My Rulebases Have Disappeared!   107

    4.11: Using the GUI over Slow Links   107

    4.12: I Cannot Fetch a Host's Interfaces   108

    4.13: SmartMap (or VPE) Crashes When Logging
        into SmartDashboard/Policy Editor   108

    4.14: FireWall-1 Error: No License for User Interface   109

Summary   109

Chapter 5   **Logging and Alerting**   **111**

SmartView Status   111

    System Status from the Command Line   116

SmartView Tracker   121
   Viewing Logs from the Command Line   124
   Viewing Rules in SmartDashboard   126
   Active Mode and Blocking Connections   127
   Audit Mode   131
Alerts   133
   A Word on Mail Alerts   136
Log Maintenance   136
Summary   140

Chapter 6   Common Issues   141

Common Configuration Questions   141
   6.1: How Do I Modify FireWall-1 Kernel Variables?   141
   6.2: Can I Direct FireWall-1 Log Messages to syslog? 142
   6.3: How Can I Disconnect Connections at a
      Specific Time?   143
   6.4: How Many Interfaces Are Supported?   143
   6.5: How Do I Create a Large Number of Objects
      via the Command Line?   143
Common Error Messages in the System Log   145
   6.6: Local Interface Anti-Spoofing   145
   6.7: Tried to Open Known Service Port, Port xxxx   145
   6.8: Virtual Defragmentation Errors   146
   6.9: Too Many Internal Hosts   146
   6.10: **Pth** SCHEDULER INTERNAL ERROR: No More
      Thread(s) Available to Schedule   147
   6.11: Target localhost Is Not Defined as an NG
      Module, Please Use the -1 Flag   147
   6.12: Invalid Value in the Access Attribute:
      Undefined: File Exists   148
   6.13: mbuf_alloc(1500): Cluster Alloc   148
   6.14: Log Buffer Is Full, Error: Lost xxx Log/
      Trap Messages   148
Service-Related Questions   148
   6.15: Why Doesn't Windows Traceroute Work? 148
   6.16: How Does FireWall-1 Support UNIX RPC?   149
   6.17: How Do I Block AOL Instant Messenger? 149
   6.18: How Do I Enable or Block Yahoo Messenger?   150

6.19: How Do I Block ICMP Packets of a Particular
       Length?   150
Problems with Stateful Inspection of TCP Connections   150
6.20: TCP Packet Out of State   151
6.21: Configuring FireWall-1 to Allow Out-of-State
       Packets for Specific TCP Services   151
6.22: SmartView Tracker Log Error: Rule 0: Reason:
       Violated Unidirectional Connection   152
6.23: th_flags X message_info SYN Packet for
       Established Connection   154
6.24: TCP Flags Do Not Make Sense   155
6.25: Unexpected SYN Response   155
6.26: Enabling the TCP Sequence Verifier   155
6.27: Adjusting TCP or UDP Timeouts on a
       Per-Service Basis   156
6.28: Disabling TCP Timeouts   156
Problems with FTP   156
6.29: Problems with Newline Characters   156
6.30: FTP on Ports Other Than 21   157
6.31: FTP Data Connections with a Random
       Source Port   157
6.32: FTP Servers Sending FIN Packets out of
       Sequence   157
6.33: FTP Servers That Require ident   157
6.34: Encrypting FTP Connections with SSL   157
Problems That Aren't the Firewall's Fault   158
6.35: Some Services Are Slow to Connect   158
6.36: The ident Service   158
6.37: Different DNS Definitions for Internet and
       Intranet   159
Summary   159

Chapter 7   **Remote Management**   **161**
The Components   161
Secure Internal Communication   163
Special Remote Management Conditions   164
Forcing a Firewall Module to Log Locally   164
Remote Management with NAT   165

What You Can Do with Remote Management   165
  Controlling Policy on a Firewall Module   166
  Viewing State Tables of Firewall Modules   167
  Updating Licenses   169
Moving Management Modules   172
  Source and Destination Management Servers Have
    Different IP Addresses   174
  Testing Your Migrated Management Module   176
  Limitations on Moving Management Stations   176
  Moving the Management Module off a Standalone
    Gateway   176
Highly Available Management Modules   178
  Failing Over to the Secondary Management   182
Troubleshooting Remote Management Issues   183
  7.1: Things to Check When Getting SIC Failures   183
  7.2: Syncing Clocks between Firewall and Management   184
  7.3: Establishing SIC with a Module Using Dynamic
    Addressing   184
  7.4: SIC General Failure (Error No. 148)   184
  7.5: Certificate Authority Errors in a Management
    HA Configuration   184
  7.6: Resetting SIC   185
  7.7: Forcibly Resetting SIC   185
  7.8: If All Else Fails, Debug   186
Large-Scale Management Issues   188
  Security Policies   188
  Number of Firewalls   189
  Number of Logs   190
  Reliance on GUI for Management   190
Summary   191

Chapter 8   **User Authentication**   **193**
Passwords   193
  FireWall-1 Password   194
  OS Password   194
  S/Key   195
  SecurID   196
  Defender   196

Remote Access Dial-In User Service (RADIUS)   197
Terminal Access Controller Access Control System
(TACACS/TACACS+)   197
Lightweight Directory Access Protocol (LDAP)   197
How Users Authenticate   198
Explaining User Authentication   198
Explaining Session Authentication   201
Explaining Client Authentication   202
Which Authentication Type Should You Use?   207
Setting Up Authentication   208
Creating Users   208
Creating Groups   218
Setting Supported Authentication Schemes   218
Global Properties Related to Authentication   220
Setting Up User Authentication   221
The Importance of Rule Order in User Authentication   223
Setting Up Session Authentication   225
Setting Up Client Authentication   227
Integrating External Authentication Servers   230
Integrating SecurID   230
Integrating RADIUS   231
Integrating TACACS/TACACS+   233
Integrating LDAP   234
Clientless VPN   243
Known Issues with Clientless VPN   246
Frequently Asked Questions   247
8.1: How Do I Use Users in an Authentication Server
without Entering Them into FireWall-1?   247
8.2: How Do I Integrate FireWall-1 into a Windows
NT Domain?   247
8.3: How Do I Allow People Access Based on Their
Windows Usernames?   248
8.4: How Do I Import or Export Users from a
FireWall-1 User Database?   248
8.5: How Do I Add My Own Custom Message for
Authentication?   249
8.6: How Do I Forward Authenticated HTTP
Requests to an HTTP Proxy?   249

8.7: Can I Use FireWall-1 as a Reverse HTTP Proxy?   250

8.8: How Do I Remove the Check Point Banner from
      Authentication?   250

8.9: Can I Use FireWall-1 as a Proxy?   250

8.10: Can I Use FireWall-1 as an FTP Proxy for My
      Web Browser?   250

8.11: How Do I Authenticate HTTP over Different
      Ports?   251

8.12: How Do I Authenticate Outbound HTTPS Traffic?   251

8.13: Can I Authenticate Access to Internal HTTPS
      Servers?   251

8.14: How Can I Authenticate with HTTP to a Site
      Requiring Its Own Authentication?   253

8.15: How Can Users Change Their Own Passwords?   253

8.16: Can a User Reset His or Her Own S/Key Chain?   253

8.17: Can I Customize the HTTP Client
      Authentication Pages?   254

Troubleshooting Authentication Problems   255

8.18: This Gateway Does Not Support X   255

8.19: The Connection Is Closed by a Session
      Authentication Agent   255

8.20: Authentication Services Are Unavailable.
      Connection Refused.   256

8.21: Session Authentication Is Not Secure   256

8.22: Using Session Authentication with Content
      Security   256

8.23: Authenticating on Each URL   256

8.24: No Client Auth Rules Available   256

8.25: Policy Install Logs Out Client Authentication Users   257

8.26: Partially Automatic Client Authentication
      Redirects Site to an IP Address   257

8.27: Users Are Not Being Prompted for Authentication   257

8.28: Request to Proxy Other Than Next Proxy Resource
      http://proxy.foo.com   257

8.29: Cannot Telnet to the Firewall   258

8.30: When Accessing Certain Sites via HTTP, the
      Connections Are Dropped with Various Error
      Messages   258

8.31: SecurID Authentication Fails after One Try   258

Summary		259
Sample Configurations		260
A User Authentication Example		260
A Session Authentication Example		263
A Client Authentication Example		265

Chapter 9   Content Security   269

The Security Servers   269
A Word about Licensing and Third-Party Products   269
CVP and UFP   270
Resources and Wildcards   271
The HTTP Security Server   271
Filtering HTTP without a UFP or CVP Server   272
UFP with the HTTP Security Server   278
CVP with the HTTP Security Server   282
Frequently Asked Questions about the HTTP
    Security Server   285
Performance Tuning the HTTP Security Server   293
Troubleshooting Issues with the HTTP Security Server 297
The FTP Security Server   299
Frequently Asked Questions about the FTP Security
    Server   300
The SMTP Security Server   302
SMTP Security Server Parameters   302
SMTP Resources   306
Frequently Asked Questions about the SMTP
    Security Server   310
Troubleshooting the SMTP Security Server   312
The TCP Security Server   316
CVP with the TCP Security Server   316
UFP with the TCP Security Server   318
General Questions about the Security Servers   318
9.29: Why Don't the Connections I Make through
        the Security Servers Appear to Originate from
        the Firewall?   318
9.30: Why Is the Security Server Used Even if the
        Rule Matched Does Not Use a Resource?   319

9.31: Can I Mix User Authentication and Content
Security?   319
9.32: Can I Mix Session Authentication and
Content Security?   319
Debugging the Security Servers   319
Summary   321
Sample Configurations   322
SMTP Content Security   322
FTP Content Security   326
HTTP Content Security   330

Chapter 10   **Network Address Translation**   **335**

Introduction to Address Translation   335
RFC1918 and Link-Local Addresses   338
How NAT Works in FireWall-1   339
The Order of Operations   341
Implementing NAT: A Step-by-Step Example   343
Determining Which IP Addresses to Use   345
Setting Up Proxy ARPs   345
Setting Up Static Host Routes   348
Creating Network Objects   349
Modifying the Anti-Spoofing Settings   350
Creating Security Policy Rules   350
Creating Address Translation Rules   350
Installing and Testing the Security Policy   351
Limitations of NAT   351
NAT Is Incompatible with Some Protocols   351
Connections That Can Bypass the Firewall   352
Troubleshooting NAT with a Packet Sniffer   355
ARPs   356
SYN Packets with No Response   357
SYN Followed by RST   359
Useful `tcpdump` Flags   361
`tcpdump` Expressions   362
Useful `snoop` Flags   363
`snoop` Expressions   364
Summary   364

Sample Configurations   365
    Creating a Simple Network with NAT   365
    Migrating to a Larger Net with NAT   369
    Using a Double-Blind Network Configuration   374

Chapter 11   **Site-to-Site VPN**   **379**
Introduction to a VPN   379
    Concepts   380
    Cryptography and Encryption   380
    Encryption Keys   380
    Entropy—the Random Pool   380
    Symmetric Encryption   381
    Asymmetric Encryption   381
    Hash Functions   382
    Fingerprints   382
    Certificate Authorities   383
    Diffie-Hellman Keys   383
    The Encryption Domain   383
A Word about Licensing   383
    VPN-1 Pro versus VPN-1 Net   384
FWZ, IPSec, and IKE   384
    FWZ   384
    IPSec   385
    IKE   386
    Security Associations   386
How to Configure Encryption   386
    Planning Your Deployment   386
    Traditional Mode or Simplified Mode?   388
    Configuring the VPN in Traditional Mode   389
    Configuring the VPN in Simplified Mode   397
    Gateway Clusters for High-Availability VPNs   401
Frequently Asked Questions about VPNs in FireWall-1   403
    11.1: Does FireWall-1 Interoperate with Third-Party
        VPN Products?   403
    11.2: Does the Gateway Clusters Feature Interoperate
        with Third-Party VPN Products?   403
    11.3: Can I Run Microsoft Networking Protocols
        through a VPN?   403

11.4: Can I Set Up a VPN with a Site without Giving It Access to All My Machines? 403

11.5: Can I Set Up More Than One VPN with Different Sites Each Using Different Encryption Schemes? 403

11.6: Can I Set Up More Than One VPN with Different Sites and Use a Different Source IP Address for Each Site? 403

11.7: Does FireWall-1 Support a Hub-and-Spoke Model Like Some VPN Hardware Devices Do? 404

11.8: How Does NAT Interact with Encryption? 405

11.9: How Can Two Sites That Use the Same Address Space Establish a VPN with One Another? 405

11.10: Can I Require User Authentication in Addition to Encryption? 406

11.11: Can the VPN Gateway Be behind Another Device That Does NAT? 406

11.12: Can a Gateway Be a Member of More Than One VPN Community? 407

Troubleshooting VPN Problems 407

11.13: General Troubleshooting Guidelines for VPN Problems 407

11.14: No Response from Peer 407

11.15: AddNegotiation: Try to Handle Too Many Negotiations 408

11.16: Debugging Interoperability Issues with IKE 408

11.17: Known Interoperability Issues 409

11.18: Encryption Failure: Packet Is Dropped as There Is No Valid SA 410

11.19: Traceroute Does Not Appear to Work through a VPN 410

11.20: VPN Fails When Transferring Large Packets 411

Summary 411

Sample Configurations 412

Creating a Three-Site VPN 412

Adding a Business Partner to the VPN Mesh 415

Switching the Seattle Firewall to a Gateway Cluster Configuration 419

Chapter 12	**SecuRemote and SecureClient**	**425**

Introduction to SecuRemote and SecureClient   425
A Word about Licensing   426
Configuring SecuRemote on FireWall-1   426
     Configuring the Gateway Object for SecuRemote   427
     Creating Users for Use with SecuRemote   428
     Defining Client Encryption Rules and Remote Access
       Community Rules   431
     Configuring Global Properties   432
     Setting Up Desktop Security   434
     Installing SecureClient   438
Office Mode   442
     Before Office Mode   442
     What Office Mode Does   443
     Configuring Office Mode   444
     Known Limitations of Office Mode   446
Microsoft L2TP Clients   446
High-Availability and Multiple Entry Point Configurations   450
Microsoft Networking and SecureClient   453
     Forwarding DNS Requests inside the Encryption
       Domain   453
     Forwarding WINS Requests inside the Encryption
       Domain   456
     Secure Domain Logon   457
SecureClient Packaging Tool   457
     Manually Creating an Installation Image   465
Frequently Asked Questions   468
     12.1: Can I Use SecuRemote if My Client Is Subject
       to NAT?   468
     12.2: Can Multiple SecureClient Users Behind the
       Same NAT Device Access the Same Firewall?   469
     12.3: How Do I Initiate an Encrypted Session to a
       SecuRemote Client?   469
     12.4: What if My SecuRemote Client Must Pass
       through a FireWall-1 Gateway?   470
     12.5: How Can I Use SecuRemote When I Am
       behind a Proxy?   471
     12.6: How Do I Disable SecuRemote at Startup?   472

12.7: How Do I Tell FireWall-1 to Use a Different
Port for SecureClient Topology Requests?   473

12.8: Can I Share an Internet Connection and Use
SecuRemote?   473

12.9: Can I Install SecureClient on the Same Machine
with a VPN Client from Another Vendor?   473

12.10: Can SecureClient Be Controlled via the
Command Line?   474

Troubleshooting   476

12.11: SecuRemote Communication Ports Are Blocked   476

12.12: ISP Uses a Custom Adapter to Connect   476

12.13: Problems Adding the New Site   476

12.14: Determining the IP Address When Using IP
Pool NAT   477

12.15: Encapsulation, Packet Sizes, and Failing
Applications   477

12.16: Windows NT and File Permissions   478

12.17: Mixing NICs and Dial-up Adapters   479

12.18: NG FP1/FP2 System Status Viewer Shows
No Response for Desktop Policy Server   480

Summary   480

Sample Configurations   481

Creating a Simple Client-to-Site VPN   481

Using SecureClient with Gateway Clusters   484

Configuring Multiple Entry Point SecureClient   488

Chapter 13   **High Availability**   **493**

State Synchronization's Role in High Availability   493

A Word about Licensing   494

The State Synchronization Protocol   494

Configuring State Synchronization   495

What Are the Limitations of State Synchronization?   498

Implementing High Availability   499

Asymmetric Routing   500

HA Solution Providers   502

Load Balancing   503

Frequently Asked Questions Regarding State Synchronization   512

13.1: How Do I Know State Synchronization Is
Working?   512

13.2: Can I Change the MAC Address Used by the
State Synchronization Mechanism? 512

13.3: Can I Perform State Synchronization between
Two Platforms of Differing Performance
Characteristics? 513

13.4: How Can I Prevent a Specific Service from
Being Synchronized via State Synchronization? 513

Error Messages That Occur with ClusterXL or State
Synchronization 514

13.5: Various Error Messages Occur during a
Full Sync 514

13.6: Error Changing Local Mode from <mode1> to
<mode2> because of ID <machine_id> 514

13.7: Inconsistencies Exist between Policies Installed
on Cluster Members on My Console 514

13.8: CPHA: Received Confirmations from More
Machines Than the Cluster Size 515

13.9: FwHaTimeWorker: Wait Failed (Status N) 515

13.10: fwha_reset_timer: Failed to Allocate Timer
DPC or Timer Object 515

13.11: There Are More Than 4 IPs on Interface
<interface name> Notifying Only the First Ones 515

13.12: fwha_create_icmp_echo_request: Failed to
Create Packet 515

13.13: fwha_receive_fwhap_msg: Received Incomplete
HAP Packet (Read <number> Bytes) 515

13.14: Inconsistencies Exist between Policies Installed
on the Cluster Members 516

13.15: Sync Could Not Start Because There Is No
Sync License 516

13.16: fwldbcast_timer: Peer X Probably Stopped 516

13.17: fwlddist_adjust_buf: Record Too Big for Sync 517

13.18: fwha_pnote_register: Too Many Registering
Members, Cannot Register 517

13.19: fwha_pnote_register: foo Already Registered (#5) 517

13.20: fwha_pnote_reg_query: Pnotes Not Relevant
in Service Mode 517

13.21: fwldbcast_update_block_new_conns: Sync in
Risk: Did Not Receive ack for the Last 410
Packets 517

13.22: fwhandle_get: Table kbufs—Invalid Handle—
Bad Entry in Pool 0   519
Summary   520

Chapter 14   **INSPECT**   **521**
What Is INSPECT?   521
Basic INSPECT Syntax   522
   Conditions   524
   Constants   526
   Registers   526
   Manipulating Table Entries   527
   Creating Your Own Tables   528
How Your Rulebase Is Converted to INSPECT   529
   Services of Type Other   536
Sample INSPECT Code   536
   Allowing Outbound Connections to SecuRemote
   Clients   536
   Point-to-Point Tunneling Protocol   537
   Allowing a Connection Based on a Previous
   Connection   537
   Different Rules for Different Interfaces 538
   Changing Your Default Filter   539
   fw monitor   540
   Examples   542
   Warnings   543
Summary   543

Appendix A   **Securing Your Bastion Host**   **545**
Securing Solaris   545
   Partitioning Your Drive   545
   Patching Your Installation   546
   Minimal Packages for SPARC Solaris 2.8 546
   Removing Unnecessary Services   550
   Logging and Tweaking   551
Securing Windows NT   552
   Network Protocols   552
   Machine Name and Domain   553
   Services   553

IP Routing   553
WINS TCP/IP   553
WINS Client   553
Services to Disable after Installation   554
Local Hosts File   554
Registry Hacks   554
Account Names Policies   555
Service Packs and Critical Updates   556
Securing Windows 2000   556
Initial Installation   556
Network Protocols and Services   556
Machine Name and Domain   557
Hotfixes   557
Services to Disable after Installation   557
IP Routing   558
DNS Registration   558
NetBIOS over TCP   558
Preventing RPC Locator from Listening   558
Securing Linux   559
Partitioning Your Hard Drive   559
Choosing the Packages to Install   559
Eliminating Services   560
Logging and Tweaking   560

Appendix B   **Sample Acceptable Usage Policy**   **563**

Appendix C   `firewall-1.conf` **File for Use with OpenLDAP v1**   **567**

Appendix D   `firewall.schema` **File for Use with OpenLDAP v2**   **571**

Appendix E   **Performance Tuning**   **575**
Number of Entries Permitted in Tables   575
Memory Used for State Tables   576
Tweaks for Specific Operating Systems   577
IPSO-Specific Changes   577
Solaris-Specific Changes   577
Windows NT–Specific Changes   577

Appendix F **Sample `defaultfilter.pf` File**   **581**

Appendix G **Other Resources**   **583**

   Internet Resources   583
   Software   584
      Third-Party Log Analysis Tools   584
      S/Key Generators   585

Appendix H **Further Reading**   **587**

Index   **589**

Frequently Asked Questions

4.1	Which Files Make Up My Security Policy?	102
4.2	How Do I Edit `objects_5_0.C` and `rulebases.fws` Manually?	102
4.3	Does Any Service Really Mean Any Service?	104
4.4	When Should I Reinstall My Security Policy?	104
4.5	Which Characters or Words Cannot Be Used When Naming Objects?	104
4.6	Are the Global Properties per Firewall or Global?	106
4.7	How Do I Enable DNS Verification When I Use the Rulebase Property to Allow DNS Queries?	106
4.8	Are the GUI Clients Backward Compatible?	106
4.9	How Do I Enable Specific Rules on Specific Interfaces?	106
4.10	My Rulebases Have Disappeared!	107
4.11	Using the GUI over Slow Links	107
4.12	I Cannot Fetch a Host's Interfaces	108
4.13	SmartMap (or VPE) Crashes When Logging into SmartDashboard/ Policy Editor	108
4.14	FireWall-1 Error: No License for User Interface	109
6.1	How Do I Modify FireWall-1 Kernel Variables?	141
6.2	Can I Direct FireWall-1 Log Messages to syslog?	142
6.3	How Can I Disconnect Connections at a Specific Time?	143
6.4	How Many Interfaces Are Supported?	143
6.5	How Do I Create a Large Number of Objects via the Command Line?	143
6.6	Local Interface Anti-Spoofing	145
6.7	Tried to Open Known Service Port, Port xxxx	145
6.8	Virtual Defragmentation Errors	146
6.9	Too Many Internal Hosts	146
6.10	**Pth** SCHEDULER INTERNAL ERROR: No More Thread(s) Available to Schedule	147
6.11	Target localhost Is Not Defined as an NG Module, Please Use the -1 Flag	147
6.12	Invalid Value in the Access Attribute: Undefined: File Exists	148

6.13	mbuf_alloc(1500): Cluster Alloc	148
6.14	Log Buffer Is Full, Error: Lost xxx Log/Trap Messages	148
6.15	Why Doesn't Windows Traceroute Work?	148
6.16	How Does FireWall-1 Support UNIX RPC?	149
6.17	How Do I Block AOL Instant Messenger?	149
6.18	How Do I Enable or Block Yahoo Messenger?	150
6.19	How Do I Block ICMP Packets of a Particular Length?	150
6.20	TCP Packet Out of State	151
6.21	Configuring FireWall-1 to Allow Out-of-State Packets for Specific TCP Services	151
6.22	SmartView Tracker Log Error: Rule 0: Reason: Violated Unidirectional Connection	152
6.23	th_flags X message_info SYN Packet for Established Connection	154
6.24	TCP Flags Do Not Make Sense	155
6.25	Unexpected SYN Response	155
6.26	Enabling the TCP Sequence Verifier	155
6.27	Adjusting TCP or UDP Timeouts on a Per-Service Basis	156
6.28	Disabling TCP Timeouts	156
6.29	Problems with Newline Characters	156
6.30	FTP on Ports Other Than 21	157
6.31	FTP Data Connections with a Random Source Port	157
6.32	FTP Servers Sending FIN Packets out of Sequence	157
6.33	FTP Servers That Require ident	157
6.34	Encrypting FTP Connections with SSL	157
6.35	Some Services Are Slow to Connect	158
6.36	The ident Service	158
6.37	Different DNS Definitions for Internet and Intranet	159
7.1	Things to Check When Getting SIC Failures	183
7.2	Syncing Clocks between Firewall and Management	184
7.3	Establishing SIC with a Module Using Dynamic Addressing	184
7.4	SIC General Failure (Error No. 148)	184
7.5	Certificate Authority Errors in a Management HA Configuration	184
7.6	Resetting SIC	185
7.7	Forcibly Resetting SIC	185
7.8	If All Else Fails, Debug	186
8.1	How Do I Use Users in an Authentication Server without Entering Them into FireWall-1?	247

8.2	How Do I Integrate FireWall-1 into a Windows NT Domain?	247
8.3	How Do I Allow People Access Based on Their Windows Usernames?	248
8.4	How Do I Import or Export Users from a FireWall-1 User Database?	248
8.5	How Do I Add My Own Custom Message for Authentication?	249
8.6	How Do I Forward Authenticated HTTP Requests to an HTTP Proxy?	249
8.7	Can I Use FireWall-1 as a Reverse HTTP Proxy?	250
8.8	How Do I Remove the Check Point Banner from Authentication?	250
8.9	Can I Use FireWall-1 as a Proxy?	250
8.10	Can I Use FireWall-1 as an FTP Proxy for My Web Browser?	250
8.11	How Do I Authenticate HTTP over Different Ports?	251
8.12	How Do I Authenticate Outbound HTTPS Traffic?	251
8.13	Can I Authenticate Access to Internal HTTPS Servers?	251
8.14	How Can I Authenticate with HTTP to a Site Requiring Its Own Authentication?	253
8.15	How Can Users Change Their Own Passwords?	253
8.16	Can a User Reset His or Her Own S/Key Chain?	253
8.17	Can I Customize the HTTP Client Authentication Pages?	254
8.18	This Gateway Does Not Support X	255
8.19	The Connection Is Closed by a Session Authentication Agent	255
8.20	Authentication Services Are Unavailable. Connection Refused.	256
8.21	Session Authentication Is Not Secure	256
8.22	Using Session Authentication with Content Security	256
8.23	Authenticating on Each URL	256
8.24	No Client Auth Rules Available	256
8.25	Policy Install Logs Out Client Authentication Users	257
8.26	Partially Automatic Client Authentication Redirects Site to an IP Address	257
8.27	Users Are Not Being Prompted for Authentication	257
8.28	Request to Proxy Other Than Next Proxy Resource http://proxy.foo.com	257
8.29	Cannot Telnet to the Firewall	258
8.30	When Accessing Certain Sites via HTTP, the Connections Are Dropped with Various Error Messages	258
8.31	SecurID Authentication Fails after One Try	258
9.1	Can I Filter HTTP on Other Ports (e.g., Port 81)?	285
9.2	Can the HTTP Security Server Forward Requests to a Caching Proxy Server?	286
9.3	Why Do I Get the Error "Request to Proxy Other Than Next Proxy Resource http://proxy.foo.com" When Filtering Traffic to a Proxy Server?	286

9.4   How Do I Redirect People to a Usage Policy Page?   286

9.5   How Do I Prevent People from Downloading Files or Accessing Streaming Media via HTTP?   287

9.6   Can I Allow Certain Users to Download Files Provided They Authenticate?   287

9.7   How Can I Set Up FireWall-1 to Support Content Security for Outbound HTTPS?   288

9.8   Can I Block the Use of KaZaA, Instant Messages, and Other Applications That Can Tunnel over HTTP?   288

9.9   Why Do I Have Problems Accessing Some Sites When the HTTP Security Server Is Enabled?   290

9.10   How Can I Permit Schemes Other Than FTP and HTTP through the HTTP Security Server?   291

9.11   How Can I Customize the Error Messages Given by the HTTP Security Server?   292

9.12   The HTTP Security Server Won't Work   297

9.13   My Users See the Error Message "FW-1 at Kyle: Unknown WWW Server"   297

9.14   My Users See the Error Message "Failed to Connect to WWW Server"   297

9.15   I Have Problems When I Try to Use Internet Explorer (or Other Browsers That Support HTTP 1.1) through FireWall-1   298

9.16   I Can't Access Certain Web Sites through the HTTP Security Server   298

9.17   The Memory Usage of `in.ahttpd` Keeps Growing   298

9.18   Why Won't the FTP Security Server Let Me Use Certain FTP Commands?   300

9.19   Why Do I Always Have Problems with Certain Sites When Using the FTP Security Server?   301

9.20   Why Do I Have a Problem FTPing to Any Site with the FTP Security Server?   302

9.21   When I Use the SMTP Security Server, to What Should the MX for My Domain Point?   310

9.22   Can I Have the Firewall Be the MX for My Domain?   310

9.23   Why Won't the SMTP Security Server Use the MX Records?   311

9.24   Can I Use the SMTP Security Server to Help Fight Incoming Spam?   311

9.25   Can the SMTP Security Server Accept E-mails of Any Size?   312

9.26   When Does CVP Get Performed on E-mails in the SMTP Security Server?   312

9.27   I See the Message "Connection to Final MTA Failed" in the SmartView Tracker/Log Viewer   312

9.28 Mail Appears to Get Stuck in the SMTP Security Server Spool Directory   313

9.29 Why Don't the Connections I Make through the Security Servers Appear to Originate from the Firewall?   318

9.30 Why Is the Security Server Used Even if the Rule Matched Does Not Use a Resource?   319

9.31 Can I Mix User Authentication and Content Security?   319

9.32 Can I Mix Session Authentication and Content Security?   319

11.1 Does FireWall-1 Interoperate with Third-Party VPN Products?   403

11.2 Does the Gateway Clusters Feature Interoperate with Third-Party VPN Products?   403

11.3 Can I Run Microsoft Networking Protocols through a VPN?   403

11.4 Can I Set Up a VPN with a Site without Giving It Access to All My Machines?   403

11.5 Can I Set Up More Than One VPN with Different Sites Each Using Different Encryption Schemes?   403

11.6 Can I Set Up More Than One VPN with Different Sites and Use a Different Source IP Address for Each Site?   403

11.7 Does FireWall-1 Support a Hub-and-Spoke Model Like Some VPN Hardware Devices Do?   404

11.8 How Does NAT Interact with Encryption?   405

11.9 How Can Two Sites That Use the Same Address Space Establish a VPN with One Another?   405

11.10 Can I Require User Authentication in Addition to Encryption?   406

11.11 Can the VPN Gateway Be behind Another Device That Does NAT?   406

11.12 Can a Gateway Be a Member of More Than One VPN Community?   407

11.13 General Troubleshooting Guidelines for VPN Problems   407

11.14 No Response from Peer   407

11.15 AddNegotiation: Try to Handle Too Many Negotiations   408

11.16 Debugging Interoperability Issues with IKE   408

11.17 Known Interoperability Issues   409

11.18 Encryption Failure: Packet Is Dropped as There Is No Valid SA   410

11.19 Traceroute Does Not Appear to Work through a VPN   410

11.20 VPN Fails When Transferring Large Packets   411

12.1 Can I Use SecuRemote if My Client Is Subject to NAT?   468

12.2 Can Multiple SecureClient Users Behind the Same NAT Device Access the Same Firewall?   469

12.3 How Do I Initiate an Encrypted Session to a SecuRemote Client?   469

12.4   What if My SecuRemote Client Must Pass through a FireWall-1 Gateway?   470

12.5   How Can I Use SecuRemote When I Am behind a Proxy?   471

12.6   How Do I Disable SecuRemote at Startup?   472

12.7   How Do I Tell FireWall-1 to Use a Different Port for SecureClient Topology Requests?   473

12.8   Can I Share an Internet Connection and Use SecuRemote?   473

12.9   Can I Install SecureClient on the Same Machine with a VPN Client from Another Vendor?   473

12.10   Can SecureClient Be Controlled via the Command Line?   474

12.11   SecuRemote Communication Ports Are Blocked   476

12.12   ISP Uses a Custom Adapter to Connect   476

12.13   Problems Adding the New Site   476

12.14   Determining the IP Address When Using IP Pool NAT   477

12.15   Encapsulation, Packet Sizes, and Failing Applications   477

12.16   Windows NT and File Permissions   478

12.17   Mixing NICs and Dial-up Adapters   479

12.18   NG FP1/FP2 System Status Viewer Shows No Response for Desktop Policy Server   480

13.1   How Do I Know State Synchronization Is Working?   512

13.2   Can I Change the MAC Address Used by the State Synchronization Mechanism?   512

13.3   Can I Perform State Synchronization between Two Platforms of Differing Performance Characteristics?   513

13.4   How Can I Prevent a Specific Service from Being Synchronized via State Synchronization?   513

13.5   Various Error Messages Occur during a Full Sync   514

13.6   Error Changing Local Mode from <mode1> to <mode2> because of ID <machine_id>   514

13.7   Inconsistencies Exist between Policies Installed on Cluster Members on My Console   514

13.8   CPHA: Received Confirmations from More Machines Than the Cluster Size   515

13.9   FwHaTimeWorker: Wait Failed (Status N)   515

13.10   fwha_reset_timer: Failed to Allocate Timer DPC or Timer Object   515

13.11   There Are More Than 4 IPs on Interface <interface name> Notifying Only the First Ones   515

13.12   fwha_create_icmp_echo_request: Failed to Create Packet   515

13.13 fwha_receive_fwhap_msg: Received Incomplete HAP Packet
(Read <number> Bytes)   515

13.14 Inconsistencies Exist between Policies Installed on the Cluster Members   516

13.15 Sync Could Not Start Because There Is No Sync License   516

13.16 fwldbcast_timer: Peer X Probably Stopped   516

13.17 fwlddist_adjust_buf: Record Too Big for Sync   517

13.18 fwha_pnote_register: Too Many Registering Members, Cannot Register   517

13.19 fwha_pnote_register: foo Already Registered (#5)   517

13.20 fwha_pnote_reg_query: Pnotes Not Relevant in Service Mode   517

13.21 fwldbcast_update_block_new_conns: Sync in Risk: Did Not Receive
ack for the Last 410 Packets   517

13.22 fwhandle_get: Table kbufs—Invalid Handle—Bad Entry in Pool 0   519

Preface

Every book should have some introductory text that explains it. This book is no exception. After reading this preface, you should know the following:

- How this book came to be
- What this book is and what it's not
- What typographical conventions are used in this book
- Some of the people who made this book possible

How This Book Came to Be

After spending two years on the first edition of this book, I was relieved to finally have the book done. However, Check Point played a cruel trick on me and released FireWall-1 NG around the same time that my book came out in October 2001. That book was mostly on FireWall-1 4.1, so my book was already obsolete! People kept asking me, "So when are you going to update your book for NG?"

Another thing happened right around that time: My wife and I decided to move to the Seattle area from Spokane and build a new house. We had to live in a much smaller apartment for several months until the house was completed.

After moving twice and finally finding the motivation to do this again, I began the task of turning *Essential Check Point FireWall-1* into *Essential Check Point FireWall-1 NG* in July 2002. Unlike the last attempt at this, I knew this was going to be a solo project. This didn't bother me. After all, I did it once.

What This Book Is and Is Not

What you are holding in your hands now is a book about Check Point FireWall-1 NG. It covers the essentials of the product. Each chapter discusses a major feature of the product or a specific topic that will help you plan for or maintain your FireWall-1 NG installation. You get step-by-step configuration instructions for many features in FireWall-1 complete with screenshots and several sample configurations you can try. The book also includes lots of information from my FireWall-1 Frequently Asked Questions (FAQs) on http://www.phoneboy.com.

Not every feature of FireWall-1 is covered in this text. The "essential" features I have chosen to cover are based on my experience as someone who has supported this product since 1996. Other peripheral topics, like encryption and network security, are covered briefly as they relate to FireWall-1 but are not covered in great detail. I feel that other authors do a better job of covering these topics—some examples are provided in Appendix H.

A summary of the chapters in this book follows. Note that where sample configurations are said to exist in a chapter, it means there are step-by-step examples you can follow to set up your own equipment, provided you have it.

Chapter 1, Introduction to Firewalls, briefly discusses firewalls in general, the different technologies used in today's firewalls, and how they are used in FireWall-1.

Chapter 2, Planning Your Firewall-1 Installation, talks about the issues that should be considered prior to installing a firewall, such as understanding your current network topology, establishing a formalized security policy, and reviewing the various types of licenses that exist in FireWall-1.

Chapter 3, Installing FireWall-1, walks you through the initial configuration of FireWall-1 when it is loaded for the first time. This chapter also covers the basics of preparing your system for a firewall installation.

Chapter 4, Building Your Rulebase, explains the basics of creating a security policy within FireWall-1 and includes how to use the Policy Editor application.

Chapter 5, Logging and Alerting, explains how logging and alerting work in FireWall-1. Details about how to use the Log Viewer and System Status Viewer applications are also provided.

Chapter 6, Common Issues, is a collection of FAQs that may come up once you have set up your firewall and become familiar with the SmartView Tracker/Log Viewer application. These FAQs are not specific to features covered in future sections of the book.

Chapter 7, Remote Management, explains how to manage multiple firewall modules from a single management console. Sample configurations are provided in this chapter.

Chapter 8, User Authentication, explains how you can provide access control for services based on individual users. Sample configurations are provided in this chapter.

Chapter 9, Content Security, explains how you can restrict the kind of content that enters or leaves your network via HTTP, FTP, and SMTP. Sample configurations are provided in this chapter.

Chapter 10, Network Address Translation (NAT), explains what NAT is, why it is a necessary evil, and how to configure NAT within FireWall-1. Sample configurations are provided in this chapter.

Chapter 11, Site-to-Site VPN, explains what a Virtual Private Network (VPN) is and how to configure FireWall-1 to support this feature. Sample configurations are provided in this chapter.

Chapter 12, SecuRemote and SecureClient, builds on Chapter 11. It explains how to establish client-to-site VPNs using Check Point's Windows-based VPN client called Secure Client, which is also known as SecuRemote. Sample configurations are provided in this chapter.

Chapter 13, High Availability, explains State Synchronization and how it plays a role in highly available firewalls. Also covered are the problems that arise when implementing multiple firewalls in parallel along with some ideas on how to overcome these problems.

Chapter 14, INSPECT, is an overview of the language that is the heart of Check Point FireWall-1. Several examples of working INSPECT code are provided in the chapter as well as in the appendixes.

The appendixes cover topics such as hardening an operating system, sample INSPECT code, performance tuning, recommended books, and Web sites on the Internet where you can obtain software and more information.

Conventions

FireWall-1 runs on multiple operating systems, but there are two basic kinds of platforms: UNIX and Windows NT. My personal bias is UNIX; therefore, all pathnames and the like, unless otherwise specified, are always given in their UNIX form. For those of you who use Windows NT and are not familiar with UNIX conventions, the following paragraph describes how to convert the paths from a UNIX form to a Windows form.

Almost all paths given include FWDIR, which is an environment variable that should be defined and points to the directory under which FireWall-1 is installed. To reference this variable on a UNIX platform, it is preceded by a dollar sign (e.g., $FWDIR). On a Windows platform, the variable is surrounded by percent signs (e.g., %FWDIR%). Path components on a UNIX platform are separated by forward slashes (e.g., /), whereas on Windows, they are separated by back slashes (e.g., \).

To convert the path $FWDIR/bin to its Windows equivalent, replace $FWDIR with %FWDIR% and replace the forward slash with a back slash. On Windows, the path should look like this: %FWDIR%\bin.

Unless otherwise specified, all commands mentioned throughout the text should work on both UNIX and Windows. Examples of commands that you type in (and their output) appear in `Courier` font. I also use this font for filenames and daemon processes. The commands you type in appear in a **`bold Courier`** font. If what you type in does not echo back on the screen (usually because it is a password), this is reflected in a ***`bold italic Courier`*** font.

To put it all together, the following sample output results from running the UNIX **`passwd`** command to change my password:

```
# passwd dwelch
Enter login password: abc123
New password: def456
Re-enter new password: def456
passwd (SYSTEM): passwd successfully changed for dwelch
#
```

The pound/hash sign (#) is the UNIX prompt and is typically used for the Super-User account. I type in the command **`passwd dwelch`** (which echoes to the screen). I am then prompted to enter my old password, ***`abc123`***, which does not echo to the screen. Next, I am prompted to enter a new password, ***`def456`***, which also does not echo to the screen. I am then asked to confirm my new password as my password choice, which means I type it again. Finally, I am told my password has been changed successfully.

Numbered FAQs appear starting in Chapter 4. For a full listing of these questions see the list starting on page xxiii.

Acknowledgments

Thanks to:

- My wife, Alisa, and my son, Jaden, who put up with this book process a second time.
- Derin Mellor for providing me with several ideas that I used in Chapter 13.
- Lance Spitzner for allowing me to use his "Armoring Solaris" whitepaper as the basis for Appendix A.
- My editors: Karen Gettman, Jessica Goldstein, and Elizabeth Ryan.
- My reviewers: Tina Bird, Robert Bruen, Jed Daniels, Joseph Dell, Matthew Gast, Brad C. Johnson, Paul Keser, Marcus Leech, Valerie LeVielle, and Tom Warfield. Your reviews were invaluable to this process.
- Folks at Nokia: Paul Esch, Matthew Gulbranson, Steve Merchant, Qian Zhao, John Kobara, Karl Danz, Ed Ingber, Claudio Basegra, Scott McComas, Venkat Cheemalakonda, Bihn Vo, Pavla Thatcher, Patrick Miller,

Chris Morosco, the guys who work in Support, and anyone else who puts up with me on a semi-regular basis.
- Folks at Check Point: Adam Pearlman, Gil Carmon, Hanan Levin, Nimrod Vered, Yaniv Kaul, and Scott McFarlane.
- A bunch of people whom I'm sure I've forgotten to name.
- And finally, to the rest of you who have visited my Web site, contributed to the process, kept me employable, and bought the first edition.

Dameon D. Welch-Abernathy
a.k.a. PhoneBoy
dwelch@phoneboy.com
PGP Fingerprint: 72A2 8D9D BDC0 98D2 1E5D 3A2D 09D0 A5C1 597F 5D2A
November 2003

Chapter

1

Introduction to Firewalls

This chapter provides a brief overview of firewalls—what they can and cannot do. It is not meant to comprehensively cover the topic of firewalls or network security in general. These topics are better covered by more general texts. In this chapter, you will explore some of the technologies used in firewalls, investigate which technologies are used by FireWall-1, and establish why FireWall-1 is the right firewall for you. Examples of how a given technology handles a specific service are also provided.

By the end of this chapter, you should be able to:

- Understand what a firewall is and is not capable of
- Understand what technologies firewalls typically employ
- Discuss the pros and cons of different firewall technologies
- Understand why FireWall-1 is the right firewall for the job

What Is a Firewall?

A firewall is a device that allows multiple networks to communicate with one another according to a defined security policy. They are used when there is a need for networks of varying levels of trust to communicate with one another. For example, a firewall typically exists between a corporate network and a public network like the Internet. It can also be used inside a private network to limit access to different parts of the network. Wherever there are different levels of trust among the different parts of a network, a firewall can and should be used.

Firewalls are similar to routers in that they connect networks together. Firewall software runs on a host, which is connected to both trusted and untrusted networks. The host operating system is responsible for performing routing functions, which many operating systems are capable of doing. The host operating system should be as secure as possible prior to installing the firewall software.

This not only means knowing how the operating system was installed but also making sure that all of the security patches are applied and that unnecessary services and features are disabled or removed. More details about these security issues are provided in Chapter 3.

Firewalls are different from routers in that they are able to provide security mechanisms for permitting and denying traffic, such as authentication, encryption, content security, and address translation. Although many routers provide similar capabilities (such as high-end devices from Cisco), their primary function is to route packets between networks. Security was not part of their initial design but rather an afterthought. A firewall's primary function is to enforce a security policy, and it is designed with this in mind.

What a Firewall Cannot Do

It is important to realize that a firewall is a tool for enforcing a security policy. If all access between trusted and untrusted networks is not mediated by the firewall, or the firewall is enforcing an ineffective policy, the firewall is not going to provide any protection for your network. However, even a properly designed network with a properly configured firewall cannot protect you from the following dangers.

- *Malicious use of authorized services:* A firewall cannot, for instance, prevent someone from using an authenticated Telnet session to compromise your internal machines or from tunneling an unauthorized protocol through another, authorized protocol.
- *Users not going through the firewall:* A firewall can only restrict connections that go through it. It cannot protect you from people who can go around the firewall, for example, through a dial-up server behind the firewall. It also cannot prevent an internal intruder from hacking an internal system. To detect and thwart these kinds of threats, you may need a properly configured intrusion detection/prevention system.
- *Social engineering:* If intruders can somehow obtain passwords they are not authorized to have or otherwise compromise authentication mechanisms through social engineering mechanisms, the firewall won't stop them. For example, a hacker could call your users pretending to be a system administrator and ask them for their passwords to "fix some problem."
- *Flaws in the host operating system:* A firewall is only as secure as the operating system on which it is installed. There are many flaws present in operating systems that a firewall cannot protect against. This is why it is important to properly secure the operating system and apply the necessary security patches before you install the firewall and on a periodic basis

thereafter. It also explains why "appliance" firewalls such as those provided by Nokia and NetScreen, which contain a purpose-built, hardened operating system, are becoming more popular.

- *All threats that may occur:* Firewall designers often react to problems discovered by hackers, who are usually at least one step ahead of the firewall manufacturers.

An Overview of Firewall Security Technologies

Many companies engage in marketing hype to try to prove that their technology is better. Despite the hype, all firewall security technology can be broken down into three basic types: packet filtering (stateful or otherwise), application layer gateways, and Stateful Inspection.

Packet Filters

Packet filters screen all network traffic at the network and transport layer of the TCP/IP packet. This means they look at source and destination IP addresses, protocol number, and, in the case of TCP and UDP, source and destination port numbers. Packet filtering is built into routers as well as some UNIX kernels. Usually, when site administrators start thinking about network security, they start with packet filtering because it is inexpensive. Most routers on the market today, even consumer-grade models, support some form of packet filtering. Because routers are needed to connect different networks together (especially when connecting to the Internet), the additional cost for using this technology is minimal. Packet filtering requires very little extra memory and processing power, so even a low-end router can handle a fairly moderate load. Packet filtering is also fairly transparent to legitimate users.

Traditional packet filtering is static, that is, the only criteria for allowing packets are whether or not the IP addresses or port numbers match those specified in the packet filter configuration. Many packet filters today implement some concept of the "state" of a connection, using a table and additional information in the TCP headers to track previously allowed packets within a connection. This makes it much easier to allow only, for instance, outbound connections from a trusted network to an untrusted network without inadvertently allowing unrelated packets from the untrusted network to the trusted network.

The biggest downside to packet filters is that they are difficult to maintain. Although this point is certainly arguable, even an expert can have trouble configuring a moderately complex set of access lists or Linux `ipchains` rules. Many consumer-grade routers that have packet filtering do not have an adequate interface or are very limited in what they can filter.

Packet filters also do not screen above the network and transport layers. This means they cannot do things like:

- Provide content security (e.g., virus scanning or filtering based on specific sites and Web pages accessed)
- Authenticate services (i.e., make sure only authorized users use a service)
- Dynamically open and close ports for applications as they require them (necessary for applications like RealAudio, FTP, and H.323 applications)
- Validate a particular port that is used only for a specific service (e.g., making sure that only valid HTTP traffic traverses port 80)

Application Layer Gateways

Application layer gateways, also known as *proxies* or *application proxies,* take requests from clients and make them connect to servers on the client's behalf. In some cases, the client explicitly connects to the proxy server. In other cases, the proxy intercepts the connection with help from the underlying operating system or network architecture. Because an application proxy is usually specific to the network service, it can be fully aware of the session. This means the proxy can do content screening, provide authentication, and ensure that only the particular service is used (e.g., an HTTP proxy can make sure that only HTTP traffic is allowed through), or it can provide other application-specific services such as caching. It also provides a well-formed connection to servers on the other side of the firewall because it opens up connections on behalf of the clients.

However, this extra capability comes at a price. Application proxies require memory and CPU cycles just like any other application. Generally speaking, application proxies use more memory and CPU cycles than packet filtering, although how much they use depends on the specific circumstances. If you want to use application proxies to provide services to the Internet, each application you want to run through your firewall must have a proxy written for it, or the application must be compatible with a "generic" proxy that will work with simple TCP or UDP connections. Because many applications are not being developed to work with an application proxy, some applications simply cannot be proxied. The client/server model is somewhat broken by application proxies because the application proxy will always originate the connection from the server's point of view.[1] In large environments, the poor throughput of application proxies is another drawback.

---

1. Some would argue that this is actually not a problem. Whether or not this is a problem depends on the specific application and what you are trying to track down.

Another important drawback of a proxy, particularly for internal use, is that it becomes very difficult to track who is going where for how long because the proxy often masks the original source or destination of the traffic. You might be able to track this on the firewall, but from any other vantage point on the network, how do you know?

Stateful Inspection

Stateful Inspection combines the best features of stateful packet filtering and application layer gateways. Check Point's Stateful Inspection engine rests between the data link and network layers (e.g., between the network interface card and the TCP/IP driver). TCP/IP packets from the network layer and higher are scanned according to your security policy and will be either allowed through or stopped. The TCP/IP stack will not see dropped or rejected packets, which can provide an extra layer of protection. Stateful Inspection can look at the entire packet and make security policy decisions based on the contents and the *context* of the packet, using a state table to store connection state and using knowledge of how specific protocols are supposed to operate. In the case of FTP, FireWall-1 can dynamically open ports between two hosts so that the communication will succeed and then close the ports when the connection is done. Stateful Inspection is what gives FireWall-1 "Application Intelligence" (e.g., NG with Application Intelligence, or NG AI).

Stateful Inspection requires slightly more memory and CPU cycles than packet filtering because it has to do more, but it takes substantially less memory and CPU usage than does an application proxy. Stateful Inspection is best when the engine is made aware of how a protocol functions, although Check Point does not make use of Stateful Inspection for every protocol. Because Stateful Inspection does track connection state regardless of the service, it is better than a packet filter, but you are limited to opening specific ports and allowing the traffic through without further checking.

Technology Comparison: Passive FTP

It is useful to compare how the different technologies handle complex connection types. One such connection type is Passive FTP, which is used by Web browsers when they initiate an FTP connection. Passive FTP requires:

1. A TCP connection from a client to port 21 on the FTP server.
2. A TCP connection from a client to some random high port on the FTP server for data communication. The ports used for this communication are communicated to the client when it requests passive mode via the PASV command.

For this comparison, assume that the FTP server is behind your firewall and that you need to allow people on the Internet to FTP to this machine.

Packet Filters

Packet filtering can handle standard FTP quite nicely because it uses fixed TCP ports (20 and 21). However, in order to allow Passive FTP, the packet filter has to open all TCP ports above 1024 to allow Passive FTP to work with the FTP server. This is a gaping hole that can be used by programs other than FTP to compromise your systems.

Application Proxies

An application proxy is aware of the FTP connection and opens all the necessary ports and connections to complete the FTP connection. However, each TCP or UDP connection through an application proxy requires twice the normal number of connections on the proxy server (one for each side of the connection). A normal Passive FTP connection requires two open connections on a client machine. On the application layer gateway, this translates to four open TCP connections.

Most operating systems have a limit to the number of simultaneous connections they can handle. If enough connections are going through the machine at the same time, this limit will be reached, and no further connections will be allowed through. In high-performance, high-capacity networks, using a proxy for FTP connections is simply asking for trouble.

Stateful Inspection

Stateful Inspection understands connection context. When the PASV command is sent from the client to the server, Stateful Inspection reads the server's response and opens the ports necessary to complete the connection. It also restricts the IP addresses that can use these ports to the client and server. The connection then goes through the firewall normally. Because Stateful Inspection allows the native operating system to route, no connections are established on the firewall itself. Once the connection is terminated, the ports opened by the PASV command are closed.

Technology Comparison: Traceroute

Traceroute is used to show the particular path a connection will take through the various routers and gateways within the network and gives you a basic idea of the latency between any two hosts on a network. It is a common troubleshooting tool used by network administrators. There are two varieties of traceroute:

UDP and ICMP. UDP traceroute is used by almost every UNIX implementation. ICMP traceroute is typically used by Microsoft operating systems, though some UNIX implementations also allow you to perform an ICMP traceroute. How traceroute functions can be used to show the strengths of Stateful Inspection and the weaknesses of packet filters and application proxies.

UDP traceroute involves sending out packets to high-numbered ports above 31000—the actual ports used will vary based on the implementation. ICMP traceroute uses ICMP Echo Requests instead. In both cases, the client generates a number of packets (usually three) over a period of time (usually one second) to the server using a time to live (TTL) value of 1. Each subsequent set of packets will have an increasingly higher TTL value, which allows the packets to get closer and closer to the server.

During a traceroute session, any of the following can occur.

- The server responds with an ICMP Echo Reply message or an ICMP Port Unreachable packet (i.e., the traceroute has finally reached the server).
- An intermediate router or gateway gets a packet with a TTL value of 1; it decrements the TTL to 0. Because a router or gateway cannot route a packet with a TTL of 0, it sends back an ICMP Time Exceeded message.
- An intermediate router or gateway determines it has no route to the server and sends back an ICMP Destination Unreachable message.
- An intermediate router or gateway fails to respond either because it is configured to not respond to or pass traceroute traffic or because it is down.
- The client decides it has sent too many sets of traceroute packets (the default is 30) and stops.

For any firewall solution to securely allow traceroute through,[2] it must take all of these situations into account. Let's explore how each of the firewall technologies can address passing traceroute.

Packet Filters

With packet filtering, you would have to allow the following types of traffic to pass through your packet filter:

- All UDP ports above 31000
- ICMP Echo Request

---

2. Most firewall administrators do not want to allow traceroute into their network from the outside but do wish to allow internal hosts to initiate it outbound and then allow only appropriate reply traffic back in.

Conversely, you would also have to allow the following types of packets to enter your network from any host:

- ICMP Echo Reply
- ICMP Time Exceeded
- ICMP Destination Unreachable
- ICMP Port Unreachable

Although these rules would allow legitimate traceroute traffic, they can also allow network access by packets that were not in response to a valid traceroute request. In the past, these kinds of unsolicited packets were used in denial-of-service (DoS) attacks. It is important that you allow in only those packets that are in response to a traceroute or ping query. Packet filtering alone is not an adequate tool to allow traceroute to function yet protect you from possible DoS attacks. It is important to note that the UDP ports allowed could also be used for something other than traceroute.

Application Proxies

UDP can be proxied to some degree, but due to its nature, ICMP cannot be proxied, though some versions of SOCKS can proxy ICMP using special SOCKS-aware ICMP programs. In a relatively small, controlled, homogeneous environment, this may be feasible. In a large, heterogeneous environment protected by application proxies, it may not be possible to allow all clients to traceroute through the firewall.

Stateful Inspection

With Stateful Inspection, you can watch for either a UDP packet with a low TTL value or an ICMP Echo Request packet coming from a particular client. Once this happens, you can temporarily permit the necessary ICMP packets to return to the client initiating the outgoing traceroute request. After you have received the appropriate response (i.e., an ICMP Echo Reply, Port Unreachable, or Destination Unreachable message) and/or after a specific period of time (e.g., 60 seconds), you can stop allowing the necessary ICMP packets to the client.

FireWall-1 statefully inspects ICMP.

What Kind of Firewall Is FireWall-1?

Check Point advertises FireWall-1 as primarily a Stateful Inspection firewall. Although this is certainly FireWall-1's biggest strength, FireWall-1 uses both Stateful Inspection and application proxies. Application proxies are used when content security or user authentication is necessary for HTTP, Telnet, rlogin, FTP, and SMTP. Stateful Inspection is used for all other security functions. To be fair, most commercial and even homegrown firewalls employ some combination of these two technologies because none of the technologies can provide all the necessary functionality.

FireWall-1 also offers some other interesting capabilities, many of which are covered in future chapters:

- Site-to-site VPNs
- Client-to-site VPNs
- Content filtering (with the help of third-party products)
- Address translation
- Authentication (integrated with third-party authentication servers)
- Enterprise-wide policy management
- High availability (with the help of third-party products)
- INSPECT, a language with which you can modify Check Point's Stateful Inspection engine

Do You Really Need FireWall-1?

Whether or not you really need FireWall-1 might seem like a strange question to ask in a book about FireWall-1. One of the important points I make in this book is that FireWall-1 is simply a tool used to enforce a security policy. In some cases, using this tool may be overkill. In other cases, this tool is just one of many that are used.

Let's look at a one- or two-person site. In this case, whether or not to use a firewall depends on what the network connection is and what needs to be protected. If the connection is an analog dial-up connection to the Internet that does not stay up a majority of the time, a firewall may not be entirely necessary. If the connection is something more permanent, like a leased line, Digital Subscriber Line (DSL), or cable modem, or if what goes on at this site is highly sensitive or valuable, a firewall may be necessary. If the people who occupy this site are technically savvy, perhaps they will set up their external router with an access list, set up a multihomed host using a BSD or Linux-based operating system, use one of the many consumer-grade firewall devices on the market, or install personal firewall software on the computers. Depending on what the site's needs are, these solutions may be sufficient.

Now let's look at a slightly larger site, say, one that employs 25 to 50 people. This type of site is likely to have some sort of permanent Internet connection.

It may even have an externally accessible server or two like a mail server and a Web server. Again, as mentioned previously, this type of site could probably get away with setting up a multihomed host using a BSD or Linux-based operating system running their built-in filtering mechanisms, or an access list on a router. Perhaps the site also needs to allow one or two people access to the internal network from home. At this point, a few "holes" would be added to the firewall. At a later time, a few other people might want to use some sort of specialized application through the firewall and a few more holes would get added. Pretty soon, the firewall starts to look like Swiss cheese.

Now let's talk about a large corporate site with thousands of people. A site like this could use a firewall or two. One obvious place to put a firewall would be at the external connection to the world, but firewalls could also be used internally to protect certain sensitive departments like human resources, research and development, or accounting. And perhaps this corporate site is also responsible for some smaller remote offices. These remote offices likely need secure access into the internal network at the corporate site. Also, the corporate site might like to be able to manage the security policy for the remote sites. And, of course, there are those who want to work from home or who need secure access to the corporate network from the Internet.

People tend to think of security needs in terms of the size of the network involved. The preceding examples are typical of what I have experienced in the real world. What type of firewall you require, if any at all, really comes down to your specific needs or the needs of an organization. A one- or two-person site might be developing source code that could potentially be worth millions of dollars; thus network security becomes important. Another example might be a university network with thousands of students, where an open environment is far more important than a secure environment—although you can bet that certain parts of the network, like admissions and finance, require very tight security. The main question you have to ask when considering a firewall is, "What is at stake if an unauthorized person gains access to my network?"

FireWall-1 is an appropriate solution for networks of all shapes and sizes. This is because FireWall-1 is one of the few firewalls that can grow with your needs. In a network with few needs, FireWall-1 can start out as a simple Internet firewall. As your needs change, you can easily add firewalls and still be able to easily keep track of and manage your corporate-wide security policy. As your network grows, you can readily upgrade or change the platform on which FireWall-1 is installed and add functionality, such as a VPN, quite easily. Because FireWall-1 works the same on all supported platforms, you will not have to spend a significant amount of time reconfiguring or relearning the product. Adding new functionality is usually as simple as adding a new license string and modifying your configuration to support the new feature. With the added functionality of INSPECT, you can program FireWall-1 to securely support just about any service.

With the help of this book, you will be able to effectively use FireWall-1 in just about any network environment in which you work.

More Information

Many other network security topics could have been covered in this chapter, and even the topics covered could have been covered in greater depth. However, the focus of this book is not on general security topics but rather on FireWall-1. Many of the general topics are covered in depth in other books by other authors. Appendix G includes a list of Web sites with more information on interesting software. Appendix H includes a list of recommended books.

Chapter

2

Planning Your FireWall-1 Installation

Careful planning should precede the installation of any firewall. In this chapter, I first discuss how to determine the current state of your network by developing a network topology. Next, I discuss how to discover "zones of trust" and figure out where to put your firewalls. I then show you how to set down some basic security policies in writing. And finally, I cover one of the trickiest parts of a FireWall-1 installation: licensing.

By the end of this chapter, you should be able to:

- Explain what a security policy is and how it applies to your organization
- Break down a security policy into three critical components: what, who, and how
- Develop an overall firewall architecture and rulebase design using your organization's security policy as a guide
- Understand what license types are available, how they are enforced, and how to get them

Network Topology

Before you begin to think about installing a firewall, or any other security device for that matter, you should document what your network looks like. This means generating a map of the network, which illustrates all of the major points of interest, and diagramming how they all logically connect together. Although it is not necessary to document individual workstations, you should document:

- WAN connections
- Dial-up connections
- Internet connections
- Routers

- Firewalls
- Important servers (either individually or as a group)

There are a few automated tools that may be able to help with this. For example, Microsoft Visio provides some automatic mapping functionality. Lumeta seems to be one of the most promising. Their maps of the Internet (available at http://www.lumeta.com/mapping.html) have appeared in magazines such as *Wired*. There are others, but even if you use one of these tools to generate your map, you'll still need to do some additional manual work to identify all of the points of interest.

Because a firewall is a perimeter-based security device, it is most effective when the number of entry and exit points is limited. The process of documenting these entry points into the network may prompt you to reorganize your network in such a way as to limit the number of entry or exit points. This is not entirely a bad thing.

In a multisite company (i.e., a company that occupies more than one physical location), getting a complete network topology may be difficult or impossible. Someone at each physical location should be responsible for maintaining a local network map. A cloud, or a similar symbol, can represent a remote network. This is what is typically used to represent the Internet.

Once you have a clear understanding of the components in your network, you can begin to determine where the different zones of trust are. Many people tend to think of only two zones: everything outside the firewall and everything inside the firewall. Although this is certainly a start, it is a bit more complicated than that. If you have servers that are externally accessible from the Internet, you could consider creating a demilitarized zone (DMZ) or service network. Servers in the DMZ are typically accessible from any network, so they should be secured at the host and application levels to protect against possible compromise. The purpose of a DMZ is to isolate all servers that are accessible from untrusted sources, like the Internet, so that if someone compromises one of those servers, the intruder will have only limited access to externally accessible servers. Servers in the DMZ should be fortified and secured as much as possible and should have a limited ability to initiate connections to internal systems, if any.

In many networks, there are several levels of trust. For instance, sensitive human resources or accounting functions may take place in a separate part of the network that is inaccessible to all but authorized users. There may be parts of the network that contain users who cannot be trusted, or they may contain machines of unknown danger. For example, there may be experimental sections of the network where it is important to set up servers and machines quickly as well as training labs where "guest" access to parts of the network is provided.

Each network and each situation are different. You may need to interview managers and even individual users to determine where these zones of trust should be. Once you have determined what the zones of trust are, the most effective locations of firewalls will become self-evident.

A Word about Subnetting and VLANs

Keep in mind that a firewall is a device similar to a router in that traffic is passed from one interface to another. Like any router, each interface must be connected to a logically different network. This means that if you want to insert a firewall into an existing network, you must make sure that each physical interface of the firewall is on a unique subnet. There are two notable exceptions to this.

1. The Nokia IP51, a device no longer sold, supports a bridging mode that allows the same subnet to be on the WAN and LAN interfaces.
2. IPSO 3.7, used on Nokia platforms, has a transparent mode where two or more interfaces can be connected to the same logical network segment. It does layer 2 forwarding and MAC address learning like an Ethernet bridge would do, but it does not do loop detection or spanning tree. Refer to Resolution 15992 in Nokia's Knowledge Base for more details.

Depending on your existing network, this may mean subnetting existing network space, adding address space, or employing Network Address Translation (NAT). (See Chapter 10 for more information.) For network segments that are accessible only inside the firewall, RFC-1918 address space can be added easily. NAT is only necessary if those segments access a public network like the Internet.

Each zone of trust should also be on a separate physical network. Physically different and unconnected switches or hubs are preferred to virtual LANs (VLANs) on a switch, which are VLAN segments created by software in a switch. The problem with the VLAN approach is that if the switch is misconfigured or somehow compromised, traffic can get from one zone to another without going through the firewall. There is nothing wrong with VLANs—just make sure that a physical switch does not occupy more than one zone of trust.

Developing a Site-Wide Security Policy

A security policy is the critical first step toward securing your organization's network. It lays the overall foundation of how your organization approaches security issues. It explains what resources are important, who is responsible for those resources, and the general guidelines on how your organization will protect those resources. It does not go into detail about how this policy is *enforced,* which is often decided by the security administrators.

Firewalls are a technical tool used to enforce the security policy. A firewall is not the only tool that can be used to enforce a security policy, but it plays a major role in many organizations. With a clearly defined policy, you will know precisely who will maintain your firewalls and what kinds of changes will be allowed. Without a policy, it is not clear what the purpose of the firewall is, nor is it clear what kinds of changes to the policy are allowed. As a result, different people will enforce different rules, which may often conflict with one another. What was enforced one day may be changed the next. Rules might be randomly added and dropped with no real, coherent plan. The outcome would be an effective tool configured ineffectively.

The sort of security policy discussed in this section has nothing to do with FireWall-1, at least not yet. A security policy is a written document that should be simple to read and states what resources should be secured and under what conditions access will be provided or denied. It does not provide details on what needs to be done to secure the organization.

Senior Management Buy-In

Regardless of how you attack this problem, unless the senior managers in your organization approve of and support the implementation of a security policy, all attempts at implementing and enforcing the security policy will likely be futile. Discuss the issue with your senior managers. Get them to allocate the necessary resources to craft the security policy, which includes representatives from each functional area within the organization. Involving actual end users is also important because the results of those policies will be most visible to them.

The What, Who, and How

Once you have support from senior management, the next challenge is creating a simple document that everyone can use. Too often, extensive security policies are created, which cover every conceivable situation. These documents become so large and cumbersome that no one has time to either read or understand them. By keeping the document short and simple, you will have a usable document that can be understood by all.

As stated earlier, there are three general areas you want to include in your security policy: what is important, who is responsible for it, and guidelines on how to protect it. You should first identify the assets you need to protect, the value of which often determines what steps are reasonable and prudent to protect them. For most companies, specific types of information have to be protected from unauthorized access. Often, people protect servers, systems, and/or users. Although this is often necessary in the course of protecting the data, keep in mind that the primary goal is to protect the information. When the information moves from one system to another, you may have to update your security policy on the firewall or other devices to ensure that data remains protected.

The second area of security policies is ownership, namely, who is responsible for what. Ownership and responsibility should begin at the upper management levels of your organization and work down from there. It is critical that all parts of your organization have someone who is held accountable for that area. For example, most organizations have someone in charge of financial affairs, marketing, sales, and customer service. This is just as true for network security. The security policy needs to define someone responsible for both the administration of the firewall and the approval of the policy the firewall is intended to enforce. The individual rules configured into your firewall can have a major impact on your organization. Someone in your organization should be responsible for approving all requests for the rulebase to be changed. In organizations where this administrator is not defined, one person may add a rule, and then another person might remove the same rule. If there is only one person (or group of persons) responsible for approving rulebase changes, you can avoid these problems.

The security policy should not name specific individuals but instead name positions. Individuals come and go. If John Doe is responsible for the firewalls, as defined by the security policy, what happens when John Doe leaves the company or moves to a new position? All positions should be defined by a title, such as Chief Security Officer (CSO) or Firewall Administrator. The positions themselves should be clearly defined in this policy as well.

Finally, the security policy should cover basic guidelines on how to secure its assets, which may include the types of devices necessary to perform this function. For example, a policy document might state that a firewall should be used to mediate access between the organization's network and the Internet. This is reasonable. The document might also state that the firewall should support certain features or carry a particular certification, such as Common Criteria EAL4, FIPS 140-1 level 2, ITSEC E3, or ICSA. However, the document should not state that Check Point FireWall-1 should be used. Why? Technology changes too rapidly to be detailed in a security policy. The security policy should provide only guidelines or basic standards as to what will be implemented. The technical details of implementing the security policy should be left to those who must implement it (i.e., the security team).

To give another example, your organization's security policy could state that all Internet access to the company's intranet Web server must be securely authenticated using a token-based, one-time password scheme. This is *what* is required. *How* this is enforced should be left to the security team. For this book, the *how* could be enforced by Check Point FireWall-1. The firewall would intercept any HTTP requests to the intranet Web server and require authentication first. This could be done through the use of the HTTP Security Server tied into a SecurID-based authentication system. Mentioning either FireWall-1 or SecurID by name in the security policy document would be inappropriate because those are references to specific products.

It is your security policy that guides your firewall implementation and maintenance. A firewall is just part of the technical implementation of that security policy. If you and your organization do not understand your security policy, you will not be able to properly implement and maintain your firewall, not to mention other items that make up the security infrastructure in your organization.

Implementing Firewalls without a Written Security Policy

Your organization may not have a security policy or, if a security policy does exist, it may be poorly documented or understood. The problem then is that the firewall must be implemented and maintained, but without much guidance on what it is supposed to enforce. Normally in these situations, a firewall is quickly constructed, and rules are added as needed. No prior planning is done. If you find yourself or your organization in this situation, there are steps you can take to prevent problems.

The best solution is to create a security policy as soon as possible. If this cannot be done, you can take some short-term measures. First, be careful. If you are responsible for maintaining the firewall, including implementing the firewall rules, you could be held responsible if something happens. Even if you were told by someone from a different department to create a new rule (e.g., the marketing department requested access to its internal Web server from the Internet), you could be liable for a security breach.

In order for network security to be properly implemented, you must educate the managers and get them to buy into the process. This may mean spending some time with members of upper management explaining to them the importance of network security. Without support from upper management, all attempts to implement proper network security are doomed to fail. It is highly recommended that someone in upper management (perhaps your boss) be responsible for security. Ask him or her to identify someone to approve the firewall rules and make sure that person has adequate authority with which to do this. Organizations that already have a clear security policy will have already defined these policies and procedures. Unfortunately, if your organization does not have a security policy, or the security policy does not cover firewalls, you will have to do much of this yourself.

Once you have identified areas of responsibility and procedures for approving and maintaining the firewall, your life will become a lot less stressful, with less liability falling on your shoulders.

An Example of a Security Policy

Instead of reviewing an entire security policy, I present a portion of a security policy here. It is designed to give you an idea of how a security policy document might look. Keep in mind that no two security policies are alike. Every organization's policy document has its own unique format and issues. This example not only gives you a better idea of how a security policy can look but also provides specific examples of what to look for in relation to firewalls. As covered earlier, a security policy should be general in nature, covering who is responsible for what. The particular section shown here describes the management and procedures for implementing and maintaining Company X's firewalls. A sample Acceptable Usage Policy can be found in Appendix B of this book.

Company X Information Security Policy

Section 010: Firewall Implementation and Management

SUMMARY

Firewalls are a critical security asset used to protect Company X's information resources. It is critical that all firewalls be configured, implemented, and maintained in a standardized and secure fashion. In response to the risks, this document describes Company X's official policy regarding firewall implementation and management.

I. CONFIGURATION AND IMPLEMENTATION

A. *Operating System:* Before a firewall can be installed on an operating system, that operating system must be fully secured and tested in accordance with the Chief Security Officer. See Company X Operating System Standards document for more information.

B. *Responsibility:* Before implementation, an administrator must be identified as responsible for the firewall. This administrator is fully responsible for maintaining both the firewall software and the underlying operating system. The administrator may select up to two other individuals to assist in maintaining the firewall. However, these individuals must be approved by the Chief Security Officer.

C. *Access:* Only the administrator and approved assistant(s) may access the firewall or operating system. Thus, there can be no more than three accounts for the firewall and operating system. Only the firewall administrators may have administrative access to the operating system and firewall software.

D. *Default Rule:* All of Company X's firewalls are based on this premise: That which is not expressly permitted is denied.

(continued)

---

continued

II. MAINTENANCE

A. *Logs:* The firewall administrator is responsible for ensuring the daily review and archiving of firewall logs.

B. *Rules:* Only the firewall administrator is authorized to make any changes in the firewall rulebase. All requests must be forwarded to the firewall administrator and be approved by the Chief Security Officer prior to the enactment of any changes.

This section of the sample security policy covers the policies and procedures of maintaining the organization's firewalls. It is highly recommended because it helps define who is responsible for what. Notice that specific names are not used, only positions. This ensures that as people change positions, the security policy does not have to be continually updated. In addition, this section states the overall policy for firewall rulebases, specifically: That which is not expressly permitted is denied. The firewall can enforce this policy by denying all traffic. The rulebase is then modified to allow only that which is expressly permitted.

Other samples can be found at The SANS Institute (http://www.sans.org). This organization maintains several sample security policy documents that cover a wide variety of situations and are based on common best practices. You can use them as templates to craft your own document. SANS also provides links to other locations that provide sample security policies.

Fun with Check Point Licensing

Perhaps one of the more challenging aspects of FireWall-1 is licensing the product. Even those who have been selling and supporting FireWall-1 for a number of years tend to get tripped up by Check Point's licensing. Throughout the book, I will mention where specific licenses are needed to perform certain functions. In this section, I specifically discuss where license considerations come into play during the initial planning and installation.

The major components that require licensing are listed below:

- Firewall module
- Management console
- Management GUI applications, that is, SMART Clients

A firewall module enforces your security policy and sends log information to a management console. This is typically referred to as *the firewall.* The management console is responsible for storing, compiling, and pushing the security policies out to the firewall modules. It also receives logging information from the firewall modules and processes alerts. The Management GUI applications allow you to view, edit, and install security policies; view logs; and see the status of all installed firewall modules. The Management GUIs communicate with the management console, which does all of the actual work.

With some exceptions, which I will note in the following sections, each of these components may exist on separate systems. You can even mix and match the platforms on which each of these components exist.[1] For example, you can have the firewall on a Nokia platform, the management console on Solaris, and the Management GUIs on Windows.

Types of Licenses

In the following subsections, I describe the types of licenses you can get for FireWall-1.

Node-Limited Firewalls

Node-limited firewall licenses are restricted in terms of the number of IP addresses that can be behind the firewall. FireWall-1 listens for any IP-based traffic on all interfaces except for external one(s). When you define the gateway object within FireWall-1 that represents the gateway, you specify which interface(s) is/are external. Anytime it hears hosts talking to each other with an address on a nonexternal interface, it notes the IP addresses. Once FireWall-1 has heard n IPs (plus a 10% fudge factor), connections from the $n+1$ hosts generate e-mails to root and messages to syslog or the event viewer. When the license is exceeded by a large number of hosts on a busy network, FireWall-1 consumes itself with logging and mailing out messages about exceeding your license. In many cases, this causes the firewall to process traffic very slowly, if at all.

So what are the implications of how FireWall-1 enforces a node-limited license? *Anything* behind your firewall with an IP address will eventually be found out. This includes noncomputer components like printers, coffeemakers,[2] and so on. Anything with an IP address that talks on your LAN will be heard, eventually. Also, machines with multiple IP addresses will most likely be counted more than once. Peripherals that do not use TCP/IP should not be counted. Machines that only use AppleTalk, IPX, NetBEUI, and so on should also not be counted. Because FireWall-1 only looks for IP traffic, it should safely ignore these machines.

---

1. In a High Availability configuration, each firewall in the cluster must be on the same platform.

2. There's even an official Request for Comment (RFC) related to coffeepots connected to the Internet. See RFC2328 at http://www.faqs.org or another source for Internet RFCs.

Node-limited licenses are appropriate for use only where you can guarantee the number of hosts behind a single gateway. While it is trivial to fool the firewall into believing there are fewer hosts behind it than there are, Check Point's End User License Agreement forbids using any means to circumvent its licensing mechanisms. As stated in section 2.5 of the End User License Agreement that comes with FireWall-1 NG Feature Pack 3 (FP3):

> The License permits the use of the Product in accordance with the designated number of IP addresses [. . .]. It is a violation of this End User License Agreement to create, set-up or design any hardware, software or system which alters the number of readable IP addresses presented to the Product with the intent, or resulting effect, of circumventing the Licensed Configuration.

In FireWall-1 4.1 and earlier, node-limited licensed gateways were permitted to have only a single external interface. In FireWall-1 NG, you can have more than one external interface defined. However, routing between external interfaces is not permitted.

Single-Gateway Products

A single-gateway product (also referred to as a *firewall Internet gateway*) is a node-limited firewall module bundled with a management console. This management console is only capable of managing a single-firewall module, and the firewall module must be installed on the same host as the management console. Because a single-gateway product includes a node-limited firewall license, it has the same restrictions as those stated in the previous section.

Secure Server (FireWall-1 Host)

One license type is designed to protect a single host. It has all the functionality of a standard firewall module except that it is not allowed to forward packets.

SMART Console and SMART Center (Management Console)

SMART Console in FireWall-1 NG with Application Intelligence[3] (NG AI) is the same thing as SMART Center in FireWall-1 NG FP3, which is Check Point's marketing name for the management console. If your single-gateway product does not include a management console, you need to obtain a separate license for the management console. You can install the management console on the same platform as the firewall. If you plan to manage multiple firewalls or use High Availability, having your management console on a different platform is recommended. For more information on remote management, see Chapter 7.

---

3. NG AI is Feature Pack 4. Check Point decided to give it a spiffy new marketing name.

Motif GUI

A separate license is needed if you want to use the Management GUIs on any platform other than a Windows platform.[4] This is because Check Point must pay a licensing fee to the company that provides Check Point with the tool-kit used to make the GUI for these platforms. These licenses were free for Fire-Wall-1 4.0, but they require additional payment for FireWall-1 4.1 and later. The license is tied to the IP address or hostid of your management console and will be installed on your management console.

Check Point Express (Small-Office Products)

After the release of NG AI, Check Point decided to change how it sells products geared toward small-office environments. Check Point Express is targeted for companies with sites of 50 to 500 users, and it supports multiple sites. Essentially, anything you can get in an enterprise edition (which typically supports unlimited users) can be obtained in a Check Point Express version. Check Point Express runs on the same type of hardware that "normal" Check Point licenses run on, but Check Point Express supports a limited number of users and costs less. Check Point Express licenses require the use of NG AI with a special patch that enables the Check Point Express licensing (available at http://www.checkpoint.com/techsupport/express.html). NG AI R55 and later will support Check Point Express directly.

VPN-1 Embedded NG (Safe@ Products)

SofaWare is a wholly owned subsidiary of Check Point that makes security devices aimed more at the consumer market and priced accordingly. These are referred to as Safe@ appliances. The hardware devices are similar to a Linksys or D-Link home router in form factor and features, though the number of users supported is limited by license—five users at the low end, unlimited users on the higher-end hardware. These devices support most cable/DSL providers, using DHCP with dynamic addressing and PPP over Ethernet (PPPoE) support. They do not run Check Point FireWall-1 but rather what Check Point calls VPN-1 Embedded NG under a Linux operating system. The devices can be locally managed or can be integrated into an existing Check Point environment, supporting content security and VPN access (both client-to-site and site-to-site). NG FP3 and later include a management plug-in that allows limited management of these devices.

---

4. If you use a copy of Crossover Office v2.1 or above, you can install and use the SmartConsole applications on Linux, albeit with a few minor glitches. For more information on Crossover Office, see http://www. codeweavers.com.

A number of companies sell platforms that run VPN-1 Embedded NG: VPN Dynamics (V4), Nokia (IP30 and IP40), Intrusion (PDS500), and Celestix (Orion series). Check Point sells its own version of these products under the VPN-1 Edge and SofaWare S-box labels.

SmartDirectory (LDAP Account Management)

If you plan to integrate FireWall-1 with a Lightweight Directory Access Protocol (LDAP) server (see Chapter 8 for details), you need to purchase an additional license for this feature.

VPN, SecuRemote, and SecureClient

All VPN functionality in FireWall-1, whether for site-to-site or client-to-site, requires additional licenses to be installed on the management and firewall modules. The software to support this functionality is included in the installation—the license activates that functionality. The SecureClient endpoints do not require licenses to be installed on them.

Getting Licenses

Each product you purchase will be given a certificate key. This certificate key, once registered at http://usercenter.checkpoint.com, can be used to obtain your permanent license key for your product. The actual process, if everything goes well, is very straightforward. Not only will you be given the license information on a Web page, you will also be sent e-mail with the same information. Save this e-mail and print the license page. You will need this information when installing the product. You will also need the certificate key when you upgrade at a later date because the same certificate key will be used for the updated product (provided you purchase a software subscription, which should be activated at the same time the product is licensed).

There are two types of licenses: *local licenses* (i.e., tied to the specific module) and *central licenses* (i.e., tied to the management console). Local licenses are the more traditional type that's been in use in FireWall-1 since the beginning. Central licenses are new in NG and allow you to easily move a license between modules without having to have the license reissued. Central licenses are tied to the management station, so if that gets moved, you will need new licenses. Central licenses are required for modules with a dynamic IP address.

There are two ways to license a FireWall-1 installation: on a hostid or on an IP address. The hostid is an ID number based on information burned onto the motherboard. Hostid-based licensing can occur only on SPARC Solaris because this hardware type actually supports this type of license. On AIX, you can use a hostid-based license, but the hostid of an AIX box is actually based on an IP address, so there is no point to doing so. Windows, Linux, and Nokia do not allow hostid-based licenses and can be licensed only by IP addresses. For central licenses, the IP or hostid to which the license must be generated is the management module. For a local license, you use the module's IP or hostid.

Licenses based on an IP address require that the IP address noted in the license be associated with an interface that is active when FireWall-1's kernel-loadable module loads at boot time. On a Solaris or Linux platform, the licensed IP address must be associated with the physical interface (i.e., it cannot be an interface alias).

It is relatively easy to get evaluation licenses to do the testing and even the initial deployment of your firewall. Your Check Point reseller can obtain an evaluation license for you. Also, with each "eval pack" (which contains a CD and some documentation), you get a certificate key that can be used to generate two 30-day evaluation licenses. Also, fresh installations of the software since NG FP2 also contain a 15-day embedded license that is activated when Secure Internal Communication (SIC) is initialized on the platform. This happens during the initial configuration.

In some cases, it has taken many months to get the correct permanent licenses, especially when upgrading from one version of FireWall-1 to the next, so do not be surprised if this happens to you. Unfortunately, there is no magic to this process. Making sure you have copies of your certificate keys and software subscription IDs helps tremendously but does not guarantee success in obtaining a permanent license quickly. Be prepared to work with both your Check Point reseller and Check Point itself to resolve licensing issues. If you find you must run a production firewall on an evaluation license, make sure that you request new evaluation licenses at least a week before you actually need them. It may take at least that long to hunt down another license you can use. The same is true with an upgrade of permanent licenses: Request the upgrade at least a week (or more) before you need them.

There are two kinds of evaluation licenses: those that are tied to an IP address or hostid and those that are not (which are sometimes called *floating evals*). Licenses of the latter type display the word eval where an IP address or hostid would be. Check Point does not generally distribute these licenses, though these licenses are still used within Check Point and occasionally make their way into the outside world. These licenses are good only for a limited period of time. They usually have a start date of some sort; if the system is dated before this time, the license will be invalid. As such, you cannot backdate your system to use one of these licenses indefinitely.

During the FireWall-1 3.0 time frame, Check Point changed to a system where evaluation licenses were tied to a specific IP or hostid, which is still in use today. The dirty little secret about these licenses was that they are actually *permanent* licenses that have an expiration date. It appeared that you can backdate the system to use these licenses. However, I am quite certain that this is against Check Point's Licensing Agreement.

Summary

Although it is impossible to describe every situation you might encounter during the planning phase of installation, this chapter covered the basic elements you need to know to ensure that your installation process is successful. Making sure you understand your existing network structure, establishing a written security policy, and understanding how Check Point licenses work are key to the success of your initial installation.

Chapter

3

Installing FireWall-1

This chapter discusses the installation of FireWall-1, from building the system to loading the software. The actual configuration of FireWall-1 is covered in later chapters.

By the end of this chapter, you should be able to:

- Select the operating system that is best for your environment
- Properly harden an operating system
- Install the firewall software

Selecting an Operating System

The first step in building your firewall is selecting the operating system on which the application will run. With FireWall-1, you have several options:

- Windows NT/2000 Server
- Sun Solaris (SPARC)
- AIX
- Nokia IP Security Platform (IPSO)
- Linux and Secure Platform (SPLAT)

Each operating system has its advantages and disadvantages. Some of the advantages and disadvantages are listed in the sections that follow, where each operating system is discussed. However, no one operating system is best for every environment. The single most important criteria for choosing an operating system should be the skill set of your administrators. Whichever operating system you select, make sure your security staff is knowledgeable in that particular operating system. Even if you select the best operating system in the world, you will have problems if you lack the skilled personnel to build and maintain it. Your firewall will not be as secure or as stable as it should be without a properly configured operating system.

The following subsections discuss the various operating systems on which FireWall-1 will run.

Windows NT/2000

The assumption in this subsection is that Windows NT 4.0 Server or Windows 2000 Server/Advanced Server will be used. Check Point supports FireWall-1 only on Windows NT Server or Windows 2000 Server/Advanced Server. Windows NT Workstation and Windows 2000 Professional can be used in test environments, but they are not recommended in a production environment because Microsoft has limited each product to ten concurrent connections and doesn't support advanced routing capabilities. Windows NT Server and Windows 2000 Server/Advanced Server also include additional capabilities not present in Windows NT Workstation, such as mirrored drives. In this text, comments regarding Windows NT also apply to Windows 2000 unless otherwise specified.

You might wonder why I mention Windows NT at all, considering that Microsoft has declared it will no longer support Windows NT after the end of 2003. The fact is that a lot of people still use Windows NT. Not for firewalls, necessarily, but it is still in use and will probably still be in use long after Microsoft has decided to stop supporting it.

Advantages

Some of the advantages of using Windows NT Server and Windows 2000 Server/Advanced Server include the following.

- *Ease of use:* Windows has a GUI interface that many people are familiar with. This makes installation and maintenance of the operating system and firewall more user-friendly.
- *Widely used:* Windows is widely deployed. Windows 2000 is a popular choice for FireWall-1 installations these days, and Windows NT was historically a popular choice. There is plenty of documentation on both Windows NT/2000 and FireWall-1 on Windows NT/2000.
- *Lots of third-party software:* If FireWall-1 does not provide a particular function, it's likely that a third-party application does.

Disadvantages

Some of the disadvantages of using Windows NT Server and Windows 2000 Server/Advanced Server include the following.

- *Remote administration:* Compared to UNIX, Windows is more difficult to remotely administer because most administration tasks can be performed only with a GUI. This can be mitigated somewhat by installing third-party software such as Terminal Server or VNC, but these may introduce additional security issues. Even with these tools, the most essential remote administration tool ends up being a car.

- *Command-line access:* Windows lacks a powerful command-line interface. This makes advanced troubleshooting more difficult for both the operating system and the firewall software. Many of the advanced troubleshooting methods covered in this book are more difficult to perform on Windows than on other platforms.

SPARC Solaris

The original versions of FireWall-1 ran on SunOS and Solaris. Needless to say, Solaris is well supported both in terms of FireWall-1 and in terms of third-party applications.

Note that I am differentiating here between SPARC Solaris, which runs on SPARC processors, and Solaris x86, which runs on Intel-based hardware. The latter used to run FireWall-1, but Check Point currently does not support FireWall-1 on Solaris x86.

Advantages

The advantages of using SPARC Solaris include the following.

- *Widely used:* Solaris is widely used and is a popular choice for FireWall-1 installations. There is plenty of documentation on both Solaris and FireWall-1 on Solaris.
- *Primary development platform for Check Point:* The majority of Check Point's development work occurs on Solaris.
- *Command-line access:* UNIX systems have a strong command-line interface. This makes troubleshooting both the operating system and the firewall application easier, especially by remote.
- *High-end hardware support:* Solaris tends to support high-end hardware including lots of memory and large disk drives. This means Solaris is a very scalable platform.
- *Third-party software:* Although not as big of an advantage as on Windows, many applications you may need to use in conjunction with FireWall-1 will also run on Solaris.

Disadvantages

The disadvantages of using SPARC Solaris include the following.

- *Training:* Solaris, like most flavors of UNIX, requires more skill and training. It takes an experienced administrator to optimize the operating system. Not only can good Solaris administrators be difficult to find, but they may also cost more.

- *Policy Editor costs:* Policy Editor requires extra costs to deploy on Solaris. You are better off running Policy Editor from a Windows platform and connecting to a management console, which can run on any platform.

AIX

IBM makes a version of UNIX, called AIX, on which FireWall-1 can run.

Advantages

Some of the advantages of using AIX include the following.

- *Command-line access:* UNIX systems have a strong command-line interface. As mentioned above, this makes troubleshooting both the operating system and the firewall application easier, especially by remote.
- *High-end hardware support:* AIX tends to support high-end hardware including lots of memory and large disk drives. This means AIX is scalable.

Disadvantages

Some of the disadvantages of using AIX include the following.

- *Deployment and resources:* Compared to Solaris, AIX is not as widely deployed. As such, good information on AIX is harder to find, not to mention the lack of information on using either of these operating systems with FireWall-1.
- *Not a first-tier operating system:* New FireWall-1 features do not appear on AIX right away. In fact, they often appear on AIX last because the vast majority of users choose other platforms. In December 2002, NG was available only as a beta, and it was Feature Pack 1 at that (FP3 was shipping at that time). NG with Application Intelligence (NG AI) is now available on AIX.
- *Training:* Similar to Solaris, AIX requires more training to administer. Good AIX administrators can be difficult to find and may also cost more.
- *Third-party software:* Due to the small installed base of FireWall-1 on this platform, vendors may not release versions of their software for either operating system. If they do, it is almost always after Windows and Solaris versions are released.

Nokia IP Security Platform (IPSO)

The Nokia IP Security Platforms (IPxxx[1]) are platforms specifically designed to run specialized applications, such as FireWall-1. The operating system that runs on this hardware is a modified version of FreeBSD called IPSO. IPSO began life as an ATM switching operating system at a company called Ipsilon Networks. In fact, IPSO used to stand for IP Switching Operating system. Nokia acquired Ipsilon Networks in 1998. The terms *Nokia platform* and *IPSO* are used interchangeably throughout this text.

Advantages

Some advantages of using IPSO include the following.

- *Ease of use:* Configuration of the operating system is performed with a standard Web browser.
- *Command-line access:* Although much of the configuration is done with a standard Web browser, a standard UNIX command line is available to perform troubleshooting and monitoring—where I feel the use of the command line is most important. IPSO 3.6 also introduced a supported configuration command-line interface as well.
- *Hardened operating system:* Most of what is considered insecure has been removed from the operating system or is relatively easy to disable in Voyager, the Web-based interface for configuring IPSO.
- *Widely used:* Among hardware vendors that sell prepackaged solutions with FireWall-1 installed, Nokia sells more boxes than anyone else. In fact, in 2003, Check Point derived more than 40% of its revenue from sales on Nokia platforms.
- *More thoroughly tested product:* Both Nokia and Check Point test the operating system, firewall, and hardware together for quality assurance.
- *Easier to upgrade:* The operating system and applications on IPSO are designed to be relatively easy to upgrade or downgrade as needed.
- *Rack-mountable:* Most Nokia application platforms are rack-mountable and are suitable for use in a secured machine room. The IP100 series platforms are wall-mountable.
- *Easy to manage:* In addition to the easy-to-service hardware design, the operating system can be centrally managed with a product called Network

---

1. The Nokia IP30 and IP40 platforms use a Linux-based operating system and use VPN-1 Embedded NG. The IP40 has a command-line interface very similar to what you would find on other Nokia platforms. The IP71 is also based on Linux but is no longer sold. The Nokia IP51 and IP55 are based on VxWorks and are also no longer sold.

Horizon Manager. This is a boon for companies with a large number of IP Security Platforms to manage.

- *Support:* A single vendor provides support for both FireWall-1 and IPSO. In addition, Nokia's Technical Assistance Centers have achieved Support Center Practices certification.

Disadvantages

Some disadvantages of using IPSO include the following.

- *Customization:* What you gain in terms of a good user experience, you lose in terms of the ability to customize the box. Some consider the lack of customization a good thing; others do not. Nokia does have a Software Development Kit (SDK) and a Developers Alliance. However, these items are not free.
- *Cost:* Nokia platforms have a higher acquisition cost than similar hardware and software combinations from other vendors. In addition, Nokia support agreements tend to be more expensive than other hardware and software options.
- *Command-line access:* IPSO 3.6 and later provide a command-line interface through which you can make configuration changes, but it is nonstandard, at least with respect to how most UNIX systems operate.
- *Third-party applications:* Few third-party applications run on IPSO. Nokia is increasing the number of vendors that run applications on the platform, but certainly not at the rate that applications are being made available on other UNIX platforms.

Linux and Secure Platform

Linux is a UNIX-like operating system made available under the GNU Public License (GPL), meaning that you have free access to the source code and can make any modifications you like.[2] Many Linux distributions, such as Red Hat, are similar to Solaris in administration. Most UNIX administrators can easily convert to a Linux environment.

Due, in part, to its popularity and cost, Check Point has released what is referred to as the "Black CD," a.k.a. Secure Platform or SPLAT. It is basically a stripped-down version of Red Hat Linux with FireWall-1 preloaded on it. The idea is this: Take a totally blank system with supported hardware, load this CD, and you have a firewall that's ready to go. There are a number of OPSEC Plat-

---

2. The Linux kernel itself is under the GPL; various other programs included with most Linux distributions are either GPL or other similar open-source licenses.

form vendors that sell packaged hardware that can either sit on the desktop or be rack-mounted similar to a Nokia platform.

For the purposes of this comparison, Linux and Secure Platform are treated the same way. There are some differences, which are highlighted below.

Advantages

The advantages of using Linux and Secure Platform include the following.

- *UNIX features:* Linux shares the same advantages of most versions of UNIX—strong remote management and a command-line interface.
- *Lower cost of acquisition:* Because you do not have to pay nearly as much for the operating system (it can be free!) and can use commodity PC hardware for your system, the overall cost of acquisition is less.
- *Ease of installation:* If you use Secure Platform, Check Point has done all the work of hardening the operating system for you. Just plug in the CD and go!
- *Performance:* At least in many performance tests commissioned by Check Point, Linux platforms perform better than other, similarly configured platforms.
- *Support:* When using SPLAT, the operating system and firewall are supported by a single vendor.
- *Open source:* You get not only the operating system free of charge but also the source code.

Disadvantages

The disadvantages of using Linux include the following.

- *Distribution specific:* FireWall-1 is supported only on Red Hat Linux using specific versions of the kernel. The exact versions supported depend on what version of FireWall-1 you are using. A few folks have made it work on other versions of Red Hat and even other distributions like Mandrake, SuSE, and Debian. I have run an NG FP3 management station on Debian, though management stations aren't as sensitive to kernel versions as firewall modules are.
- *Customization:* Any customization (i.e., adding software packages) done on Secure Platform makes the operating system component entirely unsupported by Check Point.
- *Limited interface support:* Not every type of interface is supported. Ethernet and various types of PPP interfaces appear to be supported. In Secure Platform, getting a device driver for a nonsupported device working with

the operating system is difficult. If Secure Platform does not recognize your hardware out of the box, you are better off installing the appropriate version of Red Hat Linux instead.

- *Not easily upgradable:* The reliance on specific kernel versions makes it difficult to upgrade the kernel with a security patch yet still have that kernel work with the FireWall-1 kernel loadable module. The "upgrade" from NG FP2 Secure Platform to NG FP3 Secure Platform required a complete reinstall, thus it really wasn't an upgrade. Check Point is supposedly improving this.

- *Secure Platform missing key functionality:* I've seen numerous complaints in public forums that Check Point stripped out too much stuff from Red Hat for Secure Platform to be entirely usable. For instance, Check Point did not include a Secure Shell (SSH) daemon, which is standard on Solaris, IPSO, and even Red Hat Linux. Later versions of Secure Platform appear to have more packages, including the routing daemon Zebra in NG AI.

Installing the Operating System

Once you have chosen an operating system, you should make sure you have the necessary hardware, software, and configuration information to install it. You can then install it, taking extra care to make sure you install and configure only what you need and disable what you don't.

Preparing for the OS Installation

After selecting your operating system, you can begin to plan your build. Before the actual build process begins, you need to confirm some preliminary information and resources. The following checklist covers most of the important considerations. Complete this checklist before you begin the installation process—it will simplify the build process and identify any configuration issues before you begin building the box(es).

- Do you have the required hardware?
    - Ensure that you have enough network interface cards. It never hurts to have extra network ports handy in case your network grows.
    - Ensure that you have the disk space for logs on your management console.
- Do you have the operating system installation media?
    - Ensure that you also have a proper license for your operating system (if necessary).

- Determine which version of the operating system you are going to install.
- Obtain the latest system patches or service packs.
- Do you have the FireWall-1 installation media or can you get it from an accessible FTP server?
  - Obtain the proper licenses.
  - Obtain the latest service/feature packs for FireWall-1.
  - If installing via FTP, determine the IP address of the FTP server.
  - If installing via FTP, determine the username and password necessary to access this software.
  - If installing via FTP, ensure that it is accessible from where you plan to install the platform.
- How will you configure the operating system? Establish the system configuration by determining the following information:
  - System name
  - Name, IP address, and netmask of all interface cards
  - IP address of the DNS server
  - Default router and additional network routes
  - Routing protocols (BGP, OSPF, RIP)
  - Disk partitions
  - User accounts and passwords
- How will you configure the firewall? Determine the following information for the firewall configuration:
  - IP address(es) of machine(s) that will run the GUI client
  - IP addresses of remote modules or management module (if required)
  - Accounts for firewall administration

Guidelines for the OS Installation

Once you have identified the required information, you can begin the build process. The first step in building your operating system is to start with a new installation. Never trust previous installations of an operating system. By installing and configuring the operating system from scratch, you know exactly how it has been configured and can better trust it. Each operating system has its own unique installation process. You will want to build an installation checklist for your particular operating system.

When you receive a Nokia IP Security Platform from the factory, it comes preinstalled with IPSO and a fresh configuration you must configure via a console cable. These installations can generally be trusted, but it is likely that an earlier version of either FireWall-1 or IPSO is loaded on the platform. You can either upgrade the existing software or simply reinstall the system from scratch from an FTP server where you have loaded all of the necessary software bits.

During the installation and build procedure, ensure that the system is never attached to a live network. Attaching an unsecured operating system to a network exposes it to a variety of risks. It is quite possible to have a system probed, attacked, and compromised within 15 minutes of being connected to the Internet! If you need to add software to your system, such as OS patches or additional software, use an intermediate system to download the required software. You can then either burn the software to a CD or directly connect the two systems over a private, secured network.

Once the operating system has been installed, the next step is to configure it for your environment. This usually consists of adding system accounts (in a secure manner discussed in Securing the Operating System, below) and configuring all networking including DNS. This is where the preceding checklist comes in handy. Remember, the operating system—not FireWall-1—is responsible for all networking and routing. The firewall only determines what can and cannot happen. Once a session has been approved or authenticated by the firewall, it is up to the operating system to send the packets in the correct direction. You must ensure that you set up networking properly, or traffic will not reach its destination. Each operating system has its own specific ways of setting up interfaces and routing. If you are employing address translation, refer to Chapter 10 for additional notes about changes to routing that might need to be made.

Once the system has been fully secured and configured, build a lab network that replicates the network point your firewall will protect. Have lab equipment replicate the routers and networks the firewall will route from and to. This way your network configurations can be tested before being implemented. Unfortunately, many organizations do not have the luxury of a lab to test their configurations. A second technique is to verify the system configuration during the implementation phase. Once the system is ready and the firewall has been installed and configured, the box is deployed on the network. Once plugged into the network, turn off both the firewall and routing on the box (do this only with a fully armored system). Then, from the box, attempt to ping every network that should be accessible from the firewall, including the Internet. The key point is to confirm that the operating system is properly configured before turning on the firewall. If the system can ping every network it is supposed to, more than likely, the system is properly configured. If you cannot ping a network that should be accessible, fix the problem before turning on the firewall. Once again, use this method only with a fully armored system and IP routing turned off. You won't be able to test routing through the firewall in this configuration, but you can ensure that the firewall knows how to get everywhere it is supposed to.

Securing the Operating System

The entire purpose of a firewall is to secure your resources. However, a firewall is only as secure as the operating system it resides on. If the operating system is compromised, so is the firewall, defeating your organization's security. Therefore, you need to build the operating system as securely as possible. Each operating system has unique and specific issues. For detailed examples on how to properly build a secure system for a firewall, see Appendix A. However, there are standard concepts that apply to every operating system; these are described here.

The OS hardening process begins with the installation. Most UNIX systems allow the user to select the applications or packages to install during the installation process. By selecting the minimal installation possible, you can limit the vulnerabilities present in the new operating system. With other operating systems, such as Windows 2000, lots of unnecessary components are installed by default, and no choice is given as to whether or not to install them. Once the installation is complete, additional services, such as Workstation and Server, need to be removed or disabled.

Once the operating system has been loaded, you should remove any unnecessary applications and software that were installed. If the firewall does not require a particular application, remove it. The new system should be a dedicated firewall. Do not run other applications on it, such as DNS, a Web server, a mail server, a Windows domain controller, and so on. The more applications you have on your system, the greater the risk for compromise. If an application is not installed, it cannot be compromised. As discussed earlier, this armoring process begins during installation, where you install only the bare minimum of software required. Once the installation is complete, ensure that all other unnecessary services are turned off. You can verify that services are not running by running `netstat -na` and making sure that you can account for all the ports shown as listening. You can also run a port scanner against the system to validate what `netstat -na` shows you. Even if a service is not running, binaries remaining on the operating system can be locally exploited; these need to be removed. Several of the descriptions in Appendix A explain how to remove binaries for unused programs (e.g., removing packages in Linux/Solaris).

The firewall should be as isolated as possible from other components within the network. This means that a firewall operating system should not participate in any network logon scheme such as a Windows Domain/Active Directory or Network Information Service (NIS). These kinds of services not only increase the risk of compromise but also create the possibility you will not be able to log into the firewall if the authentication server is down. All authentication should be done locally using strong passwords (abc123 is *not* a strong password), or perhaps authenticating against a one-time password system such as S/Key or even SecurID. For name resolution, you can't entirely get away from DNS, but it is important that the local host file on the firewall operating system contain entries for critical servers within the infrastructure. This will reduce the delays that will occur in interaction with the firewall when DNS is offline.

The next step is to patch the operating system. New exploits and vulnerabilities are constantly being identified for all operating systems. Patches help protect against these known vulnerabilities. Make sure the new system is fully patched after the initial installation. For Windows, this requires the latest service packs and hotfixes. For Solaris, it is advised to install the latest recommended patch cluster from Sun. Patching an operating system is not a one-time event; due diligence must be exercised to ensure that all the latest security patches are applied. Security Focus (http://www.securityfocus.com) is an excellent source for this information. As new vulnerabilities are discovered, vendors release new patches to update their operating systems.

After you have applied all the latest patches and hotfixes, you should update and secure whatever services and applications you are running on the box just as you would your operating system. Most services can be secured to some extent. If the service cannot be secured, you may want to replace it with an alternative or eliminate it all together. For example, if you are running Telnet or FTP daemons on UNIX systems, you will want to install TCP wrappers to limit who can access these services. Replacing these services with more-secure applications is an even better solution. SSH can be used like Telnet and FTP to log on to a system and transfer files to a system. It also provides stronger authentication and encryption than Telnet or FTP alone. Regardless, ensure that any additional applications you are running on the operating system are current and secured.

Logging is another critical feature. Just like the firewall, most operating systems log user and kernel activity on the system. Make sure your operating system is logging important events. This helps you troubleshoot better because logs can often warn you if something is going wrong. They can also let you know if someone is trying to break in, because logon failures are usually logged. Logs also leave an audit trail, telling you who did what, which is especially important when something goes wrong. Many organizations use a dedicated log server to store system logs. The firewall operating system can be configured not only to log all system information locally but also to send the logs over the network to the dedicated log server. This ensures two sources of logging information in case one source becomes corrupted or inaccessible. Regardless of which options you choose, ensure that your operating system is logging all system and user activity.

However, also note that too much logging can slow the system down, so although logging is a good thing overall, judicious use is best.

In addition, you should secure user access to the operating system. More than one person, but not too many, should have access to the system. Limit the access to a small group of people who are trusted—three is a good number. The more people who have access to the operating system, the greater the chance that something can go wrong. These accounts should have hard-to-guess passwords or even require a one-time password scheme. You should also establish these accounts on the local system only. Do not use any network login scheme like NIS or a Windows Domain Logon, but SecurID or some other one-time password scheme is acceptable.

Never use a generic account for the initial login. Often, part of breaking into a system is choosing the right username to try. A hacker tries common usernames like admin, root, fwadmin, guest, and so on because they are highly likely to exist on a system. Disable these logins, if possible, and require a login that identifies a specific user. This same rule applies to the firewall administrator account used to access the FireWall-1 Management GUIs (more about these in Chapter 4).

Always require users to first authenticate themselves; then allow them to gain the necessary access. This procedure builds in at least two layers of authentication (which is more secure) and leaves an audit trail of who is doing what. Windows 2000 provides a RunAs feature that allows you to run commands with greater privilege. Windows NT also has similar functionality through the use of third-party applications. Make sure users have only the access they absolutely require. Do not give them root or administrator access if they do not require it to administer or maintain the system. The same is true for the FireWall-1 Management GUIs.

As far as routing goes, I generally recommend using static routes on a firewall. If you must use dynamic routing, which makes sense in complex environments, ensure that you have enabled authentication within the routing protocol to limit the possibility of importing spoofed routes, and log any authentication failures. Avoid using RIP, if at all possible, because it's relatively easy to pollute a RIP routing table. Additionally, you can use FireWall-1 to restrict who is allowed to send routing updates.

Beginning the FireWall-1 Installation

Once you have properly installed, configured, and secured your operating system, you are ready to proceed with installation of the firewall software. The installation instructions included in the Getting Started guide as part of your

Check Point documentation explain the specific steps necessary to load the software from the CD or from a tarball downloaded from Check Point's Software Subscription section. Check Point now distributes complete releases with each feature pack and does not require you to install a "base" release for a new installation.[3]

When downloading the software from Check Point's Software Subscription site, there are two ways to download it: as individual packages or as a "wrapper." Usually, installation via the wrapper is best because it will automatically load selected packages in the correct order. On the other hand, the wrapper contains every single package in the Check Point suite—some of which you may not use.

> NOTE!   There appears to be a problem with the NG FP3 installation wrapper on IPSO: It will not correctly install the Desktop Policy Server for Secure Client. In this case, you will need to uninstall the Desktop Policy Server package and reinstall the Desktop Policy Server from the individual package. The package will then install correctly.

For the purposes of demonstration, I will show the process for installing NG FP3 on a separate management console and firewall module. The management console will be loaded on a Windows 2000 platform. The firewall module will be loaded on a Nokia IP350. While it may seem strange that I don't show the process on other platforms as well, I can assure you the questions asked of you during installation will be almost identical.

Installing an NG FP3 Management Console on Windows 2000

In this example, NG FP3 is being installed via the installation wrapper. Installing the individual packages is basically the same except that you must choose to install each package manually. First, you would install the SVN Foundation package. Next, you would install the VPN-1/FireWall-1 package. Finally, you would install other packages as needed.

The installation wrapper allows you to choose which packages you wish to install. After clicking on the NG FP3 `setup.exe` for the wrapper installation, you are prompted to install Gateway Components or Desktop Components. Select Gateway Components. Then you can choose which components you want to install. A dialog similar to Figure 3.1 appears. For this example, you're installing a management station on this platform and not a firewall module, so the only checkboxes you need to select are VPN-1 & FireWall-1 and SMART Clients.

---

3. A notable exception to this is NG FP2: While it is possible to install NG FP2 as a standalone release, it actually installs NG FP1 first, then upgrades it to NG FP2. On a Nokia platform, you will see NG FP1 and NG FP2 packages loaded on your platform. Removing the NG FP1 packages is a bad idea.

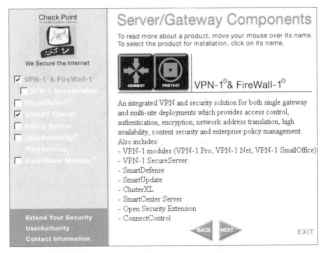

Figure 3.1   Choosing the components to install

After clicking Next, you see a screen similar to Figure 3.2, which simply confirms your choices. Click Next.

You then are presented with a screen similar to Figure 3.3. You can choose whether this is a firewall module, a management server, or a log server. A log server is a platform on which only logs are stored. A management server is also a log server, so that option is redundant when you've selected a management server. A machine can be both a firewall module and a management server. This is actually required for some licenses. In this case, select only the management server. Click Next.

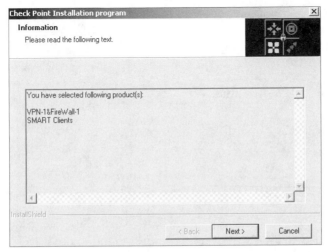

Figure 3.2   Verifying the components you wish to install

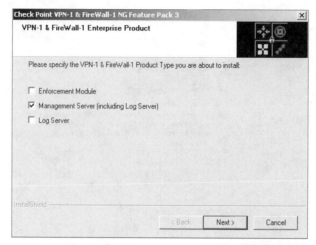

Figure 3.3   Choosing the management console and/or the FireWall-1 module

Figure 3.4 shows the next screen, which allows you to choose whether this is a primary management station or a secondary management station. In most cases, you will select primary. If you are using Management High Availability and this is a secondary management station, you will select the secondary option instead. Click Next.

Figure 3.5 shows the next screen, which allows you to choose whether to install the Backward Compatibility package. This option is necessary only if your management station will be used to manage FireWall-1 4.1 firewalls. In this

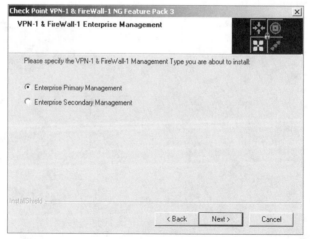

Figure 3.4   Specifying a primary management station

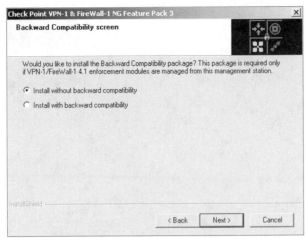

Figure 3.5   Choosing to install FireWall-1
without backward compatibility

case, select the option "Install without backward compatibility." The management station thus will not manage FireWall-1 4.1 firewalls. Click Next.

The next screen, shown in Figure 3.6, allows you to select an installation directory for FireWall-1. The default is usually what you want to specify, but if you decide not to install in the default location, make sure you choose an installation path that does not contain any spaces or you will likely have difficulties later. Click Next.

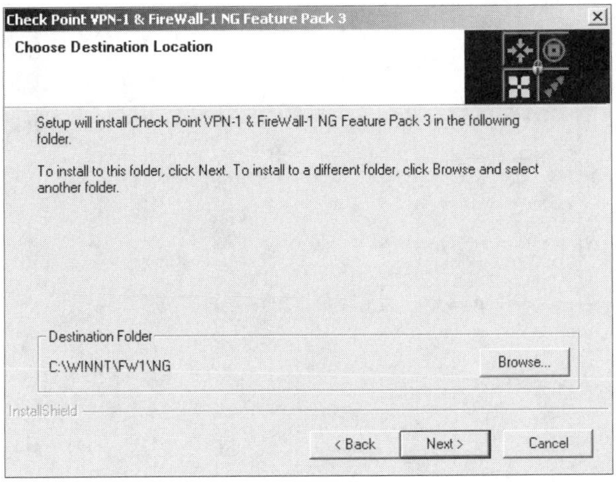

Figure 3.6   Choosing an installation directory for FireWall-1

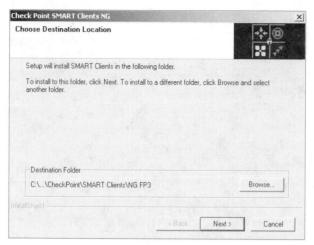

Figure 3.7   Choosing an installation directory for SMART Clients

After the VPN-1 & FireWall-1 software load, you are presented with a choice of installation directory for the SMART Clients, as shown in Figure 3.7. This may be installed anywhere you choose. Click Next.

Figure 3.8 shows that you are then presented with several choices for which GUI applications to install. It is generally safe to install all the GUI applications, however, you may not wish to for one reason or another. Select the applications appropriate for your installation and click Next.

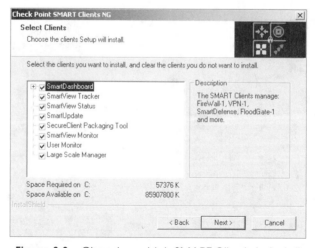

Figure 3.8   Choosing which SMART Clients to install

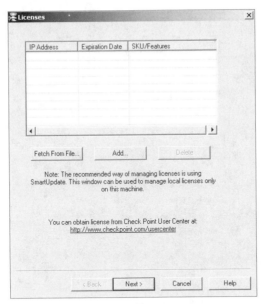

Figure 3.9   Installing licenses

Next, you are presented with a screen to add licenses, as shown in Figure 3.9. If you do not have a license to add, a 15-day evaluation license will be generated later and you can click on Next. If you do have a license, click on the Add button and enter the details, similar to what is shown in Figure 3.10. Click OK, then Next.

Now add an administrative user so that the initial policy can be constructed; see Figure 3.11. (The role of this administrative user is described in Chapter 4.) Click OK, then Next.

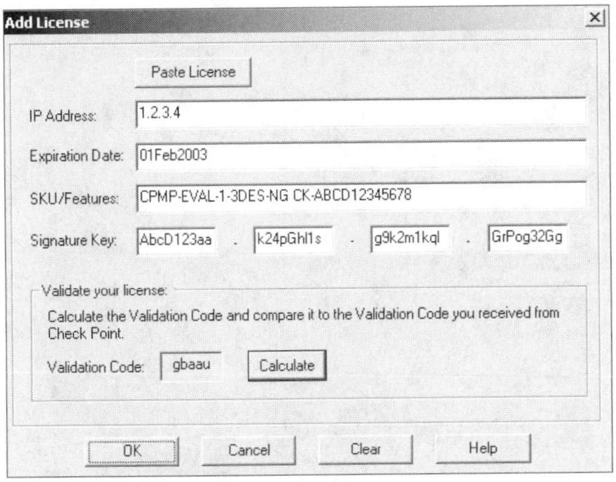

Figure 3.10   Adding a new license

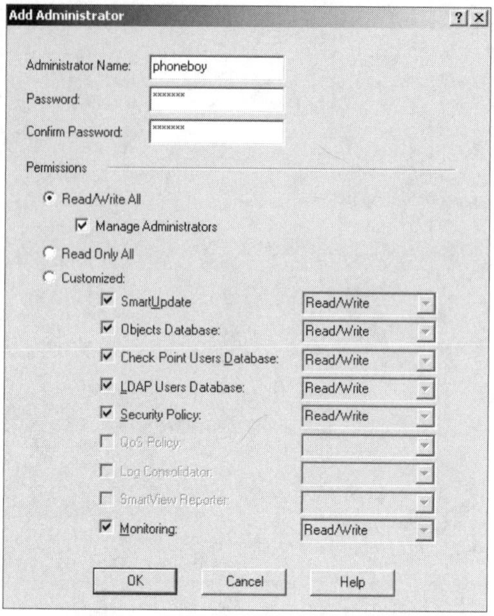

Figure 3.11   Adding a new administrator

You want to add the IP addresses of any client machines that will have the SMART Clients loaded on them and will require access to the management station, as shown in Figure 3.12. The local management console is already included, so you need not specify it here. Click Next.

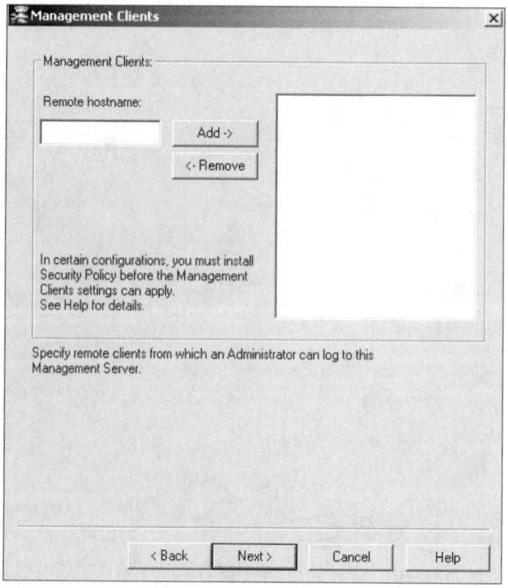

Figure 3.12   Adding remote management IP addresses

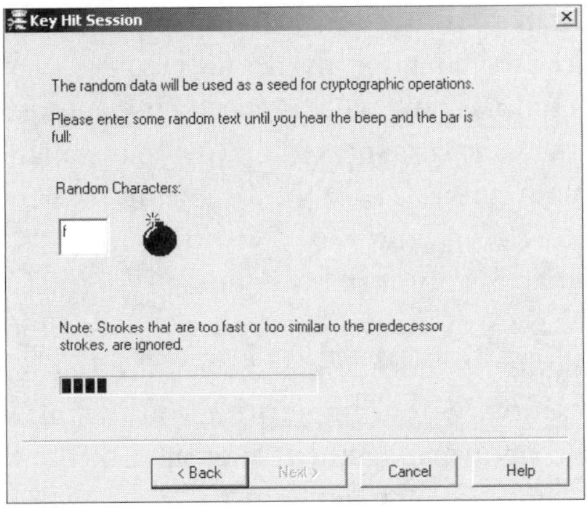

Figure 3.13   Random keystroke session

You are then prompted to type a bunch of random keystrokes, as shown in Figure 3.13. This seeds the random number generator for internal certificate authority functions, such as those needed by the Secure Internal Communication (SIC) process, which is described in more detail in Chapter 7. Click Next.

You need to click on the Initialize and Start Certificate Authority button, as shown in Figure 3.14. This is necessary for SIC to be used, which is needed to establish communication with other Check Point modules. The Internal Certificate Authority (ICA) is also used for issuing VPN-related certificates.

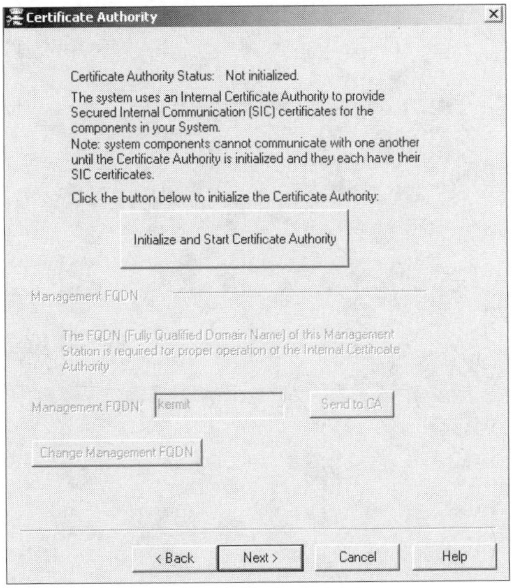

Figure 3.14   Establishing the Internal Certificate Authority

If you did not install a license, you will see a dialog similar to Figure 3.15. A 15-day evaluation license generated by the software is used in this case. Get a permanent license as soon as possible if you see this message.

In this example, the hostname picked up by the installation program was not a fully qualified domain name (FQDN). To ensure that the ICA will function correctly, you need to change the FQDN shown in the Certificate Authority window to match what is appropriate for your system. Click on the Change Management FQDN button. In the example shown in Figure 3.16, I have set the name to kermit.phoneboy.com. Click on Send to CA. Click on Next.

Now you are presented with a fingerprint you can use to validate that you have connected to the right management station with the SMART Clients. An example is shown in Figure 3.17. Click Finish.

Figure 3.15   Dialog showing the 15-day evaluation license message

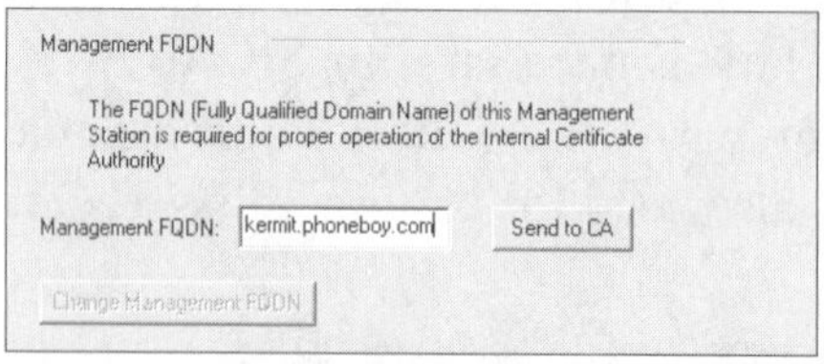

Figure 3.16   Changing the FQDN of the management station

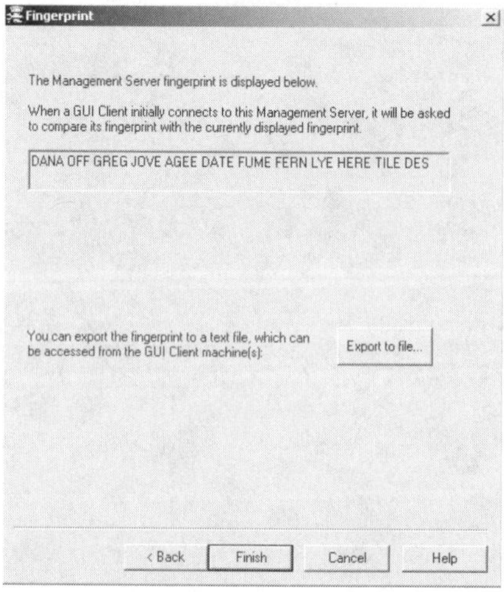

Figure 3.17   Fingerprint of the management station

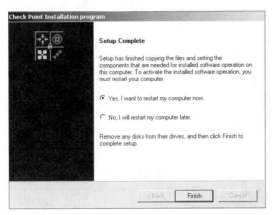

Figure 3.18 Installation completed

When the installation is completed, you will see a dialog similar to Figure 3.18. If you are going to install a hotfix (e.g., NG FP3 Hotfix-2 or a Hotfix Accumulator), do not reboot, and install it now. After the installation, reboot your computer. Otherwise, select the Yes radio button and reboot now.

Installing an NG FP3 firewall module on an IP350

In this example, we will use the installation wrapper for IPSO to load NG FP3 as a firewall module on an IP350. On other UNIX platforms, the installation wrapper presents a text-based installation screen where you can choose which package(s) you want to install. In IPSO, all of the packages are automatically loaded, but only SVN Foundation and VPN-1/FireWall-1 are *enabled* by default. The other packages may be enabled as necessary in Voyager. For the purposes of this example, we do not need to configure anything in Voyager because the default packages suffice.

If the packages were loaded by the command line (e.g., **newpkg**), you will need to log out of your terminal session and log back in as admin or root. If the command **echo $CPDIR** shows something like /opt/CPshared-50-03, you are ready to proceed. If not, the package load did not proceed correctly. In IPSO, ensure that CPShared and FireWall-1 are actually marked as *active*.

Now type the command **cpconfig**. You are then presented with a license agreement. Once you have read and accepted the license agreement, you are presented with several choices for installation type, as shown below.

```
Select installation type:
- - - - - - - - - - - - --

(1) Enforcement Module.
(2) Enterprise Management.
```

```
(3) Enterprise Management and Enforcement Module.
(4) Enterprise Log Server.
(5) Enforcement Module and Enterprise Log Server.
```

```
Enter your selection  (1-5/a-abort) [1]:
```

Since this will be a firewall module only, select Enforcement Module, option 1.
   Next, you will be asked:

```
Would you like to install a Check Point clustering product (CPHA,
CPLS or State Synchronization)? (y/n) [n] ?
```

If you plan to install this firewall module in a HighAvailability (HA) pair using
VRRP, IP Clustering) or a Check Point HA product,[4] you should select "yes"
here. In this example, I would choose "no" because the module I am installing
this on will not be used for HA.
   Next, you will be told several things.

```
IP forwarding disabled
Hardening OS Security: IP forwarding will be disabled during boot.
Generating default filter
Default Filter installed
Hardening OS Security: Default Filter will be applied during boot.
```

In order, these items mean the following.

1. The system has disabled IP forwarding. This means that the underlying
   operating system will not forward packets that aren't destined for itself.
2. To go one step further, the system has disabled IP forwarding at boot
   time. This means the system will not forward packets until FireWall-1 has
   loaded with a nondefault security policy.
3. The system has loaded a default filter, which blocks all traffic to the firewall unless it is a response to a valid connection originating from the firewall.
4. The system will load this new default filter at boot time.

   The next step is to enter the licenses. The following example shows how to
enter the license and the details manually. Central licensing is discussed in
Chapter 7.

---

4. Check Point HA products, except those built into VPN-1/FireWall-1 or IPSO itself, are not available on
   Nokia platforms. This is for the more general case on other UNIX-type platforms.

```
Configuring Licenses...
========================
Host              Expiration  Signature                    Features

Note: The recommended way of managing licenses is using SmartUpdate.
cpconfig can be used to manage local licenses only on this machine.

Do you want to add licenses (y/n) [y] ? y

Do you want to add licenses [M]anually or [F]etch from file: m
IP Address: 1.2.3.4
Expiration Date: 01Feb2003
Signature Key: dfMBwazxr-tbbHRxN2v-DnxgHNJkA-LQAXycV3i
SKU/Features: CPMP-EVAL-1-IKE3DES-NG CK-ABCD1234567890

License was added successfully
```

Now you have to generate some system entropy, that is, the random pool that will be used for various cryptographic functions, including authentication between the firewall and management server. Randomly press letter keys at random intervals until the system tells you to stop.

```
Configuring Random Pool...
===========================
You are now asked to perform a short random keystroke session.
The random data collected in this session will be used in
various cryptographic operations.

Please enter random text containing at least six different
characters. You will see the '*' symbol after keystrokes that
are too fast or too similar to preceding keystrokes. These
keystrokes will be ignored.

Please keep typing until you hear the beep and the bar is full.

    [...................]

Thank you.
```

Finally, you must establish a one-time password for SIC, which will be used to authenticate the management station to the firewall module. Once this one-time password is used, all further authentication will be done with certificates.

```
Configuring Secure Internal Communication...
=============================================
The Secure Internal Communication is used for authentication between
Check Point components
```

```
Trust State: Uninitialized
Enter Activation Key:
Again Activation Key:

The Secure Internal Communication was successfully initialized
```

A new default filter will be compiled—one that permits management traffic to the firewall module. This policy will apply until the first real security policy is installed from the management station.

```
initial_module:
Compiled OK.

Hardening OS Security: Initial policy will be applied
until the first policy is installed
```

Finally, you must reboot the system to properly install FireWall-1.

```
In order to complete the installation
you must reboot the machine.
Do you want to reboot? (y/n) [y] ? y
```

Upgrading from FireWall-1 4.1

Upgrading FireWall-1 from one release to the next has never been a walk in the park unless you have a relatively simple configuration. My advice is to *not* attempt to upgrade. The reason is simple: Quite a lot has changed between FireWall-1 4.1 and FireWall-1 NG, more so than, say, an upgrade from version 3.0 to version 4.1. In the vast majority of cases, you are much better off simply recreating the configuration from scratch.

In case you decide to ignore my advice and attempt to upgrade anyway, here are a few pointers.

1. Make sure that you've upgraded to 4.1 SP6 before attempting any upgrades. Upgrades from previous versions are known to fail. NG AI supposedly supports upgrades from 4.1 SP5 and above, but I have not tried that.

2. Before you even think about upgrading, make a backup of your current $FWDIR on your management station first. In fact, you might want to back up at each step *just in case*. If you upgrade to NG AI, Check Point will offer to make a backup of your management station before upgrading. Take advantage of that too.

3. Analyze all of your workstation objects. All object names should be fewer than 18 characters long and should start with a letter. Underscores were allowed in previous versions of FireWall-1 but are not allowed under NG.

4. Analyze all of your services, especially ones you have added. Compare the service names with a list of predefined services in the version of NG you plan to upgrade to. Upgrades to NG will fail if the services you have created happen to match a predefined service (either in name or in port). An easy way to get a list of predefined services is to load the appropriate version of the GUI client on a workstation and log in using the Demo mode or with the *local trick (see Chapter 4).

5. Check that all the policy names in your system start with a letter. Numbers were permitted in previous versions, but not in NG. The upgrade will succeed in this case, but you will have problems working with the policy—even to save it to a different name!

6. Remove any unnecessary policies and objects. The fewer policies that the upgrade process has to deal with, the better.

7. Remove the services VDO-live, cooltk, and the group CoolTalk. The conversion process will say they are being removed, but you will be asked to manually remove these services when you verify a policy. You won't be able to remove them because they won't be listed as services.

8. Obtain a copy of the Upgrade Verification Utilities, available from http://www.checkpoint.com/techsupport/downloadsng/utilities.html. These programs are designed to catch some of the items mentioned above and a few other things not mentioned here. There are pre-upgrade and post-upgrade utilities, both of which should be run at the appropriate time to ensure a smooth(er) upgrade.

Summary

Although this chapter did not cover every contingency or situation you may encounter during your installation, it provided you with a guided procedure for completing the initial installation of FireWall-1. Configuration of the rulebase and other options in FireWall-1 are covered in later chapters.

4

Building
Your Rulebase

This chapter covers how to build a basic rulebase. I begin by discussing how to set up access to the FireWall-1 Management GUIs (i.e., SMART Clients). I then discuss the different kinds of objects you can create. Next, the various components that make up your rulebase, including the rulebase properties and anti-spoofing, are explained. Finally, I cover the topic of making a rulebase, including certain rules that should appear in every rulebase.

By the end of this chapter, you should be able to:

- Understand what the Management GUIs do
- Control access to the Management GUIs
- Understand the order in which anti-spoofing, rulebase properties, and the rules themselves are actually applied
- Determine which rules should be in every rulebase
- Create a rulebase

The Management GUIs

The Management GUIs allow you to create and edit your security policy as well as view policy logs and system status. Several distinct applications make up the Management GUIs. In NG FP3, Check Point decided to rename all of the Management GUI client programs using the Smart moniker. To reduce confusion and to give a sense of familiarity for readers who are familiar with earlier versions of FireWall-1, I refer to these programs by both names in the list below and throughout the book. In NG AI, Check Point collectively refers to the Management GUIs as SmartConsole.

- *SmartDashboard/Policy Editor:* Allows you to view and modify your security policy. This application is covered in this chapter.

- *SmartTracker/Log Viewer:* Allows you to view your firewall logs. This application is covered in Chapter 5.
- *SmartView Status/Status Manager:* Allows you to view basic system status and display alerts from your firewalls. This application is also covered in Chapter 5.
- *SecureClient Packaging Tool:* Allows you to create custom Secure Client installation bundles. This application is covered in Chapter 12.
- *SmartUpdate/SecureUpdate:* Allows you to manage Check Point software installed on remote modules. This application is covered in Chapter 7.
- *SmartView Monitor/Traffic Monitoring:* Allows you to get real-time data on the amount and kinds of traffic going through the firewall. Since this application relates to FloodGate-1, this application is not covered in this book.
- *Reporting Tool:* Allows you to run reports on logged firewall activity.
- *User Monitor:* Allows you to monitor which users are currently using Secure Client and data about those clients.
- *Large Scale Manager:* Allows you to view the status and install policy on a large number of gateways. This application is discussed in Chapter 7, but it is not explicitly covered.

The SMART Clients, as Check Point has referred to them since FireWall-1 NG FP3, view data stored on the management console via a TCP connection on port 18190. They do not store any information locally except for preferences for the application itself. The most common (and recommended) platform on which to run the GUIs is Windows (95, 98, NT, or 2000). A Motif version exists for Solaris. It uses the same code as the Windows platform and is nearly identical in appearance, but it runs on an emulation layer that, at least in the past, has been slow and known to be buggy and leak memory. To add insult to injury, Check Point charges extra for the use of this GUI, reportedly because Check Point has to pay a licensing fee to the company that provides the emulation layer.

Introducing SmartDashboard (a.k.a. Policy Editor)

Before discussing how to control access to the administrative interfaces, I want to briefly talk about the most often used administrative interface: SmartDashboard (a.k.a. the Policy Editor). The introduction of the NG version of FireWall-1 brought forth massive changes in all the Management GUI applications, but the most striking changes are in what Check Point now calls SmartDashboard. Figure 4.1 shows a sample of how it looks after you initially authenticate.

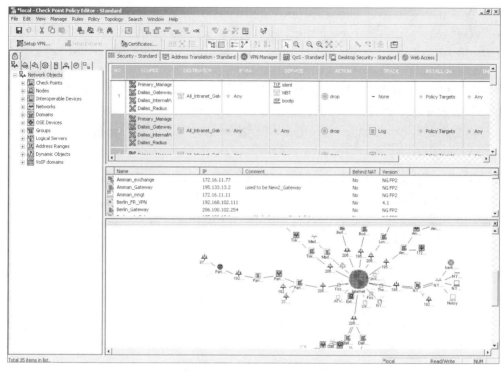

Figure 4.1   SmartDashboard

The familiar toolbar and menus are along the top. On the left, you see what is referred to as the *objects tree*. From here, you can see all the different types of objects, each in its own tab. Within these tabs, you can view the objects in a hierarchical fashion as well as create and edit the objects by right-clicking on the object or category and selecting the appropriate menu options. You can also drag and drop objects from this area into the rulebase, which is the top window in the main portion of the screen with headings such as Source, Destination, Service, Action, and so on.

Just below the rulebase, there is an area called the *objects list*. As you change to different categories in the objects tree, the objects list changes to give you a summary listing of all the objects of that category. Like the objects tree, you can right-click to create or edit an object as well as drag and drop objects into the rulebase.

Below the objects list is the Visual Policy Editor (VPE). From here, you can see the various objects you have created and how they interrelate with one another. You can move objects around in this view and connect them to other objects, creating a network map similar to what you would see in Visio or similar applications.

When you create gateways and define the interfaces they have, pseudo-objects get created for each network. VPE allows you to "actualize" these pseudo-objects into real objects by right-clicking on the object and selecting Actualize. This is one of my favorite features of VPE. Another nice thing is that VPE can be undocked from the main Policy Editor screen to give the other parts of the Policy Editor more room.

The downside to VPE is that it costs extra—it is not included with a basic FireWall-1 license.

Configuring Management Users via `fwm` or `cpconfig`

It is important to note that the users mentioned in this section can authenticate only to the Management GUIs. They do not in any way correspond to specific user accounts on the operating system or to users who authenticate for other services through the firewall. The latter type of users is discussed in Chapter 8.

In order to configure users for the Management GUIs, you can do one of the following things.

- Add users via **cpconfig**.
- Run **fwm -a** on the command line.
- Add administrative users via the Policy Editor.

> NOTE! The user database in the Policy Editor is different from the database maintained by `cpconfig` or `fwm`. If a user exists in both databases, the user in the `fwm` database takes precedence.

The permissions you can enter depend on which version of FireWall-1 you are using. You can assign permissions to not only FireWall-1/VPN-1 functions but also to other applications in the Check Point Suite. If you add a user via **cpconfig** on Windows NT, a screen that looks like Figure 4.2 appears (see the next subsection).

If you add a user via the command line, you will be prompted for the same permissions. Note that while I am using **fwm** commands in the following example, you would see essentially the same behavior if you ran **cpconfig** and selected the appropriate option to add users.

```
# fwm -a
Administrator name: dwelch
Password: abc123
Verify Password: abc123
Permissions for all Management Clients (Read/[W]rite All,
[R]ead Only All, [C]ustomized) w
```

```
Administrator dwelch was added successfully and has
Read/Write permission to all management clients
```

The preceding example creates a user who can do anything. The user being created in the following example can perform limited functions.

```
# fwm -a
Administrator name: jerald
Password: def456
Verify Password: def456
Permissions for all Management Clients (Read/[W]rite All,
[R]ead Only All, [C]ustomized) c
      Permissions for SecureUpdate (Read/[W]rite,
      [R]ead Only, [N]one) r
      Permissions for Check Point Users Database (Read/[W]rite,
      [R]ead Only) w
      Permissions for LDAP Users Database (Read/[W]rite,
      [R]ead Only, [N]one) w
      Permissions for Security Policy (Read/[W]rite,
      [R]ead Only, [N]one) w
      Permissions for QoS Policy (Read/[W]rite, [R]ead Only, [N]one) n
      Permissions for Monitoring (Read/[W]rite, [R]ead Only, [N]one) n
Administrator jerald was added successfully and has
Read Only permissions for SecureUpdate
Read/Write permissions for Check Point Users Database
Read/Write permissions for LDAP Users Database
Read/Write permissions for Security Policy
```

A password must be no more than eight characters in length. If you want to change the password of an existing user, run **fwm -a** again or use **cpconfig** to make the change. Table 4.1 lists some of the other command-line options for the **fwm** command.

Table 4.1   Command-line options for fwm

Flag	Description
-a foo	Adds or updates the username foo
-s abc123	Sets the user's password to abc123 (requires -a)
-r foo	Removes the user foo
-p	Prints a list of administrative (GUI) users
-g rulebase.W	Imports the file rulebase.W into the rulebases.fws file, which contains all the rulebases on your management console

Configuring Management Users via Policy Editor

In the NG version of FireWall-1, Check Point added the ability to manage management users via the Policy Editor application. You do this by either pulling down the Users and Administrator option from the Manage menu or clicking on the following icon in the objects tree: ⌗ . If you did the latter, find the Administrators subtree, right-click with your mouse, and pull down New Administrator. If you did the former, you will see a screen like Figure 4.2. From here, push the New button and select Administrators. Either set of steps will get you to Figure 4.3.

Figure 4.2 Managing users and administrators

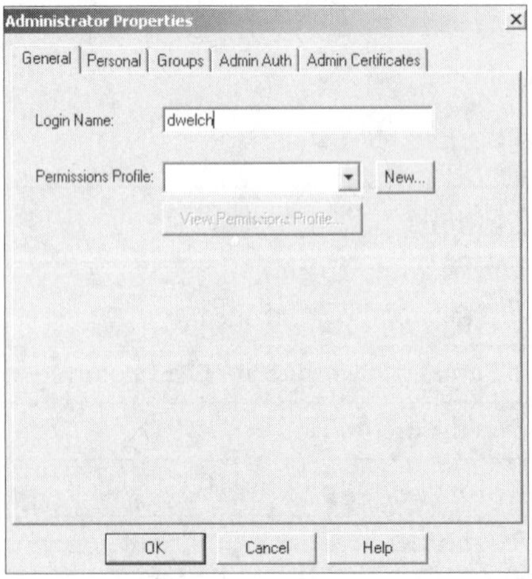

Figure 4.3 Administrator Properties, General tab

The login name is the name by which the user identifies him- or herself when logging into an administrative GUI. A permissions profile determines what permissions this administrative user has. Since no permissions profiles exist, we must create a new one. Click on the New button in the Administrator Properties window. Figures 4.4 and 4.5 show the Permissions Profile Properties, General tab and Permissions tab, respectively; these are fairly self-explanatory.

NOTE!   Administrative users cannot have the same name as normal users. They also cannot function as normal users (e.g., in user authentication).

WARNING!   Be sure you get your permissions profile correct the first time. Once you create it, you will have no way to edit or remove it!

Figure 4.4   Permissions Profile Properties, General tab

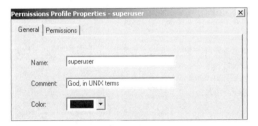

Figure 4.5   Permissions Profile Properties, Permissions tab

After creating your permissions profile, set the Personal options for the administrative user, as shown in Figure 4.6.

The important thing to set here is the expiration date for the user. Optionally, you can specify a comment or color. I prefer to put the real name associated with the user as a comment, but you can do anything you like.

The next things to configure are the groups this user is in, how this user authenticates, and the user's certificate. These are shown in Figures 4.7 through 4.9. The authentication types shown in Figure 4.8 are explained in Chapter 8.

Figure 4.6   Administrator Properties, Personal tab

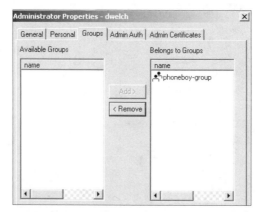

Figure 4.7   Administrator Properties, Groups tab

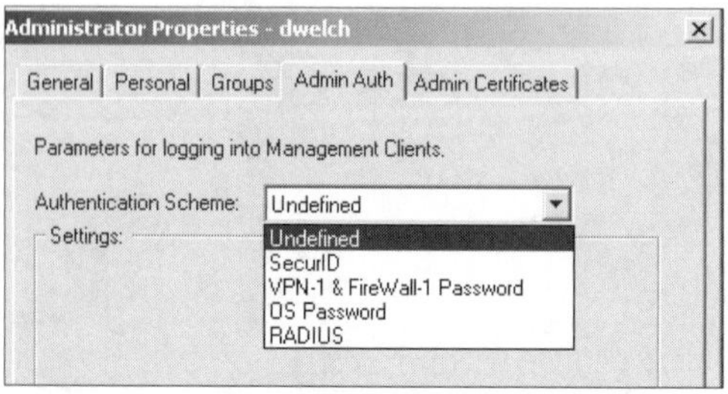

Figure 4.8   Administrator Properties, Admin Auth tab

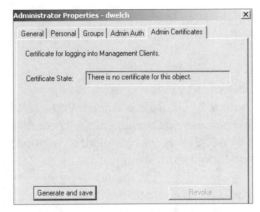

Figure 4.9   Administrator Properties, Admin Certificates tab

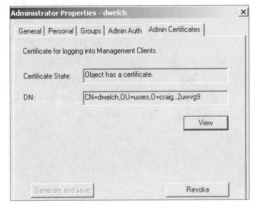

Figure 4.10   Administrator Properties, Admin
Certificates tab with certificate defined

When an administrative user has a certificate defined, the screen will look similar to Figure 4.10. The user presents that certificate during the initial authentication process with the GUI. If both an authentication scheme and a certificate are defined, either one can be used to authenticate to the Management GUIs.

Configuring Which Hosts Can Use Management GUIs

Once you know how to create a specific user for the Management GUIs, you need to tell your management console which IP addresses are allowed to use them. The IPs that are allowed to connect are configured in the file $FWDIR/ conf/gui-clients. The file contains a simple list: one IP address or DNS hostname per line. You can specify a range of IP addresses using a * wildcard (e.g., 192.168.0.*).

The localhost (i.e., the management console) is always allowed to connect regardless of the contents of this file, although a proper username and password must still be entered.

> NOTE! Where the management console and firewall module are on the same system, if you use the "Accept VPN-1 & FireWall-1 control connections" property (discussed later in this chapter) to permit access via the SMART Clients, you will need to reinstall your security policy before any changes to $FWDIR/conf/gui-clients will take effect.

> NOTE! When you use * as a wildcard in $FWDIR/conf/gui-clients, the "Accept VPN-1 & FireWall-1 control connections" property will not allow access to the management station. An explicit rule must be created, similar to what Figure 4.38 shows later in this chapter.

Being able to manage your security policy from *any* machine on your internal network may be desirable. Listing all possible IPs your clients may come from may not be. A highly recommended way to get around the limitation is to install an SSH server on the management console and use port forwarding on the SSH client. Port forwarding works by forwarding data from a local port to the remote host or port. On your SSH client, you would configure the port forwarding as follows:

• Local port 18190
• Remote hostname is management-console
• Report port is 18190

In your GUI, you would connect to localhost (127.0.0.1) instead of the management console's hostname or IP. Your SSH client will forward the communication over the SSH connection (which is, of course, encrypted) to the management console. The SSH daemon on the management console will then send the connection to port 18190 on the localhost. The management console will see the connection coming from localhost, which is always allowed.

Now you can effectively manage your FireWall-1 security policy from anywhere. While FireWall-1 now provides both strong encryption and authentication to the Management GUIs, this was not always the case. SSH also provides another encryption layer and strong authentication (using an RSA or DSA key). An alternative to SSH for people using Windows NT/2000 for a management console is ZeBeDee, which is similar to SSH in that it provides many of the same functions, but the client and the server run under both Windows and UNIX platforms.

Files Modified by SmartConsole

SmartConsole directly reads from and writes to the following files on the management console. If any of these files require manual editing, make sure that no one is connected via the GUI. You can do this by killing the `fwm` process via the command **`fw kill fwm`**.

- `$FWDIR/conf/objects_5_0.C`: Your network objects and services
- `$FWDIR/conf/rulebases_5_0.fws`: Your FireWall-1/VPN-1 rulebases
- `$FWDIR/conf/slprulebases_5_0.fws`: Your Desktop Security policies for SecureClient (see Chapter 12)
- `$FWDIR/conf/fgrulebases_5_0.fws`: Your FloodGate-1 policies
- `$FWDIR/conf/fwauth.NDB*`: Your user database and encryption keys[1]

The Management GUI also reads from, but does not directly write to:

- `$FWDIR/log/fw.log`: Security policy log
- `$FWDIR/log/fw.alog`: Accounting log
- `$FWDIR/log/fw.vlog`: Active log
- `$FWDIR/log/fw.*ptr`: Log pointer files

SmartDashboard/Policy Editor Restrictions

Only one user can be logged in to the Security Policy Editor in read-write mode at any given time. This prevents multiple managers from overwriting each other's changes. This also means that a user with only Users-Edit privileges can prevent an administrator with read-write from logging in using read-write mode. When this occurs, you will get the error message shown in Figure 4.11.

Figure 4.11 Logging into Management GUI when another administrator is connected

---

1. On UNIX/IPSO platforms, `fwauth.NDB` is simply one file. On Windows NT, `fwauth.NDB` contains a number that points to a file named `fwauth.NDBx`.

GUI Demonstration Mode

If you have to demonstrate FireWall-1 and do not have easy access to a management console, you can use a demonstration mode built into the Security Policy Editor and the Log Viewer. If you are using a pre-FP2 version of FireWall-1 NG, you can log in with any username and password to hostname *local.

This demonstration mode allows you to work with the files installed in the same directory as your GUI. They are demo versions of `objects_5_0.C`, `rulebases_5_0.fws` and other files. Although not all parts of the GUI will be available in demonstration mode, it is perfect for demonstrating the GUI to others without having to use it on a live system.[2] It is also possible to edit objects via the GUI or replace the included demo files with your own. The files you need to modify include but may not be limited to the following.

- `rules.fws`: Contains all defined rulebases. It is exactly the same format as `$FWDIR/conf/rulebases.fws` on the management console.
- `objects.fws`: Contains all users and services. It is exactly the same format as `$FWDIR/conf/objects.C` on the management console.
- `users.fws`: Contains users and groups for the demo rulebases. Note that this file is of a different format than `$FWDIR/conf/fwauth.NDB`. To get a feel for the format, create some users in *local mode and view the file.
- `lv_recs.fws`: Contains demonstration log entries.

The Rulebase Components

A *rulebase* is a representation of a policy that determines who can do what and when. In SmartDashboard/Policy Editor, several elements make up this policy: objects, rules, topology, and the global properties. This section covers the creation and composition of these components.

Objects

You can create several types of objects in FireWall-1. The important ones for constructing an initial policy are covered here; others are covered elsewhere in the book.

Check Points and Nodes

In NG FP1 and previous versions, objects representing nodes running components of the Check Point Suite were grouped together with regular nodes as

---

2. Many of the screenshots generated for this book were done in demonstration mode.

workstation objects. Now Check Point has created a specific object type for these nodes. In general, objects of type Check Point are very similar to node objects and share many common attributes. Both types of objects are explained in this subsection.

You create Check Points or node objects by selecting network objects from the Manage menu. From here, click on the New button; you will then see Check Points, nodes, and other options. You can also click on this icon in the objects tree: 🖳. From here, you can select the appropriate type of object (Check Points, nodes, and so on). When you right-click on the appropriate object type, you will see a New option, where a number of different types of gateways are specified.

> NOTE! Throughout the text, I will interchange the terms *workstation object* and *node object*. They are the same.

Check Point Gateways

A Check Point gateway object is meant to define a multihomed node in your network running a Check Point product (e.g., FireWall-1). Figure 4.12 shows the main components of these objects. Note that other components make up a workstation object. These components are covered in other sections of the book as they are needed; only the critical ones are covered in this section.

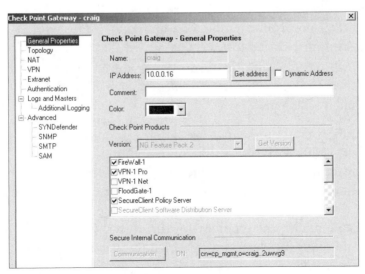

Figure 4.12   Check Point Gateway, General Properties frame

You can specify the following settings on the General Properties frame.

Name: Indicates the name you give the object. It should be a name that is different from any other object. Avoid the names fw or fw1 because they have been known to cause problems. If the name is greyed out as it is in Figure 4.12, it means the object was created as part of the initial installation and cannot be renamed or removed.

IP Address: Indicates the object's primary IP address. If you are defining a firewall, this IP address should be the external, routable IP address. The Get address button allows you to get an IP address if the object name is resolvable via DNS.

Dynamic Address: Indicates whether the object has a dynamic or fixed IP address. If the host represented by this object does not have a fixed IP address (i.e., the host gets the address via DHCP), check the Dynamic Address box. Note that this is not supported for management modules that manage other platforms.

Comment: Describes the object in more detail. This is optional.

Color: Specifies the object's color.

Check Point Products: Specifies the Check Point products installed on this node and the version. If the object shows the version dimmed out as in Figure 4.12, the object is for the management console itself and cannot be changed. When you update to different versions, this option will change accordingly.

Version: Specifies the FireWall-1 version. Use the Get Version button to obtain the version from a remote firewall module. This works only if Secure Internal Communication (SIC) is established.

Secure Internal Communication: Allows you to check the status of SIC, which is used to authenticate modules to each other. SIC is described in more detail in Chapter 7.

For any object that represents a firewall, the Topology frame is *vital* for correct operation. Figure 4.13 shows this configuration.

For newly created Check Point objects, click on Get Topology. A connection will be made to that node via SIC, assuming SIC is established. The appropriate node's interfaces will be queried and the routing table will be interrogated. This will be used to establish the topology for the object, which is necessary for setting up anti-spoofing and determining which interface is external.

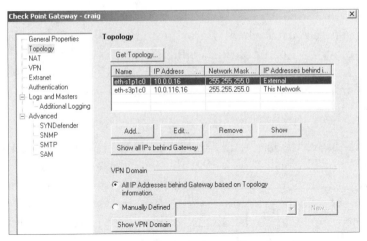

Figure 4.13   Check Point Gateway, Topology frame

> **NOTE!** The external interface for licensing purposes on node-limited licenses is taken from the definitions given in the Topology frame.

Topology settings include the following.

Name: Indicates the physical name of the interface. It should match the name given in `ifconfig -a` (in UNIX or IPSO) or `ipconfig` (in Windows NT).

IP Address: Indicates the interface's IP address. You must specify the interface's physical IP address. You cannot specify an interface alias.

Network Mask: Indicates the netmask for the interface's IP address.

IP Addresses behind interface: Shows what IP addresses are protected by this interface.

More details about the Topology frame of Figure 4.13 appear in the Topology and Anti-Spoofing subsection later in this chapter. The VPN Domain is discussed in Chapter 11.

Check Point Nodes

Check Point nodes are similar to Check Point gateway objects except that they are not multihomed machines. They are typically used for management consoles and machines running Check Point Secure Server. For these objects, the General Properties section is generally the only one that requires configuration. Topology is not relevant on nodes without more than one interface.

Gateway Clusters

Gateway clusters are used when two or more firewall modules participate in a High Availability or Load Sharing configuration. Nodes that participate in a gateway cluster have "shared" properties, which are defined in the gateway cluster object. These objects are discussed in more detail in Chapters 11 and 13.

Embedded Devices

These are hardware devices that run an "embedded" version of Check Point FireWall-1. As of FireWall-1 NG FP2, the only devices supported here are the Nokia IP51 and certain Xylan switches. Nokia has discontinued the IP51, and Xylan no longer sells the embedded version of FireWall-1 in its switches. Therefore, this object type will not be discussed. However, the configuration for these objects is similar to other Check Point gateways.

Externally Managed Gateways and Nodes

These types of objects are identical to regular Check Point gateways and nodes except that these are objects not managed by your current management console. You would define these if you were trying to set up a VPN with another site that also ran Check Point FireWall-1 (4.0 or later).

Node Gateways and Hosts

These are objects for nodes that do not run Check Point FireWall-1 and will not interoperate with Check Point VPN functions. For node host objects, only the general properties are relevant. For node gateway objects, the topology is also relevant, but only if you are using VPE.

Network

The network object is used to specify a network or a subnet thereof. The IP address and netmask define the network, as shown in Figure 4.14.

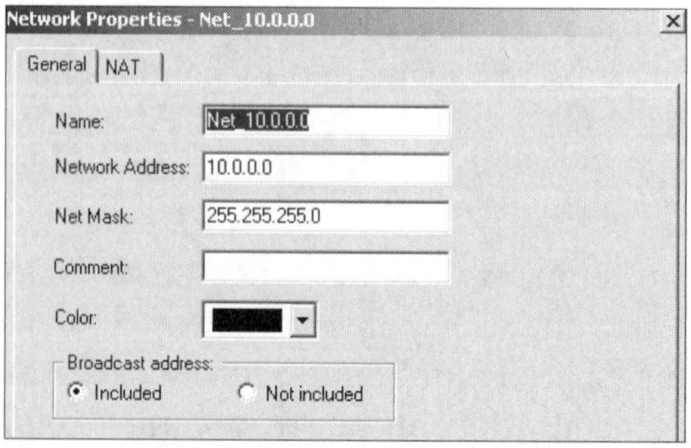

Figure 4.14 Network Properties, General tab

The General tab settings for the Network Properties section include the following.

> **Name:** Indicates the name you give the network.
>
> **Network Address:** Indicates the network's IP address. You should use the first IP address of the network.
>
> **Net Mask:** Indicates the network's netmask.
>
> **Comment:** Describes the network in more detail.
>
> **Color:** Specifies the object's color.
>
> **Broadcast address:** Determines whether or not to include the broadcast address of the network in the network definition.

The NAT tab for the Network Properties section is discussed in Chapter 10.

> NOTE! You are not allowed to create a network object with a netmask of 255.255.255.255. You must create these kinds of objects as workstation objects.

Domain

The domain object is used to specify a particular DNS domain. FireWall-1 determines whether an IP address fits within this domain by performing a reverse DNS lookup on the appropriate IP address (i.e., it performs an IP-to-name translation). This means that the host that enforces the security policy must be able to perform DNS queries. If it cannot do so for whatever reason, that IP address is not considered part of this domain. To specify a particular domain, provide a domain name beginning with a dot (.). For example, to specify phoneboy.com as a domain name, use ".phoneboy.com".

Domain objects are not recommended because DNS is typically not considered a reliable source of information (i.e., it can easily be spoofed), although I suppose once the Secure DNS extensions are widely deployed, this will be less of an issue. However, domain objects also cause a performance hit for all connections because their IP addresses must be looked up.

OSE Device

OSE device object types are used only when you want to manage an access control list on a router or use the Check Point FireWall-1 features that can be embedded into certain vendors' switches. These features are not in wide use and therefore are not covered in this book. Unless you plan to use these features, you will not need to create these types of objects.

Interoperable Device

Interoperable devices are ones that will participate in a VPN with your Check Point gateway and are otherwise identical to node gateway objects.

Groups

Group objects combine multiple objects so you can refer to them as a single entity. For example, if the network objects net-10.0.10.0-24 and net-10.0.11.0-24 represent your internal network, you can group them together and call them internal-net. An example of a simple group is shown in Figure 4.15.

Check Point added a new type of group in the NG version of FireWall-1: group with exclusion. This allows you to exclude items in one group from another group. For example, if you wanted to create a network object that represented all the hosts in your internal network except for a few restricted hosts, you would create two simple groups: one for your internal network (internal-networks) and one for your restricted hosts (restricted-hosts). You could then create a group with exclusion of the form "internal-networks *except for* restricted-hosts." A sample group with exclusion is shown in Figure 4.16.

Exclusion groups also allow you to exclude from the Any group, so you can define the Internet as "Any *except for* internal-networks."

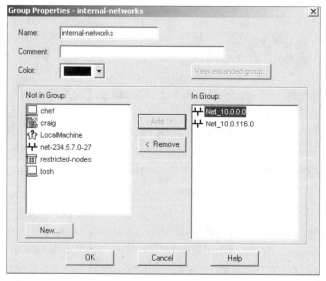

Figure 4.15   Simple group

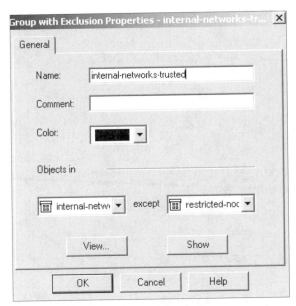

Figure 4.16   Group with Exclusion Properties

Address Range

Address range objects are used to define a range of addresses. They cannot be used for any purposes other than address translation rules. These objects are discussed in Chapter 10.

Services

You can create seven types of services: TCP, Compound TCP, UDP, RPC, ICMP, DCE-RPC, or Other. Similar to network objects, you can also group these services. Most services you will need are already predefined in FireWall-1, but sometimes you will need to define your own.

You can create your own service by selecting Services from the Manage menu, then clicking on the New button and choosing the appropriate type of service. Or you can click on this icon in the objects tree: ⬦. From here, right-click on the appropriate type of service, and select New. Figure 4.17 shows a definition for SSH.

The General tab settings for the TCP Service Properties section include the following.

> **Name:** Indicates the name you give the service. The port number can automatically be filled in with the Get button (see below) if the name matches the service's file entry on the management console.

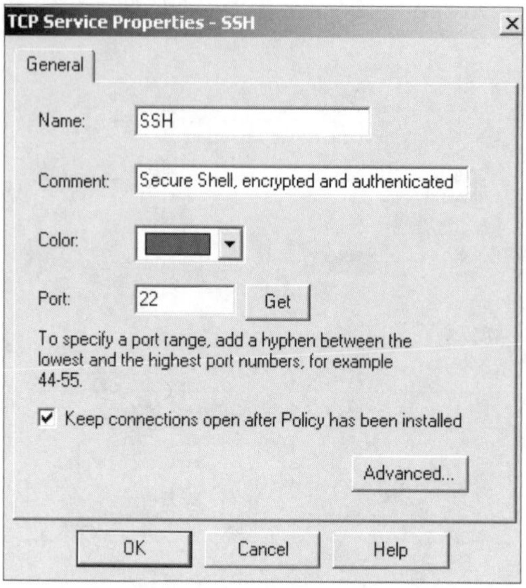

Figure 4.17   TCP Service Properties

Comment: Describes the service in more detail.

Color: Specifies the object's color.

Port: Indicates the port number that corresponds to the service. In the case shown in Figure 4.17, it is 22. You can also specify a port range (x-y) as well as ports above or below a certain number (e.g., >1024, <1024). The Get button attempts to resolve the service name against the management console's services file (`/etc/services` for UNIX platforms, `%SystemRoot%\system32\ drivers\etc\services` for NT platforms).

The Advanced button brings up some additional options, shown in Figure 4.18.

The additional options include those listed below.

Source port: Specifies the source port (the port the client uses to connect to the service) or range of source ports permitted by this service. Normally, any source port is allowed. However, if you want to restrict the source port to a specific range, you can do that by using this setting.

Protocol Type: Specifies the protocol type. For most services, this is left as None. Services that require special treatment that FireWall-1 supports are specified here. Supported protocols include DNS, FTP, FW1_CVP, H.323, HTTP, IIOP, Netshow, PNA, Rshell, RTSP, SMTP, SQLNET2, and Winframe. If you are using this service in conjunction with Content Security, set the protocol type accordingly (see Chapter 9).

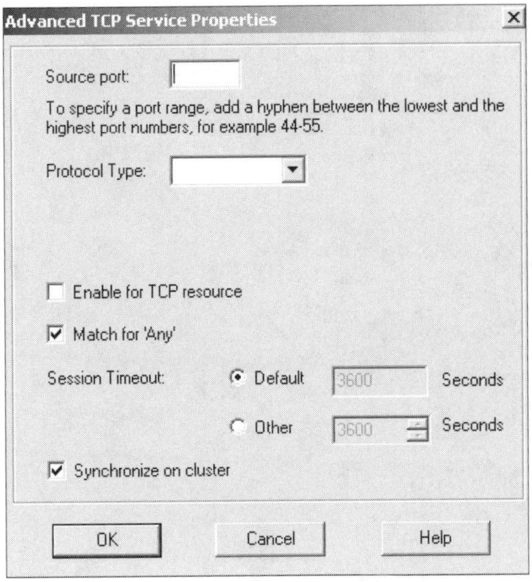

Figure 4.18   Advanced TCP Service Properties

Enable for TCP resource: Indicates whether or not you wish to use the Content Security features of FireWall-1 on this particular TCP service. If you do, this option will need to be checked. See Chapter 9 for more details.

Match for 'Any': Indicates whether the service will be included in the definition for the Any service. When a rule specifies the Any service, services with this checkbox selected will be included in that definition. If you want to allow the service to be included in the definition only when explicitly listed in a rule, uncheck this box.

Session Timeout: Specifies the amount of inactivity permitted for this service before FireWall-1 expires the connection from the connection tables. Note that when a session is removed from the connection tables, any further traffic on that connection will result in TCP Packet Out of State messages in the logs (see Chapter 6). The timeout can be set to Default, which sets the timeout to use either the timeout specified in the Global Properties screen (see Global Properties later in this chapter) or a service-specific value. The maximum amount of time you can specify is 86,400 seconds (24 hours). The minimum amount of time you can specify is 60 seconds.

Synchronize on cluster: Synchronizes connections using this service to other members in the cluster when using State Synchronization (see Chapter 13). To increase performance, this should be disabled for services that generate a large number of connections in a short period of time (e.g., HTTP).

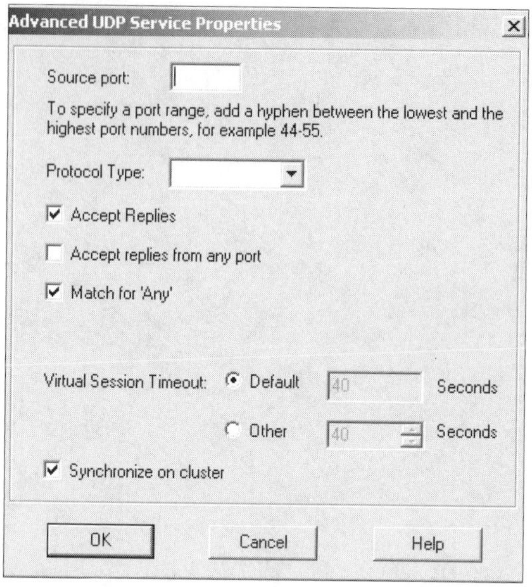

Figure 4.19 Advanced UDP Service Properties

For UDP connections, the options on the General tab are the same as those for TCP. Clicking on the Advanced button brings up some additional options (see Figure 4.19), most of which are similar to the properties for TCP services.

However, some advanced options for UDP connections are different, as listed below.

Accept Replies: This option enables FireWall-1's Virtual Session capability for this UDP service. If a client initiates a UDP packet from source port X to the server on destination port Y, packets that come from the server from source port Y to the client on destination port X are considered part of the same "virtual" session. Most well-behaved UDP-based applications operate in this manner. If this feature is not desired for this particular UDP service, then by unchecking the box, you prevent reply packets from being accepted unless an explicit rule is defined permitting it.

Accept Replies from Any Port: Some UDP-based applications do not follow the model in the previous option but instead generate a reply packet from a different source port (i.e., a reply packet comes from source port Z instead of Y as above). Generally, you should keep this option disabled, but if you run into a UDP-based application with this behavior, check this box.

Virtual Session Timeout: Unlike with TCP, there is no way for FireWall-1 to determine whether or not a UDP "session" has ended. Instead, FireWall-1

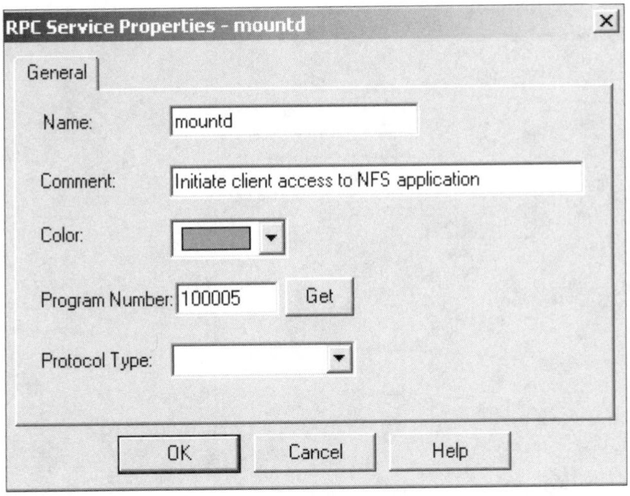

Figure 4.20　RPC Service Properties

assumes that if there has been no activity on that session for a period of time, the session is over. The timeout can be set to Default, which sets the timeout to use either the timeout specified in the Global Properties screen (see Global Properties later in this chapter) or a service-specific value. The maximum amount of time you can specify is 86,400 seconds (24 hours); the minimum is 10 seconds.

For RPC, you simply define a name and an RPC program number, as shown in Figure 4.20. The Get button acquires the needed information from the RPC file on a UNIX platform. Protocol type is currently empty, which could change in the future.

For services of type ICMP, you simply define a name, an ICMP type, and an ICMP code. The ICMP types and codes are defined in RFC792. For services of type Other, you need to write INSPECT code. These kinds of services are discussed in Chapter 14.

Time

Time objects are created to define different time periods of the day. These objects allow certain activities to take place at certain times of the day and/or on certain days but not others. You create these objects by selecting Time from the Manage menu or by selecting the clock icon in the objects tree, then right-clicking on Time and selecting New. Figure 4.21 shows an example of a time object.

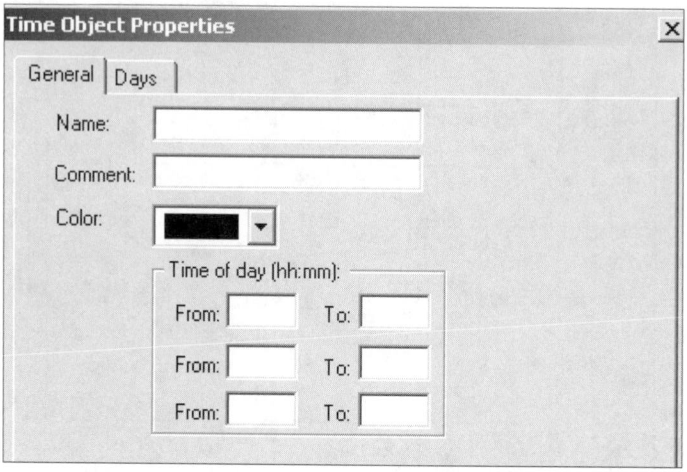

Figure 4.21   Time Object Properties, General tab

The General tab settings for the Time Object Properties section include the following.

Name: Indicates the name you give the time period.

Comment: Describes the time period in more detail.

Color: Specifies the object's color.

Time of day: Specifies up to three different time periods in a 24-hour format. Note that this controls only when the connection can *start;* if the connection continues past these time frames, it will still be allowed.

Figure 4.22 shows the Days tab. On the Days tab you can specify the following settings.

Days specification: "None" means every day. "Day in month" allows you to specify a specific date or dates in a particular month. "Day in week" allows you to specify particular days of the week.

Days in month: If you selected "Day in month," you can specify particular days in a month.

Day in week: If you selected "Day in week," you can specify certain days of the week.

Month: If you selected "Day in month," you can specify a specific month.

There is also a scheduled event type of time object, which is used specifically to tell Check Point when certain events should occur (e.g., log rotation). Figure 4.23 shows an example. You may set it for either a specific time or an interval of every *x* period of time.

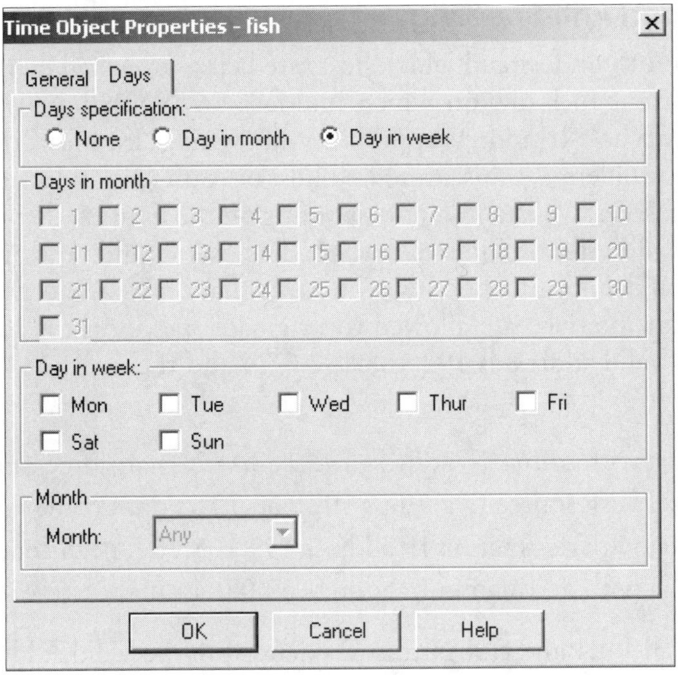

Figure 4.22   Time Object Properties, Days tab

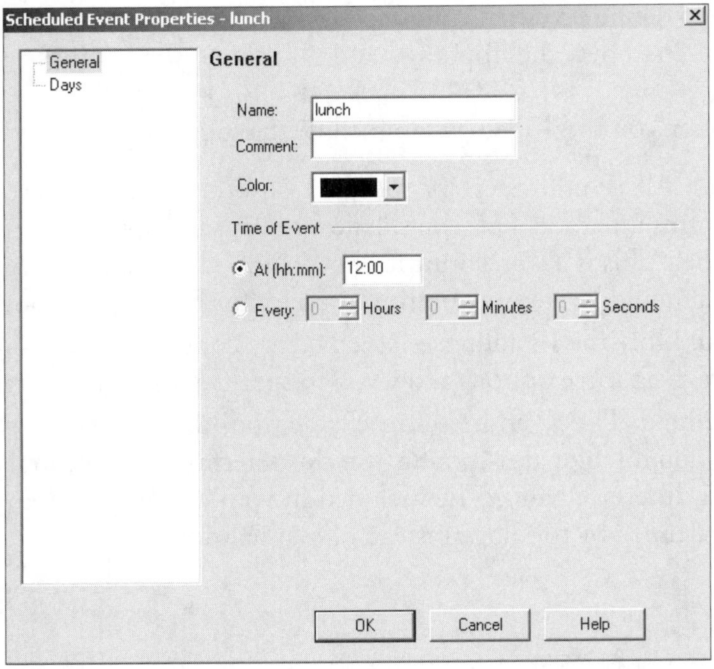

Figure 4.23   Scheduled Event Properties

Topology and Anti-Spoofing

It is important to understand which hosts are being protected by the firewall. It is also important to know on which interface any given host is supposed to appear. When a host IP address appears on the "wrong" interface, this is a potentially serious problem—a misconfigured host or router, or an intruder! To catch these sorts of issues, we establish anti-spoofing on the firewall, that is, preventing the use of IP addresses on interfaces where the hosts should not appear.

When you define anti-spoofing, you assert that only packets with source IPs defined for an interface are allowed to originate traffic on the interface.[3] For example, if a valid address is 192.168.182.0/24 and the interface is le0, the following are true.

- A packet with source IP address 192.168.182.4 can come into le0.
- A packet with source IP address 192.168.1.8 cannot come into le0.
- A packet with destination IP address 192.168.182.4 can come into le0.
- A packet with destination IP address 10.0.0.4 cannot come into le0.

In FireWall-1 4.1 and earlier, this was defined in the Valid Address setting in the Interface portion of the gateway object. In the NG version, the setting is now called Topology, and we define it in the Topology frame of the gateway object. Unlike the Valid Address setting in FireWall-1 4.1, the Topology setting is also used to define "external" interfaces, which is important for licensing.

Figure 4.24 shows the Topology and Anti-Spoofing settings for a specific interface.

The options on the Topology tab include the following.

External: All IP addresses *not* specified on other interfaces are considered valid on this interface. This is similar to the "others" option in FireWall-1 4.1 and earlier. This is also relevant for node-limited licenses in that it indicates no hosts should be counted on this interface for licensing purposes.

Internal: Only the IP addresses specified are considered valid on this interface. The next three options allow you to specify which IPs are valid.

Not Defined: The IP addresses reachable from this interface are undefined. This option disables anti-spoofing on this interface. In addition, any IPs behind this interface will *not* be included in your encryption domain, assuming it is defined by topology instead of manually.

---

3. This is different from FireWall-1 4.1, which also validated that a packet being *routed* to a specific interface was also valid. This caused all sorts of problems with address translation.

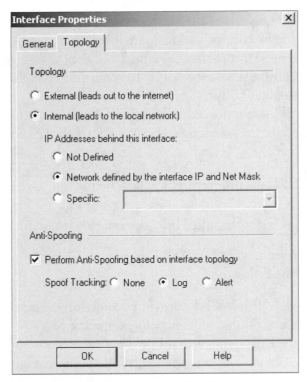

Figure 4.24 Interface Properties, Topology tab

Network defined by the interface IP and Net Mask: This option specifically means "the logical network this interface is on." It is defined by the interface's IP address and netmask per the configuration screen. All other networks are not considered valid. In FireWall-1 4.1 and earlier, this option was titled the more confusing This Net.

Specific: This option refers to a defined group of network objects (networks, hosts) that make up the valid addresses for this interface. This is typically used where there are multiple networks reachable from this interface.

Perform Anti-Spoofing based on interface topology: If this option is checked, anti-spoofing will be performed on this interface, assuming that Not Defined is not selected. If unchecked, anti-spoofing will not be performed on this interface. Spoof tracking can be set to None (no logging), Log, or Alert. If you enable anti-spoofing, it is *highly* recommended that you enable logging of this property. All anti-spoofing drops will log as Rule 0 (see Chapter 6). If you want to log IP Options drops, go to the Log and Alert frame of the Global Properties screen and enable IP Options Drop logging (see the next section).

Global Properties

The Properties screens control various parts of the rulebase. It is important to understand what these properties are and how they affect your rulebase. To access the global properties, select Global Properties from the Policy menu in SmartDashboard/Policy Editor.

All implied rules are enforced eitherbound (both inbound and outbound) and can be applied in the following ways.

- **First:** The property is applied before any rules listed in the rulebase.
- **Before Last:** The property is applied before the last rule listed in the rulebase.
- **Last:** The property is applied *after* the last rule listed in the rulebase.

The global properties for FireWall-1 are shown in Figure 4.25. The options available include the following.

Accept VPN-1 & FireWall-1 control connections: This option allows various FireWall-1 modules to communicate via FireWall-1 communication ports. A complete list of ports that FireWall-1 uses is covered in Tweaking the Global Properties later in this chapter, particularly in Figures 4.38 through 4.40.

Accept outgoing packets originating from gateway: This property refers to packets originated by the gateway itself (e.g., an administrator on the gateway executing **ssh** to a different host). This property eliminates the need to add an explicit rule to allow access from the firewall itself.

Accept RIP: If you are running Routing Information Protocol (RIP) on your firewall and you require the ability to communicate with other routers via RIP, you can select this property to permit the necessary traffic, although you can also create explicit rules. Most people who run dynamic routing protocols run Open Shortest Path First (OSPF), so this property can generally be safely disabled in the vast majority of cases. Note that enabling this property does not allow you to move RIP packets from one interface to another, nor does it allow RIP to function if your firewall does not have the appropriate routing daemon present and running.

Accept Domain Name over UDP (Queries): This option permits all UDP port 53 traffic from anywhere to anywhere. This is actually a very dangerous setting and should be disabled because non-DNS traffic (such as Back Orifice) could easily use UDP port 53. See FAQ 4.7 later in this chapter for information on how to enable DNS verification, which makes this property far less dangerous.

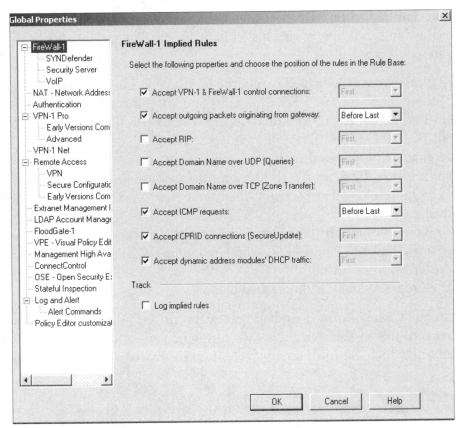

Figure 4.25   Global Properties, FireWall-1 Implied Rules frame

Accept Domain Name over TCP (Zone Transfer): This option is necessary only if your primary and secondary DNS servers are separated by your firewalls. As with the preceding option, this is a dangerous default that should be disabled unless DNS verification is enabled.

Accept ICMP requests: In order to accept reply packets for ICMP requests (e.g., an echo reply for an echo request), this property needs to be enabled. However, many people have found this property does not work properly.

Accept CPRID connections (SecureUpdate): This allows SmartUpdate/ SecureUpdate to remotely upgrade your firewall modules.

Accept dynamic address modules' DHCP traffic: This permits DHCP requests to originate from the firewall. It also allows the appropriate DHCP response packets into the firewall. This is useful if you are using modules with dynamic addressing.

Log implied rules: By checking this box, you indicate that anything enabled in this property screen should be logged. Anything that gets logged will show up as Rule 0.

IP Options are a rarely used part of the IP protocol. The features provided by IP Options allow, among other things, IP Spoofing. Most legitimate end-user applications do not use IP Options. As such, most firewalls automatically block packets with IP Options. FireWall-1 is no exception.

To enable IP Options drop logging, go to the Log and Alert frame, which is shown in Figure 4.26. Set the IP Options drop setting to Log (or Alert) if you want IP Options logging to occur. Other options on this screen are discussed in Chapter 5.

One other important set of properties to look at is the Policy Editor customizations shown in Figure 4.27. Note than in FireWall-1 NG FP1 and earlier, this option does not exist.

The properties include those listed below.

Create Check Point installed gateways using: Allows you to choose between the "classic" screens shown throughout this book and the "wizard" screens, which ask you a series of questions to answer when creating objects.

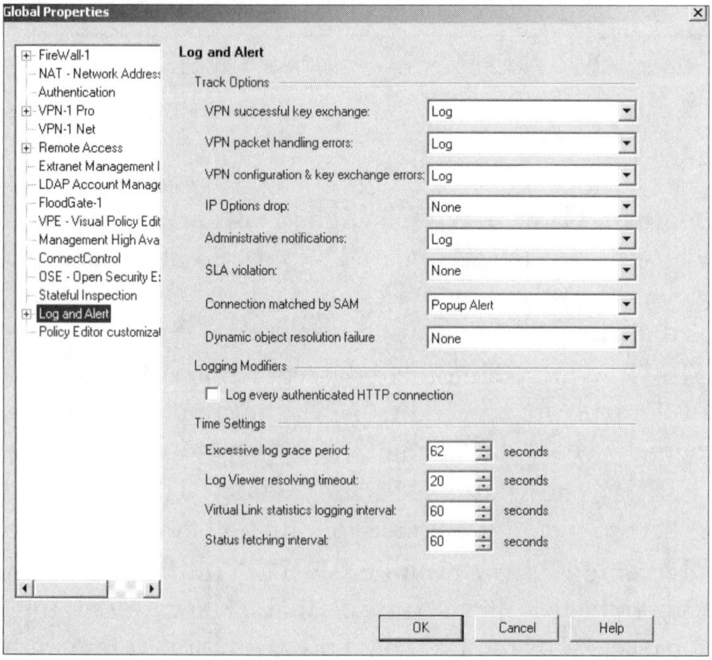

Figure 4.26   Global Properties, Log and Alert frame

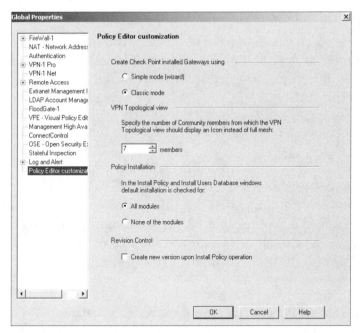

Figure 4.27   Global Properties, Policy Editor customization frame

VPN Topological view: Allows you to specify the number of objects that require separate representation in a meshed VPN configuration. This is relevant only when using VPN configurations in Simplified mode.

Policy Installation: Specifies whether or not all modules are selected for installation when you choose to install a new security policy to a firewall module.

Revision Control: Allows you to create a revision of your security policy each time it is loaded into a firewall module (see Chapter 7).

The Rulebase

In order to determine who can do what, you must create rules. The rules are created in terms of objects and services as defined in the previous section. Rules should be listed in the order you want them enforced. In the following subsections, I discuss the actual order in which rules are applied, but for the sake of discussion at this point, let's assume they will be enforced in the order shown in the rulebase.

The Parts of a Rule

Each rule has several elements. In many cases in this book, I will not show all the elements because they are not always relevant. However, in this section, I discuss all of them.

Source and Destination

In the Source and Destination parts of the rule, you input the hosts that will be allowed to originate a connection or will be an allowed destination for a connection. Multiple objects can be listed in this part of the rule. If there are multiple sources or destinations listed in a rule, they are treated as an OR, meaning that any host that matches will be allowed.

If Via

A VPN Community is specified in this column, which will be present when Simplified mode is enabled in the Global Properties screen for VPN-1 Pro. The If Via part of the rule indicates that this rule will apply if the connection is coming from or going to a member of the VPN Community specified (i.e., it will be encrypted or decrypted). If this column contains Any (the default), no encryption will be used for this rule. Chapter 11 covers this in more detail.

Service

In the Service part of the rule, you input the services that are allowed between the source(s) and destination(s) listed in the rule. If there are multiple services listed, they are treated as an OR, meaning that any service listed in the rule will match.

Action

If the source, destination, and services match, an action is applied. The Action part of the rule can have the following values.

- **Accept:** Allow the connection through the firewall.
- **Drop:** Do not allow the connection through the firewall; give no notification to the sender.
- **Reject:** Do not allow the connection through the firewall; notify the sender with a TCP Reset message or an ICMP Destination Unreachable message as appropriate.
- **User/Client/Session Auth:** Allow the connection through the firewall provided the user successfully authenticates. See Chapter 8 for more details on these actions.
- **Encrypt/Client Encrypt:** Allow the connection through the firewall and encrypt or decrypt the packet. This option will show up only if Traditional VPN mode is used and is covered in Chapters 11 and 12.

Track

After an action is taken on the packet, you need to determine how to log it. There are several options you can choose; more details about these options appear in Chapter 5.

- **None:** Do not log.
- **Log:** All available information about the packet is written to the log.
- **Account:** This is usually used with a rule using an action of accept. The number of bytes and length of the connection are logged to the accounting log file as well as a normal long log entry, which is written to the normal log. *Do not use this option lightly* because it can significantly increase the amount of CPU time FireWall-1 uses to log the information.
- **Alert/Mail Alert/SNMP Trap/User Defined:** Make a long log entry and execute an action to notify the administrator.

Install On

In the Install On part of the rule, you indicate which gateway(s) will be responsible for enforcing this rule. These can be gateways (the default), integrated firewalls, a specific target, or Src or Dst. Src causes the rule to be installed on all gateways and enforced only in the outbound direction. Dst causes the rule to be installed on all gateways and enforced only in the inbound direction.

Time

In the Time part of the rule, you select a time object that represents when this rule will apply. If the time/date does not match, the rule does not apply.

Comment

The Comment part of the rule contains a description of the rule. In some versions of FireWall-1, a carriage return in a comment can cause problems, so try to avoid using carriage returns. Also, it is unwise to use characters that are not typically ASCII characters (like umlauts) because they can sometimes cause a policy installation to fail.

Sample Rules

Figure 4.28 shows a sample rule that is fairly common in most installations. This rule permits the internal network to use HTTP, HTTPS, and SSH to any host not on the internal network.[4] Another common rule is shown in Figure 4.29.

---

4. You might wonder why I did not choose Any in the Destination field. Typically, you do not need the firewall to reach the internal network. Any, although a setting even I use in a rulebase from time to time, is considered insecure. For more details about this setting, consult the Black Hat 2000 Security briefing on FireWall-1, which can be found at http://www.dataprotect.com/bh2000/. There is also a mirror of this document at http://www.phoneboy.com/docs/bh2000/.

SOURCE	DESTINATION	IF VIA	SERVICE	ACTION
Internal-Networks	Internal-Networks	Any	TCP http / TCP https / TCP SSH	accept

Figure 4.28 Rule to permit services from internal network

SOURCE	DESTINATION	SERVICE	ACTION	TRACK
Internal-Networks	email-server	TCP smtp	accept	Log

Figure 4.29 Rule to permit SMTP from the Internet to the e-mail server

SOURCE	DESTINATION	IF VIA	SERVICE	ACTION	TRACK
Any	Any	Any	Any	drop	Log

Figure 4.30 Rule to drop all traffic

Figure 4.30 shows another rule you will commonly see. This rule drops all packets and logs the packets. It shows up as the last rule in your rulebase. It is commonly referred to as the Cleanup rule.

Order of Operations

Established connections are allowed provided they are listed in the state tables and are accepted and address translated as necessary. For new connections, FireWall-1 and surrounding pieces follow this order of operations:

1. Inbound anti-spoof check (verifies that the source IP is included in the interface's Topology setting)
2. Inbound check against the rulebase (includes properties)
3. NAT, if appropriate properties are enabled (see Chapter 10)
4. Outbound check against the rulebase (includes properties)
5. NAT, if appropriate properties are not enabled (see Chapter 10)

The rulebase is applied in the directions specified in rules by the Install On field. In most cases, it means both entering and leaving the gateway. However, if a rule specifies Src (outbound) or Dst (inbound), the rule applies only in that direction. Once a packet matches a rule, it performs the action listed in the Action field, and no further rulebase processing occurs on that packet. For authenticated connections not going through Security Servers, the rules and properties are processed in the following order.

1. Rulebase properties listed as First are processed. Matches are accepted and not logged.
2. Rules 1 through n–1 (assuming n rules) are processed and logged according to their individual settings.
3. Rulebase properties listed as Before Last are then processed. Matches are accepted and not logged.
4. Rule n is processed and logged according to its setting.
5. Rulebase properties listed as Last are then processed. Matches are accepted and not logged.
6. The Implicit Drop rule is matched (no logging occurs).

Figure 4.31 shows a diagram of the preceding sequence, which helps demonstrate what happens during this process. Note that dropped packets may be logged prior to reaching the end of the flowchart, depending on the circumstances and configuration.

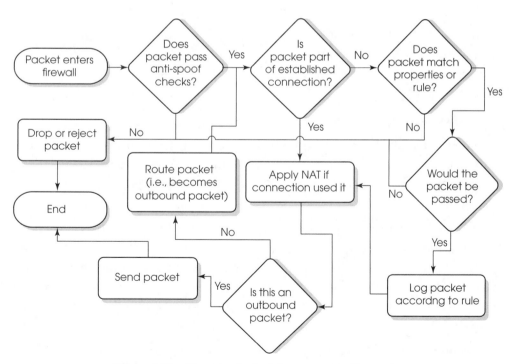

Figure 4.31   Flowchart of rulebase evaluation order

Various versions of the FireWall-1 documentation state that the rules are examined in the sequence they are presented in the rulebase. This is generally correct, but you must also take into consideration what is permitted by the settings on the Properties screens. The rules that result from the Properties settings (i.e., the Properties rules) will be enforced appropriately with respect to your rulebase. This means the Properties rules marked First will be applied before your rulebase, Before Last will be applied between rules $n-1$ and n, and Last will be applied after your last rule.

There is one case where FireWall-1 does not process the rules in order but instead uses the rule that is most permissive: when authentication for HTTP, FTP, Telnet, and rlogin is used and such a rule is matched in the rulebase. If a user authentication rule matches the packet (i.e., the source, destination, and service match), then before authentication occurs, all rules in the rulebase are evaluated. The least restrictive rule will be used. An example of this is shown in Chapter 8.

So what is a good rule of thumb when ordering the rules in your rulebases? The following list shows how I typically order my rulebase based on action types:

1. Client Encrypt rules
2. FireWall to FireWall Encryption rules
3. Incoming (from Internet) Accept rules
4. Outgoing (to Internet) Accept rules
5. Client Authentication rules
6. Session Authentication rules
7. User Authentication rules
8. Cleanup rule (drop all)

Note that any rules that will be used heavily should be moved as close to the top of the rulebase as possible because it will improve performance, particularly if there are more than 30 rules.

Making Your First Rulebase

Now that the various components have been discussed, I will talk about making a rulebase. As mentioned earlier, the rulebase is what determines who can do what, where, and when. In order to make a rulebase, you need to create and configure the various components that make up the rulebase. Follow this order of business.

1. Get a map of the network(s) the firewall is designed to protect. It does not need to be a totally detailed map, but it needs to cover the major points of

interest: physical and logical network segments being protected, any special hosts (externally accessible hosts or any hosts that require special access or restrictions), and all routers one hop away from the firewall.

2. Create network objects for each network segment and special hosts. Do not create the firewall at this step.

3. Create groups that make up all the networks on each leg of the firewall. This is for anti-spoofing, as well as for creating a much more readable rulebase later.

4. Create the Check Point gateway object(s) and configure anti-spoofing.

5. Adjust rulebase properties as appropriate.

6. Install the security policy.

You might think you should create the Check Point gateway object first. However, the reason you create it *last* is so you can define anti-spoofing at the same time you create the Check Point gateway object.

Knowing Your Network

Knowing what you are protecting is half the battle. If you do not have a network map, the process of generating one should give you an idea of how the various parts of your network talk to one another. You need to find out what network segments (physical and logical) are present, how they talk to one another, what routers are present, and so on. Although there are programs that claim to be able to automatically map a network for you, the best approach is to sit down and just figure it out. In some situations, this is fairly easy because there are only a couple of network segments. However, in large networks, figuring out the entire network may be too large a task for a single person to do. In this case, delegate responsibility to people who are in the best position to know how their part of the network is configured.

Regardless of how you collect all the information, generate a network map of some kind. Although it is not required, having a visual representation of your network is extremely helpful when crafting policy. To guide you through the rest of the steps, let's use the network pictured in Figure 4.32. This network has two segments: an internal segment with PCs and workstations, and a DMZ with e-mail and WWW servers.

NOTE! In the sample network diagrams throughout this book, I use RFC1918 address space to "protect the innocent." I am treating the 192.168.0.0/16 address space as if it were routable on the Internet, though it normally is not.

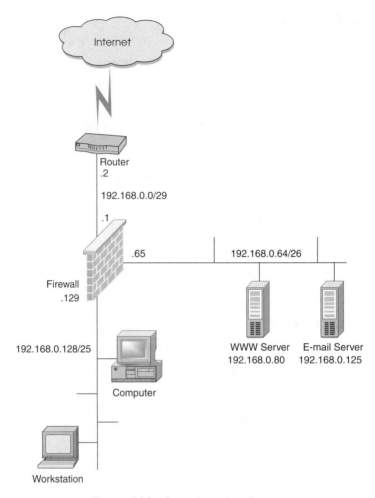

Figure 4.32 Sample network map

Defining Objects

Seven network objects need to be created:

- A network object for 192.168.0.128/25, called net-192.168.0.128-25
- A network object for 192.168.0.64/26, called net-192.168.0.64-26
- A group object called net-internal, which contains net-192.168.0.128-25
- A group object called net-dmz, which contains net-192.168.0.64-26
- A workstation object for the WWW server, called www-server
- A workstation object for the e-mail server, called email-server
- A Check Point object for the firewall/management console itself, called firewall

You will note that I stated that a group should be created for both the internal and DMZ networks even though they contain only one object each. I did this for two reasons: It makes a more readable rulebase, and it allows easier expansion later.

Unless you are allowing access to or from hosts outside of the DMZ or the internal segment, it is not necessary to define anything in addition to these objects. Figures 4.33 through 4.36 show how the net-192.168.0.64-26, net-dmz, email-server, and firewall objects are defined.

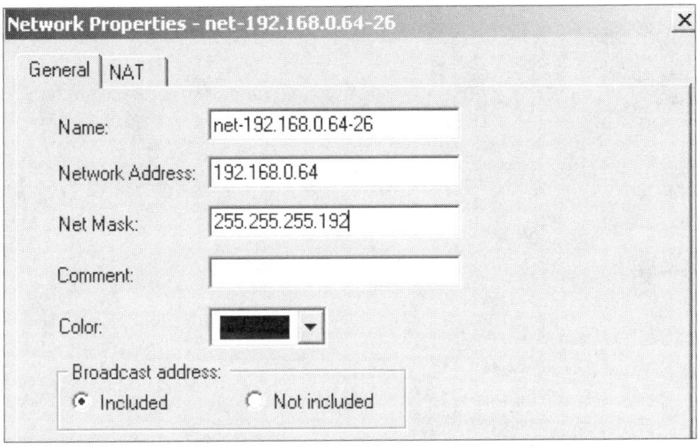

Figure 4.33   Network Properties for net-192.168.0.64-26

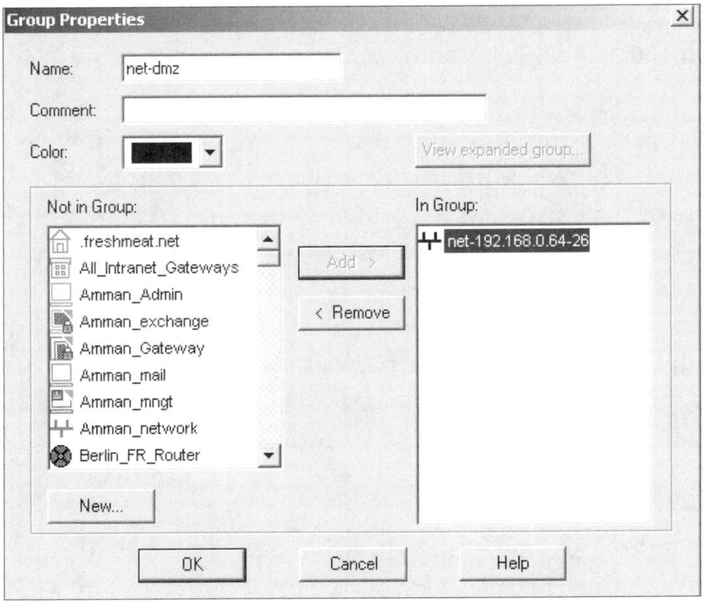

Figure 4.34   Group Properties for net-dmz

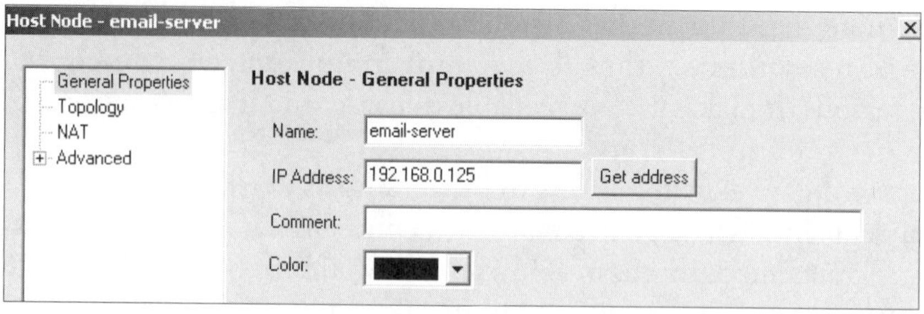

Figure 4.35   Host Node, General Properties frame for email-server

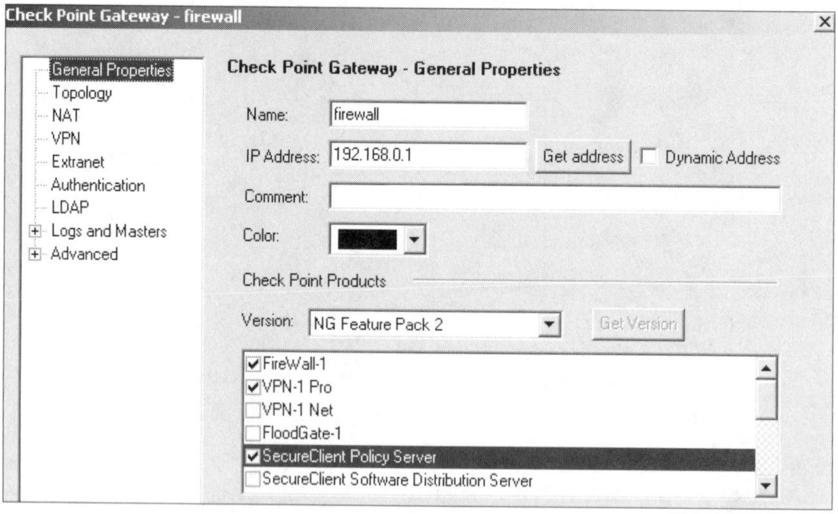

Figure 4.36   Check Point Gateway, General Properties frame for firewall

The last object is the most important to discuss, especially with regard to how it is created. The other objects are fairly self-explanatory.

The name of the Check Point gateway object should match the hostname of the box. The name should not be a reserved word or a defined service name, and it should not contain any illegal characters. (See the Frequently Asked Questions section later in this chapter for more details.) The IP address listed should be the external, routable IP address of the firewall. The name of the object should be resolvable to this IP address via the local hosts file. The licensed IP address of the firewall should also be the same as the IP address.

Defining the Rules

In Chapter 2, I discussed defining a site-wide security policy. If you have a policy document, generating the rules for your security policy in FireWall-1 should be relatively straightforward. If you do not have such a document, it might be a good idea to generate one now. One way to create this document is to sit down with some department heads in a conference room, draw the network on the whiteboard, and define some rules. When I used to install FireWall-1 at customer sites, part of my installation process was exactly that: sketch the network on a whiteboard and make a list of requirements of who needs to do what, where, and when. The result of this process should be a list of simple-to-understand statements that can easily be turned into rules in FireWall-1.

Using the sample network shown in Figure 4.32 and some arbitrary business rules, the following set of statements can be generated. The business rules will obviously be different for each network.

1. Everyone can access the e-mail server via SMTP. Access to this service will not be logged on the firewall.
2. Everyone can access the WWW server via HTTP. Access to this service will not be logged on the firewall.
3. Hosts on the internal network (192.168.0.128/25) can access the SMTP server via POP3. Access to this service will be logged.
4. Hosts on the internal network can access the HTTP server via SSH. Access to this service will be logged.
5. Hosts on the internal network can access the Internet via HTTP, HTTPS, and FTP. Access to these services will be logged.
6. Except for the preceding rules, all other traffic should be dropped. All dropped packets will be logged.

These business rules translate to the rules in the rulebase pictured in Figure 4.37.

NO.	SOURCE	DESTINATION	SERVICE	ACTION	TRACK
1	✱ Any	🖥 email-server	TCP smtp	🕸 accept	– None
2	✱ Any	🖥 www-server	TCP http	🕸 accept	– None
3	⊞ net-internal	🖥 email-server	TCP pop-3	🕸 accept	📋 Log
4	⊞ net-internal	🖥 www-server	TCP SSH	🕸 accept	📋 Log
5	⊞ net-internal	⊠ net-dmz	TCP http TCP https TCP ftp	🕸 accept	📋 Log
6	✱ Any	✱ Any	✱ Any	◎ drop	📋 Log

Figure 4.37   Sample rulebase for the network shown in Figure 4.32

Tweaking the Global Properties

The following list contains some guidelines for setting the various properties as well as rules to use in place of these settings. All of the following properties are in the FireWall-1 portion of the Global Properties screen except for one.

Accept VPN-1 & FireWall-1 control connections and Accept CPRID connections: Even though Check Point has tightened these properties over the years to make them safer, some people still feel these properties are dangerous. These two properties enable over 30 different rules, so I understand people's concerns. Enabling these properties and selecting Implied Rules from the View menu shows a complete list of these rules. I have combined many of these rules into groups of implied rules, shown in Figures 4.38 through 4.40. Accept CPRID connection only enables the FW1_CPRID service as shown in Figure 4.38. Note that I did not list implied rules for products not covered in this book.

SOURCE	DESTINATION	SERVICE	ACTION	TRACK	INSTALLATION	TIME	COMMENT
mgmt-modules	firewall-modules	TCP FW1 TCP FW1_ica_push TCP CPD TCP FW1_ica_services TCP FW1_CPRID	accept	– None	*	*	Allows management modules to push security policy to firewall modules
firewall-modules	mgmt-modules	TCP FW1_log TCP FW1 TCP FW1_ica_pull TCP FW1_ica_services	accept	– None	*	*	Allows firewall modules to log to their management module and fetch policy
mgmt-clients	mgmt-modules	TCP CPMI TCP CP_redundant	accept	– None	*	*	Allows GUI-clients to connect to management module using Policy Editor, etc.
mgmt-modules	firewall-modules	TCP FW1_sam	accept	– None	*	*	Allows management modules to perform Suspicious Activity Monitoring functions
mgmt-modules	mgmt-modules	TCP CPD_amon	accept	– None	*	*	Allows highly available management modules to monitor each other

Figure 4.38 General replacement rules for Accept control connections and Accept CPRID connections properties

SOURCE	DESTINATION	SERVICE	ACTION	TRACK	INSTALLATION	TIME	COMMENT
* Any	mgmt-modules	TCP FW1_key	accept	– No	*	*	Allows management modules to be connected to for the purpose of exchanging encryption keys
* Any	firewall-modules mgmt-modules	TCP FW1_pslogon_NG TCP FW1_topo UDP tunnel_test	accept	– No	*	*	Allows SecureClient users to obtain policy and log into the Policy Server
* Any	firewall-modules	UDP tunnel_test UDP FW1_scv_keep_alive IKE IKE_tcp IPSEC	accept	– No	*	*	Tunnel test is used for SecureClient to "phone home" periodically to keep the VPN tunnel active.
mgmt-modules firewall-modules	firewall-modules	TCP CP_Exnet_PK TCP CP_Exnet_resolve	accept	– No	*	*	Allows Check Point's Extranet (VPN) functions to operate.

Figure 4.39 VPN replacement rules for Accept control connections property

SOURCE	DESTINATION	SERVICE	ACTION	TRACK	INSTALL ON	TIME	COMMENT
firewall-modules	c_v_p-servers u_f_p-servers	TCP FW1_cvp TCP FW1_ufp	accept	– None	*	*	Allows FireWall-1 to communicate with CVP and UFP servers
firewall-modules	authentication-ser	UDP RADIUS UDP TACACS TCP TACACSplus securid TCP AP-Defender TCP ldap	accept	– None	*	*	Allows firewall modules to communicate to external authentication servers

Figure 4.40   Authentication replacement rules for Accept control connections property

Accept outgoing packets originating from gateway: This property is generally safe to leave enabled. The one reason you might not leave this property enabled is for logging purposes. In this case, you can create a rule permitting all traffic from the firewall with the Track field set to Log. Figure 4.41 shows an example. If you think that not enabling this property or adding this rule will keep a hacker from using your firewall to break into other systems, consider this: If a hacker has that kind of access to your firewall, chances are he can probably disable the firewall.

Accept RIP: Figure 4.42 shows an example of a replacement rule you could use for this property if you wanted to disable the property and still use RIP. This property allows RIP packets that originate from anywhere, which I view as dangerous. RIP2-ROUTERS.MCAST.NET is a host object with IP address 224.0.0.9 and is needed only if RIPv2 is being used.

Accept Domain Name over UDP (Queries): This property allows UDP-type DNS packets to and from anywhere. Should you wish to disable this property, which is very dangerous to leave enabled, see Figure 4.43 for an example replacement rule for this property. If you leave this property enabled,

SOURCE	DESTINATION	SERVICE	ACTION	TRACK	INSTALL ON	TIME	COMMENT
firewall-modules	* Any	* Any	drop	Log	*	*	Log traffic originating from the firewall module

Figure 4.41   Rule to allow connections from the firewall

SOURCE	DESTINATION	SERVICE	ACTION	TRACK	INSTALL ON	TIME	COMMENT
Internal-Networks	Internal-Networks RIP2-ROUTERS.MCAST.NET	rip rip-response	accept	– None	*	*	Allow internal networks to exchange RIP information

Figure 4.42   Rule to allow RIP on internal networks

SOURCE	DESTINATION	SERVICE	ACTION	TRACK	INSTALL ON	TIME	COMMENT
Internal-Networks	dns-servers	UDP domain-udp	accept	– None	*	*	Allow clients to query known DNS servers

Figure 4.43   Rule to allow DNS queries from clients to DNS servers

I highly recommend that you enable stateful DNS queries, explained in FAQ 4.7 later in this chapter.

Accept Domain Name over TCP (Zone Transfer): This property allows TCP-type DNS packets to and from anywhere. Should you wish to disable this property, which is very dangerous to leave enabled, see Figure 4.44 for an example replacement rule for this property. Note that unless your primary and secondary DNS servers are separated by your firewall, neither the property nor the rule is necessary. If you leave this property enabled, I highly recommend that you enable stateful DNS queries, explained in FAQ 4.7 later in this chapter.

Accept ICMP requests: This property allows ICMP requests from any location. This includes echo requests, timestamp requests, information requests, and mask requests. This property is considered dangerous and should be disabled. If you wish to allow outbound ping or traceroute, consider using a rule similar to Figure 4.45. Note that replies to these ICMP packets are controlled by a different property.

Accept Stateful ICMP Replies: This property is actually in the Stateful Inspection frame of the Global Properties screen, which will be explained in more detail in Chapter 6. The property is mentioned here because it is necessary to have this property enabled for ICMP to work correctly. By default, it should be.

Accept dynamic address modules' DHCP traffic: This property permits DHCP packets that originate from a firewall marked as having a dynamic address and any replies to it. Unless you have a firewall that uses DHCP in any way, this property can be disabled.

Log Implied Rules: If you have any implied rules enabled and want their activity logged, check this box.

NO.	SOURCE	DESTINATION	SERVICE	ACTION	TRACK	INSTALLON	TIME	COMMENT
1	dns-servers	dns-servers	TCP domain-tcp	accept	– None	*	*	Allows DNS servers to exchange zone info

Figure 4.44   Rule to allow DNS servers to perform zone transfers

SOURCE	DESTINATION	SERVICE	ACTION	TRACK	INSTALLON	TIME	COMMENT
Internal-Networks	Internal-Networks	ICMP echo-request ?? traceroute	accept	– None	*	*	Allows ping and traceroute to the Internet

Figure 4.45   Rule to allow outbound ping and traceroute to the Internet

Rules That Should Be in Every Rulebase

Some specific rules should be included in your rulebase regardless of what your security policy states. These rules are common in many installations, and there are good reasons for them.

The first rule that should be part of your rulebase is the last rule in your rulebase: the Cleanup rule, shown in Figure 4.30 earlier in this chapter. Even if this rule is not specified, it is always *implied*. However, you should add a rule explicitly with logging so you know about all unauthorized traffic.

Another good rule is a rule that denies all traffic to the firewalls, what many people refer to as the Stealth rule (see Figure 4.46).

It may seem strange to explicitly drop traffic to your firewall if your last rule is "deny all" anyway. However, this separates that traffic so you can more easily see what traffic is being directed at your firewall. You can also perform a different tracking option, such as an alert. Normally, the Stealth rule goes at or near the top of your rulebase. However, it should appear *after* any rule that permits traffic directly to the firewall. Figure 4.47 shows an example of such a rule. This rule allows VRRP to the firewall, which is relevant to Nokia platforms.

This rule permits VRRP and IGMP packets from the hosts in the Firewalls group to the firewalls and the special address vrrp.mcast.net. This rule will be enforced on all gateways, and packets that match this rule will not be logged. It is a common rule found on a pair of Nokia firewalls running VRRP.

I typically like to add to rulebases a rule that rejects ident packets, as shown in Figure 4.48. Ident is used by some services to identify the remote end of the

SOURCE	DESTINATION	SERVICE	ACTION	TRACK	INSTALL ON	TIME	COMMENT
✱ Any	firewall-modules	✱ Any	⦿ drop	▤ Log	✱	✱	Drop all traffic to the firewall (i.e., the stealth rule)

Figure 4.46   Stealth rule

SOURCE	DESTINATION	IF VIA	SERVICE	ACTION	TRACK
Firewalls	Firewalls vrrp.mcast.net	✱ Any	vrrp igmp	🛡 accept	– None

Figure 4.47   Rule to permit VRRP to function on Nokia platforms

SOURCE	DESTINATION	SERVICE	ACTION	TRACK
✱ Any	✱ Any	TCP ident	⊖ reject	– None

Figure 4.48   Rule to reject ident traffic

connection, although it is relatively easy to spoof. Internet Relay Chat (IRC) and SMTP are the most common services that use ident. Most SMTP servers can live without ident information, whereas most IRC servers are configured to deny a connection if ident doesn't return information. If you simply drop incoming ident packets, these services will appear to hang until the attempted ident connection times out. By rejecting the packets instead of dropping them, you can avoid this delay.

Installing the Policy

Once you have created a good policy, you need to install it. You do this by selecting Install from the Policy menu or by clicking this button in the GUI: 📥. A series of dialog boxes are then displayed, informing you about various aspects of your security policy that might need correction. In addition, you will see a screen where you can select which gateways to install the policy on and some conditions for installing that policy (i.e., it must install successfully on all selected gateways or members of a cluster). If the installation is done correctly, you should see something similar to the screen shown in Figure 4.49.

If an error or problem is encountered, you might receive one of the following error messages. Note that this list does not contain every possible problem you might encounter, but it does contain the most common errors.

No machines eligible for Policy Installation! If you forgot to define an internal gateway with FireWall-1 installed, you will see this message. Make sure at least one object is defined in this manner before attempting to install a policy.

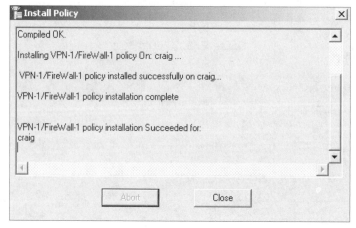

Figure 4.49   Policy installation status screen

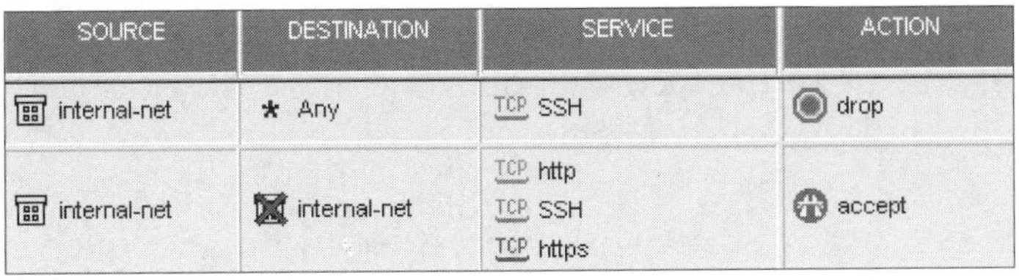

SOURCE	DESTINATION	SERVICE	ACTION
internal-net	＊ Any	TCP SSH	drop
internal-net	internal-net	TCP http TCP SSH TCP https	accept

Figure 4.50 Rule with conflicts

Rule x hides/conflicts with Rule y for Services z: This message means that Rule x is constructed in such a way that Rule y would *never* apply. Consider the example shown in Figure 4.50. The first rule would deny the internal network access via SSH before the second rule could allow it. Therefore, the second rule could never allow SSH from the internal network.

Authentication for command load failed: This error message displays when your management module and firewall module are on separate platforms, and you have not established an authenticated control connection between them. See Chapter 7 for more details.

External interface not set by this loading: This error occurs on node-limited licenses when you have not defined your external interface in the topology of your Check Point gateway object. Go back to the gateway object, view the topology definition, and make sure at least one interface is defined as "external."

Connection timed out or refused: A "connection timed out" message occurs if the remote firewall module is disconnected from the network or has a policy loaded on it that prevents the management module from communicating with it. To resolve problems with the policy, log into the firewall module and run the command **fw unloadlocal**. This will unload the current policy on your firewall module. A "connection refused" message may occur for a similar reason but also occurs when the fwd process is no longer active. On a UNIX/IPSO platform, type **fw kill fwd; fwd**. On a Windows NT platform, restart the FireWall-1 service in the Windows NT/2000 Services Manager.

Frequently Asked Questions

This section contains some questions that are frequently asked in terms of general policy configuration. Specific features have their own subsections. The FAQs are numbered so the text can refer to them more easily.

4.1: Which Files Make Up My Security Policy?

The user-defined part of the security policy lives in `$FWDIR/conf`. Specifically, these files include the ones listed below.

- `objects_5_0.C`: All network objects, services, and rulebase properties are stored in this file.
- `fwauth.NDB*`: This is the user database file, which also stores the encryption keys used for the VPN features of FireWall-1.
- `rulebases_5_0.fws`: This file contains all security policies for FireWall-1 and VPN-1.
- `slprulebases_5_0.fws`: This file contains all security policies for Secure Client, that is, Desktop Security policies.
- `*.W`: This file contains individual policy files that get converted to `.pf` files, which are installed on your firewall module.
- `*.pf`: This file contains "compiled" policy files. These files are not really compiled in the conventional sense, but they are turned into INSPECT code. You can edit this file directly if you would like; any changes you make to this file will be overwritten any time you reload this policy from the GUI.

Other files also make up your security policy in `$FWDIR/lib/*.def`. You can edit these files, but normally you do not edit these files unless instructed to do so by your support provider (or as directed in this book).

4.2: How Do I Edit `objects_5_0.C` and `rulebases.fws` Manually?

To modify `objects_5_0.C` and `rulebases.fws` manually (which several sections of this book tell you to do to enable or disable features), kill the `fwm` process on your management console by using the command **fw kill fwm**, which terminates any GUIs that may be connected. Once you edit these files, make sure you delete `objects_5_0.C.bak` and `objects_5_0.C.sav`. If these files have a more recent timestamp, `fwm` will use these files instead of your edited `objects_5_0.C`. Check Point recommends executing **cpstop** on the management console, making the changes, and then typing **cpstart** to restart the software.

All modifications to these files, unless otherwise specified, will always occur on the management console only, not the firewall modules. Once you have made changes to these files, you need to reinstall the security policy for the changes to take effect on the firewall modules.

An alternate approach to manually editing `objects_5_0.C`, and the suggested approach for most of the changes needed in this book, is to use **dbedit** or the GUIdbedit tool. A sample session with **dbedit** follows.

```
C:\Download>dbedit
Enter Server name (ENTER for 'localhost'): 10.0.0.16
Enter User Name: dwelch
Enter User Password: abc123
Please enter a command, -h for help or -q to quit:
dbedit> modify properties firewall_properties
nat_dst_client_side_manual true
dbedit> update properties firewall_properties
firewall_properties updated successfully.
dbedit> quit
```

To make the same change with GUIdbedit, log into the GUIdbedit utility, which presents a login screen similar to that of the Policy Editor. Once you've logged in, you can navigate to the appropriate setting and make the change. Figure 4.51 shows the same change being made that was made with **dbedit** above.

WARNING! **dbedit** does not work correctly when run from an IPSO platform prior to NG FP3. You should either run **dbedit** from a different platform or use the GUIdbedit tool.

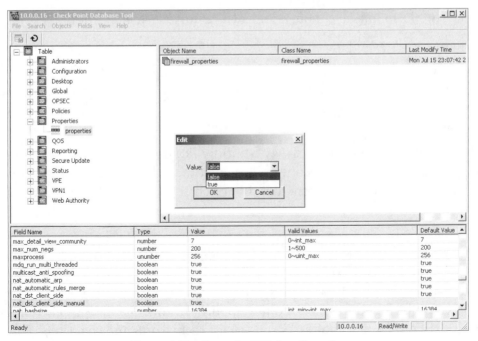

Figure 4.51   Sample GUIdbedit session

Table 4.2. Services that do not work with the Any service

snmp-trap	snmp-read	sip_any	sip	http_mapped	ftp_mapped
smtp_mapped	tunnel_test_ mapped	ftp-port	ftp-pasv	AT-Defender	dhcp-req-localmodule
sqlnet2-1521	H323_any	H323_ras			

4.3: Does Any Service Really Mean Any Service?

Prior to FireWall-1 NG, it was not possible to easily "see" which services would not apply when the Any service is specified. In NG, it is now possible to define a service in the GUI so that Any does not include that particular service. This means the service in question must be *explicitly* listed in any accept rule. In NG FP2, the predefined services defined without the Match for Any flag set include those shown in Table 4.2.

To obtain a current list of services for your installation, create a file called Servername with the following three lines in it:

```
localhost
-t services -pf
-q
```

Then run the following command on a UNIX management station:

```
# more ServerName | queryDB_util | awk '/Object Name/ {host=$3}
/include_in_any/ {print host,":"$2}' > include.txt
```

The file include.txt will now include services that are included in the Any service based on their property settings.

4.4: When Should I Reinstall My Security Policy?

You should reinstall your security policy anytime you make a change to a network object, the rulebase properties, the rulebase, or any of the files that make up the security policy.

4.5: Which Characters or Words Cannot Be Used When Naming Objects?

The most current list of characters or words that cannot be used when naming objects can be found in Check Point Support's Knowledge Base article number 36.0.89127.2471605. Tables 4.3 and 4.4 list these words and characters.

Table 4.3 Illegal characters

Space	+	*	?	!	(
)	{	}	?	[	]
#	<	>	,	:	;
ë	ì	`	\	/	@
$	%	^	|	&	

 NOTE! In Table 4.4, any capitalization of these words is also illegal.

Table 4.4 INSPECT reserved words

accept	account	alert	all	and	any	apr
April	aug	august	auth	authalert	black	blue
broadcasts	call	date	day	debug	dec	December
deffunc	define	delete	direction	do	domains	drop
dst	duplicate	dynamic	expcall	expires	export	feb
February	firebrick	foreground	forest green	format	fri	Friday
from	fwline	fwrule	gateways	get	gold	gray
green	hashsize	hold	host	hosts	if	ifaddr
ifid	implies	in	inbound	interface	interfaces	intrap
insecdata	ipsecmethods	is	jan	January	jul	july
jun	june	kbuf	keep	limit	log	long
magenta	mail	mar	march	may	mday	medium
modify	mon	Monday	month	mortrap	navy	netobj
netof	nets	nexpires	not	nov	November	oct
October	or	orange	origdport	origdst	origsport	origsrc
other	outbound	outrap	packet	packetid	packetlen	pass
r_arg	r_cdir	r_cflags	r_ckey	r_connarg	r_ctype	r_entry
r_pflags	r_proxy_action	r_tab_status	r_xlate	record	red	refresh *(continued)*

Table 4.4   *continued*

reject	resourceobj	routers	sat	Saturday	sep	September
servers	servobj	set	short	skipmen	snmptrap	spoof
spoofalert	sr	src	static	sun	Sunday	sync
targets	thu	Thursday	to	tod	tracks	tue
Tuesday	ufp	userdefined	vanish	wasskipped	wed	Wednesday
xlatedport	slatedst	slatemethod	xlatesport	xlatesrc	xor	year

4.6: Are the Global Properties per Firewall or Global?
Rulebase properties apply to all gateways managed by the management console. Many properties that used to be global have moved to the individual firewall.

4.7: How Do I Enable DNS Verification When I Use the Rulebase Property to Allow DNS Queries?
In **dbedit**, explained in FAQ 4.2, execute the following commands:

```
dbedit> modify properties firewall_properties fw_dns_verification true
dbedit> update properties firewall_properties
```

Similar changes can be made via the GUIdbedit tool.

4.8: Are the GUI Clients Backward Compatible?
You can manage FireWall-1 4.1 firewalls from an NG management console, but you cannot use an NG GUI to connect to a 4.1 management console. SMART Clients are *not* backward compatible, that is, you can use only the version of the GUI that came with the version of your software.

4.9: How Do I Enable Specific Rules on Specific Interfaces?
SmartDashboard/Policy Editor was not set up to allow you to bind specific rules to specific interfaces of a firewall. Rules are processed in order. Rules that do not apply are skipped. Processing a rule takes a near-zero amount of time, so unless you have a few hundred rules, there's little reason to do it this way.

   If it is an absolute requirement that certain rules are active only on certain interfaces, it can be done, but the technique is not elegant. Take the generated .pf file from a policy install in the GUI (it should be called rulebase-name.pf, located in $FWDIR/conf on the management console) and modify it so that the rules in question are installed only on the interface in question.

Chapter 14 explains how you might go about that. You can then install it with the **fw load** command.

Note that every time you change your security policy in the GUI, you will need to go into the generated .pf file, manually reapply the changes, and **fw load** the modified .pf file. It's not elegant, but that's what you have to do to make it do what you want.

Troubleshooting

SmartDashboard/Policy Editor does not have too many issues. However, a few problems come up from time to time. Note that the issues described in the following subsections continue the numbering system used in the FAQs in the previous section.

4.10: My Rulebases Have Disappeared!

There are times when it appears that all of your rulebases have disappeared. This is because the rulebases.fws file is corrupt. You can simply recreate this file by closing any GUI connected to the management console and performing the following steps:

On UNIX:

```
# cd $FWDIR/conf
# fwm -g *.W
```

On Windows NT:

```
c:\> cd %FWDIR%\conf
c:\WINNT/FW/conf> for %i in (*.W) do fwm -g %i
```

There are some differences between these commands.

- On UNIX, the * is interpreted as a wildcard and includes all .W files.
- On Windows NT, the * is not interpreted as a wildcard, so you must list the .W files individually (thus the for loop).

When importing rulebase files, if objects referenced in a specific rulebase no longer exist, the rulebase in question will not be successfully imported. This happens with particularly old rulebases. You will see errors to this effect when you run this command: These errors are normal.

4.11: Using the GUI over Slow Links

If you are using the GUI over a particularly slow link or have a particularly large number of rulebases or network objects, you may see a lot of Server Not

Responding messages when you attempt to use the GUI. The GUI tries to download `objects_5_0.C` and all the rulebases used. If this takes longer than the timeout value (which is 25 seconds), you will get this message.

In FireWall-1 NG, a new "compressed connection" feature was added. By default, the SmartDashboard/Policy Editor application should have this option enabled. However, it's possible it might have been disabled. On the SmartDashboard/Policy Editor logon screen, ensure that the "Use compressed connections" option is enabled. It will be listed if you click on the "More options" link.

Although not much can be done for the size of `objects_5_0.C`, the number of rulebases can certainly be reduced. Remove some unused rulebases. You can also adjust the timeout for the GUI client connection as follows.

- **UNIX:** Set the environment variable `SERVER_TIMEOUT` before running **fwpolicy** (e.g., `setenv SERVER_TIMEOUT 60` to set the timeout to 60 seconds).
- **Windows:** Create the following Registry entry as a DWORD, specifying the desired number of seconds for the timeout: `HKEY_LOCAL_MACHINE/SOFTWARE/CheckPoint/Policy Editor/5.0/server_timeout`.

4.12: I Cannot Fetch a Host's Interfaces

When you are editing a workstation object, you may be trying to do a **GET** to automatically fill in the interfaces on the Interfaces tab. This may fail. You can only fetch the interfaces on a host that has either FireWall-1 installed or SNMP installed. Depending on the object in question and the version of FireWall-1 being used, you will either have to troubleshoot this as a remote management issue (see Chapter 7) or as an SNMP issue.

4.13: SmartMap (or VPE) Crashes When Logging into SmartDashboard/Policy Editor

After upgrading FireWall-1 4.1 to FireWall-1 NG FP3 (management server), sometimes SmartDashboard crashes after logging in to it. It seems to be the SmartMap that generates this problem.

The solution for this problem is to edit the objects file (don't do this manually!) by using **dbedit** as shown below.

```
c:\> dbedit
Enter Server name (ENTER for 'localhost'): <ip management server>
Enter User Name: <username>
Enter User Password: <pass>
Please enter a command, -h for help or -q to quit:
```

```
dbedit> modify properties firewall_properties totally_disable_VPE true
dbedit> update properties firewall_properties
firewall_properties updated successfully.
dbedit> quit
```

Now when you try to log in to the SmartDashboard, you'll be able to manage your firewall and policy but without the SmartMap.

4.14: FireWall-1 Error: No License for User Interface

There are several possible causes for this error:

- Check that the `$FWDIR/conf/gui-clients` file on the management console is defined correctly.
- If you are using the GUI from a UNIX platform, you must have the motif license feature. In FireWall-1 4.1 and later, this feature costs extra.
- Make sure that the host specified at the login screen is actually the management console, not the remote firewall module. Keep in mind that the SmartConsole applications, the Management Module, and firewall module can all reside on separate machines, so make sure you specify the correct machine.
- Check that the license is bound to the correct address on the Windows platform. (Run **ipconfig** from the DOS prompt.)
- Remember that the licensed IP address must be the primary address of its interface. If the licensed IP address is bound to a virtual interface, FireWall-1 will not work.
- Check that there are no other licensing irregularities. For example, an expired eval or demo license can cause various errors, including this one. Reinstall your currently valid licenses. Also ensure the licenses you have are appropriate for the topology you are using. For example, if you have a separate management license and you've installed a standalone configuration, this won't work. You must either request the appropriate licenses or change your topology to fit the licenses you have.

Summary

Although it is impossible to describe every situation you might encounter during the initial configuration of your security policy, this chapter covered the basic elements you need to know. Each element that is written into your security policy was detailed, including the rulebase properties and anti-spoofing. Different situations you might commonly encounter along the way as well as some common configuration questions were answered.

Chapter

5

Logging and Alerting

Logs and alerts are critical aspects of your firewall; they tell you what is going on with various aspects of your firewall. In this chapter, I focus on how logging and alerting work. I also show you what you are likely to see in the Log Viewer and SmartView Tracker/Status Manager as well as suggest some strategies for managing your log files.

By the end of this chapter, you should be able to:

- Determine what information is displayed in SmartView Status/Status Manager
- Determine what information is displayed in SmartView Tracker/Log Viewer
- Identify where logging and alerting actually occur

SmartView Status

SmartView Status, also known as the Status Manager in FireWall-1 NG FP2 and earlier, allows you to see the current state of all your Check Point modules. In FireWall-1 4.1, this application was called the System Status Manager and only told you about the firewall. Now the application tells you about any Check Point product running on the platform and gives a great deal more information about what is running. Figure 5.1 shows an example of Status Manager on one of my boxes. Though it is from a FireWall-1 NG FP2 installation, it shows the same information and looks the same as SmartView Status in NG FP3 and above.

You can click on individual installed components and get detailed information about that component. For instance, if you click on FireWall-1, you see something like Figure 5.2.

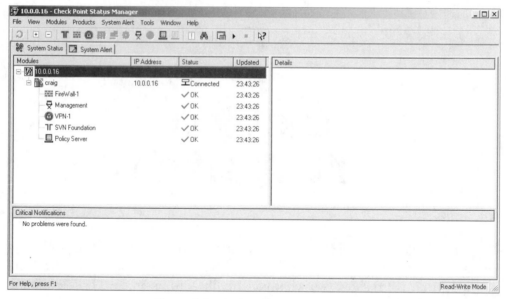

Figure 5.1 System Status for Craig

NOTE! The packet counters are reset at each successful policy installation.

FireWall-1 Details	
Status:	OK
Policy Name:	Standard
Installed At:	Fri Aug 2 23:29:34 2002
Packets	
Accepted:	406
Dropped:	14
Logged:	10
UFP Cache	
Hit ratio (%):	0
Connections inspected:	0
Hits:	0
Hash Kernel Memory	
Total memory allocated:	0 bytes using 0 blocks in 1 pools
Total memory used:	342392 bytes used (0%); peak was 371820 bytes
Total blocks used:	110 blocks used (0%); peak was 119 blocks
Allocations:	556416
Allocation failures:	0
Frees:	553859
Free failures:	0
System Kernel Memory	
Total memory used:	7140304 bytes used; peak was 7631864 bytes
Allocations:	74816
Allocation failures:	0
Frees:	74675
Free failures:	0

Figure 5.2 System Status, FireWall-1 Details screen

The Management status tells you whether or not the management software is up, the status of High Availability (if applicable), and which clients are connected. This is shown in Figure 5.3.

Figure 5.4 shows the status and counters related to the VPN module.

Figure 5.5 shows the status of the SVN Foundation, which includes information about the operating system, memory, and disk utilization.

```
Details
Status:                     OK
Started:                    yes
Synchronization status:     N/R (Self synchronization is not relevant)
Active status:              N/A
Connected clients:          2
   Client 1
      Administrator:        dblock
      Host:                 calhost
      Database locked:      false
      Application type:     Status Manager
   Client 2
      Administrator:        dwelch
      Host:                 CARTMAN
      Database locked:      false
      Application type:     Status Manager
```

Figure 5.3   System Status, Management Details screen

```
Details
Status:                OK
Packets
   Encrypted:          0
   Decrypted:          0
Errors
   Encryption errors:  0
   Decryption errors:  0
   IKE events errors:  0
Hardware
   HW Vendor Name:     None
   HW Status:          Off
```

Figure 5.4   System Status, VPN Details screen

```
SVN Foundation Details
Status:                 OK
Version:                NG Feature Pack 2 (Build 52213)
OS Information
   OS Name:             IPSO
   OS Version:          3.5
   OS Build:            N/A
   OS SP:               N/A
   OS Level:            3.5-FCS6 releng 1005  05.02.2002-024900 i386
CPU
   Usage:               8%
   User time:           4%
   System time:         4%
   Idle time:           93%
Memory
   Total virtual memory:    2638756 KB
   Active virtual memory:   2633704 KB
   Total real memory:       126656 KB
   Active real memory:      61036 KB
   Free real memory:        5052 KB
Disk
   Free space:          79%
   Total free space:    496 MB
   Available free space: 446 MB
   Total space:         623 MB
```

Figure 5.5   System Status, SVN Foundation Details screen

Table 5.1 States for Check Point modules in the SmartView Status/Status Manager

State	Description
Waiting	The management console is in the process of establishing a connection to the module.
Connected	A connection was successfully established to the module.
Disconnected	The module is not responding to requests for status update. The module might be disconnected from the network, a loaded security policy might be preventing the query, or some other condition might be causing the problem.
Untrusted	A connection was established to this module, but Secure Internet Communication (SIC) failed to this module. This may be because SIC is not configured on the module, it is out of sync with the management console, or this module is managed by a different management console.

 NOTE! The disk statistics are relevant only to the drive/partition on which FireWall-1 is installed. On UNIX platforms, including IPSO, this is /opt.

A module can have four different states (see Table 5.1). An application on a module can have seven different states (see Table 5.2). Specific details regarding failure alerts can be seen in the Critical Notifications portion of the SmartView Status/Status Manager screen.

Alerts can be defined for the different applications on your module. After clicking on the System Alert tab, you can set alerts for the different applications. These alerts refer to conditions that might occur on a specific module (e.g., a change in application state, a potential failure condition on the module). Alerts can be defined on a per-module basis or they can be defined globally. If you select your module name on the left of the window, on the right you will see three choices for how System Alerts are defined.

- **Same as Global:** This module will use the Global Alerts settings.
- **Custom:** This module will have uniquely defined alert conditions.
- **None:** This module will not generate any alerts.

Figure 5.6 shows the global alerts you can set for the SVN Foundation application, which are the same as those available on individual modules. The type of

Table 5.2 States for Check Point applications in the SmartView Status/Status Manager

State	Description
Waiting	The management console is in the process of establishing a connection to the application.
OK	A connection was successfully established to the application and everything appears to be functioning normally.
Unknown	The application is not responding to requests for status update. The module might be disconnected from the network, a loaded security policy might be preventing the query, a Check Point agent is not installed on this module, or some other condition might be causing the problem.
Untrusted	A connection was established to this module, but Secure Internet Communication (SIC) failed to this module. This may be because SIC is not configured on the module, it is out of sync with the management console, or a different management console manages this module.
No response	There is no Check Point software installed on this machine, or it is present but corrupted.
Attention	In a cluster configuration, one or more nodes in the cluster is experiencing a problem. At least one node is functioning correctly, however, and is serving the traffic.
Problem	The application is responding but is reporting an unusual condition. What this problem is will vary by product. In FireWall-1, for instance, this status can mean that no policy is installed.

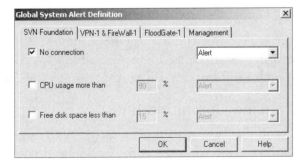

Figure 5.6 Global System Alert Definition, SVN Foundation tab

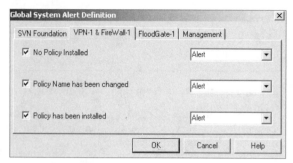

Figure 5.7   Global System Alert Definition, VPN-1 & FireWall-1 tab

alert that will occur, which you can set for each alert condition, is explained later in this chapter.

The alerts you can set on the SVN Foundation tab are listed below.

No connection: This refers to losing connectivity to the module.

CPU usage more than: If the CPU utilization on the module goes above the specified percentage, issue the specified alert type.

Free disk space less than: If the available disk space becomes less than the specified percentage, issue the specified alert. Remember that this is only for the drive/partition on which FireWall-1 is installed.

Figure 5.7 shows the global system alerts for VPN-1 and FireWall-1, which also happen to be the same alerts as for FloodGate-1. The alerts are listed below.

No Policy Installed: If the policy becomes uninstalled for any reason, issue the specified alert type.

Policy Name has been changed: If the policy that was previously installed has a different name than the policy just installed, issue the specified alert type.

Policy has been installed: When a policy is installed, issue the specified alert type.

The global system alerts for the management module specify an alert only for synchronization. If you are using High Availability for Management Modules and you lose synchronization for any reason, display the appropriate alert.

System Status from the Command Line

If you have command-line access to your management module, you can also get System Status information from the command line. If you are working with remote firewalls, these commands will work only if you have established an authenticated control connection with the remote firewall as described in Chapter 7.

To check the status of the local firewall, use the following command:

```
# fw stat
HOST        POLICY      DATE
localhost template    21Dec2000 12:59:23 :   [>eth-s1p1c0] [<eth-s1p1c0]
```

Here's how to look at the status of a remote firewall:

```
# fw stat mrhat mrtwig
HOST        POLICY      DATE
mrhat       av          21Nov1999 15:23:59 :   [>eth-s1p4c0]
[<eth-s1p4c0] [>eth-s1p1c0] [<eth-s1p1c0] [>eth-s1p3c0]
mrtwig      av          21Nov1999 15:28:17 :   [>eth-s1p4c0]
[<eth-s1p4c0] [>eth-s1p1c0] [<eth-s1p1c0] [>eth-s1p3c0]
```

This output[1] tells you which policy is loaded (av is loaded on both mrhat and mrtwig), the date the policy was loaded on each box, and which interfaces have seen traffic inbound and outbound. In this example, both firewalls have seen traffic on eth-s1p4c0 and eth-s1p1c0 in both directions. The eth-s1p3c0 interface has seen traffic only in the outbound direction.

To get more detailed statistics, run **fw stat -long**:

```
# fw stat -long mrhat
HOST     IF         POLICY  DATE                 TOTAL REJECT  DROP ACCEPT  LOG
mrhat    >eth-s1p4c0 av     21Nov1999 15:23:59   72    0       0    72      1
mrhat    <eth-s1p4c0 av     21Nov1999 15:23:59   57    0       0    57      0
mrhat    >eth-s1p1c0 av     21Nov1999 15:23:59   180   0       14   166     1
mrhat    <eth-s1p1c0 av     21Nov1999 15:23:59   170   0       0    170     0
mrhat    >eth-s1p3c0 av     21Nov1999 15:23:59   90    0       90   0       1
```

The eth-s1p2c0 interface is missing from this list because it has not seen any traffic. To show this interface, use the -inactive parameter:

```
# fw stat -long -inactive mrhat
HOST     IF         POLICY  DATE                 TOTAL REJECT  DROP ACCEPT  LOG
mrhat    >eth-s1p4c0 av     21Nov1999 15:23:59   72    0       0    72      1
mrhat    <eth-s1p4c0 av     21Nov1999 15:23:59   57    0       0    57      0
mrhat    >eth-s1p1c0 av     21Nov1999 15:23:59   184   0       17   167     1
mrhat    <eth-s1p1c0 av     21Nov1999 15:23:59   171   0       0    171     0
mrhat    >eth-s1p2c0 av     21Nov1999 15:23:59   0     0       0    0       0
mrhat    <eth-s1p2c0 av     21Nov1999 15:23:59   0     0       0    0       0
```

---

1. Yes, I know this output looks dated, given when this book was written. However, I can assure you the format of the output of these commands hasn't changed in a very long time.

```
mrhat    >eth-s1p3c0 av    21Nov1999 15:23:59  90  0    90       0       1
mrhat    <eth-s1p3c0 av    21Nov1999 15:23:59   0  0     0       0       0
```

The preceding examples of monitoring have been present in FireWall-1 since at least version 2.1. **cpstat** allows you to check on the status of various modules within the Check Point suite and also gives you the ability to monitor various parts of the operating system, giving you far more details than in previous versions. The usage for **cpstat** is:

```
cpstat [-h host][-p port][-f flavour][-o polling [-c count]
       [-e period]] [-d] application_flag
```

The flags for **cpstat** are described in more detail in Table 5.3. The applications you can query with **cpstat** are listed in Table 5.4. The flavors for os, fw, and vpn are specified in Tables 5.5, 5.6, and 5.7, respectively.

Table 5.3 Flags for cpstat

Flag	Description
-h host	Specifies a resolvable hostname, dotted notation IP address, or Dynamic IP hostname. The default, if none specified, is localhost.
-p port	Specifies which port to connect to if you are running the AMON process on a different port. The default is port 18192.
-f flavor[a]	Specifies which "flavor" of the particular type of application you want to look in. These are specified by application type in Table 5.4. The default is to use the first flavor listed in the configuration file for that module, which is a .cps file in the module's conf directory ($FWDIR/conf for FireWall-1 related modules, $CPDIR/conf for modules associated with SVN Foundation, and $FGDIR/conf for FloodGate-related modules).
-0 interval	Specifies the number of seconds between polls of the specified module. The default is 0, meaning show the results only once.
-c count	Specifies the number of times to poll the specified module. The default is 0, meaning poll only once.
-e period	Specifies the amount of time over which statistical counters are computed. This is ignored for other types of counters.
-d	Enables debugging, which is useful for troubleshooting why the command might have failed.
application_flag	Specifies which application to query (see Table 5.4).

a. In English-speaking countries, it's -f flavour. In American-speaking countries, it's -f flavor. Israel is an English-speaking country, despite strong ties to the United States.

Table 5.4 Applications that can be queried with `cpstat`

Application	Description
os	Parameters specific to the operating system. Flavors are specified in Table 5.5.
persistency	A parameter specific to application persistence, i.e., whether or not the application will automatically start on reboot.
polsrv	Parameters specific to Policy Server. The `default` flavor shows only the number of licensed and connected users. The `all` flavor shows whether or not the Policy Server is up in addition to the number of users.
fw	Parameters specific to FireWall-1. Flavors are specified in Table 5.6.
vpn	Parameters specific to VPN-1. Flavors are specified in Table 5.7.
ha	Parameters specific to High Availability. The `default` flavor shows the current state of High Availability. The `all` flavor shows this in addition to the current state of all modules in the cluster.
ls	Parameters specific to Load Sharing.
mg	Parameters specific to Management Module.
fg	Parameters specific to FloodGate.

Table 5.5 Application flavors for `os`

Flavor	Description
default	Shows SVN Foundation build numbers and OS version/service pack levels
routing	Shows the routing table on the specified module
memory	Shows statistics on memory usage, both real and virtual memory
old_memory	Shows statistics on memory usage, both real and virtual memory at the last policy installation
cpu	Shows statistics related to CPU utilization, similar to what you might find in a UNIX **vmstat**
disk	Shows statistics related to disk usage; only shows partition where SVN Foundation is installed
perf	Acts as a combination of `memory`, `cpu`, and `disk`
average_cpu	Shows average CPU utilization
average_memory	Shows average memory utilization
statistics	Shows both `average_cpu` and `average_memory`
all	Shows everything about the operating system covered in previous flavors

Table 5.6 Application flavors for `fw`

Flavor	Description
`default`	Shows the policy name, when it was installed, and packet statistics on a per-interface basis
`policy`	Same as `default`, but also shows the number of connections (current and peak)
`totals`	Shows the number of total packets accepted, denied, and logged
`hmem`	Shows statistics related to `halloc` memory, i.e., where FireWall-1 state tables are stored
`kmem`	Shows statistics related to FireWall-1's use of kernel memory
`inspect`	Shows statistics related to FireWall-1's INSPECT engine
`cookies`	Shows statistics related to cookie[a] processing
`chains`	Shows statistics related to chain processing
`fragments`	Shows statistics related to fragmented packet processing
`ufp`	Shows URL Filtering Protocol statistics
`http`	Shows HTTP Security Server statistics
`ftp`	Shows FTP Security Server statistics
`telnet`	Shows Telnet Security Server statistics
`rlogin`	Shows rlogin Security Server statistics
`smtp`	Shows SMTP Security Server statistics
`perf`	Shows a listing of counters from `hmem`, `kmem`, `inspect`, `cookies`, `chains`, `fragments`, `ufp`, `http`, `ftp`, `telnet`, `rlogin`, and `smtp`
`all`	Shows all flavors

a. Note that a cookie in this context is how FireWall-1 represents a packet in a platform-independent manner, not a cookie that you might experience on a Web site or a cookie that a certain blue monster on *Sesame Street* might like to eat.

Table 5.7 Application flavors for `vpn`

Flavor	Description
`product`	Shows the version of VPN-1
`general`	Shows basic packet statistics for VPN-1
`IKE`	Shows IKE statistics
`ipsec`	Shows IPSec statistics

(continued)

Table 5.7   *continued*

Flavor	Description
fwz	Shows FWZ statistics (obsolete on modules in FireWall-1 NG FP2 and above)
accelerator	Shows statistics related to the encryption accelerator (Broadcom, Chrysalis)
nic	Shows statistics related to network interface cards
all	Shows all information related to the VPN-1 module

SmartView Tracker

In FireWall-1 NG FP2 and before, the application is called the Log Viewer or Log Manager. In NG FP3 and later, it is called SmartView Tracker. I discuss SmartView Tracker specifically in this section. Figure 5.8 shows how SmartView Tracker looks after you authenticate.

When you load up the SmartView Tracker, you will see a number of things. Along the top of the screen, three tabs are shown: Log, Active, and Audit. Log is

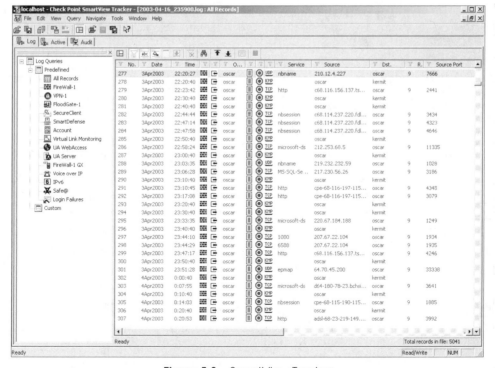

Figure 5.8   SmartView Tracker

for rulebase and event logging from Check Point modules, Active means currently active connections, and Audit is for logging the actions of administrators.

Table 5.8 shows the various log fields used by FireWall-1, VPN-1, SecureClient, and SmartDefense.

Table 5.8 Entries in Log Viewer

Entry	Description
No.	The log entry number.
Date	The date the log entry was generated.
Time	The time the log entry was generated.
Product	The product for which this log entry is relevant.
Interface	The interface on which the packet being logged came in or went out (with direction) or indicates "daemon" if the message came from a FireWall-1 daemon (e.g., the security servers, fwm).
Origin	The firewall module that generated the log entry.
Type	Log (normal rulebase logging), Alert (for alert log entries), or Control (changes to policy or logging on a firewall).
Action	The action taken on the packet (Drop, Reject, Accept, and so on).
Service	The service of the packet (HTTP, Telnet, and so on), which is usually based on the destination TCP/UDP port.
Source	The source IP address of the connection or packet.
Destination	The destination IP address of the connection or packet.
Proto	The protocol of the IP packet (TCP, UDP, ICMP, and so on).
Rule No.	The rule number that this connection or packet matched in the rulebase.
NAT rule num.	The NAT rule number that this connection or packet matched in the rulebase.
Nat add. rule num.	The number of an additional NAT rule if one was applied.
Source Port	The source port of the packet if TCP or UDP. For other protocols, this field is gibberish.
User	The appropriate username if the action was an authorization or de-authorization or was the result of an authenticated connection (with or without encryption).
SrcKeyID	The source's KeyID if the action was encrypt or decrypt. *(continued)*

Table 5.8 *continued*

Entry	Description
DstKeyID	The destination's KeyID if the action was encrypt or decrypt.
Elapsed	The amount of time the connection was active (Accounting mode only).
Bytes	The number of bytes for the connection in question (Accounting mode only).
XlateSrc	The source IP address the connection will have after NAT is applied.
XlateDst	The destination IP address the connection will have after NAT is applied.
XlateSPort	The source port the connection will have after NAT is applied.
XlateDport	The destination port the connection will have after NAT is applied.
Partner	The name of the partner site making a connection if an extranet is defined.
Community	The name of the community to which this log entry relates if a VPN Community is used.
Enc Scheme	The encryption scheme used for this connection (usually IKE, but may be others if managing FireWall-1 4.1 boxes).
VPN Peer Gateway	The gateway that sent or received the encrypted packet.
IKE Initiator Cookie	Information relating to the IKE communication.
IKE Responder Cookie	Information relating to the IKE communication.
IKE Phase 2 Msg Id	The ID of the IKE negotiation.
Encryption Methods	Lists all the encryption methods used in both encryption and data integrity.
Info	More information about this log entry. For most packets or connections, it will simply show "len X," where X is the number of bytes in the packet. This entry also shows useful information on encrypt/decrypt log entries and drops or rejects on Rule 0.

If you have a serious amount of traffic flowing through the firewall, you will have many log entries. It is very important that you examine your logs on a regular basis to make sure that proper security is maintained. However, it can be difficult to look through a few thousand log entries. The following list contains a few hints that might save you some time.

- Limit the number of entries that appear in the log. Do not log on *every* rule, but instead log judiciously. Log only important information (e.g., all unauthorized traffic). Creating rules to catch noise services to drop and not log is one way to do this.

- Rotate your logs frequently. The SmartView Tracker/Log Viewer does not function very well when the log contains more than a few hundred thousand entries. Although you can rotate your logs manually in the GUI, it is recommended that you set up log rotation on a schedule. This is discussed in the Log Maintenance section later in this chapter.
- Use the selection criteria to limit the displayed items or to find the entries you are most interested in.
- Use some of the third-party log analysis tools listed in Appendix G.

Selection criteria are chosen by right-clicking the column title in question and selecting Edit Filter. The options presented depend on the field you click. The following list contains a few notes regarding selection criteria.

- Selection criteria are cumulative; if you use more than one selection criteria, they will be ANDed together.
- The SmartView Tracker/Log Viewer *remembers* previous selection criteria, so you could possibly end up excluding all log entries. Before applying selection criteria, click the Current Selection Criteria button, and make sure all the selection criteria are deleted if necessary.
- The option Show Null Matches on the Options screen affects how log entries are displayed in the selection criteria. You will see Show Null Matches as an icon above the log entries in FireWall-1 NG FP3 or in the Options section under the Selection menu. This shows entries that are neither included nor excluded by the current selection criteria. For example, if you are selecting entries based on the Action field and you have control entries in your log, they will neither be included nor excluded because control log entries do not have Action entries.
- Right above the list of log entries are three icons that control whether or not the selection criteria are applied, whether or not IPs are resolved to names, and whether or not services are resolved to names. In FireWall-1 NG FP1 and FP2, these are listed under the Tools menu.

Viewing Logs from the Command Line

You can also view logs from the command line on the management module by using the command **fw log**. This command shows the logs in ASCII text. Note that not all fields are shown, only relevant fields. Check Point has improved the output of this command so that it is easier to read. It should also be easier to parse with a variety of tools. Output from **fw log** looks something like this:

Date: Aug 24, 2002

```
 1:15:02 ctl    craig.phoneboy.com >daemon sys_message:
installed defaultfilter; product: VPN-1 & FireWall-1;

 1:15:02 ctl    craig.phoneboy.com >daemon sys_message:
The eth-s3p1c0 interface is not protected by the
anti-spoofing feature. Your network may be at risk;
product: VPN-1 & FireWall-1;

 1:15:02 ctl    craig.phoneboy.com >daemon sys_message:
The eth-s2p1c0 interface is not protected by the
anti-spoofing feature. Your network may be at risk;
product: VPN-1 & FireWall-1;

 1:15:02 ctl    craig.phoneboy.com >daemon sys_message:
The eth-s1p1c0 interface is not protected by the
anti-spoofing feature. Your network may be at risk;
product: VPN-1 & FireWall-1;

 1:43:20 ctl    craig.phoneboy.com >daemon sys_message:
installed phoneboy-traditional; product: VPN-1 & FireWall-1;

 1:43:20        craig.phoneboy.com >daemon cp_message:
Parameter 'Connections hash table size' changed from
65536 to 32768;

12:34:08 drop   craig      >eth-s2p1c0 product: VPN-1
& FireWall-1; src: Alpha-Cluster-Inside.foo.com; s_port:
IKE; dst: craig; service: 876; proto: udp; rule: 5;

12:48:17 accept craig      >eth-s1p1c0 product: VPN-1
& FireWall-1; src: cartman.phoneboy.com; s_port: 2343;
dst: craig; service: https; proto: tcp; rule: 1;

12:48:22 accept craig      >eth-s1p1c0 product: VPN-1
& FireWall-1; src: cartman.phoneboy.com; s_port: 2344;
dst: craig; service: https; proto: tcp; rule: 1;

12:48:55 accept craig      >eth-s1p1c0 product: VPN-1
& FireWall-1; src: cartman.phoneboy.com; s_port: 2345;
dst: craig; service: https; proto: tcp; rule: 1;
```

There are plenty of options you can use with **fw log** to help you find the log entries you want to examine. Table 5.9 lists the options for this command. Here's the usage information for the **fw log** command:

```
fw log [-f [-t]] [-n] [-l] [-o] [-c action] [-h host]
[-s starttime] [-e endtime] [-b starttime endtime]
```

Table 5.9 Options for the `fw log` command

Flag	Description
-f	Shows the log forever if no file is specified. Entries are shown as they are generated.
-t	Used with -f to show only new log entries (i.e., entries added after **fw log** was executed).
-l	Includes the date in each line's log entry instead of printing out the date separately.
-s start-time	Used with -f to show log entries generated after the specified date or time (hh:mm format).
-e end-time	Used with -f to show log entries generated before the specified date or time (hh:mm format).
-b timea timeb	Used with -f to show log entries generated between the specified times.
-o	Shows detailed log chains, i.e., all entries in a log record.
-c action	Shows only entries of a specific action type: accept, drop, reject, ctl.
-u filename	Specifies the unification scheme file name.
-m mode	Specifies the unification mode: semi, raw, initial. The latter is the default.
-a	Shows only accounting log entries.
-k alert-type	Shows only the specified alert_type (or all).
-g	Prevents delimiting of the displayed log entries, i.e., uses no colon (:) after a field name or semicolon (;) after a field value.
-h firewall	Shows log entries generated by the firewall module named "firewall."
-n	Prevents name resolution for source and destination IP addresses.
log-file	Uses the specified log file (otherwise, use $FWDIR/log/fw.log).

```
[-u unification_scheme_file] [-m (initial|semi|raw)]
[-a] [-k (alert_name|all)] [-g] [logfile]
```

Viewing Rules in SmartDashboard

When right-clicking on a log entry in SmartTracker in FireWall-1 NG FP3 and above, you have the option of selecting View Rule in SmartDashboard. This is useful because it allows you to see exactly which rule the logged packet hit. However, this works only if the currently installed security policy has a Database

Revision associated with it. In SmartDashboard, select File → Database Revision Control and create a database revision for the current policy. Install the security policy.

Future Accept log entries can be selected in SmartDashboard and the View Rule in SmartDashboard function will work.

Active Mode and Blocking Connections

So far, I have discussed only the most commonly used mode: Log mode. In the Log Manager application (NG FP3 and later), along the top of the screen beneath the icon bar is a series of tabs. In NG FP2 and before, there is a pull-down menu in the icon bar. Either mechanism allows you to change to the other two modes in the Log Viewer: Active and Audit. Because Active mode works differently than Log mode, let's take a look at how it works. Figure 5.9 shows a screen from Active mode. This mode shows connections that are currently active through the firewall (i.e., in its state tables). Table 5.10 lists the fields that are displayed and provides descriptions of each field.

The main function you can perform in Active mode is to temporarily block a connection. This is done without modifying the existing rulebase in Smart Dashboard/Policy Editor. All such blocks are active until the firewall module is unloaded (e.g., with `fw ctl uninstall`), the system is rebooted, or the block is manually removed. To block a specific connection, click on the connection, then pull down Block Intruder from the Tools menu. You will be presented with the following options.

Block only this connection: Blocks only this specific connection. If the host attempts to connect to this destination and this service port again, it will be blocked.

Block access from this source: Blocks any connection the host listed as the source attempts to make.

No.	Date	Time	C...	Product	Interface	Origin	Type	Action	Service	Source
1	24Aug2002	15:08:12	766	VPN-1 & FireWall-1	daemon	craig	Log	Accept	rip	10.0.0.251
2	24Aug2002	15:08:12	767	VPN-1 & FireWall-1	daemon	craig	Log	Accept	rip	craig
3	24Aug2002	15:08:12	768	VPN-1 & FireWall-1	daemon	craig	Log	Accept		10.0.0.252
4	24Aug2002	15:08:12	769	VPN-1 & FireWall-1	daemon	craig	Log	Accept	IKE	10.0.0.254
5	24Aug2002	15:08:12	770	VPN-1 & FireWall-1	daemon	craig	Log	Accept	ssh	10.0.0.2
6	24Aug2002	15:08:12	771	VPN-1 & FireWall-1	daemon	craig	Log	Accept	rip	10.0.0.254
7	24Aug2002	15:08:12	772	VPN-1 & FireWall-1	daemon	craig	Log	Accept	rip	10.0.0.11
8	24Aug2002	15:08:12	773	VPN-1 & FireWall-1	daemon	craig	Log	Accept	domain-udp	10.0.116.13
9	24Aug2002	15:08:12	774	VPN-1 & FireWall-1	daemon	craig	Log	Accept	rip	craig
10	24Aug2002	15:08:12	775	VPN-1 & FireWall-1	daemon	craig	Log	Accept	rip	10.0.0.252
11	24Aug2002	15:08:12	776	VPN-1 & FireWall-1	daemon	craig	Log	Accept	ssh	10.0.0.2
12	24Aug2002	15:08:12	777	VPN-1 & FireWall-1	daemon	craig	Log	Accept	CPMI	10.0.0.2
13	24Aug2002	15:08:12	784	VPN-1 & FireWall-1	daemon	craig	Log	Accept	ntp-udp	10.0.0.254
14	24Aug2002	15:08:13	786	VPN-1 & FireWall-1	daemon	craig	Log	Accept	domain-udp	10.0.116.13

Figure 5.9   Active mode in Log Manager

Table 5.10   Fields in Log Viewer Active mode

Name	Description
No.	The log entry number.
Date	The date the log entry was generated.
Time	The time the log entry was generated.
Conn. ID	A number referencing this specific connection.
Product	The product this connection is relevant for.
Interface	The name of the interface the packet came in on. Usually "daemon."
Origin	The firewall module that generated the log entry.
Type	Usually Log.
Action	The action taken on the packet, usually Accept.
Service	The service of the packet (HTTP, Telnet, and so on), which is usually based on the destination TCP/UDP port.
Source	The source IP of the packet.
Destination	The destination IP of the packet.
Proto	The IP protocol of the packet. This is usually TCP, UDP, or ICMP, but it could be any IP protocol or a number.
Source Port	The source port of the packet if it is TCP or UDP.
Elapsed	The amount of time elapsed since the connection began, for entries logged as type Accounting.
Bytes	The number of bytes that have elapsed since the connection began, for entries logged as type Accounting.
Information	More information about the entry. This is usually blank.

Block access to this destination: Blocks the connection if any host tries to reach this destination host.

Blocking Timeout: Indicates how long this block will be active. Indefinite really means until the firewall module is unloaded (via `fw ctl uninstall`), a reboot occurs, or the connections are unblocked by using `fw sam -D` or `fw sam -C`, or by selecting Clear Blocking under the Tools menu.

Force this blocking: Indicates the firewalls that will enforce the block you are requesting. By default, only the firewall the connection went through will enforce this block. This function can be pushed to all firewalls managed by this management console.

Note that you can enable these actions from the command line of the management module or firewall module using the command **fw sam**, as shown below. These command options are described in Table 5.11.

```
sam [-v] [-s sam-server] [-S server-sic-name] [-t timeout]
   [-l log] [-f fw-host] [-C] -((n|i|I|j|J) <criteria>

sam [-v] [-s sam-server] [-S server-sic-name] [-f fw-host]
   -M -ijn <criteria>

sam [-v] [-s sam-server] [-S server-sic-name] [-f fw-host] -D
```

The criteria for the **fw sam** command are described in Table 5.12.

The IP addresses in Table 5.12 may be resolvable hostnames or dotted decimal notation addresses. Service may be a resolvable service name (in the services file, like Telnet or WWW) or a service number (a TCP/UDP port number). Protocol may be a protocol name (like TCP) or a protocol number.

Table 5.11 Options for the fw sam command

Option	Description
-v	Turns on verbose mode.
-s sam_server	Specifies the Suspicious Activity Monitoring (SAM) server to be contacted. The default is localhost.
-t timeout	Specifies the timeout in seconds. The default is Never.
-f fw_gist	Specifies the firewalls to run the operation on. This command option should contain either the name of a firewalled object, the name of a group of firewalled objects, or one of the predefined names: all and gateways. The default is all.
-C	Cancels the specified option.
-n	Notifies every time a connection that matches the specified criteria passes the firewall.
-i	Inhibits connections that match the specified criteria.
-I	Inhibits connections that match the specified criteria and closes existing connections that match it.
-D	Deletes all previous operations.

Table 5.12 Criteria for the `fw sam` command

Format	Description
`src ipaddr`	Matches the source address of connections
`dst ipaddr`	Matches the destination address of connections
`any ipaddr`	Matches the source or destination address of connections
`subsrc ip netmask`	Matches the specified network by IP and netmask in the source IP of the packet
`subdst ip netmask`	Matches the specified network by IP and netmask in the destination IP of the packet
`subany ip netmask`	Matches the specified network by IP and netmask in either the source or destination IP of the packet
`srv srcip dstip service protocol`	Matches the specified source, destination, and service
`subsrv srcip netmask dstip netmask service protocol`	Matches the specified source network (IP and netmask), specified destination network (IP and netmask), service, and protocol (i.e., blocks a service between two networks)
`subsrvs srcip netmask dstip service protocol`	Matches the specified source network (IP and netmask), specified destination host, service, and protocol (i.e., blocks a specific network from accessing a particular host via a particular port/protocol)
`subsrvd srcip dstip netmask service protocol`	Matches the specified source IP, specified destination network (IP and netmask), service, and protocol (i.e., blocks a specific host from accessing a particular network using a specific port/protocol)
`dstsrv dstip service protocol`	Matches the specified destination IP, service, and protocol (i.e., blocks all access to a specific host via a specific port/protocol)
`subdstsrv dstip netmask service protocol`	Matches the specified source network (IP and netmask), service, and protocol (i.e., blocks all access to a specific network via a specific port/protocol)
`srcpr ip protocol`	Matches the specified source IP address and protocol (i.e., prevents a particular IP from originating traffic of a specified protocol type)
`dstpr ip protocol`	Matches the specified destination IP address and protocol (i.e., prevents all access to a particular host via the specified protocol)
`subsrcpr ip netmask protocol`	Matches the specified source network (IP and netmask) and protocol (i.e., prevents a particular network from originating traffic of a specified protocol type)
`subdstpr ip netmask protocol`	Matches the specified destination network (IP and netmask) and protocol (i.e., prevents all access to a particular network via the specified protocol)

For example, if you wanted to turn on additional notification for a specific action, say, accessing www.phoneboy.com, you would type:

```
# fw sam -n dst www.phoneboy.com
```

All notifications will appear as rule "sam" in the logs. If you wanted to deny all connections to www.phoneboy.com for 60 seconds, you would type:

```
# fw sam -t 60 -i dst www.phoneboy.com
```

If you wanted to deny all connections to foo.bar.com and close any existing connections, you would type:

```
# fw sam -I dst foo.bar.com
```

If you wanted to close a specific Telnet connection from host.yoursite.com to foo.bar.com and prevent further requests from that host, you would type:

```
# fw sam -I srv host.yoursite.com foo.bar.com 23 6
```

(Note that 23 is the port number for Telnet; 6 is the protocol number for TCP.) To cancel the preceding operation, you would type:

```
# fw sam -C srv host.yoursite.com foo.bar.com 23 6
```

To cancel all previous operations (i.e., unblock all blocked connections), you would type:

```
# fw sam -D
```

Audit Mode

A new feature in NG is the ability to see exactly what administrators do in the various SmartConsole applications. The most detail is shown for SmartDashboard/Policy Editor because that is where the most changes can be made. For the other GUIs, you will see when administrators log in or out only. Figure 5.10 shows a sample of Audit mode. Table 5.13 explains the fields you will see in this view.

No.	Date	Time	Origin	Application	Operation	Object Name	Changes
83	24Aug2002	2:40:03	craig	cpstat_monitor	Logged in		
84	24Aug2002	12:46:25	craig	Log Manager	Logged in		
85	25Aug2002	0:03:48	craig	Log Manager	Logged out		
86	25Aug2002	0:32:07	craig	SmartDashboard	Logged in		
87	25Aug2002	0:37:51	craig	Log Manager	Logged in		
88	25Aug2002	0:42:21	craig	SmartDashboard	Create	alpha-cluster	
89	25Aug2002	0:42:21	craig	SmartDashboard	Update	craig	use_cert: changed from 'none' to 'defaultCert' ;use_clientless_...
90	25Aug2002	0:42:21	craig	SmartDashboard	Update	phoneboy-trad...	rule 1 - action: added 'accept_action' ;rule 1 - action: removed...
91	25Aug2002	0:46:01	craig	SmartDashboard	Install Policy	firewall_applic...	
92	25Aug2002	0:46:52	craig	SmartDashboard	Logged out		
93	25Aug2002	0:46:57	craig	Log Manager	Logged out		
94	25Aug2002	19:51:04	craig	SmartDashboard	Logged in		
95	25Aug2002	23:47:14	craig	SmartDashboard	Update	craig	certificates: added 'certificate' ;
96	25Aug2002	23:50:17	craig	Log Manager	Logged in		
97	25Aug2002	23:55:55	craig	SmartDashboard	Create	alpha-cluster2	
98	25Aug2002	23:55:55	craig	SmartDashboard	Rename	alpha-cluster-vpn	Object name was changed from 'alpha-cluster2' to 'alpha-clust...
99	25Aug2002	23:55:55	craig	SmartDashboard	Create	nokia-networks	
100	25Aug2002	23:55:55	craig	SmartDashboard	Update	alpha-cluster-vpn	encdomain: changed from 'addresses_behind_gw' to 'manual' ;
101	25Aug2002	23:56:03	craig	SmartDashboard	Create	phoneboy	
102	25Aug2002	23:56:03	craig	SmartDashboard	Create	phoneboy	
103	26Aug2002	0:06:20	craig	SmartDashboard	Update	MyIntranet	ike_p1_hash_alg: changed from 'MD5' to 'SHA1' ;ike_p2_enc_a...
104	26Aug2002	0:06:20	craig	SmartDashboard	Update	RemoteAccess	ike_p1_use_shared_secret: changed from 'false' to 'true';parti...
105	26Aug2002	0:06:20	craig	SmartDashboard	Create	phoneboy-simple	
106	26Aug2002	0:06:20	craig	SmartDashboard	Update	firewall_proper...	enable_ip_pool: changed from 'false' to 'true';
107	26Aug2002	0:06:20	craig	SmartDashboard	Update	craig	certificates: added 'certificate' ;certificates: removed 'certificat...
108	26Aug2002	0:06:20	craig	SmartDashboard	Create	net_10.0.255.0	
109	26Aug2002	0:06:20	craig	SmartDashboard	Update	craig	ip_pool_securemote: changed from 'false' to 'true';certificates:...
110	26Aug2002	0:06:20	craig	SmartDashboard	Update	internal-networks	internal-networks: added 'net_10.0.255.0' ;
111	26Aug2002	0:06:20	craig	SmartDashboard	Create	phoneboy-simple	
112	26Aug2002	0:06:27	craig	SmartDashboard	Logged out		
113	26Aug2002	0:27:18	craig	Log Manager	Logged out		
114	26Aug2002	13:37:00	craig	SmartDashboard	Logged in		
115	26Aug2002	18:19:22	craig	SmartDashboard	Update	AdvancedSecu...	asm_synatk_global_override: changed from 'true' to 'false';
116	26Aug2002	18:19:22	craig	SmartDashboard	Update	AdvancedSecu...	asm_synatk_global_override: changed from 'false' to 'true';
117	26Aug2002	18:19:24	craig	SmartDashboard	Logged out		
118	26Aug2002	23:47:57	craig	Status Manager	Logged in		

Figure 5.10   SmartView Tracker, Audit mode

Table 5.13   SmartView Tracker Entries in Audit mode

Entry	Description
No.	The log entry number
Date	The date the log entry was generated
Time	The time the log entry was generated
Origin	The management module that generated the log entry
Application	The product for which this log entry is relevant
Operation	The event that is being logged (Logged in, Logged out, Create, Update, Install Policy)
Object Name	The object that was acted upon, if relevant
Changes	The changes that occurred to this object in detail
Administrator	The administrative user making the change
General Information	Other relevant information (e.g., user logged in, which policy was loaded)

Alerts

Now that I have discussed the two applications that let you look at logs and alerts, I will talk about alerts themselves; mainly, how they are generated. Aside from creating rules that have a Track of one of the alert types, you need to configure the Log and Alert frame of the Global Properties screen, which is shown in Figure 5.11. This allows you to configure some additional events that get logged. The alert types and the commands they execute are specified in the Alert Commands frame (subsection of the Log and Alert frame); see Figure 5.12. Note that all commands listed must be executable on the management console, *not on individual firewalls.*

 NOTE! All "alerted" entries also generate a log entry.

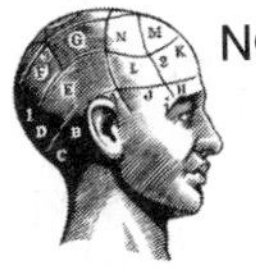

The additional activities on which you can control logging include those listed below. (The pop-up menu to the right of each item shown in Figure 5.11 controls how that action is logged or alerted.)

VPN successful key exchange: The appropriate log or alert is generated when a successful key exchange occurs for either a client-to-site VPN or a site-to-site VPN.

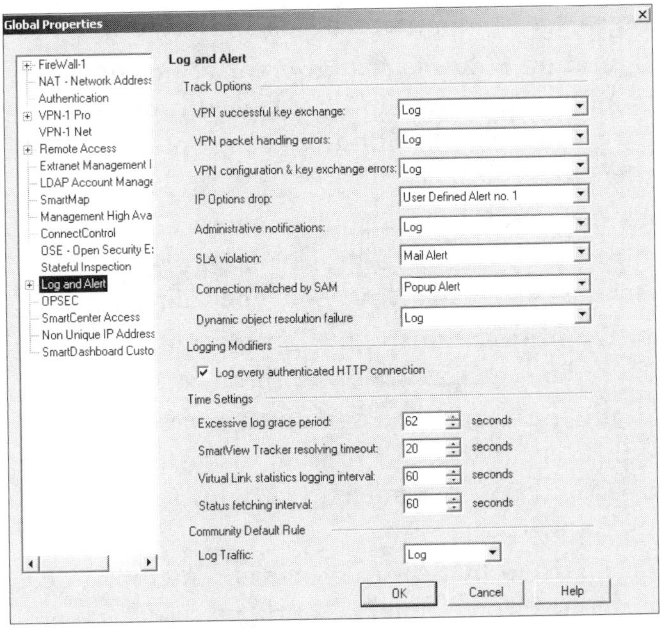

Figure 5.11 Global Properties, Log and Alert frame

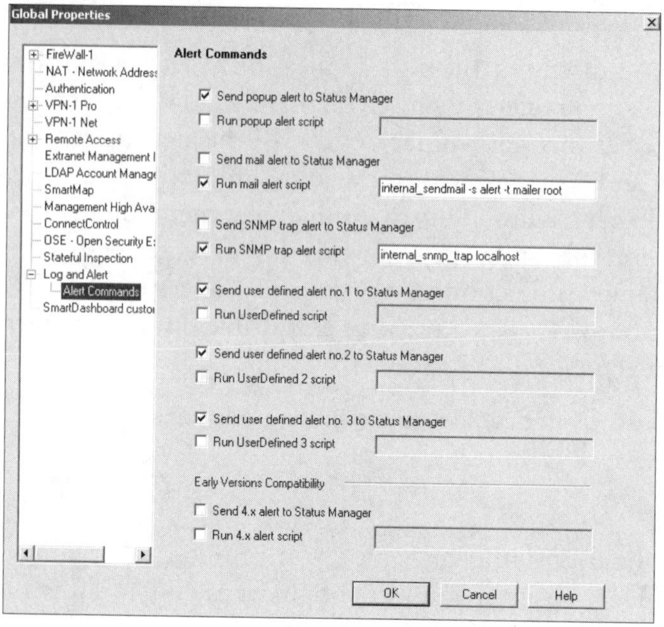

Figure 5.12   Global Properties, Alert Commands frame

VPN packet handling errors: If errors occur while processing encrypted packets (e.g., because they are malformed or come from the wrong host), this activity generates the appropriate log and/or alert.

VPN configuration & key exchange errors: A log or alert is generated if a configuration error occurs in the VPN-related configuration (e.g., attempting to encrypt to a network within your encryption domain) or if an error occurs during a key exchange.

IP Options drop: All packets containing IP Options are dropped. This entry controls how IP Options drops are logged. This is set to None by default. Why this isn't set to at least Log is beyond me.

Administrative notifications: This generates a log or alert for various administrative items, such as when a certificate is about to expire.

SLA violation: If a virtual link is defined and the availability parameters defined for that link are not met, that is, the virtual link does not meet the established Service Level Agreement (SLA), this activity generates the appropriate log or alert entry.

Connection matched by SAM: If SmartDefense/SAM determines certain packets are among its predefined network attacks, this generates the appropriate log entry or alert.

Dynamic object resolution failure: If for some reason a module is not able to resolve a dynamic object (e.g., you have not executed the appropriate commands on the module to define it), this activity generates the appropriate alert or log entry.

Log every authenticated HTTP connection: In many cases, loading a Web page requires more than one connection to be opened. If this option is checked, each and every one of those connections will be logged instead of just the first one to a particular site.

Excessive log grace period: To try to limit the number of entries logged to the log file, FireWall-1 keeps track of everything logged for a set period of time, and if a particular activity (by source, destination, service, and source port) occurs within the excessive log grace period multiple times, only one log entry is generated. By default, this option is set to 62 seconds, which in reality results in about 60 seconds. Whatever setting you choose, be sure to add 2 seconds to the value.

SmartView Tracker resolving timeout: This option indicates the number of seconds the SmartView Tracker/Log Viewer spends on attempting to resolve the IP addresses of entries shown. Note that this timeout does not always seem to be enforced on Windows when WINS is used to resolve names.

Virtual Link statistics logging interval: When virtual links are defined, this option defines how often the statistics for these links are updated.

Status fetching interval: This determines how frequently the management station queries your other Check Point modules to obtain status information.

Log Traffic (for Community Default Rule): If you have enabled the "Accept all encrypted traffic" option in any of your VPN Communities, this option controls whether or not those default rules generate log entries.

As mentioned, Figure 5.12 shows the different types of alerts and the actions taken for those alerts. There are two types of actions for each alert; you can select either, neither, or both of them.

Send alert to Status Manager: The alert is sent to the Status Manager, where it is displayed in a pop-up window.

Run script: When the alert occurs, run the indicated script from your management console. Unless a full path is specified, the command is assumed to be in your OS path.

Note that it is possible to write your own script or program that parses the input and performs an action based on that input. The script must take a single line of text from standard input (stdin). The format used is identical to how log entries are output via the command **fw log**. Once you have your program written, you simply replace the appropriate alert command with the complete pathname to the script or program on the management console.

> **NOTE!** If you make any changes to these properties, you will have to reinstall the security policy before they will take effect.

A Word on Mail Alerts

A common belief among FireWall-1 administrators is that there is some magic to e-mail alerts. There really isn't. A command is executed on your platform that sends the e-mail. UNIX platforms usually have some sort of command-line utility (e.g., **mail** or **mailx**) that can take a subject and recipient via command-line arguments and message data until an end-of-file is reached. In order for these commands to deliver e-mails to anything beyond the local system, some sort of sendmail-type application must be available. If one of these is not available or not configured correctly, I recommend installing something like sSMTP (available at http://ibiblio.org/pub/Linux/system/mail/mta/, among other places), which is nothing more than a way to relay e-mail to a proper mail hub for processing. IPSO-based platforms have everything you need to do this, provided you have configured the appropriate mail gateway and from address in Voyager.

Windows-based platforms do not generally contain a command-line mail utility, so Check Point includes a sendmail binary, which functions like a **mail** or **mailx** program on UNIX. It also allows you to use the command line to specify the SMTP server to send the message through. You will need to change the command shown in the Alert Commands frame of the Global Properties screen to:

```
sendmail -s Alert -f fw1@yourdomain -t ip-of-smtp-server
you@yourdomain
```

Log Maintenance

It is recommended that you look at your logs regularly to determine whether people are attempting to violate your security policy. Also, log files themselves tend to get rather big and need to be switched every so often. In the Log Viewer application itself, you can use the New command under the File menu in the Log Viewer to rename the old log file and the Switch Active File command under the File menu to simply delete the current log, or use the command **fw logswitch** from the management console. Optionally, you can give **fw**

logswitch an argument with a filename to switch the log to. The default is to simply stamp the previous fw.log file with the current date and time.

People often wish to rotate their logs daily or more frequently if logging is particularly heavy. I personally recommend doing a logswitch on a daily basis unless you log more than a few hundred thousand entries a day, in which case I would rotate at a regular interval as needed to keep the total number of log entries below 300,000.

FireWall-1 NG introduced many more options for automatically rotating log files, aside from automating this task with a **cron** job or the **at** scheduler in Windows. A gateway or management object can be configured to automatically rotate logs at a certain time or under certain circumstances. Figure 5.13 shows the configuration for a sample gateway object.

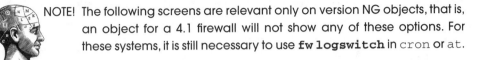 NOTE! The following screens are relevant only on version NG objects, that is, an object for a 4.1 firewall will not show any of these options. For these systems, it is still necessary to use **fw logswitch** in cron or at.

The options for the Logs and Masters tab are listed below.

Log switch when file size is: As the name implies, this automatically switches the log file when it reaches the specified size.

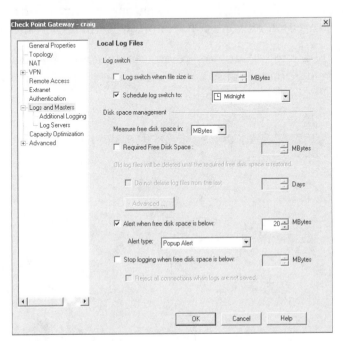

Figure 5.13 Gateway object, Logs and Masters tab

Schedule log switch to: This option allows you to specify a time to automatically rotate the log file. The selectable times here are defined as time objects of type scheduled event.

Measure free disk space in: Changing this option affects how the remaining options will be answered. The default is megabytes (MBytes). The other option is percent, which means free space is specified as a percentage of the overall disk space available.

Required Free Disk Space: This indicates the number of megabytes/percentage of free disk space that must be kept available. If this option is checked, the next option becomes available.

Do not delete log files from the last: This option specifies the number of days of logs that must be kept. All logs older than this will be deleted.

Advanced: This button allows you to specify a script that will run before logs are deleted. This script may, for instance, FTP the logs to a different location.

Alert when free disk space is below: This option executes the alert (indicated in the Alert type pull-down menu) when the disk space drops below the specified threshold.

Stop logging when free disk space is below: As the name implies, this option stops logging when disk space reaches the specified threshold.

Reject all connections when logs are not saved: In the unfortunate event that the system isn't saving logs, this option prevents any new connections through the firewall. Existing connections will still be permitted.

It is also possible to forward logs to other management or log servers via the Additional Logging frame (subsection of the Logs and Masters frame). Figure 5.14 shows those configuration options.

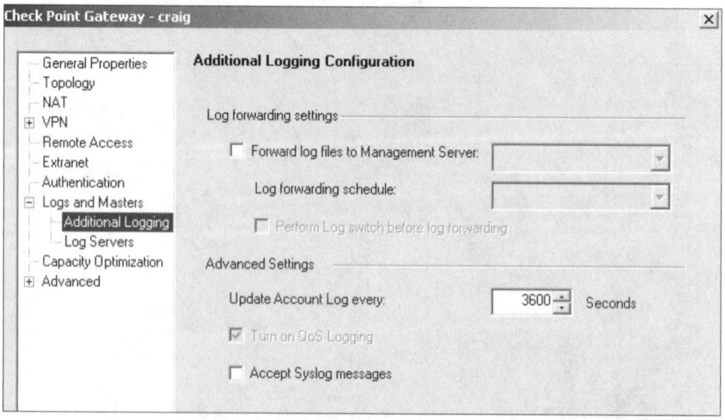

Figure 5.14 Gateway object, Additional Logging frame

The options for additional logging include those listed below.

Forward log files to Management Server: As the name implies, you can forward log files to a different management server, but you can also forward logs to a log server. Objects specified as management consoles or as log servers can be selected.

Log forwarding schedule: You must also define when this forwarding occurs by selecting a time object of type scheduled event.

Perform Log switch before log forwarding: This option performs a log switch. The log-switched file is then forwarded to the specified management server.

Update Account Log every: Any account log entries for active connections get written to the log file as frequently as this option specifies.

Turn on QoS Logging: This enables logging for FloodGate.

Accept Syslog messages: This option is present in FireWall-1 NG FP3 and later. Syslog is a remote logging mechanism used by UNIX-based platforms. This allows your module to accept syslog entries from other hosts and integrate them into the Check Point logs.

Firewall objects also have the Log Servers tab in their definition, which allows you to configure where logs are initially written. Figure 5.15 shows how this screen looks.

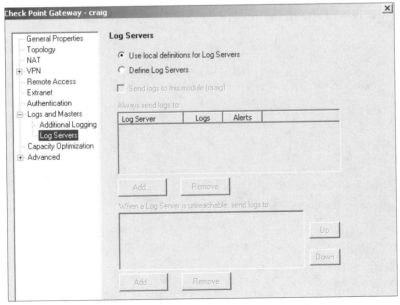

Figure 5.15   Gateway object, Log Servers frame

You can define the following options on this tab.

Use local definitions for Log Servers: This tells the firewall module to use the definitions defined in `$FWDIR/conf/masters` and `$FWDIR/conf/loggers` on the local firewall module. This also affects the Masters frame of the object, assuming it has one. This is particularly useful when the management station will be accessible only via NAT. This configuration is described in Chapter 7.

Define Log Servers: This option allows you to manually override the default logging settings.

Send logs to this module: By choosing this, you can write all logs to your local disk. If you select this option, it's recommended that you forward the logs to your management console regularly. This option won't work on systems without a local hard disk (e.g., Nokia IP71).

Always send logs to: This allows you to specify to which management console or log servers the logs are sent.

When a Log Server is unreachable, send logs to: If the primary log servers are down, use the specified alternates, in the specified order.

Summary

Understanding what is happening with your firewall is vital to maintaining the security of your networks. SmartView Tracker and SmartView Status applications are just two of the many tools you can use to do this.

Chapter

6

Common Issues

One of the weaknesses I felt the first edition of this book had was that it did not include enough Frequently Asked Questions (FAQs) of a more general nature, that is, things that might come up in the day-to-day operation of your firewall but didn't neatly fall into other chapters I've written. Since providing answers to FAQs about FireWall-1 is how I got to be well known within the FireWall-1 community in the first place, it seems fitting that I include a chapter in the book that is nothing but FAQs.

The FAQs in this chapter relate to error messages you might see in the operating system logs, on the console, and in SmartView Tracker/Log Viewer. The FAQs also cover other situations that the average firewall administrator needs to resolve that are more general in nature.

By the end of this chapter, you should be able to:

- Configure your firewall to deal with some common situations
- Diagnose common error messages that occur with your firewall
- Recognize common issues that appear to be firewall-related but are not

Common Configuration Questions

In the course of using or configuring FireWall-1, a number of common configuration questions come up from time to time. The following subsections document the most common ones.

6.1: How Do I Modify FireWall-1 Kernel Variables?

Over the years, Check Point has introduced some rather obscure features by exposing "kernel variables" that can be tweaked to change certain behavior. While this is not the most elegant solution, it involves the least amount of work because it requires no GUI changes. Modifying kernel variables is relatively straightforward once you know how. You perform the appropriate commands for your platform and reboot.

Let us assume that the kernel variable we want to modify is `fw_allow_udp_`
`port0`. For the record, this particular variable allows packets to be sent from or
to UDP port 0, which FireWall-1 normally drops. In order to allow these kinds
of packets, we need to change the value of this parameter to `1`. The value can be
specified in decimal or hexadecimal (precede with an `0x` for hexadecimal).

In general, you can substitute `fw_allow_udp_port0` and `0x1` for the variable you want to modify and the value you wish to assign it, respectively.

On Solaris machines, add the following line to the bottom of the `/etc/`
`system` file, and reboot:

```
set fw:fw_allow_udp_port0=0x1
```

On an IPSO system (VPN-1 Appliance or Nokia IPxxx), you need to get the
`modzap` utility from Resolution 1261 in Nokia's Knowledge Base. You can then
use the following command line to modify the `fw_allow_udp_port0` parameter and reboot the system:

```
nokia[admin]# modzap _fw_allow_udp_port0
                  $FWDIR/boot/modules/fwmod.o 0x1
```

 NOTE! On IPSO, all kernel variables begin with an underscore (_).

On a Linux platform, you simply add the following line to `$FWDIR/boot/`
`modules/fwkern.conf` and restart FireWall-1 (no reboot required):

```
fw_allow_udp_port0=1
```

For Windows, there is no way to modify kernel variables without getting a
special utility called `fwpatch` from Check Point support. In some cases, it is
possible to tweak registry settings.

6.2: Can I Direct FireWall-1 Log Messages to syslog?

To log specific events to syslog, I use user-defined logging for this. My user-
defined program (defined in the Global Properties section, Log and Alert frame)
is `/usr/ucb/logger -p daemon.notice`. The path to the `logger` utility
varies depending on the operating system.

Another alternative is to log everything to syslog. You can do this with the
following command:

```
# fw log -f 2>>/var/adm/fw-log.log | /bin/logger -p \
    local5.info > /dev/null 2>&1 &
```

This command runs in the background and logs everything to syslog. Note that it might be best to put this into a boot script after FireWall-1 loads so that everything is dumped to syslog.

On Windows platforms, instead of `logger`, use the Kiwi SyslogGen program, available from http://www.kiwisyslog.com.

6.3: How Can I Disconnect Connections at a Specific Time?

Active connections stay in the connections tables until they either terminate or expire. The rulebase controls only when connections start, not how long they are allowed to stay connected.

One way to block connections at a specific time is to use the **fw sam** command, which is described in Chapter 5. At a specified time, run a command via **cron** that blocks all inappropriate traffic and disconnects any active session for a specific period of time. Once the timeout for that command expires (you can set it as low or as high as you want), everything should go through your rulebase normally. The old connections should theoretically be forgotten.

6.4: How Many Interfaces Are Supported?

FireWall-1 NG up to NG FP2 supports 256 interfaces. Versions NG FP3 and above support 1,024 interfaces. However, each IP associated with the platform might get associated with the interface slot, depending on how old a version you are running.

On the Nokia platform, things are a little more complicated, depending on which version of IPSO and FireWall-1 you happen to be using. The following list shows what your interface limit is based on the versions used:

- FireWall-1 NG FP2 or earlier without VLAN hotfix: 64 interfaces
- FireWall-1 NG FP2 with VLAN hotfix: 256 interfaces
- FireWall-1 NG FP3 on IPSO 3.6: 256 interfaces
- IPSO 3.7 or above (with supported FireWall-1 version): 1,024 interfaces

What constitutes an interface varies by platform. GRE tunnels, VLANs, frame relay DLCIs, point-to-point links, permanent virtual circuits, and other similar constructs may be considered interfaces by FireWall-1.

6.5: How Do I Create a Large Number of Objects via the Command Line?

Bulk creation of objects is accomplished through the use of the command-line program **dbedit**, which provides a protected interface to the Check Point object database, along with object validation.

The **dbedit** commands used to create a simple network object are listed below. (x.y.z.w is the IP address, a.b.c.d is the netmask, and sample-network is the name of the object.)

```
dbedit> create network sample-network
dbedit> modify network_objects sample-network ipaddr x.y.z.w
dbedit> modify network_objects sample-network netmask a.b.c.d
dbedit> update network_objects sample-network
```

The **create** command is used to bring the object into existence, the **modify** command is used to change elements of that object, and the **update** command is used to push that change to the object database.

To create a simple host object (e.f.g.h is the host object IP), use these commands:

```
dbedit> create host_plain sample-host
dbedit> modify network_objects sample-host ipaddr e.f.g.h
dbedit> update network_objects sample-host
```

To group the objects together, use these commands:

```
dbedit> create network_object_group sample-group
dbedit> addelement network_objects sample-group ''
                network_objects:sample-network
dbedit> addelement network_objects sample-group ''
                network_objects:sample-host
dbedit> update network_objects sample-group
```

In the preceding example, the **addelement** command is responsible for adding the objects into the group. Since a group can potentially contain non-network objects, we have to be explicit when we add them to a group, which is why we refer to sample-network and sample-host as network_objects:sample-network and network_objects:sample-host, respectively, within the code.

You can also create a network object with automatic NAT by using the following commands:

```
dbedit> create host_plain london

dbedit> modify network_objects london ipaddr 192.168.1.1
dbedit> modify network_objects london color red
dbedit> modify network_objects london comments "This is london calling"
dbedit> modify network_objects london add_adtr_rule true
dbedit> modify network_objects london NAT NAT
dbedit> modify network_objects london NAT:valid_ipaddr 195.195.195.3

dbedit> modify network_objects london NAT:netobj_adtr_method adtr_static
dbedit> update network_objects london
```

In the preceding example, if you wanted to do hide mode NAT, replace `adtr_static` with `adtr_hide`.

By putting the appropriate **dbedit** commands in a file and invoking **dbedit** correctly, you could script the creation of network objects. To automate the process, execute something similar to the following on your management station (`dbeditcmdfile.txt` contains the **dbedit** commands).

```
# dbedit -s localhost -u admin -p adminpw -f dbeditcmdfile.txt
```

Common Error Messages in the System Log

One thing there is no shortage of in FireWall-1 is error messages. The following subsections highlight several common errors and what you can do to prevent them.

Several of these FAQs reference HFA-xxx versions. These are called Hotfix Accumulators, something Check Point Support started generating since FireWall-1 NG FP3. They are simply "jumbo hotfixes" that include fixes for a number of issues combined. These fixes can be obtained from Check Point Support, which users with a direct support agreement can do. Companies that provide support for Check Point products can also provide these hotfixes. The same applies for almost any other hotfix mentioned.

6.6: Local Interface Anti-Spoofing

Local interface anti-spoofing is a different sort of anti-spoofing than the one configured in the gateway object for the firewall. FireWall-1 drops any packet it receives with a source IP address of one of the firewall's local interfaces that the firewall did not originate. You might see this if you plug two or more physical interfaces on different logical interfaces into the same hub.

You can disable local interface anti-spoofing by changing the FireWall-1 kernel variable `fw_local_interface_anti_spoofing` to 0. For more details on how to change FireWall-1 kernel variables, see FAQ 6.1.

6.7: Tried to Open Known Service Port, Port xxxx

The error message "Host tried to open known service port" shows up with services that use multiple ports for their communication. This error is most common with FTP but can also occur with other services. By default, FireWall-1 does not allow services that negotiate data ports to choose a service that is defined in FireWall-1. This check can be disabled by editing `$FWDIR/lib/base.def` on the management console and reinstalling the security policy.

In theory, this check prevents anyone from using the control connection of an allowed service such as FTP to open a service that may not otherwise be allowed between the client and server. However, this check applies only to pre-defined services. Someone interested in subverting the firewall in this manner could just as easily choose a service port undefined in FireWall-1 and, instead of using an FTP data connection, do something else through it. Because of this, I do not see this check providing real value, and any value it does have is over-shadowed by the fact that it frequently breaks legitimate FTP usage.

In FireWall-1 NG FP1 and above, you can resolve this problem by editing $FWDIR/lib/base.def on the management station. Add the following line in the following location (the line to add is set in bold):

```
#ifndef __base_def__
#define __base_def__

#define NO_SERVER_PORT_CHECK

#include "services.def"

//
// (c) Copyright 1993-2001 Check Point Software Technologies Ltd.
// All rights reserved.
```

This line effectively disables the macros that check for defined services. The change will take effect once the security policy is pushed to the enforcement points.

6.8: Virtual Defragmentation Errors
In order to determine whether or not a fragmented packet should be allowed, FireWall-1 holds all fragments it receives until it can assemble the entire packet in memory. If the assembled packet would normally pass, FireWall-1 passes the packet but sends it out as it was received—fragmented—thus the term *virtual defragmentation*. If FireWall-1 doesn't receive all the fragments for the packet or the fragment table fills up, which may occur during a fragmentation-based denial-of-service (DoS) attack, FireWall-1 drops the fragments and does not forward them, generating log messages along the way.

6.9: Too Many Internal Hosts
This error shows up when you have a node-limited firewall license and FireWall-1 believes you have violated the license because it has "seen" too many hosts on the internal interfaces. Note that the configuration in the Topology section of the gateway object determines which interfaces are internal and external. (See Fun with Check Point Licensing in Chapter 2 for discussion of node-limited licenses and their enforcement.)

If you see this error, it means the number of discrete IP addresses protected by the firewall has exceeded the license limitation. Anything behind your firewall with an IP address will eventually be discovered, regardless of whether or not the host traverses the firewall. Machines with multiple IP addresses and machines that change their IP addresses will be counted more than once.

When the license is exceeded by a large number of hosts on a busy network, FireWall-1 will consume itself with logging and messages about exceeding your license. In extreme cases, this will cause the firewall to process traffic very slowly, if at all. Note, however, that FireWall-1 will still continue to pass traffic, even from those hosts that exceed the license count. However, performance may be severely degraded because FireWall-1 spends time notifying you that your license count has been exceeded.

You can get a count of the number of hosts by entering the command **fw tab -t host_table -s**. The entry under the #VALS heading corresponds to the number of hosts it has counted. You can see which IP addresses are currently being counted against your license by issuing the command **fw lichosts**.

You will have to reset FireWall-1 in regards to the IP addresses it has erroneously logged as internal. Remove the $FWDIR/database/fwd.h and $FWDIR/database/fwd.hosts files and restart FireWall-1. You can also reset the table with **fw tab -t host_table -x**.

6.10: **Pth** SCHEDULER INTERNAL ERROR: No More Thread(s) Available to Schedule

This error comes up during policy installations from SmartDashboard/Policy Editor. You can safely ignore this message.

6.11: Target localhost Is Not Defined as an NG Module, Please Use the -l Flag

This message also shows up during policy installations from SmartDashboard/Policy Editor. Unfortunately, this error indicates that one or more objects in the $FWDIR/conf/objects_5_0.C file have been corrupted. There are a few ways to proceed.

1. If the management station was upgraded recently, try downgrading to the prior release and use the Upgrade Verifier to ensure consistency. You can download this utility from http://www.checkpoint.com/techsupport/downloadsng/utilities.html.

2. With the management station stopped (**cpstop**), replace $FWDIR/conf/objects_5_0.C with $FWDIR/conf/objects_5_0.C.backup. Restart the management station (**cpstart**) and see if the problem still occurs.

3. Check for duplicate IP addresses in the firewall and management gateway objects.

4. Upgrade to NG FP3, HFA-306, later HFA hot fixes, or NG AI. These versions resolve this issue.

6.12: Invalid Value in the Access Attribute: Undefined: File Exists

This error occurs when the topology settings have not been defined in the FireWall-1/VPN-1 version 4.1 object interfaces. This error message is harmless, and the policy does get installed on the version 4.1 module. To correct this situation, edit the FireWall-1/VPN-1 version 4.1 object interfaces properties and configure the topology settings with the appropriate options for your network configuration.

6.13: mbuf_alloc(1500): Cluster Alloc

If the firewall policy is installed when there is heavy traffic, the "mbuf_alloc" debug message may be displayed on the console. The message can be safely ignored.

6.14: Log Buffer Is Full, Error: Lost xxx Log/Trap Messages

The kernel module maintains a buffer of waiting log messages that it gives to fwd to send to the management module. The buffer is circular, so high levels of logging may cause buffer entries to be overwritten before they can be sent to fwd. When this happens, the system log will display messages indicating that log entries are being lost.

One solution to this issue is to reduce the amount of logging done. Disable any accounting rules that you can. Eliminate as much logging as possible.

Another solution is to increase the size of this buffer. In FireWall-1 NG, you will need to change the fw_log_bufsize kernel variable. This should be set to a value of 0x40000 or higher. FAQ 6.1 explains how to set these kernel variables.

Service-Related Questions

By design, firewalls restrict the use of certain services. Some services are more problematic than others. The following FAQs relate to the use of certain services through FireWall-1.

6.15: Why Doesn't Windows Traceroute Work?

This problem originally existed in pre-4.0 versions of FireWall-1. It does not exist in 4.0 or 4.1 versions of FireWall-1. Though the reason has changed, the problem has returned in FireWall-1 NG FP1 and FP2.

With an NG FP1/FP2 firewall using hide NAT, a packet sniffer shows that the client is being sent ICMP "time exceeded" messages as it should. However, the client appears to ignore these ICMP messages and displays "Request Timed Out" messages for hops past the firewall. Analysis of these ignored packets shows both an invalid checksum and less data than was sent by the ICMP echo-request packet (56 bytes of data received versus the 64 bytes sent). These are the likely reasons the packets are being ignored.

With an NG FP1/FP2 firewall using static NAT, the ICMP "time exceeded" packets at each hop after the firewall are dropped by the firewall with the message "ICMP packet out of state" in the logs.

Check Point issued hotfix SHF_FW1_FP2_0068 to resolve this issue. Upgrading to NG FP3 or later also solves the problem.

6.16: How Does FireWall-1 Support UNIX RPC?

Each service based on Remote Procedure Call (RPC) uses its own unique program number (within each service, a version number). When an RPC-based program starts, it uses a random TCP and/or UDP port number. The portmapper is used to map each program number to a particular port used by the RPC-based program at that moment. The connection to the portmapper process must be UDP for FireWall-1 to support it—TCP connections to the portmapper are currently not supported.

FireWall-1 supports RPC by monitoring the client RPC request to the portmapper. The portmapper replies with the port number. FireWall-1 temporarily opens that port number for the connection from the client to the server. Once the connection is over, FireWall-1 closes the port.

In terms of custom applications, 99% of the time, you can simply define your custom application as a new service using the following parameters:

- Type of connection (e.g., TCP, UDP, RPC)
- Port number (for TCP and UDP)
- Program number for RPC

Once done, you can use the newly defined service like any other network services.

6.17: How Do I Block AOL Instant Messenger?

To block AOL Instant Messenger, block access to the IP addresses listed in Table 6.1.

Table 6.1.   IP addresses known to be used for AOL Instant Messenger

64.12.161.153	152.163.214.108	152.163.241.121	152.163.242.28
64.12.161.185	152.163.214.109	152.163.241.128	205.188.1.56
152.163.214.75	152.163.241.96	152.163.241.129	205.188.4.106
152.163.214.76	152.163.241.120	152.163.242.24	205.188.147.114

Table 6.2.   IP addresses known to be used for Yahoo Messenger

204.71.177.35	204.71.201.48	216.115.107.64	216.115.107.103
204.71.200.54	204.71.202.58	216.115.107.65	216.115.107.104
204.71.200.55	204.71.202.59	216.115.107.66	216.115.107.105
204.71.200.56	216.115.105.214	216.115.107.67	216.136.173.179
204.71.200.57	216.115.105.215	216.115.107.101	216.136.172.221
204.71.200.68	216.115.107.63	216.115.107.102	204.71.202.73
204.71.201.47			

6.18: How Do I Enable or Block Yahoo Messenger?

To do this, you need to allow or block access via port 5050 to the IP addresses listed in Table 6.2.

6.19: How Do I Block ICMP Packets of a Particular Length?

You can block ICMP packets by specifying a maximum acceptable length. For example, to block packets that are longer than 100 bytes, first define a service of type Other. Then set the protocol number to 1 and put the following in the Match field:

```
ip_len > 100
```

This will match any ICMP packets greater than 100 bytes in length (including headers). Create a rule with this new service to drop the packet.

Problems with Stateful Inspection of TCP Connections

The problem with using a stateful firewall is that if the applications that go through it have a slightly different concept of what proper TCP state should be, or if the firewall makes invalid assumptions, some services will cease to function. The following subsections explain what some of those errors are and how to fix them.

6.20: TCP Packet Out of State

The "TCP Packet out of state" error message means that FireWall-1 sees a TCP ACK packet for which it does not have a matching state table entry. This may occur because the connection was inactive for a period of time or the connections tables were flushed (e.g., because of a policy installation or restart).

A little history is in order here. In FireWall-1 4.0 and earlier, if FireWall-1 received a TCP ACK packet that didn't match an entry in the connections tables, it would strip off the data portion of the packet (thus making it harmless), change the TCP sequence number, and forward the packet to its final destination. Because the destination host would see an unexpected sequence number, it would send a SYN packet to resynchronize the connection. The SYN packet would then go through the rulebase. If the rulebase permitted the packet, the entries in the connections tables would be recreated and the connection would continue.

In FireWall-1 4.1 and FireWall-1 4.1 SP1, FireWall-1 allows the unsolicited TCP ACK packet only if it comes from the server. If the TCP ACK packet comes from the client (i.e., the machine that originated the connection), the TCP ACK packet is dropped.

Then someone figured out that this handling of ACK packets could be used to cause a DoS attack against both the firewall and the host behind it. Since FireWall-1 4.1 SP2, by default FireWall-1 drops ACK packets for which there are no entries in the state tables. However, in NG FP3 and above, you can revert back to the pre-4.1 SP2 behavior by going into the Global Properties frame, Stateful Inspection tab, and unchecking the "Drop out of state TCP Packets" box. In NG FP2 and before, use **dbedit** as described in FAQ 4.2 and enter the following commands:

```
dbedit> modify properties firewall_properties
            fw_allow_out_of_state_tcp 1
dbedit> update properties firewall_properties
```

NOTE! FireWall-1 NG FP2 does have the option in the GUI to make this change. However, the option doesn't entirely work due to a coding error that still uses the NG FP1 method.

6.21: Configuring FireWall-1 to Allow Out-of-State Packets for Specific TCP Services

Some application vendors use TCP connections in ways that do not follow the standards documented in RFC793. Since FireWall-1 attempts to enforce strict adherence to the standards, applications that do not comply will have difficulties communicating through FireWall-1 or any other stateful packet filter. NG FP2 and above provide a functionality that allows TCP packets for a specific port number even if they do not conform to Check Point's idea of state. This allows out-of-state TCP packets for specific services provided the packets would normally be passed by the rulebase. To do this, edit `$FWDIR/lib/user.def` on the management station and add a line of code (set in bold) within the following context:

```
#ifndef __user_def__
#define __user_def__

//
// User-defined INSPECT code
//

deffunc user_accept_non_syn() { dport = 22 };

#endif /* __user_def__ */
```

The INSPECT code between the curly braces defines the service(s) you wish to allow. The preceding example is SSH (TCP port 22). To define multiple services—for example, SSH (port 22), https (port 443), and ldap (port 389)—replace the bold line in the preceding example with this one:

```
deffunc user_accept_non_syn() { dport=22 or dport=443 or
        dport=389 };
```

To permit non-SYN packets between hosts a.b.c.d and x.y.z.w in addition to non-SYN packets on port 22, use the following:

```
deffunc user_accept_non_syn() { (src=x.y.z.w, dst=a.b.c.d) or
                                (src=a.b.c.d, dst=x.y.z.w) or
                                dport=22 };
```

(See Chapter 14 for more information on INSPECT.) If the rulebase is constructed carefully enough, the firewall should be relatively safe from an ACK-type DoS attack because all packets allowed by this change must still pass the rulebase.

6.22: SmartView Tracker Log Error: Rule 0: Reason: Violated Unidirectional Connection

FireWall-1 can mark a connection in the connections table to allow traffic to pass in one direction only. This can either be a connection that started from the inside, in which case FireWall-1 would mark the table to read that only outbound packets are allowed, or it can be a connection that originated from the outside, in which case FireWall-1 would mark the table to read that only in-bound packets are allowed. This means that data can pass in only one direction (ACK packets as part of normal TCP are acceptable). When a packet violates a unidirectional connection, Check Point logs an entry into SmartView Tracker/Log Viewer.

UDP services have an option to set a service to accept replies. In a sense, that is unidirectional. Unidirectional TCP connections occur with FTP. Some programs that use FTP do so in a nonstandard way that requires all the connections used by the FTP connection to be bidirectional.

To allow for bidirectional FTP connections in FireWall-1 NG, perform the following steps.

1. Stop the FireWall-1 management station with **cpstop**.
2. Edit `$FWDIR/lib/base.def` on the management station. Add the following bolded lines within the context shown:

```
deffunc ftp_port_code() {
ftp_intercept_port(CONN_ONEWAY_EITHER) or (IS_PASV_MSG,reject or 1)
};

deffunc ftp_pasv_code() {
ftp_intercept_pasv(CONN_ONEWAY_EITHER) or (IS_PORT_CMD,reject or 1)
};

deffunc ftp_bidir_code() {
ftp_intercept_port(NO_CONN_ONEWAY)
or
ftp_intercept_pasv(NO_CONN_ONEWAY)
};

deffunc ftp_code() {
ftp_intercept_port(CONN_ONEWAY_EITHER)
or
ftp_intercept_pasv(CONN_ONEWAY_EITHER)
};
```

3. Edit `$FWDIR/conf/tables.C` on the management station as follows (changes are set in bold):

```
: (protocols
      :table-type (confobj-dynamic)
      :location (protocols)
      :read_permission (0x00000000)
      :write_permission (0x00040000)
```

```
:queries (
        :all (*)
    )
)
```

Note that `table-type` will be changed from `confobj-static` to `confobj-dynamic`.

4. Start the FireWall-1 management station with **cpstart**.

5. Use **dbedit** to enter the following commands:

```
dbedit> create tcp_protocol FTP_BI
dbedit> update protocols FTP_BI
dbedit> modify protocols FTP_BI handler ftp_bidir_code
dbedit> modify protocols FTP_BI match_by_seqack true
dbedit> modify protocols FTP_BI res_type ftp
dbedit> update protocols FTP_BI
dbedit> quit
```

This allows you to create the bidirectional FTP service.

6. Open up SmartDashboard/Policy Editor and create a new service of type TCP. It will be on port 21. Give it a name other than FTP_BI (e.g., ftp_bidir). Click the Advanced button and select FTP_BI as the protocol type.

7. Use the new service in a rule. Install the security policy.

6.23: th_flags X message_info SYN Packet for Established Connection

This error can be seen in SmartView Tracker/Log Viewer when FireWall-1 receives a new connection from a source to a destination over the same port/service as a connection that was recently closed with a FIN or RST. FireWall-1 hangs onto these connections until the TCP end timeout is reached, which defaults to 60 seconds. This behavior is normal and expected.

The first step in alleviating this issue is to lower the TCP end timeout to see if that helps remove the connection from the connections table in time for the new connection to be received without a conflict. In FireWall-1 NG FP2 and later, the TCP end timeout can be modified via the GUI in the Stateful Inspection frame of the Global Properties section.

If the problem still occurs, the solution is to use TCP Sequence Verifier in NG FP3 to enable FireWall-1 to see the connection as a new connection, not an established one. For this to work properly, you need to run NG FP3 or above. On Nokia platforms, ensure that you have disabled flows. Contact Nokia Support for assistance.

Another option exists in hotfix SHF_FW1_FP3_0114, which is included in NG FP3 HFA-311 and above. You can change the behavior by modifying the value of the kernel variable `fw_reuse_established_conn` in three ways: change it to the TCP port number on which you need this behavior, change it to `-1` for all ports, or change it to `-2` to disable the behavior. See FAQ 6.1 for instructions on how to edit FireWall-1 kernel variables.

6.24: TCP Flags Do Not Make Sense

These errors show up in SmartView Tracker in FireWall-1 NG FP3 and above. SmartDefense is dropping packets with the SYN and RST flags set as malformed instead of as a normal RST packet.

Check Point provides a fix for this issue in hot fix SHF_FW1_FP3_0114. This fix is included in NG FP3 HFA-311 and above. After applying the fix, you can change the behavior by modifying the value of the kernel variable `fw_accept_syn_rst` to the TCP port number on which you need this behavior, to `-1` for all ports, or to `-2` to disable the behavior. See FAQ 6.1 for instructions on how to edit FireWall-1 kernel variables.

6.25: Unexpected SYN Response

These error messages show up in SmartView Tracker on FireWall-1 NG FP3 and above when the firewall receives unexpected SYN-ACK packets. To allow these packets, change the kernel variable `fw_allow_out_of_state_syn_resp` to 1. FAQ 6.1 explains how to change kernel variables.

6.26: Enabling the TCP Sequence Verifier

Prior to FireWall-1 NG FP1, FireWall-1 did not perform any checking of TCP sequence numbers. NG FP1 introduced this functionality, which validates the TCP sequence numbers used in a connection. It provides better tracking of the state of TCP connections. Enabling this feature can eliminate certain kinds of error messages in the logs and possibly create others.

To enable TCP Sequence Verifier on NG FP3 or above, in SmartDashboard, select SmartDefense from the Policy menu. The option is listed under TCP as Sequence Verifier.

To enable TCP Sequence Verifier on NG FP2, check the "Drop out of sequence packets" option under TCP Sequence Verifier in the Stateful Inspection frame in the Global Properties section.

To enable TCP Sequence Verifier on NG FP1, use **dbedit** to edit the following property to `true` in the `objects_5_0.C` file:

```
dbedit> modify properties firewall_properties fw_tcp_seq_verify 1
dbedit> update properties firewall_properties
```

6.27: Adjusting TCP or UDP Timeouts on a Per-Service Basis

In FireWall-1 NG, you can set these timeouts in the GUI directly. For both TCP and UDP services, go into the Advanced section of the service in question. For TCP services, edit the session timeout. For UDP services, edit the virtual session timeout. Reinstall the security policy.

6.28: Disabling TCP Timeouts

It is usually better to use some of the other tricks discussed to permit TCP packets that are out of state, such as the method described in FAQ 6.21. I don't even want to think about the security implications of leaving idle TCP connections open forever, but my gut tells me that this is not a good idea.

If you absolutely need to disable timeouts for a service because the vendor of your application refuses to implement a mechanism for periodically checking to see whether a connection is alive, this is how you would do it with **dbedit:**

```
dbedit> modify services service-name timeout 2147483647
dbedit> update services service-name
```

The value specified in the preceding example is used internally by the kernel to specify connections that do not time out. However, if you set any smaller number slightly less than 2,147,483,647, you still get connections that should last many years, assuming you do not stop your firewall for that long.

Problems with FTP

While FTP has been around since before the Internet ran on TCP/IP, every client and server seems to act a little differently. Stateful firewalls like FireWall-1, which expect things to happen only in certain ways, get tripped up by clients and servers that are RFC compliant, but choose to implement the RFCs differently. The following FAQs are related to FTP problems.

6.29: Problems with Newline Characters

Some FTP implementations send a PORT command in one packet and the newline character in another. By default, FireWall-1 assumes the PORT command and the newline will appear in the same packet. To enable checking for this, uncomment out the bolded #define statement (i.e., remove the // characters at the beginning of the line) in $FWDIR/lib/base.def on the management console and reinstall the security policy.

```
//    Use this if you do not want the FW-1 module to insist on a
// newline at the end of the PORT command:
// #define FTPPORT(match)        (call KFUNC_FTPPORT <(match)>)
```

Some other sites do not send out a proper newline at all. To resolve this, comment out the following line in `$FWDIR/lib/base.def` on the management console (i.e., add `//` at the beginning of the line) and reinstall the policy.

```
#define FTP_ENFORCE_NL
```

6.30: FTP on Ports Other Than 21

Some FTP servers use an alternate port for their control connection. By default, FireWall-1 knows how to handle FTP control connections only on port 21. To allow FTP using an alternate port, create a new service of type TCP. In the advanced configuration for the service, set the protocol type to FTP. Use this new service in a rule.

6.31: FTP Data Connections with a Random Source Port

Unfortunately, FireWall-1 NG does not currently allow for modification of INSPECT code to allow random FTP data port return traffic. The only existing workaround is the use of PASV transfers. Some FTP clients do not support passive mode, which means you may need to use a client that does.

6.32: FTP Servers Sending FIN Packets out of Sequence

It has been reported that Solaris clients cannot FTP to an NT SP6a platform. Microsoft's TCP/IP stack sends the FIN packets out of sequence. Installing the latest version of patch 105529 on Solaris resolves this issue.

6.33: FTP Servers That Require ident

Some FTP servers require a connection back to the FTP client on port 113 (ident). You will have to create an explicit rule permitting ident back to the client, which means that if you're using hide translation, you will simply not be able to access this FTP server.

6.34: Encrypting FTP Connections with SSL

Firewalls do not normally pass FTP connections encrypted with SSL—commonly referred to as FTP over SSL. The reason for this is simple: A firewall cannot inspect the FTP control connection because it is encrypted. FireWall-1 therefore cannot predict the FTP ports used by the FTP over SSL session.

Some people have been able to get this to work by simply applying FAQ 6.29, assuming the ports used are the standard TCP port 21 for control and 20 for data. Some variants of FTP over SSL operate over different ports—using

SOURCE	DESTINATION	SERVICE	ACTION
🖥 ftp-client	🖥 ftp-server	<u>TCP</u> ftp-ssl-control	⊕ accept
🖥 ftp-server	🖥 ftp-client	<u>TCP</u> ftp-ssl-data	⊕ accept

Figure 6.1   Rulebase for an FTP over SSL connection

port 990 for control and port 989 for data. In this case, you simply need to create the following TCP services:

- *ftp-ssl-control:* port 990
- *ftp-ssl-data:* port number higher than 1024, source port 989

In other words, ftp-ssl-data accepts connections with a destination port of any TCP high port provided the source port is 989. The rulebase to permit access would look similar to Figure 6.1.

 NOTE! In no case will FTP over SSL be supported with hide NAT. This is because FireWall-1 is unable to see the control portion of the connection—it is, after all, encrypted. Thus the ports used by the control connection cannot be modified. FTP over SSL will work with static NAT.

Problems That Aren't the Firewall's Fault

There are several issues that some people think are related to the firewall or think that their firewall should be able to do. This section documents some of these issues that have nothing to do with FireWall-1.

6.35: Some Services Are Slow to Connect

Some services are slow to connect either because the remote server is not able to do a reverse DNS lookup on the IP address you are coming from (it is timing out while looking) or because they are expecting an answer to their query on the ident port. To fix the latter problem, see FAQ 6.36. To fix the former problem, you must ask your DNS administrator to modify the reverse lookup tables so that the IP address you are coming from is resolvable.

6.36: The ident Service

When attempting to use certain services like SMTP or IRC, the server tries to send a communication back to the client on the ident service port. The ident service is typically used to provide identification for certain services. In general, it is not necessary. It is highly recommended that you create a rule that rejects all ident traffic (instead of dropping it) without logging so that services that rely on ident will start faster because they won't wait for the ident connection to time out.

6.37: Different DNS Definitions for Internet and Intranet

When you have different DNS definitions available for internal and external hosts, you want what is commonly referred to as *split-horizon DNS*.

Your external DNS servers (i.e., the ones responsible for serving DNS queries to the outside world) contain only the bare minimum information—mail exchanger (MX) records, externally accessible hosts, and reverse lookup for your IP space. The internal DNS is a superset of the external DNS server, containing both inside and outside names and IP numbers. Your internal hosts and the firewall use the internal DNS server, which may use the external DNS server as a forwarder to answer requests (i.e., resolve queries for domains outside your own).

Each DNS server should be set up on different systems. Your internal DNS server should be inside your firewall on the internal network. Your external DNS server should be either on the DMZ/service network or outside the firewall entirely (perhaps your ISP manages it). Some firewalls run a DNS server on the firewall itself. You can do this, but most people (myself included) do not recommend this configuration.

Summary

This chapter dealt with common situations that have occurred in many Fire-Wall-1 installations, some for several years. While this is not the first time most of these issues have been disclosed, it is the first time solutions to them have been made available in print.

Chapter

7

Remote Management

Large organizations often require multiple firewalls in order to keep the network secure. The ability to manage all these firewalls from a central place is desirable, as is the ability to manage the firewalls from anywhere. FireWall-1 offers this ability via a centralized management module, which Check Point calls Smart-Center in its current marketing, and GUIs that run on Solaris and Microsoft Windows—called SmartConsole. Often, in smaller environments, the firewall and management module are on the same box. This configuration masks a lot of the complexity and power of FireWall-1.

This chapter explains each of these components in detail and how they interact with one another. Remote management is then discussed. Topics in this area include the ability to manage one or more remote firewalls from a single management module, scenarios that might arise (including management module migration), and troubleshooting suggestions for these configurations.

By the end of this chapter, you should be able to:

- Understand the different components of FireWall-1 and how they interact
- Effectively manage several remote firewall modules
- Move your management module from one host to another
- Troubleshoot common problems with remote management

The Components

FireWall-1 can be broken down into three basic components:

1. **A firewall module:** A device that enforces a security policy. Also called an *enforcement point*.

2. **A management module:** A device that stores, compiles, and installs the security policy the firewall modules enforce. It also stores logs the firewalls send back and can send alerts.

3. **SmartConsole:** Programs that talk to a management module and allow you to view logs and system status, as well as modify the security policy. In NG FP2, this collection of programs are generally referred to as GUI Clients. Each component can exist on completely separate systems, or they all can exist on the same system. Figure 7.1 shows how the components communicate with one another.

How do these processes communicate with each other? The GUI connects to the `fwm` process on the management module, which listens on TCP port 18190. The IP address of the client, as well as the username and password that are supplied, are authenticated against a database of allowed IP addresses and users. If these match, the connection is allowed. The network objects, security policies, and users are downloaded to the local GUI. Depending on the access privileges, the user can view logs and system status and read, modify, and load new security policies to the firewall modules. All communication between the management module and GUI are encrypted.

The management module stores configuration about your firewall modules. This includes network objects, users, security policies, and logs. It compiles and loads rulebases to the firewall modules. The management module opens connections to the remote firewalls via TCP port 18191 on demand to load security policies. Applications are monitored over TCP port 18192.

The firewall module enforces your security policy. It accepts, drops, rejects, authenticates, and encrypts traffic. The firewall module opens a connection to its management module on TCP port 257 to send logs. It also opens a connection via TCP port 18191 to fetch the security policy at boot time. In addition, the firewall module communicates with antivirus servers, URL filters, and authentication servers as necessary.

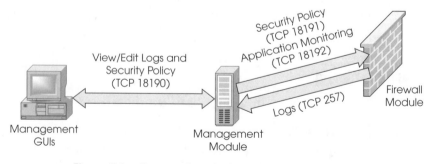

Figure 7.1 Connections between various modules

The communication between the management and firewall module is encrypted and authenticated by means of Secure Internal Communication (SIC).

Secure Internal Communication

Anyone who has managed installations of distributed FireWall-1 4.1 or earlier knows what the `fw putkey` command is. Anyone who has managed a particularly complex FireWall-1 environment has done `fw putkey` numerous times, particularly when adding a new firewall—not just for the firewall you're adding but also for all the other firewalls in your installation because the authentication between the firewalls and the management station broke. I can't tell you how many customers I've had to help with `putkey`-related problems over the years. Even customers who knew what they were doing would get tripped up by the `putkey` process.

Aside from the technical issues of getting and keeping `putkey`-type authentication working, it was unclear exactly how secure it was.

In FireWall-1 NG, Check Point decided to do away with the `fw putkey` command and created Secure Internal Communication. SIC uses Secure Sockets Layer (SSL) to encrypt all data. The management station becomes an Internal Certificate Authority (ICA) and issues all managed modules a certificate. These certificates are used to validate the identity of a node.

You may recall that during the initial installation of a firewall module, you are asked to provide a one-time password (OTP). You are not asked to configure any other information pertaining to the management station. The management module will establish an anonymous SSL session with the module and exchange OTPs. If they match, the management station will generate a signed certificate for the module, which will authenticate future communications between the management module and the firewall module. Because certificates are used for authentication, there are no longer issues related to authentication getting out of sync.

When managing FireWall-1 4.1 modules from an NG management module, authentication between modules will occur using `fw putkey`. On the NG management module, authentication is configured the same way as if the firewall module were running NG—in SmartDashboard. In the General frame of any locally managed Check Point object, there is a button called Communication under the heading Secure Internal Communication. To the right of this button, you will see a field. If it contains something similar to "CN=grover,O=snuffleupagus..ou812q," a certificate is defined for that host. If this is blank (and it will be for a newly defined object) or if you know that you need to reestablish SIC

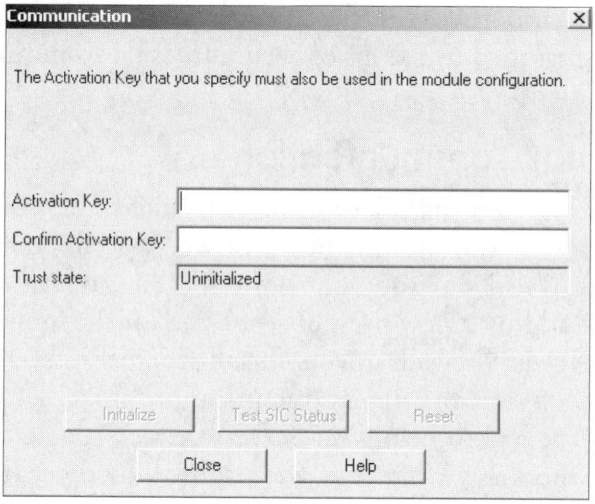

Figure 7.2   Establishing a one-time password between modules

with a particular host, click the Communication button to establish the OTP. Figure 7.2 shows the screen that appears after you click the button.

Figure 7.2 shows how the Communication screen looks for a module that has never had SIC established with it before or has had its SIC status reset. Type in the OTP in the Activation Key and Confirm Activation Key fields. Assuming this is a FireWall-1 NG module, clicking the Initialize button causes the management module to attempt to establish an encrypted session with the firewall, exchange OTPs, and generate certificates. Assuming the remote module is configured with the same OTP and FireWall-1 is up, running, and accessible, the value in the Trust state field should change to "Trust established." If there was a problem connecting to the module or the OTP was not set, you will instead see "Initialized but trust not established." In this case, the next time the module fetches policy, SIC should be established. On the management module, you can also click Initialize once the module is online and available.

Special Remote Management Conditions

The steps outlined in the previous section work if NAT is not involved. In some situations you may need to manage a firewall over the Internet, and your management module will require NAT to get to the Internet.

Forcing a Firewall Module to Log Locally

By default, when a firewall module is remotely managed, any logging is automatically sent to the management module. In some cases you may not want this to occur. One example is when a remote firewall module is accessible only via a relatively slow link, and the overhead imposed by logging across the network is undesirable. Logging is desirable, but it would be far better to do it locally.

The Log Maintenance section in Chapter 5 describes the various options for logging, which includes logging to the local firewall module and then transferring those logs to the management station on a preset schedule. These options are set on the gateway object under subsections of the Log and Alert frame.

Remote Management with NAT

There are situations where you may need to manage your firewall module from a management module subject to address translation. The actual SIC process works okay provided you configure the firewall module to use the NAT address for the management module.

On the management module, create an object of type Check Point host with the remote management's statically NATted IP address. If you are using manual NAT rules, this should already be done, though the object might be a normal workstation object. If so, delete the object and recreate it as an object of type Check Point host. In the Installed Products section of the General frame of your new Check Point host object, select Log Server.

Next, you will go into the gateway object definition. Go to the appropriate gateway object on the management station. Select the Masters frame under Log and Alert. Select the option "Use local definitions for Masters." You will get a warning about this affecting the Additional Logging frame as well. Select yes. Install the security policy.

On the firewall module, do a **cpstop**. Edit the file `$FWDIR/conf/masters`, which will look something like the following:

```
[Policy]
snuffleupagus
[Log]
snuffleupagus
[Alert]
snuffleupagus
```

Change all three instances of your management module object (snuffleupagus in this example) to the new Check Point object you created previously.

Now type in **cpstart** to bring up the firewall module. It should correctly log to the management module using the NAT address, and the management station should be able to push policy to the firewall module without problems.

What You Can Do with Remote Management

This section explains what you can do with the command line once remote management is configured correctly. Many of these commands can be executed when the management module and firewall module are on the same machine as well. See also the various command-line functions documented in Chapter 5.

Controlling Policy on a Firewall Module

A management module can load or unload a policy from a firewall module. The Security Policy Editor is normally used to do this, but this task can also be initiated from the command line on the management module. With a large and/or complex policy, you should load the policy from the command line because it takes far less time than using the GUI.

To load a policy from the management module to the firewall module, use the command **fwm load** as shown in the following example. (Note that snuffleupagus is the name of the management module and oscar is the firewall.)

```
C:\WINNT\FW1\NG\conf>fwm load pb-simple2.W oscar
pb-simple2.W: Security Policy Script generated into pb-simple2.pf
pb-simple2:
Compiled OK.

Installing Databases on: localhost

 Database installed successfully on snuffleupagus...

Database installation complete


Database installation succeeded for:
snuffleupagus

Installing CPMAD Policy On: localhost

 CPMAD policy installed successfully on snuffleupagus...

CPMAD policy installation complete


CPMAD policy installation succeeded for:
snuffleupagus

Installing VPN-1/FireWall-1 policy on: oscar ...

 Connection templates will not be offloaded to the SecureXL
accelerator due to restrictions defined in the rulebase.
 VPN-1/FireWall-1 policy installed successfully on oscar...

VPN-1/FireWall-1 policy installation complete


VPN-1/FireWall-1 policy installation succeeded for:
oscar

C:\WINNT\FW1\NG\conf>
```

To unload the policy on the remote firewall module from the management module, use the command **fwm unload** as shown in the following example.

```
C:\WINNT\FW1\NG\conf>fwm unload oscar

Uninstalling Policy From: oscar

 VPN-1/FireWall-1 policy successfully uninstalled from oscar...

VPN-1/FireWall-1 policy uninstall complete.

C:\WINNT\FW1\NG\conf>
```

On the remote firewall module, you can fetch the last installed policy from the management module by using the **fw fetch** command as shown in the following example.

```
oscar[admin]# fw fetch snuffleupagus

Fetching Security Policy From: snuffleupagus

 Local Policy is Up-To-Date.
 Reinstalling Local Policy.

Installing Security Policy pb-simple2 on all.all@oscar
 Fetching Security Policy Succeeded

oscar[admin]#
```

NOTE! If you're familiar with FireWall-1 4.1 and earlier versions, you may have noticed that fwm is now used to manipulate the policy from the management station instead of fw. You can still use fw, though you will get an error message declaring the command obsolete. For fetching a policy from the management module, however, fwm cannot be used and will generate a usage message.

Viewing State Tables of Firewall Modules

The **fw tab** commands can be run from the management module to check the state tables on a firewall module. A few tables of interest include the connections table and the address translation tables. The following command shows you the contents of the connections table on oscar:

```
# fw tab

oscar:
 - - - - connections  - - - -
dynamic, id 8158, attributes: keep, sync, expires 25,
refresh, limit 25000, hash size 32768, kbuf 16 17 18
19 20 21 22 23 24 25 26 27 28 29 30, free function a47ed69c 0
```

```
<00000000, 0a0000ff, 00000208, 0a000001, 00000208, 00000011,
28203a0a> -> <00000001, 0a000001, 00000208, 0a0000ff,
00000208>(00000011)
<00000001, 0ad02001, 00000043, ffffffff, 00000044, 00000011,
28203a0a> -> <00000000, 0ad02001, 00000043, ffffffff, 00000044>
(00000011)
<00000001, 0a0000ff, 0000007b, 0a0000fe, 0000007b, 00000011,
6c61763a> -> <00000000, 0a0000fe, 0000007b, 0a0000ff, 0000007b>
(00000011)
<00000001, 0a000002, 000011c1, 3f6f1665, 00000016, 00000006,
6f745f6b> -> <00000000, 0a000002, 000011c1, 3f6f1665, 00000016>
(00000006)
<00000001, d82f7135, 00000016, 0a000002, 000011be, 00000006,
5f41535f> -> <00000000, 0a000002, 000011be, d82f7135, 00000016>
(00000006)
<00000000, 0a000009, 00000dd7, 04164206, 00000050, 00000006,
32303128, 0a293030, 203a0a29, 54324c28, 75745f50, 6c656e6e,
6d6c5f73, 79743a0a, 28206570, 29746e69, 0001f001, 00806000,
00000006, 00000e10, 00000000, 3e8774d4, 00000000; 0001f001,
00806000, 00000006, 00000e10, 00000000, 3e8774d4; 9/20>
<00000001, 0a000001, 00000208, 0a0000ff, 00000208, 00000011,
61763a0a, 3228206c, 0a293030, 203a0a29, 73776628, 74616e79,
656d5f6b, 646f6874, 79743a0a, 28206570, 00020001, 00806000,
00000006, 00000028, 00000000, 3e8774a4, 00000000; 00020001,
00806000, 00000006, 00000028, 00000000, 3e8774a4; 17/40>
<00000001, 04164206, 00000050, 0a000009, 00000dd7, 00000006,
616e5f72> -> <00000000, 0a000009, 00000dd7, 04164206, 00000050>
(00000006)
<00000000, 3f6f1665, 00000016, 0a000002, 000011c1, 00000006,
725f7469> -> <00000000, 0a000002, 000011c1, 3f6f1665, 00000016>
(00000006)
<00000001, ffffffff, 00000044, 0ad02001, 00000043, 00000011,
61662820> -> <00000000, 0ad02001, 00000043, ffffffff, 00000044>
(00000011)
<00000000, d82f7135, 00000016, 44740502, 00006b64, 00000006,
62282065> -> <00000000, 0a000002, 000011be, d82f7135, 00000016>
(00000006)
<00000001, 44740502, 00000100, 0a000009, 00000de1, 00000006,
61645f67> -> <00000000, 0a000009, 00000de1, 44740502, 00000100>
(00000006)
<00000000, d82f7135, 00000016, 0a000002, 000011be, 00000006,
6628203a> -> <00000000, 0a000002, 000011be, d82f7135, 00000016>
(00000006)
<00000000, 3f6f1665, 00000016, 44740502, 00006b66, 00000006,
3a0a290a> -> <00000000, 0a000002, 000011c1, 3f6f1665, 00000016>
(00000006)
<00000001, 3f6f1665, 00000016, 0a000002, 000011c1, 00000006,
```

```
61636464> -> <00000000, 0a000002, 000011c1, 3f6f1665, 00000016>
(00000006)
<00000000, 0a0000fe, 0000007b, 0a000001, 0000007b, 00000011,
206c6176> -> <00000001, 0a000001, 0000007b, 0a0000fe, 0000007b>
(00000011)
...(20 More)
```

NOTE! The first six items in each connections table entry are direction (0 is inbound, 1 is outbound), source IP, source port, destination IP, destination port, and IP protocol number. They are all in hexadecimal. You can find a complete description of all other entries in the connections table in Check Point's Advanced Technical Reference Guide, available from http://www.checkpoint.com/support/technical/documents/atrg-ngfp3/pdf/cpts-doc-atrg-01-s-ngfp3.pdf. You need a valid software subscription agreement to view these documents. You may also purchase this document from Check Point Education Services via the following order form: https://www.checkpoint.com/services/education/courseware/OrderHomePage.jsp.

You can also get just a count of the number of entries in a few tables if that is all you are interested in:

```
C:\WINNT\FW1\NG\conf> fw tab -t connections -t fwx_alloc -s oscar
HOST        NAME                    ID  #VALS #PEAK #SLINKS
oscar       connections           8158    14    33    33
oscar       fwx_alloc             8187    10   107     0
```

ID is an internal identifier for the table, #VALS means the number of entries, #PEAK is the "high-water mark" for the number of entries in this table, and #SLINKS shows the number of symbolic links present in the connections table (each connection actually generates more than one entry).

WARNING! There appears to be a bug in FireWall-1 NG FP3 that causes these kinds of queries from the management station to return bogus results. Queries from the local firewall module return the correct results.

Updating Licenses

You can view, retrieve, and edit licenses for remote firewall modules from a management module. In addition to command-line functionality, it is also possible to manage licenses from SmartUpdate. Instead of presenting a table that explains the commands, I will take you through the process of replacing a license on a module for the first time, which will show you all the commands.

First we should get the licenses from all the nodes by using the command **cprlic get -all**. If we want to get licenses from a specific module, we can use the command **cprlic get modulename**. If any of the modules are running FireWall-1 4.1, we need to use the -v41 flag. In any case, this brings all of the licenses installed on these modules into the repository.

Now we should see which licenses are present. The command **cprlic print -all -x -t -a** prints all licenses installed on all platforms (-all), print signatures (-x), print license type (-t), and where the license is attached (-a). Optionally, -all can be replaced with the relevant module name. The other command-line options are optional but recommended to obtain the most information.

```
C:\ > cprlic print -all -x -t -a

The following licenses appear in the database:
=================================================
Host              Expiration Features
eval                05May2003  dZCTqLvXYp3ytGaJDe9tRxLDCAQjdMPx4Pab
CPMP-MEDIA-1-NG  CK-CP  central snuffleupagus oscar
eval                01Mar2003  d7uXL9CypXoNpAqubgjvN7N5EoE6nE6LbBff
CPMP-EVAL-1-3DES-NG  CK-CP  central oscar
```

When the preceding output was generated, the date was March 30, 2003. This means the eval license dated 01Mar2003 is expired and can be safely removed from the system. To do this, we must first detach the license from oscar (the module on which it is installed), then remove it.

To remove the license, we use the command **cprlic del oscar d7uXL9CypXoNpAqubgjvN7N5EoE6nE6LbBff**. We must specify the module name and the "signature" of the license in question. If the module has a dynamic IP address, we use the -p option and specify the current IP address of the module. When the command completes, we get a list of licenses attached to the specified module.

A **cprlic print -all -x -t -a** command now shows different output:

```
C:\> cprlic print -all -x -t -a

The following licenses appear in the database:
=================================================
Host              Expiration Features
eval                05May2003  dZCTqLvXYp3ytGaJDe9tRxLDCAQjdMPx4Pab
CPMP-MEDIA-1-NG  CK-CP  central snuffleupagus oscar
eval                01Mar2003  d7uXL9CypXoNpAqubgjvN7N5EoE6nE6LbBff
CPMP-EVAL-1-3DES-NG  CK-CP  central
```

Notice that the 01Mar2003 license is now no longer attached to oscar. Since it is no longer attached to any module, we can remove it using the **cprlic rm** command. We specify this license by signature again as shown below:

```
C:\> cprlic rm d7uXL9CypXoNpAqubgjvN7N5EoE6nE6LbBff

Are you sure you want to delete this license? [y/n] : y

Operation complete. License deleted from database.
```

Now we will add a new license to the repository for the firewall module. We do this with **cprlic add**.

```
C:\> cprlic add 10.0.0.9 30May2003 d3uDEt3jb-pPgE8ZEyd-
     hBNMH5AvT-SkCJJEMgn CPMP-EVAL-1-3DES-NG CK-1337DEADD00D

Operation Done.
```

Now we can install the license on the module with **cprlic put** as shown below:

```
C:\> cprlic put oscar 10.0.0.9 30Apr2003
d3uDEt3jbpPgE8ZEydhBNMH5AvTSkCJJEMgn CPMP-EVAL-1-3DES-NG
CK-D1790E4B08B4

Operation Done.


The following licenses are attached to oscar
===============================================
Host            Expiration Features
eval            05May2003   CPMP-MEDIA-1-NG  CK-CP
10.0.0.9        30May2003   CPMP-EVAL-1-3DES-NG  CK-1337DEADD00D
```

To make life even easier, all of these functions can be done via the Smart Update GUI as well. Figure 7.3 shows you the SmartUpdate Licenses tab in NG FP3.

To get the view shown in Figure 7.3, you must select View Repository from the Licenses menu. With the License Repository window showing, you can simply right-click anywhere in it and add new licenses, detach a license (provided you are clicking on a license), export licenses, or view the license. You can also drag and drop licenses from the License Repository window to the modules on which you wish to install the licenses. Right-clicking on a license in the License Management window allows you to detach the license or export it to a file.

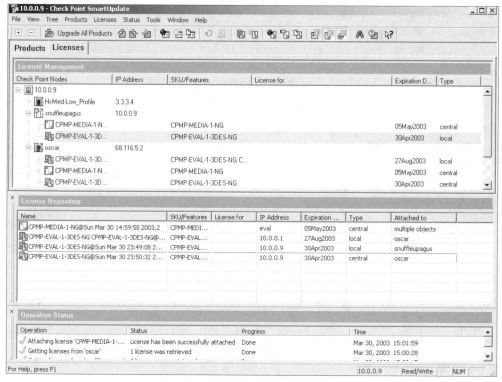

Figure 7.3   SmartUpdate Licenses tab

Moving Management Modules

As a company grows from needing one firewall to several, it may be desirable to move the management functions from the firewall platform to a separate box that functions only as a management module. Check Point has, unfortunately, made the process of doing so far more complicated in NG than it was in earlier versions.

The assumption is that the two management modules will be of the same type (i.e., they will both be UNIX-type platforms or they will both be Windows-type platforms). This is critical because there is currently no way to convert a UNIX-type registry to a Windows-type registry or vice versa. Also, both management modules should be at the same software revision level, that is, if one management module has NG FP3 with Hotfix Accumulator patch 308 (HFA-308) loaded, then the other management module needs to be at that level as well. Note that the two management modules do not ultimately have to have the same IP address. Before proceeding, perform a **cpstop** on both management servers.

For the purposes of discussion, let us assume you have a machine that has a management module installed on it. This will be the source machine. Let us also assume that you have a newer, more powerful machine that will replace the source machine. This will be the destination machine. The destination machine has had Check Point FireWall-1 loaded on it, configured as a management module. Whether these are both UNIX or Windows machines at this point is not relevant because I provide steps for both UNIX and Windows and will note any differences. What is relevant is that both management modules are the same type of platform (i.e., you cannot do this where one platform is Windows, the other a UNIX type).

If the management modules are UNIX, issue the following commands on the destination server:

```
destination# rm -rf $CPDIR/conf/* $CPDIR/database/*
destination# rm -rf $FWDIR/conf/* $FWDIR/database/* $FWDIR/log/*
```

For Windows, the commands are:

```
C:\> del /s %CPDIR%\conf\*
C:\> del /s %CPDIR%\database\*
C:\> del /s %FWDIR%\conf\*
C:\> del /s %FWDIR%\database\*
C:\> del /s %FWDIR%\log\*
```

Next, copy the contents of the following directories from the source machine to the destination machine.

- $CPDIR/conf (and all subdirectories)
- $CPDIR/database/*.C
- $FWDIR/conf/* (with subdirectories)
- $FWDIR/log/*

On the destination machine, remove the following files, if they exist. They will get recreated when FireWall-1 starts up.

- $FWDIR/conf/CPMILinksMgr.db
- $FWDIR/conf/CPMILinksMgr.db.private

Now you need to copy the SIC key from the registry on the source machine to the destination machine. These steps depend on whether the management stations are UNIX or Windows.

On a UNIX platform, edit the registry file. In NG FP1 and NG FP2, the file is $CPDIR/../registry/HKLM_registry.data. In NG FP3 and above, the file is `$CPDIR/registry/HKLM_registry.data`. On the destination management server, find the entries between the line that begins with `: (SIC` and the line that contains only a right parenthesis. Delete any entries between those two lines. For example, prior to making this change, the section in the registry file might look like the following:

```
: (SIC
        :ICAState ("[4]3")
        :ICAdn ("o=chef.phoneboy.com..iz6ech")
        :HasCertificate ("[4]1")
        :MySICname ("cn=cp_mgmt,o=chef.phoneboy.com..iz6ech")
        :CertPath ("/opt/CPshrd-50-03/conf/sic_cert.p12")
)
```

After you make the deletion, the section will look like this:

```
: (SIC
)
```

NOTE! The actual lines in the file will be indented more. The indents are reduced in this text for readability.

Once you have deleted those entries on the destination machine, copy all entries between the `: (SIC` and `)` lines in the registry file from the source machine to the same location in the destination machine's registry.

On a Windows platform, use **regedit** to export the key `HKEY_LOCAL_MACHINE\SOFTWARE\CheckPoint\SIC` from the source platform's registry and copy to the destination. If the destination machine had FireWall-1 installed to a different directory than the source, change the `CertPath` registry entry accordingly.

Next, load up new licenses on the destination platform. If the destination server's IP is different, you will need new licenses. Finally, start the destination management server.

If the source and destination servers have the same IP, you can skip to Testing Your Migrated Management Module, which follows the next subsection.

Source and Destination Management Servers Have Different IP Addresses

Assuming that a new management object was created (it should be in most cases), all instances of the source management server's object must be replaced with the destination management server's object. You can easily find all the relevant locations by selecting the source object, right-clicking, and selecting Where

Used. If a new management object was not created, simply edit the existing one to match the new configuration.

If a new management object was created, both objects now have the same SIC name. This is bad and must be corrected. Close Policy Editor/Smart Dashboard and use either **dbedit** or the Check Point Database Tool to clear the SIC name from the old object. The attribute is called sic_name. For example, if your management object were called charlie_brown, the command in **dbedit** would be:

```
dbedit> modify network_objects charlie_brown sic_name ""
dbedit> update network_objects charlie_brown
```

If you wish to delete the source management object, **cpstop** the destination management server, then edit $FWDIR/conf/objects_5_0.C (see FAQ 4.2 for guidelines). Find the source management object. Change the attribute Deleteable to true (it will be under the AdminInfo section). Save the changes. Now **cpstart** the management station, and use Policy Editor/Smart Dashboard to remove the object.

 WARNING!   If the source management station has certificates on it, deleting the source object will also delete these certificates. Also, relevant ICA certificates will also be revoked. If you intend to use this management server again and need these certificates, *do not delete the source management station.*

Next, you must adjust the fully qualified domain name (FQDN) in the ICA. This is used to generate the Certificates Revocation List (CRL) distribution point URL that is written on the ICA-generated certificates. In many cases, you will need to change the FQDN definition to the destination management module's FQDN. You do this in the **cpconfig** program on UNIX platforms or with the Check Point Configuration Tool on Windows.

When gateways managed by the management station are using VPNs with external entities (nonmanaged) and the authentication of these VPNs is done with ICA-generated certificates, changing the FQDN may not be desirable because the authentication of these VPNs will likely fail. There are two possible ways to resolve this.

1. On the destination management server, change the FQDN in the ICA to the destination machine's FQDN and generate new certificates for all relevant gateways and users.
2. Update the DNS so that the source FQDN will now be resolved to the destination management server FQDN. After doing this, change the FQDN on the source management server to avoid ambiguity.

Finally, adjust the masters and log servers for each module to point at the destination management server before attempting to install the security policy on these modules.

Testing Your Migrated Management Module

There are five actions you should perform to verify that the destination management station is functional and that the relevant firewall modules are now using it.

1. Use SmartDashboard/Policy Editor to check communication with each module using the Test SIC option.
2. Install the security policy on any module now controlled by the destination management server.
3. Use the SmartView Status/Status Manager application to check the status on all modules.
4. Use the SmartView Tracker/Log Viewer application to verify that each module is sending log entries.
5. Use the `fw fetch` command to fetch policy from each module onto which you installed policy.

If all of these steps work, congratulations—you've successfully moved a management station from one system to another.

Limitations on Moving Management Stations

There are some limitations related to moving management stations.

- If the source and destination management servers use different IP addresses and you manage FireWall-1 version 4.1 firewalls, you will need to redo putkeys with each module.
- If both management servers are used simultaneously and changes are done on both, *these changes cannot be merged automatically.* All changes need to be applied manually to both management servers.
- Changes that involve ICA modifications, which include issuing or revoking certificates, *cannot be synchronized, even manually.* For example, if you revoke a certificate on one management server, it will be added to the CRL on that server, but there is no way to add this to the other management server's CRL.

Moving the Management Module off a Standalone Gateway

Often, a small organization begins with a standalone gateway that has the firewall and management module on the same platform. However, there comes a time when the firewall needs to be "just a firewall" and the management module duties are best done on a separate platform. The following section explains how to accomplish this task.

Once the new management module is set up with the proper IP addresses and FireWall-1 is configured, you can follow the steps provided earlier. Follow the instructions for deleting the old primary management object because you will need to recreate that object as a firewall module only.

Now for the tricky part: convincing your old management plus firewall module to be just a firewall module. In this instance, Check Point recommends reinstalling the software. However, it is possible to take an unsupported shortcut here. After stopping the module with **cpstop**, you will need to edit the $CPDIR/registry/HKLM_registry.data file to do two things:

1. Remove SIC information.
2. Tell FireWall-1 it is not a management station.

To remove SIC information, look for the lines in the registry file that look like this:

```
: (SIC
      :ICAState ("[4]3")
      :ICAdn ("o=chef.phoneboy.com..iz6ech")
      :HasCertificate ("[4]1")
      :MySICname ("cn=cp_mgmt,o=chef.phoneboy.com..iz6ech")
      :CertPath ("/opt/CPshrd-50-03/conf/sic_cert.p12")
)
```

Remove everything between the first and last lines shown above so the result looks like this:

```
: (SIC
)
```

Below the SIC section is the FW1 section. In this section, the following lines will likely need to be changed:

```
:StandAlone ("[4]0")
:FWManagement ("[4]0")
:Management ("[4]0")
:LogServer ("[4]0")
:Primary ("[4]0")
:HAManagement ("[4]0")
```

On your ex-management station, one or more of these values may be set to "[4]1". All of the preceding lines should be set to "[4]0" as shown above.

At this point, you should use **cpconfig** to establish a new OTP on the firewall module. If you haven't done so already, create the new gateway object for the firewall module, and establish SIC using the OTP you specified on the firewall module.

Highly Availabile Management Modules

While Check Point has allowed highly available firewalls since the version 3.0 days, only with FireWall-1 NG has Check Point supported a way to create a highly available management station, though it does come at the cost of an additional management license. The management module machines should not also be configured as firewall machines, that is, as a distributed management setup at the same software version as the primary, including any hotfixes.

When you install FireWall-1 on the secondary management module, it should use the same operating system as your primary management module. You should also choose the module type as Secondary Management. In this kind of installation, the only major question you are asked is to provide an OTP. As for a firewall module, this is how the primary management module will authenticate itself to this secondary module.

On the primary management station, use the Policy Editor/SmartDashboard application to create a new object of type Check Point host. The object will look similar to Figure 7.4. The key thing to select in this screen is Secondary Management Station.

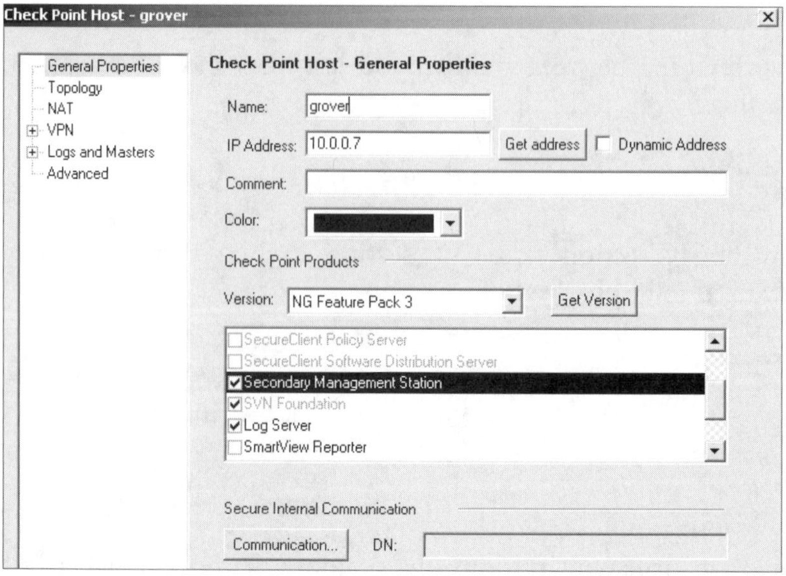

Figure 7.4 Secondary management object

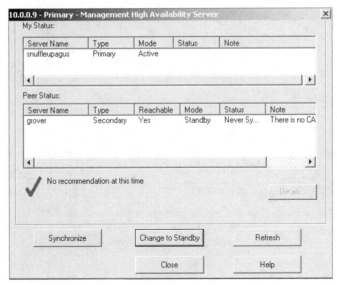

Figure 7.5   Preparing to manually sync the management modules

Next, you should establish SIC with the secondary management station. Click on the Communication button and type in the OTP you defined on the secondary management station. Click Initialize. SIC should now be established.

From the Manage menu, select Management High Availability. A window similar to Figure 7.5 appears.

You can see that the management stations shown in Figure 7.5 have never been synced. Click on the Synchronize button. A window will pop up, giving you two options.

Synchronize Configuration Files Only: This synchronizes only the database and configuration files.

Synchronize Fetch, Install, and Configuration Files: In addition to the database and configuration files, this option synchronizes files that will allow the managed firewall modules to fetch their security policies from the secondary management station. This happens only if the modules are configured to use the secondary management station as one of its masters.

For the purposes of discussion, choose the second option. Click OK. After several minutes, depending on the speed of the link between the management stations, you will see the peer status changed to Synchronized.

By default, the management stations will synchronize anytime a policy is loaded to a firewall module. In the Global Properties section under the Management High Availability frame, pictured in Figure 7.6, you can choose additional

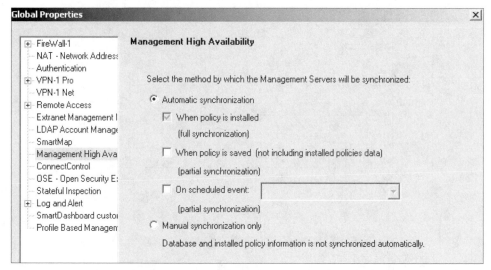

Figure 7.6 Global Properties, Management High Availability frame

options. The options here include three that relate to automatic synchronization and one for manual.

When policy is installed: This option is always checked when automatic synchronization is specified. This synchronizes all management module data when the policy is installed to a module.

When policy is saved: This option causes all database and configuration files to be synchronized when the Save button is clicked in SmartDashboard/ Policy Editor. This does not include data on policies currently installed on modules. As such, this is a partial synchronization.

On scheduled event: This option allows you to specify a time object that indicates when a partial synchronization will occur.

Manual synchronization only: With this option selected, no data will be automatically synchronized between the management stations. All synchronization must be done manually as described previously.

 WARNING!   Neither synchronization mode will synchronize manual changes to any .def files. Make sure that any changes made on one management module are also made on the other.

To ensure that either management module can push a policy to the firewall module, the gateway object must be configured for both management stations. This is done in the gateway object in the Masters subsection of the Logs and Masters frame, as shown in Figure 7.7.

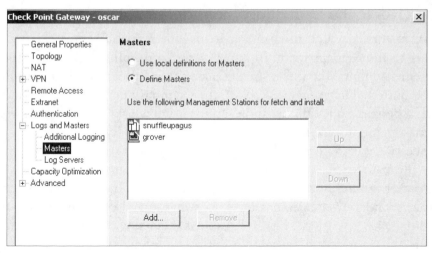

Figure 7.7   Gateway object, Logs and Masters, Masters subsection

Similarly, if you want to be able to view logs on either management module, the gateway object needs to be configured accordingly. This is done in the Log Servers subsection of the Logs and Masters frame, as shown in Figure 7.8.

Once these changes are made, the policy will need to be reinstalled on the firewall module.

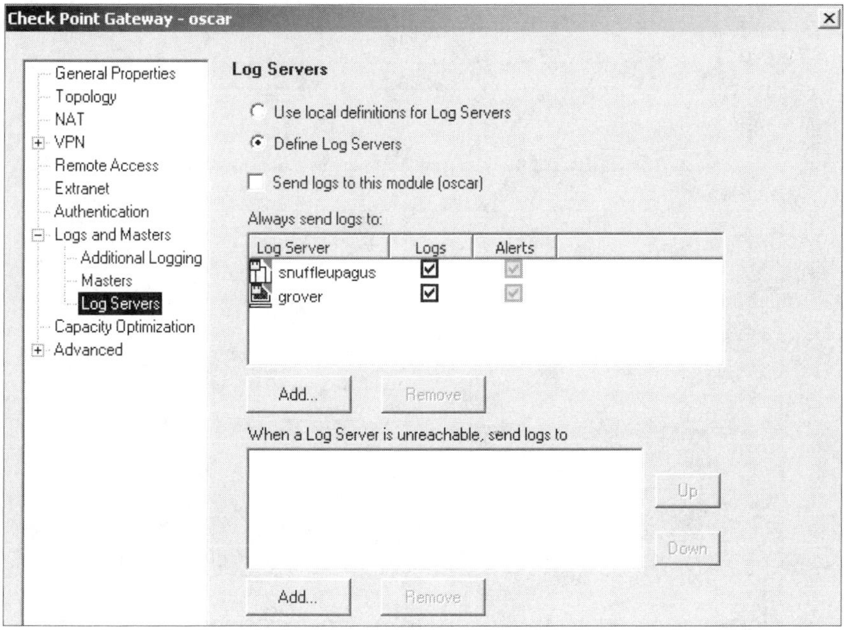

Figure 7.8   Gateway object, Logs and Masters, Log Servers subsection

Failing Over to the Secondary Management

You can manually switch the primary management station into Standby mode by going to the Manage menu in SmartDashboard/Policy Editor and selecting Management High Availability. In the dialog that appears, click the Change to Standby button. Then you can log into the secondary management station with SmartDashboard/Policy Editor and everything will work as if you are on the primary management station.

Of course, you rarely switch over your management station because you plan to. Usually, your primary management station goes down due to a hardware failure, a power failure, or some other unforeseen event. In this case, you can log into the secondary management module using SmartDashboard/Policy Editor and change to Active mode. Figure 7.9 shows the dialog that comes up after logging into the secondary management station with SmartDashboard/Policy Editor while the primary management station is down.

As you can see in Figure 7.9, the primary management station, snuffleupagus, is down. When you click on the Change to Active button, the secondary management module will attempt to become active. This process may take a few

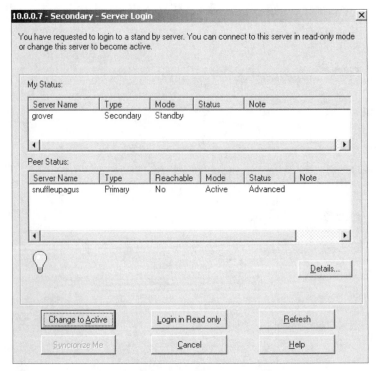

Figure 7.9   Connecting to the secondary management station when the primary one is down

minutes because the secondary management module will attempt to notify the primary management module, which will fail because it is offline.

Once the primary module comes back online, it too will believe it is in master state. This is not good. If changes were made on the secondary management module, you will need to first log into the primary management station with SmartDashboard/Policy Editor and switch it to Standby mode, then log into the secondary management station, synchronize with the primary, and change the secondary to Standby mode. That will get all the changes to the primary and make it the currently active management station.

I found that in order to change the management stations to Standby mode, I needed to kill the fwm process, and manually restart it; otherwise I would get an error message, "A Read/Write Management client is connected." You can kill the fwm process and restart it with the following two commands:

```
# fw kill fwm
# fwm
```

 WARNING!   If you made changes on the secondary management station and then initiate a synchronize action from the primary management station, all changes on your secondary module will be overwritten!

Troubleshooting Remote Management Issues

This section covers how to troubleshoot issues related to remote management.

7.1: Things to Check When Getting SIC Failures

The most obvious things to check: Is there connectivity? From one module, can you Telnet to the other module on port 18191? If a TCP connection isn't established, is there some sort of router or firewall that might be blocking this communication? Is the firewall itself blocking the communication?

If the firewall has the default filter loaded, try the command **fw unload local**. This unloads the security policy, so be careful! You will want to load a proper security policy as soon as possible after doing this.

SIC relies on a process called **cpd**, which is responsible for performing all intermodule communications. The process needs to be running on the firewall modules and listening on port 18211 (**netstat** can be used to verify this).

The next thing to check is whether or not the modules contain each other's IP addresses and hostnames in the local hosts file (/etc/hosts on UNIX, %SystemRoot%\System32\drivers\etc\hosts on Windows). If the remote module is subject to address translation, add the translated IP address to the hosts file.

The last thing to check is the date and time on the operating systems. Because SIC uses certificates that are time and date based, if one system is configured very differently than the other, relative to GMT, the generated certificates might not be valid. See the next FAQ.

7.2: Syncing Clocks between Firewall and Management

The error message "I am getting the error: SIC Error for getifs: validate: not yet valid" indicates that there is a clock synchronization problem between the management server and the module. The message indicates that the management server clock is ahead of the module's clock and that the module is not willing to accept the management server's certificate because it is in the future and thus not yet valid.

Synchronize the module's clock with the management server's clock and restart the **cpd** daemon on the module (e.g., **fw kill cpd; cpd**).

7.3: Establishing SIC with a Module Using Dynamic Addressing

Initially, you should configure the firewall module as if it did not have a dynamic IP address. This means that when creating the gateway object, you specify the module's current IP address. Enter the OTP as normal and initialize SIC. Get the interfaces under the Topology frame of the object. Finally, you can check the Dynamic IP box on the General frame of the gateway object.

7.4: SIC General Failure (Error No. 148)

This usually means there is a connectivity problem between the modules. After checking to see that the remote module is up, go to the module and unload the security policy by typing the command **fw unloadlocal**. If SIC succeeds, it is likely a problem with your security policy, or the default filter was loaded. You will want to reinstall the security policy as soon as possible after doing this.

7.5: Certificate Authority Errors in a Management HA Configuration

The error "A write operation was executed while Certificate Authority is running in read only mode. Operation failed." shows up only in a Management High Availability configuration.

If the `$FWDIR/conf/mgmtha.conf` file is corrupted or empty, the primary management server will not be able to extract information regarding the status of the local machine. To ensure that the ICA database does not get corrupted, it is locked into a read-only mode. To resolve this, follow these steps.

1. Execute **cpstop** on both primary and secondary management servers.

2. Remove `$FWDIR/conf/mgmtha.conf` and `$FWDIR/conf/mgmtha_stack` from both machines.

3. Execute **cpstart** on both primary and secondary management servers.

The preceding steps will cause the primary management server to recreate the files and allow the ICA database to load in a read-write mode.

7.6: Resetting SIC

Once a module is defined in FireWall-1 NG, you cannot change its name. The SIC certificate associated with each managed module is based on the name of the module itself. If you have to change the name of the module, you must generate a new SIC certificate. There may be other reasons when you have to regenerate certificates or reset SIC as well.

To reset SIC between a firewall and a management station, open the appropriate module object in Policy Editor/SmartDashboard, click on the Communication button, then click the Reset button in the Communication window.

To reset SIC on the management server itself, use the command **fw sic_reset** *after* you have stopped the management station with **cpstop**. This command deletes the Internal Certificate Authority, deletes the Management Server Certificate, deletes the Certificates Revocation List, and updates the objects database.

 WARNING!   This command resets SIC authentication for all modules. Authentication will need to be reestablished for all modules.

Next, you have to reinitialize the Internal Certificate Authority. This is done via the **cpconfig** utility in UNIX systems. On Windows, use the Check Point Configuration Tool and select the Certificate Authority tab. Once you have done that and restarted the management station with **cpstart**, you need to re-establish SIC with each module managed by this management module.

7.7: Forcibly Resetting SIC

There are times when FAQ 7.6 does not result in resetting SIC. The next step is to attempt to revoke your ICA certificate. Use the command **cpca_client revoke_cert -n certificate-DN** (your DN is listed in the general tab of your management station object under the SIC section). Once you have done this, proceed as in FAQ 7.6.

 WARNING!   Revoking your ICA certificate will disrupt SIC and IKE connectivity and is not recommended.

A more drastic approach is the following.

1. Stop the management station by issuing a **cpstop**.
2. Remove the `$FWDIR/conf/InternalCA.*` and `$FWDIR/conf/ICA.*` files.
3. Edit `$FWDIR/conf/objects_5_0.C` and remove the `sic_name` attribute from the primary management object.
4. Find the `internal_ca` object and remove it. It might look something like the following:

```
: (internal_ca
        :ca_type (internal)
        :cacertificate ()
        :cacertsignkey (690f1ea0d466f4b4c09c1ad9)
        :crl_cache_timeout (86400)
        :crl_cache_type (Timeout)
        :crl_http (true)
        :crl_ldap (false)
        :dn ("O=snuffleupagus..uf8rzq")
        :internal_CA_check_CRL (true)
        :permissions_strings ()
        :permissions_type (None)
        :type (ca)
)
```

5. Use **cpconfig** to reinitialize SIC and follow the rest of the steps in FAQ 7.6.

7.8: If All Else Fails, Debug

To enable debugging of SIC, issue the following commands on UNIX, assuming a C-shell-based shell is being used (the default on Nokia platforms).

```
# cpstop
# setenv OPSEC_DEBUG_LEVEL 3
# setenv TDERROR_ALL_ALL 3
# cpd -d
# cpstart
```

On a UNIX platform with an sh-based shell, use these commands.

```
# cpstop
# OPSEC_DEBUG_LEVEL=3
# export OPSEC_DEBUG_LEVEL
# TDERROR_ALL_ALL=3
# export TDERROR_ALL_ALL
# cpd -d
# cpstart
```

On a Windows platform, use the following code.

```
C:\> cpstop
C:\> set OPSEC_DEBUG_LEVEL=3
C:\> set TDERROR_ALL_ALL=3
C:\> cpd -d
C:\> cpstart
```

These commands tell **cpd** to write a debug/trace output to the $CPDIR/log/ cpd.elg file. Once you've captured what the problem is, type **cprestart** to bounce FireWall-1 and turn off **cpd** debugging.

$CPDIR/conf/sic_policy.conf is akin to $FWDIR/lib/control.map in FireWall-1 4.1 and earlier. It defines the policy that the module follows for communication via SIC (i.e., who can authenticate with what and how to authenticate when connecting). From the **cpd** debug above, you might uncover a mismatch in authentication. Editing this file might allow you to resolve that issue.

The sic_policy.conf file contains lots of helpful comments. However, there are two basic types of entries you will see: rules and aliases. Rules determine who can do what. Aliases give you a nice way to group multiple items together (think "groups" in the Policy Editor) and make rules look more readable.

There are two types of rules: inbound rules and outbound rules. Inbound rules refer to connections coming from external hosts (i.e., I am the server and a client is connecting to me). Outbound rules refer to connections being established to external hosts (i.e., I am the client connecting to a server). Rules are listed and enforced in order; the first matching rule is used.

Rules look like this:

```
<apply-to> ; <peers> ; <ports> ; <services> ; <method>
```

<apply-to> indicates for whom the rule is relevant, similar to the Install On field in the Policy Editor. ANY means apply the rule on any installation type. Otherwise, a group can be specified. If <apply-to> does not reference the local system, the rule is ignored.

<peers> specifies how the other end of the connection is referred to, which can be listed as a SIC name, an IP address, a predefined alias, a group defined in the objects database, or a user-defined alias.

<ports> refers to the port on which the server listens. This is usually left as ANY because security requirements usually do not dictate that a specific port be used.

<services> refers to the Check Point services for which this rule is relevant. Check Point services are unload, load, db_download, commit, and so on, as well as OPSEC services such as sam, lea, and cvp.

`<methods>` indicates the methods by which this service is permitted if the first four entries of the rule match. The methods are tried in the order listed, so the most desirable methods should be listed first.

Aliases take the following form:

```
<name>: <element-1>, <element-2>, ..., <element-n>
```

Aliases are listed before any rules in `sic_policy.conf`. There are many predefined aliases already listed in this file.

Large-Scale Management Issues

Check Point has historically had issues with managing a large number of firewalls. Although Provider-1 (Check Point's management product geared at large enterprise and service providers) helps somewhat, there are some inherent weaknesses in how FireWall-1 does things and how well it scales. Thus far, no really good solutions to these problems exist; however, knowing about them is half the battle, which is the purpose of this section.

Security Policies

I first need to address security policies. Although a single policy can actually be enforced on numerous firewalls, several limitations affect the ability to manage security policies in general.

Number of Network Objects

The Management GUI and the `fwm` process on the management module do not deal with a large number of objects very well (above 10,000 or so). Having lots of memory on your management module can mitigate this, but the fewer network objects you have, the better.

Number of Rules

Although FireWall-1 can (theoretically) handle any number of rules, large security policies (over 150 rules) on the whole take an extremely long time to compile and install on the various modules. Even managing the rules themselves becomes problematic.

Number of Rulebases

The Management GUI is somewhat inefficient in that each rulebase, whether or not it is actually being used on a firewall, is downloaded to the GUI. This causes some problems within the GUI, particularly if you have a large number of rulebases or even a small number of large rulebases. Although you can adjust timeouts to increase the amount of data that can be transferred, as well as enable compression in the SmartDashboard/Policy Editor application when logging in, there are inherent limitations to downloading everything to the Management GUI.

Hierarchical Management

As it stands now, anyone with read-write access to SmartDashboard/Policy Editor can change the security policy on any firewall. For large organizations with a number of sites, it is reasonable to assume there will be different needs at the different sites. The ideal structure would be to have three classes of rules in the following order:

1. *Organization-wide rules:* A global administrator would set these rules. A local site administrator would not be able to override these rules.
2. *Site-specific additions:* A local administrator could tweak these rules to his or her liking. Anything not denied in the organization-wide rules would be placed within these rules.
3. *Organization-wide default rules:* A global administrator would also set these rules. These could include rules that take effect if neither of the two previous sets of rules apply.

Some of these rule types are addressed in Provider-1, but it would be nice to see this level of granularity in the standard management product as well.

Number of Firewalls

Although there is no theoretical limit to the number of firewalls that can be managed by a single management module, there is a realistic limit. In most cases, this number is 12; however, it varies depending on the amount of logging that is taking place, the processing speed of the management module, and the network bandwidth. Many sites employ local logging on the firewalls and regular downloads of the logging information to increase the number of firewalls that can be managed. If you plan to manage more than 12 firewalls, Provider-1 may be a better choice for a management station.

Check Point has attempted to address the "number of firewalls" issue by allowing firewalls to log locally and then, at regular intervals, transfer the logs down to the management station automatically. In addition, the Large Scale Manager product allows for managing hundreds of similar gateways. Each gateway is assigned a ROBO Gateway Profile, which defines the common properties between all the gateways. This profile is defined in SmartDashboard/Policy Editor. In Large Scale Manager, you can then define the individual gateways that use this profile. Gateways that use this mechanism are referred to as ROBO Gateways.

ROBO Gateways function a little differently than other types of gateways in terms of their policy. While you can push a policy out to a specific ROBO device, a ROBO Gateway periodically fetches its security policy from the management station. This ensures the gateway is always in sync.

Each ROBO Gateway can also have a series of dynamic objects assigned to it. Within the individual ROBO Gateway definitions in Large Scale Manager, you can assign what each dynamic object means on that specific gateway.

Actual policies for the ROBO Gateways are defined in the SmartDashboard application. Each ROBO Gateway Profile can be listed as an Install-On target for rules. In addition, defined dynamic objects can also be used in the rulebase.

Number of Logs

Having a large amount of logs is not an easy problem to solve, regardless of what you use as a firewall. However, with FireWall-1, SmartView Tracker becomes a bottleneck. Some reports have suggested that more than 300,000 log entries will cause SmartView Tracker to lock up or even cause FireWall-1 to stop logging. Frequent log switches can mitigate this. Even if you could view this many log entries, would you want to? How could you analyze such large log files or even search through them to find events you are interested in?

Reliance on GUI for Management

While the SmartConsole applications are nice, many enterprise customers prefer to use a command-line interface (CLI) to configure their security devices. The main reason is that configuration via CLI can easily be scripted. When you have to create thousands of network objects and set up lots of very similar interrelationships between these objects, not to mention creating lots of very similar rules, using a GUI is very inefficient and error-prone. Imagine trying to create a thousand very similar network objects via SmartDashboard!

In FireWall-1 4.1 and earlier, Check Point provided no way to configure the firewall via a command line. In FireWall-1 NG, Check Point provides a way to do some configuration of network objects via the command line by using **dbedit**. The interface to **dbedit** is not very well documented—Check Point provides no guidance on how **dbedit** can be used to create or modify all types of network objects. Furthermore, **dbedit** does not allow you to create rules.

Check Point provides a general application programming interface (API) called Check Point Management Interface (CPMI). This provides secure access to Check Point's management server's databases. **dbedit** uses this interface. Applications developed using the OPSEC SDK can make use of this interface.

This means if you want your own CLI into Check Point's management server's databases, you could. To my knowledge, no such applications already exist. It's also unclear whether or not CPMI allows you to modify the rulebase.

Every aspect of FireWall-1 should be controllable via an easy-to-use, well-documented CLI. That isn't to say SmartConsole applications should go away—they provide a very important function. To appeal to a wide range of customers, both an easy-to-use GUI and a well-documented CLI are extremely important.

Summary

Being able to manage multiple firewalls is important in any organization. You should now understand how to establish an authenticated control connection between a firewall and a management module in a variety of situations. You can perform a number of tasks once this connection is established. When something goes wrong with this connection, you can now troubleshoot it. You also know how to move your management module from one system to another. Additionally, you understand some of the issues that come into play when managing multiple firewalls within a large network.

Chapter

8

User Authentication

It is unfortunate that some people cannot be trusted to do only what they are supposed to do. If it were not for these people, you would not need to take security measures to protect your networks. Authentication provides a mechanism for validating user identities and also provides different levels of access. FireWall-1 provides several different mechanisms for authenticating users.

In this chapter, I cover the key to all authentication schemes used within FireWall-1 today: passwords. Next, I cover the three methods of authentication supported by FireWall-1 for users, complete with a demonstration of each: User Authentication, Session Authentication, and Client Authentication. I then discuss how to actually set up FireWall-1 so it can perform authentication, including how to integrate FireWall-1 with various external authentication servers. Finally, I discuss how to troubleshoot authentication-related problems.

By the end of this chapter, you should be able to:

- Understand the difference between static and one-time password systems
- Use User, Session, and Client Authentication as a user
- Understand which authentication mechanism is the most appropriate for a given situation
- Set up User, Session, and Client Authentication
- Integrate supported third-party authentication servers into FireWall-1
- Configure Clientless VPN functionality
- Troubleshoot problems with authentication

Passwords

All multiuser computer systems have some form of login identification (or username) and some sort of password. This has been the basis for authentication on computers since multiuser computer systems came into existence. All authentication mechanisms in FireWall-1 rely on some sort of username and password, the credentials by which a user proves to the firewall who he or she is. Before proceeding, let's briefly discuss passwords.

To date, the vast majority of authentication is done with a static password. Most users, when left to their own devices, choose very simple passwords that are easy to guess. Even if a complicated password is chosen, the password, as it is being typed, can easily be picked off the wire with a packet sniffer. For these reasons, static passwords are not recommended. The risks these passwords create are somewhat mitigated by encrypting the passwords as part of the data stream (e.g., as part of SSH or HTTPS). However, most applications do not use encryption. Also, there is no point to encryption if the password is easy to guess.

One-time password (OTP) schemes were developed to solve these problems. They require a different password each time the user authenticates. Even though the network may be subject to packet tracing and may be able to see the entire challenge/response session, no information is divulged, so a hacker cannot pretend to be a particular user. OTP schemes use a secret key along with a cryptographic hash function. As long as the secret key is not divulged, the scheme is not compromised.

Passwords, regardless of whether or not they are OTPs or static passwords, can be managed a number of different ways, some inside FireWall-1 and others on external authentication servers.

FireWall-1 Password

FireWall-1 Password is a simple, static password that is maintained internally by FireWall-1. The password can be up to eight characters in length. No additional software is needed to use FireWall-1 Password. FireWall-1 Passwords are static, so use outside of a test environment is not recommended.

OS Password

FireWall-1 can use the login and password information stored in the operating system of the firewall for authentication. You are limited to what the specific operating system allows in terms of usernames and passwords (the latter are usually static passwords of limited length). No additional software is needed to use OS Password.

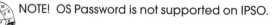 NOTE! OS Password is not supported on IPSO.

S/Key

S/Key is an OTP system that uses an MD4 or MD5 cryptographic hash function. It uses three values: a password number, a seed value (usually the same as the username), and a secret key. The password number and the seed value are transmitted in the clear as the challenge. The challenge, along with the secret key, is typed into an *S/Key generator* that resides on the user's local system. The S/Key generator then outputs a response to the challenge, which users type in to authenticate themselves. S/Key generators are widely available on the Internet free of charge.

Given the challenge and the response, it is impossible to determine what future responses need to be without knowing the secret key used to generate the S/Key chain. However, if you choose an easy-to-guess secret key, your login can easily be compromised. It is important to choose a secret key that is difficult to guess. As of version 4.1, FireWall-1 requires a secret key of at least ten characters to try to enforce a difficult-to-guess secret key.

When you log on and use S/Key, you are given a challenge such as:

```
SKEY CHALLENGE: 98 username
```

The number is the password number, which decrements after each successful login. The seed (in this case `username`) always stays the same. You type this information into an S/Key generator along with your secret key. This generates an OTP, which you then use as the response.

On a UNIX platform, the interaction with an S/Key generator looks something like this:

```
$ key 98 username
Reminder - Do not use this program while logged in via telnet or rlogin.
Enter secret password: test123
CUFF IRIS ELK JEFF ROSY GAG
```

On a Windows platform, the interaction with an S/Key generator might look similar to Figure 8.1.

Figure 8.1   Sample S/Key generator

S/Key can be used natively in FireWall-1 without having to purchase additional software. S/Key generators, and where to obtain them, for Windows and UNIX platforms are listed in Appendix G.

As of FireWall-1 NG with Application Intelligence (FP4), S/Key is no longer a supported authentication scheme. One major reason for this is that S/Key does not work where the firewalls are in a High Availability configuration. S/Key is also not widely used in corporate environments.

SecurID

SecurID uses a hardware token with a value that changes every minute or so. The card is synchronized with an ACE/Server, which validates the authentication attempt. So long as you do not lose this card, your authentication will be secure.

When you are prompted for authentication, you will be given a passcode prompt. Depending on the type of SecurID card you have, you will either type in a PIN (four to eight alphanumeric digits in length) followed by the six-digit number currently displayed on your SecurID card, or you will enter the PIN on your SecurID card, press the diamond key, and type in the number displayed on the SecurID card. Because the SecurID card and ACE/Server are in sync, the ACE/Server knows what the SecurID card should read at any given moment.

Using SecurID involves purchasing both the ACE/Server (which runs on UNIX or Windows NT workstations) and SecurID keys. The hardware keys expire after a period of time. Figure 8.2 shows a sample SecurID token.

Defender

Defender (formerly Axent Pathways Defender) is also a hardware token–based solution. You use a numeric keypad on the hardware key to punch in a challenge

Figure 8.2 Sample SecurID token

and a user-definable PIN, which gives you a response. The hardware key is programmed with an ID that is also specified on the Defender Authentication Server. This key is tied to a specific login ID and cannot be used with anyone else's login ID.

When you log in, you are prompted with a challenge (a number). You enter this number along with your PIN into the hardware key. This generates your response, which you then type into the computer.

As of FireWall-1 NG FP3, Defender is no longer a supported authentication scheme. Based on my personal experience, this is not a widely used authentication scheme. For as long as I've been supporting FireWall-1 (since 1996), only one customer has asked me about this authentication scheme. In any case, Defender has a RADIUS-compatible mode, which can be used with FireWall-1.

Remote Access Dial-In User Service (RADIUS)

Originally developed by Livingston (now a part of Lucent), RADIUS is an authentication server usually used by those providing dial-up access for authentication. RADIUS can theoretically support any sort of password scheme, whether static or OTP. A wide variety of other authentication servers (SecurID, Defender, and others) also implement a RADIUS-compatible mode to make it easy for other applications to tie in, thus making RADIUS support rather ubiquitous. Some RADIUS servers can also be used to provide authentication via an OS-level password (e.g., a Windows NT/2000 domain password). It is often far easier and more secure to use RADIUS to authenticate against a Windows NT domain than to use actual Microsoft protocols to do it.

Terminal Access Controller Access Control System (TACACS/TACACS+)

TACACS provides access control for routers, network access servers, and other networked computing devices via one or more centralized servers. BBN Technologies originally developed TACACS for use on MILNET. Cisco has built upon and enhanced TACACS. The original TACACS is no longer supported by Cisco. A newer version, called TACACS+, provides several enhancements to the original protocol, including the use of TCP (instead of UDP) and separation of functions (authentication, authorization, and accounting).

Lightweight Directory Access Protocol (LDAP)

LDAP Directories are becoming popular in midsize to large enterprises as a way to centrally store and manage information about people, places, and things. FireWall-1 allows you to use information stored in an LDAP server as well as store data specific to FireWall-1 there. This allows you to use existing LDAP tools and SmartDashboard/Policy Editor to manage users. All authentication schemes previously mentioned can be used with users defined in an LDAP server in addition to the password that is stored in each LDAP record (typically a fixed password). You also have further flexibility insofar as groups can be defined in terms of existing hierarchies that may already exist in your LDAP Directory. Users can also be defined in terms of templates. All an administrator has to do is change the template to change the attributes of all the users who use that template. LDAP requires the purchase of additional licenses in FireWall-1 in order to make use of it; you must also have an LDAP server.

How Users Authenticate

Now that I have discussed passwords, I can talk about the various ways FireWall-1 asks users for passwords. Demonstrations of each method are provided in the following subsections.

Explaining User Authentication

User Authentication allows you to provide authentication for five different services: Telnet, rlogin, HTTP, HTTPS, and FTP. FireWall-1 provides user-level authentication via the appropriate Security Server processes. These processes are invoked when FireWall-1 needs to authenticate a connection. The Security Server authenticates the session, then passes it on to the remote server.

For example, if you wanted to Telnet to 172.29.0.44 and you want FireWall-1 to require authentication, the following exchange would occur:

```
$ telnet 172.29.0.44
Trying 172.29.0.44...
Connected to 172.29.0.44.
Escape character is '^]'.
Check Point FireWall-1 authenticated Telnet server running on mrhat
User: dwelch
FireWall-1 password: abc123
User dwelch authenticated by FireWall-1 authentication
Connected to 172.29.0.44
Red Hat Linux release 6.0 (Hedwig)
Kernel 2.2.12-20 on an i486
login:
```

The following list explains the steps taken in the previous code.

1. FireWall-1 intercepts the communication between the client and the server.

2. FireWall-1 prompts for a username and password.

3. If the user successfully authenticates with FireWall-1, the connection is then passed on to the destination host. The remote host then prompts for a username and password, which will likely be different from the one given to the firewall.

Because rlogin works in almost exactly the same way, a specific rlogin example is not needed. HTTP and HTTPS use the standard authentication screen you would see in your Web browser when accessing a password-protected Web site (see Figure 8.3).

You must enter your username and password. If a specific challenge is needed before you can enter your password (e.g., for S/Key), just enter your username and click OK. You are then presented with the challenge as the "reason" shown in the dialog box.

FTP is a bit more complicated. Even though you can FTP directly to a specific host and FireWall-1 will intercept it, you must still tell the FTP Security Server where to go:

```
$ ftp 172.29.0.44
Connected to 172.29.0.44.
220 aftpd: Check Point FireWall-1 Secure FTP server running on mrhat
Name (172.29.0.44:dwelch):
```

At this point, you must enter a username in the following format: Site User@FireWall-1 User@Remote Host. If the FireWall-1 user and the FTP site user are the same, you can enter the username in this format: User@Remote Host.

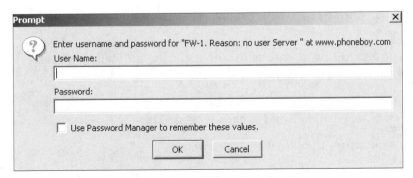

Figure 8.3 Sample HTTP authentication

Here is an example of an FTP authentication:

```
Name (172.29.0.44:dwelch): anonymous@dwelch@172.29.0.44
331 aftpd: FireWall-1 password: you can use password@FW-1-password
Password:
```

The password is in the following format: `FTP Site Password@FireWall-1 Password`.

Anonymous login to an e-mail server usually asks for an e-mail address; dwelch@phoneboy.com is the e-mail address used in the following example. Note that if either the username or password contains an @ symbol, you need to enter the @ twice.

```
Password: dwelch@@phoneboy.com@abc123
230-aftpd: User dwelch authenticated by FireWall-1 authentication
230-aftpd: Connected to 172.29.0.44. Logging in...
230-aftpd: 220 stinkpot Microsoft FTP Service (Version 3.0).
230-aftpd: 331 Anonymous access allowed, send identity (e-mail
name) as password.
230 aftpd: 230 Anonymous user logged in.
Remote system type is Windows_NT.
ftp>
```

A different interface is available by making a change via **dbedit** or the GUIdbedit tool. See FAQ 4.2 in Chapter 4 for instructions on how to do this. In **dbedit**, you would enter the following commands:

```
dbedit> modify properties firewall_properties new_ftp_interface true
dbedit> update properties firewall_properties
```

In this case, the FTP to 172.29.0.44 is a bit easier to access via the command line:

```
$ ftp 172.29.0.44
Connected to 172.29.0.44.
220 aftpd: Check Point FireWall-1 Secure FTP server running on mrhat
Name (172.29.0.44:dwelch):
```

At this point, you must enter a username in the following format: `FireWall-1 User@Remote Host`, which is used in the example below:

```
Name (172.29.0.44:dwelch): dwelch@172.29.0.44
331 aftpd: FireWall-1 password: you can use FW-1-password
```

Next, simply enter the FireWall-1 Password:

```
Password: abc123
230-aftpd: User dwelch authenticated by FireWall-1 authentication
230-aftpd: Connected to 172.29.0.44. Logging in...
```

```
230-aftpd: 220 stinkpot Microsoft FTP Service (Version 3.0).
ftp>
```

You should then be connected to the remote FTP server. You must log in by using the **user** command as follows:

```
ftp> user anonymous
331 Anonymous access allowed, send identity (e-mail name) as password.
Password: dwelch@phoneboy.com
230 Anonymous user logged in.
ftp>
```

Explaining Session Authentication

Session Authentication can be used for any service. Authentication relies on the presence of an agent on the client, which prompts users for authentication as they make the connection request. When necessary, the firewall contacts the agent, which either transparently provides authentication to the firewall or prompts the user for authentication if it cannot provide authentication. Check Point includes agents for all supported platforms (Windows, Solaris, AIX, and HP).

Figure 8.4 illustrates an example of what happens when a user tries to use Session Authentication on a Windows platform. In Figure 8.4, the user tries to access vax134.area.com via HTTP. Once the username is entered, FireWall-1 prompts the user for a password, as shown in Figure 8.5.

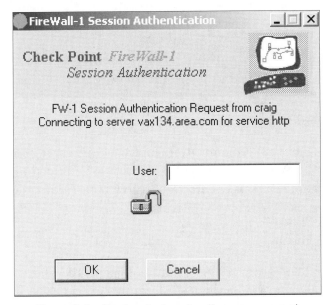

Figure 8.4 Session Authentication user prompt

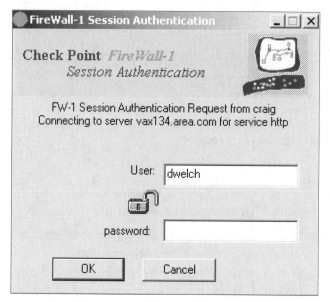

Figure 8.5 Session Authentication password prompt

Explaining Client Authentication

Client Authentication can be used to authenticate any service. The user must authenticate with the firewall before using the service. The service is then provided to the user a specific number of times and/or for a specific period of time. A user can authenticate in four ways, depending on how Client Authentication is configured:

- A Telnet connection to the firewall on port 259
- An HTTP connection to the firewall on port 900
- An HTTPS connection to the firewall on port 950
- User or Session Authentication

For the latter case, the authentication looks no different from the example shown earlier in the Explaining User Authentication subsection. However, you have two other choices to make with respect to Client Authentication:

- Standard Sign-On
- Specific Sign-On

Standard Sign-On lets users simply authenticate once and do whatever the authentication allows. Specific Sign-On requires users to specify each destination and service they want to use when they authenticate. Users are allowed to access only those services and destinations they specify, even if the rule allows for more. For simplicity's sake, most administrators are satisfied with simply allowing users to use Standard Sign-On because it requires less end-user training.

Manual authentication via Telnet using Standard Sign-On looks like this:

```
$ telnet 10.0.0.1 259
Trying 10.0.0.1...
Connected to 10.0.0.1
Escape character is '^]'.
Check Point FireWall-1 Client Authentication Server running on craig
User: dwelch
password: abc123
User dwelch authenticated by FireWall-1 authentication

Choose:

(1) Standard Sign-on
(2) Sign-off
(3) Specific Sign-on

Enter your choice: 1

User authorized for standard services (1 rules)


Connection to host lost.
$
```

As mentioned, with Specific Sign-On, users must specify each service and destination they want to access. The following example attempts to set up HTTP and FTP access to www.phoneboy.com. Only HTTP will be permitted; FTP will not.

```
$ telnet 10.0.0.1 259
Trying 10.0.0.1...
Connected to 10.0.0.1
Escape character is '^]'.
Check Point FireWall-1 Client Authentication Server running on craig
User: dwelch
password: abc123
User dwelch authenticated by FireWall-1 authentication

Choose:

(1) Standard Sign-on
(2) Sign-off
(3) Specific Sign-on

Enter your choice: 3
```

```
Service (^D to Quit): http
Host: www.phoneboy.com
Client Authorized for service

Service (^D to Quit): ftp
Host: www.phoneboy.com
User not allowed for service ftp on host

Service (^D to Quit):

Connection to host lost.

$
```

Figure 8.6   Manual Client Authentication over HTTP, username entry

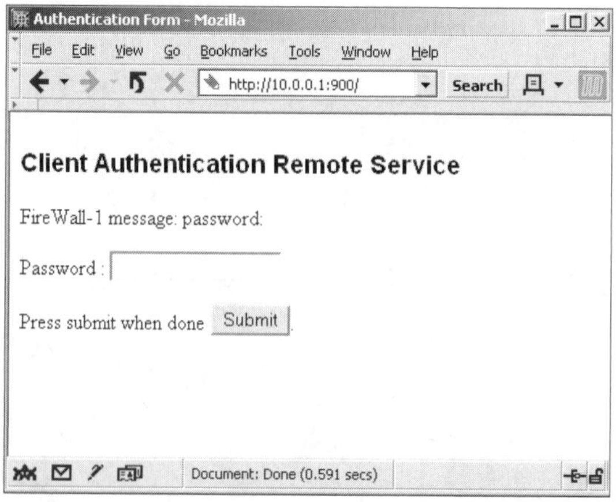

Figure 8.7   Manual Client Authentication over HTTP, password entry

HTTP authentication to port 900 on the firewall is shown in Figure 8.6. Note that a username has already been entered into the form. When you click Submit, the screen shown in Figure 8.7 appears.

Type in your password, and click the Submit button. You are then presented with the screen shown in Figure 8.8. Select Standard Sign-On and click Submit to complete the authentication, as shown in Figure 8.9.

When you select Specific Sign-On, a screen appears allowing you to enter the services and hosts you want to access. Figure 8.10 shows entries for using both FTP and HTTP to www.phoneboy.com. The response to this authentication request is shown in Figure 8.11.

Figure 8.8   Manual Client Authentication over HTTP, method selection

Figure 8.9   Manual Client Authentication over HTTP, Standard Sign-On authorization

Figure 8.10   Manual Client Authentication over HTTP, Specific Sign-On details

Figure 8.11   Manual Client Authentication over HTTP, Specific Sign-On completed

Which Authentication Type Should You Use?

Usually, the application you need to authenticate and the operating system of the client in question dictate the type of authentication you need to perform. Table 8.1 provides you with a guide to the various authentication schemes.

Client and Session Authentication have a limitation: Only a single user can come from an IP address you want to authenticate from. Typical UNIX systems and NAT gateways present situations where more than one person can potentially come from a single IP address. In the case of Client Authentication, a user who authenticates from such an IP address could potentially be letting in more users than just him- or herself. Client Authentication can be dangerous in this situation. With Session Authentication, the problem is that it is not clear whom to prompt for Session Authentication on a multiuser system. Because the Session Authentication agent typically caches the login and password information, you have a situation where either the user is constantly entering in (or having to

Table 8.1   Authentication schemes

Use This Method	Under These Circumstances
User Authentication	• The protocol in question is FTP, HTTP, HTTPS, rlogin, or Telnet. • You want to authenticate each session. • If the protocol is HTTP and you want to authenticate the session for a specific period of time. • You want to perform content security. • You need the proxy capabilities of the Security Servers.
Client Authentication	• The protocol in question is not FTP, HTTP, HTTPS, rlogin, or Telnet. • You want to authenticate for a specific period of time. • You want better performance than the Security Servers can provide. • Only one user can come from a given IP address at a time.
Session Authentication	• The protocol in question is not FTP, HTTP, HTTPS, rlogin, or Telnet. • Only one user can come from a given IP address at a time. • You want to authenticate each session. • You have a Session Authentication agent for the client platform you want to authenticate against.

cancel) authentication requests for connections he is not making or more than just the authorized user is allowed to perform a service. In these cases, the only appropriate authentication mechanism is User Authentication because each individual session is authenticated in-band, which means you are limited to what you can reasonably authenticate.

Setting Up Authentication

Now that I have discussed passwords and how the various forms of authentication work, I will discuss how to set up authentication.

Creating Users

Before you can begin to authenticate people, you need to know how to create users. In SmartDashboard/Policy Editor, click on this icon in the objects tree: 𝍤 . From here, you may create users, templates, and groups by right-clicking on the appropriate name and selecting New. You may also select Users from the Manage menu. In this case, a dialog box similar to Figure 8.12 appears. Note that all of the same functions can be performed via either interface.

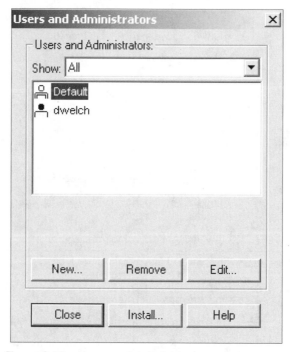

Figure 8.12   Users and Administrators, main screen

Use the buttons on the Users and Administrators main screen for the following purposes.

New: Create a new user, group, or template.

Remove: Remove the user, group, or template selected.

Edit: Edit the user, group, or template selected.

Close: Close the window.

Install: Install the user database on managed firewalls. This must be done any time the user database has been modified.

When you click New, the pop-up menu shown in Figure 8.13 appears. This menu contains several options.

User by Template: All users are initially created through a template. Default is the one created by Check Point on installation.

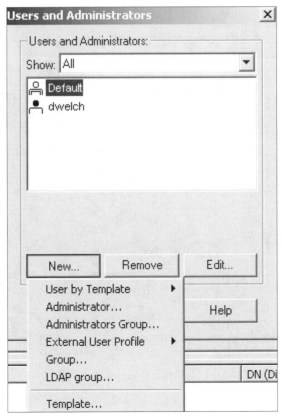

Figure 8.13   Users and Administrators, New menu

Administrator: This option creates an administrative user who can log into the Check Point SmartConsole GUI applications. These users *cannot* be used to log to authenticate at the firewall.

Administrators Group: This item creates a group of administrative users.

External User Profile: This tells FireWall-1 to forward requests by unknown users to a specific authentication server and give all of those users a common profile. This functionality supercedes the generic* functionality[1] that existed in NG FP2 and earlier. It also improves on it because you can define more than one external user profile, whereas previously you could define only one generic* user.

Group: This option allows you to create a new group within FireWall-1.

LDAP group: To reference a branch of an LDAP Directory for use in FireWall-1, use this option. This is discussed in the Integrating LDAP sub-section of this chapter.

Template: This option is used to create a template user.

For template users or external user profiles, most of the screens shown in Figures 8.16 through 8.23 are identical for both situations. The only difference is that template users or external user profiles cannot have passwords established.

For this example, select User by Template and then Default. You are then presented with the dialog shown in Figure 8.14. If you created an external user profile by domain (instead of choosing Match All Users), you will see a dialog like Figure 8.15.

The field in Figure 8.14 allows you to enter the username for the user in question. This name is what the user will authenticate to the firewall as. In Figure 8.15, you have more options.

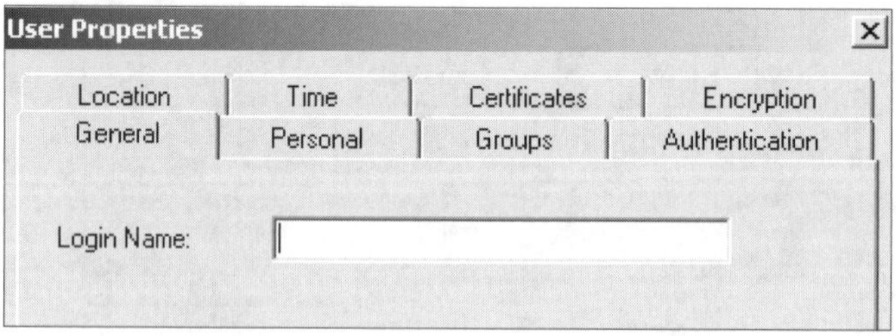

Figure 8.14 User Properties, General tab

---

1. In NG FP2 and earlier, you could create a user with the name generic*. This provided functionality similar to the External User Profile option.

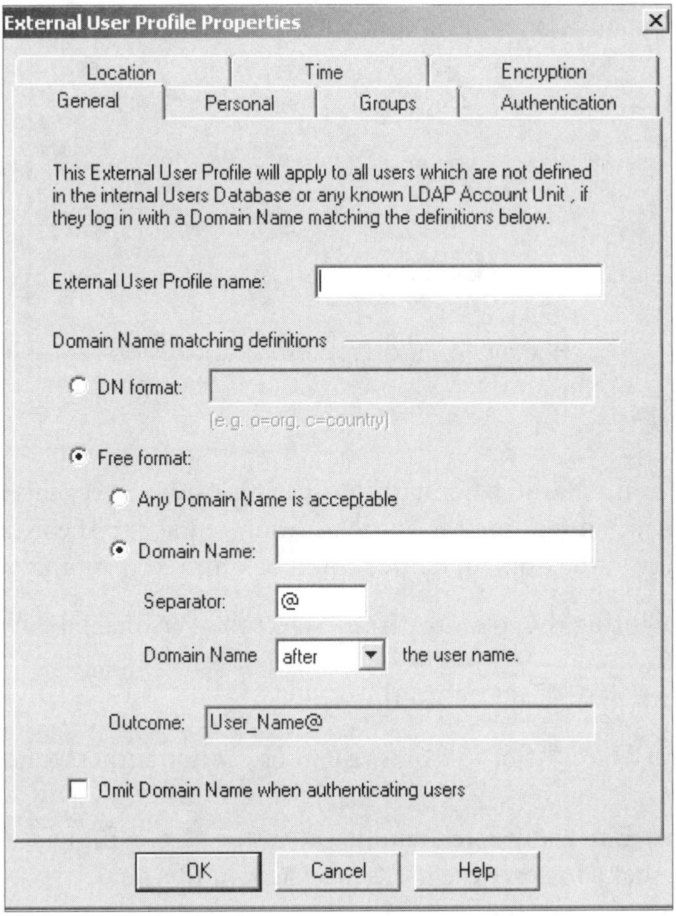

Figure 8.15 External User Profile Properties

External User Profile Name: This field provides a way to refer to the external user group.

DN Format: If you are using LDAP, this option allows you to specify the branch that is valid for this user group.

Any Domain Name is acceptable: If you select this option, the domain name specified by the user when he or she authenticates will be accepted, even if it is not valid. If you don't want the user to have to specify a domain, when creating the external user group, select Match All Users as described previously.

Domain Name: Here you specify the domain name that matches this external user group. You can also specify the separator and where the domain appears (before or after the username).

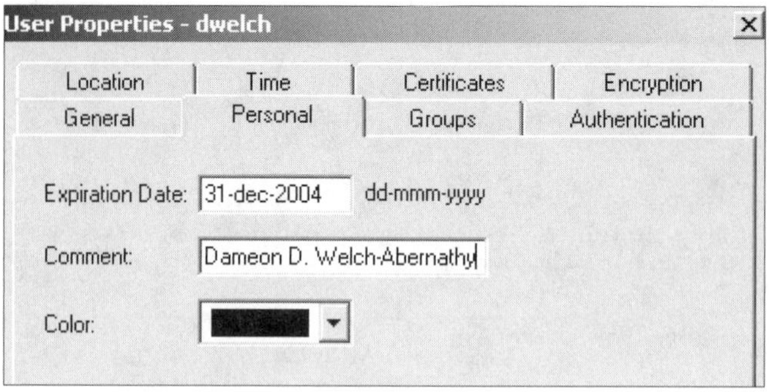

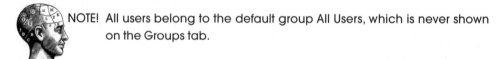

Figure 8.16 User Properties, Personal tab

Omit Domain Name when authenticating users: Select this option to indicate that when sending the authentication request to the external authentication server, the domain name should be omitted from that request.

After configuring the user properties, select the Personal tab, which is shown in Figure 8.16.
The following fields appear on this dialog.

Expiration Date: After this date, the user cannot authenticate through the firewall.

Comment: Enter any information you want as a comment. It is strongly suggested that you enter the user's full name in this field.

Color: Choose a color for this object.

Next is the Groups tab (see Figure 8.17), where you list the groups the user is a member of.

NOTE! All users belong to the default group All Users, which is never shown on the Groups tab.

Now let's look at the Authentication tab (see Figure 8.18). A user must have a form of authentication defined. Recall that the authentication types were described earlier in this chapter, although specific settings for some of these types are discussed in this section.
I'll start with S/Key (see Figure 8.19). This tab contains the following items.

Seed: This field usually contains the username, but it can be anything. The value is used as part of calculating the S/Key chain.

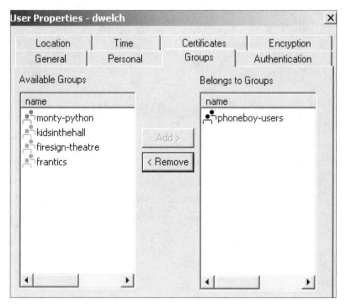

Figure 8.17   User Properties, Groups tab

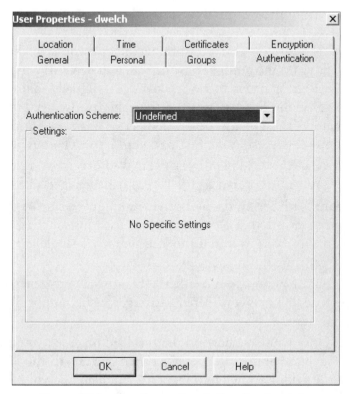

Figure 8.18   User Properties, Authentication tab

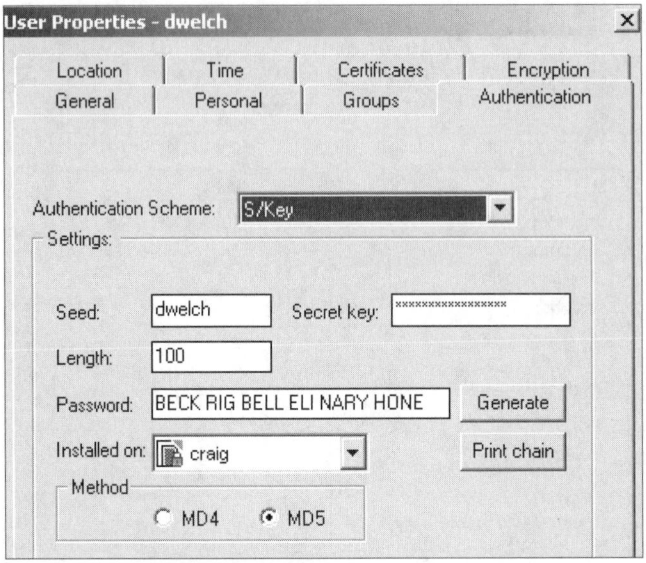

Figure 8.19 User Properties, Authentication tab, S/Key

Secret key: This field contains the password the user enters into an S/Key generator to generate the response to the S/Key challenge. It must be at least ten characters long.

Length: This field contains the number of passwords in the chain. This value also indicates the number of times the user can authenticate before his or her S/Key chain needs to be regenerated—actually, one less than this number because the first password in the chain is displayed in the GUI, so you can match the user with the printed S/Key chain (see Print chain at the end of this list). As a result, the first password in the chain is not used.

Password: Leave this field blank. It will be filled in once you click the Generate button. (When I captured Figure 8.19, I had already clicked that button.)

Installed on: With S/Key, the user can exist on only a single FireWall-1 gateway. This is to ensure that each password is used just once. The easy way to do this is to allow you to install the user on only a single gateway. In other words, you can't use this on a gateway cluster.

Method: You can choose to use either MD4 or MD5 to generate the proper S/Key response. MD5 is considered a stronger hash, but not all S/Key generators support it.

Generate: Once you have filled in the Installed on, Seed, and Length fields, click the Generate button. A password then appears in the Password field. If none of the fields are filled in (except for Installed on, which must be filled in), FireWall-1 will make up a secret key and generate a chain of 100 passwords. FireWall-1 does not tell you what the key is, so you need to click the Print chain button (below). If a user loses the printout, there is no way to recover the chain, and a new chain must be generated.

Print chain: Once you have filled in all the fields, click the Print chain button to print out the entire chain of passwords. This printout allows a user to use S/Key authentication in situations where having an S/Key generator is not desirable. Make sure your end user does not lose this piece of paper!

If you decide to use FireWall-1 Password as your authentication type, see Figure 8.20. Enter your password in the Password field. Your password is stored locally and encrypted with a mechanism similar to the one used to store UNIX passwords in /etc/passwd.

If you decide to use RADIUS as your authentication type, see Figure 8.21. This screen presents you with any server objects of type RADIUS or any groups that might contain them. By default, all RADIUS servers are queried.

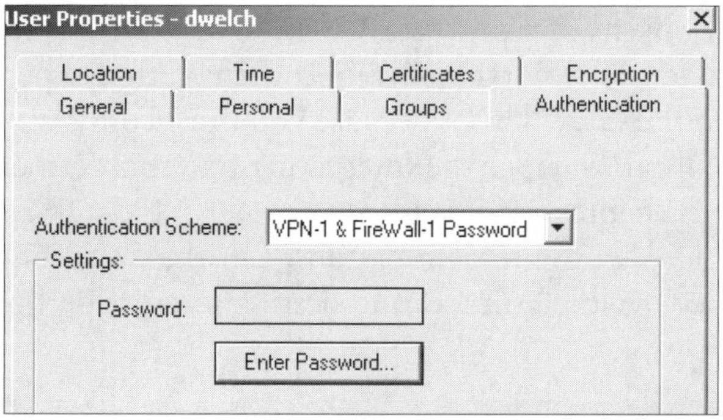

Figure 8.20   User Properties, Authentication tab, FireWall-1 Password

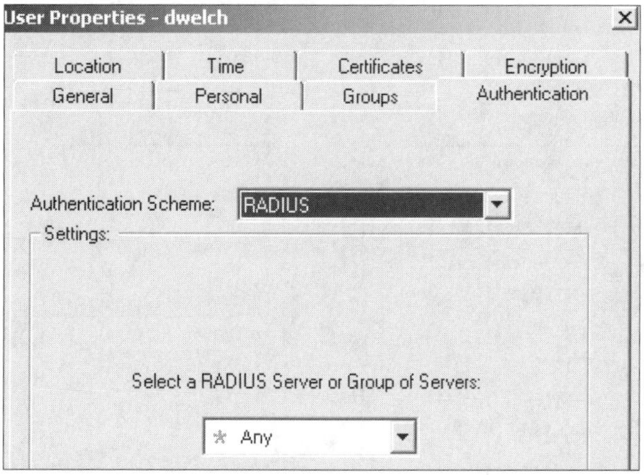

Figure 8.21   User Properties, Authentication tab, RADIUS

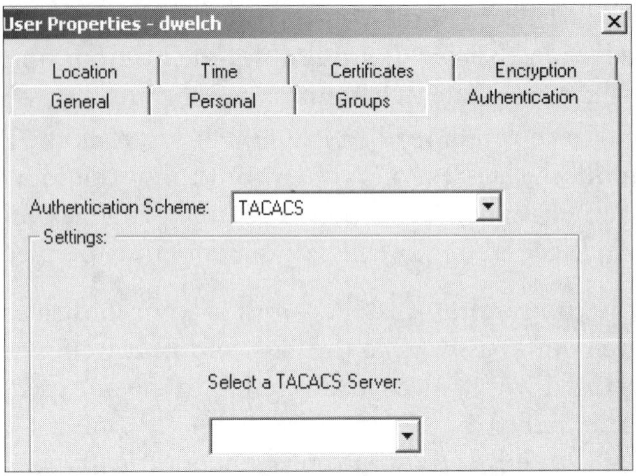

Figure 8.22   User Properties, Authentication tab, TACACS

For TACACS, you will receive a dialog similar to the one shown in Figure 8.22. Only server objects of type TACACS are shown on this screen.

If you decide to use SecurID as your authentication type, you will see no specific settings in the GUI. This is because you must configure an `sdconf.rec` file on each firewall gateway. See the Integrating External Authentication Servers section later in this chapter for details.

Let's quickly look at the remaining tabs. On the Location tab (see Figure 8.23), you can specify which sources and destinations are permitted for a partic-

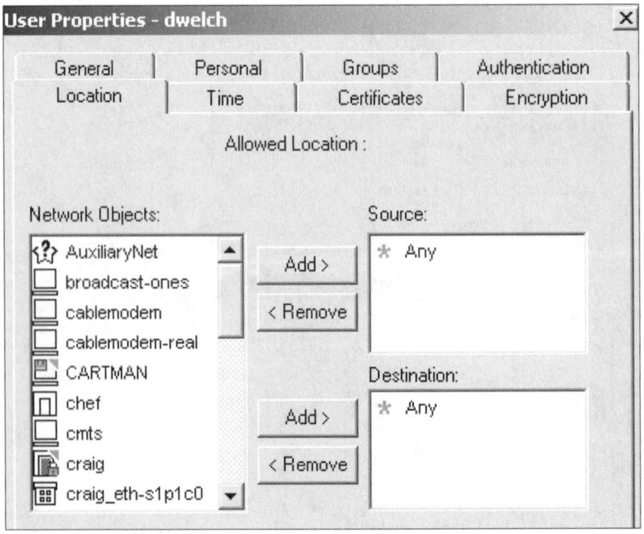

Figure 8.23   User Properties, Location tab

ular user. Note that the rulebase can specifically override this designation on a per-rule basis, as I will describe in more detail in the Setting Up User Authentication section.

The Time tab defines when a user is allowed to authenticate (see Figure 8.24). The user must still be permitted by the rulebase.

The Certificates tab (see Figure 8.25) allows you to generate a certificate for the user based on the Internal Certificate Authority (ICA). Certificates can be

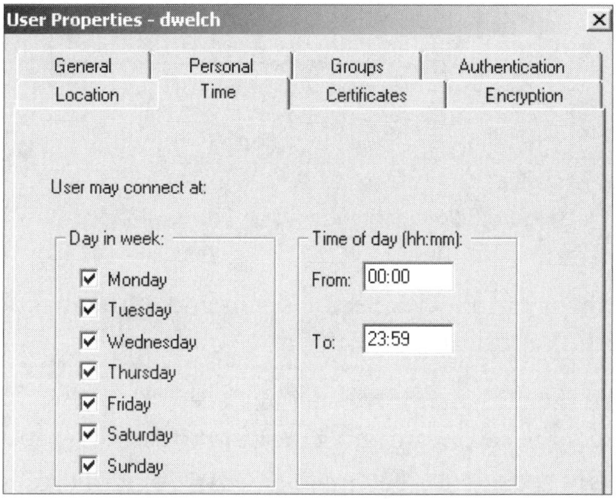

Figure 8.24 User Properties, Time tab

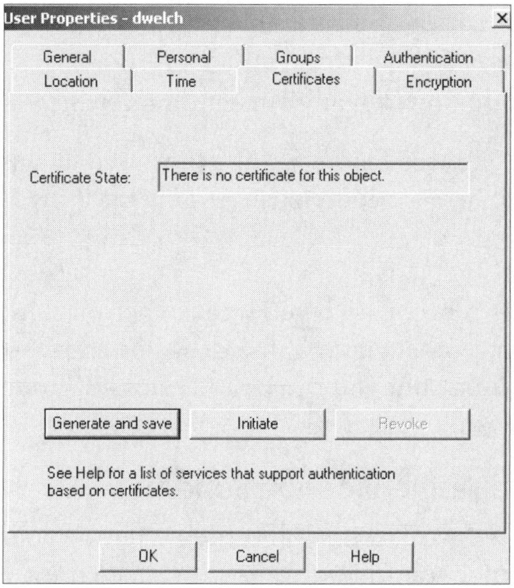

Figure 8.25 User Properties, Certificates tab

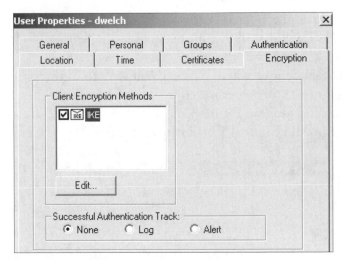

Figure 8.26   User Properties, Encryption tab

used only for authentication with SecureClient and authentication via HTTPS. The buttons on the Certificates tab offer three options.

Generate and save: This simply generates a certificate, prompting for a password to protect the certificate and a location to save it.

Initiate: This is specific for SecureClient use. A certificate is generated and stored on the management station. A registration key tied to that specific user is also issued. With the IP address or fully qualified domain name (FQDN) of the management console and the registration key, a user can obtain the certificate via SecureClient.

Revoke: This option revokes any outstanding certificates for this user.

The Encryption tab (see Figure 8.26) is not used at this point, but I've included the screenshot here for completeness. This tab is discussed in Chapter 12.

Creating Groups

Creating a new group is necessary if you want to permit some of your users to do certain things, but not others. FireWall-1 does not allow you to define rules in terms of individual users, but you can define rules for groups. The dialog looks similar to the one shown in Figure 8.27.

Setting Supported Authentication Schemes

You must configure the workstation object representing your firewall so that the authentication schemes you intend to use are enabled on your firewall object. Edit the object, and go to the Authentication frame (see Figure 8.28).

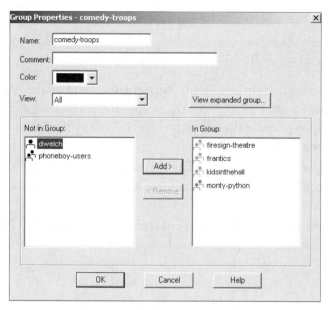

Figure 8.27 Group Properties

By default, OS Password and FireWall-1 Password are disabled. In NG FP3, S/Key is disabled by default as well. If you want to use these authentication schemes, you need to select them here. The options for using HTTP Next Proxy and setting a User Authentication session timeout are discussed in the Setting Up User Authentication section. The option to enable wait mode is discussed later in the Setting Up Client Authentication section.

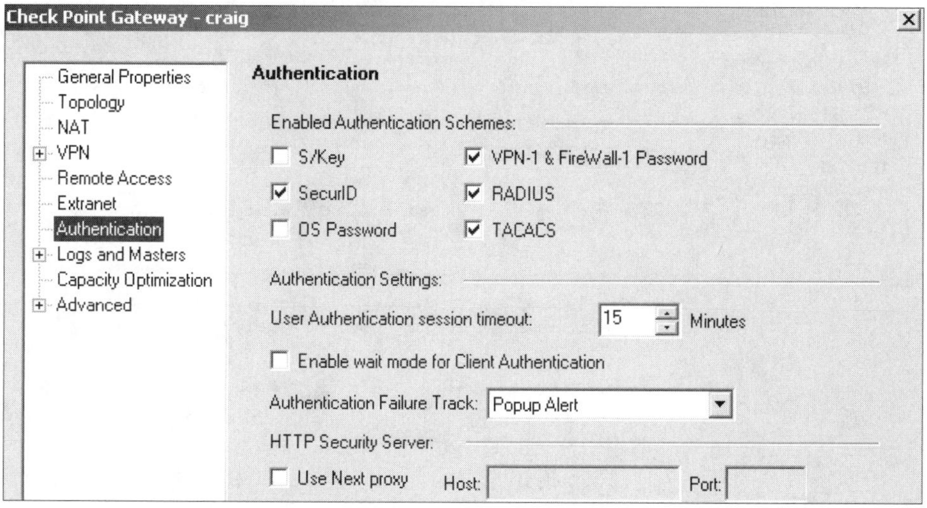

Figure 8.28 Gateway Properties, Authentication frame

Global Properties Related to Authentication

Figure 8.29 shows the Authentication frame in the Global Properties section. Several options relate to all the authentication schemes.

> **Terminate rlogin/telnet/Client Authentication/Session Authentication connections after:** If a user connects via one of the specified methods and the user fails to provide the correct credentials the specified number of times, the session will be terminated.
>
> **Authenticate internal users with this suffix only:** This option is relevant for certificate-based authentication when using the ICA. By default, this value matches the current value for your ICA.
>
> **User's certificates which were initiated but not pulled will expire after:** When a certificate is generated for a user but the user does not "pull" the certificate into SecureClient, the certificate will expire after the specified number of days.
>
> **User Authentication session timeout:** This is relevant only for FireWall-1 4.1 and earlier gateways, where this option was specified as one of the global

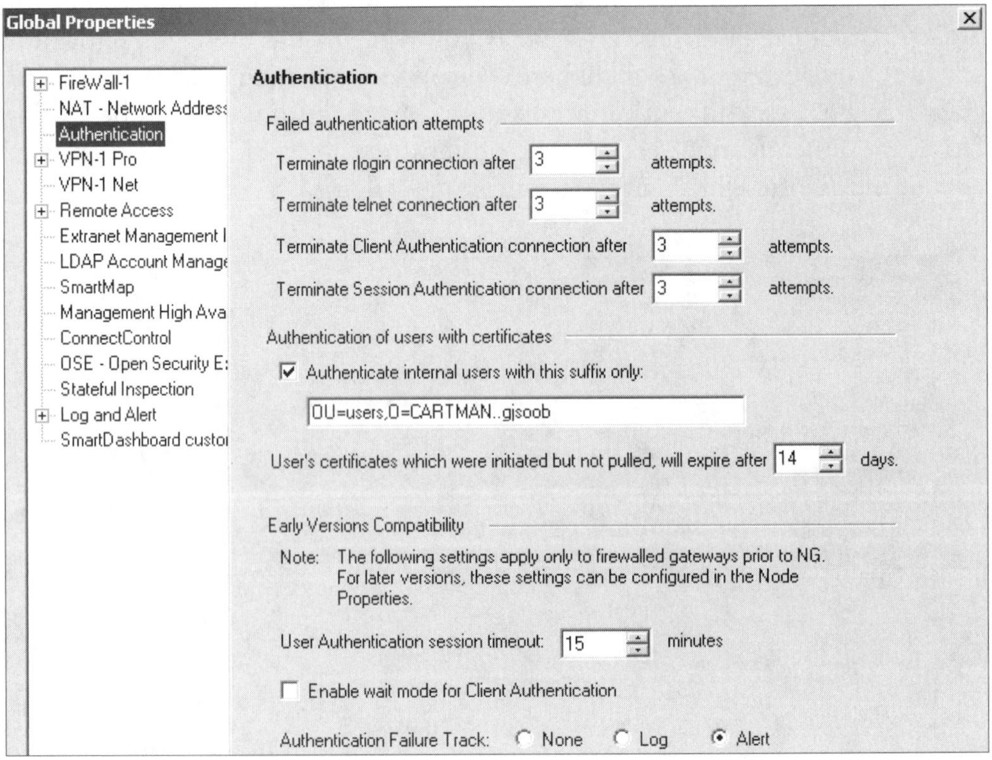

Figure 8.29   Global Properties, Authentication frame

properties instead of on a per-firewall basis. This is discussed in the Setting Up User Authentication section.

Authentication Failure Track: This is relevant only for FireWall-1 4.1 and earlier gateways, where this option was specified as one of the global properties instead of on a per-firewall basis. The Authentication Failure Track provides three options that determine what happens when a user fails to authenticate successfully. The selected alert will be generated upon failure.

Setting Up User Authentication

Set up User Authentication by following these steps.

1. Create the necessary users and groups required for authentication, then install the user database.
2. Ensure that the appropriate Security Servers are enabled in `$FWDIR/conf/fwauthd.conf`.
3. Create the appropriate rule(s) in the rulebase.
4. Configure the User Authentication action properties.
5. Configure the Rulebase Properties Authentication frame.
6. Verify and install the policy.

After creating your users, verify that the appropriate Security Servers are enabled in `$FWDIR/conf/fwauthd.conf`. By default, they should be enabled, but it never hurts to check. The lines for the servers you want to enable should be present and not commented out (i.e., the line should not begin with a #). The FTP, HTTP, Telnet, and rlogin servers are enabled if these lines are present in `fwauthd.conf` and are not commented out:

```
21      fwssd      in.aftpd      wait   0
80      fwssd      in.ahttpd     wait   0
513     fwssd      in.arlogind   wait   0
23      fwssd      in.atelnetd   wait   0
```

You then need to create the appropriate rule in the rulebase. When adding the source of the rule, right-click the source field, and select Add User Access. Select the appropriate group. The Location must also be set. The No restriction option means Any in the rulebase. The Restrict option allows you to select a network object or group that represents where you want to authenticate the connections from.

For example, if you want to authenticate all users in the group knights-of-the-roundtable from the network camelot to the host castle-anthrax via Telnet and HTTP, the rule would look like the one shown in Figure 8.30.

SOURCE	DESTINATION	SERVICE	ACTION
knights-of-the-roundtable@Any	castle-anthrax	TCP telnet TCP http	User Auth

Figure 8.30   The Knights of the Round Table can go to Castle Anthrax

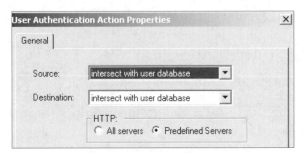

Figure 8.31   User Authentication Action Properties, General tab

You must then edit the User Authentication properties by right-clicking the Action field of the rule and selecting Edit Properties. Figure 8.31 shows the screen that appears. For both the source and the destination, you can select one of two options:

Intersect with user database: This option means that if the user who authenticates is coming from a source or destination (as appropriate) that is not allowed as defined in the user's record, the user will actually be denied, even if the rule says the user should be allowed access. This option allows you to set up fairly granular access.

Ignore user database: This option means that users who would otherwise be denied as a result of the allowed sources or destinations defined in their user record are allowed anyway.

To illustrate the way these options work, let's use the users sir-gallahad and sir-lancelot with the rule created earlier. The allowed sources and destinations for sir-gallahad are both Any. The allowed sources for sir-lancelot are Any, but his allowed destination does not include castle-anthrax (i.e., it is neither Any nor a group that includes castle-anthrax). If the User Authentication properties for the rule are defined using "intersect with user database" for the destination, when sir-lancelot tries to authenticate to access castle-anthrax, he will be denied, even if he is coming from camelot[2] and presents correct credentials. If the setting

---

2. It's only a model.

used is "ignore user database," sir-lancelot will be permitted to go to castle-anthrax, provided he supplies the correct credentials and is coming from camelot.

For the HTTP section of this screen, there are two options:

All servers: This setting should be the default for this screen. It allows you to authenticate and go to any HTTP server without having to define it in the Policy Properties Security Servers tab. Of course, the connection must still match the rulebase. Unless you are using this rule to authenticate access to internal servers only, it is highly recommended that you use this setting (otherwise, the rule won't work).

Predefined Servers: This option is the actual default. It means you can go only to servers defined in the Policy Properties Security Servers tab. Using this setting makes sense only if you are using FireWall-1 as a reverse proxy server.

As part of setting up User Authentication, you must go to the gateway object and configure some related options. Recall that in the discussion of Figure 8.28 there were some options I did not explain. Two of these options come into play now.

User Authentication session timeout: If an authenticated Telnet, FTP, or rlogin connection is inactive for the specified number of minutes, the connection will be terminated. In HTTP, this option has a different meaning. If an OTP is used, this is the amount of time the user will be authenticated before a new OTP is requested. *If a static password scheme is used with HTTP, this setting has no effect because Web browsers typically cache passwords until the client exits.*

Use Next Proxy: If you are using the firewall as a proxy for your internal Web clients, this option controls which proxy server to forward authenticated or content-screened content to.

Also on that frame, the Authentication Failure Track provides three options that determine what happens when a user fails to authenticate successfully. The selected alert will be generated upon failure.

Finally, you must configure the global properties as appropriate for your needs.

Once the rules and the rulebase properties are set to your liking, install the security policy.

The Importance of Rule Order in User Authentication

There is one case where FireWall-1 does not process the rules in order but instead uses the rule that is most permissive. This occurs when User Authentication

NO.	SOURCE	DESTINATION	SERVICE	ACTION	TRACK
1	✳ Any	🖥 web_server	TCP http TCP https	🔘 accept	– None
2	✳ Any	🖥 Email_Server	TCP smtp	🔘 accept	– None
3	✳ Any	🖥 ftp_server	TCP ftp	🔘 accept	– None
4	👤 DMZAdmins@internal-networks	🔀 DMZ_net	TCP telnet TCP ftp	👤 User Auth	📄 Log
5	👤 FWAdmins@internal-networks	🗄 Local_Gateway	TCP telnet	👤 User Auth	📄 Log
6	✳ Any	🗄 Local_Gateway	✳ Any	🔘 drop	📄 Log
7	🖩 internal-networks	✳ Any	TCP telnet TCP ftp TCP http TCP https	🔘 accept	📄 Log
8	✳ Any	✳ Any	✳ Any	🔘 drop	📄 Log

Figure 8.32 Sample rulebase

for HTTP, FTP, Telnet, and rlogin is used and such a rule is matched in the rulebase. If during the in-order rulebase evaluation the rule that matches the connection (based on source, destination, and service) is User Authentication, all rules in the rulebase are evaluated and the least restrictive one applies. Check Point refers to this as the Insufficient Information problem in the documentation.

To give you an idea of what this means, consider the security policy shown in Figure 8.32.

Based on the rules and how the rulebase rules are applied, the following list details how these rules will apply themselves.

- Everyone on the Internet will be able to access the HTTP, HTTPS, and SMTP servers without any authentication from the firewall.
- Everyone will have access via FTP to the ftp_server. Other rules (Rule 4 and Rule 7) could match this rule as well, but Rule 3 matches first because it is listed first and does not involve User Authentication. This is not a major problem, but worth noting.
- Users in the DMZAdmins group who Telnet or FTP from internal-networks to DMZ_net will not have authenticated access to all servers in DMZ_net for two reasons: Rule 3 and Rule 7. Rule 3 matches FTP connections to the FTP server before Rule 4. When Rule 4 is matched, because it is a User Authentication rule, the least restrictive rule applies and thus Rule 7 permits access.

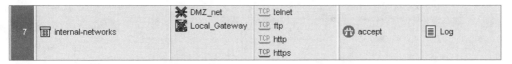

Figure 8.33   A more restrictive Rule 7

- When people Telnet to the firewall, Rule 5 matches initially, but again because of the least restrictive rule for User Authentication, Rule 7 actually permits the communication without authentication.
- Rule 7 also permits these services to the firewall as well, which may not be desirable.

The major problem in this rulebase is that Rules 4 and 5 do not provide authentication in cases where you would expect them to because Rule 7 is too permissive. You can fix this by making Rule 7 a bit less permissive by excluding DMZ_net and Local_Gateway from the allowed destinations, as shown in Figure 8.33.

Setting Up Session Authentication

The basic steps for setting up Session Authentication are similar to the steps described in the previous section for setting up User Authentication.

1. Create the necessary users and groups required for authentication, then install the user database.
2. Create the appropriate rule(s) in the rulebase.
3. Configure the Session Authentication action properties.
4. Configure the Rulebase Properties Authentication frame.
5. Verify and install the policy.

The source and destination for the rule are defined in the same way as shown in the preceding section. A Session Authentication rule might look like the one shown in Figure 8.34.

You then configure the Session Authentication action properties by right-clicking Session Auth and selecting Edit Properties. A screen similar to the one shown in Figure 8.35 appears.

Figure 8.34   Sample Session Authentication rule

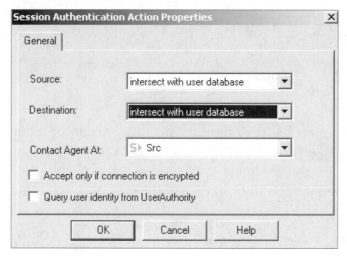

Figure 8.35 Session Authentication Action Properties, General tab

The Source and Destination fields are defined as they were for User Authentication. The Contact Agent At field tells FireWall-1 on which host to attempt to contact a Session Authentication agent. The possibilities are as follows.

Src: The IP address that is originating the connection will be contacted. This is the default value and the most common.

Dst: The IP address that the connection is destined for will be contacted. Use this option for protocols where the client/server model is reversed, such as X Windows.

Other Host: You can select which workstation will receive the authentication request.

Two other options are also available on the General tab.

Accept only if connection is encrypted: If this is checked, Session Authentication will take place only if it is able to establish an SSL connection to the agent.

Query user identity from UserAuthority: If this is selected, the user identity will be checked with a UserAuthority server when authenticating the user.

Once the rules are set up to your liking, verify that the Authentication Failure Track is set appropriately in the Policy Properties Authentication tab, and install the security policy.

NOTE!   Because the firewall will be originating a connection to port 261 on a remote host, make sure that your outbound security policy does not prohibit this.

Setting Up Client Authentication

The basic steps for setting up Client Authentication are similar to the steps used to set up User and Session Authentication.

1. Create the necessary users and groups required for authentication, then install the user database.
2. Create the appropriate rule(s) in the rulebase.
3. Configure the Client Authentication action properties.
4. Configure the Rulebase Properties Authentication frame.
5. Verify and install the policy.

The source and destination for the rule are defined in the same way as those for User Authentication. A Client Authentication rule might look similar to the screen shown in Figure 8.36.

You then configure the Client Authentication action properties by right-clicking Client Auth and selecting Edit Properties. A screen similar to the one shown in Figure 8.37 appears.

The Source and Destination fields are defined as they were for User Authentication. Due to the nature of Client Authentication, it is not possible for the Client Authentication process to know where the client may be connecting to when the Required Sign On is set to Standard (see below), so the user's allowed destinations cannot be checked.

Apply Rule Only if Desktop Configuration Options are Verified relates to SecureClient and will be discussed in Chapter 12.

Required Sign On can be set to Standard or Specific. Standard allows the user to log in and be automatically authorized for all services allowed by the rule(s). The Specific selection means that the user must manually request each service and each host he or she will be trying to contact. Examples of each of these methods were provided earlier in the Explaining Client Authentication subsection.

🖧 mice@magrathea	🖥 earth	🎛 pcANYWHERE	🔘 Client Auth	📋 Log

Figure 8.36   Sample Client Authentication rule

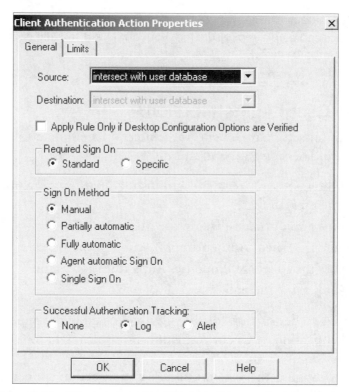

Figure 8.37 Client Authentication Action Properties, General tab

You can set the Sign On Method to one of the following options.

Manual: With this option, authentication can occur only via a Telnet to the firewall on port 259 or via HTTP to the firewall on port 900. Note that the other methods in this list also allow for manual authentication.

Partially automatic: FireWall-1 allows you to use User Authentication to perform a Standard Sign-On. This means you can Telnet, FTP, rlogin, or HTTP to a destination permitted by the rule, and FireWall-1 will use User Authentication to authenticate you when necessary.

Fully automatic: This option is the same as partially automatic, but if a non–User Authentication service is used (i.e., not Telnet, FTP, rlogin, or HTTP), FireWall-1 will use Session Authentication to authenticate the user. If the user successfully authenticates, FireWall-1 performs a Standard Sign-On.

Agent automatic Sign On: FireWall-1 attempts to use Session Authentication when the rule is matched and the user has not previously been authenticated. If the user successfully authenticates, FireWall-1 performs a Standard Sign-On.

Single Sign On: When used with Meta IP, this option allows users to sign on as a result of authenticating with Windows NT. Otherwise, this option has no effect.

You can set Successful Authentication Tracking to one of the following options.

None: Nothing is logged when a user authenticates successfully against this rule.

Log: A long log entry is generated when a user successfully authenticates against this rule.

Alert: A long log entry is generated plus an alert is sent as defined in Global Properties.

You also need to set the timeout period for the authentication in the Limits tab (see Figure 8.38).

You can set the Authorization Timeout value to a specific period of time or Indefinite. If you choose Indefinite, either the user must explicitly sign off and reload the security policy or you must stop and start FireWall-1 in order for the user to no longer be permitted. If you select Refreshable timeout, the timeout resets every time the user makes a successful connection against this rule, which means that the user has to reauthenticate only if the user has not made any new connections for a period of time.

The Number of Sessions Allowed setting refers to the number of individual connections the user is allowed to make through the firewall before the authentication expires. With HTTP (or any other service that makes lots of individual connections), the default of five connections will be used very quickly. With Telnet, the user is allowed to make five Telnet connections before the authentication expires.

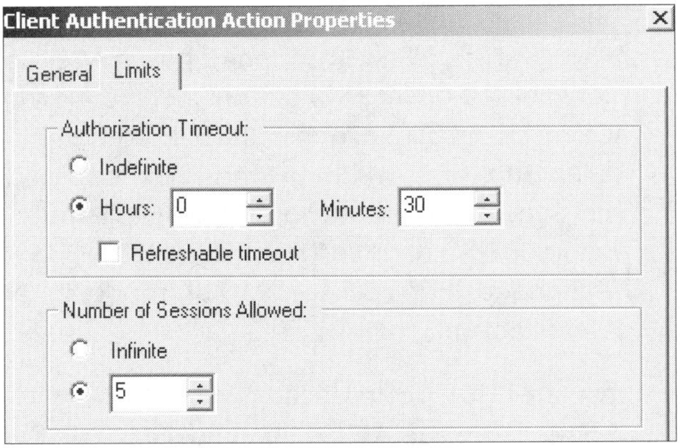

Figure 8.38 Client Authentication Action Properties, Limits tab

NOTE! If partially automatic authentication is enabled and a user uses HTTP to authenticate, there must not be a rule (such as a Stealth rule) listed before the Client Authentication rule that prohibits HTTP to access the firewall.

Once the rules are set up to your liking, verify that the gateway properties for authentication (see Figure 8.28) and the global properties for authentication (see Figure 8.29) are defined as you wish.

As promised earlier in the chapter, it's time to talk about the Enable wait mode option that appears in the Authentication frame of the Gateway Properties section. This option changes the behavior of Client Authentication via Telnet. Normally, once authentication is successful, the Telnet connection to the firewall closes. When wait mode is enabled, the connection stays open. The authentication is active as long as this connection is open. Once this connection is closed, the authentication is no longer valid. This particular option does not scale well because the firewall has to keep a connection open to each client that authenticates. At least in my experience, FireWall-1 is unable to handle more than about 20 to 30 users authenticated with this option enabled.

Once the gateway and global properties are set as desired, install the security policy.

Integrating External Authentication Servers

The following subsections describe how to integrate the various supported authentication servers with FireWall-1.

Integrating SecurID

SecurID supports native ACE mode (a proprietary mechanism) and authentication via the RADIUS protocol. The following instructions apply to setting up native ACE mode.

 WARNING! Although FireWall-1 4.1 supported native ACE mode, versions of FireWall-1 NG prior to FP3 did not include full support for native ACE mode on all platforms. Check Point came out with a hotfix to FP2 on Solaris, Windows, and Linux that fixed several issues with SecurID authentication. Native ACE mode was not supported on IPSO at all until FP3. If using NG FP0, FP1, or FP2, it is recommended that you use RADIUS mode to provide SecurID authentication.

To configure FireWall-1 for SecurID authentication, you simply need to copy the sdconf.rec file from the ACE/Server to /var/ace/sdconf.rec on UNIX or IPSO or to %SystemRoot%\System32\sdconf.rec on Windows

NT. Generating a proper `sdconf.rec` file on the ACE/Server is the tricky part of this process.

Your firewall will be defined as an ACE/Client within the ACE/Server. Be sure that the client hostname and IP address of the firewall defined in the ACE/Server agree with the firewall's own definitions. This means that the client hostname specified should be the same as the UNIX, Windows NT, or IPSO command **hostname** and that the IP address that this name resolves to is the same on both systems. The other IP addresses associated with the firewall should be listed as Secondary Nodes, which must be listed in order for the ACE/Server to accept authentication requests from the firewall. For IPSO systems, do not include the VRRP IP addresses. In addition, if using version 5.0 or later of the ACE/Server, you will need to define legacy-mode authentication that supports a defined primary server and a backup server.

SecurID is a predefined group of services. SecurID uses UDP port 5500 and TCP port 5510.

Integrating RADIUS

FireWall-1 works with RADIUS version 1 and version 2 servers. The following subsections provide an example of how to configure a UNIX-based RADIUS server to support FireWall-1.

Adding a Firewall to RADIUS Server's Clients File

The clients file (in `/etc/raddb` on UNIX stations) contains entries of the following format:

```
radius-client    shared-secret
```

The `radius-client` in this case is your firewall. Note that this name should reflect the hostname your firewall resolves as on your RADIUS server. You may need to do some debugging to determine the correct hostname.

The `shared-secret` is a password that both the RADIUS client (your firewall) and the RADIUS server will use for encryption when communicating with each other. In FireWall-1 3.x, shared secrets beginning with a number or the letter `f` have problems.

Adding Users in RADIUS Server's Users File

You may not need to add users in the users file if you already have existing RADIUS users in your database file (typically in `/etc/raddb` on UNIX). If you are setting up new users, your user entries should look something like this:

```
phoneboy    Password = "abc123", Expiration = "Dec 31 2005"
            User-Service-Type = Login-User
```

Note that you can put other entries in the users file that are not used by FireWall-1. The only entries that FireWall-1 cares about are the entries listed above. Note that if you install a RADIUS server on a UNIX or Windows machine and you want to use the existing users configured in the operating system for authentication, make sure you have an entry in the users file that looks similar to this:

```
DEFAULT   Auth-Type = System, User-Service-Type = Login-User
```

Creating a RADIUS Service (Optional)

You can use RADIUS on a nonstandard port. You will need to create a new RADIUS service as appropriate. The default port for RADIUS is UDP 1645.

Creating a RADIUS Server Object

You need to create a workstation object for your RADIUS server in your Security Policy Editor. You then need to create a new server object of type RADIUS. The dialog in Figure 8.39 shows the General tab for RADIUS Server Properties. The fields on this screen are described as follows.

Name: Enter the name you want to give the object. It should be unique.

Comment: Enter any information you would like in this field.

Color: Select whichever color is appropriate.

Host: Indicate the workstation object on which the RADIUS server runs.

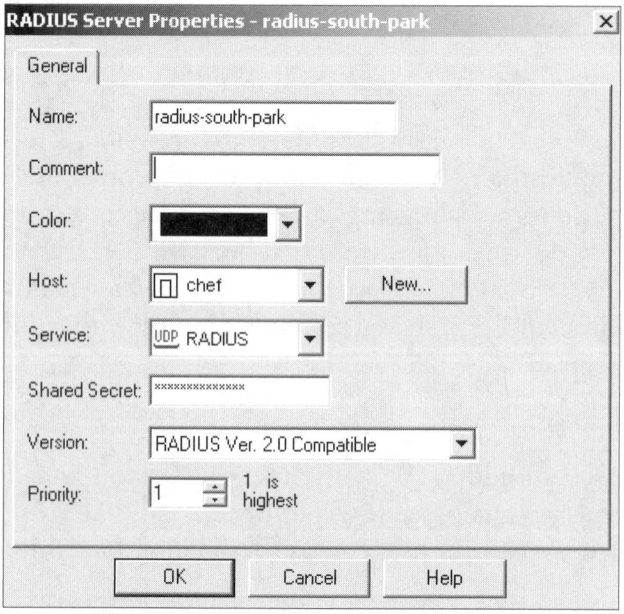

Figure 8.39   RADIUS Server Properties, General tab

Service: Indicate the port on which RADIUS runs. By default, this is port 1645 (i.e., the default RADIUS port).

Shared Secret: Indicate the shared secret. This should match the shared secret configured on the RADIUS server.

Version: Choose the appropriate version of the RADIUS server.

Priority: If you have multiple RADIUS servers, you can prioritize the order in which they are queried. The default is 1, which is the highest priority, meaning it will be queried first. Check Point recommends having only one server defined with each priority.

Once you have completed these fields, you should be able to create users of type RADIUS.

Integrating TACACS/TACACS+

The TACACS configuration is very similar to RADIUS, although it is much simpler. You must configure a server object of type TACACS after defining the workstation object on which your TACACS server runs (see Figure 8.40). The fields on this screen are described as follows.

Name: Enter the name you want to give the object. It should be unique.

Comment: Enter any information you would like in this field.

Color: Select whichever color is appropriate.

Host: Indicate the workstation object on which the TACACS server runs.

Type: Choose TACACS or TACACS+ as necessary.

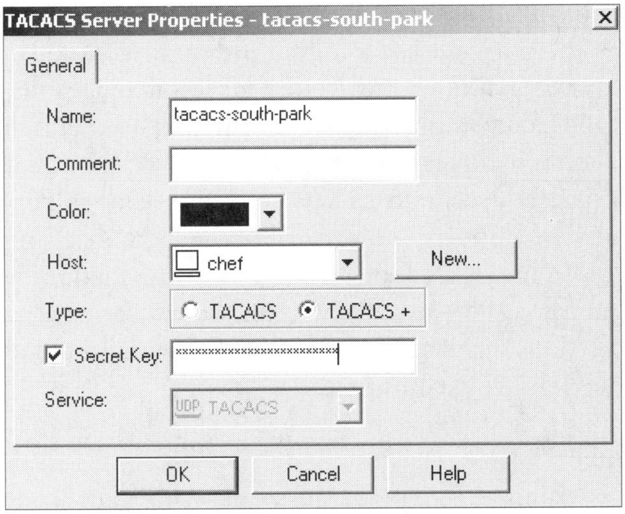

Figure 8.40 TACACS Server Properties, General tab

Secret Key: If the checkbox is activated and TACACS+ is being used, enter the secret key. This should be the same as the NAS Key defined on your TACACS+ server.

Service: Indicate the port on which TACACS is used. (This option is active only when TACACS is being used.)

Once you have completed these fields, you should be able to create users of type TACACS.

 NOTE! TACACS uses UDP port 49, and TACACS+ uses TCP port 49.

Integrating LDAP

In order to integrate FireWall-1 into an LDAP server, you need to have certain items.

- The suffix of the directory. Your LDAP administrator should be able to tell you the suffix of the directory. For the following examples, I will use "o=acmelabs, c=us".
- An account on the LDAP server that has at least read access to the parts of the directory FireWall-1 will use.
- If you want to use SmartDashboard/Policy Editor to edit users on the LDAP server, you need an account with read-write access on the LDAP server.

Once you have this information, you will want to configure the LDAP server with the schema for FireWall-1. Note that although you could simply disable schema checking, this makes your directory far less manageable. Schema checking ensures that the data you import into the directory server follows a particular format. Check Point includes a schema file in $FWDIR/lib/ldap/schema. ldif. However, it is coded in an LDAP Data Interchange Format (LDIF) file and thus can only be imported into directory servers that support modifying schemas via an LDIF file. A separate schema file is provided for Microsoft Active Directory in Windows 2000 at $FWDIR/lib/ldap/schema_microsoft_ad. ldif. Current versions of Netscape Directory Server (and possibly others) support this using the following command:

```
$ ldapmodify -D "cn=root" -w password -f schema.ldif
```

When using this command, replace **cn=root** with your rootdn name, and replace **password** with your actual password. The output of this command should continually print `"modifying entry cn=schema"` over and over without any errors.

Other LDAP servers, such as OpenLDAP versions 1 and 2, do not support schema modifications in this manner. As a result, you have to modify your schema so that it includes the FireWall-1 schema. Instructions on how to do this are provided in Appendix C for OpenLDAP version 1 and Appendix D for OpenLDAP version 2.[3]

> WARNING!   OpenLDAP is not considered an OPSEC-compliant LDAP server. This means if you call Check Point with a problem regarding communication with an OpenLDAP server, Check Point will likely refuse to support you. This being said, OpenLDAP appears to work well for many users, and Check Point even includes instructions for integrating OpenLDAP with FireWall-1 on the support site.

Once all of the previous requirements are met, you can begin to configure FireWall-1 to use LDAP. The first change you need to make is in the LDAP

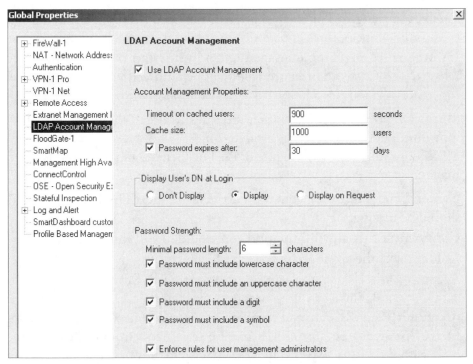

Figure 8.41   Global Properties, LDAP Account Management tab

---

3. All of the LDAP examples in this book were done against an OpenLDAP server.

Account Management frame of the Global Properties section (see Figure 8.41). In this frame you can set the following options.

Use LDAP Account Management: Select this checkbox if you want to allow FireWall-1 to use LDAP. All other options on this screen will be dimmed if this is unchecked.

Timeout on cached users: This value indicates the amount of time FireWall-1 will cache an entry it has read from the LDAP server before it attempts to reread the entry from the LDAP server.

Cache size: This value indicates the number of users FireWall-1 will attempt to keep cached in memory.

Password expires after: If this option is checked, LDAP users will be forced to change their passwords after the specified number of days.

Display User's DN at Login: If you choose Display in this section, you will be able to see your full Distinguished Name as defined in the LDAP server (e.g., `"cn=pinky, o=acmelabs, c=us"`). This allows you to verify that you are authenticating against the correct record in the LDAP database; thus it's a useful diagnostics tool.

Password Strength: This section presents various options for enforcing strong passwords. These options apply only when a user *changes* his or her password.

Enforce rules for user management administrators: If this property is selected, the Password Strength rules will be enforced when the administrator creates or modifies a VPN-1 & FireWall-1 Password.

Once you have configured these properties, you can then define an LDAP account unit, which is created as a server object. The screens used to create an LDAP account unit start with Figure 8.42. The General tab includes the following items.

Name: Enter the name you want to give to the LDAP account unit. It should be unique.

Comment: Enter any information you would like in this field.

Color: Select the appropriate color.

Account Unit Usage: You can use the Certificate Revocation Lists (CRLs are used in a Public Key Infrastructure) stored in the LDAP server. If you are using only the CRL retrieval function, you do not need to fill in the login DN or password because CRLs can be obtained through an anonymous bind with the LDAP server. The User management option allows you to use accounts stored in the LDAP server for authentication.

Profile: This field specifies the kind of LDAP server you are authenticating against. The options are Microsoft_AD (Microsoft Active Directory),

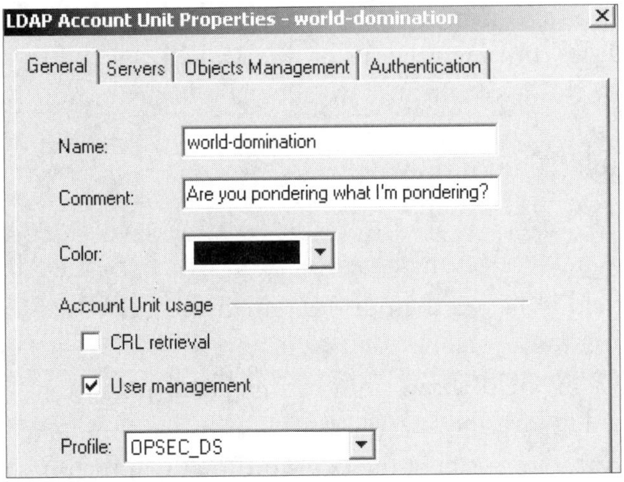

Figure 8.42   LDAP Account Unit Properties, General tab

Netscape_DS (Netscape/iPlanet Directory Server), Novell_DS (Novell Directory Server), and OPSEC_DS (all other directory servers). For OpenLDAP, use OPSEC_DS.

The Servers tab (see Figure 8.43) allows you to define the LDAP servers that make up this account unit. You may include any number of LDAP servers you have defined by clicking on the Add button. The assumption is that all LDAP

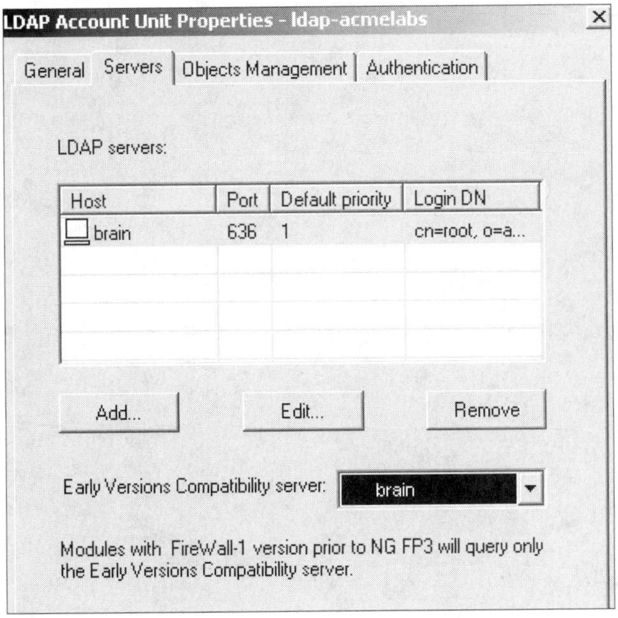

Figure 8.43   LDAP Account Unit Properties, Servers tab

servers in this account unit will have the same data (i.e., they are replicas of each other). For modules running versions of FireWall-1 prior to FP3, only one of the LDAP servers in this account unit will actually be used. You can select which one in this screen.

If you add an account unit, you will see a screen similar to Figure 8.44. You can select the following options on this tab.

Host: In this field, select the host object on which the LDAP server runs.

Port: This field indicates the port on which the LDAP server expects unencrypted communication. The default is port 389.

Login DN: This field shows the distinguished name that will be used by FireWall-1 to log into the LDAP server.

Password: Enter in this field the password that will be used by FireWall-1 to log into the LDAP server. A second password field is presented so you can validate the password you typed.

Default priority: This value reflects the priority relative to all other LDAP servers that serve this account unit. The highest priority value is 1.

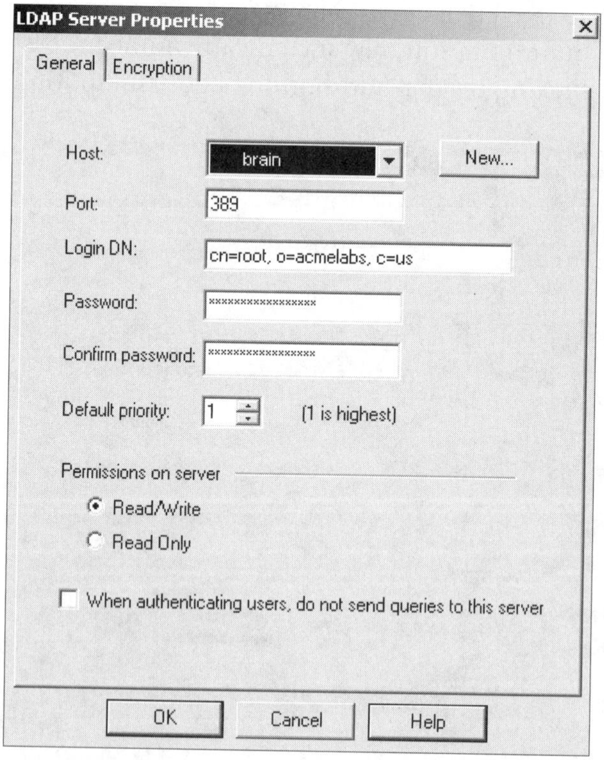

Figure 8.44   LDAP Server Properties, General tab

Permissions on server: These options indicate the permissions that the DN used by FireWall-1 to log into the LDAP server will have. The DN need not have read/write permission unless you wish to use SmartDashboard/Policy Editor to manage users on the LDAP server.

When authenticating users, do not send queries to this server: This options tells FireWall-1 not to use this particular LDAP server to authenticate users. This is useful when an LDAP server goes temporarily offline.

If you wish to communicate with the LDAP server using SSL, go to the Encryption tab (see Figure 8.45). Here you can set the following properties.

Use Encryption (SSL): If you need to use SSL to access your LDAP server, select this checkbox.

Encryption port: Indicate the port used to make the encrypted connection to the LDAP server. The default is port 636.

Verify that server has the following Fingerprints: Because FireWall-1 does not use a certificate authority to verify keys, you should obtain the server key fingerprints via some non-network method and enter them in this box. If you do not, FireWall-1 will fill in this information the first time an SSL connection is made to the LDAP server. On subsequent attempts to connect, FireWall-1 compares what it receives with what is in this box and displays an error message if there is a discrepancy.

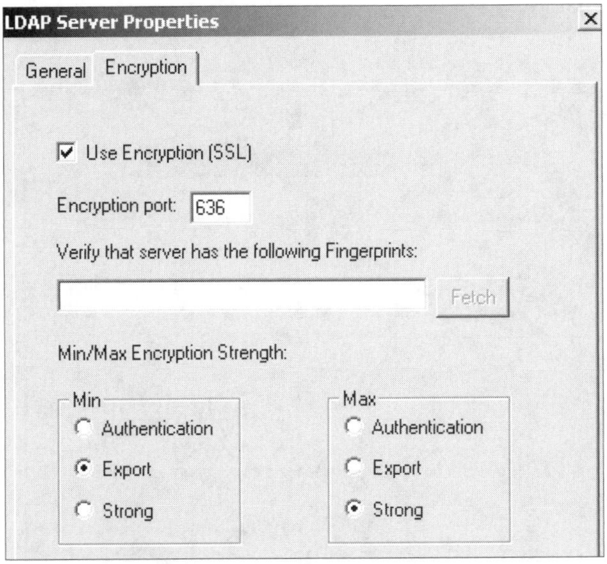

Figure 8.45   LDAP Server Properties, Encryption tab

Min/Max Encryption Strength: Set the minimum and maximum levels of encryption you want to allow for the SSL connection to the LDAP server. Export refers to 40-bit encryption. Strong refers to 128-bit encryption. Authentication means effectively no encryption.

After adding all the LDAP servers that support the account unit, you need to tell FireWall-1 what branches in the LDAP database to use. This is done via the Objects Management tab in the LDAP Account Unit Properties frame, shown in Figure 8.46. You can set the following options in this tab.

Manage objects on: If you are using multiple LDAP servers for this account unit and will be managing users via SmartDashboard/Policy Editor, this field should point to the LDAP server that is the master, that is, not the replica servers.

Branches in use: Specify in which branches of the LDAP server to look for users.

Prompt for password when opening this Account Unit: If you do not feel comfortable storing the password for your administrative login to the LDAP server, check this box. This means a password will be required anytime you want to use SmartDashboard/Policy Editor to edit objects on the LDAP server.

Return X entries: If an LDAP query could potentially return lots of entries, this option will limit how many entries will be returned.

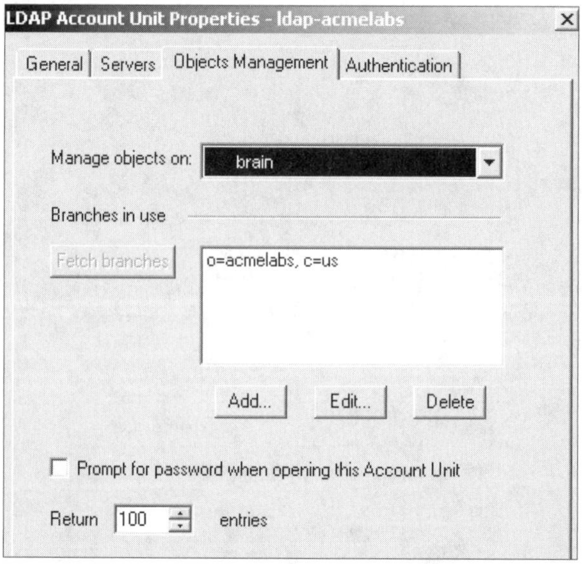

Figure 8.46 LDAP Account Unit Properties, Objects Management tab

The Authentication tab is shown in Figure 8.47. This tab contains several properties.

Use common group path for queries: If an account unit is made up of several branches, selecting this option optimizes the query to the LDAP server so that only the common elements of those branches are queried.

Allowed authentication schemes: This section defines the authentication schemes this account unit will allow. It is very similar to the specifications listed in the Gateway Properties screen for your firewall object(s).

Use user template: If an LDAP server being used does not contain information specific to FireWall-1, the missing information is filled in from the specified user template when this option is checked. Be careful to ensure that the template does not contain user-specific information (e.g., IKE with pre-shared secrets should be different for each user). If your template contains VPN-1 & FireWall-1 Password as an authentication scheme, this will be mapped to the normal LDAP password for that user.

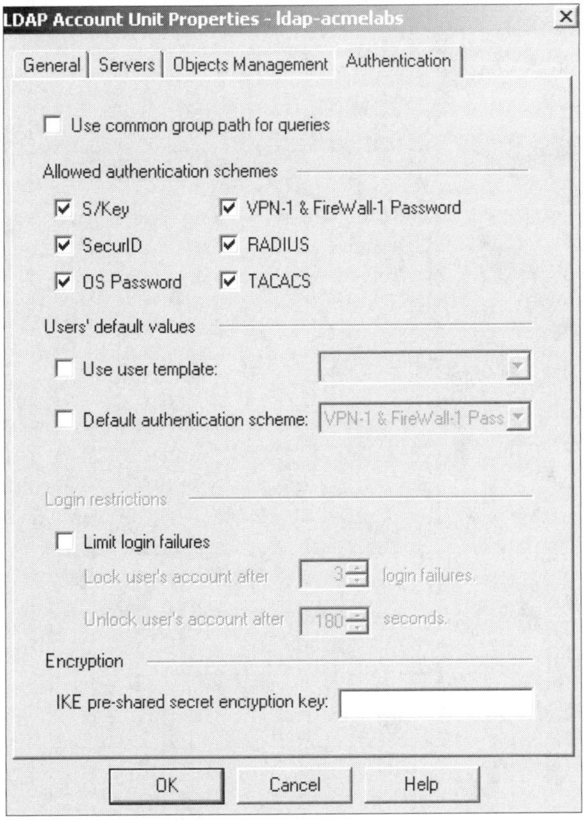

Figure 8.47   LDAP Account Unit Properties, Authentication tab

Default authentication scheme: This is similar to the previous option except that only authentication-specific information is defined. If you select RADIUS or TACACS, you will be prompted for the RADIUS or TACACS server to use. As with the previous option, VPN-1 & FireWall-1 Password maps to the normal LDAP password. S/Key is not allowed as an option because more information is needed to establish an S/Key chain.

Limit login failures: If this box is checked, a user who fails to authenticate properly the specified number of times will have his or her account temporarily locked for the specified amount of time.

IKE pre-shared secret encryption key: When IKE pre-shared secrets are defined in the LDAP server, they are stored encrypted. The value in this field is the encryption key used to store those secrets in the LDAP server.

Once you have defined the LDAP account unit, you then need to create an LDAP group via the Manage Users interface (from the Manage menu, select Users) or from the objects tree view. Figure 8.48 shows the General tab for the Group Properties screen, which includes the following properties.

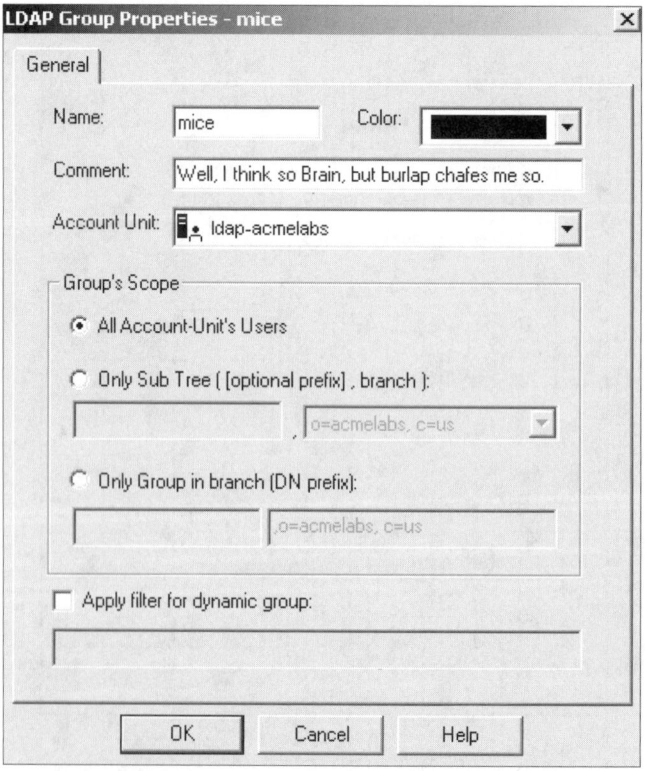

Figure 8.48 LDAP Group Properties, General tab

| mice@acmelabs | acmelabs | * Any | Client Auth | ! Alert |

Figure 8.49   Sample authentication rule with LDAP group

Name: Enter the name you want to give this external group.

Color: Choose the appropriate color for this group.

Comment: Enter any information you would like in this field.

Account Unit: Choose the LDAP account unit you defined earlier.

Group's Scope: You can further narrow the account unit specified by designating either a certain subtree or an existing LDAP group using a DN prefix.

Apply filter for dynamic group: You may specify additional LDAP criteria to filter against in this box. For example, you can check to see if certain fields contain certain values (e.g., `"objectClass=myObject or mail=*.us.acmelabs.com"`).

Once you have completed these fields, you can create a rule in terms of this new external group (see Figure 8.49).

Clientless VPN

Clientless VPN is becoming increasingly popular. The idea is to use a Web browser to provide access to an intranet, which many people already have installed on their computers for surfing the Internet. Unfortunately, this means you can access only Web-enabled applications. For some organizations, this is enough.

FireWall-1 has actually had the basic functionality for Clientless VPN since FireWall-1 4.1, though the feature was never called that and it was never enabled via the GUI. In NG FP3, Check Point added a GUI option for Clientless VPN under the VPN Advanced frame of the gateway object. In NG FP2 and before, you can enable the functionality as follows.

1. Add the following entry to `$FWDIR/conf/fwauthd.conf` on your firewall module:

```
443     fwssd     in.ahttpsd     wait     443     ec
```

2. Stop the firewall with the command **cpstop**.
3. Modify the `prompt_for_destination` property to be `true` instead of `false`. You can do this by using **dbedit** or the GUIdbedit tool, or by

manually editing `objects_5_0.C`. (See FAQ 4.2 for details.) The **dbedit** commands for this are:

```
dbedit> modify properties firewall_properties
               prompt_for_destination true
dbedit> update properties firewall_properties
```

4. Restart the firewall with the command **cpstart**.
5. Reinstall the security policy.

There are two ways to access Clientless VPN:

1. Access sites directly via HTTPS as if they were available on the Internet (e.g., https://wacko.animaniacs.com).
2. Access sites via the firewall using HTTPS (e.g., https://firewall.animaniacs.com/wacko). This is best described as the *reverse proxy method*.

In either case, you need to create a rule similar to the one shown in Figure 8.50. You must also open up the service definition for HTTPS, go to the Advanced section, and change the protocol type to HTTP.

If you decide to go the reverse proxy route, which you would want to do if not all the Web servers you want to access have a public IP associated with them, you will need to go to the Security Server frame under Global Properties. Figure 8.51 shows this screen, which includes a section called HTTP Server. Each server needs to be added to this screen.

Let's assume the firewall has the FQDN hellonurse.animaniacs.com and that three servers need to made accessible: yakko, dot, and wacko. Each one is defined as an HTTP server. The properties for each of these HTTP servers are similar to what is shown in Figure 8.52. The fields on the HTTP Server Definition screen are described below.

Logical Name: Enter the name you want to give the logical server. The server will be accessible as http://firewall-name/logical-name. In the case of Clientless VPN, it's actually https://firewall-name/logical-name.

Host: Indicate the hostname or IP address of the host that FireWall-1 will connect to when this logical server is accessed.

Port: Indicate the port of the host to access using the host in the previous field.

Figure 8.50   Sample rule for Clientless VPN

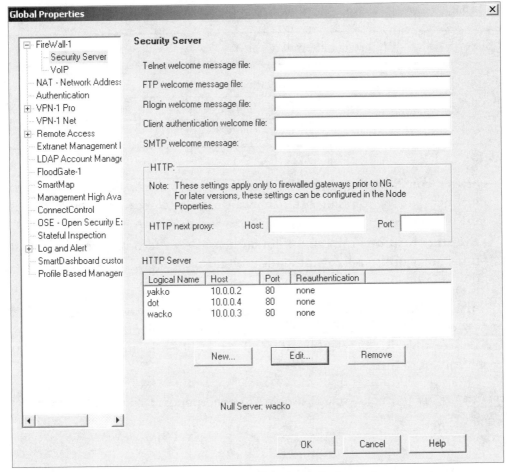

Figure 8.51   Global Properties, Security Server frame

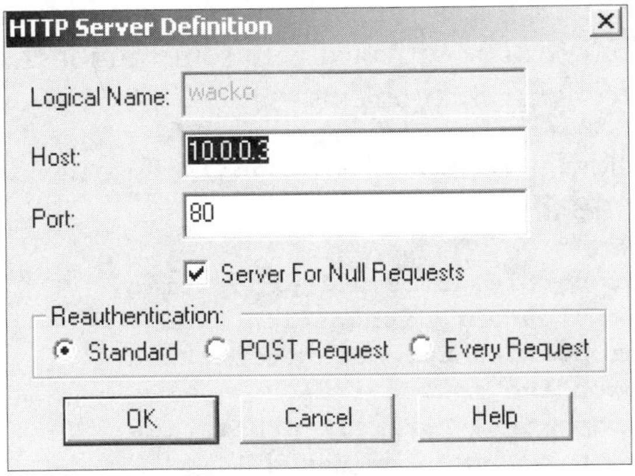

Figure 8.52   HTTP Server Definition

Table 8.2 URLs for accessing Web servers through the firewall

Site	URL through Firewall
yakko	https://hellonurse.animaniacs.com/yakko
wacko	https://hellonurse.animaniacs.com/wacko
dot	https://hellonurse.animaniacs.com/dot

Server For Null Requests: You can define only one logical server in this manner. Simply accessing http://firewall-name can access the server that is the null server.

Reauthentication: You can ask for authentication according to the normal rules. You can also ask for authentication on every request or ask for authentication only on a POST command.

After all three servers are defined, this information appears in the HTTP Server section of the Security Server frame as shown in Figure 8.51. The servers will be accessible via the URLs listed in Table 8.2. The rule shown in Figure 8.50 enables access to these servers.

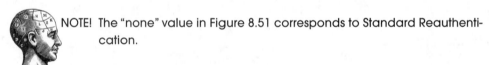 **NOTE!** The "none" value in Figure 8.51 corresponds to Standard Reauthentication.

Known Issues with Clientless VPN

Two issues that come up with Clientless VPNs—issues related to the use of Outlook Web Access and the use of the Netscape/Mozilla browser with certificate-based authentication—can be corrected with some minor changes. Perform the following steps to resolve these problems.

1. Enter the following commands in **dbedit** or use the GUIdbedit tool. See FAQ 4.2 for details.

```
dbedit> modify properties firewall_properties
        http_allow_content_disposition true
dbedit> modify properties firewall_properties
        enable_propfind_method true
dbedit> modify properties firewall_properties
              cert_req_ext_key_usage 1
dbedit> update properties firewall_properties
```

`http_allow_content_disposition` enables the use of the Content-Disposition header in FireWall-1, which is usually dropped by default. `enable_propfind_method` enables extended methods (i.e., other than GET, HEAD, and so on) used by Outlook Web Access, which are not accepted by default. `cert_req_ext_key_usage` allows FireWall-1 to accept the kinds of certificate requests used by the Netscape/Mozilla browser.

2. Modify `$FWDIR/conf/InternalCA.C` on the management station. Add the following property:

   `:ike_cert_extended_key_usage (1)`

3. Perform a **cprestart** on the management and firewall modules.
4. Generate a new VPN certificate for the gateway.
5. Edit the gateway object in the VPN Advanced frame and specify the newly generated certificate as the certificate to use.
6. Reinstall the security policy on your modules.

Frequently Asked Questions

Now that you have learned the basics of setting up authentication, take a look at the following FAQs for more information. As in previous chapters, the FAQs are numbered for easy reference.

8.1: How Do I Use Users in an Authentication Server without Entering Them into FireWall-1?

Because of the way you configure LDAP into FireWall-1, all LDAP users in the appropriate branch will appear in SmartDashboard automatically. However, if you are using RADIUS, SecurID, Defender, TACACS, or even a Windows NT domain, you need to create an external user profile in NG FP3 or later or a user with the username generic* in NG FP2 and earlier (only one such user can be defined). FireWall-1 queries the external authentication mechanism defined in the external user profile or in generic* user for users who are not defined in FireWall-1. You configure this user as you would any other user, keeping in mind that the parameters you set apply to all users not otherwise defined in FireWall-1. For users who require different parameters (for example, those who need to be in different groups), you still need to define these users individually in FireWall-1.

8.2: How Do I Integrate FireWall-1 into a Windows NT Domain?

If you have FireWall-1 on Windows NT, you can simply make the firewall system part of your Windows NT domain and set up an external user profile or generic* user to use OS Authentication. However, it is generally not recommended that you run any of the Microsoft Networking services on your firewall.

If your FireWall-1 does not run on Windows NT or you decide not to run the Microsoft Networking services on your Windows NT firewall, you can set up a RADIUS server that pulls its authentication information from Windows NT, which requires running a RADIUS server on a Windows NT server. You can easily set up FireWall-1 to authenticate against the RADIUS server. This configuration is far more secure than running Microsoft Networking services on your Windows NT firewall.

8.3: How Do I Allow People Access Based on Their Windows Usernames?

This involves using a product by Check Point called Meta IP, which is not covered in this book. For more details on this product, visit Check Point's Web site at http://www.checkpoint.com.

8.4: How Do I Import or Export Users from a FireWall-1 User Database?

The commands in question are **fw dbimport** and **fw dbexport**, respectively. The options for **fw dbimport** are described in Table 8.3. The usage is as follows:

```
fw dbimport [-m] [-s] [-v] [-r] [-k errors] [-f file] [-d delim]
```

Table 8.3 fw dbimport Options

Parameter	Description
-m	Applies if an existing user is encountered in the import file. If this option is specified, the user's default values will be replaced by the values in the template (the default value or the value given in the attribute list for that user in the import file), and the original values will be ignored. If this option is not specified, an existing user's original values will not be modified.
-s	Suppresses the warning messages issued when an existing user's values are changed by values in the import file.
-v	Enables verbose mode.
-r	Deletes all existing users (but not groups or templates) in the database.
-k nerrors	Continues processing until nerrors errors are encountered. The line count in the error messages starts from 1 including the attributes line and counts empty or commented-out lines.
-f file	Specifies the name of the import file. The default import file is $FWDIR/conf/user_def_file.
-d delim	Specifies a delimiter different than the default value (;).

Table 8.4   fw dbexport Options

Parameter	Description
-g usergroup	Specifies a group of users to be exported (others are not exported).
-u username	Specifies that only the indicated user should be exported.
-d delimiter	Specifies a delimiter different than the default value (;).
-a attributes	Specifies the attributes to export in the form of a comma-separated list between { } characters, e.g., -a {name,days}. If there is only one attribute, the { } may be omitted.
-f filename	Specifies the name of the output file. The default output file is $FWDIR/conf/user_def_file.

The **fw dbexport** options are documented in Table 8.4. The usage is as follows:

```
fw dbexport [ [-g <group> | -u <user>] [-d <delim>]
            [-a {attrib1, attrib2, ...}  ] [-f <file>] ]
```

 NOTE! FireWall-1 Passwords are stored in the output encrypted with the UNIX crypt() function using the first two characters of the actual password as the "salt" argument.

 NOTE! The fw dbimport function will not import users who are assigned to groups that do not exist in the user database. You need to create these groups manually before importing the users.

8.5: How Do I Add My Own Custom Message for Authentication?

Go to the Security Servers frame of the Global Properties screen, which is shown in Figure 8.51. You can specify welcome files for Telnet, FTP, rlogin, and Client Authentication. Specify the full path to the file, which must exist on the firewall module.

8.6: How Do I Forward Authenticated HTTP Requests to an HTTP Proxy?

In the Authentication frame of the Gateway Properties screen (see Figure 8.28 earlier in the chapter), there is a checkbox labeled Use Next Proxy. If you want FireWall-1 to send requests to a proxy server, fill in the host and the port number of the proxy server. Note that this works only when FireWall-1 is configured as the proxy server for your Web-browsing clients.

8.7: Can I Use FireWall-1 as a Reverse HTTP Proxy?

Yes, you can. The instructions for enabling this are almost exactly the same as the instructions for setting up Clientless VPN except that you can use the HTTP service instead of HTTPS. Authentication is still required.

8.8: How Do I Remove the Check Point Banner from Authentication?

The authentication daemons all show a banner identifying them as Check Point firewalls. Some people, at least those who believe in the concept of "security through obscurity," think that it is not a good idea to reveal the kind of firewall you are running. You can remove these banners by changing a parameter in objects_5.0.C (see FAQ 4.2 for details). The following commands would be entered into **dbedit:**

```
dbedit> modify properties firewall_properties undo_msg true
dbedit> update properties firewall_properties
```

 WARNING! If you use the FTP or SMTP Security Server, connections may fail after you disable the banner messages if you don't define a custom message for these servers as described in FAQ 8.5.

8.9: Can I Use FireWall-1 as a Proxy?

FireWall-1 can authenticate these connections without having to proxy. There may be environments where using FireWall-1 in a proxy capacity is necessary. FireWall-1 requires authentication for Telnet, FTP, and rlogin. HTTP can be used as a proxy without authentication using a resource.

For proxy mode to work correctly, you must enable the Prompt for Destination mode in objects_5_0.C. This is described earlier in the Clientless VPN section.

For HTTP, if you do not want to perform authentication but want to use HTTP in proxy mode, you need to create a matchall resource, as discussed in Chapter 9, and use HTTP with this resource instead of just HTTP.

8.10: Can I Use FireWall-1 as an FTP Proxy for My Web Browser?

FireWall-1 supports proxying FTP using an FTP interface. However, Web browsers expect the FTP proxy to act like an HTTP proxy. Make sure you set your browser's FTP proxy to the firewall on port 80 instead of port 21.

Note that because FireWall-1 can be used as an FTP proxy with User Authentication, FTP or HTTP cannot be denied from the firewall because the firewall has to originate these connections.

8.11: How Do I Authenticate HTTP over Different Ports?

You need to follow these five steps to enable filtering on other ports.

1. Create a service for the ports in question (e.g., http8000).
2. Add a rule with the new service.
3. Reconfigure $FWDIR/conf/fwauthd.conf.
4. Install the security policy.
5. Bounce the firewall (**cprestart**)

The following paragraphs describe the steps in more detail.

Creating the service is straightforward. Create a new service of type TCP. Set the port accordingly (e.g., 8000). Go to the Advanced settings frame, and set the protocol type to HTTP.

To reconfigure $FWDIR/conf/fwauthd.conf, you need to add a line to this file for each port on which you want to filter. For port 8000, for instance, the line would read:

```
8000    fwssd    in.ahttpd    wait    0
```

Reinstall the security policy and bounce the firewall after making these changes (e.g., **cprestart**). You can then use HTTP port 8000 in a service, authenticate against it with User Authentication, and perform content security on that port.

8.12: How Do I Authenticate Outbound HTTPS Traffic?

FireWall-1 can authenticate outbound HTTPS traffic. However, it can do so effectively only when FireWall-1 is the proxy server for HTTPS requests from the Web browser. The following line must be added to $FWDIR/conf/ fwauthd.conf:

```
443    fwssd    in.ahttpd    wait    0
```

This line ensures that the HTTP Security Server is listening on port 443 to handle HTTPS requests. Once this line is added to fwauthd.conf, FireWall-1 must be restarted (**cprestart**). Next, modify the HTTPS server so that the protocol type is HTTP (instead of None). You should then be able to add the appropriate rule and install the policy.

Note that no special certificate is necessary to authenticate outbound traffic.

8.13: Can I Authenticate Access to Internal HTTPS Servers?

Yes, you can. However, if you have Clientless VPN enabled, that will override the steps described below.

1. Make sure a certificate is generated in the VPN portion of your gateway object.
2. Modify `$FWDIR/conf/fwauthd.conf` so that the HTTP Security Server is running in SSL mode with your defined certificate.
3. Kill `fwd` on the firewall module.
4. Modify the HTTPS service to be of type HTTP.
5. Add an appropriate rule and install the security policy.

The following paragraphs describe the steps in more detail.

Go to the VPN frame of your gateway object. Generate a certificate against your certificate authority if needed. Make note of the certificate name (`default Cert` if you allow the system to generate one for you).

Next, modify the file `$FWDIR/conf/fwauthd.conf` by adding a line that enables the HTTP Security Server to run on an additional service port dedicated to HTTPS:

```
443     fwssd     in.ahttpd     wait     0 eb:defaultCert
```

The `eb:defaultCert` at the end of this line means two things: encrypt between both the client-to-firewall connection as well as the firewall-to-server connection, and `defaultCert` refers to the name of your certificate. Once this change is made, use the command **fw kill fwd** on the firewall module. Assuming `cpwatchdog` is running, `fwd` should restart on its own in a minute or two.

Next, you have to set a few parameters in `objects_5.0.C` on the management station (see FAQ 4.2 for details). Enter the following commands into **dbedit**:

```
dbedit> modify properties firewall_properties
            http_connection_method_proxy true
dbedit> modify properties firewall_properties
            http_connection_method_transparent true
dbedit> modify properties firewall_properties
            http_connection_method_tunneling true
dbedit> update properties firewall_properties
```

Modify HTTPS Service Properties so that the protocol type is HTTP. Add an appropriate rule to the rulebase (such as the rule shown in Figure 8.53), and install the security policy.

NOTE! When you connect to the server, you will get a message about the certificate not matching the name. Just accept the certificate when prompted. This is unavoidable.

SOURCE	DESTINATION	SERVICE	ACTION	TRACK
 timelords@Any	⬜ tardis	TCP https	👤 User Auth	📄 Log

Figure 8.53   Sample User Authentication rule with HTTPS

> **WARNING!**   In NG FP3 base (no hotfixes), certificates from the ICA cannot be used with a Netscape/Mozilla browser. If you want Netscape browsers to work, you must use certificates from a different certificate authority or upgrade to Hotfix-2 or above.

8.14: How Can I Authenticate with HTTP to a Site Requiring Its Own Authentication?

Enter your login as follows: remoteuser@fw1user. Then enter your password as follows: remotepass@fw1pass. FireWall-1 will strip off the @fw1user and @fw1pass portions when passing the authentication to the remote site. If the remote username or password contains an @, you need to enter the @ twice (e.g., @@).

8.15: How Can Users Change Their Own Passwords?

The short answer is they can't, at least not directly. One site I know of uses OS Password as its authentication mechanism. The company then allows its users to Telnet to the firewall, authenticate, and then change their passwords via the operating system of the firewall. This has all kinds of potential security risks involved, so it is not recommended.

If you are using an external authentication server and it has its own remote password-changing utility, you may be in luck. Check Point also supports enforcing password changes for LDAP users as long as the password is changed when prompted by FireWall-1 or is changed through SmartDashboard/Policy Editor. You may also be able to use the data from an **fw dbexport**, massage it with another application that allows you to change your password, and import it with **fw dbimport**.

8.16: Can a User Reset His or Her Own S/Key Chain?

When a user has fewer than ten S/Key passwords left, FireWall-1 will prompt the user to create a new S/Key chain if the user authenticates via Telnet, rlogin, or Client Authentication. The user will need to specify a different seed value (the default seed is the username), a new chain length to FireWall-1, and the last password in the chain.

On a UNIX machine, you would generate the new key chain as follows (assuming you want to use `seed` as the new seed value and 1000 as the chain length):

```
$ key 1000 seed
Reminder - Do not use this program while logged in via telnet or
          rlogin.
Enter secret password: foobar
JOG WAKE SUN MEND ILL COWL
```

After generating the new key chain, you can input this information into your Telnet User Authentication or Client Authentication session as follows:

```
Check Point FireWall-1 authenticated Telnet server running on mrhat
User: phoneboy
SKEY CHALLENGE: 9 phoneboy.
Enter SKEY string: MUG EMMA PI PRY HOYT MANN
User phoneboy authenticated by S/Key system

You have only 8 one-time passwords left. A new S/Key chain should be
created. If you have a new chain, you can enter it now by typing the
chain length and the last password in the chain.

Enter New Chain (y/n) ? y

Enter S/Key chain length: 1000
Enter the last string of the new chain: JOG WAKE SUN MEND ILL COWL
New S/Key chain accepted

Connected to foo
```

The password generated and entered in the preceding example is used only to initialize the S/Key chain. Future passwords will decrement from that point in the chain. Also, FireWall-1 always prompts you to use the old seed value, not the new one you entered. You need to remember to use the new seed value when using an S/Key generator or when generating your own list.

8.17: Can I Customize the HTTP Client Authentication Pages?

It may be desirable for a variety of reasons to customize these pages with a different look. The HTML files that FireWall-1 uses are located in `$FWDIR/conf/ahclientd` on the firewall module.

- `ahclientd1.html` is the first page users are greeted with (i.e., this page prompts users for a username).
- `ahclientd2.html` is the end-of-session page after a successful authentication.

- `ahclientd3.html` is the page for signing off.
- `ahclientd4.html` is the successful-login page where users choose the kind of sign-on or sign-off they desire.
- `ahclientd5.html` is the Specific Sign-On page.
- `ahclientd6.html` is the page for authentication failure.
- `ahclientd7.html` is the page that prompts users for their passwords.
- `ahclientd8.html` is another page that prompts users for their passwords.

These files contain `%s` or `%d` where FireWall-1 inserts information into these pages. Do not delete these symbols because unpredictable results will occur. You certainly can change where they appear, but do not change the order in which they appear. You must also keep the files less than 1,024 bytes in size.

Note that if you want to include any graphics, they need to be from a different Web server.

Troubleshooting Authentication Problems

The following sections contain some problem situations that you may run into and suggestions on how to resolve them. You should also see Chapter 9 for more troubleshooting hints. The troubleshooting headings are numbered for easy reference.

8.18: This Gateway Does Not Support X

When trying to log in as a specific user, the following error might appear:

```
This Gateway Does Not Support X
```

The X represents an authentication scheme (SecurID, RADIUS, and so on). This error message occurs for one of two reasons:

1. Your gateway object is not defined with this authentication scheme enabled.
2. If an LDAP user is trying to authenticate, the LDAP account unit does not have this authentication scheme configured as supported. Correct this problem, reinstall the security policy, and try again.

8.19: The Connection Is Closed by a Session Authentication Agent

If you are using Session Authentication with a protocol that opens lots of connections (like HTTP), you will see this error in your logs. In these cases, it is advisable to use Client Authentication with fully automatic authentication instead of using Session Authentication by itself.

8.20: Authentication Services Are Unavailable. Connection Refused.

This message occurs in one of two situations:

1. The appropriate Security Server is not enabled in `$FWDIR/conf/fwauthd.conf`.
2. There is more than one object with the firewall's IP address.

Fix these situations, reload the policy, restart FireWall-1, and try again.

8.21: Session Authentication Is Not Secure

This message means that communication between the firewall and the Session Authentication agent is cleartext. The same thing goes for User Authentication for Telnet, FTP, HTTP, and rlogin and Client Authentication—the password is not encrypted. If you are concerned with passwords being sniffed over the wire, use an OTP scheme like S/Key or SecurID. This way, even if the password is captured over the wire, it will not be useful.

You can also enable encrypted Session Authentication. In fact, you can force it by enabling the "Accept only if connection is encrypted" option in the Session Authentication Action Properties screen (see Figure 8.35 earlier in the chapter).

8.22: Using Session Authentication with Content Security

FireWall-1 does not support this because User Authentication can be used for any service for which Content Security is available.

8.23: Authenticating on Each URL

If FireWall-1 is used for User Authentication and the firewall is not set as the proxy in the client browser, you will be asked to authenticate at each new Web site to access because the Web browser will not use the previous authentication information entered as each new site is accessed. In these situations, you should use Client Authentication with partially automatic authentication or use Session Authentication.

8.24: No Client Auth Rules Available

This error appears when a user attempts to authenticate and there is no Client Authentication rule that matches. The source IP address, user's group, and the user's allowed sources must match the rule. The user should not have a "blank" in the allowed source or destination section.

8.25: Policy Install Logs Out Client Authentication Users

A policy install flushes certain tables, of which the `client_auth` table is one. Although this is not generally recommended for security reasons, you can open `$FWDIR/lib/table.def` on the management console and modify the following entry:

```
client_auth = dynamic sync expires AUTH_TIMEOUT kbuf 3  \
                    expcall KFUNC_CLIENT_AUTH_EXPIRE;
```

`keep` needs to be added to this line after `sync`. It should read:

```
client_auth = dynamic sync keep expires AUTH_TIMEOUT kbuf 3  \
                    expcall KFUNC_CLIENT_AUTH_EXPIRE;
```

The `keep` prevents the `client_auth` table from being flushed on a policy install. You must reinstall the security policy in order for this change to take effect. The only way to flush this table is to bounce FireWall-1 (**cprestart**).

8.26: Partially Automatic Client Authentication Redirects Site to an IP Address

The HTTP Security Server needs to be instructed to use the HTTP host header instead of the IP address. To do that, perform the following commands in **dbedit** or make the appropriate change in the GUIdbedit tool:

```
dbedit> modify properties firewall_properties
            http_use_host_h_as_dst true
dbedit> update properties firewall_properties
```

See FAQ 4.2 in Chapter 4 for instructions on how to modify `objects_5_0.C`.

8.27: Users Are Not Being Prompted for Authentication

The likely reason for this problem is that one of the rules is less restrictive than the User Authentication rule actually matched. Long logging on all rules should allow you to discover which rule is the cause. Make this rule less restrictive, and/or reorder the rules to resolve this problem.

8.28: Request to Proxy Other Than Next Proxy Resource http://proxy.foo.com

This message is a result of trying to filter traffic going to a proxy server. You need to set the HTTP Next Proxy server and port as described in FAQ 8.6. You can go to only one proxy server per firewall because it is impossible to set more than one server in the Use Next Proxy setting.

8.29: Cannot Telnet to the Firewall

Sometimes while trying to Telnet to the firewall with User Authentication, you get the Check Point Telnet banner, you authenticate successfully, but then you lose the connection. If you are attempting to allow users to Telnet to the firewall for the purpose of proxy authentication, make sure `prompt_for_destination` is set to `true` in `objects_5_0.C`. If you want to allow people to Telnet to the firewall to log on to the firewall itself, you need to make sure that the Telnet daemon is running on the firewall box. Check `/etc/inetd.conf` to see if the Telnet daemon was commented out by FireWall-1 upon installation. If it was, uncomment it, and send the `inetd` process a hangup (HUP) signal.

 WARNING!   It is not recommended that you allow users to Telnet to your firewall directly. For enhanced security, use an encrypted login mechanism like SSH.

8.30: When Accessing Certain Sites via HTTP, the Connections Are Dropped with Various Error Messages

Check Point's HTTP Security Server disallows some HTTP behaviors. As a result, some sites do not function when accessed through the HTTP Security Server. FAQ 9.9 gives some suggested settings for `objects_5_0.C` to eliminate these errors.

8.31: SecurID Authentication Fails after One Try

In this situation, SecurID authentication is set up, but after one successful authentication attempt, all future attempts fails. You might see the error message "[LOG_ERR] ACEAGENT: The message entry does not exist for message ID: 100x" when this occurs.

The ACE agent inside of FireWall-1 embeds a hash of its IP address in the authentication request packet before passing it to the ACE/Server. The ACE/Server will run a hash on the expected source IP of the ACE agent and compare it to the received hash. The ACE/Server uses the defined primary host agent IP to derive this hash. If the two hashes do not match, the authentication request is denied.

This method is problematic when an ACE agent is multihomed. The ACE agent may derive a hash from one of its other IP addresses. When this behavior occurs, it is necessary to create an `sdopts.rec` file in the `/var/ace` directory. The `sdopts.rec` file forces the ACE agent to use a specific IP address to derive its hash. Follow these steps.

1. Create the `sdopts.rec` file in the `/var/ace` directory.
2. Using **vi**, edit the `sdopts.rec` file and insert the following line:

```
CLIENT_IP=ip.addr.of.ace-agent
```

3. Restart FireWall-1 using **cprestart**.

Summary

Authentication is an important part of any security infrastructure. You now know the three methods used by FireWall-1 to provide authentication, the conditions under which you can apply each method, how to configure each method, and how to troubleshoot when things go wrong. You can also integrate FireWall-1 with various external authentication servers.

Sample Configurations

The following subsections present three situations that build on each other as the network and the needs of the enterprise change. Each type of authentication is demonstrated.

A User Authentication Example

The Situation

Consider the situation pictured in Figure 8.54. Assuming that all IPs used are routable (i.e., no NAT is necessary), let's implement the security policy listed below.

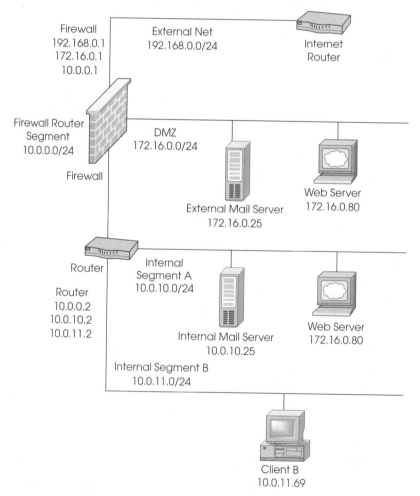

Figure 8.54 Network for sample configurations

The Goals

- The Web server in the DMZ will be accessible via HTTP from anywhere.
- The e-mail server in the DMZ will be accessible via SMTP from anywhere and via POP-3 from the internal networks.
- Users bob and dan can FTP or Telnet from the internal network to any host on the DMZ segment provided they authenticate.
- Users bob, dan, doug, and joe can access the Intranet Web server from anywhere via HTTP provided they authenticate.
- Internal users on Segment A and B (dubbed "Internal") can access hosts on the Internet via HTTP, FTP, and HTTPS.
- All other traffic should be denied.
- Authentication timeouts should be enabled for at least 30 minutes.
- All users will authenticate with S/Key and have a chain length of at least 1000.

The Checklist

- Create the necessary network objects.
- Create the necessary users and groups required for authentication, and install the user database.
- Ensure that the appropriate Security Servers are enabled in `$FWDIR/conf/fwauthd.conf`.
- Create the appropriate rule(s) in the rulebase.
- Configure the User Authentication action properties.
- Configure the Rulebase Properties Authentication frame.
- Verify and install the policy.

The Implementation

After creating all the network objects that represent your network, create the users bob, dan, doug, and joe. Make sure the expiration date for each user is set far enough in the future. Next, create the group WebAdmins and add bob and dan to this group.

In this situation, the Security Servers you will be using are for Telnet, FTP, and HTTP. As such, you should verify in `$FWDIR/conf/fwauthd.conf` that these servers are enabled:

```
21      fwssd       in.aftpd        wait    0
80      fwssd       in.ahttpd       wait    0
23      fwssd       in.atelnetd     wait    0
```

NO.	SOURCE	DESTINATION	SERVICE	ACTION	TRACK
1	* Any	External_Web_Server	TCP http	accept	— None
2	* Any	External_Mail_Server	TCP smtp	accept	— None
3	DMZAdmins@internal-networks	DMZ_Net	TCP telnet TCP ftp	User Auth	Log
4	* Any	firewall	* Any	drop	Log
5	All Users@Any	Intranet_Web_Server	TCP http	User Auth	— None
6	internal-networks	External_Mail_Server	TCP pop-3	accept	— None
7	internal-networks	DMZ_Net	TCP telnet TCP ftp TCP http TCP https	accept	Log
8	* Any	* Any	* Any	drop	Log

Figure 8.55 Rulebase for the User Authentication sample configuration

If you see the preceding lines without a comment character (#) in front of them, the servers are enabled. If the lines are missing or commented out, add them or uncomment them, and bounce FireWall-1 (`cprestart`).

As for the rulebase, you need to make sure that the rules do not allow more than they should. These rules should allow authenticated access to the appropriate hosts without permitting nonauthenticated access. The proper rulebase is shown in Figure 8.55.

Next, you need to configure the User Authentication action properties for both rules that use User Authentication. For each rule, right-click User Auth (in the Action part of the rule). Figure 8.56 shows the screen that appears for each rule.

You also need to configure the Authentication section of the firewall object so that the User Authentication timeout is 30 minutes, as shown in Figure 8.57.

Once this configuration is set up, verify and install the security policy.

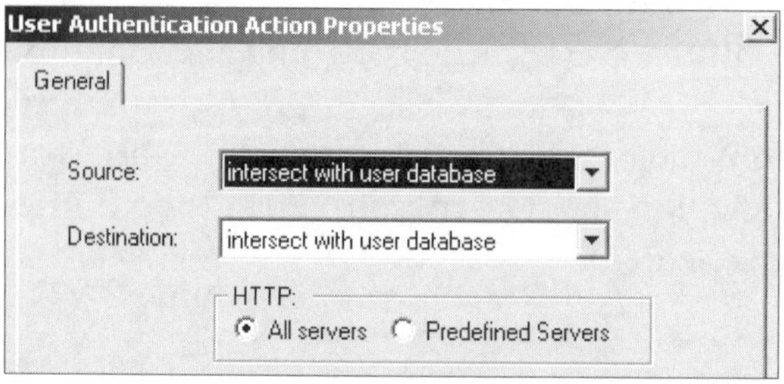

Figure 8.56 User Authentication Action Properties, General tab

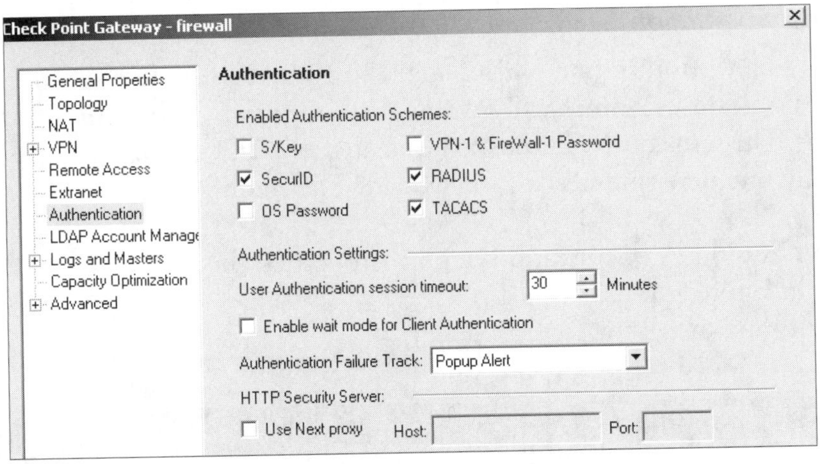

Figure 8.57 Gateway Properties, Authentication frame

A Session Authentication Example

The Situation

The same network as in the previous example is used in this situation except a new server has been added to the DMZ (172.16.0.42). This server needs to be administered via a program called VNC, which uses TCP port 5900. VNC does not provide strong enough authentication, so it was decided to use Session Authentication to authenticate this service. A new user (michael) will be the only user permitted to access this service on the internal network. This user will also be able to use FTP or Telnet from the internal network to any host on the DMZ segment provided he authenticates.

The Goals

- Create new user michael.
- Create a new group for michael called VNCAdmins.
- Add michael to the groups VNCAdmins and WebAdmins.
- Permit michael to use VNC to access the new machine via Session Authentication.

The Checklist

- Create the necessary network objects.
- Create the necessary users and groups.
- Create the appropriate rule(s) in the rulebase.
- Configure the Session Authentication action properties.
- Verify and install the policy.

The Implementation

Create a new workstation object for 172.16.0.42. Create the group VNC Admins. Create user michael. Add michael to group VNCAdmins and Web Admins. The service VNC needs to be created as a TCP service on port 5900.

Only one new rule needs to be added. The modified rulebase is shown in Figure 8.58.

The Session Authentication action properties should be the defaults, as shown in Figure 8.59.

Verify and install the security policy.

NO.	SOURCE	DESTINATION	SERVICE	ACTION	TRACK
1	✳ Any	🖥 External_Web_Server	TCP http	🕸 accept	– None
2	✳ Any	🖥 External_Mail_Server	TCP smtp	🕸 accept	– None
3	👥 DMZAdmins@internal-networks	⊹ DMZ_Net	TCP telnet TCP ftp	🔒 User Auth	📋 Log
4	👥 VNCAdmins@internal-networks	🖥 VNC_Server	TCP VNC	🔄 Session Auth	📋 Log
5	✳ Any	🔲 firewall	✳ Any	⦿ drop	📋 Log
6	👥 All Users@Any	🖥 Intranet_Web_Server	TCP http	🔒 User Auth	📋 Log
7	🔳 internal-networks	🖥 External_Mail_Server	TCP pop-3	🕸 accept	– None
8	🔳 internal-networks	✖ DMZ_Net	TCP telnet TCP ftp TCP http TCP https	🕸 accept	📋 Log
9	✳ Any	✳ Any	✳ Any	⦿ drop	📋 Log

Figure 8.58   Rulebase for the Session Authentication sample configuration

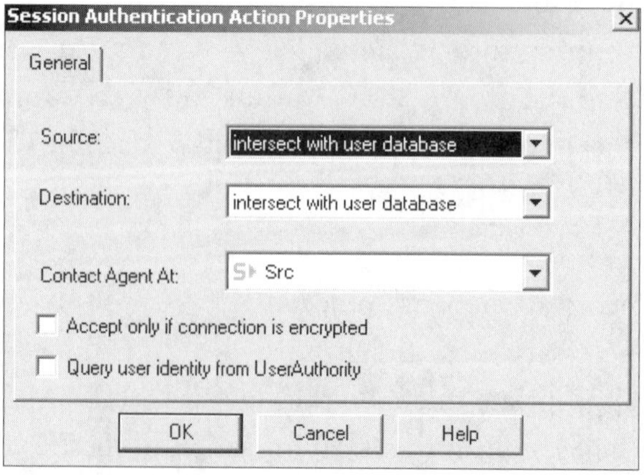

Figure 8.59   Session Authentication Action Properties, General tab

A Client Authentication Example

The Situation

Once again, the same basic network shown in Figure 8.54 is used in this situation. Due to a recent change in company policy, all outbound Internet access must be authenticated. Because of the way User Authentication works with HTTP and because it is not desirable to set the proxy in the browser, Client Authentication seems the most appropriate choice. It is also desirable to switch the existing User Authentication rules to Client Authentication. Users should reauthenticate after 30 minutes of inactivity. Also, user michael would like to be authenticated to use VNC as a result of authenticating for HTTP as well as via the Session Authentication agent.

The Goals

- Change Rules 3 and 6 from the previous situation (see Figure 8.58) to Client Authentication.
- Allow both Client and Session Authentication for VNC.

The Checklist

- Change the actions of Rules 3 and 6 to Client Authentication.
- Add a new rule allowing VNC to be authenticated by Client Authentication.
- Configure Client Authentication action properties for each of these rules.
- Verify and install the policy.

The Implementation

After changing the action of the rules, your rulebase should look like the one shown in Figure 8.60.

Each of the Client Authentication actions should have the properties set as shown in Figures 8.61 and 8.62.

Verify and install the policy.

Notes

The Client Authentication rule is listed before the Session Authentication rule because there is no reason to ask for Session Authentication if user michael is already authenticated via Client Authentication.

NO.	SOURCE	DESTINATION	SERVICE	ACTION	TRACK
1	✳ Any	🖥 External_Web_Server	TCP http	🕸 accept	− None
2	✳ Any	🖥 External_Mail_Server	TCP smtp	🕸 accept	− None
3	👤 DMZAdmins@internal-networks	DMZ_Net	TCP telnet TCP ftp	🔲 Client Auth	📋 Log
4	👤 VNCAdmins@internal-networks	DMZ_Net	TCP VNC	🔲 Client Auth	📋 Log
5	👤 VNCAdmins@internal-networks	🖥 VNC_Server	TCP VNC	🔄 Session Auth	📋 Log
6	✳ Any	🧱 firewall	✳ Any	⬤ drop	📋 Log
7	👤 All Users@Any	🖥 Intranet_Web_Server	TCP http	🔲 Client Auth	📋 Log
8	🔢 internal-networks	🖥 External_Mail_Server	TCP pop-3	🕸 accept	− None
9	🔢 internal-networks	✖ DMZ_Net	TCP telnet TCP ftp TCP http TCP https	🕸 accept	📋 Log
10	✳ Any	✳ Any	✳ Any	⬤ drop	📋 Log

Figure 8.60 Sample rulebase for the Client Authentication sample configuration

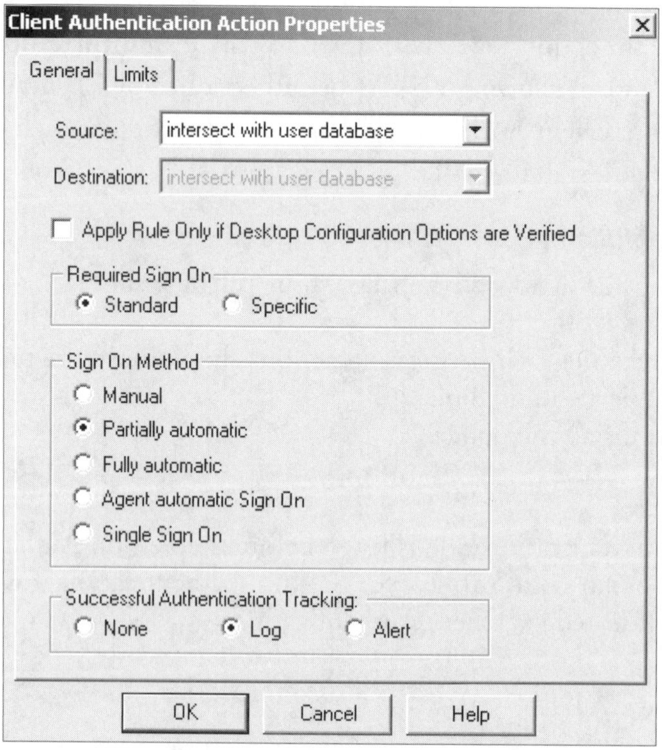

Figure 8.61 Client Authentication Action Properties, General tab

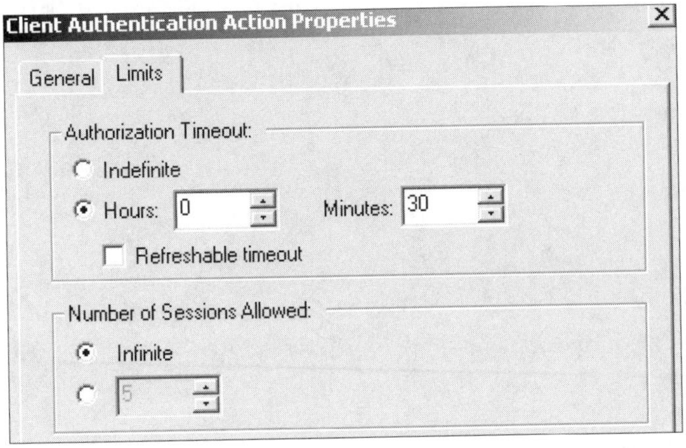

Figure 8.62   Client Authentication Action Properties, Limits tab

Chapter

9

Content Security

In the last chapter, I talked about restricting access based on the user; in this chapter, I talk about restricting access to certain kinds of content. Such restrictions include not allowing people to access certain kinds of sites (e.g., pornography, news), preventing people from accessing specific types of content (e.g., RealAudio, MP3), and scanning content for viruses. I also discuss the various Security Servers for HTTP, FTP, SMTP, and TCP in some detail.

By the end of this chapter, you should be able to:

- Know what CVP and UFP are used for
- Restrict content for HTTP, FTP, SMTP, and generic TCP services
- Understand the performance issues inherent in Content Security
- Understand how to tune your FireWall-1 installation to perform well
- Troubleshoot problems with Content Security

The Security Servers

FireWall-1 normally relies on Stateful Inspection. However, like authentication, the business of virus and content filtering requires more capabilities than can be provided by Stateful Inspection alone. In these cases, FireWall-1 uses the various Security Servers to perform the necessary tasks. In the last chapter, I discussed how they were used for authentication. In this chapter, I look at each individual Security Server a bit more closely and explain how to configure them.

A Word about Licensing and Third-Party Products

All firewall modules can use Content Security. Certain kinds of embedded firewalls cannot use Content Security. However, in order to use more than the rudimentary functions of Content Security in FireWall-1, third-party software is required. Check Point maintains a list of compatible applications and software vendors at http://www.opsec.com.

CVP and UFP

Inevitably, Check Point recognized that it could not do everything in terms of providing security. Consequently, Check Point created a program called Open Platform for Security (OPSEC), which allows third-party products to "hook in" to Check Point FireWall-1 and provide services. Two of these protocols, Content Vectoring Protocol (CVP) and URL Filtering Protocol (UFP), are discussed in this section. Some of the other OPSEC functions include the following:

- *Suspicious Activity Monitoring Protocol (SAMP):* Provides for intrusion detection
- *Log Export API (LEA):* Offers the ability to analyze firewall logs
- *Event Log API (ELA):* Helps other applications tie into Check Point's alerting mechanisms
- *OPSEC Management Interface (OMI):* Allows third-party products to access the security policy
- *Public Key Infrastructure (PKI):* Enables Check Point to use third-party certificate authorities for authentication and encryption
- *Secure Authentication API (SAA):* Allows Check Point to use a variety of authentication mechanisms such as hardware-based tokens and biometric authentication
- *High Availability (HA):* Provides for highly available firewall servers
- *User-to-Address Mapping (UAM):* Helps authenticate and track users more effectively
- *User Authority API (UAA):* Offers the ability to pass authentication information to other servers in order to reduce the number of authentication prompts

CVP is used to scan content. It is typically used to scan for viruses, but it can also be used to scan for malicious Java applets or ActiveX controls, depending on which CVP server you decide to use. CVP works this way: A content stream is intercepted by one of the Security Servers. FireWall-1 determines that the content needs to be scanned by the CVP server before allowing the content to be given to the end user. As the content is downloaded through the firewall, it is sent to the CVP server, which typically runs on a separate server from the firewall. The CVP server then takes one of three actions toward the content (this action is configured in the security policy).

1. Send the content as is, without any modifications.
2. Send corrected content, with the virus or other offending content removed.
3. Do not send the content at all.

Table 9.1   Wildcards usable in all resources

Character	Description
*	Matches any string of any length. For example, *@phoneboy.com matches all e-mail addresses at phoneboy.com.
+	Matches any single character. For example, pink+@acmelabs.com would match pinky@acmelabs.com but not pinkie@acmelabs.com.
{,}	Matches any of the listed strings. For example, brain@{acmelabs,animaniacs}.com would match both brain@acmelabs.com and brain@animaniacs.com.

UFP is used to filter HTTP traffic destined for the Internet based on URLs and the categories under which they fall. As a user requests a URL in his or her Web browser, FireWall-1 uses the HTTP Security Server to check that URL against a UFP server, which returns the category for the URL. Based on that category and the defined security policy, FireWall-1 either permits the connection to the URL or rejects it. This allows, say, Christian organizations to filter non-Christian content or for workplaces to filter pornography.

Resources and Wildcards

Resources are simply a way to match a specific kind of content and then perform some action on it. Some resources are matched based on a query to a UFP server. Others are matched based on specific resources that you define.

The wildcards listed in Table 9.1 can be used in all resources. SMTP provides an additional wildcard, which is discussed in the SMTP Security Server section later in this chapter.

The HTTP Security Server

Of all the Security Servers in FireWall-1, the HTTP Security Server is used most often. Because the HTTP Security Server can be used with both CVP and UFP, I will cover how to set up both types of Content Security.

The HTTP Security Server is enabled when the following situations are true.

- There is a line that permits `in.ahttpd` to start up in `$FWDIR/conf/fwauthd.conf`. This is normally present by default.

- A resource is used in your security policy or in a rule that involves User Authentication for HTTP.

Refer to Chapter 8 for information on authentication. Defining resources is first discussed in the Filtering HTTP without a UFP or CVP Server subsection. The proper line for the HTTP Security Server in $FWDIR/conf/fwauthd.conf should have no comment symbol (#) at the beginning of the line and should look like this:

```
80      fwssd       in.ahttpd     wait    0
```

The first argument is the port on which the HTTP Security Server runs (port 80). The second argument states that it uses the binary `fwssd` to run the Security Server. The third argument specifies which server it will be. In this case, it is the HTTP Security Server (i.e., `in.ahttpd`). The fourth argument, which is usually `wait`, is used to indicate one of two things: which port it listens on (if greater than or equal to zero) or how many instances of the server to run (if negative). I discuss the latter point in the Performance Tuning section later in this chapter. The only time you want the Security Server listening on a particular port is when users will use the firewall as a nontransparent proxy for HTTP. If this line is not present or is commented out, the HTTP Security Server will not run, and any process that relies on it will fail.

Filtering HTTP without a UFP or CVP Server

FireWall-1 has some rudimentary filtering features that can be used without a UFP or CVP server. These features should be used only for the most basic of filtering needs. Anything too complex should be done with a UFP or CVP server.

You can use these filtering features by creating URI resources. From Smart Dashboard/Policy Editor, select Manage, then choose Resources or click on the ⌕ icon in the objects tree, right-click on URI, and select New URI. Next, select New, and then choose URI. You are presented with the window shown in Figure 9.1.

You can set the following properties on the General tab.

Name: In this field, enter the name of the resource (must be unique).

Comment: Enter any information you like in this field.

Color: Select a color to represent the resource.

Use this resource to: This choice allows you to determine the resource's primary goal: logging URLs that users access (Optimize URL logging) or providing content security (Enforce URI capabilities, which also logs URLs that people access). The latter relies on the HTTP Security Server; the former operates directly in the kernel and thus is faster. In NG with Application Intelligence, this tab also presents the option Enhance UFP performance. This allows you to move UFP functions into the kernel module to increase

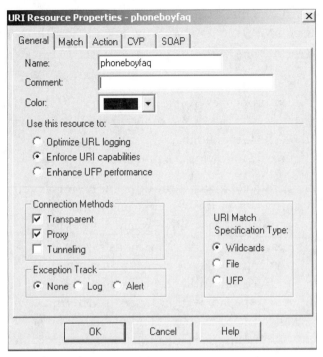

Figure 9.1   URI Resource Properties, General tab

performance but prevents you from using UFP caching (explained later in this chapter), CVP, or authentication. It also removes the ability to perform certain HTTP protocol checks, such as validating HTTP methods and content length.

Connection Methods: In this section of the tab you can specify when this resource is applied. Transparent means that the user will use the service normally, and FireWall-1 will transparently intercept the communication. Proxy means that this resource is applied when people specify the firewall as the proxy in their browser. Tunneling is used when FireWall-1 (defined as the proxy to the client's Web browser) cannot examine the content of the request, only the hostname and port number. An example of this is HTTPS. Only the hostname and port number are sent in cleartext; the rest of the content is encrypted. The hostname and port number are the only specifications that can be filtered on using the Tunneling connection method. If Tunneling is specified, all Content Security options in the URI specification are disabled.

URI Match Specification Type: This option specifies how you define this resource: as type Wildcards, File (which requires that you create a URI file), or UFP. The first two methods are discussed later in this subsection. The last method is discussed in the UFP with the HTTP Security Server subsection.

Exception Track: Here you can specify how to log anything this resource acts upon.

After setting these properties, you must then specify which URLs to filter by clicking on the Match tab. Figure 9.2 shows how it looks when the Wildcards option is selected on the General tab.

You can configure the following parameters.

Schemes: This parameter matches the different protocols you can use through the HTTP Security Server. It is relevant only if the firewall is specified as the proxy for these protocols. Normally, it is safe to just select the http checkbox.

Methods: This parameter specifies methods for HTTP. GET is used when you request a particular page (or element on a page); POST is used when sending data to a Web site (filling out forms and so on); HEAD is usually used by caching servers and Web browsers to determine whether or not an element has changed (and thus to decide whether or not to download it); PUT is a less commonly used method for uploading files via HTTP. If another method is required, you can specify it in the Other field. To allow any method, use * in the Other field.

Host, Path, Query: These fields break down the various parts of the URL into filterable components. For example, in the URL http://www.phoneboy. com/search/wwwwais/wwwwais.cgi?keywords=content+security, the host part of the URL is www.phoneboy.com, the path is /search/wwwwais/ wwwwais.cgi, and the query is basically everything else (usually for CGI scripts such as search engines). You can filter on any part of the URL.

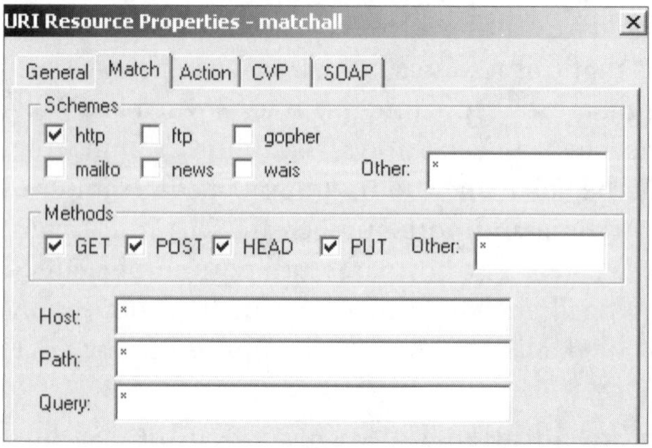

Figure 9.2 URI Resource Properties, Match tab

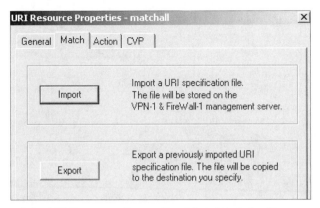

Figure 9.3   URI Resource Properties, Match tab for File resources

If you selected the File option under URI Match Specification Type on the General tab to create a resource of type File (i.e., to filter URIs based on a file) rather than Wildcards, the Match tab shown in Figure 9.3 appears.

A URI specification file is a series of lines in the following format:

```
ip-addr    /path    0
```

`ip-addr` is the IP address of the Web server you want to match against. For sites that resolve to multiple IP addresses, you need to list each one specifically. You can also use fully qualified domain names in this file, though it requires that DNS be enabled and configured on the firewall. `/path` is optional. If you want to restrict a certain subdirectory of a site (or a certain URL), enter it here. `0` (or any hexadecimal number) is required at the end of each line.

Here is a sample file:

```
10.0.146.201 0
10.251.29.12 0
10.91.182.100 /support.d 0
10.184.151.198 /support 0
```

There must also be a blank line at the end of the file. Once you have created this file, click the Import button and specify the path to this file on your Smart Console system. It will then be uploaded to your management console.

You then need to specify the action to take if this resource matches, so click the Action tab (see Figure 9.4).

On this tab, you can configure the following parameters.

Replacement URI: If the rulebase action this resource is used in is dropped or rejected, the user should be redirected to this URL. This could, for

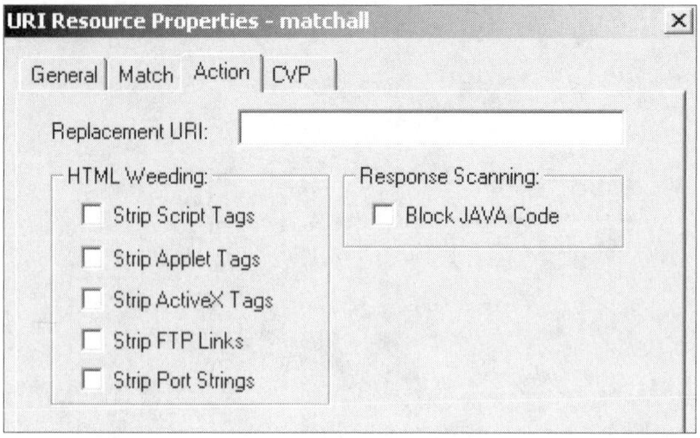

Figure 9.4   URI Resource Properties, Action tab

instance, be a policy document telling people the rules and regulations of Web usage.

HTML Weeding: In this section of the tab you can select which tags to strip out if the action is accepted. The HTTP Security Server does not really strip them but rather comments out the offending HTML so that the tags are not active when downloaded. A user could theoretically save the HTML and reload a modified, local copy.

Block JAVA Code: FireWall-1 can block the download of any Java code if you select this checkbox. It does not match JavaScript, which is done with the HTML Weeding option Strip Script Tags.

Figure 9.5 shows the CVP tab, where you can specify whether or not this resource will enforce virus scanning and the parameters that control how it is done.

This tab includes the following options.

Use CVP: Enable the use of CVP in this resource. If this property is un-checked, all other fields on this screen will be greyed out.

CVP server: Select an OPSEC Application server that has CVP in it. I will show how these are defined in the CVP with the HTTP Security Server sub-section.

CVP server is allowed to modify content: This allows the CVP server to attempt to disinfect a file that has a virus. If this option is not checked and the content is determined to have a virus, the communication will be rejected.

Send HTTP Headers/requests to CVP server: These options allow the CVP server to make security or filtering decisions based on data contained in the HTTP request headers.

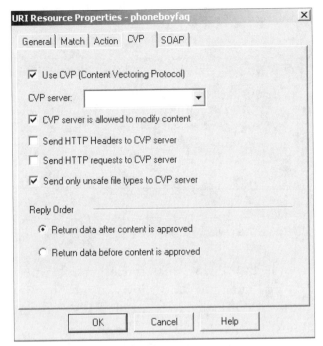

Figure 9.5 URI Resource Properties, CVP tab

Send only unsafe file types to CVP server: This option was introduced in NG with Application Intelligence. Normally, FireWall-1 sends all traffic through the CVP server. If this option is enabled, FireWall-1 inspects the content of the traffic to determine whether it is a kind of file that may contain a virus—FireWall-1 does not trust file extensions or MIME types for these checks. Graphic or movie files are considered "safe" and thus are not sent to the CVP server. Executable and Microsoft Office documents are sent to the CVP server for virus scanning.

Return data after content is approved: Data is sent to the CVP server for approval. Only after all the data has been received and scanned is it sent back from the CVP server. The problem with this option is that with large files on slow links, this can cause the client connection with the server to take a very long time before any data is returned. The client may time out in this case.

Return data before content is approved: This allows the CVP server to scan and correct content "on the fly." This option solves the problem of transferring large files over slow links, but it may mean the client receives part of a file that the CVP server will ultimately reject because, for instance, it finds a virus it cannot disinfect.

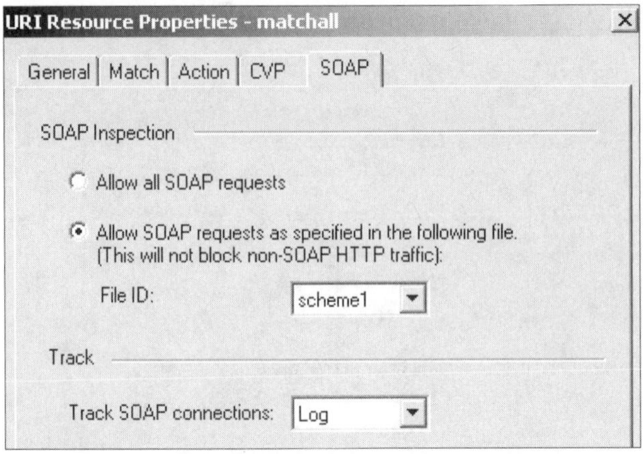

Figure 9.6 URI Resource Properties, SOAP tab

Figure 9.6 shows the SOAP tab, which is relevant only when using Wildcard URI types and NG FP3 and later. This allows you to filter and/or log Simple Object Access Protocol (SOAP) requests over HTTP. You may either allow all SOAP requests or filter for specific ones.

The schemes you can select are defined in files in `$FWDIR/conf/XML` on the management console. There are several files in this directory (`scheme1` through `scheme10`) where you can define specific sets of allowed SOAP requests. The files must contain entries of the following format:

```
namespace          method
```

For example:

```
http://tempuri.org/message/ EchoString
http://tempuri.org/message/ SubtractNumbers
```

You can then use this resource in a rule, as shown in Figure 9.7.

UFP with the HTTP Security Server

The UFP server is a third-party application that should be run on a different platform from the firewall. A variety of UFP servers available for FireWall-1 run on Windows or Solaris. I will not cover their setup in this book. It is sufficient to say that once they are set up correctly, FireWall-1 can then communicate with them on TCP port 18182.

SOURCE	DESTINATION	SERVICE	ACTION	TRACK
internal_network	✱ Any	HTTP http->phoneboyfaq	⊖ reject	🗐 Log

Figure 9.7 Sample HTTP resource rule

To configure UFP to work with FireWall-1 and the HTTP Security Server, perform the following steps.

1. Define the workstation object on which the UFP server is running (if necessary).
2. Define the OPSEC Application object that represents the UFP server.
3. Define a URI resource of type UFP.
4. Add a rule using the resource, and install the policy.

Let's assume you have created a workstation object named babyike where the UFP server is installed. In SmartDashboard/Policy Editor, do one of the following.

- Select Manage and then choose OPSEC Applications.
- Click on the following icon in the objects tree: ⚙. Then right-click on OPSEC Application, and select New OPSEC Application.

Figure 9.8 shows the resulting screen.

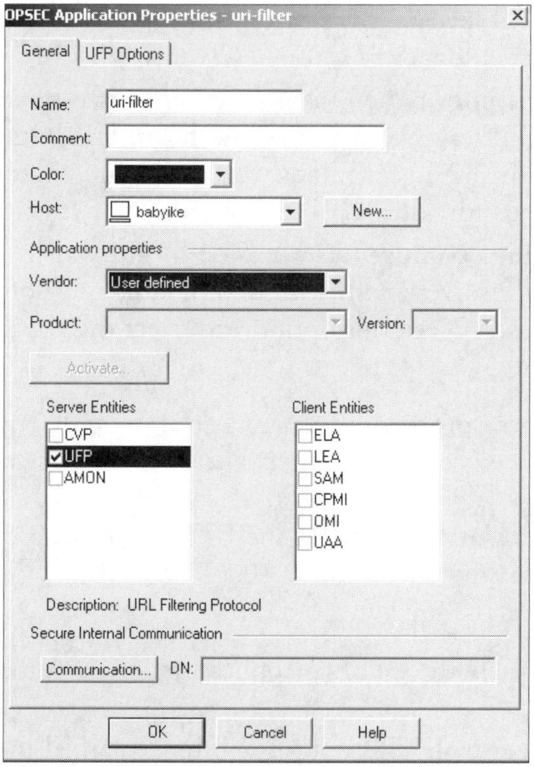

Figure 9.8   OPSEC Application Properties, General tab

The General tab contains the following options.

Name: Enter the name of the resource (must be unique).

Comment: In this field, you can add a note about this OPSEC Application server.

Color: Select whichever color you would like.

Host: This is the workstation object on which the UFP server is running.

Application properties: In this section of the tab, select the vendor of the application, the product, and the version as appropriate. If your vendor isn't listed, you may want to select User defined. In this case, make sure that UFP is checked under Server Entities.

Secure Internal Communication: In FireWall-1 NG FP1 and later, SIC is used to authenticate communications with third-party OPSEC applications. This is where you configure the one-time password used during the initial certificate exchange. Additional steps will need to be performed in your OPSEC application to perform this exchange.

Figure 9.9 shows the UFP properties described below.

Service: This field specifies the service used to communicate with this server. Normally, this should be FW1_ufp (TCP port 18182).

Dictionary: The information in this section is used to validate the connection to your UFP server. Categories are shown if a connection can be successfully established. You can choose the actual categories that are allowed or disallowed in the individual URI resource.

Use early versions compatibility mode: In FireWall-1 4.1, authentication between the UFP server and the firewall module uses something other than SIC. In these cases, check this option and select the appropriate authentication method.

After setting these properties, you can create your URI resource. For this example, the resource is called uri-filter. The URI resource needs to be of type UFP.

Next, go to the Match tab, select the UFP Server websense, and select the Blocked category, as shown in Figure 9.10.

This tab contains the following options.

UFP server: Specify the OPSEC Application object you created that defines the UFP server.

UFP caching control: This option will be explained in the UFP Caching subsection later in this chapter.

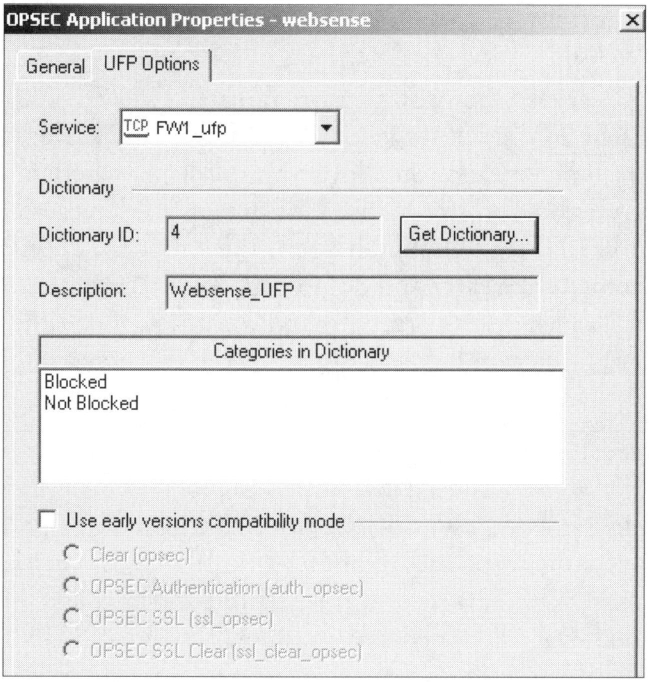

Figure 9.9   OPSEC Application Properties, UFP Options tab

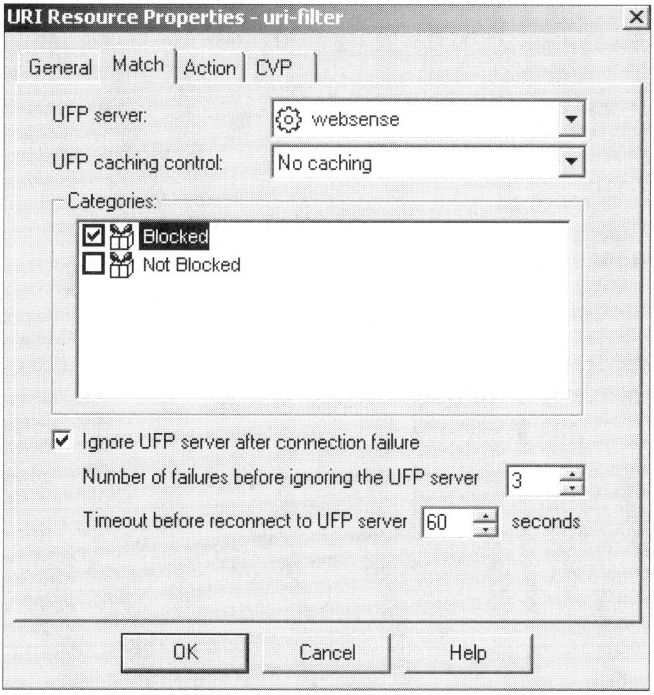

Figure 9.10   URI Resource Properties, Match tab

Categories: Specify the categories on the UFP server to which this URI will apply. For Websense servers, this should be Blocked.

Ignore UFP server after connection failure: FireWall-1 will continually connect to the UFP server. If for some reason the UFP server fails to respond in a timely fashion, this option allows you to specify whether to "fail closed" (i.e., keep trying to connect to the UFP server until successful, meanwhile blocking all HTTP traffic) or "fail open" (i.e., after the specified amount of time, ignore the UFP server and do not categorize the traffic). You can specify the number of failures permitted and the amount of time between each communication attempt before it ignores the UFP server.

If you wanted to, you could go to the Action tab and specify other filtering options, but instead, for this example, let's move on to create the rules to block Web sites that Websense has been configured to block (see Figure 9.11).

The first rule is created by using the Add with Resource option for the Service column, selecting http, and then selecting uri-filter. This rule catches all Websense-filtered URLs. The second rule permits URLs that are not filtered by Websense. This second rule is necessary to allow access to all URLs except those prohibited by Websense.

CVP with the HTTP Security Server

The CVP server is a third-party application that should be run on a different platform from the firewall. A variety of CVP servers available for FireWall-1 run on Windows or Solaris. I will not attempt to cover their setup in this book. It is sufficient to say that once they are set up correctly, FireWall-1 can then communicate with them on TCP port 18181.

To configure CVP to work with FireWall-1 and the HTTP Security Server, perform the following steps.

1. Define the workstation object on which the CVP server is running (if necessary).
2. Define the OPSEC Application object that represents the CVP server.
3. Define a resource that uses the CVP server (or modify an existing one).
4. Use the rule with the resource, and install the policy.

SOURCE	DESTINATION	SERVICE	ACTION	TRACK
internal_network	Any	http->uri-filter	reject	Log
internal_network	Any	http	accept	Log

Figure 9.11   Sample rules for URI filtering

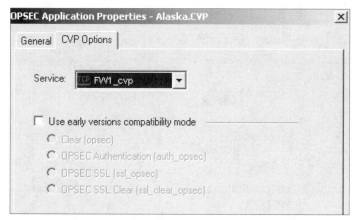

Figure 9.12   OPSEC Application Properties, CVP Options

As in the UFP example above, let's assume you have created a workstation object named babyike where the CVP server is installed. In SmartDashboard/ Policy Editor, do one of the following.

- Select Manage and then choose OPSEC Applications.
- Click on the following icon in the objects tree: ⚙. Then right-click on OPSEC Application, and select New OPSEC Application.

A screen similar to Figure 9.8 (shown earlier) appears. For this example, the OPSEC Application object is named f-secure-cvp.

Since a CVP server is being defined, choose the relevant options for CVP— choose the correct CVP server information or select User defined in the Vendor field, and make sure CVP is checked under Server Entities. Also define SIC, if relevant.

Figure 9.12 shows the CVP Options tab.

The properties are listed below.

Service: Select the service used to communicate with this server. Normally, this should be FW1_cvp (TCP port 18181).

Use early versions compatibility mode: In FireWall-1 4.1, authentication between the CVP server and the firewall module uses something other than SIC. In these cases, check this option and select the appropriate authentication method.

You then need to create a resource that performs CVP. Create a new resource called virusscan (see Figure 9.13), which matches all URIs and performs virus scanning.

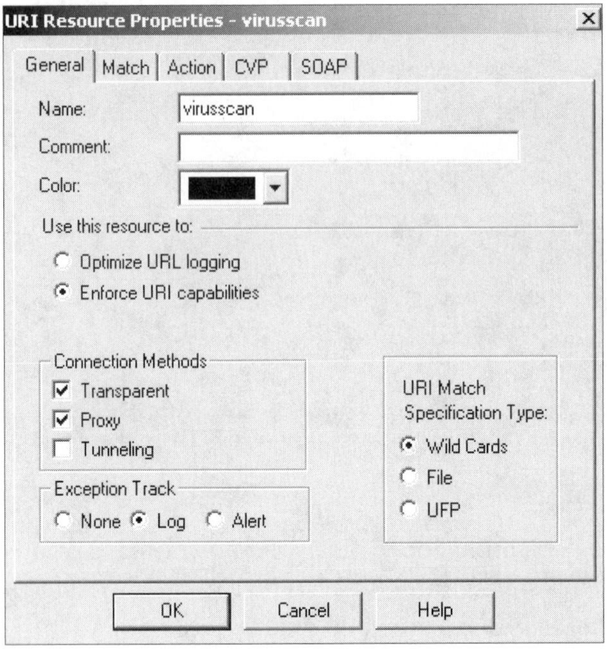

Figure 9.13   URI Resource Properties, General tab

The Match tab, shown in Figure 9.14, shows the settings used to make this resource match all URLs.

The CVP tab, shown in Figure 9.15, is where you define which CVP resource to apply. You then need to add this resource to a rule. You can combine it with the UFP example so that both URLs and content are filtered (see Figure 9.16).

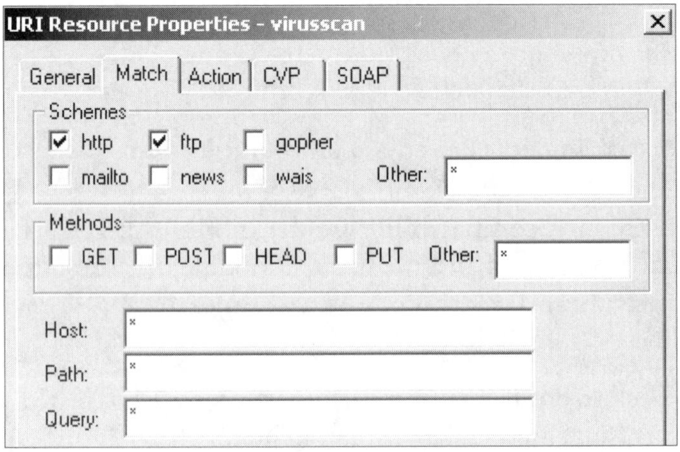

Figure 9.14   URI Resource Properties, Match tab

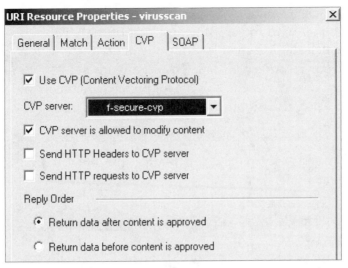

Figure 9.15   URI Resource Properties, CVP tab

SOURCE	DESTINATION	SERVICE	ACTION	TRACK
ᛁᛁ internal_network	* Any	HTTP http->virusscan	🜨 accept	🗒 Log

Figure 9.16   Sample rule with CVP

Frequently Asked Questions about the HTTP Security Server

To keep all the information about a particular Security Server together, I provide a corresponding FAQs subsection at the end of each Security Server section.

9.1: Can I Filter HTTP on Other Ports (e.g., Port 81)?

There are five steps necessary to enable filtering on other ports.

1. Create a TCP service for the port in question (e.g., http81), and make it of type URI.
2. Add a rule with a resource using the new service.
3. Install the security policy.
4. Reconfigure `$FWDIR/conf/fwauthd.conf` to run the Security Server on that port.
5. Bounce the firewall (**cprestart**).

Creating the service is straightforward. Create a new service of type TCP. Set the Protocol Type to HTTP and the port as necessary (e.g., port 81). If you add a resource by right-clicking in the Service part of a rule, you can associate a resource with the new service you created (e.g., http81). If you filter with wild-card resources, you need to enter the host part of the URL as `host:port`. For example, to match all, instead of entering `*`, you need to type it as `*:*`. If you do not do this, your resource will fail. To reconfigure `$FWDIR/conf/fwauthd.conf`, you need to add a line to this file for each unusual port you want to filter on. For port 81, for instance, the line would read as follows:

```
81  fwssd   in.ahttpd    wait    0
```

Reinstall the security policy, and bounce the firewall after making these changes (**cprestart**).

9.2: Can the HTTP Security Server Forward Requests to a Caching Proxy Server?

Yes, but only if your clients are configured to use the firewall as their proxy server. Set the Use Next Proxy setting in your gateway object definition, Authentication frame.

9.3: Why Do I Get the Error "Request to Proxy Other Than Next Proxy Resource http://proxy.foo.com" When Filtering Traffic to a Proxy Server?

Set the Use Next Proxy setting in your gateway object definition, Authentication frame, to point at the proxy server. This setting only allows you to filter traffic to one HTTP proxy server.

9.4: How Do I Redirect People to a Usage Policy Page?

The assumption here is that end users are redirected to a policy page only when they try to access a site that is against the usage policy. You can take one of two approaches.

- Create a resource that matches the sites you *do not want* to allow access to. Use this resource in a rule as shown earlier in the chapter, setting the replacement URL accordingly in this resource.
- Create a resource that matches the sites you *want* to allow access to. If you want to then redirect users to a policy page when they try to load a page they are not allowed to access, use the matchall resource and set the replacement URL accordingly. If you want to allow users access to only the sites matched by the resource allowedsites and deny access to every-thing else (via a matchall resource), the rules would look like those shown in Figure 9.16.

NOTE! If you use the replacement URL in conjunction with User Authentication and a user is redirected to a policy page, the user will get FireWall-1's Authentication Failed page with a link to the redirected page.

9.5: How Do I Prevent People from Downloading Files or Accessing Streaming Media via HTTP?

You can use the HTTP Security Server to deal with both of these issues. If you have CVP, you may be able to use the CVP server to screen out those MIME types. If you are not using a CVP server, you can do this with a wildcard URI. In the Path section of the Match tab, you can specify all file extensions that you do not want people to download.

- To block Real Audio/Real Video, enter *.{ra,ram,rm,rv}.
- To block most downloads, enter *.{exe,zip,com,bat,sit,tar,tgz,tar.gz,lha, rar,r0+}.

You would then create a rule that uses this resource and denies access to anything matching this resource. Place this rule before your other rules that permit HTTP.

WARNING!   Attempting to filter based on file extension or even MIME type is futile. There are plenty of ways to get around these filters by using different extensions or different MIME types, which are merely suggestions for how the file should be treated. In order to filter out all the files you don't want, you will likely filter some files that you *do* want (throwing the baby out with the bath water).

9.6: Can I Allow Certain Users to Download Files Provided They Authenticate?

In order for this to work correctly, all users need to authenticate, even to use normal HTTP. The rules to do this are shown in Figure 9.17.

SOURCE	DESTINATION	SERVICE	ACTION
All Users@internal-net	internal-net	http->bad-file-types	User Auth
internal-net	internal-net	http->bad-file-types	drop
All Users@internal-net	internal-net	http	User Auth

Figure 9.17   Rules to allow file downloads with authentication

Once a packet potentially matches a User Authentication rule—that is, the source, destination, and service match what is specified in the rule—the least restrictive rule in the rulebase is the one that will actually apply. Therefore, it is important to place the rule that denies access to downloads before the rule that allows everyone to use HTTP.

9.7: How Can I Set Up FireWall-1 to Support Content Security for Outbound HTTPS?

Due to the nature of HTTPS, it is possible to authenticate or provide Content Security for HTTPS only when the client specifies the firewall as the proxy for HTTPS. Some other steps must be performed as well.

First, ensure the following line exists in `$FWDIR/conf/fwauthd.conf`:

```
443     fwssd    in.ahttpd    wait    0
```

If this line does not exist or it is commented out, add/uncomment it, and bounce FireWall-1. Second, modify the predefined service HTTPS. Change the protocol type from None to http. You can then use HTTPS for authentication or Content Security as appropriate provided the client is configured to use the firewall as a proxy for HTTPS requests.

9.8: Can I Block the Use of KaZaA, Instant Messages, and Other Applications That Can Tunnel over HTTP?

These applications are difficult to filter because they can use legitimate HTTP requests. However, a closer inspection of these HTTP request headers reveals telltale traces of what kinds of applications they are. FireWall-1 NG FP3 and later have a way to filter this traffic by using the HTTP Security Server and some properties that you need to add manually to `$FWDIR/conf/objects_5_0.C` on the management console. (See FAQ 4.2 in Chapter 4 for caveats on editing this file.)

The following example shows patterns that block KaZaA and Gnutella. Several other patterns may also already exist in your `objects_5_0.C` file.

```
(firewall_properties:
:fields (

    . . .

        :http_header_detection (
              :http_detect_header_pattern_mode (true)
              :http_detect_header_pattern_log (alert)
```

```
:http_header_names (
        : (
                :match_string (X-kazaa)
                :regular_exp (X-Kazaa)
          )
    )
:http_header_names_values (
        : (
                :match_string (Server)
                :regular_exp ([kK]a[zZ]a[aA])
          )
        : (

                :match_string (Host)
                :regular_exp ([kK]azaa)
          )
        : (

                :match_string (User-Agent)
                :regular_exp ([gG]nu)
          )
        )
)
```

The properties used in these patterns are described below.

http_detect_header_pattern_mode: This property determines whether or not header detection is enabled. By default, it is `false`. To enable header detection, set this property to `true`.

http_detect_header_pattern_log: This one determines what kind of log to generate when one of the defined patterns is detected. Valid values are `none` (log nothing), `log` (generate a log entry), and `alert` (generate an alert).

http_header_names: This property specifies the header names to watch for. Each header you wish to filter has a stanza with two elements: `match_string` (simply for your reference, not actually used by FireWall-1) and `regular_exp` (to specify the regular expression that matches the desired header).

http_header_names_values: Similar to the previous one, but with this property you can look for a header that has a specific value, as specified in `match_string`. If this header is found, the specified `regular_exp` is compared against the header's value.

Once you have added these patterns, you need to use the HTTP Security Server to perform this filtering. This can be done with a simple matchall resource. For Gnutella specifically, you need to add GNUTELLA* to the match field of the resource and make sure the resource is used in a drop or reject rule.

9.9: Why Do I Have Problems Accessing Some Sites When the HTTP Security Server Is Enabled?

This happens because the HTTP Security Server requires tweaking to access many popular sites. Table 9.2 shows the various `firewall_properties` tweaks you can perform by using **dbedit** on the management server or by manually editing the `objects_5_0.C` file (see FAQ 4.2 for details).

Table 9.2   Recommended `firewall_properties` tweaks for the HTTP Security Server

Property	Setting	Description of Property
http_enable_uri_queries	true	If this is set to `false`, FireWall-1 will strip ASCII encoding of certain characters.
http_allow_content_ disposition	true	Content disposition is a way to let the Web browser know what it is about to receive. This could potentially allow people to download a type of file that the security policy may not allow them to download.
http_log_every_connection	true	This enables logging of all sites an authenticated user visits.
http_buffer_size	32768	This allows you to specify the buffer size used by the HTTP Security Server to process connections; 32768 is the maximum, and 4096 is the minimum.
http_sup_continue	true	This enables the HTTP Security Server to support the HTTP 1.1 CONTINUE command.
http_force_down_to_10	true	This forces the HTTP connection version down to 1.0. You need to do this when working with CVP servers.
http_avoid_keep_alive	true	This forces the HTTP Security Server to ignore the "keep-alive" directive in HTTP 1.1. You need to do this when working with CVP servers.
http_cvp_allow_chunked http_weeding_allow_chunked http_block_java_allow_ chunked http_allow_ranges	true	These properties allow the HTTP Security Server to handle requests that occur as byte ranges, often used in HTTP 1.1 requests. *(continued)*

Table 9.2   *continued*

Property	Setting	Description of Property
`http_use_host_h_as_dst`	true	After authentication with partially automatic Client Authentication, the user is normally redirected to the site's IP address instead of the name. With this property set to `true`, the user will instead be redirected to the host as shown in the HTTP host header (which reflects the host that is being accessed).
`http_disable_content_enc` `http_disable_content_type` `http_allow_ranges`	true	Web browsers like Mozilla and Web servers like Apache support "compressed" encoding types. The page and the elements are sent to the client compressed in order to save bandwidth. Enabling these properties allows those kinds of pages to be sent through the HTTP Security Server.
`http_max_url_length` `http_max_header_length`	n	Enabling these properties prevents FireWall-1 from truncating long URLs. n refers to the number of characters allowed in the URL (for the first property listed) and in HTTP headers (for the second).
`http_max_auth_redirected_ num`	n	This allows you to increase the number of partially automatic Client Authentication connections the firewall can process at one time.
`http_check_request_ validity` `http_check_response_ validity`	false	Disabling these checks allows Internet Explorer to browse URLs that contain characters not between ASCII 32 and ASCII 127. Normally, FireWall-1 would reject any URLs that contain these characters.

9.10: How Can I Permit Schemes Other Than FTP and HTTP through the HTTP Security Server?

Enable the following properties by modifying the appropriate `firewall_ properties` section in `objects_5_0.C`:

```
:http_allow_double_slash (true)
:http_use_default_schemes (true)
```

The first property enables the HTTP Security Server to accept double slashes (//) in a substring of a URL. In order to allow this, the Security Server defines a set of schemes that it will accept, which is what the second property covers.

The default set includes prospero, gopher, telnet, finger, mailto, http, news, nntp, wais, file, and ftp. You may also define new schemes to add to this set. This requires manual editing of `objects_5_0.C`. For example, to add the schemes fish and trouble to the permitted list, add the following code to the `firewall_properties` section of `objects_5_0.C`. (Note that the colons are needed.)

```
:scheme (
        : ("fish:")
        : ("trouble:")
)
```

9.11: How Can I Customize the Error Messages Given by the HTTP Security Server?

On the firewall module, edit the file `$FWDIR/conf/cspc/cspc.en_us`. This enables you to modify just about any message that any of the Security Servers generate. Some common messages to edit include:

- "FW-1 at host"
- "Failed to connect to the WWW server"
- "Unknown WWW server"

Each line in `$FWDIR/conf/cspc/cspc.en_us` is of the following format:

```
IDENTIFIER    size    string
```

`IDENTIFIER` is a unique string that identifies the message to FireWall-1. Do not change this. `size` is the maximum number of characters the message can be. Do not change this either. `string` is the actual string that FireWall-1 will display. It may contain some special words surrounded by # signs, such as `#host#` or `#html#`.

For the three examples listed above, the lines look like this:

```
CPSC_HTTP_FW_AT_HOST            1024      "FW-1 at #host#:"
CPSC_HTTP_CONN_FAIL_ERR         1024      "\n#local_host# Failed
to connect to the #.40server#."
CPSC_HTTP_UNKNOWN_SERVER_ERR 1024         "\n#local_host# Unknown
WWW server."
```

These lines could be changed so they read:

```
CPSC_HTTP_FW_AT_HOST            1024      "Message from firewall:"
CPSC_HTTP_CONN_FAIL_ERR         1024      "\n#local_host# Failed
to connect to the #.40server#. This may be a transient
problem, in which case simply reloading the page will work.
```

If this problem persists, it may be a problem with the
remote server."
CPSC_HTTP_UNKNOWN_SERVER_ERR 1024   "\n#local_host# Unknown
WWW server. This could mean you typed an incorrect URL or
there was a problem looking up the site in DNS. If the URL
is correct and the problem persists, contact your
administrator."

Performance Tuning the HTTP Security Server

One of the most common complaints about Content Security is performance. This is partially the result of the HTTP Security Server running in user space, versus the kernel space where much of FireWall-1 lives. Some of the performance issues can be overcome by tuning the platform on which the HTTP Security Server is running. However, there are some inherent limitations in the Security Servers in terms of the number of users who can go through a single system because Content Security overall requires significantly more resources than simply passing traffic. Personally, I would not use the HTTP Security Server for more than 1,000 users. Check Point has always claimed it is making strides in this area, and the company has increased performance in some circumstances by moving stuff to the kernel. However, I continually hear complaints from administrators who attempt to implement the HTTP Security Server in a large enterprise setting and end up doing something else.

In this subsection, I talk about what you need to do to improve performance of the Security Servers, which will increase the efficiency of the HTTP Security Servers. You should also apply the general performance-tuning suggestions in Appendix E.

Increasing the Number of Allowed Entries in `proxied_conns`

By default, the number of entries in `proxied_conns` (a table that stores connections via the Security Servers) is 25,000. For best performance, you should modify this number to twice the number of connections you actually expect to handle. In `$FWDIR/lib/table.def` on the management console, modify the following line:

```
proxied_conns = dynamic expires AUTH_TIMEOUT kbuf 4;
```

To modify the line to support 50,000 connections, for example, make it read:

```
proxied_conns = dynamic limit 50000 expires AUTH_TIMEOUT kbuf 4;
```

Increasing the HTTP Buffer Size

The default size is 4,096 bytes. It can be increased to a maximum of 32,768. A larger buffer size means fewer system calls; however, each connection will take up that much more memory, so there is a trade-off. See Table 9.2 in FAQ 9.9 for the property that sets the buffer size.

Increasing the Number of Security Server Instances

It's usually necessary to increase the number of Security Server instances for the HTTP Security Server, but you can do it for any Security Server. If you have multiple processors on your firewall, increasing the number of instances allows you to take advantage of these processors. You can use this trick if you are using a single processor system, too.

To increase the number of instances for any Security Server, you need to modify its line in the `$FWDIR/conf/fwauthd.conf` file, which has the following format:

```
<listen-port><binary><daemon-name>wait -<instances>
```

For example, if you want to run four instances of `in.ahttpd`, which will all listen on port 80, the corresponding line should look like this:

```
80     fwssd     in.ahttpd    wait    -4
```

Connections from the same HTTP client will always be directed to the same daemon within the authenticated session timeout. Connections begin to use alternate daemons only after the previous daemon fills up. All connections from a client will always be handled by the same daemon.

UFP Caching

When an HTTP request is made, the IP address of the destination is checked against the cache. If the IP address is in the cache, the category associated with that IP address is used. If it is not in the cache, the HTTP Security Server sends the request to the UFP server, which returns the appropriate category information and is then cached. Caching can be controlled by FireWall-1 or by the UFP server. Check Point recommends the latter method, which is thought to be more accurate.

If FireWall-1 controls the caching, FireWall-1 uses two methods to update the cache.

- *One-request method:* FireWall-1 takes the information returned by the UFP server and writes it to the cache.
- *Two-request method:* FireWall-1 makes a second request to the UFP server to determine whether the IP address of the site could match multiple categories. Only if the entire site uses the same category is the data written to the cache.

The one-request method is more aggressive in caching at the expense of cache integrity. The two-request method is slower, but the cache integrity is significantly improved.

Where the UFP server controls the caching, information necessary to update the cache is returned with each request looked up.

To enable UFP caching, create a URI resource, or edit an existing one. Go to the Match tab and enable the caching accordingly. Use the new URI resource in a rule.

Kernel URL Logging

Kernel URL logging allows you to log URLs without having to divert the connection to the HTTP Security Server. This improves overall performance in these situations. Kernel URL logging is enabled in a resource on the General tab by selecting Optimize URL logging (see Figure 9.1 earlier in this chapter). This resource cannot also be used for Content Security or URL filtering.

Adding More Memory, Physical and Virtual

The HTTP Security Server requires lots of memory, especially when it is busy. I have personally witnessed a busy `in.ahttpd` process on a Nokia platform handling just 1,024 concurrent connections require as much as 87MB of memory! Memory usage for `in.ahttpd` has proven to be similar on other platforms. The more physical memory you have, the better. Also, your swap size should be fixed (preferably on a dedicated device) and should be twice the size of the amount of physical memory you have.

 NOTE! On a Nokia platform that was running a version of IPSO prior to 3.4 and then upgraded, the system will have a swap partition size of only 256MB. For systems newly installed with IPSO 3.4 and later, the swap partition was increased to the lesser of a quarter of the overall available disk space or 1GB. A fresh reinstallation of IPSO from boot manager or boot floppy is required to obtain this larger swap size.

Adjusting File Descriptors Globally and Per Process

On a UNIX platform, there is a limit to the number of file descriptors available both to a specific process and globally. When started, `in.ahttpd` attempts to reserve the maximum number of file descriptors allowed by the operating system. On Solaris, this is 1,024. On IPSO, this is 2,048. Windows NT does not have this issue.

An HTTP connection going through the Security Server requires two sockets: one for the connection from the client and one for the client to the server.

Each socket requires a file descriptor. A limit of 2,048 file descriptors means that fewer than 1,024 concurrent active connections can go through each instance of the in.ahttpd daemon. Other things like logging require file descriptors as well. When the maximum number of file descriptors has been reached, a "Too many open files" error is entered in $FWDIR/log/ahttpd.elg.

Allowing each in.ahttpd daemon to handle more than 1,024 concurrent connections is *not* recommended. Another factor to consider is the amount of memory that each process requires. Recall that earlier I stated that an instance of in.ahttpd handling 1,024 connections took 87MB of memory. Limiting the file descriptors to 1,024 (thus 512 connections per process) reduces the memory utilization to 47MB. The more concurrent connections each process can handle, the larger the process will get. In some cases, it might actually be better to decrease the number of file descriptors and increase the number of processes running.

On IPSO, the number of file descriptors allowed is limited by two kernel variables: kern:maxfiles (global limit) and kern:maxfilesperproc (per-process limit). The limits are 8,096 and 2,048, respectively. To modify these values, use the **ipsctl** command:

```
# ipsctl -w kern:maxfiles 4X
# ipsctl -w kern:maxfilesperproc X
```

X is the number you want to modify these values to; 4X means four times the value you choose for X. Because these values are set to their defaults at boot time, you need to add these commands to /var/etc/rc.local so they are changed at each startup.

On Solaris, add the following line to /etc/system and reboot:

```
set rlim_fd_max = X
```

On Linux, you need to do two things. In /etc/security/limits.conf, add the following lines:

```
* soft nofile 1024
* hard nofile X
```

These lines allow users to set their own file descriptor limits on login. You also need to change the system-wide limits by executing the following commands. (Add these to a startup script to be done on each reboot.)

```
# echo X >/proc/sys/fs/file-max
# echo 3X >/proc/sys/fs/inode-max
```

Troubleshooting Issues with the HTTP Security Server

Many of the following issues also apply to authentication because Security Servers are used for authentication. In this subsection, I talk about how to resolve common problems with the HTTP Security Server. A separate section on gathering debug information from Security Servers (Debugging the Security Servers) appears later in this chapter.

9.12: The HTTP Security Server Won't Work

A Security Server cannot share the same port as another application. For example, if you are using the HTTP Security Server bound to a specific port (say, port 80) and you have something else bound to that port (such as Voyager on a Nokia platform), one of the services must be moved.

9.13: My Users See the Error Message "FW-1 at Kyle: Unknown WWW Server"

This message could mean a few different things.

- The URL typed was incorrect.
- The firewall is not configured to use DNS for name resolution. The HTTP Security Server requires that the firewall be configured to use DNS.
- FireWall-1 timed out when it attempted to look up the name for the site.
- Your DNS server is configured to cache negative responses to DNS requests so that the same request is not made again. The client may also be running a name service–caching daemon that does something similar. You may want to consider disabling these features or setting the timeouts sufficiently high so that proper time is given to resolve the DNS queries.

If desired, you can change the error message text as described in FAQ 9.11.

9.14: My Users See the Error Message "Failed to Connect to WWW Server"

There are two possible reasons for this message.

- Connection to the site timed out or was refused at the remote end. In this case, you can usually do a refresh and the page will load correctly.
- The remote site either has a missing or inconsistent reverse DNS entry for its IP address.

Check Point considers the latter a security risk and does not allow these sites to be contacted through the HTTP Security Server. Check Point also does not allow you to turn off this feature. You have the following workaround options.

- Contact the administrators of the remote site in question to ask them to fix the site's reverse DNS entry.
- Add an entry in your firewall's local host file, and have the system resolve against the host file first.
- Exclude the site in question from going through the Security Server by adding a rule above your Security Server rule that permits normal HTTP to the site.

If desired, you can change the error message text as described in FAQ 9.11.

9.15: I Have Problems When I Try to Use Internet Explorer (or Other Browsers That Support HTTP 1.1) through FireWall-1

To solve this issue, enable the following properties as described in FAQ 9.9 (Table 9.2).

```
:http_cvp_allow_chunked (true)
:http_weeding_allow_chunked (true)
:http_block_java_allow_chunked (true)
:http_allow_ranges (true)
:http_force_down_to_10 (true)
:http_sup_continue (true)
:http_avoid_keep_alive (true)
```

9.16: I Can't Access Certain Web Sites through the HTTP Security Server

Various sites have issues when they are accessed via the HTTP Security Server. If you've enabled the properties suggested previously and are still having problems, do not use the HTTP Security Server for these sites. Place a rule that permits access to these sites above any rule that uses the HTTP Security Server.

9.17: The Memory Usage of `in.ahttpd` Keeps Growing

In just about every version of the HTTP Security Server that I've seen, heavy use of the HTTP Security Server seems to cause the process to grow without bounds until the system crashes. This and performance issues are the reasons I hesitate to recommend that large sites use the HTTP Security Server. You may have to write a script to monitor `in.ahttpd`'s memory usage and kill this process when it grows beyond a certain limit (25MB is the limit several of my customers have used).

The FTP Security Server

The FTP Security Server is used to restrict people from uploading or downloading files as well as to virus scan all FTP file transfers. The FTP Security Server is enabled when the following situations are true.

- There is a line that permits `in.aftpd` to start up in `$FWDIR/conf/fwauthd.conf`. This line is usually present by default.
- A valid resource is defined in your security policy or in a User Authentication rule involving FTP.

The proper line for the FTP Security Server in `$FWDIR/conf/fwauthd.conf` looks like this (with no comment character, `#`, at the beginning of the line):

```
21     fwssd          in.aftpd       wait    0
```

If this line is not present or is commented out, the FTP Security Server will not run, and any process that relies on it will fail.

To filter FTP, you need to create a resource of type FTP and use it in the rulebase. Let's create a resource called ftp_downloads to allow FTP downloads through the HTTP Security Server. From SmartDashboard/Policy Editor, select Manage and then Resources. Next select New, and choose URI. You may also click on the ⚲ icon in the objects tree, right-click on FTP, and select New FTP. Then create a new resource of type FTP, as shown in Figure 9.18.

The General tab is fairly self-explanatory, so let's move on and look at the Match tab, shown in Figure 9.19.

Path refers to a specific location on the FTP server. For instance, you could allow some people to upload to a specific directory but deny that directory to others. An example of this is shown in the Sample Configurations section later in this chapter.

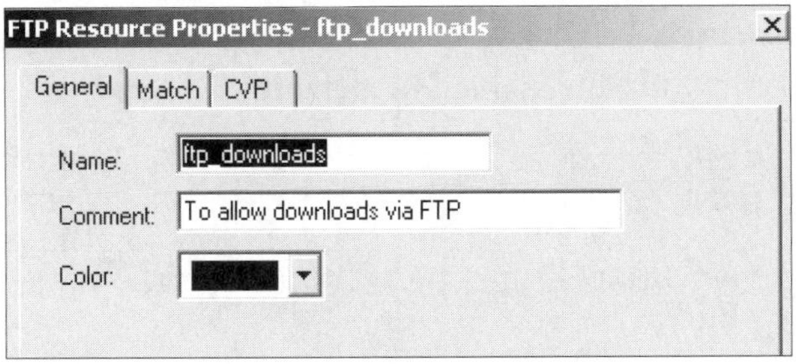

Figure 9.18 FTP Resource Properties, General tab

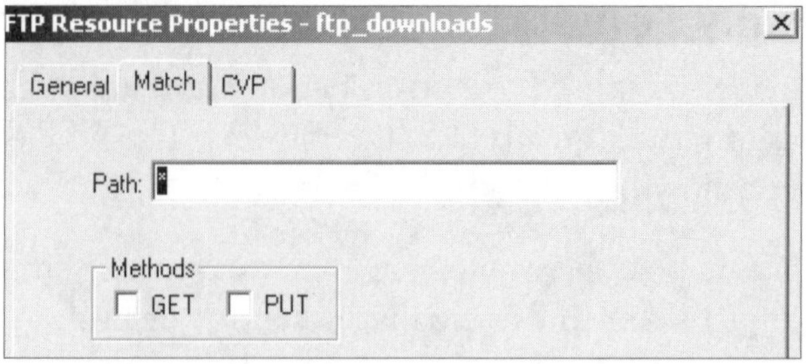

Figure 9.19 FTP Resource Properties, Match tab

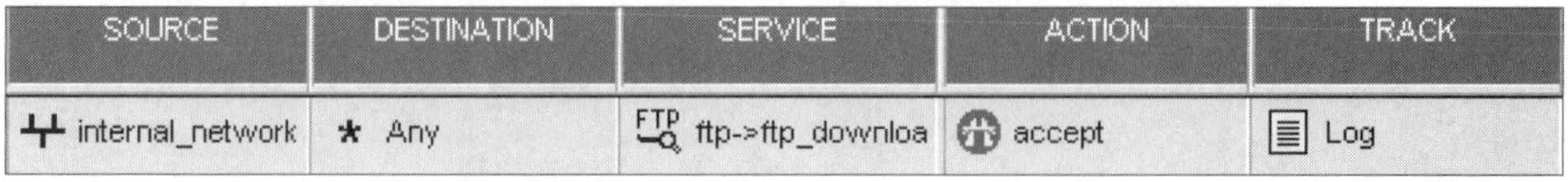

Figure 9.20 Sample FTP rule with CVP

You can match two types of methods: GET and PUT. Aside from matching the GET command, allowing GET commands also allows RETR, RNFR, and XMD5 commands. Aside from matching the PUT command, allowing PUT commands also allows STOR, STOU, APPE, RNFR, RNTO, DELE, MKD, and RMD commands. Most other commands are passed to the FTP server for execution.[1]

The CVP tab is where you specify the CVP server to use, if any. This is similar to what was shown earlier in Figure 9.5 except that the CVP tab under FTP Resource Properties excludes the HTTP-specific options.

After setting these properties, you can add a rule with this resource to the rulebase, as shown in Figure 9.20.

Frequently Asked Questions about the FTP Security Server

9.18: Why Won't the FTP Security Server Let Me Use Certain FTP Commands?

The following commands are enabled by default:

```
USER PASS ACCT REIN BYE QUIT BYTE SOCK PASV TYPE STRU MODE PORT
RETR STOR STOU APPE ALLO REST RNFR RNTO ABOR DELE LIST NLST SITE
MLFL MAIL MSND MSOM MSAM MRSQ MRCP CWD PWD RMD MKD HELP NOOP CDUP
SYST XMKD XCWD XRMD XPWD XCUP XMD5 FIND MDTM SIZE MACB FW1C
```

---

1. For details on these and other FTP commands, see RFC959, which you can obtain from http://www.rfc-editor.org, among other places.

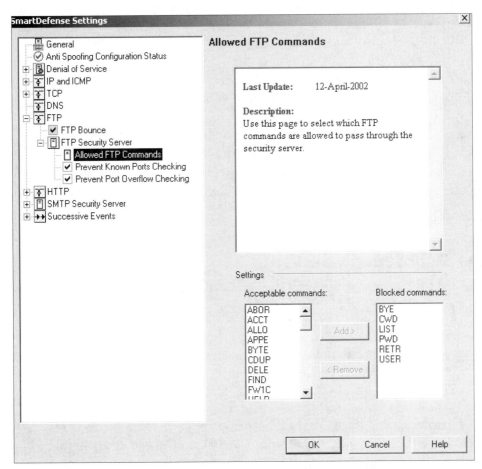

Figure 9.21   SmartDefense Settings, Allowed FTP Commands frame

The list of allowed commands is stored in the property `ftp_allowed_cmds`, which can be edited with **dbedit** or by manually editing `$FWDIR/conf/objects_5_0.C` on the management console. (See FAQ 4.2 for guidelines on how to edit `objects_5_0.C`.) You can also edit this property in SmartDefense, available in FireWall-1 NG FP2 with SmartDefense supplement or NG FP3 and later. Figure 9.21 shows how to do this.

9.19: Why Do I Always Have Problems with Certain Sites When Using the FTP Security Server?

When the user issues a **get**, **put**, **delete**, **mkdir**, or **rename**, the FTP Security Server issues a PWD command in order to get the full path. The FTP server must respond to the PWD command with a 257 message, which, according to RFC 959, must contain the absolute path in quotes. If the PWD command is disabled on the remote server or the PWD does not respond in the correct manner, the FTP Security Server will deny the request. See the previous question for how to allow PWD replies without quotes.

9.20: Why Do I Have a Problem FTPing to Any Site with the FTP Security Server?

If name service caching is occurring, particularly if the name server is caching negative responses to DNS requests, the FTP Security Server will have a problem. This may occur on the DNS server itself or on the firewall (e.g., nscd). The problem with the specific site should resolve once the cached entry expires or you disable name service caching.

The SMTP Security Server

The SMTP Security Server is used to prevent certain types of mail from passing your gateway. The SMTP Security Server is enabled when the following situations are true.

- There is a line that permits in.asmtpd to start up in $FWDIR/conf/ fwauthd.conf. This line is present by default.
- A valid resource is defined and used in your security policy.

The proper line for the SMTP Security Server in $FWDIR/conf/fwauthd. conf looks like this (with no comment character, #, at the beginning of the line):

```
25      fwssd     in.asmtpd      wait    0
```

If this line is not present or is commented out, the SMTP Security Server will not run, and any process that relies on it will fail.

The SMTP Security Server acts a bit differently than the other Security Servers. There are actually two separate processes involved: in.asmtpd and mdq. in.asmtpd intercepts SMTP connections and spools the messages to disk. That is all they do. The mdq process periodically scans the spool directory and delivers the messages to their final destinations, performing the necessary filtering, header rewriting, and content rewriting. This is more secure than attempting to do everything in one process. Figure 9.22 shows a diagram of this.

SMTP Security Server Parameters

Aside from using resources, the SMTP Security Server has parameters that are configured in $FWDIR/conf/objects_5_0.C. Descriptions of these parame-

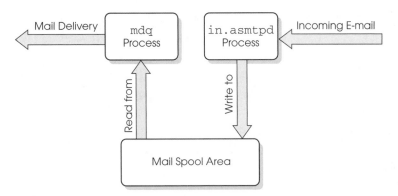

Figure 9.22   How in.asmtpd and mdq interact

ters and their default settings follow, using their names as shown in objects_
5_0.c. A few of these parameters can be modified via the gateway object definition in the SMTP frame (under the Advanced frame; see Figure 9.23).

The items you can modify in objects_5_0.C include those listed below.

timeout: This is the amount of time (in seconds) FireWall-1 will spend on
CVP scanning a message and delivering it to the Mail Transfer Agent
(MTA). It is recommended that this value be at least 90 seconds (the default
setting), if not longer. If you change this parameter, it is recommended that
you reboot in order for it to take effect. (Corresponds to "Connection timeout" in Figure 9.23.)

scan_period: This is the amount of time (in seconds) that mdq will check
the spool directory for e-mail to be delivered. By default, mdq checks for mail
every 2 seconds. Mail found during this scan is delivered. mdq will take a
number of e-mails based on the max_conns and max_conns_per_site
parameters. Once max_load is reached, mdq stops taking mail messages from
the spool directory. (Corresponds to "Dequeuer scan period" in Figure 9.23.)

resend_period: This is the amount of time (in seconds) that a message
that previously failed to be delivered will be resent from the SMTP Security
Server. The default is 600 seconds (10 minutes). (Corresponds to "Mail
resend period" in Figure 9.23.)

abandon_time: This is the amount of time (in seconds) that a message is
allowed to live in the spool directory before FireWall-1 returns the message
to the sender. The default is 432,000 seconds (5 days). The error server
defined in the specific resource matched by the rule the message was
accepted under is used to deliver the message. (Corresponds to "Mail abandon time" in Figure 9.23.)

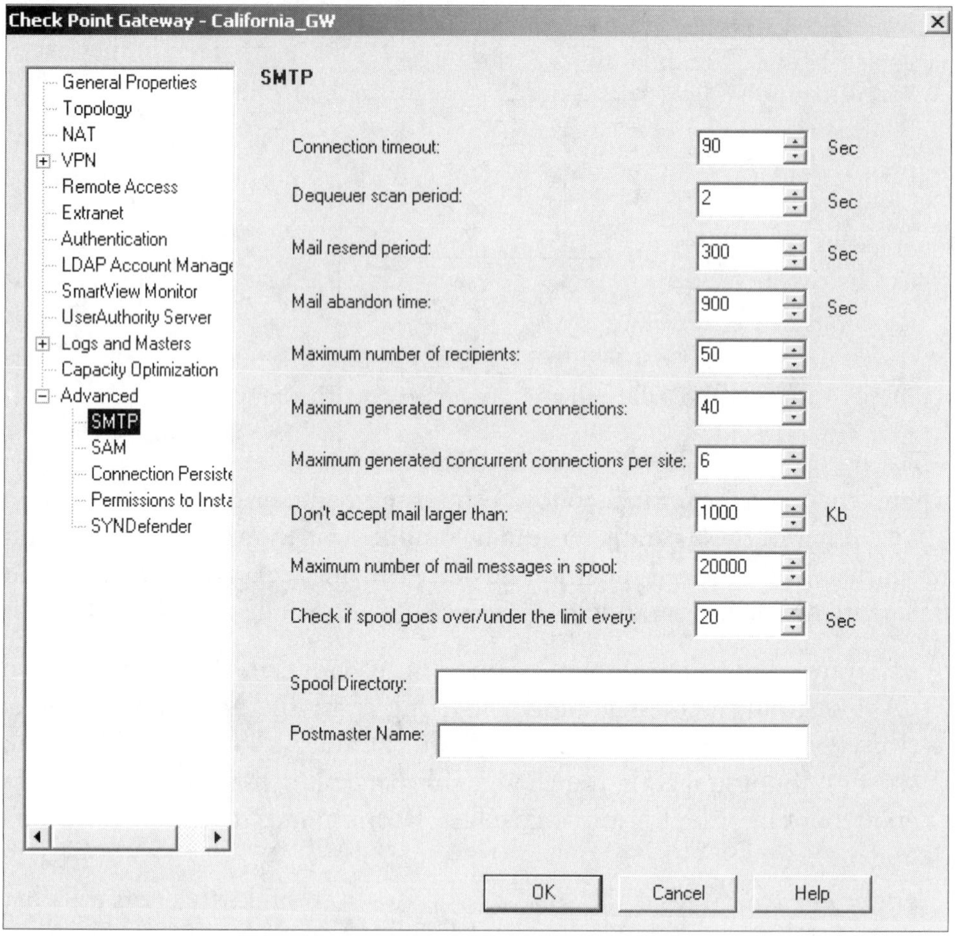

Figure 9.23 Gateway Objects, SMTP frame

rundir: This is the location where FireWall-1 spools incoming e-mail. The default is $FWDIR/spool. If you expect to process lots of e-mail, make sure this is on a partition with lots of disk space. Specify a path to the new spool directory (this must exist). (Corresponds to "Spool Directory" in Figure 9.23.)

spool_limit: This allows you to specify the maximum number of messages allowed in the spool directory. Incoming messages that exceed this limit will be rejected. (Corresponds to "Maximum number of mail messages in spool" in Figure 9.23.)

spool_limit_scan_period: This specifies how frequently to check to see that the spool_limit has been reached. (Corresponds to "Check if spool goes over/under the limit every" in Figure 9.23.)

detailed_smtp_err_mail: If this parameter is set to a value other than 0 (the default), an error mail will be generated when the SMTP Security Server cannot deliver the e-mail to some of the recipients. The error mail includes information regarding which users could not receive the original mail and a reason for each recipient. This mail message is sent only when the "Notify sender on error" flag (see the SMTP Resources subsection) is enabled in the resource that matches the incoming message. (As of NG FP3, can be tweaked only via **dbedit**.)

detailed_av_err_mail: When this parameter is set to a value other than 0 (the default) and a mail fails a Content Security check, the generated error mail will include a notification of the failure as well as the explanation message received from the Content Security Server. Note that in case of a malicious attempt to insert a virus into an organization, it may be preferable not to use this flag because it allows the generator of the mail containing the virus to receive feedback on the malicious attempt. This error mail is sent only when the "Notify sender on error" flag is enabled in the resource that matches the incoming message. (As of NG FP3, can be tweaked only via **dbedit**.)

detailed_rb_err_mail: When this parameter is set to a value other than 0 (the default) and mail message would not be allowed by the rulebase, the sender is notified. (As of NG FP3, can be tweaked only via **dbedit**.)

max_conns: This is the maximum number of connections that the SMTP Security Server will generate to SMTP servers to deliver e-mail. (Corresponds to "Maximum generated concurrent connections" in Figure 9.23.)

max_conns_per_site: This is the maximum number of connections that the SMTP Security Server will generate to a single SMTP server to deliver e-mail. (Corresponds to "Maximum generated concurrent connections per site" in Figure 9.23.)

max_mail_size: This is the maximum number of kilobytes that the SMTP Security Server will allow a message to be. (Corresponds to "Don't accept mail larger than" in Figure 9.23.)

max_mails_per_conn: This is the maximum number of e-mails the SMTP Security Server will attempt to send on a single connection to a remote SMTP server. (As of NG FP3, can be tweaked only via **dbedit**.)

max_mx_node_per_mail: A domain can have multiple MX records associated with it. This property tells the SMTP Security Server how many MX records to attempt to use to deliver a message. (As of NG FP3, can be tweaked only via **dbedit**.)

max_ips_per_mx_node: An MX record for a domain may have more than one IP associated with it. For each MX record processed by the SMTP Security Server, this is the maximum number of IP addresses it will attempt to use per MX record. (As of NG FP3, can be tweaked only via **dbedit**.)

maxrecipients: This is the maximum number of recipients an e-mail message can contain. The SMTP Security Server will reject messages that contain more recipients than specified in this parameter. (Corresponds to "Maximum number of recipients" in Figure 9.23.)

postmaster: This specifies the e-mail address of the postmaster. This e-mail address is sent copes of any messages returned for nondelivery. (Corresponds to "Postmaster Name" in Figure 9.23.)

 WARNING! In FireWall-1 4.1, these parameters were changed by editing `$FWDIR/conf/smtp.conf` on the firewall module. On an NG module, this file will be overwritten on a policy installation. It is not recommended that you edit `smtp.conf` any longer.

To modify any of these parameters, you can either edit `$FWDIR/conf/objects_5_0.C` manually on the management console, use **dbedit**, or use **Database Tool**. To edit the properties in **dbedit**, use the following commands:

```
dbedit> modify network_objects craig
             firewall_settings:smtp:detailed_smtp_err_email
             true
dbedit> update network_objects craig
```

In the preceding example, craig is the relevant firewall object, `detailed_smtp_err_mail` is the property, and `true` is the value it was set to.

SMTP Resources

To filter SMTP, you need to create a resource of type SMTP. From SmartDashboard/Policy Editor, select Manage and choose Resources. Next select New, and then choose SMTP. You may also click on the ⌕ icon in the objects tree, right-click on SMTP, and select New SMTP. You are presented with the window shown in Figure 9.24.

The options on this tab are described below.

Name: Enter the name of the SMTP resource object (must be unique).

Comment: In this field, you can describe the resource in more detail.

Color: Select whichever color you like.

Mail Delivery Server: If the server in this field is specified and this resource is matched, the e-mail will be forwarded to this server. If nothing is specified,

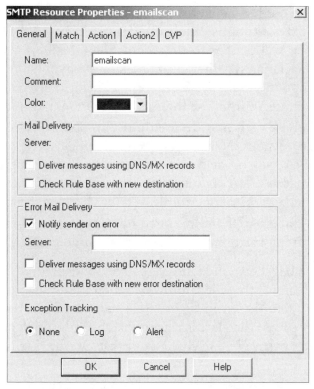

Figure 9.24 SMTP Resource Properties, General tab

the e-mail will be forwarded to the server the message was originally being sent to. To specify multiple mail servers to attempt, use the form {mailserver1, mailserver2,...}.

Error Mail Delivery Server: If the SMTP Security Server is not able to deliver the message within the abandon time and "Notify sender on error" is selected, the message will be sent through this e-mail server. If nothing is specified, the e-mail will be forwarded to the server the message was originally being sent to. To specify multiple mail servers to attempt, use the form {mailserver1,mailserver2,...}.

Notify sender on error: This setting indicates whether or not to notify the originator of the message when a delivery problem occurs. If this option is enabled, "bounce" messages will be generated if an e-mail is not successfully delivered. The level of detail of these error reports depends on `objects_5_0.C` modifications discussed in the previous subsection.

Deliver messages using DNS/MX records: This option exists for both the Mail Delivery Server and the Error Mail Delivery Server. If this option is enabled under the Mail Delivery section, Check Point will attempt to look up the MX record for the destination address and deliver to the IP(s) specified there. If this option is enabled under the Error Mail Delivery section, error messages will be sent to the originating e-mail via the domain's MX record. The operating system of the firewall must be configured with DNS enabled. This option should be used for e-mail being delivered to the Internet. For e-mail coming in from the Internet, this option may not be necessary.

Check Rule Base with new destination: This option is also available under both Delivery sections. Normally, any e-mail initially accepted by the SMTP Security Server will be delivered by the firewall without being matched against the rulebase. You can force this delivery connection to go through the rulebase for either normal or error delivery by checking the appropriate box.

Exception Tracking: If the resource finds anomalous behavior, you can either log that information, generate an alert, or do nothing.

The Match tab is shown in Figure 9.25. The Sender and Recipient fields can be matched with any of the wildcards listed earlier in the chapter.

The Action1 tab, shown in Figure 9.26, allows you to rewrite the e-mail headers. The left part of each line is what is matched (the original); the right part is its replacement (what you are changing it to). On the original side, you can

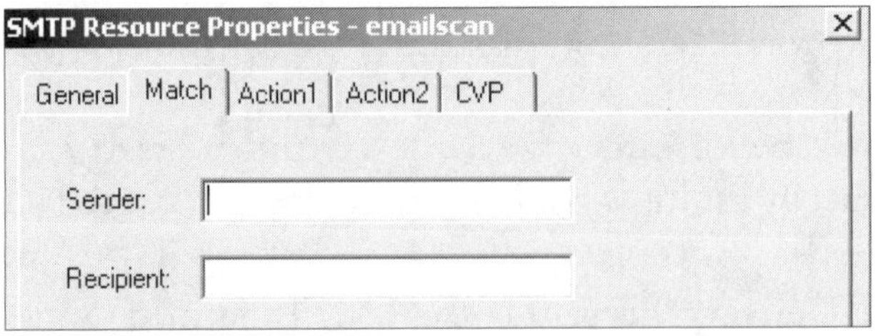

Figure 9.25   SMTP Resource Properties, Match tab

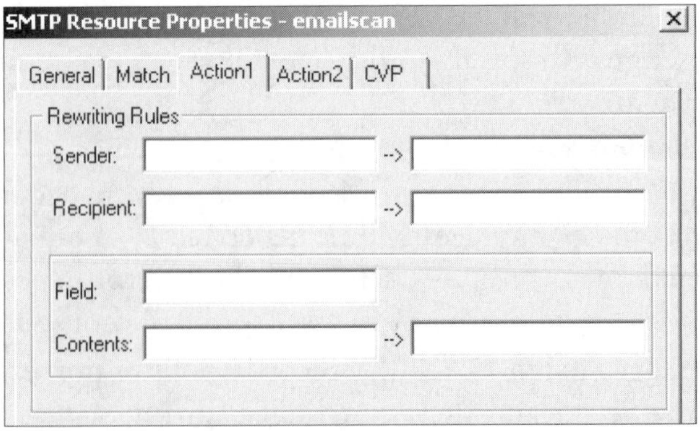

Figure 9.26   SMTP Resource Properties, Action1 tab

use normal wildcards. If you want to make what you matched part of what you translate it to, use the & wildcard to signify that. For example, if you want to rewrite all addresses of the form user@smtp.weirdal.com to user@weirdal.com, on the left side you would specify *@smtp.weirdal.com, and on the right, you would specify &@weirdal.com.

You can do this for a custom field as well. If you want to eliminate a field (say, the Received: lines), on the left enter *, and leave the right side blank.

Figure 9.27 shows the Action2 tab. If you do not want to allow certain MIME types or files with certain extensions, you can specify them on the Action2 tab. You can specify multiple MIME types or files using the normal wildcards (see Table 9.1 earlier in the chapter). Filtering on MIME types or file extensions is an inexact science at best because the e-mail client can use any MIME type it wants, and different e-mail clients use different MIME types for the same type of document. For instance, application/msword can be used for Microsoft Word documents. UNIX machines often send these kinds of docu-ments as application/octet-stream, which can also be used for applications or

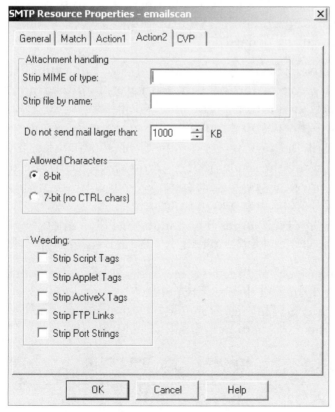

Figure 9.27   SMTP Resource Properties, Action2 tab

any binary file. On the Action 2 tab you can also restrict message size and strip out undesirable HTML tags from e-mails.

Some examples of how to use the SMTP Security Server are described in the next subsection.

Frequently Asked Questions about the SMTP Security Server

The following FAQs are provided for events that may occur with the SMTP Security Server.

9.21: When I Use the SMTP Security Server, to What Should the MX for My Domain Point?

Your MX records should point to your normal SMTP server. Provided your rules are set up correctly, FireWall-1 will intercept this traffic automatically. You do not have to change anything with respect to your MX records for your domain.

9.22: Can I Have the Firewall Be the MX for My Domain?

Usually, the SMTP Security Server intercepts communications destined for an internal SMTP server. In some cases you may want to have the firewall be the mail exchanger. You can do this with the proper SMTP resource, making sure the following fields are defined.

- **Mail Delivery Server** (on the General tab): Enter the IP address of your inbound server in this field. If you have more than one SMTP server, enter each in the format {ip-address-1,ip-address-2,...}. If your DNS is correctly defined, you can use the DNS/MX records option instead.
- **Error Mail Delivery Server** (on the General tab): Select this option if you want to notify the sender that his or her message has been rejected or in case of some other problem. If your DNS is correctly defined, you can use the DNS/MX records option instead.
- **Don't accept mail larger than** (on the SMTP frame): This option should be set appropriately. The default is 1,000KB (or roughly 1MB).

Once you have defined the resource, add a rule similar to the one shown in Figure 9.28, and reinstall the security policy.

Note that your SMTP Server should be responsible for delivering outbound messages. See the next question for more details.

SOURCE	DESTINATION	SERVICE	ACTION	TRACK
✳ Any	🖪 firewall	⬛ SMTP smtp->store_and_forward	🌐 accept	🗐 Log

Figure 9.28 SMTP Security Server rule

SOURCE	DESTINATION	SERVICE	ACTION	TRACK
✱ Any	🖥 smart-smtp-server	TCP smtp	🌐 accept	📄 Log
🖥 smart-smtp-server	🖥 Internal_Mail_Server	SMTP smtp->smtp_inbound_from_dmz	🌐 accept	📄 Log
🖥 smart-smtp-server	✱ Any	TCP smtp	🌐 accept	📄 Log
🖥 internal-smtp-server	✱ Any	SMTP smtp->smtp_outbound	🌐 accept	📄 Log

Figure 9.29   Rules for a "smart" SMTP server

9.23: Why Won't the SMTP Security Server Use the MX Records?

You might think this FAQ was meant for the previous version of my book, where I covered FireWall-1 4.1 and earlier. It's true that the SMTP Security Server did not use MX records and thus was unsuitable for use in delivering outbound e-mail. Sadly, even if the MX record option is enabled, it may not work correctly for all domains. Check Point released hotfixes for this issue in NG FP2 and possibly other releases.

A workaround, and what I consider to be "best practice," is to use a "smart" SMTP server—that is, a conventional SMTP server that knows how to properly handle MX records. This SMTP server should probably be in your DMZ. You have to make sure that any SMTP traffic from this host destined to the Internet does not get processed by any SMTP resources. To ensure that this does not happen and to have the most secure setup, use the rules shown in Figure 9.29.

The first rule matches all SMTP traffic from the Internet to the smart SMTP server (which is the MX for your domain). The second rule forces all SMTP traffic from the smart SMTP server to the internal network through the SMTP Security Server using the smtp_inbound_from_dmz resource. This resource should have the mail server configured to point to the internal SMTP server(s) and perform any necessary checking. The third rule allows the smart SMTP server to communicate to any SMTP server without going through the SMTP Security Server. The fourth rule forces your internal SMTP server to communicate through the SMTP Security Server. This last rule is optional, but you should use it if you want to perform virus scanning on any outbound e-mail.

9.24: Can I Use the SMTP Security Server to Help Fight Incoming Spam?

Spam is a notoriously difficult nuisance to filter properly. Many individuals and companies have written various programs to attempt to filter spam. Although not specifically designed to handle this task, FireWall-1 does have some features that can be used to help, namely, the SMTP Security Server.

Your inbound SMTP server is likely to be a better tool to stop spam. Most SMTP servers (with the notable exception of Microsoft Exchange 5.0 and earlier) have the capability to turn off unauthorized relaying and/or implement some checks to prevent unauthorized use. You can even subscribe to the Mail Abuse Prevention System (MAPS) or a similar system that maintains a blacklist of known bad sites.

If you are going to use the SMTP Security Server to filter spam, your SMTP resources should have the recipient and the sender defined. The recipient should be *@yourdomain.com. If you have multiple domains, it should read *@{yourdomain.com,yourotherdomain.com,...}. The send should be configured with a * to match all incoming mail.

9.25: Can the SMTP Security Server Accept E-mails of Any Size?

You should be able to type a number into the appropriate field. Keep in mind that you need to have sufficient disk space on your firewalls to accept these e-mails.

Personally, if a user wants to e-mail a large file, I feel he or she should use FTP or something similar. All e-mailed files are encoded in a 6-bit format for transmission over SMTP, which expands the file size by at least 33%.

9.26: When Does CVP Get Performed on E-mails in the SMTP Security Server?

This action is actually done as the SMTP message is being delivered to the remote SMTP server. This means the timeout value specified in the SMTP configuration on the gateway object is long enough for both tasks to occur.

Troubleshooting the SMTP Security Server

The following solutions are provided for problems that occur with the SMTP Security Server.

9.27: I See the Message "Connection to Final MTA Failed" in the SmartView Tracker/Log Viewer

This message shows up when the SMTP Security Server is unable to connect to the remote MTA (i.e., the SMTP server) to deliver that message. This may simply be a transient problem, or the remote SMTP server may simply no longer exist. The next subsection shows you how to resolve that problem.

9.28: Mail Appears to Get Stuck in the SMTP Security Server Spool Directory

Make sure your rules are ordered in such a way as to not use the SMTP Security Server when not necessary. The following subsections contain some other events that will cause messages to back up.

Maximum Concurrent Sent Mails Limit Reached

You might see the following message in the `mdq.elg` file. It means that the number of recipients specified in the mail header has exceeded the limit.

```
[195@firewall] max concurrent sent mails limit reached -
 spool scanning stops
```

The number of messages that can be sent at one time is specified with the `max_conns` and `max_conns_per_site` parameters, described in the SMTP Security Server Parameters subsection earlier in this chapter.

Messages Continue to Fail on Delivery Attempts

If sending an e-mail continues to fail (or takes a long time), the whole spool will be held up until the troubled e-mail times out. Decreasing the `abandon_time` parameter from its default of 432,000 seconds (5 days) to 3,600 seconds (1 hour) clears out the spool more quickly, returning error messages to the sender stating that the e-mail could not be delivered. (See the SMTP Security Server Parameters subsection earlier in the chapter.)

Forcing the Queue to Empty Out

You can force a queue run by using the command **fw mdq**. However, the only way to fix this (short of letting FireWall-1 attempt to deliver these messages until they expire) is to edit each individual file in `$FWDIR/spool` (or whatever `rundir` is set to), so that the destination it tries to contact is an SMTP server that will deliver the message. There are actually three directories under `$FWDIR/spool`, which contain the individual files.

- `D_resend`: This directory contains all the messages that the SMTP Security Server had problems delivering in the initial attempt. The SMTP Security Server attempts to resend messages from this directory until the message has been around longer than the `abandon_time`. Files in this directory are of the form `Rxxxxxxxx` (for messages not yet expired) or `Exxxxxxxx` (for messages that have expired).
- `D_state`: This directory contains all the messages currently being received by the SMTP Security Server, that is, partial e-mails. Once the messages are received fully, they are copied into the `D_sender` directory.

- `D_sender`: This directory contains messages that the SMTP Security Server has fully received and is about to send for the first time. If a message is not successfully sent, it is copied over to the `D_resend` directory.

In all cases, the beginning of a spool file looks like this:

```
AV_SETTING:        none
AV_IPADDR:         0.0.0.0
AV_PORT:           0
AV_HEADERS:        0
COMPOUND:          0
SRC:     192.168.230.24
SPORT:   3446
DST:     10.158.5.2
DPORT:   25
ERR_SERVER:        10.158.5.2
RULE:    11
RULEACT:           16
ERRMAIL:           0
ACCT:    0
LOG_OK:            MDQ_LOG
LOG_BAD:           MDQ_LOG
LOG_ERR:           MDQ_ALERT
```

The headers are described as follows.

AV_SETTING (none|check|cure): A header that indicates whether or not this message will be checked for viruses. none means do not scan, check means do not send if it contains a known virus, and cure means clean out any known viruses in the message before sending.

AV_IPADDR (a.b.c.d): The IP address of the antivirus scanner. This should list 0.0.0.0 if no virus checking is to be done.

AV_PORT (n): The port used for CVP, normally 18181 or 0.

AV_HEADERS (0|1): A header that indicates whether or not the CVP server is to be sent the SMTP headers. If so, then this is set to 1, otherwise 0.

COMPOUND (?): Unknown, but usually set to 0.

SRC (a.b.c.d): The source IP address of the machine that sent the e-mail.

SPORT (n): The source port used for the connection to the SMTP Security Server from the source IP address listed.

DST (a.b.c.d): The destination IP address of the machine to send the e-mail to. This is the IP address of the mail server that the source IP was originally trying to send to unless the matching resource or the default_ server parameter is set to some other value, in which case, this value reflects that instead. This is the IP address that FireWall-1 will use to deliver this message.

DPORT (n) : The destination port that will be used to send the mail to. Normally this is 25.

ERR_SERVER (a.b.c.d) : The SMTP server that will be used to attempt to deliver the failure notice if a message has been in $FWDIR/spool beyond the abandon_time. If no error_server is defined in the appropriate resource, this will be the same as the SRC setting.

RULE (n) : The rule number by which this message was originally accepted. When the message is actually delivered, this is the rule number that will be logged.

RULEACT (?) : Unknown. The value of this is usually 16.

ERRMAIL (0|1) : A header that determines whether an actual error e-mail is sent out if the mail errors out. This corresponds to the "Notify sender on error" checkbox in the appropriate resource. The value of this header is 1 if it will attempt to deliver an error, 0 if not.

ACCT (0|1) : A header that indicates whether to perform accounting tracking on this connection (value of 1) or not (value of 0).

LOG_OK (MDQ_LOG|MDQ_ALERT) : A header that specifies how to log the successful delivery of a message.

LOG_BAD (MDQ_LOG|MDQ_ALERT) : A header that specifies how to log an unsuccessful delivery attempt (e.g., a transient failure). This corresponds to Exception Tracking on the appropriate resource (see Figure 9.23 earlier in the chapter). This line will not exist in the file if Exception Tracking is set to None.

LOG_ERR (MDQ_LOG|MDQ_ALERT) : A header that specifies how to log that an error mail needs to be sent (because the message has passed the abandon time). This corresponds to the "Notify sender on error" checkbox in the appropriate resource.

Below these entries in the spool file, you will find two sets of e-mail headers: the original headers (as they were sent with the message) and the modified headers, which are what FireWall-1 will actually send to the remote SMTP server.

You can move the R file with the lowest numerical value of the spool directory, enabling the mdq process to work with the next file. The idea is that you can either modify or relocate the problem files, enabling the forwarding of the rest of the spool directory.

Once you have done this to all the files, you can type either

```
# fw mdq
```

or

```
# fw kill fwd
```

to force the SMTP Security Server to reprocess the mail spool.

 WARNING! **fw kill fwd** kills the `fwd` process, which will prevent FireWall-1 from logging, using the Security Servers, or performing encryption tasks. The `cpwatchdog` process should restart `fwd` within a minute or so of executing this command.

The TCP Security Server

The TCP Security Server allows you to perform Content Security on any TCP service by sending the raw data stream to the CVP server. The CVP server inspects the content stream and returns the results to the TCP Security Server, which then takes the specified action in the resource. The TCP Security Server can also do URL filtering, though only the destination IP address will be sent to the UFP server.

CVP with the TCP Security Server

To have the TCP Security Server perform CVP on a particular TCP service, start by creating a new TCP Resource. From SmartDashboard/Policy Editor, select Manage and then Resources. Next select New, and choose SMTP. Or you may click on the ⚲ icon in the objects tree, right-click on TCP, and select New TCP. You are presented with the window shown in Figure 9.30. Give the resource a name (tcp-virusscan is used in this example), and set the type to CVP.

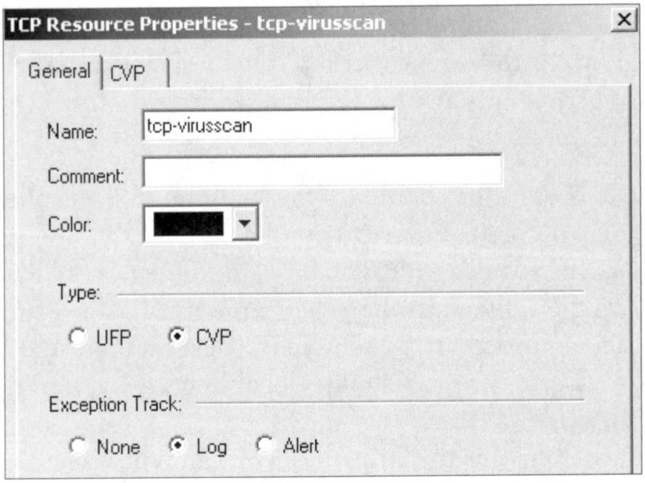

Figure 9.30 TCP Resource Properties, General tab

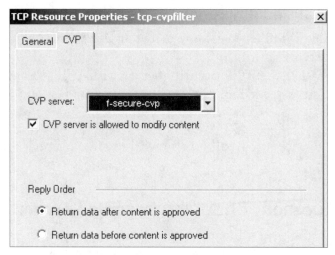

Figure 9.31   TCP Resource Properties, CVP tab

SOURCE	DESTINATION	SERVICE	ACTION	TRACK
⊥ internal_network	✱ Any	🔍 AOL->tcp-cvpfilter	🛡 accept	📄 Log

Figure 9.32   Sample rule with TCP resource

Figure 9.31 shows the CVP tab. The options here are similar to those de-scribed in the HTTP Security Server section. Once you've created the resource, edit the TCP service on which you want to enable CVP scanning. In the Ad-vanced configuration, check the "Enable for TCP resource" box.

Create a rule similar to the one shown in Figure 9.32, and push the security policy.

You must now configure the firewall module to listen on the TCP service port in question. For AOL, used in this example, the port is 5190. To do this, edit `$FWDIR/conf/fwauthd.conf` on the firewall module and add the follow-ing line to this file:

```
5190      fwssd     in.genericd     wait     0
```

Once you have done that, bounce the `fwd` process with the command **fw kill fwd**.

WARNING!   **fw kill fwd** kills the `fwd` process, which will prevent FireWall-1 from logging, using the Security Servers, or performing encryp-tion tasks. The `cpwatchdog` process should restart `fwd` within a minute or so of executing this command.

UFP with the TCP Security Server

Before proceeding with this, make sure that your UFP server can handle IP-based URLs (not all servers can).

The steps to use the TCP Security Server with UFP scanning are almost identical to the steps needed for CVP, with the following exceptions:

1. Create the TCP resource as type UFP instead of CVP.
2. You do not need to modify the firewall module to listen on the specified TCP port.

General Questions about the Security Servers

Most of the questions regarding the Security Servers are specific to each Security Server used. However, a few questions relate to the use of Security Servers in general. These FAQs cover such issues.

9.29: Why Don't the Connections I Make through the Security Servers Appear to Originate from the Firewall?

If you're familiar with FireWall-1 4.1 and earlier versions, you know that whenever the Security Servers were used, all connections through them appeared to come from the firewall. Some administrators designed their networks around this feature. In FireWall-1 NG, the firewall no longer appears to originate these connections, so designs that rely on packets originating from the firewall no longer hold true. To get the old behavior back, do one of two things:

- Create NAT rules hiding the communications behind the firewall's IP address. (NAT is discussed in Chapter 10.)
- Change a few parameters by using **dbedit** or by manually editing objects_5_0.C. (See FAQ 4.2 for details.) The parameters in question are in the firewall object properties: http_transparent_server_connection, ftp_transparent_server_connection, rlogin_transparent_server_connection, and telnet_transparent_server_connection. An example of how to edit these settings is shown below. Note that craig is the name of my firewall object.

```
dbedit> modify network_objects craig
        firewall_settings:http_transparent_server_connection
        false
dbedit> update network_objects craig
```

The notable exception to all of this is the SMTP Security Server, which still functions as it did in FireWall-1 4.1 and earlier.

9.30: Why Is the Security Server Used Even if the Rule Matched Does Not Use a Resource?

In this situation, a prior rule using the Security Servers needed evaluation by the Security Server in order to determine whether or not the rule applied. Refer to Figure 9.11 earlier in this chapter for an example.

If the connection originates from the internal network and requires HTTP, the Security Server becomes involved because it must determine whether or not the URL meets the criteria specified in the resource. If it does, the connection is rejected. If not, the HTTP is allowed by the second rule. However, because the packet required evaluation by the HTTP Security Server to determine that it did not meet the previous rule's criteria, the HTTP Security Server processes the connection even though the second rule does not explicitly use a resource.

If you want to ensure that the Security Server is not used in a particular case, you need to place a rule above any other rules that avoids using the Security Servers (i.e., no resources or User Authentication).

9.31: Can I Mix User Authentication and Content Security?

For HTTP and FTP, yes. Simply use an action of User Authentication where it is appropriate.

9.32: Can I Mix Session Authentication and Content Security?

No, you cannot. The Security Servers are required for Content Security anyway, so it makes no sense to use the Session Authentication in conjunction with Content Security. You can certainly use Session Authentication for other services, just not the ones where Content Security is required.

Debugging the Security Servers

In FireWall-1 4.1 and earlier, in order to debug the Security Servers, you were required to set environment variables and restart the fwd process. In FireWall-1 NG, you can now perform debugging without restarting any processes. When these variables are set, FireWall-1 logs the information generated into the various files in $FWDIR/log. Each Security Server has its own file with a .elg extension (e.g., the HTTP Security Server has ahttpd.elg, the FTP Security Server has ftpd.elg, and so on).

To enable debugging for the HTTP Security Server, issue the following command from your firewall module:

```
# fw debug on in.ahttpd FWAHTTPD_LEVEL=3
```

To disable debugging, issue the following command from your firewall module:

```
# fw debug off in.ahttpd FWAHTTPD_LEVEL=3
```

To enable debugging for the other Security Servers, use similar syntax. Table 9.3 shows the variables to set for the Security Servers. You can assign the variables values of 1 through 3. The larger the number, the more verbose the debugging information.

This method permits setting only one environment variable at a time, which means multiple Security Servers cannot be debugged. If you need to debug multiple Security Servers, you need to manually set the environment variables on the command line. The following example on a UNIX-based firewall using a Bourne-type shell shows you how to enable debugging for the HTTP Security Server and the SMTP mdq process.

```
# fw kill fwd
# FWAHTTPD_LEVEL=3; export FWAHTTPD_LEVEL
# FWMDQ_LEVEL=3; export FWMDQ_LEVEL
# fwd
```

Table 9.3 Debug variables for the Security Servers

Variable	Description
FWAHTTPD_LEVEL	Debug information from the HTTP Security Server (in.ahttpd)
FWAFTPD_LEVEL	Debug information from the FTP Security Server (in.aftpd)
FWACLIENTD_LEVEL	Debug information from the Client Authentication daemon over Telnet (in.aclientd)
FWAHCLIENTD_LEVEL	Debug information from the Client Authentication daemon over HTTP (in.ahclientd)
FWASMTPD_LEVEL	Debug information from the SMTP Security Server receiving process (in.asmtpd)
FWMDQ_LEVEL	Debug information from the SMTP Security Server mail dequeuer process (mdq)
FWARLOGIND_LEVEL	Debug information from the rlogin Security Server (in.arlogind)
FWATELNETD_LEVEL	Debug information from the Telnet Security Server (in.atelnetd)
FWGENERICD_LEVEL	Debug information from the TCP Security Server (in.genericd)

To do this on a Windows-based firewall, use the following commands.

```
> fw kill fwd
> SET FWAHTTPD_LEVEL=3
> SET FWMDQ_LEVEL=3
> fwd
```

Summary

Content Security provides additional control over what can be accessed through your firewalls. The HTTP, FTP, SMTP, and TCP Security Servers provide the means to filter content in FireWall-1. Resources are what tell the Security Servers how to filter content.

CVP, a feature present in all of the Security Servers, provides a mechanism for third-party products to scan content for viruses and Trojan horses. UFP, present only in the HTTP Security Server, provides a way for third-party applications to filter users' attempts to access various Web sites.

Sample Configurations

The following subsections present three situations that build on each other as the network and the needs of the enterprise change.

SMTP Content Security

The Situation

Your company wants to gradually roll in Content Security throughout its enterprise. One of the most prevalent sources of viruses has been incoming e-mail, so the managers decide to start with e-mail. Both incoming and outgoing e-mail will be scanned. HTTP and FTP traffic will eventually be scanned. (This functionality will be added in the next two situations.) The CVP and UFP servers are sitting in the DMZ. Figure 9.33 shows the network diagram for this company.

The Goals

- The Web server in the DMZ will be accessible via HTTP from anywhere.
- The e-mail server in the DMZ will be accessible via SMTP from anywhere and can send e-mail to anywhere on the Internet.

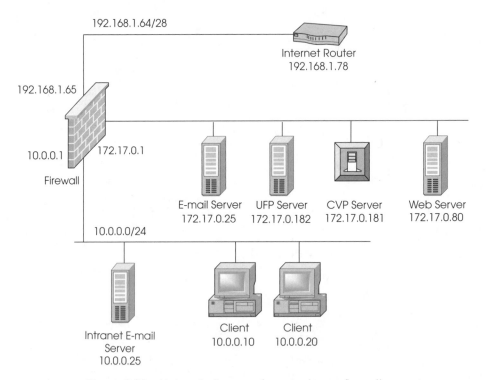

Figure 9.33   Network diagram for sample configuration

- The e-mail server in the DMZ can talk to the internal e-mail server via SMTP and vice versa. In either case, all traffic will be scanned for viruses.
- Clients on the internal network can talk to any host via HTTP and FTP.
- The UFP and CVP servers need to access their respective vendors' Web sites via HTTP to download updates (www.cvp-vendor.com and www. ufp-vendor.com).
- All other traffic should be denied.

The Checklist

- Create the necessary network objects.
- Ensure that the SMTP Security Server is enabled in `$FWDIR/conf/ fwauthd.conf`.
- Create two SMTP resources to handle inbound and outbound e-mail between the internal and the DMZ e-mail servers and scan viruses.
- Create the appropriate rule(s) in the rulebase.
- Verify and install the policy.

The Implementation

The proper line for the SMTP Security Server in `$FWDIR/conf/fwauthd.conf` looks like this (with no comment character, #, at the beginning of the line):

```
25            fwssd           in.asmtpd       wait    0
```

On most systems, this line is enabled by default, but it never hurts to make sure that this line exists and is not commented out.

The two resources then need to be created. The first resource is for e-mail coming from the DMZ-based e-mail server that forwards it to the internal e-mail server. All incoming e-mail should be forwarded to the internal SMTP server. Any errors generated should go to the DMZ-based e-mail server so they can be sent to the sender. Figure 9.34 shows how this resource looks.

You *can* leave the Match tab blank if you want because the internal and DMZ-based e-mail servers can do address checking on their own. For this example, let's leave the Action1 tab alone as well because there is no need to do any address rewriting.

In the Action2 tab, shown in Figure 9.35, strip out all messages of MIME type message/partial because it is used for sending a file across more than one message. This makes it difficult, if not impossible, to scan the file for viruses. The default message size should also be increased from 1,000KB to 5,000KB as a courtesy to users. However, I generally do not recommend sending large files

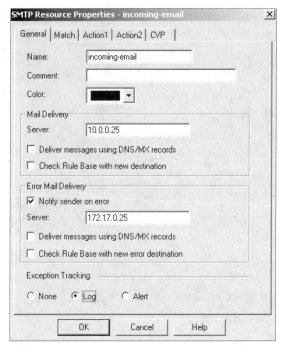

Figure 9.34 Incoming e-mail SMTP resource, General tab

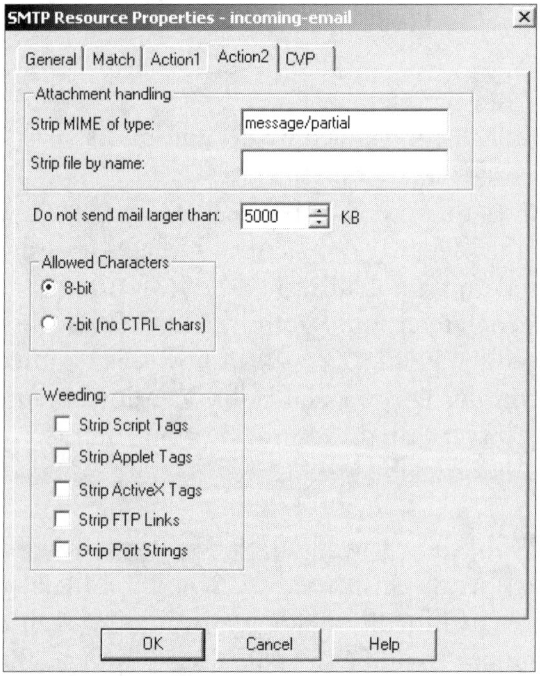

Figure 9.35 Incoming e-mail SMTP resource, Action2 tab

by e-mail because e-mailed files are actually *bigger* than they are if downloaded from an FTP or HTTP server. In order to e-mail binary files, they must be turned into a nonbinary format, which increases the overall file size.

Configure the CVP tab as shown in Figure 9.36.

Then create the outbound resource as shown in Figure 9.37.

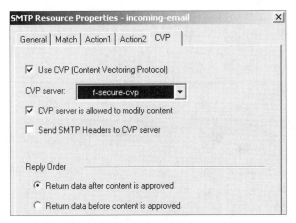

Figure 9.36   Incoming e-mail SMTP resource, CVP tab

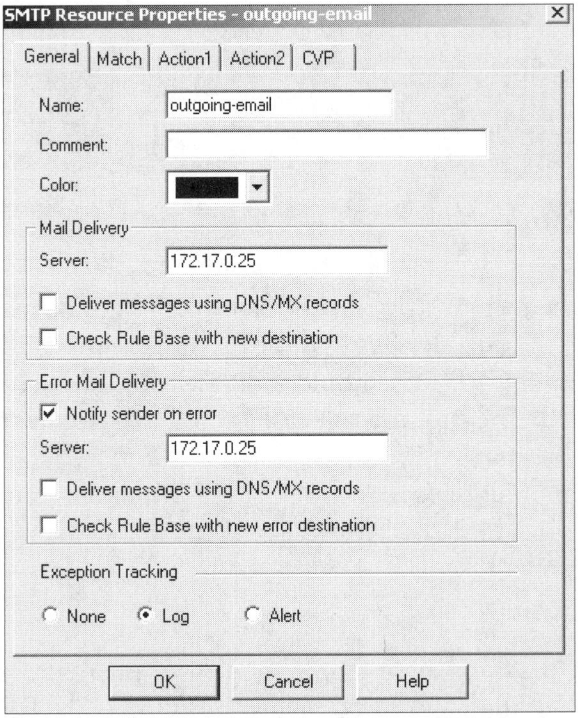

Figure 9.37   Outgoing e-mail SMTP resource, General tab

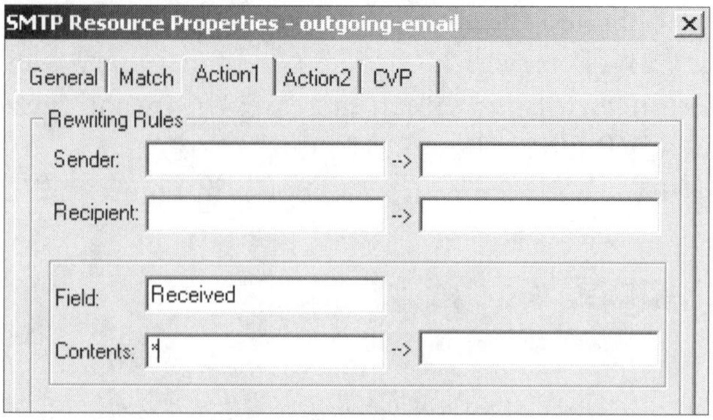

Figure 9.38   Outgoing e-mail SMTP resource, Action1 tab

NO.	SOURCE	DESTINATION	SERVICE	ACTION	TRACK
1	✱ Any	Web_Server	TCP http	accept	– None
2	Email_Server_Internal	Email_Server_DMZ	SMTP smtp->outgoing-email	accept	Log
3	net-10.0.0.0-24	Email_Server_DMZ	TCP smtp	accept	Log
4	Email_Server_DMZ	net-10.0.0.0-24	SMTP smtp->incoming-email	accept	Log
5	Email_Server_DMZ	net-10.0.0.0-24	TCP smtp	accept	Log
6	net-10.0.0.0-24	✱ Any	TCP http / TCP ftp	accept	Log
7	CVP_Server	www.cvp-vendor.com	TCP http	accept	– None
8	UFP_Server	www.ufp-vendor.com	TCP http	accept	– None
9	✱ Any	✱ Any	✱ Any	drop	Log

Figure 9.39   Rulebase for SMTP Security Server sample configuration

It might also be nice to strip out the "received" lines of messages being sent from the inside to the outside. This is done on the Action1 tab (see Figure 9.38).

The Action2 and CVP tabs should look identical to what was used for the inbound resource. In the end, the rulebase should look similar to the one shown in Figure 9.39.

Once this configuration is set up, verify and install the security policy.

FTP Content Security

The Situation

The next step in the company's Content Security plan is to turn on Content Security for FTP. Additionally, the company wants to use the FTP Security Server to allow people to upload files only to a specific directory on the Web server.

The Goal

- Create and implement resources to perform the necessary Content Security for FTP.

The Checklist

- Ensure that the FTP Security Server is enabled in `$FWDIR/conf/fwauthd.conf`.
- Create an FTP resource to scan for viruses.
- Create an FTP resource to scan for viruses and restrict access to a specific directory on the Web server.
- Create an FTP resource to allow people to download files from the Web server.
- Modify the rulebase to use these FTP resources.
- Verify and install the policy.

The Implementation

The proper line for the FTP Security Server in `$FWDIR/conf/fwauthd.conf` looks like this (with no comment character, #, at the beginning of the line):

```
25          fwssd          in.aftpd     wait    0
```

On most systems, this line is enabled by default, but it never hurts to check.

The first resource you need to create is the more general one to match everything and allow users to upload and download as they please, with the exception that all file transfers will be scanned for viruses. This configuration is shown in Figure 9.40.

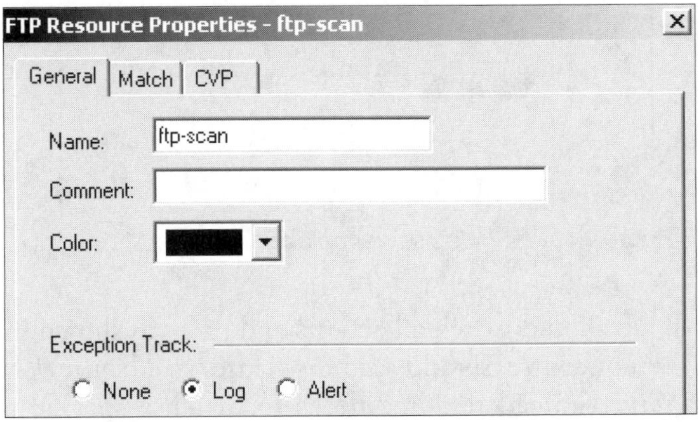

Figure 9.40 FTP scan resource, General tab

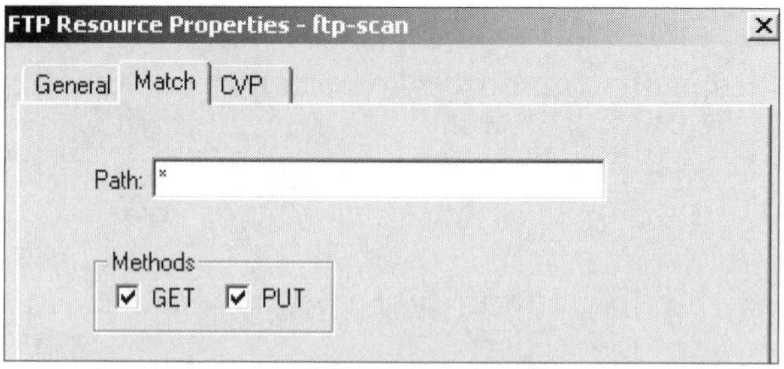

Figure 9.41   FTP scan resource, Match tab

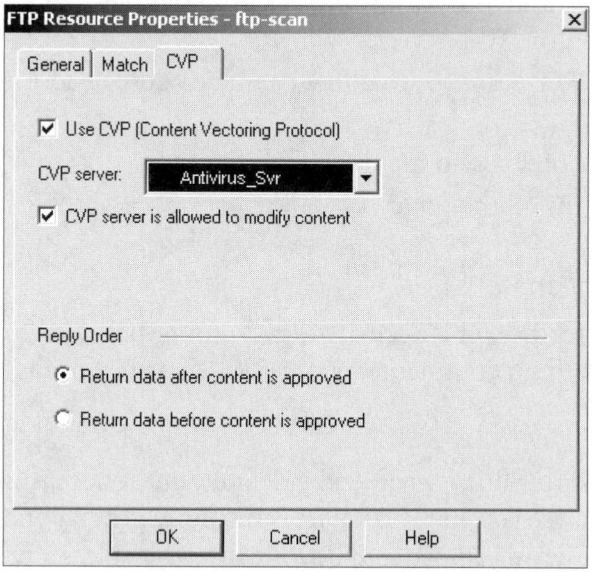

Figure 9.42   FTP scan resource, CVP tab

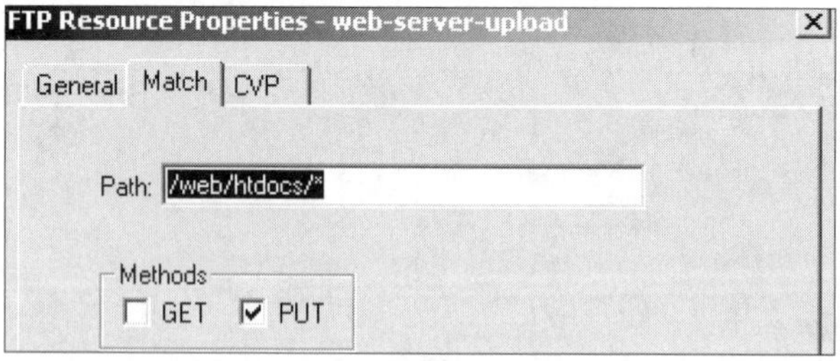

Figure 9.43   FTP Web server upload resource, Match tab

The Match tab should match all actions and paths as shown in Figure 9.41. The CVP tab, of course, should scan for viruses (see Figure 9.42).

The Web server upload resource needs to match a specific path. Use the Match tab as shown in Figure 9.43.

You are going to virus scan anything uploaded to make sure you do not pass any viruses to the outside world. The CVP tab for this configuration is shown in Figure 9.42.

Finally, you need to create a resource to allow the internal users to download from the Web server. Because you are not terribly concerned about where on that server users download from, the Match tab should match any path for GET commands, as shown in Figure 9.44.

Once the resources are created, you can modify the existing policy to use them. The rulebase should look similar to the one shown in Figure 9.45. Rules 6, 7, and 8 were added to the previous rulebase (pushing the original Rules 6 through 9 shown in Figure 9.39 into their new positions as Rules 9 through 12 in Figure 9.45).

After updating the rulebase, verify and install the security policy.

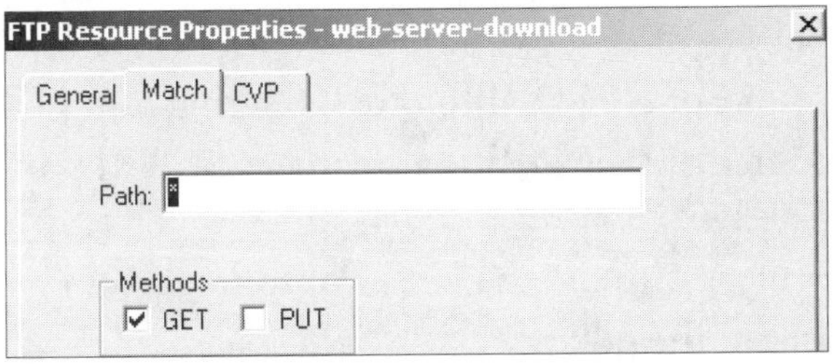

FTP Resource Properties - web-server-download

General Match CVP

Path: *

Methods
☑ GET ☐ PUT

Figure 9.44 FTP Web server download resource, Match tab

NO.	SOURCE	DESTINATION	SERVICE	ACTION	TRACK
1	✱ Any	Web_Server	TCP http	accept	— None
2	Email_Server_Internal	Email_Server_DMZ	SMTP smtp->outgoing-email	accept	Log
3	net-10.0.0.0-24	Email_Server_DMZ	TCP smtp	accept	Log
4	Email_Server_DMZ	net-10.0.0.0-24	SMTP smtp->incoming-email	accept	Log
5	Email_Server_DMZ	net-10.0.0.0-24	TCP smtp	accept	Log
6	net-10.0.0.0-24	Web_Server	FTP ftp->web-server-upload	accept	Log
7	net-10.0.0.0-24	Web_Server	FTP ftp->web-server-download	accept	Log
8	net-10.0.0.0-24	Web_Server	FTP ftp->ftp-scan	accept	Log
9	net-10.0.0.0-24	✱ Any	TCP http	accept	Log
10	CVP_Server	www.cvp-vendor.com	TCP http	accept	— None
11	UFP_Server	www.ufp-vendor.com	TCP http	accept	— None
12	✱ Any	✱ Any	✱ Any	drop	Log

Figure 9.45 Rulebase with SMTP and FTP Security Server sample configuration

HTTP Content Security

The Situation

The final step in implementing the company's Content Security plan is to implement both virus scanning and URL filtering for HTTP traffic.

The Goals

- Create and implement a resource for URL filtering and Content Security for HTTP.
- Make sure Content Security is *not* performed for internal users accessing the DMZ.

The Checklist

- Ensure that the HTTP Security Server is enabled in `$FWDIR/conf/fwauthd.conf`.
- Create a resource of type URI for URL filtering for HTTP.
- Create a resource of type URI that matches all URLs and does virus scanning.
- Modify the rulebase to use the HTTP resources.
- Verify and install the policy.

The Implementation

The proper line for the HTTP Security Server in `$FWDIR/conf/fwauthd.conf` looks like this (with no comment character, #, at the beginning of the line):

```
25            fwssd            in.ahttpd       wait    0
```

On most systems, this line is enabled by default, but it never hurts to check.

You first need to create a resource to filter URLs, as shown in Figure 9.46.

The Match tab should match the categories of Web sites you do not want the employees to view (see Figure 9.47).

Configure the settings on the Action tab (see Figure 9.48) to redirect rejected URLs to a policy page.

This completes the setup for the URL filtering resource. You then need to do virus scanning on any URL that is accepted. A second resource must be created, as shown in Figure 9.49.

The Match tab settings should match all URLs, and the CVP tab settings should filter viruses (see Figures 9.50 and 9.51, respectively).

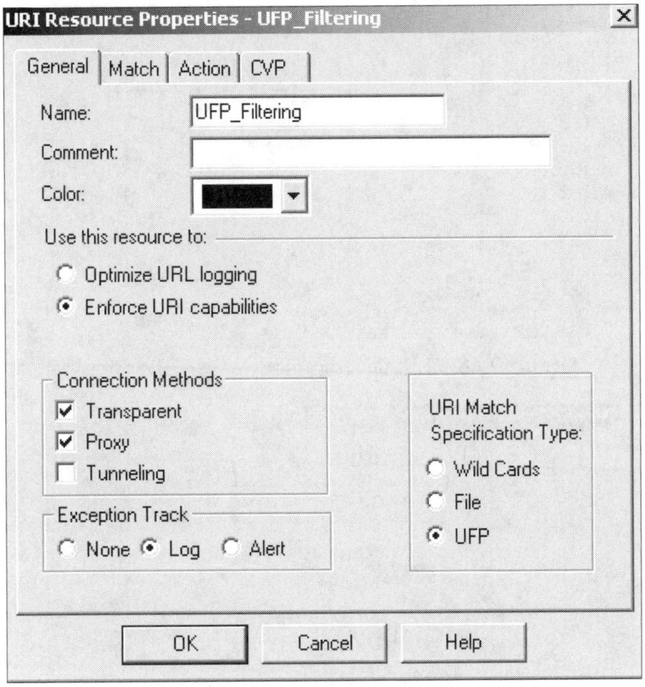

Figure 9.46   URI-filtering resource, General tab

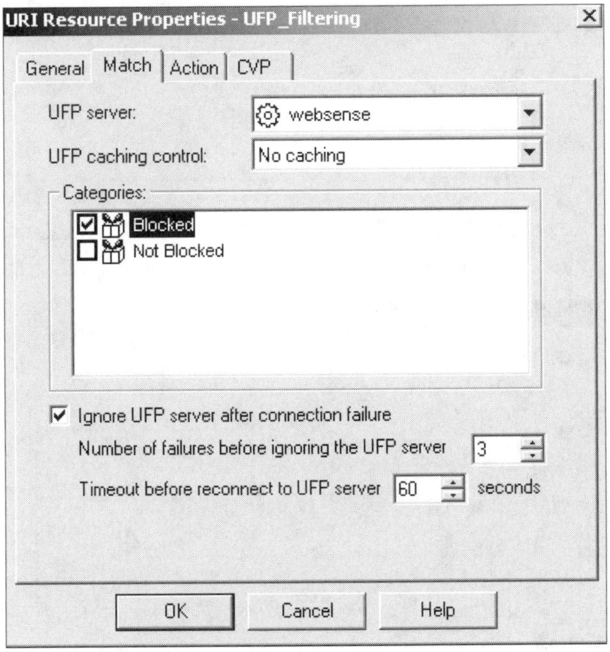

Figure 9.47   URI-filtering resource, Match tab

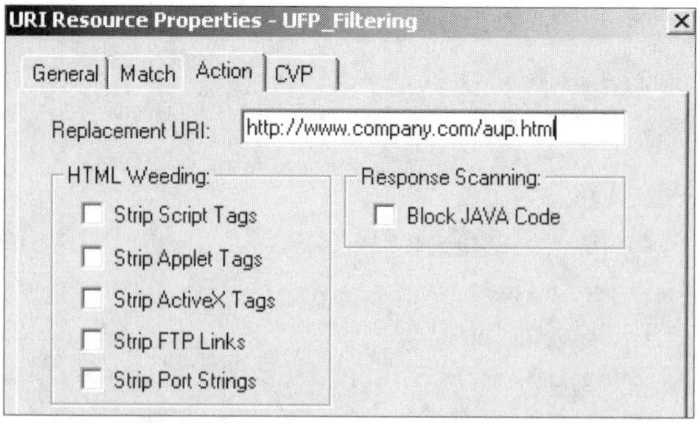

Figure 9.48 URI-filtering resource, Action tab

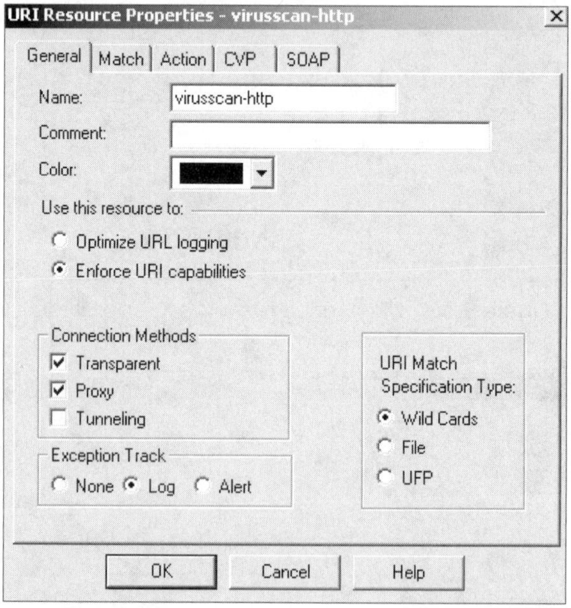

Figure 9.49 HTTP virus-scanning resource, General tab

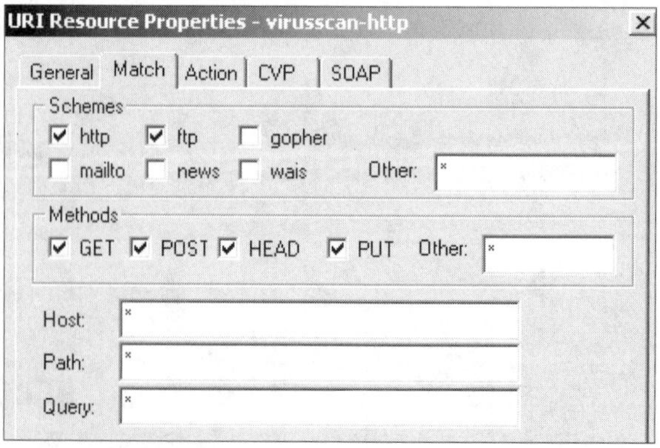

Figure 9.50 HTTP virus-scanning resource, Match tab

You then implement these resources in the rulebase, as shown in Figure 9.52. Rule 9 in the previous rulebase was replaced by a different Rule 9, and a new rule was added in the Rule 10 position, shifting down the remaining rules. After making these changes, verify and install the policy.

Notes

Rule 1 also matches internal users' attempts to access the Web server on the DMZ.

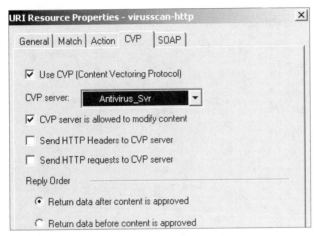

Figure 9.51   HTTP virus-scanning resource, CVP tab

NO.	SOURCE	DESTINATION	SERVICE	ACTION	TRACK
1	* Any	Web_Server	TCP http	accept	— None
2	Email_Server_Internal	Email_Server_DMZ	SMTP smtp->outgoing-email	accept	Log
3	net-10.0.0.0-24	Email_Server_DMZ	TCP smtp	accept	Log
4	Email_Server_DMZ	net-10.0.0.0-24	SMTP smtp->incoming-email	accept	Log
5	Email_Server_DMZ	net-10.0.0.0-24	TCP smtp	accept	Log
6	net-10.0.0.0-24	Web_Server	FTP ftp->web-server-upload	accept	Log
7	net-10.0.0.0-24	Web_Server	FTP ftp->web-server-download	accept	Log
8	net-10.0.0.0-24	Web_Server	FTP ftp->ftp-scan	accept	Log
9	net-10.0.0.0-24	* Any	HTTP http->UFP_Filtering	reject	Log
10	net-10.0.0.0-24	* Any	HTTP http->virusscan-http	accept	Log
11	CVP_Server	www.cvp-vendor.com	TCP http	accept	— None
12	UFP_Server	www.ufp-vendor.com	TCP http	accept	— None
13	* Any	* Any	* Any	drop	Log

Figure 9.52   Rulebase with SMTP, FTP, and HTTP Security Servers sample configuration

Chapter

10

Network Address Translation

This chapter discusses the topic of Network Address Translation (NAT). I first discuss the reasons NAT was created and how NAT is implemented in FireWall-1. Next, I show a step-by-step example of how to implement NAT in a network. I then talk about some of the inherent limitations of NAT and discuss a couple of ways to work around them. Finally, I talk about troubleshooting NAT with a packet sniffer.

By the end of this chapter, you should be able to:

- Understand why NAT is necessary
- Identify what NAT actually does
- Identify why NAT does not always work
- Effectively troubleshoot NAT problems with a packet sniffer
- Implement a NAT configuration

Introduction to Address Translation

Back in the old days of the Internet, the TCP/IP address space defined by IP version 4 (IPv4, the version used today) was thought to be more than enough. Organizations could reserve their own address spaces through the Internet Assigned Numbers Authority (IANA), now called the Internet Corporation for Assigned Names and Numbers (ICANN), and anyone who wanted a block of IP addresses generally got them.

Since the early 1990s, various people have been predicting that the IPv4 address space will simply run out of available addresses. This is partially due to the explosive growth of the Internet, but it is also due to how the IPv4 address space is divided. Many organizations that were allocated address spaces early on simply have more address spaces allocated to them than they are using on the Internet. There are also parts of the IPv4 address space that are not legal for hosts to be assigned to on the Internet, namely, the multicast (224.0.0.0/240.0.0.0 mask) and the Class E (240.0.0.0/240.0.0.0) address spaces.

As organizations are connecting to the Internet, some are discovering that their internal networks do not connect well. The main reason for this is usually a conflict in addressing. Long before the Internet was a household word, some corporations set up their internal networks using made-up addresses. However, you cannot simply make up addresses and use them on the Internet. You must use IP addresses assigned by IANA or an ISP. Renumbering a large, internal network would be a daunting task, not to mention that your ISP or IANA is not likely to give you enough addresses to cover all your hosts. Then again, does every host on your internal network really need to be uniquely addressable on the Internet?

IPv6 (the next version of IP) has far more address space—128 bits of address space versus the 32 provided by IPv4 (in wide use today)—which will solve this problem. However, most of today's Internet is still running IPv4 and probably will be for some time to come. A solution is needed that will help extend the IPv4 address space used today.

Network Address Translation does exactly this. It is a technology that allows hosts to transparently talk to one another with addresses that are agreeable to each other. To put it another way, NAT allows hosts with illegal or private address spaces to talk with hosts on a public network and vice versa. It is a godsend for network managers who have limited address space or want to make better use of the address spaces they have without having to subnet, thus reducing the number of IPs that can be used. NAT can also be perceived as a security enhancement because a firewall is required for communication between the hosts. NAT, as it is commonly implemented today, is described in RFC3022.[1]

NAT is implemented as part of the FireWall-1 kernel module that sits between the data link and network layers. As such, NAT can be provided transparently without the client's or the server's knowledge. Application proxies, by their nature, can also provide this functionality because they originate all connections coming from the internal network. However, proxies usually are not transparent and do not usually give you the level of control you have over FireWall-1's NAT functionality. You can modify the source, destination, and service port of any connection going through FireWall-1.

Consider the following example (see Figure 10.1). Let's say your ISP gives you a /29 block of addresses (netmask 255.255.255.248). If you were to use this

---

1. You can get copies of RFCs from http://www.rfc-editor.org, among other places.

Table 10.1   Breakdown of 192.168.0.0/29 address space

Host Number	Description
.0	Network identifier (cannot be used by hosts)
.1	Internet router
.2	Firewall
.3	Available
.4	Available
.5	Available
.6	Available
.7	Broadcast address (cannot be used by hosts)

address space between your Internet router and your firewall, the address space would break down into the host numbers listed in Table 10.1.[2]

Between the broadcast address, the network identifier, your firewall, and your Internet router, you have a grand total of four IP addresses you can use for other purposes. With NAT, you can do the following.

- Give your e-mail, intranet Web server, and Web server externally reachable IP addresses.
- Allow all your clients to access the Internet using the firewall's external IP address.
- Have all of your computers protected by your firewall.
- Change ISPs without having to renumber your internal network.

Figure 10.1 illustrates a sample network.

Although NAT does add an extra layer of protection and gives you flexibility, there are some downsides to NAT.

- Using NAT is like using proxies in that NAT must be updated to handle new applications. As a result, it is not compatible with every application that exists today or in the future.

---

2. If you are unfamiliar with subnetting and how it affects address space, you might want to read *LAN Technologies Explained* by Philip Miller and Michael Cummins [2000], *TCP/IP Illustrated* by W. Richard Stevens and Gary R. Wright [1993–95], or any other appropriate TCP/IP book.

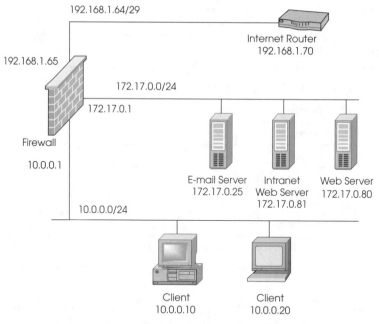

192.168.1.64/29

Internet Router
192.168.1.70

192.168.1.65

172.17.0.0/24

172.17.0.1

Firewall

10.0.0.1

E-mail Server
172.17.0.25

Intranet
Web Server
172.17.0.81

Web Server
172.17.0.80

10.0.0.0/24

Client
10.0.0.10

Client
10.0.0.20

Figure 10.1   Sample network

- NAT requires additional work to maintain. This is discussed in more detail later in this chapter in Implementing NAT: A Step-by-Step Example.
- Only so many connections can be hidden behind a single IP address.
- NAT requires extra memory and CPU on the gateway. In most cases, this is negligible, but it starts becoming noticeable when over 20,000 connections through a single gateway are subject to NAT.

More information about the disadvantages of using NAT is documented in RFC3027.

RFC1918 and Link-Local Addresses

RFC1918 (which was originally described in RFC1597) sets aside specific ranges of IP addresses that cannot be used on the Internet. Instead, these addresses are to be used internally within an organization or network. If hosts with RFC1918 addresses want to communicate with a network like the Internet, they must go through some form of NAT because no host on the Internet will know how to route RFC1918 addresses. The addresses assigned by RFC1918 are as follows:

- 10.0.0.0/8 (netmask 255.0.0.0)
- 172.16.0.0/12 (netmask 255.240.0.0, which covers 172.16.0.0–172.31.255.255)
- 192.168.0.0/16 (netmask 255.255.0.0)

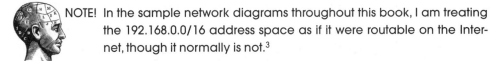 **NOTE!** In the sample network diagrams throughout this book, I am treating the 192.168.0.0/16 address space as if it were routable on the Internet, though it normally is not.[3]

Another set of address spaces that can be used for NAT is 169.254/16 (net-mask 255.255.0.0). This address space is specified in an Internet Draft called "Dynamic Configuration of IPv4 link-local addresses" (available at http://files. zeroconf.org/draft-ietf-zeroconf-ipv4-linklocal.txt). Essentially, Microsoft Dynamic Host Configuration Protocol (DHCP) clients use this method to assign an address when they are unable to communicate with a DHCP server. This address space is reserved specifically for this purpose, so it will not be in use anywhere on the Internet and is thus safe to use for NAT.

If your situation requires the use of NAT, it is strongly advised that you use address space within the recommended ranges. If you are using someone else's address space within your internal network and you need to communicate with an Internet host that happens to use the same address range, you may find yourself not being able to do so because the network traffic may never leave your internal network.

How NAT Works in FireWall-1

NAT is configured via the Address Translation tab in the Security Policy Editor. Two types of rules will show up here: *manual rules,* created by the administrator, and *automatic rules* that are created when NAT is configured on individual workstation, network, and address range objects. My personal preference is for manual rules because of the control you have over when these rules might apply.

If a packet does not match any rule in the address translation rules, the packet is not translated. If a packet does match a rule, the packet is translated, and no further processing occurs unless the "Allow bi-directional NAT" property in the NAT frame of the Global Properties section is enabled and automatic NAT rules exist. In this case, multiple automatically generated NAT rules can apply to a particular packet, which allows for both the source and destination IP addresses to be translated.

Four types of NAT are available in FireWall-1, and they can be mixed and matched as necessary: Source Static, Source Hide, Destination Static, and Destination Port Static.

1. *Source Static:* Translates the source IP address in an IP packet to a specific IP address. This is a one-to-one address translation. Return traffic, as

---

3. If you happen to recall that I also mentioned this in Chapter 4, give yourself a cookie for being astute.

necessary, is allowed back through without additional NAT rules. However, if you need to initiate connectivity from either side of the firewall, a corresponding Destination Static NAT rule is needed.

2. *Source Hide:* Makes more than one host appear as a single host (i.e., a many-to-one translation). In the text, I will refer to this simply as *hide mode.* This is perfect for hosts that require access to the Internet but should not be accessed *from* the Internet. In order to accomplish this, FireWall-1 changes the source TCP or UDP port of the packet so that it can keep track of which host the connection belongs to (and, consequently, know where to send reply packets). For ICMP packets, the data portion of the packet is modified (the data portion of an ICMP packet usually isn't used). For other IP protocols, hide mode does not work because there are no ports or data that can be modified. Most standard applications (e.g., Telnet, HTTP, FTP, HTTPS) work fine, but any application that requires a connection initiated from the outside or requires that a connection happen on a specific source port will not work in hide mode. An example of such is how Internet Key Exchange (IKE) is implemented in some VPN products.

3. *Destination Static:* Translates the destination IP address in an IP packet to a specified IP address. This is a one-to-one address translation for connections. Return traffic, as necessary, is allowed back through without additional NAT rules. However, if you need to initiate connectivity from either side of the firewall, a corresponding Source Static NAT rule is needed.

4. *Destination Port Static:* Translates only the destination (or service) port number to a different port. This, for example, allows you to transparently request going from port 8080 to port 80. It also allows you to make services on other machines accessible from the firewall's IP address.

NAT rules apply to all interfaces and cannot be applied on a per-interface basis. Usually, rules can be crafted in such a way that per-interface rules are not necessary. You can *hide* connections behind the IP 0.0.0.0, which is a special IP that tells FireWall-1 to use the interface the packet has routed out as opposed to a fixed IP address. When using the NAT frame of an object to define address translation (i.e., automatic rules), you can specify hiding behind the interface of the install-on gateway.

Even though NAT can be configured in SmartDashboard/Policy Editor, you generally need to configure the host operating system in order to support NAT.

The Order of Operations

In order to understand how to implement NAT, it is best to review the order of operations as it relates to FireWall-1 and passing traffic in general. Consider the following case, where Client A wants to communicate with Client B (see Figure 10.2).

 NOTE! In this example, NAT is not configured.

Client A determines that in order to communicate with Client B, the packet must be routed through the firewall. Client A needs to know the Media Access Control (MAC) address for the firewall's IP address (10.20.30.1), so it sends out a request via the Address Resolution Protocol (ARP) requesting the address. The firewall responds with its MAC address. Client A is then able to forward the packet to the firewall for processing.

Note that all of these events happen without any aid from FireWall-1. It is important to be aware of this exchange because when you do address translation, you must be sure that all of the translated IP addresses you set up through FireWall-1 get routed back to the firewall for processing. If the translated IP address is on the same subnet as the firewall, you need to set up a proxy ARP or static host route for that address. Otherwise, routes to those addresses will be necessary.

FireWall-1 NG has added a mechanism called Automatic ARP Configuration in the Global Properties (in the NAT frame). When this is enabled, in theory at least, the operating system of the firewall will not have to be configured to

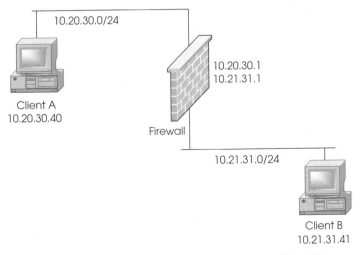

Figure 10.2 Client A communicates with Client B

proxy ARP for any addresses it is using for NAT. This property, according to the documentation, works only for automatically generated NAT rules. Even so, I have seen a number of reports that this property doesn't work with automatic rules either. I feel more comfortable making the changes to the ARP tables manually.

Once the packet is received at the firewall, FireWall-1 processes the packet according to the following steps.

1. The firewall checks to see if the packet is part of an established connection. Because this is a new connection, there is no record of the packet in the connections table, so the connection must be checked against the security policy.
2. The firewall checks IP Options. If the packet is denied because of this check, you will see a drop on Rule 0 in the SmartView Tracker/Log Viewer, assuming that IP Options logging is enabled.
3. The firewall performs an anti-spoofing check on the 10.20.30.1 interface. The source of the packet (10.20.30.40) is compared against the valid address setting. If the packet is denied because of this check, you will see a drop on Rule 0 in the SmartView Tracker/Log Viewer, assuming that anti-spoof logging is enabled on that interface. The remote end of the connection will see a "connection timed out" message.
4. The firewall checks properties and the rulebase.
5. The operating system routes the packet. The operating system determines that in order to communicate with Client B, it needs to route the packet out the 10.21.31.1 interface.
6. The firewall checks properties and the rulebase. Properties are always checked outbound as well as inbound. A rule's check depends on how you have installed it and how you are enforcing gateway rules.
7. The packet proceeds through the address translation rules. If there is a matching NAT rule, this is where NAT takes place. In this example, NAT is not occurring, so translation is not performed.
8. The packet is sent directly to Client B.

The important detail to note in this process is that NAT is not done until near the very end—that is, after the packet has been routed and has gone through the security policy, but before the packet leaves the gateway. That is, of course, unless you've turned on the Translate Destination on Client Side option.

This particular option is set in the NAT frame of the Global Properties section. With this option, when a destination IP address needs to be translated, the firewall performs the NAT operation before the packet is routed, that is, on the client side of the connection (between steps 4 and 5 above). This has two important side effects.

- Routing entries are no longer necessary on the firewall to account for NAT.
- It is possible to map ports on your firewall to servers on your internal network.

In FireWall-1 NG FP2 and before, this property is specific to automatically generated NAT rules only. In NG FP3 and above, there are separate options for both manual and automatic rules. In NG FP2 and before, you need to enable the option by using the following commands in **dbedit**:

```
> modify properties firewall_properties nat_dst_client_side_manual
        true
> update properties firewall_properties
```

Implementing NAT: A Step-by-Step Example

The following sample configuration involves NAT. I show what you need to do step-by-step to configure FireWall-1 to support this configuration (see Figure 10.3).

The security policy is defined as follows.

- Allow the external mail server and the Web server to be reached from anywhere via SMTP and HTTP, respectively.
- Allow the external mail server to send e-mail to anywhere on the Internet and to the internal mail server.
- Allow a second Web instance of a Web server (running on port 81) to be accessible via a separate IP address on port 80.
- Allow clients on segment A and segment B to browse the Internet via HTTP or HTTPS hiding behind a single IP address.
- Allow an intranet Web server to be accessible on the Internet via HTTP. The Web server will provide its own authentication, so no authentication is necessary by FireWall-1.
- Except for the former requirements, deny all other traffic.

The preceding policy is specially crafted for demonstration purposes only. Generally speaking, it is not wise to permit traffic from the Internet all the way into the internal network without some sort of encryption. Let's take the following steps to set this up.

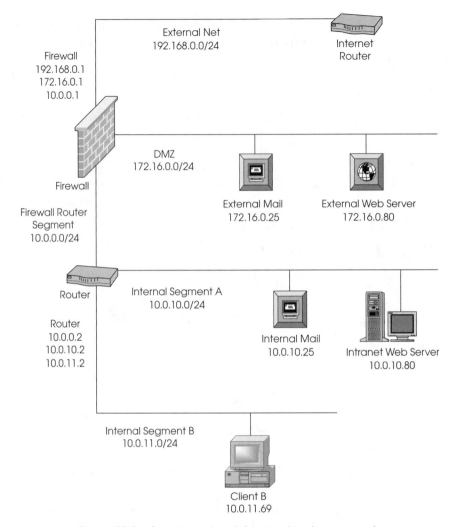

Figure 10.3 Sample network for step-by-step example

- Determine which IP addresses will be used for translation.
- Set up the necessary proxy ARPs.
- Set up the necessary static host routes.
- Create the necessary network objects.
- Make the necessary modifications to anti-spoofing.
- Create the necessary rulebase rules to permit the desired traffic.
- Create the NAT rules.
- Install the security policy, and verify that everything works as planned.

The subsections below describe these steps further.

Determining Which IP Addresses to Use

The legal addresses include everything in 192.168.0.0/24 except for the firewall (.1) and the router (.2). You can choose any other IP address in the range. The hosts for this setup will use the following static mappings:

- *External mail server:* 192.168.0.10
- *Web server:* 192.168.0.11
- *Web server (instance on port 81):* 192.168.0.12
- *Intranet Web server:* 192.168.0.13

For the browsing that segment A and segment B hosts will need, use the firewall's external IP address of 192.168.0.2.

Setting Up Proxy ARPs

Before you begin, you need to determine which MAC address you are going to use to ARP for the translated IP addresses. You know that all of the translated addresses are on the same subnet as the external interface of the firewall. You simply need to determine what the MAC (or physical) address of the external interface is and use that address. To do this, use one of the following commands:

- On UNIX and Nokia platform: `ifconfig -a`
- On Windows NT/2000: `ipconfig /all`

On a UNIX platform, you will see something like this[4]:

```
lo0: flags=849 <UP,LOOPBACK,RUNNING,MULTICAST> mtu 8232
             inet 127.0.0.1 netmask ff000000
le0: flags=863 <UP,BROADCAST,NOTRAILERS,RUNNING,MULTICAST> mtu 1500
        inet 192.168.0.1 netmask ffffff00 broadcast 192.168.0.255
             ether 0:11:22:33:44:55
le1: flags=863 <UP,BROADCAST,NOTRAILERS,RUNNING,MULTICAST> mtu 1500
        inet 10.0.0.1 netmask ffffff00 broadcast 10.0.0.255
             ether 0:c0:78:2:0:d6
le2: flags=863 <UP,BROADCAST,NOTRAILERS,RUNNING,MULTICAST> mtu 1500
        inet 172.16.0.1 netmask ffffff00 broadcast 172.16.0.255
             ether 0:c0:78:20:0:6d
```

---

4. On a Solaris platform, it is likely that you will see the same MAC address on all Ethernet interfaces. The default behavior is to use a hostid-based MAC address and not the hardware MAC. So long as two or more interfaces are not on the same physical network, this should not be a problem. You can change the MAC address on a per-interface basis with the `ifconfig` command.

On a Nokia platform, the output is slightly different:

```
loop0c0:  flags=57<UP,PHYS_AVAIL,LINK_AVAIL,LOOPBACK,MULTICAST>
        inet6 mtu 63000 ::1  -> ::1
        inet mtu 63000 127.0.0.1  -> 127.0.0.1
        phys loop0
eth-s1p1c0:  lname eth-s1p1c0 flags=e7<UP,PHYS_AVAIL,LINK_AVAIL,
BROADCAST,MULTICAST>
        inet mtu 1500 192.168.0.1/24 broadcast 192.168.0.255
        phys eth-s1p1 flags=133<UP,LINK,BROADCAST, MULTICAST,PRESENT>
        ether 0:11:22:33:44:55 speed 100M full duplex
eth-s2p1c0:  lname eth-s2p1c0 flags=e7<UP,PHYS_AVAIL,LINK_AVAIL,
BROADCAST,MULTICAST>
        inet mtu 1500 10.0.0.1/24 broadcast 10.0.0.255
        phys eth-s2p1 flags=133<UP,LINK,BROADCAST,MULTICAST,PRESENT>
        ether 0:c0:78:2:0:d6 speed 100M full duplex
eth-s3p1c0:  lname eth-s3p1c0 flags=e7<UP,PHYS_AVAIL,LINK_AVAIL,
BROADCAST,MULTICAST>
        inet mtu 1500 172.16.0.1/24 broadcast 172.16.0.255
        phys eth-s3p1 flags=133<UP,LINK,BROADCAST,MULTICAST,PRESENT>
        ether 0:c0:78:20:0:6d speed 100M full duplex
```

On a Windows NT/2000 platform, you will see this:

```
Ethernet adapter 3C5x91:

        Description . . . . . . . . : 3Com 3C5x9 Ethernet Adapter
        Physical Address. . . . . . : 00-11-22-33-44-55
        DHCP Enabled. . . . . . . . : No
        IP Address. . . . . . . . . : 192.168.0.1
        Subnet Mask . . . . . . . . : 255.255.255.0
        Default Gateway . . . . . . : 192.168.0.254

Ethernet adapter 3C5x92:

        Description . . . . . . . . : 3Com 3C5x9 Ethernet Adapter
        Physical Address. . . . . . : 00-C0-78-20-00-6D
        DHCP Enabled. . . . . . . . : No
        IP Address. . . . . . . . . : 10.0.0.1
        Subnet Mask . . . . . . . . : 255.255.255.0
        Default Gateway . . . . . . :

Ethernet adapter 3C5x93:

        Description . . . . . . . . : 3Com 3C5x9 Ethernet Adapter
        Physical Address. . . . . . : 00-0C-87-02-00-D6
        DHCP Enabled. . . . . . . . : No
        IP Address. . . . . . . . . : 172.16.0.1
        Subnet Mask . . . . . . . . : 255.255.255.0
        Default Gateway . . . . . . :
```

Use the ether or physical address of the system's external interface. In this case, you will use 00:11:22:33:44:55. Now that you know what the MAC address is, you can set up the ARPs. On UNIX systems, this is done as follows:

```
# arp -s 192.168.0.10 00:11:22:33:44:55 pub
# arp -s 192.168.0.11 00:11:22:33:44:55 pub
# arp -s 192.168.0.12 00:11:22:33:44:55 pub
# arp -s 192.168.0.13 00:11:22:33:44:55 pub
```

In order for these ARPs to be available on reboot, you need to add them to a file that executes on startup. Do not add them to the `/etc/rc3.d/S95fire wall1` script, which gets overwritten during an upgrade. Create a new startup script like `/etc/rc3.d/S94nat`.

Windows NT does not have a proxy ARP facility, so Check Point has included it as part of the software. Create the file `%FWDIR%\state\local.arp`, and enter the following information:

```
192.168.0.10      00-11-22-33-44-55
192.168.0.11      00-11-22-33-44-55
192.168.0.12      00-11-22-33-44-55
192.168.0.13      00-11-22-33-44-55
```

These ARPs will not become active until a policy reload is performed. In some cases, it may be necessary to stop and start FireWall-1.

In Windows 2000, proxy ARP is broken, particularly if you use the Routing and RAS service. Microsoft has a hotfix for this proxy ARP issue. Refer to article ID Q282312 in Microsoft's Knowledge Base. After you have that hotfix, you need a special utility from Check Point called fwparp, which is available from Check Point's Knowledge Base, article sk699. This program needs to be run after each reboot, so it is not terribly convenient. For Windows 2000 deployments, it is recommended that you do proxy ARPs on a different device or configure static routes for each of those addresses on the upstream router.

On the Nokia platform, add these ARPs via the Voyager interface as Proxy-Only type. In a VRRP configuration, configure both firewalls and use the VRRP MAC address instead of the network card's MAC. You may also configure the NAT IPs as VRRP backup IPs, thus eliminating the need for proxy ARPs.

NOTE! In IPSO, there is an option to allow connections to VRRP IP addresses. Make sure this option is disabled if you plan to configure the NAT IPs as VRRP IPs.

Setting Up Static Host Routes

The only translations for which you need to set up static host routes are those that involve a destination static translation (i.e., where the destination IP address needs to be translated). In our example, you need to set up static host routes for all of them because they will all be connected by their translated IP address.

You need to determine where the real hosts for the virtual IPs are in relation to the firewall. This is so you can determine the next hop for the static host routes you will set up. Using Figure 10.3, you know the following information.

- The external mail and external Web servers are on the same subnet as the firewall. In this case, you simply use the real host's IP address as the next hop.
- The intranet Web server is not on the same subnet as the firewall. In this case, you want to use the next hop IP address, which is the router that is connected to segment A—the segment on which the intranet Web server is connected. This is 10.0.0.2.

On UNIX platforms (not IPSO), you would add the static routes like this:

```
# route add 192.168.0.10 172.16.0.25 1
# route add 192.168.0.11 172.16.0.80 1
# route add 192.168.0.12 172.16.0.80 1
# route add 192.168.0.13 10.0.0.2 1
```

Like the previous ARPs, these lines need to go into a startup file so that they are available after a reboot.

On Windows NT platforms, the static routes you add are similar to UNIX:

```
> route add 192.168.0.10 172.16.0.25 -p
> route add 192.168.0.11 172.16.0.80 -p
> route add 192.168.0.12 172.16.0.80 -p
> route add 192.168.0.13 10.0.0.2 -p
```

Note that on Windows NT/2000, if you use the -p flag, the routes are persistent; that is, they are stored in the Registry and will stay there until they are deleted, even after a reboot.

On the Nokia platform, you can use Voyager to add these routes. Additionally, in IPSO 3.6 and later, you can use the following commands from **clish:**

```
NokiaIP380:10> set static-route 192.168.0.10/32 nexthop gateway
               address 172.16.0.25 priority 1 on
NokiaIP380:11> set static-route 192.168.0.11/32 nexthop gateway
               address 172.16.0.80 priority 1 on
NokiaIP380:12> set static-route 192.168.0.12/32 nexthop gateway
               address 172.16.0.80 priority 1 on
```

```
NokiaIP380:13> set static-route 192.168.0.13/32 nexthop gateway
               address 10.0.0.2 priority 1 on
```

In IPSO 3.5 and earlier, there is no supported manner in which to add routes via the command line.

Creating Network Objects

You must create network objects for both translated and untranslated objects; see Table 10.2.

Table 10.2. Network objects to create

Name	Object Type	IP/Mask/Group Objects	Description
net-dmz	Network	172.16.0.0/255.255.255.0	Your DMZ
smtp-dmz	Node, host	172.16.0.25	Mail server in the DMZ
smtp-dmz-ext	Node, host	192.168.0.10	Translated version of smtp-dmz
web-server	Node, host	172.16.0.80	Web server in the DMZ
web-server-ext	Node, host	192.168.0.11	Translated version of web-server (for port 80)
web-server-ext2	Node, host	192.168.0.12	Translated version of web-server (for port 81)
net-router-segment	Network	10.0.0.0/255.255.255.0	Segment shared by firewall segment and internal router
net-segment-a	Network	10.0.10.0/255.255.255.0	Segment A
web-intranet	Node, host	10.0.10.80	Intranet Web server
web-intranet-ext	Node, host	192.168.0.13	Translated version of web-intranet
smtp-internal	Node, host	10.0.10.25	Internal SMTP server
net-segment-b	Node, host	10.0.11.0/255.255.255.0	Segment B
valid-dmz	Group	net-dmz	Represents your DMZ interface's valid addresses for anti-spoofing
valid-internal	Group	net-segment-a + net-segment-b + net-router-segment	Represents your internal interface's valid addresses for anti-spoofing
firewall	Check Point gateway	192.168.0.1	Your firewall

Table 10.3 Valid address settings for the firewall

Interface	Valid Address Setting
DMZ	Interface defined by IP and netmask
Internal	Specific: valid-internal
External	External

Modifying the Anti-Spoofing Settings

When configuring your firewall object, set your topology according to the settings shown in Table 10.3. These settings are configured in the Topology frame in the firewall object. Also, make sure that each interface has Spoof Tracking set to Log to catch any errors in the anti-spoofing configuration.

Creating Security Policy Rules

The rules shown in Figure 10.4 are based on the security policy defined earlier.

Creating Address Translation Rules

Once the security policy is defined, NAT rules must be defined, as shown in Figure 10.5. Before you begin, make sure you define a service for port 81. It will be a service of type TCP. In Figure 10.5, it is referred to as http81, so you can do the

NO.	SOURCE	DESTINATION	SERVICE	ACTION	TRACK
1	∗ Any	web-server-ext web-server-ext2 web-intranet-ext	TCP http	accept	Log
2	valid-internal	smtp-dmz-ext	TCP smtp	accept	Log
3	smtp-dmz-ext smtp-internal	smtp-internal smtp-dmz-ext	TCP smtp	accept	Log
4	smtp-dmz-ext	valid-internal	TCP smtp	accept	Log
5	net-segment-a net-segment-b	∗ Any	TCP http TCP https	accept	Log
6	∗ Any	∗ Any	∗ Any	drop	Log

Figure 10.4 Sample security policy rulebase

NO.	ORIGINAL PACKET			TRANSLATED PACKET			INSTALL ON
	SOURCE	DESTINATION	SERVICE	SOURCE	DESTINATION	SERVICE	
1	✱ Any	🖥 web-server-ext	✱ Any	≡ Original	🖥 web-server	≡ Original	✱ Policy Targets
2	✱ Any	🖥 web-server-ext2	✱ Any	≡ Original	🖥 web-server	TCP http81	✱ Policy Targets
3	✱ Any	🖥 web-intranet-ext	✱ Any	≡ Original	🖥 web-intranet	≡ Original	✱ Policy Targets
4	✱ Any	🖥 smtp-dmz-ext	✱ Any	≡ Original	🖥 smtp-dmz	≡ Original	✱ Policy Targets
5	🖥 smtp-dmz	✱ Any	✱ Any	🖥 smtp-dmz-ext	≡ Original	≡ Original	✱ Policy Targets
6	⊣⊢ net-segment-a	✱ Any	✱ Any	🖳 firewall	≡ Original	≡ Original	✱ Policy Targets
7	⊣⊢ net-segment-b	✱ Any	✱ Any	🖳 firewall	≡ Original	≡ Original	✱ Policy Targets

Figure 10.5   Sample NAT policy rulebase

port translation that the security policy requires. Note that at the lower right of some of the icons used in the figure, the "S" refers to static rules, and the "H" refers to hide rules.

Installing and Testing the Security Policy

Initiate a connection to exercise each rule and ensure that each one is functioning as you expect. Test access from inside and outside the network.

Limitations of NAT

NAT does not work in all cases. The following subsections document some of the instances where NAT will not work as expected.

NAT Is Incompatible with Some Protocols

The main components that NAT changes are the IP addresses in the TCP/IP headers and possibly the TCP or UDP ports. This works for some applications, but many applications embed IP addresses in the data portion of the packet (e.g., Microsoft Networking[5]) or expect packets to come from a particular source port (e.g., IKE negotiations for IPSec). In these cases, NAT has to act somewhat like an application proxy in that it must understand the underlying protocol and make intelligent changes to the packets so that the protocol will work despite undergoing NAT.

FireWall-1 understands certain protocols like FTP, RealAudio, and Microsoft Networking (if support is specifically enabled). There are plenty of applications that do not work correctly with FireWall-1's NAT, not necessarily because

---

5. Microsoft used to say that Microsoft Networking was incompatible with NAT and that NAT, if present in your network, should be removed. It would not surprise me if the company still stood by this claim.

it is impossible to make them work but because Check Point has not added support for them. However, some protocols are simply impossible to make work with NAT. Any protocol that uses IP datagram types other than TCP or UDP often fails when NAT is applied. In fact, Check Point does not NAT packets that aren't TCP, UDP, or ICMP. Protocols that validate the IP packet headers between source and destination (such as the Authentication Header mechanism of IPSec) will not work with NAT. To a protocol that protects network traffic from man-in-the-middle attacks—attacks where the headers or payload changes in transit—NAT looks like a hacker. The bottom line: NAT breaks end-to-end connectivity and should be employed only in instances where you can live with the limitations.

Connections That Can Bypass the Firewall

NAT is problematic in situations where the firewall is not placed between both the source and the destination. Using the example in the previous step-by-step configuration (see Figure 10.3), consider the situation where a host on segment B (10.0.11.69) tries to access the intranet Web server via the translated IP address (192.168.0.13). The host 10.0.11.69 tries to initiate a connection to 192.168.0.13. Routing will eventually take this packet to the firewall. The packet is accepted by the firewall's security policy and is then processed by NAT. The first NAT rule that matches the packet is Rule 3, which translates the destination of the packet from 192.168.0.13 to 10.0.10.80. The "source" of the packet is not changed (the rule says not to touch it). The packet is then routed back to 10.0.10.80 via 10.0.0.2.

When 10.0.10.80 sends its reply, it is sent to 10.0.11.69 (the "source" of the connection attempt). The reply is routed to 10.0.10.2 and then directly to 10.0.11.69. The host 10.0.11.69 expects replies from 192.168.0.13 (which it tries to connect to), not 10.0.10.80, so the reply packets are ignored.

What would happen if the rule hid 10.0.11.0/24 behind the firewall's external IP address? When 10.0.11.69 tried to access 10.0.10.80, the packet would get routed to the firewall and passed through the rulebase. NAT then would rewrite the source of the packet to be 192.168.0.2. The destination of the packet would still be 192.168.0.13 (i.e., it would not get translated), but it would get routed out the internal interface. The Internet router would see this packet and route it back to the firewall (it is an external address, after all). The packet would ping-pong back and forth until the packet's time to live (TTL) value expired.

One reason you might connect to the translated IP address is because your internal client's DNS server resolves the host's name to the external address. You can solve this problem by implementing *split-horizon DNS*, that is, maintaining an internal version of your DNS and an external version of your DNS, typically on separate servers. The external DNS is accessible from the Internet and contains only a subset of names and addresses contained in the internal DNS server. An internal DNS contains all the names used internally and reflects the internal IP address for a host. The external DNS server reflects the externally resolvable IP addresses for the host.

Other than implementing split-horizon DNS, can you get around this problem? Yes, there are two tricks you can use, which are documented in the following subsections. However, it is highly recommended that you not place yourself in a position where you have to use these tricks.

Dual NAT (Translating Both Source and Destination)

FireWall-1 allows you to translate both the source and destination IP address at once. It is simply a matter of crafting the correct rules and placing them in the right order. In the preceding case, if you want to allow your internal network to access the internal host via its translated IP address, modify your NAT rules so they read as shown in Figure 10.6. The two rules that were added to the rulebase shown earlier in Figure 10.5 are shown with white backgrounds in Figure 10.6 and will hide the source address behind the firewall's IP address and modify the destination IP to be the web-intranet address.

In this particular case, there is another issue to contend with: ICMP Redirects. Because the firewall will be routing a packet out the same interface from which it was received, the system sends the client an ICMP Redirect, giving it a more direct route to the host. Depending on the exact circumstances, the ICMP Redirect will cause the connection either to never take place or to take a long time to establish because the client will be trying to communicate directly to a

NO.	ORIGINAL PACKET			TRANSLATED PACKET			INSTALL ON
	SOURCE	DESTINATION	SERVICE	SOURCE	DESTINATION	SERVICE	
1	∗ Any	web-server-ext	∗ Any	= Original	web-server	= Original	∗ Policy Targets
2	∗ Any	web-server-ext2	∗ Any	= Original	web-server	TCP http81	∗ Policy Targets
3	net-segment-a	web-intranet-ext	∗ Any	firewall	web-intranet	= Original	∗ Policy Targets
4	net-segment-b	web-intranet-ext	∗ Any	firewall	web-intranet	= Original	∗ Policy Targets
5	∗ Any	web-intranet-ext	∗ Any	= Original	web-intranet	= Original	∗ Policy Targets
6	∗ Any	smtp-dmz-ext	∗ Any	= Original	smtp-dmz	= Original	∗ Policy Targets
7	smtp-dmz	∗ Any	∗ Any	smtp-dmz-ext	= Original	= Original	∗ Policy Targets
8	net-segment-a	∗ Any	∗ Any	firewall	= Original	= Original	∗ Policy Targets
9	net-segment-b	∗ Any	∗ Any	firewall	= Original	= Original	∗ Policy Targets

Figure 10.6 NAT policy with dual NAT rules

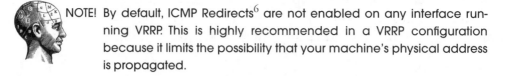

SOURCE	DESTINATION	SERVICE	ACTION	TRACK
▦ firewall-modules	✻ Any	ICMP redirect	◉ drop	− None

Figure 10.7 Rule to block ICMP Redirects

host using an IP address it knows nothing about. There are a few ways around this situation.

- Bind the translated IP address to the server's loopback interface. See the next subsection for details.
- Block ICMP Redirects. You can block outgoing ICMP Redirects in Fire-Wall-1 with the FireWall-1 rule shown in Figure 10.7.
- On some operating systems, there is an option to disable sending ICMP Redirects. On Solaris, you do this by typing:

```
# /usr/sbin/ndd -set /dev/ip ip_send_redirects 0
```

On a Nokia platform, you can do this on a per-interface basis by typing:

```
# ipsctl -w interface:<phys-if>:family:inet:flags:icmp_no_rdir 1
```

where you replace `<phys-if>` with the physical interface name (e.g., `eth-s1p1`).

> NOTE! By default, ICMP Redirects[6] are not enabled on any interface running VRRP. This is highly recommended in a VRRP configuration because it limits the possibility that your machine's physical address is propagated.

Assuming this trick works, a side effect can occur, which makes traffic traverse your network twice: once to the firewall and once to the server. This could add to an already congested network.

Binding the NAT IP Address to the Loopback Interface

The basic idea is to bind the translated IP address to the loopback interface of the server. On Windows NT, you need to add the MS Loopback interface (a software-only network adaptor) and add the IP address to this interface with a netmask of 255.255.255.255. In IPSO, you can simply add an IP address to the

---

6. It is my opinion that any network architecture that relies on ICMP Redirects to route packets is fundamentally flawed.

loop0c0 interface via Voyager. On UNIX machines, use a command such as the following:

```
# ifconfig lo0:0 204.32.38.25 up
```

If packets come into the system for the translated IP address (because, for instance, they did not come to the firewall), the system will respond to packets for this IP address. This method does require slightly more administration because you must also maintain the NAT on the individual servers.

Troubleshooting NAT with a Packet Sniffer

To troubleshoot NAT, you should first verify that each necessary step has been performed.

- Validate that an ARP entry exists for the translated IP (or that the translated IP is somehow being routed to the firewall).
- Validate that a static host route exists on the firewall to route the translated IP address to either the untranslated address or the next hop address if the real system is more than one hop away from the firewall.
- Validate that the rules are set up correctly. Set any security policy rule that applies to a NATted host to track long, and ensure that address translation is happening as you expect.

Wherever a verification of the configuration fails, a packet sniffer can be your friend. The remainder of this section shows you what you should see in a packet sniffer, what you shouldn't, and how to fix it.

Although there are plenty of external packet-sniffing devices, they can be expensive and inconvenient to use. Fortunately, some operating systems come with their own packet sniffers. Solaris comes with a tool called **snoop**. IPSO, Linux, and AIX come with **tcpdump**. Both of these tools will be discussed briefly in this chapter. Windows NT/2000 machines come with a limited packet sniffer in Network Monitor, but you can obtain a free copy of Ethereal (from http://www.ethereal.com), which works far better and reads in data files from **snoop** and **tcpdump**.

Since version 4.0, FireWall-1 has also come with its own packet-sniffing utility called **fw monitor**. Because it works at the same level as FireWall-1 (i.e., just after the MAC layer and before the network layer), its use in troubleshooting NAT issues is limited. **fw monitor** relies on INSPECT code and is discussed in Chapter 14.

Consider the network and configuration that were used in the earlier step-by-step example (see Figure 10.3). Let's assume that host 192.168.42.69 is attempting to connect to 192.168.0.13, the intranet Web server, which really resides at 10.0.10.80.

With a successful connection, a **tcpdump** of the external interface should show you the following output (-i specifies an interface to listen to).

```
# tcpdump -i eth-s1p1
tcpdump: listening on eth-s1p1
18:51:20.806020 arp who-has 192.168.0.13 tell 192.168.0.2
18:51:20.806020 arp reply 192.168.0.13 is-at 0:11:22:33:44:55
18:51:54.135062 192.168.42.69.1777 > 192.168.0.13.80: S
1184222758:1184222758(0) win 16384 <mss 1460,nop,wscale 0,
nop,nop,timestamp[|tcp]> (DF) [tos 0x10]
18:51:54.135062 192.168.0.13.80 > 192.168.42.69.1777: S
1332216451:1332216451(0) ack 1184222759 win 32120 <mss 1460,
nop,nop,timestamp 2739310[|tcp]> (DF)
18:51:54.415021 192.168.42.69.1777 > 192.168.0.13.80: . ack 1
win 17376 <nop,nop,timestamp 11362405 2739310> (DF) [tos 0x10]
```

If you were to use **snoop**, you would see the following output (-d on **snoop** specifies an interface to listen to).

```
# snoop -d hme0
Using device /dev/hme (promiscuous mode)
192.168.0.2 -> (broadcast)   ARP C Who is 192.168.0.13 ?
192.168.0.1 -> 192.168.0.2 ARP R 192.168.0.13 is 0:11:22:33:44:55
192.168.42.69 -> 192.168.0.13 HTTP C port=1777
192.168.0.13 -> 192.168.42.69 HTTP R port=1777
192.168.42.69 -> 192.168.0.13 HTTP C port=1777
```

Note that you may not necessarily see the ARP packets, especially if the originator of the packet already has the MAC address in its ARP cache. If you see SYN, SYN/ACK, and ACK packets, the connection should be established.

ARPs

The first part of the communication you should see is the request for MAC addresses via an ARP packet. When everything is working correctly, you will see an exchange like the following on the external interface with **tcpdump:**

```
18:13:20.806020 arp who-has 192.168.0.13 tell 192.168.0.2
18:13:20.806020 arp reply 192.168.0.13 is-at 0:11:22:33:44:55
```

With **snoop**, it looks like this:

```
192.168.0.2 -> (broadcast)   ARP C Who is 192.168.0.13 ?
192.168.0.1 -> 192.168.0.2 ARP R 192.168.0.13 is 0:11:22:33:44:55
```

If you do see only the first packet over and over again (e.g., the ARP "who is"), this means that nobody owns or is proving a proxy ARP for the translated address. Add a proxy ARP as described previously. In some cases (especially when Windows is the firewall), you may need to add a static host route on the external router.

SYN Packets with No Response

You should then see the SYN packet, which looks something like this with **tcpdump**:

```
18:13:22.040132 192.168.42.69.1777 > 192.168.0.13.80: S
3911298019:3911298019(0) win 16384 <mss 1460,nop,wscale
0,nop,nop,timestamp[|tcp]> (DF) [tos 0x10]
```

With **snoop**, it looks like this:

```
192.168.42.69 -> 192.168.0.13 HTTP C port=1777
```

If this packet repeats over and over again, one of four things may be wrong.

- The security policy is dropping the packet. Check your logs for drops.
- The packet is being sent to the wrong MAC address.
- The packet is not being routed properly.
- The packet isn't actually getting translated, thus it is getting ignored.

Verify that the MAC address the packet is being sent to is correct (in this case, it should be 0:11:22:33:44:55). In **tcpdump**, you do this with the -e flag, which adds the MAC address to the output. In **snoop**, the only way to do this is with the -v flag, which unfortunately is extremely verbose.

Also, you can show only packets going to or coming from host 192.168.0.13 by adding host 192.168.0.13 to the end of your **tcpdump** or **snoop** command line.

```
# tcpdump -e -i eth-s1p1 host 192.168.0.13
tcpdump: listening on eth-s1p1
18:21:49.201680 0:aa:bb:cc:dd:ee 0:55:44:33:22:11 ip 82:
192.168.42.69.2000 > 192.168.0.13.80: S 90360382:90360382(0)
win 16384 <mss 1460,nop,wscale 0,nop,nop,timestamp[|tcp]>
(DF) [tos 0x10]
18:21:54.240965 0:aa:bb:cc:dd:ee 0:55:44:33:22:11 ip 82:
192.168.42.69.2000 > 192.168.0.13.80: S 90360382:90360382(0)
win 16384 <mss 1460,nop,wscale 0,nop,nop,timestamp[|tcp]>
(DF) [tos 0x10]
18:22:07.209125 0:aa:bb:cc:dd:ee 0:55:44:33:22:11 ip 82:
192.168.42.69.2000 > 192.168.0.13.80: S 90360382:90360382(0)
win 16384 <mss 1460,nop,wscale 0,nop,nop,timestamp[|tcp]>
(DF) [tos 0x10]
```

```
# snoop -v -d hme0 host 192.168.0.13
Using device /dev/hme (promiscuous mode)
ETHER:   - -- Ether Header  - --
ETHER:
ETHER:  Packet 27 arrived at 16:47:50.83
ETHER:  Packet size = 58 bytes
ETHER:  Destination = 0:55:44:33:22:11,
ETHER:  Source     = 0:aa:bb:cc:dd:ee,
ETHER:  Ethertype = 0800 (IP)
ETHER:
IP:   - -- IP Header  - --
IP:
IP:   Version = 4
IP:   Header length = 20 bytes
IP:   Type of service = 0x00
IP:         xxx. .... = 0 (precedence)
IP:         ...0 .... = normal delay
IP:         .... 0... = normal throughput
IP:         .... .0.. = normal reliability
IP:   Total length = 44 bytes
IP:   Identification = 47535
IP:   Flags = 0x4
IP:         .1.. .... = do not fragment
IP:         ..0. .... = last fragment
IP:   Fragment offset = 0 bytes
IP:   Time to live = 245 seconds/hops
IP:   Protocol = 6 (TCP)
IP:   Header checksum = f23f
IP:   Source address = 192.168.42.69
IP:   Destination address = 192.168.0.13
IP:   No options
IP:
TCP:   - -- TCP Header  - --
TCP:
TCP:  Source port = 2000
TCP:  Destination port = 80 (HTTP)
TCP:  Sequence number = 90360382
TCP:  Acknowledgement number = 0
TCP:  Data offset = 24 bytes
TCP:  Flags = 0x02
TCP:         ..0. .... = No urgent pointer
TCP:         ...0 .... = No acknowledgement
TCP:         .... 0... = No push
TCP:         .... .0.. = No reset
TCP:         .... ..1. = Syn
TCP:         .... ...0 = No Fin
TCP:  Window = 8760
TCP:  Checksum = 0xda2b
TCP:  Urgent pointer = 0
```

```
TCP:  Options: (4 bytes)
TCP:    - Maximum segment size = 1460 bytes
TCP:
```

In the preceding case, MAC 0:aa:bb:cc:dd:ee (which is the MAC of the external router) is trying to send to MAC 0:55:44:33:22:11, which is not the correct MAC. You can usually resolve this problem by flushing the ARP cache on the external router and retrying the test.

If the packet is not being routed properly, you could see a reset (RST) packet (see the next subsection), or you could see an ICMP Destination Unreachable packet. Verify that the static host route for 192.168.0.13 is pointing to the next hop address (10.0.0.2, as shown in Figure 10.3).

If the packet is not actually being translated, you will see it very clearly in a **tcpdump** or **snoop** on the internal interface, as demonstrated below.

```
# tcpdump -i eth-s1p2 host 192.168.42.69
tcpdump: listening on eth-s1p2
18:13:22.040132 192.168.42.69.1777 > 192.168.0.13.80: S
3911298019:3911298019(0) win 16384 <mss 1460,nop,wscale
0,nop,nop,timestamp[|tcp]> (DF) [tos 0x10]
18:18:25.040168 192.168.42.69.1777 > 192.168.0.13.80: S
3911298019:3911298019(0) win 16384 <mss 1460,nop,wscale
0,nop,nop,timestamp[|tcp]> (DF) [tos 0x10]
18:40:30.040342 192.168.42.69.1777 > 192.168.0.13.80: S
3911298019:3911298019(0) win 16384 <mss 1460,nop,wscale
0,nop,nop,timestamp[|tcp]> (DF) [tos 0x10]
```

```
# snoop -d hme0
Using device /dev/hme (promiscuous mode)
192.168.42.69 -> 192.168.0.13 HTTP C port=1777
192.168.42.69 -> 192.168.0.13 HTTP C port=1777
192.168.42.69 -> 192.168.0.13 HTTP C port=1777
```

Normally, you should see the translated IP address on the internal interface. If you do not see translated packets, check your NAT rules.

SYN Followed by RST

Sometimes the packet that follows the SYN is an RST packet, as shown in the output below. (With **snoop**, you need -v to see the TCP flags.)

```
# tcpdump -i eth-s1p1 host 192.168.0.13
tcpdump: listening on le0
18:13:22.040132 192.168.42.69.1777 > 192.168.0.13.80: S
3911298019:3911298019(0) win 16384 <mss1460,nop,wscale
0,nop,nop,timestamp[|tcp]> (DF) [tos 0x10]
18:13:22.040132 192.168.0.13.80 > 192.168.42.69.1777: R
 0:0(0) ack 3911298020 win 0 [tos 0x10]
```

```
# snoop -V -d hme0
Using device /dev/hme (promiscuous mode)
_____
192.168.42.69 -> 192.168.0.13 ETHER Type=0800 (IP), size = 58 bytes
192.168.42.69 -> 192.168.0.13 IP   D=192.168.0.13 S=192.168.42.69
LEN=44, ID=47247
192.168.42.69 -> 192.168.0.13 TCP D=80 S=1777 Syn Seq=3052932309
Len=0 Win=8760 Options=<mss 1460>
192.168.42.69 -> 192.168.0.13 HTTP C port=1777
_____
192.168.0.13 -> 192.168.42.69 ETHER Type=0800 (IP), size = 60 bytes
192.168.0.13 -> 192.168.42.69 IP   D=192.168.42.69 S=192.168.0.13
LEN=40, ID=61295
192.168.0.13 -> 192.168.42.69 TCP D=64836 S=80 Rst Ack=3052932310
Win=0
192.168.0.13 -> 192.168.42.69 HTTP R port=1777
```

If this happens, one of two things is wrong.

- The remote server is not running the service specified (in this case, port 80, HTTP).
- The packet is being routed incorrectly.

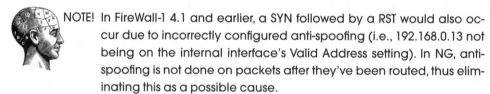 **NOTE!** In FireWall-1 4.1 and earlier, a SYN followed by a RST would also occur due to incorrectly configured anti-spoofing (i.e., 192.168.0.13 not being on the internal interface's Valid Address setting). In NG, anti-spoofing is not done on packets after they've been routed, thus eliminating this as a possible cause.

If the remote server isn't actually running the service, you will see the following in a **tcpdump** and **snoop**, respectively, on the internal interface:

```
# tcpdump -i eth-s1p1 host 10.0.10.80
tcpdump: listening on le0
18:13:22.040132 192.168.42.69.1777 > 10.0.10.80.80: S
3911298019:3911298019(0) win 16384 <mss 1460,nop,wscale
0,nop,nop,timestamp[|tcp]> (DF) [tos 0x10]
18:13:22.040132 10.0.10.80.80 > 192.168.42.69.1777: R
0:0(0) ack 3911298020 win 0 [tos 0x10]
```

```
# snoop -V -d hme0
Using device /dev/hme (promiscuous mode)
_____
192.168.42.69 -> 10.0.10.80 ETHER Type=0800 (IP), size = 58 bytes
192.168.42.69 -> 10.0.10.80 IP   D=10.0.10.80 S=192.168.42.69
LEN=44, ID=47247
192.168.42.69 -> 10.0.10.80 TCP D=80 S=1777 Syn Seq=3052932309
Len=0 Win=8760 Options=<mss 1460>
```

```
192.168.42.69 -> 10.0.10.80 HTTP C port=1777
```

```
192.168.0.13 -> 192.168.42.69 ETHER Type=0800 (IP), size = 60 bytes
192.168.0.13 -> 192.168.42.69 IP  D=192.168.42.69 S=10.0.10.80
LEN=40, ID=61295
192.168.0.13 -> 192.168.42.69 TCP D=64836 S=80 Rst Ack=3052932310
Win=0
192.168.0.13 -> 192.168.42.69 HTTP R port=1777
```

The internal interface should see the untranslated packets (10.0.10.80 is the system's real IP). If the packet is being routed to the wrong interface, you will also see the same behavior as in the preceding output. Verify that the static host route is set up correctly.

NOTE! In FireWall-1 4.1, you would also likely see a reject on Rule 0 in the logs, provided your anti-spoofing was configured correctly.

Useful `tcpdump` Flags

Table 10.4 contains a list of some useful flags for **tcpdump**, which takes commands in the following format:

```
tcpdump -i interface-name [other-flags] [expression]
```

Table 10.4 tcpdump flags

Flag	Description
-e	Displays MAC addresses with each packet.
-i interface	Specifies an interface to listen on (required).
-l	Indicates to not buffer stdout, which is useful for piping **tcpdump** output to other programs.
-n	Disables name resolution on the packets shown.
-p	Indicates to not put the interface in promiscuous mode (i.e., show only the packets destined for the host).
-r filename	Reads **tcpdump** capture from the specified file.
-s N	Captures N number of bytes for each packet (useful with -x and -X). The default is 68.
-S	Prints absolute TCP sequence numbers instead of relative ones.
-w filename	Writes captured packets to the specified file.
-x	Performs a hex dump of received packets.
-X	Performs a hex and ASCII dump of received packets (IPSO only).

`tcpdump` Expressions

All **tcpdump** commands can be followed by an expression that filters the displayed (or saved) packets to show only the packets that are interesting. Some useful expressions are shown in Table 10.5.

Table 10.5. `tcpdump` expressions

Expression	Description
`port 80`	Shows all packets with source or destination port 80 (TCP or UDP).
`host 192.168.0.3`	Shows all packets coming from or going to host 192.168.0.3.
`host 192.168.0.3 and tcp port 80`	Shows all packets coming from or going to host 192.168.0.3 that are TCP packets with a source or destination port of 80.
`proto vrrp`	Shows all VRRP packets. On non-IPSO platforms, use `ip proto 112`.
`icmp`	Shows all ICMP packets.
`\(src host 192.168.0.1 or src host 192.168.0.2\) and proto vrrp`	Shows all VRRP packets that originate from 192.168.0.1 and 192.168.0.2 (the \ before the parenthesis is to escape it for the shell).
`ether host aa:bb:cc:dd:ee:ff`	Shows all packets that come from or go to the specified MAC address.
`ip proto 50`	Shows all packets of IP Proto 50, which by definition are IPSec AH packets.
`ip[2:2] > 576`	Shows IP packets that are longer than 576 bytes. `[2:2]` refers to the specific byte location in the TCP header and its length.
`tcp[13] & 0x12 != 0`	Shows only TCP SYN/ACK packets. `tcp[13]` refers to the 13th byte in the TCP header of the packet.
`icmp[0]`	Shows ICMP type 0 packets (i.e., echo reply). `icmp[0]` refers to the 0th byte in the ICMP header.
`icmp[0] = 3 and icmp[1] = 4`	Shows ICMP type 3, code 4 packets. These happen to be a response to receiving a packet that is too large to process and has the Don't Fragment bit set.

Useful **snoop** Flags

Table 10.6 contains a list of some useful flags for **snoop**, which takes commands in the following format:

```
snoop [flags] [expression]
```

Table 10.6. snoop flags

Flag	Description
-d interface	Specifies an interface to listen on.
-v	Enables verbose mode. All packet data is displayed for each packet. When using this option, it is recommended that you pipe the output of the **snoop** command to a file or you run the risk of not being able to easily terminate your **snoop** command.
-V	Enables a less-verbose verbose mode. A summary line is displayed for each layer in the ISO model.
-n	Disables name resolution on the packets shown.
-P	Indicates to not put the interface in promiscuous mode, which means to show only the packets actually destined for this host (not useful on a switched segment).
-i filename	Reads packets previously captured from the file filename.
-o filename	Writes packets to capture the file named filename.
-s numbytes	Captures numbytes bytes for each packet. Normally, all bytes in the packet are captured.
-p x,y	Shows packets numbered between x and y. The first packet captured is 1.
-t [a|d|r]	Sets the timestamp format: a (absolute, i.e., wall clock time), d (delta, since capture was started), and r (relative time).

Table 10.7. `snoop` expressions

Expression	Description
`port 80`	Shows all packets with source or destination port 80 (TCP or UDP).
`host 192.168.0.3`	Shows all packets coming from or going to host 192.168.0.3. You can also omit the `host` qualifier.
`host 192.168.0.3 and tcp port 80`	Shows all packets coming from or going to host 192.168.0.3 that are TCP packets with a source or destination port of 80.
`icmp`	Shows all ICMP packets.
`from 192.168.0.1 or to 192.168.0.2`	Shows all packets that originate from 192.168.0.1 or are destined for 192.168.0.2.
`ether aa:bb:cc:dd:ee:ff`	Shows all packets that come from or go to the specified MAC address.
`ip proto 50`	Shows all packets of IP Proto 50, which by definition are IPSec AH packets.
`greater 576`	Shows packets longer than 576 bytes. You can use the word `less` instead of `greater` to show packets smaller than 576 bytes.
`tcp[13] & 0x12 != 0`	Shows only TCP SYN/ACK packets. `tcp[13]` refers to the 13th byte in the TCP header of the packet.

snoop Expressions

All **snoop** commands can be followed by an expression that filters the displayed (or saved) packets to show only the packets that are interesting. Table 10.7 presents some useful expressions. Note that many of the expressions are similar to those for **tcpdump**.

Summary

NAT is necessary because organizations and individuals need the ability to allow more hosts to communicate with the Internet than their address space allows. Specific blocks of IP addresses have been set aside to accommodate NAT.

NAT also provides a way to more efficiently use address space without the overhead imposed by subnetting. However, NAT imposes restrictions of its own, and it may not be appropriate for every situation.

Sample Configurations

The following three situations are representative of those I have encountered in the real world. Each is designed to demonstrate what people typically do with NAT and how the situations would be implemented on the chosen platform.

Creating a Simple Network with NAT

The Situation

You work for a small company with a few hosts on a flat network segment. Your firewall runs on a Windows NT platform. The ISP has given you only a /29 net block, which effectively gives you six hosts you can use on the outside segment. Because the firewall and Internet router each need a unique IP address, this leaves a total of four addresses that can be used for other hosts (see Figure 10.8).

The Goals

- Allow Internet users access to the mail and Web servers via SMTP and HTTP, respectively. In the future, these services will be provided on separate systems, so setting up each service with a unique IP is desirable to make future migration easier.
- Allow internal users to access anything on the Internet. All outbound users will be hidden behind a single IP address; however, this IP address should be different from the firewall.

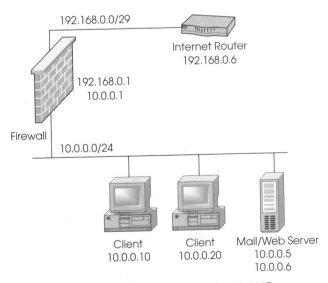

Figure 10.8 Simple network with NAT

The Checklist

- Determine which IP addresses will be used for translation.
- Set up the necessary proxy ARPs.
- Set up the necessary static host routes.
- Create the necessary network objects.
- Make the necessary modifications to anti-spoofing.
- Create the necessary rulebase rules to permit the desired traffic.
- Create the NAT rules.
- Install the security policy.

The Implementation

You must first determine which IPs you will use. Your usable IPs are 192.168.0.2–192.168.0.5. Let's use 192.168.0.2 as the IP for your external clients to hide behind, 192.168.0.3 for the SMTP server, and 192.168.0.4 for the HTTP server.

Next, set up the static ARPs for the translated addresses. In order to do this, you need to determine the MAC address of your external interface. Use the command **ipconfig /all** to determine this address:

```
Ethernet adapter 3C5x91 :

        Description . . . . . . . . : 3Com 3C5x9 Ethernet Adapter
        Physical Address. . . . . . : 00-22-44-66-88-AA
        DHCP Enabled. . . . . . . . : No
        IP Address. . . . . . . . . : 192.168.0.1
        Subnet Mask . . . . . . . . : 255.255.255.248
        Default Gateway . . . . . . : 192.168.0.6

Ethernet adapter 3C5x92:

        Description . . . . . . . . : 3Com 3C5x9 Ethernet Adapter
        Physical Address. . . . . . : 00-00-87-20-66-69
        DHCP Enabled. . . . . . . . : No
        IP Address. . . . . . . . . : 10.0.0.1
        Subnet Mask . . . . . . . . : 255.255.255.0
        Default Gateway . . . . . . :
```

The external MAC is 00-22-44-66-88-AA, which you will enter along with the IP addresses in the %FWDIR%\state\local.arp file:

```
192.168.0.2 00-22-44-66-88-AA
192.168.0.3 00-22-44-66-88-AA
192.168.0.4 00-22-44-66-88-AA
```

The 192.168.0.3 and 192.168.0.4 addresses each need a static host route. The 192.168.0.2 address does not need one because users should never be directly connecting to 192.168.0.2. The Web/mail host has two unique IP addresses associated with it. This is necessary because NAT requires a direct one-to-one mapping of IPs. This host is on the same subnet as the firewall, so the static route should be directed at the host itself:

```
> route -p add 192.168.0.3 10.0.0.5
> route -p add 192.168.0.4 10.0.0.6
```

Because you are using the -p option, these routes will be available after a reboot; they will be stored in the Registry.

Table 10.8 lists the network objects you will create.

When configuring your firewall object, set your valid address settings according to those shown in Table 10.9. Use the Topology frame of your gateway object. Also, make sure that each interface has the Spoof Tracking set to Log to catch any errors in the anti-spoofing configuration.

Table 10.8 Network objects for sample configuration 1

Name	Object Type	IP/Netmask/ Group Objects	Description
net-internal	Network	10.0.0.0/255.255.255.0	The network that represents the internal network
web-server	Node, host	10.0.0.6	The mail/Web server on the internal network
mail-server	Node, host	10.0.0.5	The mail/Web server on the internal network
mail-ext	Node, host	192.168.0.3	The translated IP for the mail server
web-ext	Node, host	192.168.0.4	The translated IP for the Web server
external-hide	Node, host	192.168.0.2	The IP that users will hide behind when going out
valid-internal	Group	net-internal	Your internal interface's valid addresses for anti-spoofing
firewall	Check Point gateway	192.168.0.1	Your firewall

Table 10.9 Valid address settings for the firewall in sample configuration 1

Interface	Valid Address Setting
3C5x91	Specific: valid-internal
3C5x92	External

The rulebase should look similar to the one shown in Figure 10.9. The NAT rules should look like those shown in Figure 10.10.

Save and install the policy.

Notes

It is not a wise idea to have your internal hosts on the same LAN segment as hosts that are accessible from an untrusted network like the Internet. However, this is a situation that, for various reasons, all too many security administrators find themselves in. From a security standpoint, you are much better off trying to move externally accessible servers to a DMZ. It will cost a couple hundred dollars to purchase an extra LAN adapter, an extra switch or hub, and a few extra cables, but the extra security gained will be well worth it.

NO.	SOURCE	DESTINATION	SERVICE	ACTION	TRACK
1	✳ Any	🖥 web-ext	TCP http	🛡 accept	📄 Log
2	✳ Any	🖥 mail-ext	TCP smtp	🛡 accept	📄 Log
3	🏢 net-internal	⊠ net-internal	✳ Any	🛡 accept	📄 Log
4	✳ Any	✳ Any	✳ Any	⊘ drop	📄 Log

Figure 10.9 Security policy for sample configuration 1

NO.	ORIGINAL PACKET			TRANSLATED PACKET		
	SOURCE	DESTINATION	SERVICE	SOURCE	DESTINATION	SERVICE
1	✳ Any	🖥 web-ext	✳ Any	= Original	🖥 mail-server	= Original
2	✳ Any	🖥 mail-ext	✳ Any	= Original	🖥 web-server	= Original
3	🏢 net-internal	✳ Any	✳ Any	🖥 external-hide	= Original	= Original

Figure 10.10 Address translation policy for sample configuration 1

You will not be able to access the mail/Web server from the internal segment via its translated addresses without some additional configuration, which is left as an exercise. (Hint: look at the "white" rules in Figure 10.6.)

Migrating to a Larger Net with NAT

The Situation

The company you work for has grown. Your ISP has given you an external segment with a few more addresses (192.168.1.64/28), and you have a separate LAN segment for your DMZ, which now also has a few more hosts in it. Your firewall platform has also changed from Windows NT to Solaris.

A certain amount of backward compatibility needs to be maintained with the old setup; that is, certain hosts need to be reachable by their old addresses. For the external addresses, the ISP is continuing to route the 192.168.0.0/29 segment to you until such time as the address space is no longer needed (see Figure 10.11).

The Goals

- Allow Internet users access to the mail and Web servers via SMTP and HTTP, respectively. Note that the servers will have to be accessible by their old IPs as well as their new ones.

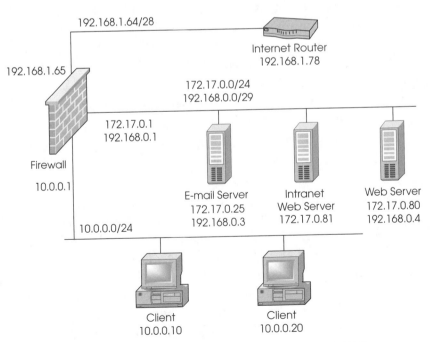

Figure 10.11   Migrating to a larger network with NAT

- Allow internal users to access anything on the Internet. All outbound users will be hidden behind a single IP address; however, this IP address should be different from the firewall.
- Allow internal users to access the intranet Web server by its old IP address (10.0.0.5). This server will not be accessible from the Internet.

The Checklist

- Determine which IP addresses will be used for translation.
- Set up the necessary proxy ARPs.
- Set up the necessary static host routes.
- Create the necessary network objects.
- Make the necessary modifications to anti-spoofing.
- Create the necessary rulebase rules to permit the desired traffic.
- Create the NAT rules.
- Install the security policy.

The Implementation

To simplify your NAT configuration a bit, assign the 192.168.0.0/29 network to the DMZ. Make sure the external router is configured to route all requests for this network to the firewall. You also need to give the firewall an IP address of 192.168.0.1 on the DMZ interface. In Solaris, you add an /etc/hostname.qe3:1 file with this IP address. You also have to modify /etc/netmasks so that 192.168.0.0 has the correct netmask (255.255.255.248). So that you don't have to reboot for this to take effect, execute the following set of commands:

```
# ifconfig qe3:1 plumb
# ifconfig qe3:1 inet 192.168.0.1 netmask 255.255.255.248
        broadcast 192.168.0.7 up
```

The SMTP and HTTP servers need to have secondary IP addresses of 192.168.0.3 and 192.168.0.4, respectively. Similar steps need to be taken on these servers.

You must then determine which IPs you will use for translation. Your new usable address range is 192.168.1.66–192.168.1.77. Let's make 192.168.1.66 the IP you use for your external clients to hide behind, 192.168.1.67 the new IP for your SMTP server, and 192.168.1.68 the new IP for your HTTP server. You are also translating 10.0.0.5 to 172.17.0.81.

Next, set up the static ARPs for the translated addresses. Because you are translating both internal and external addresses to the DMZ, you need both the internal and external interfaces' MAC addresses. An **ifconfig -a** command shows you the following:

```
lo0: flags=849 <UP,LOOPBACK,RUNNING,MULTICAST> mtu 8232
     inet 127.0.0.1 netmask ff000000
le0: flags=863 <UP,BROADCAST,NOTRAILERS,RUNNING, MULTICAST> mtu 1500
     inet 192.168.1.65 netmask fffffff0 broadcast 192.168.1.79
     ether 0:12:34:56:78:9a
qe0: flags=863 <UP,BROADCAST,NOTRAILERS,RUNNING, MULTICAST> mtu 1500
     inet 10.0.0.1 netmask ffffff00 broadcast 10.0.0.255
     ether 8:0:20:6d:0:20
qe3: flags=863 <UP,BROADCAST,NOTRAILERS,RUNNING,MULTICAST> mtu 1500
     inet 172.17.0.1 netmask ffffff00 broadcast 172.17.0.255
     ether 8:0:20:20:0:6d
qe3:1 flags=863 <UP,BROADCAST,NOTRAILERS,RUNNING, MULTICAST> mtu 1500
     inet 192.168.0.1 netmask fffffff8 broadcast 192.168.0.7
```

The external MAC is 00:12:34:56:78:9a, and the internal MAC address is 8:0:20:20:0:6d. You would do the following ARPs:

```
# arp -s 192.168.1.66 0:12:34:56:78:9a pub
# arp -s 192.168.1.67 0:12:34:56:78:9a pub
# arp -s 192.168.1.68 0:12:34:56:78:9a pub
# arp -s 10.0.0.5      8:0:20:20:0:6d  pub
```

Static routes are as follows:

```
# route add 192.168.1.67 172.17.0.25 1
# route add 192.168.1.68 172.17.0.80 1
# route add 10.0.0.5      172.17.0.81 1
```

(Note that you still need static routes for the "old" addresses, even if you don't need ARPs for them.) Because this is a UNIX platform, these ARPs and routes will disappear after a reboot. You need to add these routes and ARPs to a startup file. It is recommended that you create a new script for this purpose (such as /etc/rc3.d/S94addroutes) and add the preceding commands to this file.

Table 10.10 shows the network objects that will be created.

When configuring your firewall object, use the Topology frame to set your valid address settings according to those shown in Table 10.11. Also, make sure that each interface has the Spoof Tracking set to Log to catch any errors in the anti-spoofing configuration.

Table 10.10   Network objects for sample configuration 2

Name	Object Type	IP/Netmask/Group Objects	Description
net-internal	Network	10.0.0.0/ 255.255.255.0	The network that represents the internal network
net-dmz	Network	172.17.0.0/ 255.255.255.0	The network that represents the DMZ
net-external-old	Network	192.168.0.0/ 255.255.255.248	The old external network now on the DMZ
mail-server	Node, host	172.17.0.25	The mail server
mail-server-ext	Node, host	192.168.1.67	The translated IP for the mail server
mail-server-ext-old	Node, host	192.168.0.3	The translated IP for the mail server (historical)
web-server	Node, host	172.17.0.80	The Web server
web-server-ext	Node, host	192.168.1.68	The translated IP for the Web server
web-server-ext-old	Node, host	192.168.0.4	The translated IP for the Web server (historical)
intranet-web-server	Node, host	172.17.0.81	The intranet Web server
intranet-web-server-int	Node, host	10.0.0.5	The translated IP for the intranet Web server
external-hide	Node, host	192.168.1.66	The IP that users will hide behind when going out
valid-dmz	Group	net-dmz + net-external-old	Your DMZ interface's valid addresses for anti-spoofing
valid-internal	Group	net-internal	Your internal interface's valid addresses for anti-spoofing
firewall	Check Point gateway	192.168.1.65	Your firewall

Table 10.11   Valid address settings for the firewall in sample configuration 2

Interface	Valid Address Setting
qe3	Specific: valid-dmz
qe0	Specific: valid-internal
le0	External

The rulebase should look similar to the ones shown in Figure 10.12. The NAT rules should look like those shown in Figure 10.13.

Save and install the policy.

Notes

Sites on the DMZ should be accessible by their translated IP addresses, even from the internal network. This is because the communication is now mediated by the firewall. In the previous example, this was not the case.

NO.	SOURCE	DESTINATION	SERVICE	ACTION	TRACK
1	✳ Any	web-server-ext web-server-ext-old	TCP http	⊕ accept	▤ Log
2	✳ Any	mail-server-ext mail-server-ext-old	TCP smtp	⊕ accept	▤ Log
3	net-internal	net-internal net-dmz	✳ Any	⊕ accept	▤ Log
4	net-internal	intranet-web-server-int	TCP http	⊕ accept	▤ Log
5	✳ Any	✳ Any	✳ Any	⊙ drop	▤ Log

Figure 10.12   Security policy for sample configuration 2

NO	ORIGINAL PACKET			TRANSLATED PACKET		
	SOURCE	DESTINATION	SERVICE	SOURCE	DESTINATION	SERVICE
1	✳ Any	web-server-ext	✳ Any	= Original	mail-server	= Original
2	✳ Any	mail-server-ext	✳ Any	= Original	web-server	= Original
3	net-internal	intranet-web-server-int	✳ Any	= Original	intranet-web-server	= Original
4	net-internal	✳ Any	✳ Any	external-hide	= Original	= Original

Figure 10.13   Address translation policy for sample configuration 2

Using a Double-Blind Network Configuration

The Situation

There is a device within your network that has a faulty IP implementation and can talk to only those hosts on the same subnet it is on (i.e., it has no concept of routing).[7] Because it is also not desirable to allow everyone to access this host, a firewall is necessary to restrict access to this host. The host is using nonroutable addresses and cannot be seen by the rest of the network. It must be given a routable address so that it can be accessed. Because neither side of the connection can know the true IP address of its peer, this is referred to as a *double-blind* network configuration.

A Nokia IP330 will be used to protect this device, which will be directly connected to the device via a crossover cable. The rest of the network (the entire 10.0.0.0/8) is used internally. Figure 10.14 shows only the relevant parts of the network.

The Goals

- Allow FTP and Telnet access to 10.20.30.6 (the translated IP address for this device).
- Allow HTTPS access to the IP330 for management purposes from a specific management console (10.250.0.5, not pictured here).
- Allow SSH access to the IP330 for management purposes from anywhere.

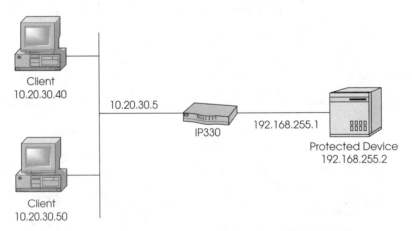

Figure 10.14   Network diagram for double-blind NAT

---

7. I've actually run into this configuration with a PBX at a college campus. As Dave Barry would say if he were writing this book, I'm not making this up.

The Checklist

- Determine which IP addresses will be used for translation.
- Set up the necessary proxy ARPs.
- Set up the necessary static host routes.
- Create the necessary network objects.
- Create the necessary rulebase rules to permit the desired traffic.
- Create the NAT rules.
- Install the security policy.

The Implementation

From the preceding goals, you know that you will be translating 10.20.30.6 to 192.168.255.2. You also know that all access to this protected device must appear to be coming from a device on the same subnet. The firewall is appropriate in this case.

You need to create an ARP for 10.20.30.6 using the MAC address of the external interface of the IP330. You can easily do this in Network Voyager. Figure 10.15 shows the Proxy ARP Entries section, where you can add a proxy ARP using a specific interface's MAC address, which is what we want. For 10.20.30.6, we will use eth-s3p1c0 as the interface. Click the Apply button at the bottom of the page.

Go to the bottom of the static route page in Voyager. Use the quick-add static routes to add a static route to route 10.20.30.6 to 192.168.255.2 (see Figure 10.16).

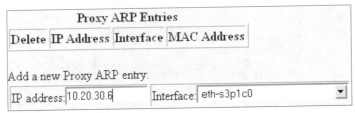

Figure 10.15   Proxy ARP Entries section in Network Voyager

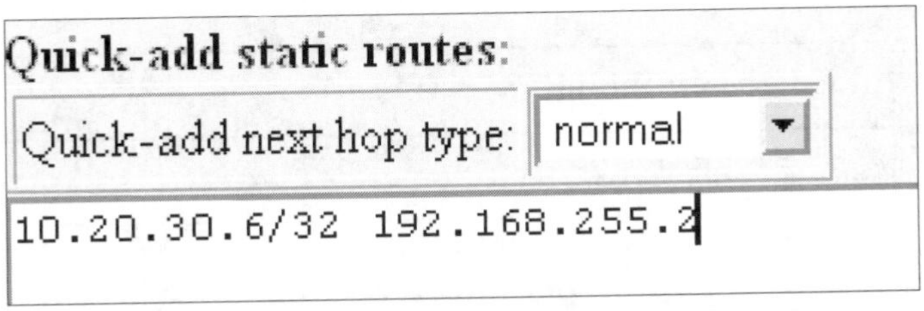

Figure 10.16   Quick-add static routes in Network Voyager

Click Apply, and then click Save. This configuration is now active across reboots.

The network objects you will create are shown in Table 10.12. When configuring your firewall object, set your valid address settings according to those shown in Table 10.13. These settings are configured in the Topology frame. Also, make sure that each interface has the Spoof Tracking set to Log to catch any errors in the anti-spoofing configuration.

Table 10.12   Network objects for sample configuration 3

Name	Object Type	IP/Netmask/ Group Objects	Description
net-protected-device	Network	192.168.255.0/ 255.255.255.0	The network on which the protected device resides
net-internal	Network	10.0.0.0/255.0.0.0	The internal network
protected-device	Node, host	192.168.255.2	The protected device's internal IP
protected-device-xlate	Node, host	10.20.30.6	The translated IP for the protected device
management-device	Node, host	10.250.0.5	The host allowed to connect to IP330 via HTTP
firewall-eth-s4p1	Node, host	192.168.255.1	A host object that represents the system's interface facing the protected device.
valid-eth-s4p1	Group	net-protected-device	The valid address setting for eth-s4p1, the interface to which the protected device is hooked
firewall	Check Point gateway	10.20.30.5	Your firewall

Table 10.13   Valid address settings for the firewall in sample configuration 3

Interface	Valid Address Setting
eth-s4p1c0	Specific: valid-eth-s4p1
eth-s3p1c0	External

NO.	SOURCE	DESTINATION	SERVICE	ACTION	TRACK
1	✷ Any	🖥 protected-device-xlate	TCP telnet TCP ftp	🔘 accept	📄 Log
2	🖥 management-device	🖼 firewall	TCP https	🔘 accept	📄 Log
3	✷ Any	🖼 firewall	TCP ssh	🔘 accept	📄 Log
4	✷ Any	✷ Any	✷ Any	🔘 drop	📄 Log

Figure 10.17 Security policy for sample configuration 3

NO.	ORIGINAL PACKET			TRANSLATED PACKET		
	SOURCE	DESTINATION	SERVICE	SOURCE	DESTINATION	SERVICE
1	🖩 internal-net	🖥 protected-device-xlate	✷ Any	🖥 firewall-eth-s4p1	🖥 protected-device	≡ Original

Figure 10.18 Address translation policy for sample configuration 3

The rulebase should look similar to the rules shown in Figure 10.17. The NAT rules should look like the one shown in Figure 10.18.

Save and install the policy.

Notes

You could do this in the reverse direction as well (i.e., have the protected device access hosts on the other side of the firewall as if they were on the same subnet), but this sample configuration shows the connections occurring in only one direction.

Chapter

11

Site-to-Site VPN

This chapter is designed to be a practical guide to planning and configuring site-to-site Virtual Private Networks (VPNs) with FireWall-1. I briefly cover a few key terms and concepts and jump right into what can be done in FireWall-1 and how to do it. This chapter is not meant to comprehensively cover encryption or encryption technologies.

By the end of this chapter, you should be able to do the following:

- Plan for a VPN
- Determine which key exchange and encryption schemes FireWall-1 uses
- Set up a VPN with FireWall-1
- Understand what a gateway cluster is and what functions it provides
- Troubleshoot VPN problems

Introduction to a VPN

A VPN is a technology that allows two or more locations to communicate securely over a public network while maintaining the security and privacy of a private network. Encryption, authentication, and packet integrity checks are key enablers of VPNs; they ensure that the data is private and the integrity of the data is maintained. The main reason for using VPNs is that private networks are expensive to acquire and maintain. Companies are finding VPNs a cost-effective way to connect sites to one another.

Given that firewalls are designed to be the gatekeepers between public and private networks, it makes sense to integrate VPN capabilities into a firewall. You can not only filter traffic but also subject VPN usage to a security policy that is integrated with your existing one. In FireWall-1, there is no separate place to create a VPN rulebase; it is simply part of your existing security policy. This makes it really easy to implement a VPN in FireWall-1.

Concepts

Many generic concepts are used throughout this chapter and are briefly defined in the following subsections. Because this chapter is not meant to comprehensively cover encryption, these descriptions may seem inadequate. For a more detailed description of these concepts, refer to Bruce Schneier's *Applied Cryptography* [1996].

Cryptography and Encryption

Cryptography is the art and science of keeping messages secure. Encryption is the actual process of transforming data into a nearly random form that can be reversed only in specific circumstances. Encryption ensures privacy by keeping information hidden from anyone for whom it is not intended, even those who have access to the encrypted data. Without encryption, a VPN would not be possible.

Encryption Keys

An encryption key is used to either encrypt data, decrypt data, or both. The kind of key used depends on the type of encryption algorithm used. The number of bits in this key plays a role in determining how strong the encryption is, though the encryption algorithm and the implementation thereof arguably play a bigger role. The fewer the bits, the easier it is to guess the encryption key by brute force (i.e., by simply trying each possible key).

Entropy—the Random Pool

Computers are deterministic: They do exactly what you tell them to do. This makes it difficult to have computers do something randomly, though personal experience might suggest otherwise. Unfortunately, there is no really good way to have a computer do something like, for instance, come up with a random encryption key. If the encryption keys aren't random or are relatively easy to work out, it doesn't matter what your encryption scheme is—someone's going to be able to read your encrypted message.

Pseudo-random number generators used in cryptography need to have two properties to be cryptographically secure.

1. The output they generate looks random. This means the output can pass all statistical tests of randomness that we can find.
2. The output must be unpredictable. This means it must be computationally infeasible to predict what the next random number will be, given the knowledge of the algorithm in use and all previously generated numbers.

One way that pseudo-random number generators are able to meet these criteria is to employ methods of obtaining entropy, or randomness from various sources. These random sources must be relatively difficult to reproduce and/or influence in a particular manner. Recall that when you first installed FireWall-1, it asked you to enter a bunch of random text. FireWall-1 uses the timing between keystrokes and the keys entered as a way to gather some initial entropy to use for the encryption processes. Other programs or operating systems may use certain kinds of network traffic, messages in system logs, or various counters from the system to gather entropy.

Symmetric Encryption

Symmetric encryption uses the same key for encrypting and decrypting data. The encryption key needs to be kept secret and should be exchanged via some sort of secure mechanism. Symmetric encryption is generally used for bulk data encryption because it is faster than other methods. Examples of symmetric encryption include the Data Encryption Standard (DES), Blowfish, the recently approved Advanced Encryption Standard (AES), and FWZ.

Asymmetric Encryption

Asymmetric encryption uses different keys for encrypting and decrypting data. Asymmetric encryption schemes are approximately 1,000 times slower than symmetric encryption schemes on similar hardware and are used only to exchange small amounts of data (e.g., encryption keys for a symmetric algorithm).

All public-key cryptography systems, such as RSA,[1] are asymmetric algorithms. In these systems, each node has a public key (which is widely distributed) and a private key (which is kept secret). A node's public and private keys have a peculiar property in that they effectively cancel out each other's effects, thus allowing you to encrypt and decrypt them in combination with another person's keys.

Consider the following example: The source node can encrypt a message using the destination node's public key, and only the destination node can decrypt it. More importantly, a source node can encrypt the message with its private key *and* the destination node's public key. The destination node can decrypt it using its own private key and the source node's public key. Aside from encrypting the message, the process provides verification that the source node was the correct node, another important function.

---

1. RSA is an encryption and authentication system that uses an algorithm developed in 1977. It is named for its authors: Ron Rivest (the R), Adi Shamir (the S), and Leonard Adleman (the A).

Hash Functions

A hash function is a one-way function that takes a variable-length input and converts it to a fixed-length string. One-way functions have the unique property of being difficult to reverse, meaning that, given the function and its output, it is computationally unfeasible to determine what value(s) was originally plugged into the function to give that output. One-way functions suitable for cryptographic use need to be collision-free, that is, it must be hard to create any two inputs that generate the same output.

Although they do not encrypt data per se, the hash functions themselves are based in cryptography and provide a very important purpose in the encryption process: validation. When data is placed through a hash function, the result is sort of a "checksum." Because it is highly unlikely that any two inputs to a hash function will give the same result, you can be reasonably confident that the data has not been tampered with.

Within the context of a VPN, the sender encrypts a packet, then passes it through a hash function, the result of which is encrypted with a symmetric algorithm such as RSA. The encrypted packet and the encrypted hash are forwarded to the recipient. Prior to decrypting, the recipient computes a hash on the encrypted packet, then decrypts the received hash and verifies that the computed and received hashes are identical. If the two hashes match, the message must have been sent by the claimed sender.

Examples of hash functions include MD5 and SHA-1.

Fingerprints

Public keys are run through a hash function to generate a result called the fingerprint. This is used to verify that you are working with the correct key. For example, I placed the fingerprint to my Pretty Good Privacy (PGP) key in the preface of this book. If you find what appears to be my PGP key on the Internet, you can download it and ask your PGP application to display this key's fingerprint. If PGP shows the same fingerprint as printed in the preface, you most likely have my correct PGP key because it is unlikely that two different PGP public keys will yield the same PGP fingerprint.

To use an example more relevant to FireWall-1, during installation of the management station, you are shown a fingerprint. The first time you connect to the management station with SmartDashboard/Policy Editor, the management station sends the public key. SmartDashboard/Policy Editor runs this key through the same hash function and displays a fingerprint for you to verify. The fingerprint shown during the initial installation should match what is shown in SmartDashboard/Policy Editor.

Certificate Authorities

A certificate authority (CA) is a trusted third party that certifies public keys. The CA has its own public and private keys. The CA takes prudent steps to verify the authenticity of a public key. The CA then signs the node's public key by encrypting it with its private key, which is then widely distributed. A node can verify it has the correct public key by decrypting using the CA's public key.

A firewall management console has its own CA, the Internal Certificate Authority (ICA). Certificates are used for authentication between managed modules. They can also be generated for firewalls to use with Internet Key Exchange (IKE) encryption as well as to identify end users. FireWall-1 does support third-party CAs.

Diffie-Hellman Keys

Diffie-Hellman (DH) keys are essentially public- and private-key pairs used in an asymmetric encryption algorithm. To verify that the keys have not been tampered with, they are typically signed by a CA key.

The Encryption Domain

The encryption domain is a concept that is not entirely unique to FireWall-1, but the term is. Generally speaking, it contains everything on the private side of the network (i.e., all hosts behind the gateway in question). Note that this does not mean that every host in the encryption domain is allowed to communicate through a VPN. This is controlled by the defined security policy. The encryption domain just defines the *potential* for encryption. You must include all translated IP addresses for internal hosts. In general, the firewall is not part of the encryption domain but can be. It should be if the firewall is being used as the *hide* address for internal hosts.

A Word about Licensing

The VPN features of FireWall-1 require licenses that enable VPN. In FireWall-1 4.1 and earlier, you also had to have the appropriate binaries. In NG, there is only one version of the binaries, which all support encryption. With the release of NG AI R55, Check Point removed fire-wall only licenses from their price list, thus newly purchased licenses will be VPN enabled. Older licenses may need an upgrade (at extra cost) to support VPN functions.

To ensure that you have licenses capable of supporting the appropriate level of encryption, check Table 11.1 against your license string, which includes the product SKU as listed on Check Point's price lists. This will tell you what level of encryption you have purchased, if any.

Table 11.1 FireWall-1 NG SKUs and encryption strength

SKU	Encryption Strength
3DES	Strongest encryption available
DES	56-bit encryption and lower
FWZ1	48-bit encryption and lower
40bit	40-bit encryption only

VPN-1 Pro versus VPN-1 Net

Check Point has introduced a new type of VPN license in NG: VPN-1 Net. VPN-1 Pro is the more traditional license, which supports a custom security policy and can be licensed by the number of protected nodes. VPN-1 Net allows for relatively simple security and VPN policies that cannot be customized; it is licensed by the number of tunnels created, not by the number of hosts. A VPN-1 Net license is far less expensive than a comparable VPN-1 Pro license, though the VPN-1 Net is less functional.

The vast majority of this chapter covers VPN-1 Pro, not VPN-1 Net.

FWZ, IPSec, and IKE

Previous versions of FireWall-1 supported a variety of key-management schemes. In NG, the only supported scheme is IKE. FireWall-1 NG FP1 and earlier also support the FWZ scheme, which Check Point deprecated in NG FP2. I briefly describe FWZ here mostly for historical reasons—its use is not described in this book.

FWZ

FWZ is Check Point's proprietary key-management system and has been available since Check Point made VPN technology part of FireWall-1 in version 2.0. FWZ incorporates the following:

- A CA (a FireWall-1 management console)
- Asymmetric encryption for the exchange of CA, DH, and per-session encryption keys
- Symmetric encryption for actual data encryption using FWZ1, a proprietary Check Point algorithm that encrypts at 48 bits, or DES, the U.S. government's data encryption standard at 56 bits

- Optional data integrity checking with an MD5 hash
- Out-of-band management of encryption keys with the RDP protocol (which runs on UDP port 259)

Unlike most encryption methods, which encrypt the entire packet (data and headers) and encapsulate it in a new packet, FWZ encrypts only the data portion of the packet, leaving the original IP headers intact. This means that little additional transmission overhead is incurred. However, it also means that if you want other hosts to access nonroutable address space behind your firewall, you must also perform NAT in order to participate in a VPN.

Due to the numerous issues with FWZ, including the fact it is nonstandard and supports only weak encryption algorithms, Check Point decided to drop FWZ in FireWall-1 NG FP2 and later.

IPSec

IPSec is a set of standards designed by the Internet Engineering Task Force (IETF), which define how hosts communicate with one another in a secure manner. In tunnel mode (which is what FireWall-1 uses), all communication between any two hosts is completely encapsulated (both IP headers and data) in new packets, which adds up to 100 bytes per packet.

IPSec has two main protocols: an Authentication Header (AH), which is designed to provide integrity and authentication without confidentiality to IP datagrams, and the Encapsulating Security Payload (ESP), which is designed to provide integrity, authentication, and confidentiality to IP datagrams. AH and ESP can be used together or separately, but AH is rarely used in IPSec because ESP provides everything that AH provides plus encryption. In fact, FireWall-1 NG does not even support AH, though you could configure ESP with no encryption and effectively get the same result.

Many different encryption algorithms are used in IPSec for both encryption and data integrity checking. Some of them include the following:

- 3DES (168-bit)[2]
- DES (40-bit and 56-bit)
- AES (128-bit and 256-bit)
- CAST (40-bit)

---

2. 3DES is essentially the DES algorithm run at 56 bits with three separate passes using two different encryption keys. Although many people claim this is 168-bit encryption ($3 \times 56 = 168$), there are really only 112 bits of secret key.

NOTE! Not all of these encryption algorithms are part of the IPSec standard. Extra care should be taken when setting up a VPN with third-party products.

For data integrity purposes, FireWall-1 uses these algorithms:

- RSA (768-bit, 1024-bit, and 1536-bit)
- DH (768-bit, 1024-bit, and 1536-bit)

IKE

IKE is the standard IPSec key-management scheme in use today. It supports automated key exchange and Public Key Infrastructure (PKI), which allows encryption keys to be managed by a separate central server (e.g., the ICA). A "pre-shared secret" (effectively a password) can also be established between two nodes.

Security Associations

Used as part of IPSec, security associations (SAs) are security policies defined for communication between two hosts or subnets. A key represents the relationship between these two. The IKE protocol is used to securely communicate these SAs.

How to Configure Encryption

As you will find, the steps in configuring encryption are very similar regardless of which encryption scheme you use. Throughout this section, I refer to the proposed VPN setup in Figure 11.1.

NOTE! As noted previously in the book, I treat 192.168.x.x as *routable address space* even though it is generally not considered routable per RFC1918.

Planning Your Deployment

You need the following information when planning a VPN based in FireWall-1:

- Which hosts and/or networks the remote site will be able to access through the VPN (your encryption domain)
- Which hosts and/or networks will be accessible at the remote site (the partner's encryption domain)
- Whether certificates or pre-shared secrets will be used

Site A has networks 10.0.0.0/8 and 172.16.0.0/16 behind its gateway. The encryption domain for Site A should include these networks along with any

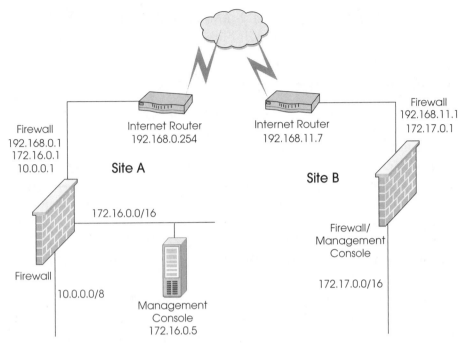

Figure 11.1   Sample VPN configuration

translated IP addresses for hosts on these networks. Likewise, Site B has the network 172.17.0.0/16 behind its gateway. The encryption domain for Site B should include these networks along with any translated IP addresses for hosts on this network.

Note that it may not be desirable for every host within the various networks to be accessible. This is okay. It is possible to restrict which hosts are accessible via the security policy. The encryption domain simply contains every network and host that could potentially be accessed through the VPN. The security policy determines which hosts can *actually* be accessed.

Should you use certificates or pre-shared secrets? The only time to consider using a pre-shared secret is when you are interoperating with either a pre-NG version of FireWall-1 or a third-party VPN. The version of FireWall-1 and how you define the VPN will determine which method(s) you can use. See the next subsection for details.

For certificates, the decision is very easy if the same management station manages all gateways in the VPN and they all run NG: Use certificates, which will be basically automatic. If a different management station manages one or more of the gateways, you will have to exchange CA keys so that your certificates can be validated. The current example demonstrates this.

Now that you know the necessary information about the different sides of the VPN, let's talk about how to set this up—in Traditional mode or Simplified mode.

Traditional Mode or Simplified Mode?

Traditional mode means defining VPNs the way it was always done in FireWall-1 4.1 and earlier versions, namely, with rules that use the action "encrypt." Simplified mode uses a VPN Community, which is similar to a group. It contains all the firewalls and encryption domains that will participate in a VPN. The community also defines which encryption methods will be used between the gateways, which simplifies configuration dramatically. A Simplified mode rulebase has a new column, If Via, which allows you to restrict certain types of traffic to be within the context of a VPN (e.g., site-a can talk to site-b only in an encrypted manner). This also makes for a far simpler rulebase, particularly when you get into a several-site VPN.

Simplified mode has an important limitation in FireWall-1 NG FP2 and before: You cannot set a pre-shared secret for IKE. If you are using NG FP2 and are setting up VPNs with non–Check Point endpoints (i.e., those endpoints represented as interoperable devices), you will need to use encryption rules.

You can determine whether new rulebases are created to use Simplified or Traditional mode by going into the Global Properties section, VPN-1 Pro frame, in SmartDashboard/Policy Editor, as shown in Figure 11.2.

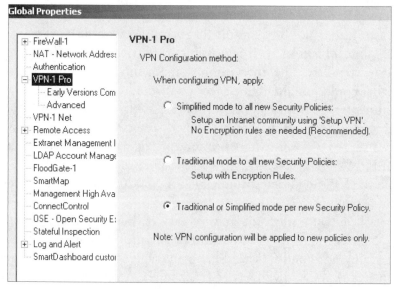

Figure 11.2   Global Properties, VPN-1 Pro frame

Until you have decided which method of creating a VPN is right for you, it is advisable to select the third option listed, Traditional or Simplified mode per new Security Policy. Once you have decided to go one way or the other, set the appropriate option.

> NOTE! This setting determines the mode only for newly created security policies. Old security policies maintain their existing Simplified or Traditional states when you change this setting in the VPN-1 Pro frame.

It is possible to convert an existing Traditional mode rulebase into a Simplified mode policy using the conversion tool present in FireWall-1 NG FP3 and later within SmartDashboard/Policy Editor. However, you cannot convert from a Simplified configuration to a Traditional one. If you decide to convert back to encryption rules, you will need to remove all of your gateways from all VPN communities or your VPN will not function correctly.

I show how to set up the VPN using both Traditional and Simplified rules in this chapter. The next subsection explains how to configure the VPN in Traditional mode; the subsection after that covers Simplified mode configuration.

Configuring the VPN in Traditional Mode

You first need to define the encryption domain for Site A and Site B on both gateways. Site A's encryption domain includes:

- 10.0.0.0/255.0.0.0 (or 10.0.0.0/8)
- 172.16.0.0/255.255.0.0 (or 172.16.0.0/16)

Define network objects for both of these networks. Put them into a group called SiteA-encdomain. Similarly, for Site B, the encryption domain contains a network object for 172.17.0.0/255.255.0.0 (or 172.17.0.0/16), which needs to be created. Even though it is only one object, place it into a group called SiteB-encdomain. This makes it easier to expand later.

Once you have done this, you must configure Site A and Site B's local firewall workstation object so that they have the correct encryption domain. Edit the gateway object and select the Topology frame. Site A's gateway object is shown in Figure 11.3.

There are two options for the VPN domain: use topology or use a specific group that you have defined. If you follow recommendations made in Chapter 4 and create anti-spoofing and topology when you initially define the gateway objects, you can use topology, which is recommended. However, it is still advisable to create a group that encompasses your encryption domain. If you want

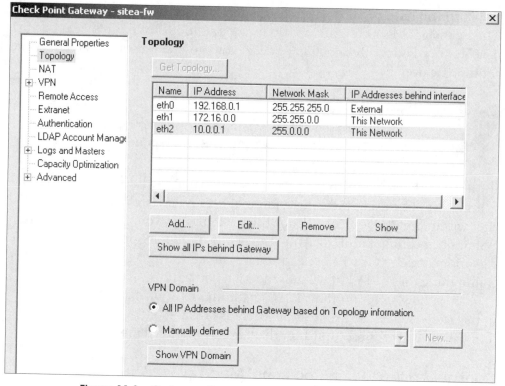

Figure 11.3   Gateway Properties, Topology frame for sitea-fw

your VPN domain to be something else, you can manually define it and assign it the appropriate group object.

Next, switch over to the VPN frame in the gateway object. Click on Traditional Mode Configuration. A dialog similar to Figure 11.4 appears.

You can choose which key exchange and data integrity methods are supported by this gateway. In general, it is best to use the defaults for these properties, though a corporate security policy may dictate that some algorithms never be used. In that case, disable the appropriate methods. Note that the actual methods used will be determined by the encrypt rule used.

We'll use the Public Key Signatures option in our example VPN. If you click on the Specify button, a dialog similar to Figure 11.5 appears. Generally speaking, it is safe to leave this as the default shown in Figure 11.5. However, if you have multiple certificates generated by different CAs and want to force the gateway to use a specific one, you can do that here.

The advanced configuration options for IKE (see Figure 11.6), which you find by clicking on the Advanced button in the Traditional mode IKE properties dialog, are generally left as the defaults unless you are interoperating with a

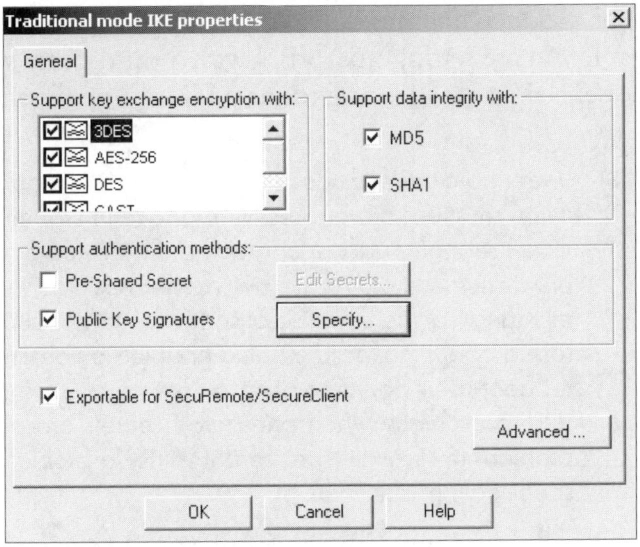

Figure 11.4 Traditional mode IKE properties

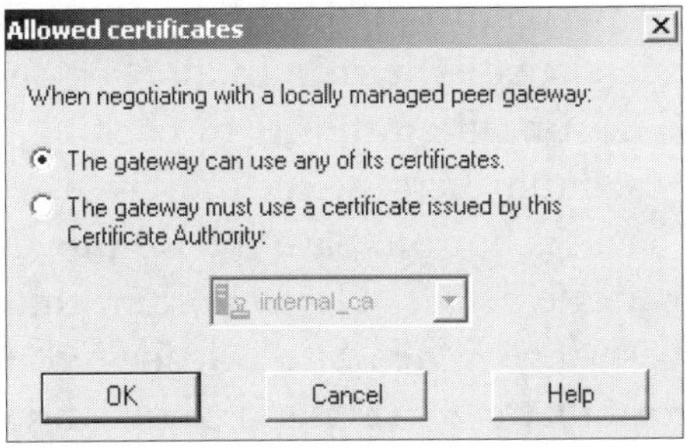

Figure 11.5 Allowed certificates for IKE

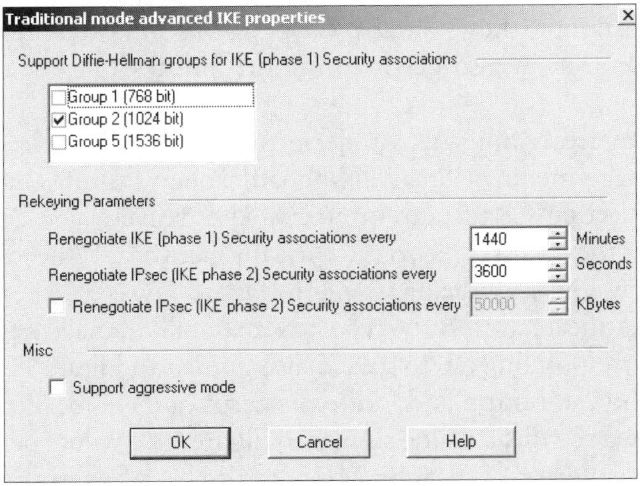

Figure 11.6 Traditional mode advanced IKE properties

third-party VPN product. In these cases, you may need to change these advanced settings. If you are setting up a VPN with a third-party site, you should validate that these settings are identical to the ones used by the third-party VPN product.

> **WARNING!** Under no circumstances should you enable aggressive mode. If you must enable aggressive mode to interoperate with a device, I strongly suggest upgrading the device or using a different device entirely. Aggressive mode uses a far less intense key exchange at the expense of some security. Security alerts were raised about this feature being enabled by default in FireWall-1 4.1 because it could be used to compromise the integrity of the VPN, particularly when pre-shared secrets are used. It's not a problem in FireWall-1 per se but rather a problem with the IKE specification itself.

Now it is time to exchange certificate authority keys. Each site needs to export its CA key and send it to the other party. First, you must get to the ICA certificate. Either select Servers from the Manage menu in SmartDashboard/ Policy Editor and double-click on internal_ca, or click on the Servers icon in the objects tree ⬚, expand Certificate Authority by clicking on it (if necessary), and double-click internal_ca. From here, select the Local Management Server tab and then click on the Save As button. Save the ICA to a file. Click on the View button to view the certificate details. The important things to note here are the MD5 and SHA-1 fingerprints. When Site B loads Site A's certificate (and vice versa), they should verify that the MD5 and SHA-1 fingerprints match, to ensure the certificate wasn't tampered with in transit.

After exchanging certificates, it is time to import the other site's CA key. The following example shows Site B's CA key being imported into Site A's management station. Site A also needs to import Site B's CA key using a similar procedure.

You need to create a new CA object. You can do this by selecting Servers from the Manage menu in SmartDashboard/Policy Editor, clicking the New button, and selecting Certificate Authority. Alternatively, you can click on the Servers icon in the objects tree, right-click on Certificate Authority, and select New. Either way, you see a dialog similar to Figure 11.7.

Set the Certificate Authority type to "External Management server" and click on the corresponding tab to see a dialog similar to Figure 11.8.

Click on the Get button and locate the certificate file for Site A's CA. Once you have selected the file, a dialog similar to Figure 11.9 will appear. Scroll down in this window and verify that the MD5 and SHA-1 fingerprints match what Site A has for its CA key. Click OK.

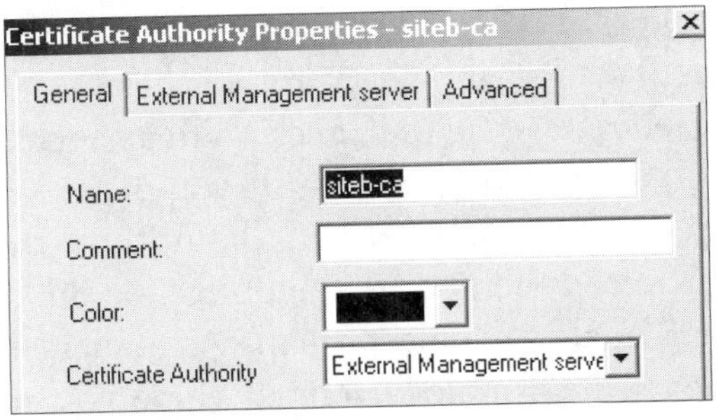

Figure 11.7   Certificate Authority Properties, General tab for siteb-ca

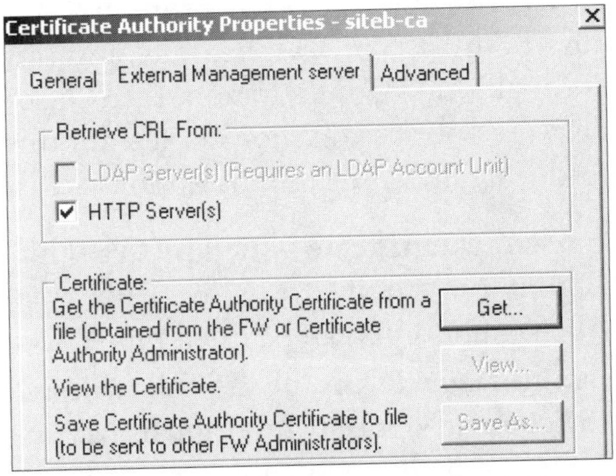

Figure 11.8   Certificate Authority Properties, External Management
server tab for siteb-ca

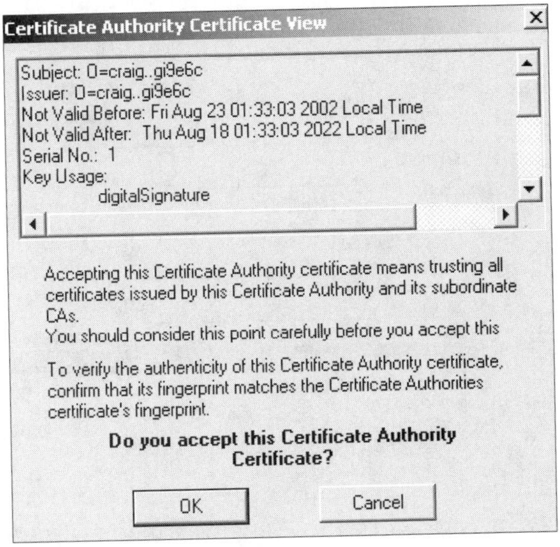

Figure 11.9   Certificate Authority Certificate View

Now that the CA keys are correctly imported, Site B's gateway can be created on Site A's management station and vice versa. In the objects tree, select the Network Objects icon, then right-click on Check Point and select New Check Point, followed by Externally Managed Gateway. Or you may select Objects from the Manage menu, click on New, select Check Point, and then select Externally Managed Gateway. You can then create the object for the remote gateway. Figure 11.10 shows Site B's gateway object on Site A's management station.

Figure 11.11 shows the Topology frame, where you manually choose the encryption domain to be the group siteb-encdomain, a group object created earlier.

Finally, you need to configure the VPN properties, specifically to require that Site B's certificate be from Site B's certificate authority. Go to the VPN frame, click on Traditional Mode Configuration, then click on Matching Criteria. Figure 11.12 shows the options you should select for this example.

In general, the certificate matching criteria options are those listed below.

Gateway must present a certificate issued by CA: This gateway must present a certificate from the specified CA for VPN-related operations. CA objects and LDAP account units can be listed in the options.

The certificate should match any of the following: The certificate must contain one of the checked options. DN (for the distinguished name) usually refers to "CN=fully-qualified-domain-name." IP Address means the cer-

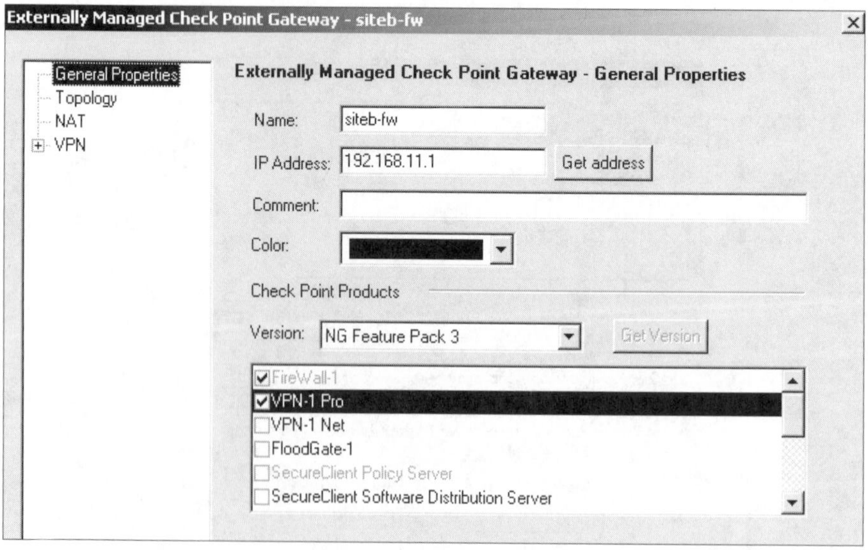

Figure 11.10 Gateway Properties, General Properties frame for siteb-fw

tificate must include the gateway's IP address as defined in the general properties. Some certificates are also generated with an e-mail address.

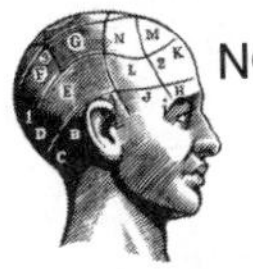

NOTE! It is not necessary to go into the Traditional mode configuration on Site B's firewall object because certificates are enabled by default.

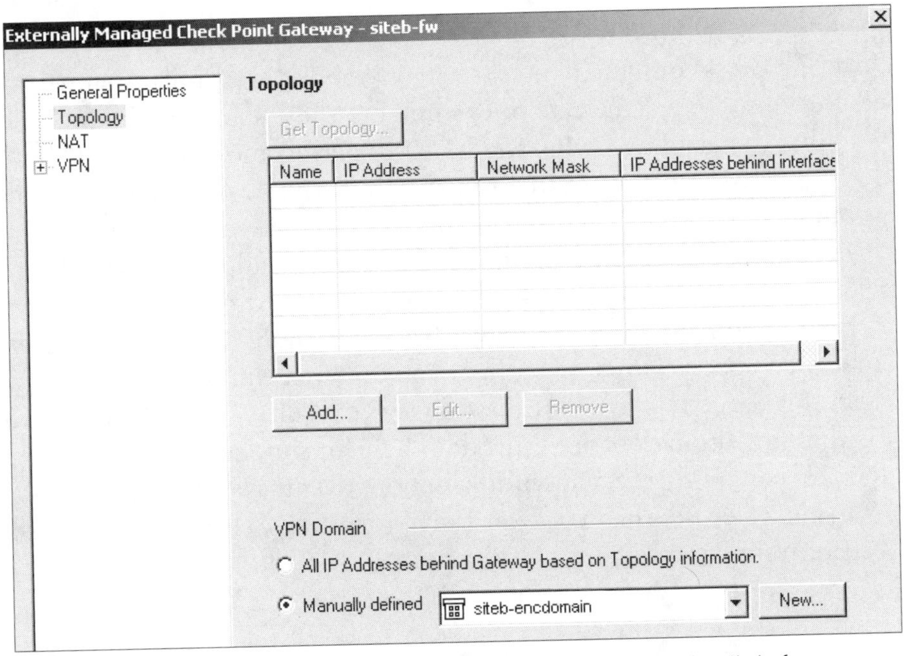

Figure 11.11   Gateway Properties, Topology frame for siteb-fw

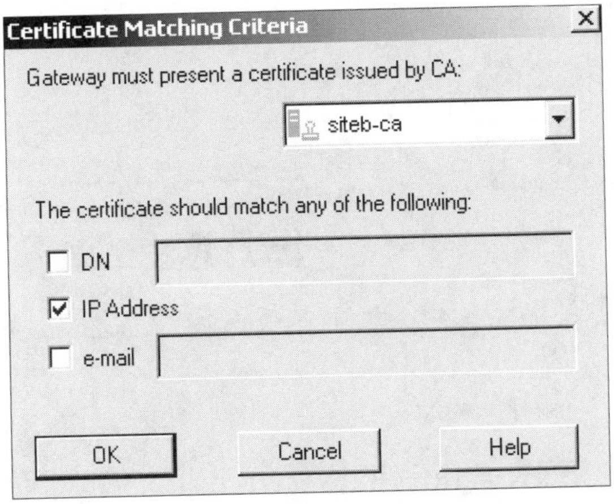

Figure 11.12   Certificate Matching Criteria for siteb-fw

SOURCE	DESTINATION	SERVICE	ACTION	TRACK
sitea-encdomain	siteb-encdomain	✳ Any	🔒 Encrypt	▤ Log
siteb-encdomain	sitea-encdomain	✳ Any	🔒 Encrypt	▤ Log

Figure 11.13   Encryption rules

Once Site B has configured Site A's gateway object in a similar manner as described previously, you can create rules similar to those shown in Figure 11.13.

Note that there are two rules listed: one to permit the traffic from Site A to Site B and one to permit the traffic from Site B to Site A. Although you can certainly combine the two rules into one, I do it this way to suppress the error message "Encryption Failed: gateway connected to both endpoints," which occurs when you use two rules instead of one. The two rules permit everything between the encryption domains. You can make these rules more restrictive by adding a specific service, specific hosts, or both, or you can even eliminate one of the rules to restrict this to a one-way VPN. Nothing says you have to allow access to all hosts in the encryption domain; I just do it here for simplicity.

Now to configure the encryption action. Right-click on both Encrypt actions in the rulebase, then click on Edit Properties. Select IKE and click on Edit. A screen similar to Figure 11.14 appears.

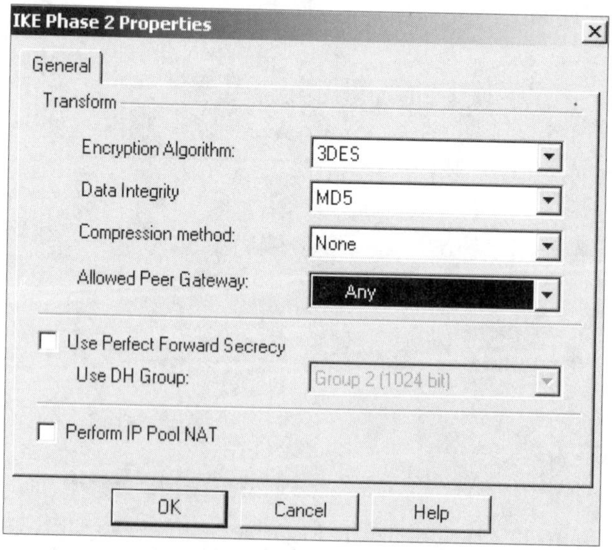

Figure 11.14   IKE Phase 2 Properties for encryption

The options you can specify here include the following.

Encryption Algorithm: This specifies what algorithm will be used to encrypt the data. In most cases, you should use AES-128 or AES-256. If you have a cryptographic accelerator, use 3DES because, as of January 2003, none of the cryptographic accelerator cards support AES.

Data Integrity: The default here is MD5, but SHA-1 is usually a better choice. However, on the performance tests I've seen on Nokia IP Security Platforms, MD5 performs a little better.

Compression method: If you wish to compress the VPN data stream, it is enabled here. Deflate is the only option you can choose.

Allowed Peer Gateway: You can specify which gateways are allowed for this rule.

Use Perfect Forward Secrecy: This option ensures that an eavesdropper who uncovers a long-term encryption key cannot use it to decrypt past captured traffic. It is highly recommended that you enable this option; it is disabled by default.

Perform IP Pool NAT: If enabled, VPN connections bound for the local gateway will be subject to IP Pool NAT. The specific pool of addresses that will be used is defined in the local gateway object under the NAT frame. The configuration for IP Pool NAT is described in Chapter 12 in the High-Availability and Multiple Entry Point Configurations section.

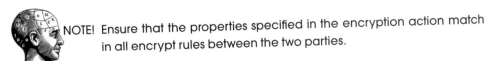

NOTE! Ensure that the properties specified in the encryption action match in all encrypt rules between the two parties.

Now that you've defined everything, it's time to install the security policy and test the VPN by trying to communicate through it.

Configuring the VPN in Simplified Mode

As in Traditional mode, you must configure the local topology of a VPN in Simplified mode so that it actually contains the encryption domain. This means creating the networks and adding them to sitea-encdomain and siteb-encdomain. You will also need to import the remote site's CA key and configure the remote gateway's matching criteria so that it will allow only certificates signed by the remote site's CA key. Since the steps are identical to the previous example, at least up to the point of creating actual rules, they are not repeated here.

After creating the gateways and setting the encryption domains, you need to create a VPN Community. There are two types of VPN Communities: Meshed

Communities and Star Communities. In a Meshed Community, all participating gateways can talk to each other. In a Star Community, you can specify two types of gateways: central gateways and satellite gateways. Central gateways all talk to one another as they do in a Meshed Community. Satellite gateways can talk only to the central gateways, not other satellite gateways. However, with VPN Routing in FireWall-1 NG FP3 and later, satellites can talk to each other via a central gateway. See FAQ 11.7 later in this chapter for details on how to implement this.

 NOTE! FireWall-1 NG FP1 allows only a single VPN Community to be used.

Click on this icon 🔒 in the objects tree, right-click on Site-to-Site, and select New, then Meshed. Alternatively, select VPN Communities from the Manage menu, click on New, and select Site-to-Site, then Meshed. Either way, you see a screen similar to Figure 11.15.

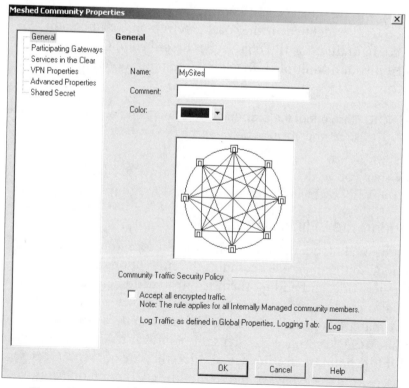

Figure 11.15   Meshed Community Properties, General frame

The options available in this frame are listed below.

Name: Enter the name you wish to give to the VPN Community.

Comment: In this field you can further describe the VPN Community.

Color: Choose an appropriate color for your VPN Community.

Accept all encrypted traffic: This property is present in NG FP3 and later. If this property is enabled, it will not be necessary to create an explicit rule to allow traffic between members of the community. All traffic is logged by default, though this can be changed in the Global Properties section, Log and Alert frame.

Figure 11.16 shows the Participating Gateways frame, where you can specify which gateways are part of the VPN Community. From this screen, you can add gateways, select gateways and edit them, remove gateways from the community, and create new gateway objects. The gateways for both Site A and Site B need to be added to the VPN Community.

As of NG FP3, VPN Communities may also allow "services in the clear," which means that the specified services will *not* be encrypted through the VPN Community. This may be useful for troubleshooting purpose (i.e., permitting ICMP through the VPN Community) or for services that are already encrypted

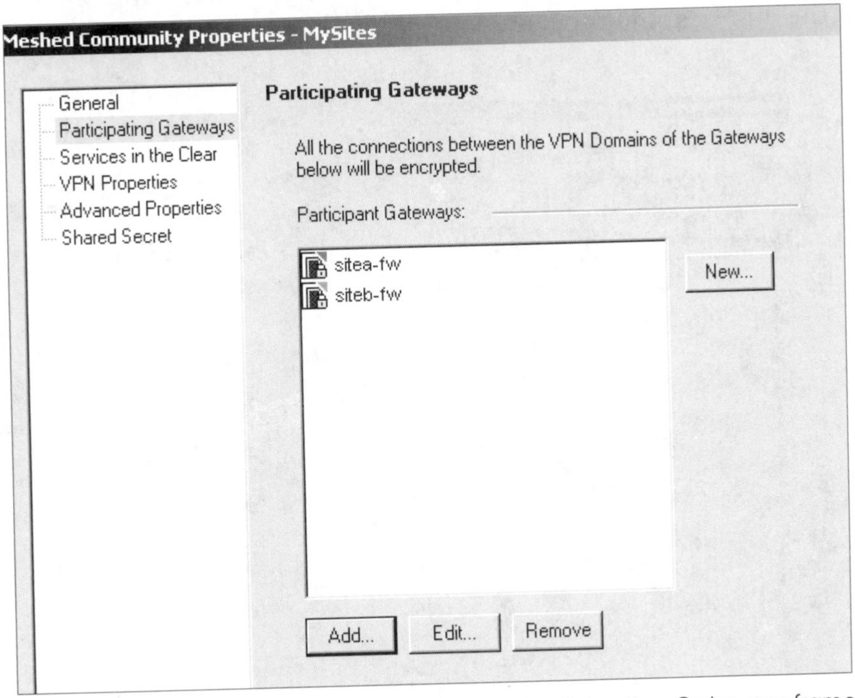

Figure 11.16   Meshed Community Properties, Participating Gateways frame

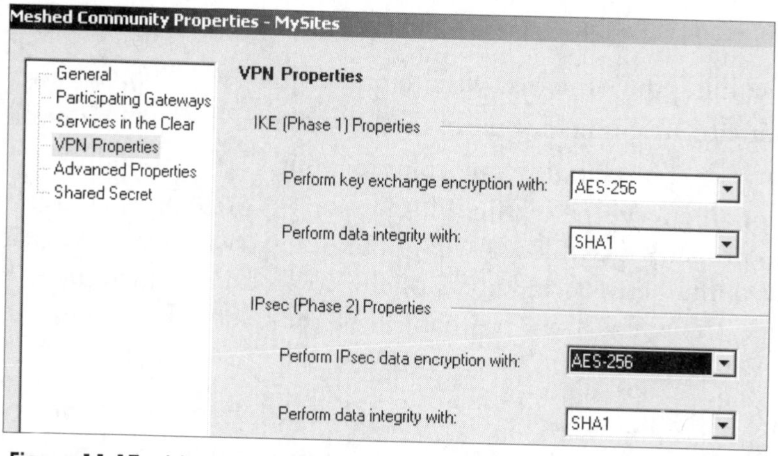

Figure 11.17 Meshed Community Properties, VPN Properties frame

(e.g., SSH, https). However, you cannot add services of type INSPECT to these groups.

In the VPN Properties frame, shown in Figure 11.17, you specify the encryption properties that will be used for all members of the VPN Community.

In the Advanced Properties frame, shown in Figure 11.18, you can specify additional properties. A new property in NG FP3 and later is the "Disable NAT inside the VPN community" property, which means that you do not have to

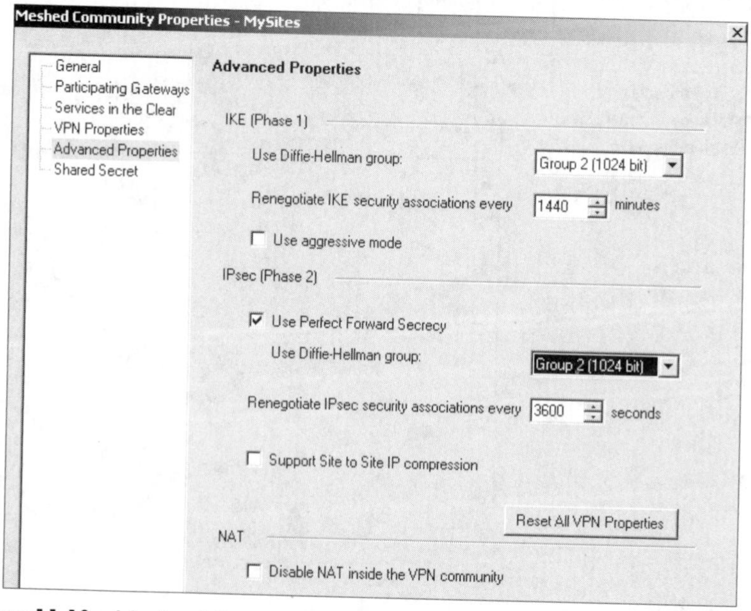

Figure 11.18 Meshed Community Properties, Advanced Properties frame

SOURCE	DESTINATION	IF VIA	SERVICE	ACTION	TRACK
✳ Any	✳ Any	🏠 MySites	✳ Any	🛡 accept	📄 Log

Figure 11.19 Simplified VPN rulebase configuration

explicitly define rules that disable address translation as was necessary with Traditional mode.

The nice thing is that these properties have to be configured in only one place—the VPN Community. This is somewhat simpler than the Traditional mode method, which required configuring each individual gateway with the correct options.

FireWall-1 NG FP3 and later also allow you to include non–Check Point devices as part of a VPN Community by allowing IKE pre-shared secrets for all externally managed VPN gateways. This is because not all third-party devices support certificate-based authentication, or at least a type that is compatible with FireWall-1. In NG FP2 and prior, if you had to establish a VPN with a device on which you could not perform certificate-based authentication, you had to use Traditional mode. You can define these secrets in the Shared Secret frame of the Meshed Community Properties section.

Figure 11.19 shows how the rulebase looks. As stated previously, you can easily restrict this by service or source/destination if you want. I am doing it the "easy" way for simplicity.

One particularly attractive thing about this configuration: As the number of sites in the VPN Community grows, the rulebase doesn't change unless it is necessary to limit access through the VPN by source, destination, or service. In the simplest configuration (allow everything), you can use exactly the same rule and it doesn't have to change at all!

Gateway Clusters for High-Availability VPNs

Gateway clusters allow for High-Availability (HA) VPNs, which, along with FireWall-1's State Synchronization mechanism, allow for a secondary gateway to be able to process encrypted traffic in the event the primary firewall fails. The gateway cluster object can be used only if an underlying HA solution is present. This could be Stonesoft's Stonebeat Full Cluster, IPSO's VRRP or Clustering, Rainfinity's Rainwall, or Check Point's own HA Module. You also need to have your management console on a separate platform from the systems that you intend to configure into a gateway cluster.

A gateway cluster is nothing more than a virtual firewall. It takes two or more firewalls in an HA configuration and makes them appear as a single entity for the purposes of installing a security policy and encryption. The mechanics of establishing a gateway cluster are described in Chapter 13.

Setting up a VPN involving gateway clusters is not very different from setting up a VPN involving a single gateway. The moment you make a firewall workstation object part of a gateway cluster, many of the tabs in the workstation properties simply disappear. This configuration needs to be done from the gateway cluster object. When you configure the VPN-related parameters for the firewall, you configure them on the gateway cluster object, not on the workstation object for the firewalls that are members of the gateway cluster.

When you are defining the remote end of the VPN and it uses a gateway cluster, you simply treat it as if it were a single firewall object. You can simply refer to a remote gateway cluster with a single workstation object. However, you need to define the Interfaces tab. Include all of the IP addresses on all gateways in the gateway cluster, including the gateway cluster IP address, similar to Figure 11.20. The interfaces' names and the netmasks are not important because you are not using this as a basis for enforcing anti-spoofing. What is important is that you enter all of the IP addresses.

 WARNING!   Despite Figure 11.20 showing you to enter the interface names in a gateway cluster object, entering anything into the Interfaces tab on a gateway cluster object may cause problems in some NG FP3 configurations. See FAQ 11.6 for details. In NG AI, you should use the actual interface names.

Due to how gateway clusters work, some interoperability issues arise with gateway clusters and third-party VPN products. These issues, along with solutions, are documented in the next section.

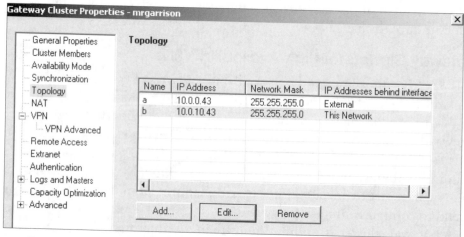

Figure 11.20   Entering interface IP addresses for a gateway cluster object

Frequently Asked Questions about VPNs in FireWall-1

This section addresses some questions that are frequently asked about VPNs in FireWall-1.

11.1: Does FireWall-1 Interoperate with Third-Party VPN Products?

Generally, yes. It is usually a matter of making sure the settings match on both ends of the VPN. This is made somewhat difficult because each vendor refers to a particular setting with a slightly different name. For known interoperability issues with some third-party VPN products, see FAQ 11.17.

In NG FP2 and FP3, there is an issue that requires a hotfix for interoperating with a Cisco PIX. For FP3, request hotfix SHF_FW1_FP3_0006 from Check Point Support. For FP2, request hotfix SHF_FW1_FP2_0248.

11.2: Does the Gateway Clusters Feature Interoperate with Third-Party VPN Products?

This feature should interoperate with third-party products. On IPSO, there have been problems with failovers with gateway clusters and third-party VPN products. These can sometimes be resolved by enabling the `ifwd` process in Voyager.

11.3: Can I Run Microsoft Networking Protocols through a VPN?

Yes, you can. You can run just about any protocol you'd like through the VPN.

11.4: Can I Set Up a VPN with a Site without Giving It Access to All My Machines?

Even though your encryption domain typically contains everything behind your gateway, you can set up the rules in such a way that the other site can access only certain machines. Note that this does not prevent the site from using the allowed services and destination to access other machines inside your network.

11.5: Can I Set Up More Than One VPN with Different Sites Each Using Different Encryption Schemes?

Yes, you can.

11.6: Can I Set Up More Than One VPN with Different Sites and Use a Different Source IP Address for Each Site?

If the sites are accessible from the same interface, no. If each site is using a different interface, then it should work. In a gateway cluster configuration, this approach works in NG FP3 or above provided the Interfaces tab is defined on the gateway cluster object. This means that all IP addresses associated with the gateway cluster (the "shared" IPs) should be manually defined. However, in NG FP3, it may cause the platform to stop responding to ARP requests.

11.7: Does FireWall-1 Support a Hub-and-Spoke Model Like Some VPN Hardware Devices Do?

In a hub-and-spoke model, all remote sites know about only the main hub site. When a remote site (a spoke) wants to communicate with another site, including the main site or even the Internet, the data is encrypted and sent to the main site. The main site knows how to get to every spoke. The data is decrypted, reencrypted if necessary, and sent on to the appropriate site. This makes configuration of the spoke sites very easy, although it adds additional overhead because the data must traverse two sites.

FireWall-1 NG FP3 and later support this with a feature called VPN Routing. In FireWall-1 NG AI, create a Star-type VPN Community, as shown in Figure 11.21.

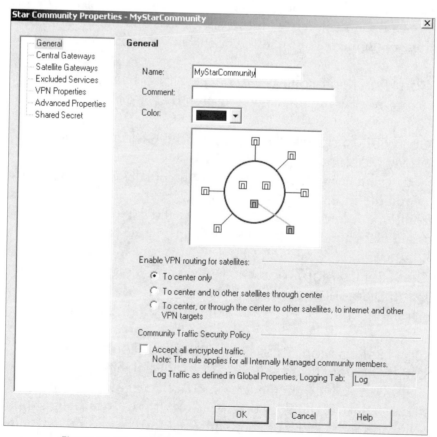

Figure 11.21 Star-type VPN Community, General frame

The General frame shows three options for VPN Routing.

To center only: This option allows a satellite gateway to talk to only the central gateway.

To center and to other satellites through center: Any satellite gateway in the VPN Community may talk to any other satellite by going through a central gateway.

To center, or through the center to other satellites, to internet and other VPN targets: A satellite gateway may communicate via a VPN to a central gateway, through which the gateway can access other VPN endpoints outside the VPN Community. Furthermore, all Internet access from a satellite site is routed through a central gateway. This allows for finer-grained control over Internet access.

In NG FP3, VPN Routing is manually defined on the management station in a file called `$FWDIR/conf/vpn_route.conf`. The format of the file is explained in embedded comments in the file. You will add lines that specify the destination network object (can be a network, gateway, host, or group object), the route packets destined for the network object should travel, and the gateway or group of gateways on which this route should be installed. Any changes to this file require reinstallation of the security policy on all managed nodes.

11.8: How Does NAT Interact with Encryption?

NAT is applied either before a packet is encrypted or after decryption. I usually suggest either that you create rules in your NAT rulebase that do not NAT any traffic between the encryption domains or that you use the "Disable NAT inside the VPN community" property discussed earlier in this chapter. Figure 11.22 shows an example of a rule you would use on Site A's security policy.

If you do decide to use NAT, make sure you include any translated addresses in the encryption domain.

11.9: How Can Two Sites That Use the Same Address Space Establish a VPN with One Another?

There is one situation where you will want to use NAT with a VPN: when two sites use the same address space within their encryption domains. In this case,

ORIGINAL PACKET			TRANSLATED PACKET		
SOURCE	DESTINATION	SERVICE	SOURCE	DESTINATION	SERVICE
sitea-encdomain	siteb-encdomain	✱ Any	= Original	= Original	= Original

Figure 11.22 Sample No-NAT rule for encryption

NO.	ORIGINAL PACKET			TRANSLATED PACKET		
	SOURCE	DESTINATION	SERVICE	SOURCE	DESTINATION	SERVICE
1	net-172.16.0.0-24	net-10.0.0.0-24	✱ Any	net-172.31.0.0-24	≡ Original	≡ Original
2	net-10.0.0.0-24	net-172.31.0.0-24	✱ Any	≡ Original	net-172.16.0.0-24	≡ Original

Figure 11.23 Site A's address translation rules

NO.	ORIGINAL PACKET			TRANSLATED PACKET		
	SOURCE	DESTINATION	SERVICE	SOURCE	DESTINATION	SERVICE
1	net-172.16.0.0-24	net-172.31.0.0-24	✱ Any	net-10.0.0.0-24	≡ Original	≡ Original
2	net-172.31.0.0-24	net-10.0.0.0-24	✱ Any	≡ Original	net-172.16.0.0-24	≡ Original

Figure 11.24 Site B's address translation rules

you will need to perform address translation to communicate with hosts in the remote site as well as provide address translation so they can talk to your hosts.

Let us assume Site A and Site B have the same encryption domain: 172.16.0.0/24. Let us also assume that Site A will translate its address space to 10.0.0.0/24 when talking with Site B. Similarly, Site B will translate its address space to 172.31.0.0/24 when communicating with Site A. Site A should define the encryption domain for itself as 172.16.0.0/24 and 10.0.0.0/24. Site A's definition for Site B's encryption domain should be 172.31.0.0/24. Site B should define its own encryption domain as 172.31.0.0/24 and 172.16.0.0/24. Site B's definition for the encryption domain for Site A should be 10.0.0.0/24.

The rules you define in this situation are identical to those for any other situation except for the NAT rules. The rules for Site A should be like those shown in Figure 11.23; for site B, like those shown in Figure 11.24. Note that no proxy ARPs or static routes should be necessary in addition to these rules.

11.10: Can I Require User Authentication in Addition to Encryption?

Yes, you can. The Sample Configurations section of this chapter includes an example of how to do this.

11.11: Can the VPN Gateway Be behind Another Device That Does NAT?

Yes. For example, assuming gw1 is subject to static NAT and gw2 is establishing a VPN with gw1, you can configure an automatic NAT rule on gw2 (*not* gw1) for gw1's nonroutable address to gw1's routable address. Additionally, configure the routable address of gw1 into the interfaces list.

11.12: Can a Gateway Be a Member of More Than One VPN Community?

Absolutely. However, gateways cannot have more than one VPN Community in common with each other.

Troubleshooting VPN Problems

The following is a list of common problems and resolutions that relate to establishing a VPN. Note that any error messages you see in the SmartView Tracker/Log Viewer are documented in the Check Point manuals. Some of the more common errors follow.

11.13: General Troubleshooting Guidelines for VPN Problems

Ensure that the appropriate kinds of traffic are being permitted between the two endpoints. If there are any filtering routers along the way, make sure they permit the following protocols:

- IP protocols 50 and 51 (for any IPSec-related scheme)
- UDP port 500 (for IKE)

Also, you should make sure that NAT is not being performed on any of the packets.

Sometimes you may need to put explicit rules in the firewall permitting this traffic. In most cases, this isn't necessary. The rules are shown in Figure 11.25.

You may also want to use a packet sniffer (e.g., `tcpdump`, `snoop`, `fw monitor`) to verify that packets are reaching the gateway. If the packets are not reaching the gateway, FireWall-1 cannot encrypt or decrypt them.

11.14: No Response from Peer

The "No response from peer" error message usually points to one of the following problems.

- The encryption domains are not correct. The encryption domain for firewall A should contain all the hosts behind firewall A and any translated IP

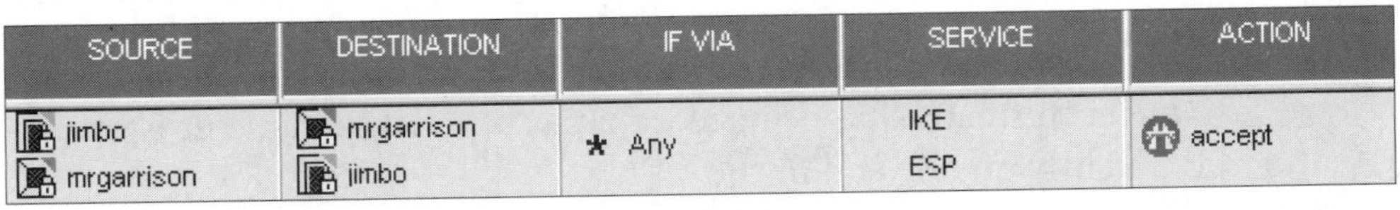

SOURCE	DESTINATION	IF VIA	SERVICE	ACTION
jimbo mrgarrison	mrgarrison jimbo	✱ Any	IKE ESP	accept

Figure 11.25 Rules to permit IKE and ESP to the firewall

addresses (including hides). The firewall should be included if it is used as the hide address. The same is true for firewall B—its encryption domain should contain all the hosts behind firewall B, any translated IP addresses, and firewall B itself if it is used as a hide address.

- The remote end does not currently have a rule that will decrypt the packet.
- The remote firewall is not set up with encryption.
- Something is blocking communication between the VPN endpoints. Check to make sure the remote firewall is properly receiving the IP packets by using a packet sniffer. Look for IP protocol 50 or UDP port 500 packets.

11.15: AddNegotiation: Try to Handle Too Many Negotiations

A key negotiation occurs when a connection is first established from one host to another. If you see this "AddNegotiation" message, it means that FireWall-1 is handling more than 200 key negotiations at once. Connections that have this message associated with them in the log will fail. In NG FP3, you can configure a firewall to support more IKE negotiations by editing the gateway object and going to the Capacity Optimization frame. Set the maximum concurrent IKE connections there.

11.16: Debugging Interoperability Issues with IKE

Everyone has a different interpretation about how to follow standards. As a result, when third-party products talk to one another, communication doesn't always work. One way to debug is to turn on IKE debugging.

In FireWall-1 4.1, it was necessary to stop and restart FireWall-1 in order to enable debugging. In NG, you can enable this on the firewall module with a simple command: **vpn debug ikeon**. You can also disable it with **vpn debug ikeoff**. When you enable debugging, $FWDIR/log/ike.elg gets created. This file contains the results of all IKE negotiations that occur. This file is a little difficult to read on its own. Fortunately, Check Point has a tool called IKEView that allows you to view this file in a more readable form. Unfortunately, it is available only to Check Point Certified Service Partners.

Most interoperability issues actually come down to one of the following things.

- A parameter mismatch has occurred, that is, one IKE parameter is configured differently on one end of the VPN.
- There is a topology or encryption domain mismatch.

11.17: Known Interoperability Issues

The following subsections detail some known interoperability issues, with fixes where appropriate.

FireWall-1 NG FP2/FP3 and Cisco PIX

In NG FP2 and FP3, you may experience a problem when trying to establish a VPN with a Cisco PIX firewall. Check Point released a hotfix to address this problem. For NG FP3, request hotfix SHF_FW1_FP3_0006 from Check Point or your support provider. For NG FP2, request SHF_FW1_FP2_0248.

Nokia Crypto Cluster

In NG FP3 and before, there are several interoperability issues with the Nokia Crypto Cluster (CC) product line, which are likely to show up in other situations as well. In some cases, you will need to take the following steps.

- Disable ISAKMP Commit Processing in the CC.
- Enable Defer Main Mode Deletion in the CC.
- Ensure that you do not restrict access to the VPN based on services on the CC. FireWall-1 is not RFC compliant in how it negotiates an IKE SA[3] because it always assumes all services are permitted, whereas the CC products negotiate the allowed services as part of the SA,[4] just as the RFCs state *must* be done.
- If you are using a version of FireWall-1 prior to NG FP3 Hotfix-2, define your encryption domain in terms of the largest possible subnets because FireWall-1 tends to simplify the encryption domains down to the largest possible subnets. This is despite having an option in `objects_5_0.C` that supposedly turns this off (see FAQ 11.18).

IPSec SAs Are Not Reestablished Properly after IKE Rekey with Cisco and/or Sonicwall

The initial VPN tunnel is established and VPN traffic flows. The subsequent IPSec rekeys work fine. However, when one end is VPN-1/FireWall-1 and the other end is either a Cisco or Sonicwall device, VPN traffic fails after an IKE rekey until an IPSec rekey is done.

---

3. In my conversations with Check Point on this issue, the representatives with whom I spoke did not believe that negotiating the allowed services in the SA is secure because it essentially advertises what is allowed. A valid point, but the behavior is not interoperable with devices acting in an RFC-compliant manner. What part of "not RFC compliant" do they not understand?

4. At least one developer who worked on the CC products actually wrote the Internet RFCs related to IPSec.

RFC2408 (Section 5.15), the relevant RFC for IKE, states: "The receiving entity SHOULD clean up its local SA database." Check Point interprets this section to mean that upon IKE rekey, ISAKMP Delete should be sent or acknowledged in order to clean up the IPSec SAs at the same time. Cisco and Sonicwall have not taken this approach and maintain the IPSec SAs across the IKE SA rekeys. This difference in behavior is what causes VPN traffic to fail.

To determine whether this behavior is occurring, display the IPSec SPI numbers before and after an IKE SA rekey operation on the third-party device. If the SPIs are the same, the device is preserving the IPSec SA across IKE rekeys. VPN traffic will fail until the next IPSec rekey.

11.18: Encryption Failure: Packet Is Dropped as There Is No Valid SA

You might see this error message when both ends of the VPN do not have the same definition for the encryption domain. First ensure that both ends of the VPN are defined with the same encryption domain. If they are the same, you should create objects that are exactly the same size as what is created on the remote end.

One annoying behavior FireWall-1 NG exhibits that FireWall-1 4.1 and earlier did not is the automatic simplification of subnets in IPSec SAs. For example, if your encryption domain contains explicit objects for 192.168.0.0/24 and 192.168.1.0/24, Check Point would attempt to negotiate an IPSec SA with 192.168.0.0/23 instead of generating SAs based on the network objects you created. To eliminate this behavior, use **dbedit** to make the following changes on your management console (see FAQ 4.2 for details on editing `objects_5_0.C`):

```
dbedit> modify properties firewall_properties
            ike_use_largest_possible_subnets false
dbedit> update properties firewall_properties
```

You must then reload the security policy for this change to take effect.

11.19: Traceroute Does Not Appear to Work through a VPN

Traceroute works by sending out packets with successively larger time to live (TTL) values (see Chapter 1). Each hop along the way generally returns an ICMP Time Exceeded message, an ICMP Destination Unreachable message, or an ICMP Echo Reply.

In an IPSec VPN, all communication between the sites is encapsulated. When FireWall-1 encapsulates a traceroute packet, the new packet inherits the TTL value of the packet being encapsulated. As a result, each hop between the firewalls sends an ICMP Time Exceeded packet back to the firewall. These packets are ignored by the firewall. Users will see these messages in their traceroute as "request timed out."

Interestingly enough, with SecureClient on NG, all hops between the firewall and client are skipped, so traceroute appears to work.

11.20: VPN Fails When Transferring Large Packets

Some applications set the Don't Fragment bit on certain packets. When the IPSec headers are added to the already large packet, the packet requires fragmentation in order to pass through the firewall. When Check Point creates the IPSec packet, the Don't Fragment bit from the original packet is maintained. FireWall-1 creates a fragmented packet that has the Don't Fragment bit set, so it cannot be fragmented and thus gets dropped at the next router.

You can force FireWall-1 to clear the Don't Fragment bit by changing the `ipsec_dont_fragment` property in `objects_5_0.C` to `false`. You can do this with the following commands in **dbedit** on the management console (craig is the firewall in this example):

```
dbedit> modify network_objects craig VPN:ipsec_dont_fragment
            false
dbedit> update network_objects craig
```

Alternatively, you can use the GUIdbedit tool to change the parameter. Either way, you must then reinstall the security policy for this change to take effect.

Summary

VPNs are an increasingly important technology as companies expand, merge, acquire, and partner with others. Having a basic understanding of the terminology is important. There are many different ways you can establish a VPN with FireWall-1, and some ways you cannot. You now know how to establish a site-to-site VPN in FireWall-1 and troubleshoot when things go wrong.

Sample Configurations

The following three situations are representative of those I have experienced in the real world. Each is designed to demonstrate what people typically do with site-to-site VPNs and how the situations are implemented on the chosen platform. All of the sample configurations are done in Simplified mode.

Creating a Three-Site VPN

The Situation

You are the firewall administrator for a company that has several sites. The main sites are in Seattle (the corporate headquarters), Sacramento, and London. Until recently, a private WAN was used to connect the various sites to one another. It is now desirable to use a VPN based on Check Point FireWall-1 to connect these sites because this choice is more cost-efficient. The main management console in Seattle manages the firewalls at the remote sites. No NAT is involved. Assume that all IPs are routable. Figure 11.26 shows a simplified network diagram.

The Goals

- Allow all hosts behind each of the three networks to communicate with each other unencumbered.
- Allow the remote firewalls to be remotely managed over the Internet.
- All sites are allowed to access sites on the Internet via FTP, HTTP, or HTTPS.
- SMTP can originate from predefined SMTP servers inside the Seattle network to the Internet (they are in a group called SMTP-Servers).
- SMTP can go to the external-smtp server from anywhere (external-smtp-server is already defined).
- Deny all other traffic.

The Checklist

- Define the encryption domains for each site.
- Define the firewall workstation objects for each site.
- Configure the firewall workstation objects for the correct encryption domain.
- Create and configure a VPN Community.
- Create the necessary encryption rules.
- Install the security policy.
- Make the appropriate changes to the internal routing to allow traffic to flow through the firewalls across the VPN.

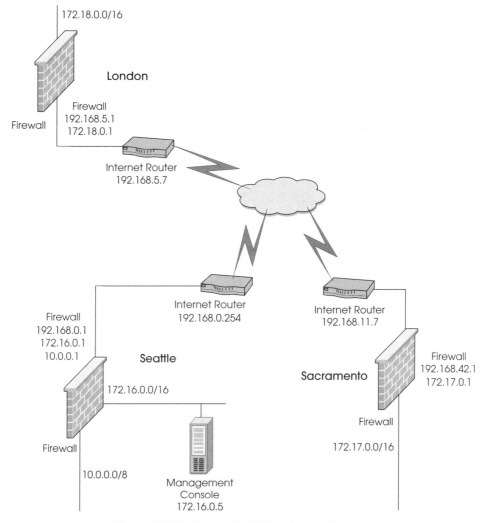

Figure 11.26 Three-site VPN network diagram

The Implementation

You first need to define the encryption domain for the three sites. Seattle's encryption domain is:

- 10.0.0.0/255.0.0.0 (or 10.0.0.0/8)
- 172.16.0.0/255.255.0.0 (or 172.16.0.0/16)

Define network objects for both of these networks. Place them in a group called seattle-encdomain.

Similarly, for Sacramento, the encryption domain contains 172.17.0.0/ 255.255.0.0 (or 172.17.0.0/16). Define a network object for this network. Even though it is only one object, place it into a group called sacramento-encdomain. This makes it easier to expand later.

Similarly, for London, the encryption domain contains 172.18.0.0/255.255.0.0 (or 172.18.0.0/16). Define a network object for this network. Place it into a group called london-encdomain.

Chances are, these firewalls have been remotely managed, so you probably do not need to create the Check Point gateway objects. However, you need to modify the objects to ensure they have the correct encryption domains.

Now create a VPN Community called MyIntranet. Add the Seattle, London, and Sacramento gateways into the encryption domain. For maximum security, configure the VPN Community with the settings shown in Figures 11.27 and 11.28.

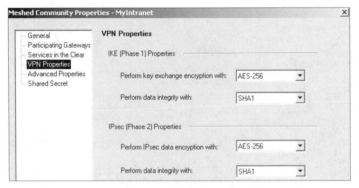

Figure 11.27 Meshed Community Properties, VPN Properties frame

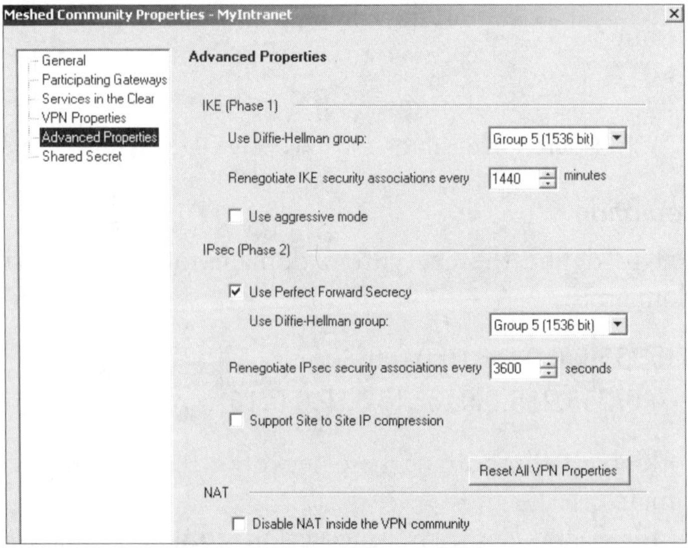

Meshed Community Properties - MyIntranet

General
Participating Gateways
Services in the Clear
VPN Properties
Advanced Properties
Shared Secret

Advanced Properties

IKE (Phase 1)

Use Diffie-Hellman group: Group 5 (1536 bit)

Renegotiate IKE security associations every 1440 minutes

☐ Use aggressive mode

IPsec (Phase 2)

☑ Use Perfect Forward Secrecy

Use Diffie-Hellman group: Group 5 (1536 bit)

Renegotiate IPsec security associations every 3600 seconds

☐ Support Site to Site IP compression

Reset All VPN Properties

NAT

☐ Disable NAT inside the VPN community

Figure 11.28 Meshed Community Properties, Advanced Properties frame

NO.	SOURCE	DESTINATION	IF VIA	SERVICE	ACTION	TRACK
1	Primary-Mgmt	sacramento-fw london-fw seattle-fw	⋆ Any	TCP FW1 TCP FW1_ica_push TCP CPD TCP FW1_CPRID	accept	– None
2	sacramento-fw london-fw seattle-fw	Primary-Mgmt	⋆ Any	TCP FW1 TCP FW1_log TCP FW1_ica_pull	accept	– None
3	sacramento-fw seattle-fw london-fw	sacramento-fw seattle-fw london-fw	⋆ Any	IKE ESP	accept	Log
4	⋆ Any	⋆ Any	MyIntranet	⋆ Any	accept	Log
5	sacramento-encdomain seattle-encdomain london-encdomain	⋆ Any	⋆ Any	TCP telnet TCP http TCP https	accept	– None
6	SMTP-Servers	⋆ Any	⋆ Any	TCP smtp	accept	– None
7	⋆ Any	external-smtp-server	⋆ Any	TCP smtp	accept	– None
8	⋆ Any	⋆ Any	⋆ Any	⋆ Any	drop	Log

Figure 11.29 Three-site VPN rulebase

You can then create all the necessary rules, which are shown in Figure 11.29.

Notes

This is a somewhat simplified example. Most sites have far more complex security policies. Just make sure your VPN rules are listed before any rules that allow outbound traffic to the Internet.

Adding a Business Partner to the VPN Mesh

The Situation

A business partner would like to be able to come in and update information on a particular UNIX Web server at the Seattle site's DMZ (172.16.0.80). The information would be transferred via Telnet or FTP. Because the information is very confidential in nature, it would be desirable to do this in a secure fashion. Because the business partner also uses FireWall-1, a site-to-site VPN is desired. To make the configuration easier, the company will use pre-shared secrets. There is no reason to access the partner site through the VPN, so only one-way access is needed. In addition to being encrypted, strong authentication is desired. It is deemed impractical to do the authentication on the UNIX Web server, so the firewall needs to be able to provide this functionality. SecurID will be used to provide authentication.

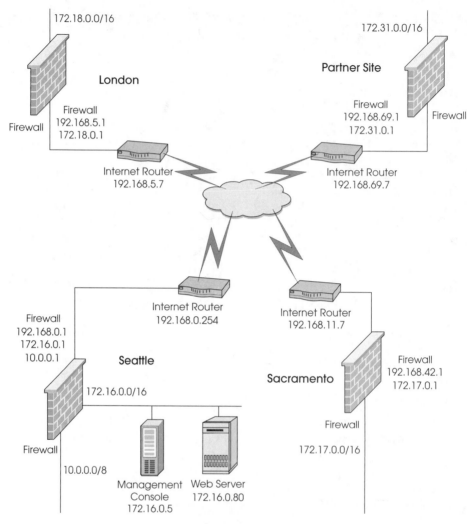

Figure 11.30 Adding a partner to the VPN

In the context of this sample configuration, the local site refers to Seattle, and the remote site refers to the partner site. Figure 11.30 shows the new network map.

The Goals

- Maintain the previous security policy as much as possible (from the previous configuration).
- Allow the remote site to access 172.16.0.80 via FTP and Telnet with authentication using SecurID authentication, and encrypt the communication.

The Checklist

- Define the encryption domains for each site.
- Define the firewall workstation objects for each site.
- Configure the gateway objects for the correct encryption domain.
- Configure the extranet community with the appropriate gateways and objects.
- Create the necessary encryption rules.
- Configure the encryption properties for each encryption rule.
- Install the security policy.

The Implementation

On the local site's management station, you need to create an encryption domain for the remote site's encryption domain, which is 172.31.0.0/16. For this example, call it partner-encdomain. Create an externally managed Check Point gateway object called partner-fw. Define it with its external IP and check the VPN-1 Pro box. Go to the Topology frame and configure the encryption domain to be the group partner-encdomain.

At the partner site, you need to create an encryption domain for the remote site (which, in this case, is Seattle). Even though the only host that will be accessed is the Web server at 172.16.0.80, you need to add everything on that network segment to the encryption domain or you will have problems establishing the VPN. Create an object for the network 172.16.0.0/16 and add it to the group seattle-encdomain.

On both management consoles, create a new VPN Community called Extranet. Both Seattle's firewall and the partner site's firewall are added to this community. Set the VPN Properties and Advanced Properties frames as shown earlier in Figures 11.27 and 11.28. Go to the Shared Secret frame and check the "Use only Shared Secret for all External Members" box. Select the other firewall, click on Edit, type in the shared secret that was exchanged in a secure channel with the administrator of the partner site, and click OK.

At the partner site, the administrator simply needs to create a rule permitting VPN access within the community (see Figure 11.31).

At the Seattle site, the configuration is a little more complicated. You have to create users for the partner site. Let's say two people are going to be performing

Figure 11.31   Rule to add to Partner Site

NO.	SOURCE	DESTINATION	IF VIA	SERVICE	ACTION	TRACK
1	Primary-Mgmt	sacramento-fw london-fw seattle-fw	✱ Any	TCP FW1 TCP FW1_ica_push TCP CPD TCP FW1_CPRID	accept	— None
2	sacramento-fw london-fw seattle-fw	Primary-Mgmt	✱ Any	TCP FW1 TCP FW1_log TCP FW1_ica_pull	accept	— None
3	sacramento-fw seattle-fw london-fw partner-fw	sacramento-fw seattle-fw london-fw partner-fw	✱ Any	IKE ESP	accept	Log
4	✱ Any	✱ Any	MyIntranet	✱ Any	accept	Log
5	partner-encdomain	web-server	Extranet	TCP http TCP telnet	User Auth	Log
6	sacramento-encdomain seatte-encdomain london-encdomain	✱ Any	✱ Any	TCP telnet TCP http TCP https	accept	— None
7	SMTP-Servers	✱ Any	✱ Any	TCP smtp	accept	— None
8	✱ Any	external-smtp-server	✱ Any	TCP smtp	accept	— None
9	✱ Any	✱ Any	✱ Any	✱ Any	drop	Log

Figure 11.32 Four-site VPN rulebase

the updates, Ren and Stimpy. Create the users with SecurID authentication. Place the two users into a group called partner-users. (The Creating Groups subsection of Chapter 8 explains why you need to do this.) Next, create the appropriate rules. Figure 11.32 shows the complete rulebase.

The new rule in this rulebase is Rule 5, which performs authentication and encryption. Make sure you right-click on the User Auth action, edit the properties, and make sure "All servers" is selected. (The Setting Up User Authentication section of Chapter 8 explains why you need to do this.) Also note that Rule 3 was modified to include the partner site.

Install the security policy and test the new configuration.

Notes

While it seems unlikely that one business partner might issue SecurID cards to another, it does happen.

Switching the Seattle Firewall to a Gateway Cluster Configuration

The Situation

This configuration uses the previous configuration except a pair of Nokia IP530s is replacing the Seattle firewall, configured in a gateway cluster configuration for High Availability and redundancy.

All other configurations remain identical. The network map is also identical except that the Seattle-FW site has two firewalls instead of one. The new "virtual" firewall created by the gateway cluster will have the same IPs as the old firewall, so only minimal changes will be necessary at the remote sites. Figure 11.33 shows the new network diagram.

The Goals

- Convert the Seattle site into a gateway cluster configuration.
- Maintain the security policy from the previous configuration as much as possible.

The Checklist

- Create a gateway cluster object for the Seattle site, defining encryption parameters.
- Define the gateway objects for Firewall A and Firewall B, making them part of Seattle's gateway cluster.
- Modify the VPN Community to include the gateway cluster.
- Install the security policy.

The Implementation

As part of bringing the gateway cluster into existence, you must also configure VRRP Monitored Circuits or Clustering on the Nokia Security Platforms. This should be done first. Although not covered in this text, Resolution 1214 in Nokia's Knowledge Base covers configuring VRRP sufficiently well. For the purposes of this exercise, Firewall A is the primary firewall, and Firewall B is the secondary firewall (i.e., it will take over if Firewall A fails). A crossover cable will be used between the two platforms, with IP addresses 172.30.0.2 and 172.30.0.3 for Firewall A and Firewall B, respectively. This will be the network where State Synchronization runs.

You have to create new gateway objects for Firewall A (seattle-fwa) and Firewall B (seattle-fwb). Configure them as if they were standalone firewalls, but don't add them to any VPN Communities. Before Firewall A and Firewall B can be added to the gateway cluster object, you need to remove them from any VPN

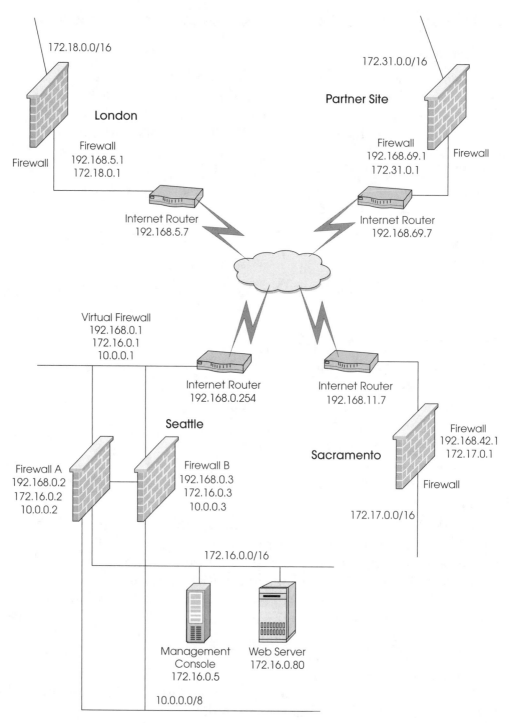

172.18.0.0/16

London

Firewall
192.168.5.1
172.18.0.1

Firewall

Internet Router
192.168.5.7

172.31.0.0/16

Partner Site

Firewall
192.168.69.1
172.31.0.1

Firewall

Internet Router
192.168.69.7

Virtual Firewall
192.168.0.1
172.16.0.1
10.0.0.1

Internet Router
192.168.0.254

Internet Router
192.168.11.7

Seattle

Firewall A
192.168.0.2
172.16.0.2
10.0.0.2

Firewall B
192.168.0.3
172.16.0.3
10.0.0.3

Sacramento

Firewall
192.168.42.1
172.17.0.1

Firewall

172.17.0.0/16

172.16.0.0/16

Management
Console
172.16.0.5

Web Server
172.16.0.80

10.0.0.0/8

Figure 11.33   Three-site VPN with partner site and gateway cluster

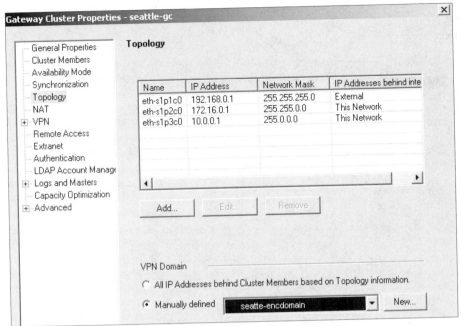

Figure 11.34 Configuring the topology of the Seattle gateway cluster

Communities they might be in. This won't be an issue for newly created objects, but if you simply renamed your old seattle-fw object as seattle-fwa and didn't remove it from its VPN Community, you would not be able to add seattle-fwa to a cluster because it would still be a member of a VPN Community.

Now create the gateway cluster object, adding seattle-fwa and seattle-fwb to it. Configure the Topology frame. Add the VRRP IP addresses on each interface to the Topology frame, as shown in Figure 11.34.

Configure state synchronization in the State Synchronization frame. Configure the 172.30.0.0/24 network as the synchronization network in the gateway cluster object (see Figure 11.35).

Go to the Authentication frame and verify that SecurID is set on the Authentication tab of this object (remember that the partner site must authenticate with HTTP or Telnet using SecurID authentication). You will have to exit the gateway cluster object definition and reenter it in order to add the object to the Extranet and MyIntranet VPN Communities.

In FireWall-1 NG FP3 and above, the gateway objects for seattle-fwa and seattle-fwb will completely disappear from the objects tree. This is perfectly normal.

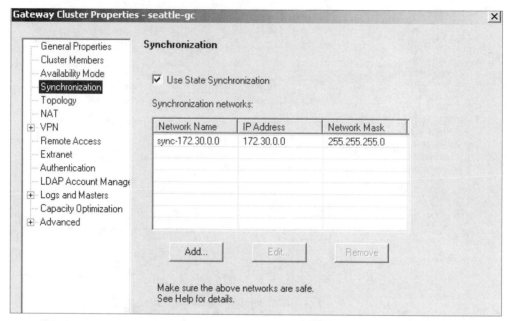

Figure 11.35 Configuring the synchronization network for the Seattle gateway cluster

The rulebase essentially remains the same on both sides except that all references to seattle-fw are replaced with seattle-gc.

I have not discussed the changes that need to be made on the partner end of the VPN. All you need to do is define the Interfaces tab on the seattle-fw workstation object so that it includes all IP addresses on both members of the cluster, including VRRP addresses. The interfaces' names and netmasks are not important because you are not setting up anti-spoofing (that is a bit difficult to do on a firewall you do not control!). The Topology frame should look something like Figure 11.36 when you are done.

Once both sets of changes are made, you can install and test the security policy.

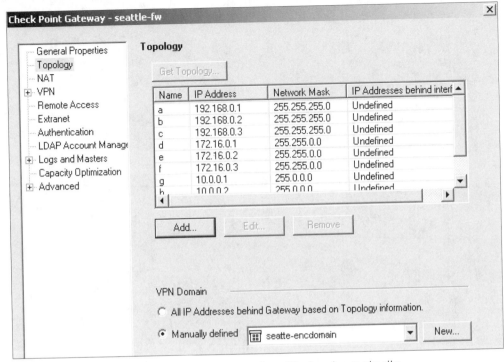

Figure 11.36   Definition of seattle-fw at remote site

Chapter

12

SecuRemote
and SecureClient

This chapter is designed to be a practical guide to planning and configuring client-to-site VPNs in FireWall-1. A few key terms and concepts are discussed throughout the chapter. It is not meant to comprehensively cover encryption or encryption technologies.

By the end of this chapter, you should be able to:

- Identify the differences between SecuRemote and SecureClient
- Configure your firewall to support SecuRemote and SecureClient
- Install SecuRemote and SecureClient
- Identify an Office Mode configuration and why you would want to use it
- Configure a Windows-based L2TP client to work with FireWall-1
- Identify a Multiple Entry Point configuration and its features
- Determine where SecuRemote and SecureClient can and cannot be used
- Troubleshoot SecuRemote problems

Introduction to SecuRemote and SecureClient

SecuRemote and SecureClient are really just two different names for the same piece of software: Check Point's VPN client software for Microsoft Windows. This software is designed to allow a single Windows client to transparently initiate a client-to-site VPN with a Check Point firewall. This chapter builds on the concepts discussed in Chapter 11. It is a separate chapter because the setup and troubleshooting for SecuRemote are different than those for site-to-site VPNs.

References to SecuRemote also include SecureClient, which has some additional features that allow network administrators to enforce a security policy on the client. If the client has a policy that does not match the one prescribed or is configured in an undesirable manner, the client can be denied access to the

VPN. Thus references to SecuRemote include SecureClient, but not necessarily the other way around.

Much like FireWall-1 on Microsoft Windows, SecuRemote binds to the Windows TCP/IP stack. This allows it to intercept connections destined for a remote encryption domain and encrypt them. Likewise, it can decrypt incoming encrypted packets. There is also a user-level process that allows you to fetch the remote encryption domain, be authenticated, and otherwise control SecuRemote. This manifests itself on the client as a little envelope in the Windows taskbar.

Much of the planning that goes into using SecuRemote is pretty much the same as planning for site-to-site encryption; that is, you still have to define an encryption domain and configure network objects. However, you can do things on a user-by-user basis. For example, some users can use different encryption parameters. You can restrict some users from going some places but not others. You get all the flexibility of User Authentication with encryption.

One issue you do have to worry about with SecuRemote is end-user support. Although the client is generally easy to install and use, sometimes it does not go well. While most general installation problems have gone away, exotic network configurations or hardware can sometimes confuse SecuRemote or cause issues with your TCP/IP stack. I've encountered more than my share of destroyed TCP/IP stacks over the years. Also, users may not know what to do when various dialog boxes appear or even fully understand what is going on, especially if they are behind a NAT device.

A Word about Licensing

As with a site-to-site VPN, SecuRemote requires both binaries that support it and the licenses to enable it. The basic SecuRemote functionality is provided as part of a standard encryption license, although you must specifically request the functionality when requesting your license. The SecureClient functionality comes at an additional charge beyond an encryption license.

If you have CPVP-VSR as part of your license string, you have SecuRemote functionality. If you have CPVP-VSC as part of your license string, you have SecureClient functionality. The number that appears after either of these designations is the number of users your license permits.

Configuring SecuRemote on FireWall-1

The general steps for configuring FireWall-1 to use SecuRemote are listed below and described in the subsections that follow.

1. Configure the gateway object for SecuRemote.
2. Create SecuRemote users.
3. Define the client encryption rules and Remote Access community rules.
4. Configure the global properties.
5. Configure the Desktop Security policy and other relevant options.
6. Install the security policy.

Configuring the Gateway Object for SecuRemote

Several areas of the FireWall-1 configuration relate to SecuRemote. At this time, I am going to touch on only what is necessary for basic SecuRemote functionality.

Similar to site-to-site encryption, you must configure the firewall object with the appropriate encryption types and encryption domain. If using the simplified VPN setup, you also need to add the gateway object to the Remote Access community. The Remote Access community was created by default. Traditional mode provides a checkbox for the Exportable for SecuRemote/ SecureClient option, as shown in Figure 12.1. Exportable for SecuRemote is somewhat of a misnomer because selecting this option actually means that when a SecuRemote client connects to the management console to request topology (i.e., the encryption domain), this firewall's encryption domain will be provided to the SecuRemote client. If this checkbox is not enabled, a SecuRemote client will not be able to download the encryption domain.

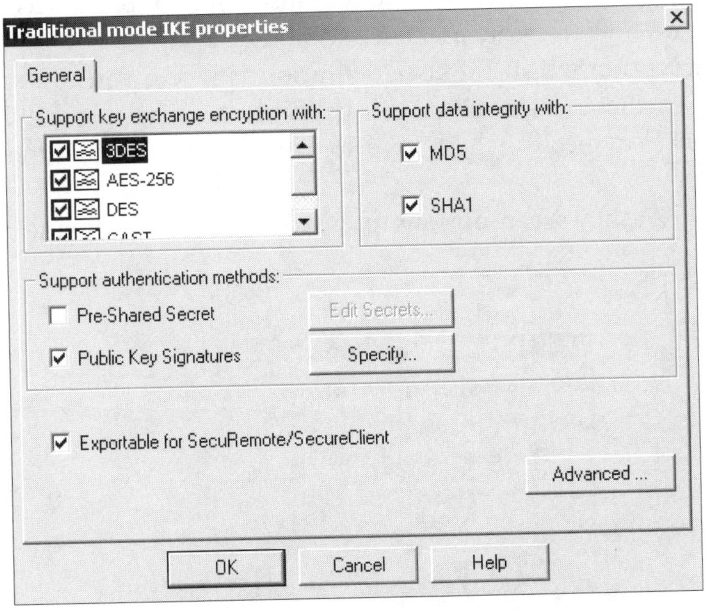

Figure 12.1   Traditional mode IKE properties

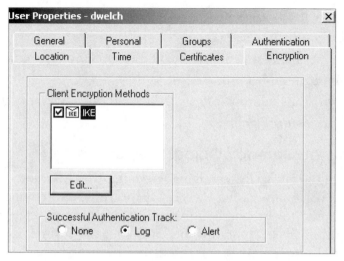

Figure 12.2 User Properties, Encryption tab

In Traditional mode, you need only enable the appropriate type of authentication (Pre-Shared Secret or Public Key Signatures options). The actual parameters specific to each user are defined in each user's definition.

Creating Users for Use with SecuRemote

You can employ the same users you created for User Authentication for outbound access to authenticate SecuRemote users for inbound access. For more information on how to create users, see Chapter 8.

The Encryption tab in the user definition is where you can specify which encryption schemes are defined for this particular user (see Figure 12.2). On this tab, you can also specify whether to log or alert when this user logs in via SecuRemote.

Figure 12.3 shows the options presented for the authentication of IKE sessions.

Figure 12.3 IKE Phase 2 Properties, Authentication tab

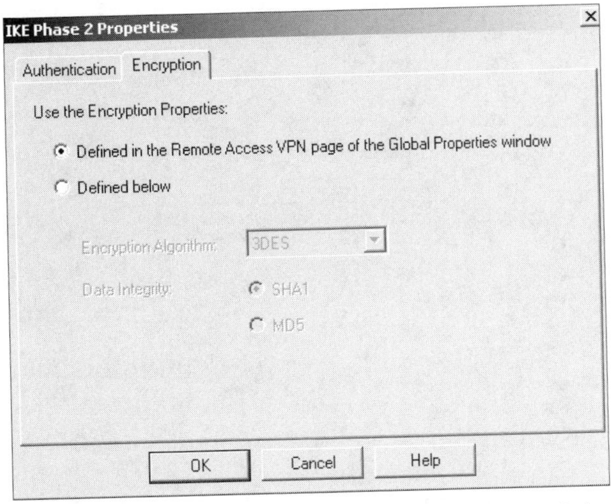

Figure 12.4   IKE Phase 2 Properties, Encryption tab

On the Authentication tab, you specify which authentication methods are supported: passwords (authentication based on a pre-shared secret) or public keys (authentication based on certificates). You would select the Password option only if you want to use a fixed password. If you want to use an external authentication server, like SecurID or RADIUS, leave this box unchecked. Ensure that the Hybrid Mode option is enabled in the Global Properties section, Remote Access, VPN Basic frame.

On the Encryption tab, shown in Figure 12.4, you get to choose how this user will have his or her data encrypted in the IPSec session. (IKE parameters are defined on a per-gateway basis.)

A global property affects what encryption parameters users will have, specifically in the Remote Access, VPN Advanced frame (see Figure 12.5). If the Enforce Encryption Algorithm and Data Integrity option is checked, users on NG FP2

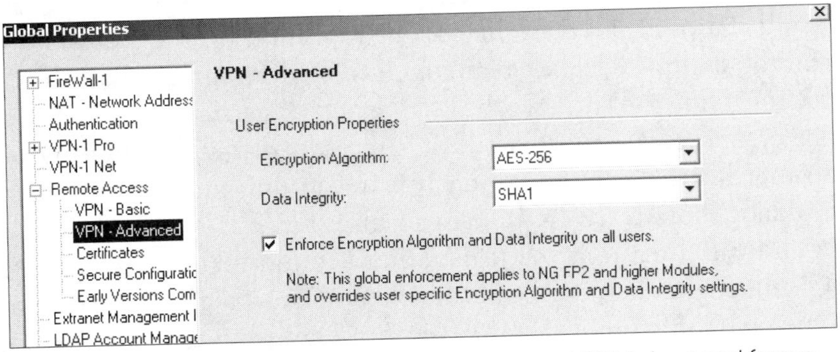

Figure 12.5   Global Properties, Remote Access, VPN Advanced frame

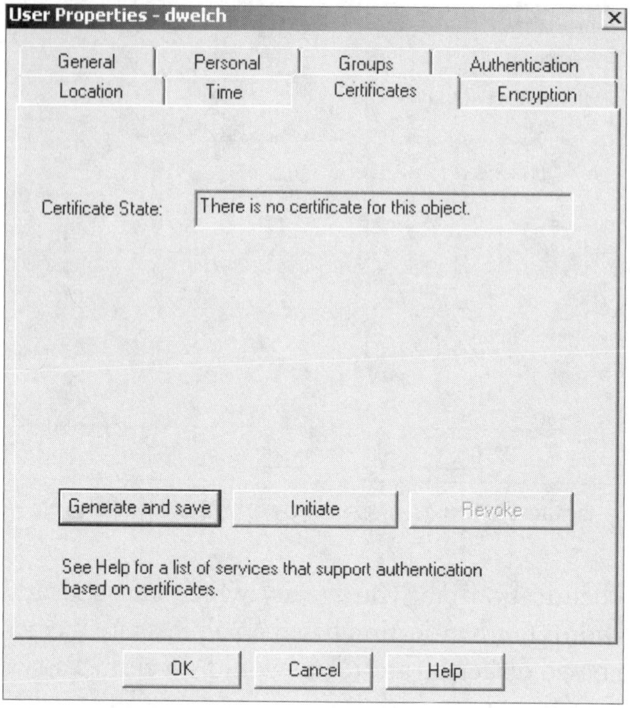

Figure 12.6 User Properties, Certificates tab

and above will be given these properties regardless of their individual settings. For pre-NG FP2 modules, they will be given whatever individual parameters they have defined.

If you wish to define a certificate for a user, click the user's Certificates tab to display the screen shown in Figure 12.6.

There are two ways to issue a certificate for a user: as a certificate file or as a reservation. In the former case, the certificate is generated on the management console and a copy is saved in the specified location on the SmartDashboard/ Policy Editor station (click Generate and save). The administrator is then responsible for giving the end user the certificate. For certificates issued as reservations, the certificate is generated but is "reserved" for the end user to download from SecureClient. Clicking on the Initiate button and clicking OK in the warning dialog shows a screen similar to Figure 12.7.

The end user then uses the registration key to obtain the certificate using SecureClient. Right-click on the SecureClient envelope in the desktop tray and select Open or Configure. From the Certificates menu, select Check Point Certificates, then Create. A wizard takes you through saving the certificate to a file

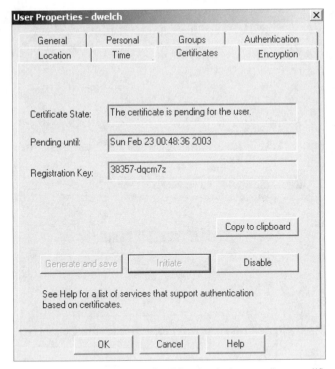

Figure 12.7   User Properties, Certificates tab, pending certificate

or smart card, then specifying the gateway IP and registration key. The certificate is then downloaded to the client and marked as usable in the management station.

Defining Client Encryption Rules and Remote Access Community Rules

The rules defined for client encryption are very similar to the rules you created for combining authentication and encryption in Chapter 11 except the action used for the rule is Client Encrypt. These types of rules are used in Traditional mode policies. With a Simplified mode policy, you instead create a rule in terms of the Remote Access community.

The first rule shown in Figure 12.8 permits your SecuRemote clients to fetch the topology from the management console. The FW1_topo service (TCP port 264) is what allows this. If you also are using the Policy Server functionality, FW1_pslogon_NG (TCP port 18231) allows this communication.

The second rule allows VPN1_IPSEC_encapsulation, IKE, and ESP, which are all the various protocols used for encryption. This is necessary if the Enable FireWall-1 Control Connections property is unchecked.

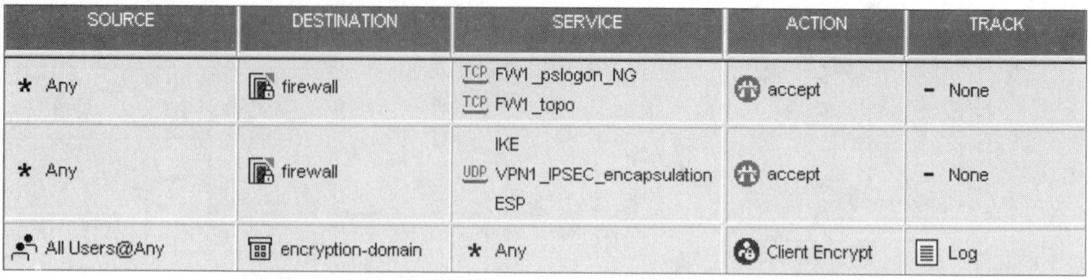

SOURCE
DESTINATION
SERVICE
ACTION
TRACK
Any
firewall
TCP FW1_pslogon_NG
TCP FW1_topo
accept
None
Any
firewall
IKE
UDP VPN1_IPSEC_encapsulation
ESP
accept
None
All Users@Any
encryption-domain
Any
Client Encrypt
Log

Figure 12.8 Traditional rulebase for SecuRemote access

User Encryption Action Properties
General
Source:
intersect with user database
Destination:
intersect with user database
Apply Rule Only if Desktop Configuration Options are Verified

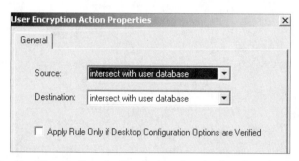

Figure 12.9 User Encryption Action Properties for the Client Encrypt action

SOURCE
DESTINATION
IF VIA
SERVICE
ACTION
TRACK
Any
firewall
Any
TCP FW1_pslogon_NG
TCP FW1_topo
accept
None
Any
firewall
Any
UDP VPN1_IPSEC_encapsulation
IKE
ESP
drop
None
All Users@Any
encryption-domain
Remote_Access_Community
Any
accept
Log

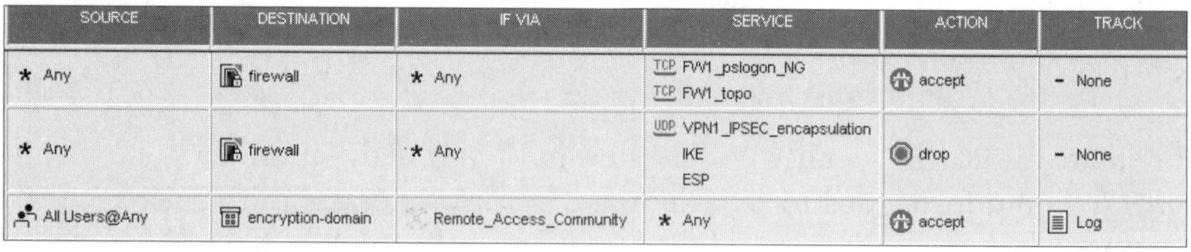

Figure 12.10 Simplified rulebase for remote access

The third rule actually permits the SecuRemote users to enter your encryption domain. The Client Encrypt action (see Figure 12.9) has properties that look very similar to those used for User Authentication. The only difference between this screen and the User Authentication screen is the checkbox, which for Client Encrypt requires that the desktop configuration options be set correctly on SecureClient. You can set these options in the Global Properties screen, Remote Access, Secure Configuration Verification frame (see the Setting Up Desktop Security section).

Figure 12.10 shows a simplified rulebase for remote access.

Configuring Global Properties

A number of items in the Global Properties screen affect client-to-site VPNs. Let's begin with the Remote Access frame, shown in Figure 12.11.

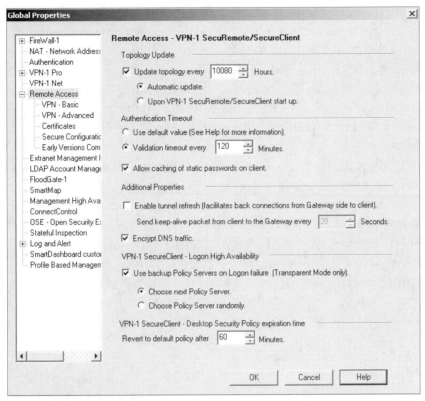

Figure 12.11   Global Properties, Remote Access frame

The list below outlines the options available in this screen.

Topology Update: The options in this section control how often a client will attempt to update the topology of this site. This does not prevent the client from updating this information on its own. Automatic means that the client will poll at the specified interval to get an update. Upon startup refers to when the client system is initially booted. If the end user cancels the update request (which is possible), the topology will be updated on first connection to the site.

Authentication Timeout: The options in this section control how often a user must supply his or her credentials to remain authenticated to the VPN. If you choose to use the default value, authentication occurs as follows: Certificate users need not reauthenticate until SecuRemote starts because certificate passwords will be cached on the desktop. Static password users (FireWall-1 password and Hybrid IKE) need not reauthenticate until SecuRemote starts if you indicate that caching of static passwords on the client is allowed; otherwise, static password users must reauthenticate as one-time password users.

Enable tunnel refresh: If enabled, this option forces the client to send periodic "hello" packets back to the gateway. This facilitates connections to connected clients from within the encryption domain.

Encrypt DNS traffic: This option tells SecureClient to forward DNS traffic relating to configured domains to the encryption domain, encrypting the communication. In an Office Mode configuration where DNS servers are assigned, all DNS queries will be encrypted and forwarded to the configured DNS server(s).

Use backup Policy Servers on Logon failure: This tells a SecureClient system in Transparent mode to try other policy servers in the specified fashion. More information on Transparent mode is presented in the section on Office Mode configuration later in this chapter.

VPN-1 SecureClient—Desktop Security Policy expiration time: If SecureClient is unable to connect to a policy server after the specified period of time, and the client has a policy loaded, the client will revert to the "default policy," which is all Desktop Security rules that do *not* relate to a specific group or have Encrypt as an action.

Setting Up Desktop Security

To use the Desktop Security options, you must have the Policy Server component loaded on your firewall module(s) and have the gateway object configured with the Policy Server as being present on the module. A user group that is allowed to access the Policy Server must be specified in the Authentication frame (see Figure 12.12).

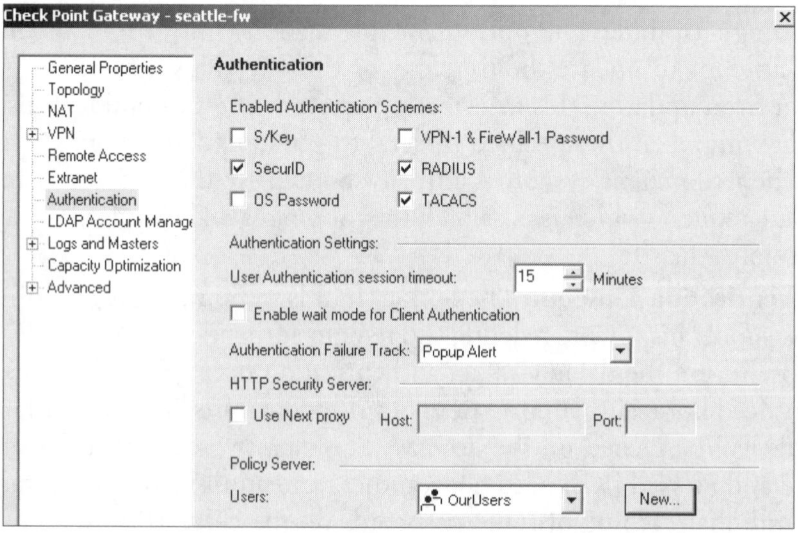

Figure 12.12 Defining a user group for the Policy Server

In the General Properties frame, ensure that SecureClient Policy Server is checked, as shown in Figure 12.13.

In the Global Properties screen, the Remote Access Secure Configuration Verification (SCV) frame has some additional relevant options (see Figure 12.14).

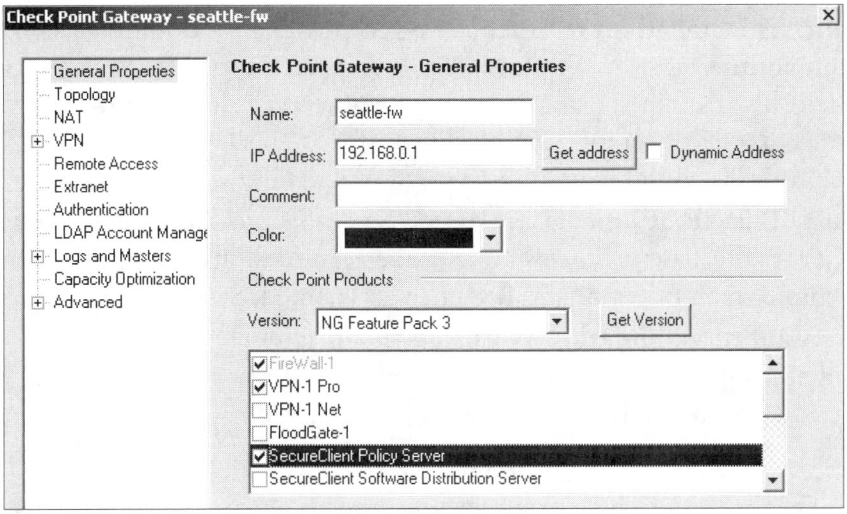

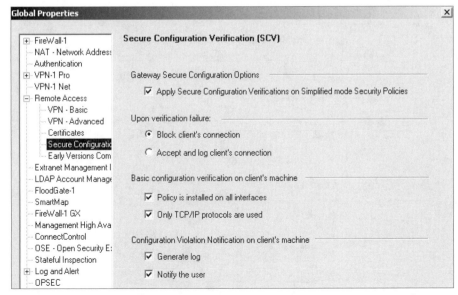

Figure 12.13   SecureClient Policy Server enabled in the gateway object

Figure 12.14   Global Properties, Secure Configuration Verification frame

These options are listed below.

Apply Secure Configuration Verifications on Simplified mode Security Policies: All Simplified mode policies with the Remote Access community require all SCV checks to pass.

Upon verification failure: In this section of the frame in NG AI, you can either block any attempt by clients that fail SCV checks or allow them anyway.

Policy is installed on all interfaces: It is possible to "unbind" SecureClient from an interface. In Windows 2000, you can simply uncheck the Secure-Client box from a specific interface. In other Windows platforms, you can either disable or remove the bindings. If this check is enabled and Secure-Client is not bound to all interfaces, SCV will fail.

Only TCP/IP protocols are used: Since SecureClient works only with TCP/IP, alternate protocols are considered undesirable. If another protocol is bound to an interface and this check is enabled, SCV will fail.

Configuration Violation Notification on client's machine: This section presents options for notifying the administrator (by generating a log) and/or the end user when an SCV violation has occurred.

Once you've defined these property screens, you need to define a Desktop Security policy. If you did not specify this type of policy when you initially created your policy, you can select New from the File menu and simply add Desktop Security to an existing policy, as shown in Figure 12.15.

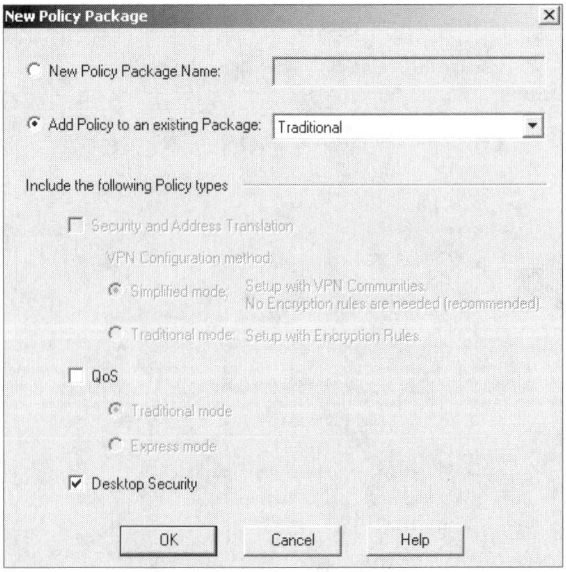

Figure 12.15 Adding Desktop Security to an existing policy

Now the Desktop Security tab is present in SmartDashboard/Policy Editor. You need to create both inbound (to the client) and outbound (from the client) rules. The rules are similar to the standard security policy rules except for the following differences.

- Inbound rules always assume a client is the destination and outbound rules always assume a client is the source. You can place restrictions on where that client is, however.
- You cannot specify a VPN Community.
- The actions are limited to Accept, Block, and Encrypt.
- Logging is limited to being either on or off for a specific rule.

Figure 12.16 shows a rulebase that permits encrypted access only to the encryption domain and not to the Internet. To allow the client to access other Internet hosts as well, change Rule 4 so that its action is Accept, as shown in Figure 12.17.

Inbound Rules

NO.	SOURCE	DESKTOP	SERVICE	ACTION	TRACK
1	encryption-domain	All Users@Any	* Any	Encrypt	- None
2	* Any	All Users@Any	* Any	Block	Log

Outbound Rules

NO.	DESKTOP	DESTINATION	SERVICE	ACTION	TRACK
3	All Users@Any	encryption-domain	* Any	Encrypt	Log
4	All Users@Any	* Any	* Any	Block	- None

Figure 12.16 Sample Desktop Security policy for allowing encrypted access only

Inbound Rules

NO.	SOURCE	DESKTOP	SERVICE	ACTION	TRACK
1	encryption-domain	All Users@Any	* Any	Encrypt	- None
2	* Any	All Users@Any	* Any	Block	Log

Outbound Rules

NO.	DESKTOP	DESTINATION	SERVICE	ACTION	TRACK
3	All Users@Any	encryption-domain	* Any	Encrypt	Log
4	All Users@Any	* Any	* Any	Accept	- None

Figure 12.17 Sample Desktop Security policy for allowing outgoing and encrypted access

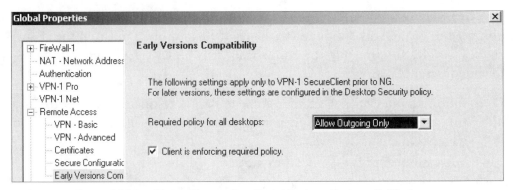

Figure 12.18   Global Properties, Early Versions Compatibility frame

These are, of course, simplistic examples. If you manage some FireWall-1 4.1 gateways or have end users who still use SecureClient 4.1, the allowed policy must be a simple one. Figure 12.18 shows the Early Versions Compatibility frame (under Remote Access in the Global Properties section) where you can define this policy.

You can choose from the following policies.

Allow All: Enforce no specific policy.

Allow Outgoing and Encrypted: The user can initiate communication to the Internet (unencrypted) or the VPN.

Allow Outgoing Only: The user can initiate a connection to the Internet but not to the VPN.

Allow Encrypted Only: The user can initiate a connection to the VPN but not to the Internet.

The checkbox for enforcing required policy, if selected, means that the user will not be allowed into the network and the SecuRemote client will be configured with a different policy than what is specified in this frame. The client receives an error to this effect when he or she authenticates.

Installing SecureClient

Users must install SecuRemote before they can use it. There are different versions of SecureClient for Windows 9x/ME, Windows NT/2000, and Windows XP because the TCP/IP stacks are very different in these three versions of Windows. Make sure the correct version for your particular operating system is installed. Before running the enclosed `setup.exe`, read the README file to make sure you are about to install the correct version. You should also ensure that the version you are installing is the same as or later than your FireWall-1 installation (e.g., if your firewall is NG AI, SecureClient should be too).

During installation, you will be asked if you want to install SecuRemote or SecureClient. Installing SecuRemote provides basic VPN functionality only. There is no reason not to include support for the Desktop Security features by also installing SecureClient, even if you do not plan to use it right away.

Another question you will be asked during installation is if you would like to install only on the dial-up adapters or on all adapters. FireWall-1 recognizes only standard Microsoft Dial-up Adapters (or RAS in Windows NT/2000) as dial-up adapters, so if you need to use a special adapter (for AOL, for instance), install on All Adapters. During the installation process, your only choices are all or nothing; that is, you cannot choose to install interfaces only on specific adapters. In Windows 9x/ME, 2000, and XP, you can easily change the interfaces SecuRemote is bound to by modifying the network properties after Secure Client has been installed. Windows NT does not provide a way to change the interfaces to which SecureClient is bound.

What does it mean if SecuRemote is bound to a particular interface? Simply put, if SecuRemote is bound to the interface, it can send encrypted traffic through it. This may have unintended consequences in some circumstances. Generally, binding SecuRemote only to those interfaces you intend to use to communicate with a remote encryption domain is the right thing to do. Binding SecuRemote to an interface does not preclude you from using that interface for nonencrypted traffic. Note that an administrator can change this behavior with the Desktop Security features.

You must reboot in order for SecuRemote to be usable. In some cases, you will not be able to reboot correctly after installing SecuRemote. These problems are discussed in the Troubleshooting section later in this chapter.

Once Windows comes up and you log in, you will see an icon in your taskbar that looks like this: 🖳. It lets you know that SecuRemote is active. The icon animates when encrypted data is being sent to a remote site. Right-click on this icon and select Open or Configure, depending on which mode the client was installed in. You will see a screen similar to Figure 12.19.

This figure shows a blank configuration with no sites. To add a site, select Create New from the Sites menu or click the New Site icon. Enter the site IP address (which is usually the firewall) and a "nickname" for the site, as shown in Figure 12.20. Click OK.

At this point, you will be prompted for authentication. Enter the appropriate username or password or specify a certificate. Figure 12.21 shows the dialog for the username and password.

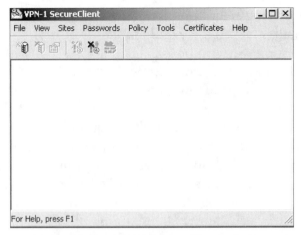

Figure 12.19 VPN-1 SecureClient window

Figure 12.20 Starting to create a new site

Figure 12.21 Authenticating with SecureClient

Figure 12.22 shows a fingerprint validation screen that appears the first time you connect. This fingerprint should match what is shown in the ICA (or other certificate authority) certificate when "viewed" in SmartDashboard/Policy Editor. If it does match, accept it by clicking OK.

After you have authenticated successfully, you will see a dialog similar to Figure 12.23 that says what method was used to authenticate you (in this example, FireWall-1 Password).

Finally, you can click OK in the Create New Site dialog when you see the Last Update field (see Figure 12.24).

Figure 12.22   Verifying the certificate fingerprint

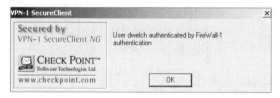

Figure 12.23   Successful SecureClient authentication

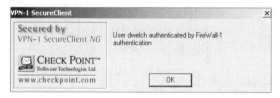

Figure 12.24   Creating a new site after the topology download

Now that you've added the site, you can attempt to connect to it. Depending on whether the site requires login to a policy server or uses Office Mode, you might need to change the connection mode in the client. From the SecureClient menu, select Configure Client Mode from the Tools menu. You can choose either Transparent mode or Connect Mode. For a policy server login or Office Mode configuration, you need to configure the client in Connect Mode. If you change modes, you will have to restart the client. Select Stop VPN-1 SecureClient from the File menu to do this.

There are a couple of options you can configure on the client that affect how the VPN connection takes place, such as forcing UDP encapsulation, IKE over TCP, or Visitor Mode. These options are discussed in the Troubleshooting section.

All of this might be confusing to an end user. Fortunately, you can prepackage a custom version of SecureClient with the site definition and appropriate settings. The SecureClient Packaging Tool, discussed later in this chapter, enables you to do this.

Office Mode

An important enhancement to SecureClient is Office Mode, which allows you to assign your remote access client an IP address, DNS, and WINS information as if the client were on the local network. To understand why this is a big step forward, a bit of history is in order.

Before Office Mode

In FireWall-1 4.1, a VPN client initiates a connection to the encryption domain simply by attempting to access the encryption domain. It is "transparent" in the sense that no interaction with the SecuRemote application is required to bring up the VPN. Once the VPN is established, the client may communicate with the encryption domain. Packets appear to be sourced from the client's IP address. If the client is sitting behind a NAT device, this is the client's non-routable IP address. This creates a number of problems.

- *IP address conflicts:* What happens when two or more VPN clients use the same private address space? With a number of NAT router vendors choosing 192.168.0.x as their internal DHCP address range and most of them assigning 192.168.0.2 *first*, you end up with a lot of clients using the same address. The firewall doesn't deal with this very well and drops clients. What about when the 192.168.0.x network is used in your encryption domain? SecuRemote doesn't work in this configuration.

- *Asymmetric routing:* In particularly large networks that span multiple sites, there may be more than one way out of the internal network depending on where you are. As a result, you might come in one gateway and go out the other. Most firewalls don't cope very well with asymmetric routing, even when VPN access is not involved. In a VPN situation, it is vital to enter and exit the same set of firewalls. IP Pool NAT attempts to resolve this problem but breaks applications that aren't NAT friendly.

- *Routing of Internet addresses in the internal network:* For a variety of reasons, it is not always desirable to allow Internet IP addresses on the internal network. It becomes especially difficult when trying to perform access control on items within the network. IP Pool NAT partially helps, but again, it is subject to the limitations of NAT.

- *Lack of integration with dial-up networking:* In some instances, it is useful to allow a VPN connection only when dialed up to the Internet. In FireWall-1 4.1, there was no way to cleanly bring up dial-up networking and the VPN connection simultaneously.

- *Disconnection from the encryption domain:* In a Transparent mode configuration, the only way to "log out" of a site (i.e., to prevent the client from sending encrypted packets to the encryption domain) is to disable or remove the site from the configuration.

- *Use of SecuRemote from within the encryption domain:* You might want to use SecuRemote to always talk to a firewall, regardless of whether or not you are in the internal network. Furthermore, your client might be using IP address space your encryption domain contains. SecureClient 4.1 and earlier did not work in this configuration.

At the end of the day, VPN access was more problematic for many people than dialing in.

What Office Mode Does

Office Mode provides solutions to all of these issues.

- *Connect Mode:* The client now provides a new way to initiate a VPN connection. Connect Mode acts a bit like dial-up networking—the interface is even similar. You must explicitly tell SecureClient to connect to the VPN domain. As part of that process, you can specify which dial-up networking connection to bring up as well. You can also *disconnect* from the VPN domain easily.

- *Client IP addresses assigned on authentication:* In Office Mode, the firewall assigns the client an IP address. The administrator can choose which IP addresses the firewall will assign or choose to obtain the IP address via an internal DHCP server. The client uses one of these IP addresses for all communications to the encryption domain, which will be assigned to a virtual adapter that appears in your Windows configuration. This eliminates problems with external addresses on the internal network as well as with NAT.

- *No client IP address conflicts:* Because the client is assigned a unique IP during the initial IKE negotiation, the client's local IP address can be almost anything it needs to be. The various types of IP address conflicts discussed earlier are essentially eliminated. There are a few cases where you will still have issues, for example, with clients located directly behind the gateway.

- *No asymmetric routing:* Each gateway has a unique set of client IP addresses associated with it. Internal routing should be set up so that these IPs will route to the appropriate gateway.

These Office Mode features make a client-based VPN much easier to deploy on a wide scale.

Configuring Office Mode

In NG AI, Office Mode is configured in the gateway object in the Remote Access Office Mode frame, as shown in Figure 12.25. In NG FP3 and earlier, it is in the gateway object's Office Mode frame (under Remote Access).

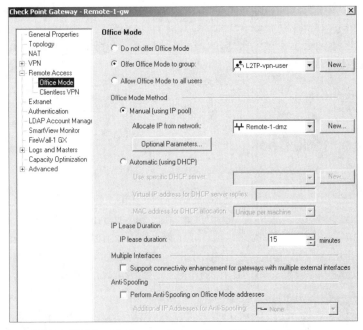

Figure 12.25   Gateway Properties, Office Mode frame

The settings here are described below.

Do not offer Office Mode: Do not use Office Mode. All properties on this page will be disabled if you select this option because Office Mode will not be used.

Offer Office Mode to group/Allow Office Mode to all users: You can allow Office Mode as a choice either for a specific group of users or for all users. Note that this doesn't require users to use Office Mode. However, your particular network configuration might make Office Mode the only thing that actually works.

Office Mode Method, Manual: This option tells FireWall-1 to automatically assign an IP address for a pool of IP addresses. In the optional parameters, you can define up to three DNS servers, three WINS servers, and the DNS domain of your client. In NG FP3 and before, ensure that the IP address space chosen is *outside* of your encryption domain.

Office Mode Method, Automatic: This option tells FireWall-1 to send a request to an internal DHCP server to obtain configuration information. You need to tell FireWall-1 which DHCP server to forward the request to and an IP address to originate the requests from. The DHCP server uses this IP address as a "hint" to determine which subnet to allocate IP addresses from. As with the previous method, ensure that the IP addresses assigned by the DHCP server are outside of your encryption domain. In NG AI, you can also specify how the MAC address will be generated to be used as part of the DHCP request. The routing on your internal network should ensure packets destined for this IP address get routed to the firewall.

IP Lease Duration: When FireWall-1 allocates a client to an IP, this is how long that IP should be given to a particular client unless the client requests that it be renewed. Provided there's a connection between the client and server, this should always be the case.

Support connectivity enhancement for gateways with multiple external interfaces: In NG AI, this checkbox might be better described as "Make Office Mode work with more than one external interface." This option affects performance, so check this box only if you have more than one external interface.

Perform Anti-Spoofing on Office Mode addresses: In NG AI, this option tells FireWall-1 to ensure that a packet that appears to be coming from an Office Mode address is really coming from a client operating in Office Mode. If address space is being allocated by a DHCP server, the address range(s) need to be specified in the Additional IP Addresses for Anti-Spoofing field.

Once you have made the appropriate configurations here, install the security policy. Now ensure that an explicit route for the chosen Office Mode network is specified on the gateway(s). This route will point to your "next hop" toward the Internet (i.e., the default route). Check Point suggests this route be added even if your routing table would normally route the packets that direction anyway. Other hosts and/or routers on the internal network need a similar route.

The Office Mode networks themselves won't really exist within your network, though for all intents and purposes, the networks exist within the firewall. Within your internal network, ensure that packets destined for these networks are routed to the firewall.

On the client side, you need to ensure that the client is installed in Secure-Client mode and that Connect Mode is enabled. Right-click on the Secure-Remote envelope icon and select Configure. From here, select Connect Mode from the Tools menu. If necessary, change the mode to Connect Mode, and restart the client. Select Stop VPN-1 SecureClient from the File menu. Then navigate to the Start menu, select Programs, then Check Point VPN-1 Secure-Client, then SecureClient. This starts the client again.

Known Limitations of Office Mode

Office Mode has a few minor limitations.

- *There is no Windows 9x/ME support:* Office Mode does not work on Windows 9x/ME platforms. Considering that Microsoft is ending support for these platforms in January 2004, it is unlikely Check Point will ever support this feature on these platforms.
- *One Office Mode client cannot connect to another prior to NG AI:* Two client machines connected into the same firewall cannot communicate with one another through the VPN in NG FP3 and earlier. NG AI supports this functionality.
- *Office Mode also allocates an IP Pool NAT address:* If you have IP Pool NAT configured, your Office Mode clients will also be allocated an IP Pool NAT address.

Microsoft L2TP Clients

Configuring FireWall-1 to work with L2TP clients[1] is fairly straightforward. First, you must set up Office Mode as described in the previous section. Addi-

---

1. They are also commonly referred to as PPTP (Point-to-Point Tunneling Protocol) clients. However, Check Point does not support PPTP mode. FireWall-1 requires the use of IPSec over L2TP.

tionally, make sure that the L2TP-specific options are configured accordingly. This is configured in the gateway object in the Remote Access frame. The L2TP Support checkbox allows you to use L2TP clients in place of SecureClient. Specify the authentication method for the *user-based* portion of the authentication and the certificate FireWall-1 will present to the clients. MD5 Challenge uses a username and password for authentication purposes versus a certificate. If MD5 Challenge is used, make sure that users are configured with IKE pre-shared secrets. The IKE pre-shared secret is the password the user enters when prompted by the client. In your rulebase, ensure that the L2TP service is permitted to the firewall.

L2TP also requires machine-level authentication, which is always done with a certificate. This means each L2TP client machine requires its own certificate. The Check Point documentation is unclear about how to create a certificate for these machines, though it seems to suggest two *different users* be created—one for the machine and one for the user. In practice, you only need one user and one certificate, though you end up needing to install the certificate in two different locations if you use certificate-based authentication, only one with MD5 Challenge.

Before any client certificates are issued, an adjustment needs to be made to how FireWall-1 generates certificates. This is necessary because Windows requires that specific attributes be set in the certificates, and FireWall-1 does not set these by default. On the management console, if using the ICA to generate L2TP certificates, perform the following steps.

1. Type **cpstop**.
2. Edit `$FWDIR/conf/InternalCA.C` by adding the following lines:

```
:ike_cert_extended_key_usage (1)
:user_cert_extended_key_usage (2)
```

The first line tells the ICA to generate IKE certificates for gateways with the Server Authentication purpose. The second line says to generate user-certificates with the Client Authentication purpose.

3. Type **cpstart**.

If you're using an OPSEC CA instead, log into the management station with **dbedit** (or use Database Tool) and issue the following commands:

```
dbedit> modify properties firewall_properties
             cert_req_ext_key_usage 1
dbedit> update properties firewall_properties
```

Now restart the management console with **cprestart**.

Client certificates can be issued with the correct attributes. Go into the appropriate user(s), then generate and save the certificate to your local system. You then have to somehow give the certificate and the associated passphrase to the end user. The end user installs this certificate into his or her platform. To install the certificate into Windows 2000 and XP, follow these steps.

1. Log into the desired platform as a user with local administrator privileges.

2. Copy the certificate onto the desired platform into a known location. For the purposes of these steps, let's assume the certificate file is copied to the path `c:\data\fish.p12`.

3. From the command prompt (or from the Start menu, select Run), run the command `mmc` (i.e., the Microsoft Management Console).

4. From the Console menu, select Add/Remove Snap-in.

5. In the Add/Remove Snap-in window, click on Add.

6. In the Add Standalone Snap-in window, select Certificates and click on Add.

7. In the Certificates Snap-in window, select Computer Account and click on Next.

8. In the Select Computer window, select Local Computer and click on the Finish button. If you are using MD5 Challenge for authentication, skip to step 11.

9. In the Add/Remove Snap-in window, click on Add.

10. In the Add Standalone Snap-in window, select My user account and click on Finish.

11. Click on Close in the Add Standalone Snap-in window

12. Click on Close in the Add/Remove Snap-in window.

13. Double-click on Certificates (Local Computer) and you will see a list of certificate types in the Logical Store Name frame.

14. Double-click on Personal in the Logical Store Name frame. That frame should be replaced with one called Object Type.

15. Right-click in the Object Type frame and select All Tasks, then Import.

16. Click on Next in the resulting Certificate Import Wizard screen.

17. Specify the path to the certificate file, which in this case is `c:\data\fish.p12`.

18. In the next screen, type in the passphrase used by the administrator to protect the certificate. Check the Mark Private Key as Exportable checkbox. Click on Next.

19. When prompted for a certificate store, select Automatically, then click on Next, then Finish. Click on OK in the dialog that notifies you the import was successful. If you are using MD5 Challenge for authentication, skip to step 22.

20. Double-click on Certificates—Current User and you will see a list of certificate types in the Logical Store Name frame.

21. Repeat steps 14 through 19.

22. From the Console menu, select Save.

23. Specify a file with a `.msc` extension, e.g., `Console1.msc`. Click Save.

24. Exit the Microsoft Management Console.

The client will now have the ability to use the certificate for authenticating the L2TP session. The next step is to ensure that the IPSec policy agent is running, which can easily be checked by typing the command **net start "IPSEC Policy Agent"** into a command prompt to see if it says the policy agent is already started. If it is, chances are it is enabled by default as well. If this command starts up the IPSec policy agent, you will need to go into Services (under the Administrative Tools section of the Control Panel) and set the IPSec policy agent to start automatically.

Now you will create a new connection for the L2TP connection. Perform the following steps.

1. Right-click on My Network places on the Windows desktop and choose Properties. The Network and Dial-up Connections window should be displayed.

2. Double-click on the Make New Connection icon and click Next.

3. Choose "Connect to a private network through the Internet" and click Next.

4. Choose whether or not to dial up an initial connection. You would do this if you needed to use dial-up to establish an Internet connection.

5. Enter the gateway's DNS resolvable name or IP address and click Next.

6. Choose whether you wish to make this connection available to all users or not and click Next.

7. Enter a name for this connection and click Finish.

8. Right-click on the connection icon just created and select Properties.

9. Click on the Networking tab. Specify the VPN server type as L2TP.

10. Click on the Security tab, choose Advanced security options and click on Settings.

11. Under Logon Security, select Use Extensible Authentication Protocol (EAP). Under the pull-down menu, select Certificate or MD5 Challenge depending on what was specified on the gateway.

12. If you chose Certificate, click on Properties and Certificate. Uncheck Validate Server Certificate unless you wish to export the ICA key and import it into the workstation. Click OK.

13. Click OK two more times.

Now your client should be able to connect using this new network connection profile. When it is activated, you will either enter your username and IKE pre-shared secret or select your certificate and click OK. Assuming everything was configured correctly, the connection should come up.

 NOTE! Microsoft's L2TP Client appears to not work correctly in a NAT environment. Microsoft has issued an update for the L2TP clients on Windows 2000 and Windows XP. Refer to Microsoft Knowledge Base Article 818043. The update is also available through Windows Update.

High-Availability and Multiple Entry Point Configurations

If your firewall is configured into a High-Availability (HA) configuration, it is possible to use the Gateway Cluster feature to provide seamless failover of SecuRemote connections. Simply configure your gateway objects for each member of the cluster, then add them to the gateway cluster object. You configure all of your encryption schemes and keys within this object. When the SecuRemote client fetches the encryption domain, all of the physical IPs plus the virtual IP of the gateway cluster will be included as part of the gateway definition. This allows any system in the cluster to be used to process a SecuRemote connection.

In addition, it is now possible to have multiple firewalls responsible for the same encryption domain. This allows you to have different firewalls in different physical locations provide access to the same encryption domain. This is useful for large companies that have multiple ways to reach the Internet through different firewalls at (possibly) physically different locations.

The Multiple Entry Point feature also provides a level of High Availability. Although it does not provide for transparent failover (i.e., if the primary gateway fails, connections will not fail over), it does allow you to automatically use a secondary gateway in the event of a failure.

The biggest challenge to overcome in HA environments is to make sure that the same firewall is used for both incoming traffic and outgoing traffic for the client. Office Mode configurations should not have this problem because each client is assigned a unique IP address specific to the gateway being connected to.

If you do not have the appropriate licenses for Office Mode, you can use IP Pool NAT. IP Pool NAT is a sort of "reverse NAT" for incoming SecuRemote connections. As SecuRemote users authenticate and connect into the encryption domain, the client is allocated an IP address from a pool of addresses on a first-come, first-served basis. All packets coming from that SecuRemote client are then statically NATted to that IP address. The pool of addresses chosen must be unique for each firewall. If the pool of IP addresses is on the same subnet as the firewall's internal interface, proxy ARPs must be present for each IP in the pool to ensure that packets are forwarded to the firewall. The preferred method would be to use one or more subnets of nonroutable address space and ensure that internal routing routes these subnets to the correct firewall.

It may be desirable to allow SecuRemote users to access certain resources where you want to allow access only from within the internal network (e.g., the access is restricted by other firewalls or router access control lists). Office Mode is one way to resolve this issue. IP Pool NAT is another. Each incoming SecuRemote user is allocated a unique IP address on the internal network, "masking" the external IP address from internal firewalls or router access control lists.

To enable IP Pool NAT, you must first go to the Global Properties section, NAT frame, and enable IP Pool NAT as shown in Figure 12.26.

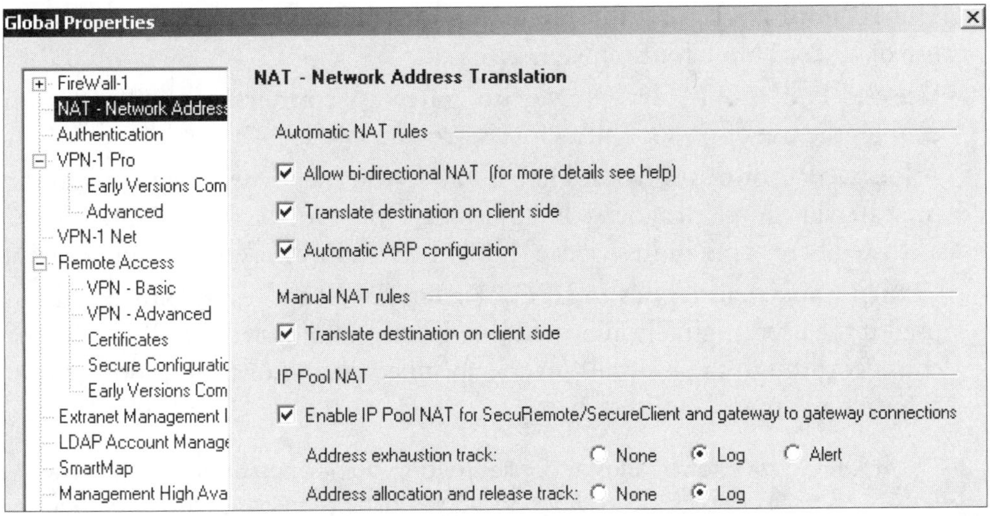

Figure 12.26 Global Properties, NAT frame

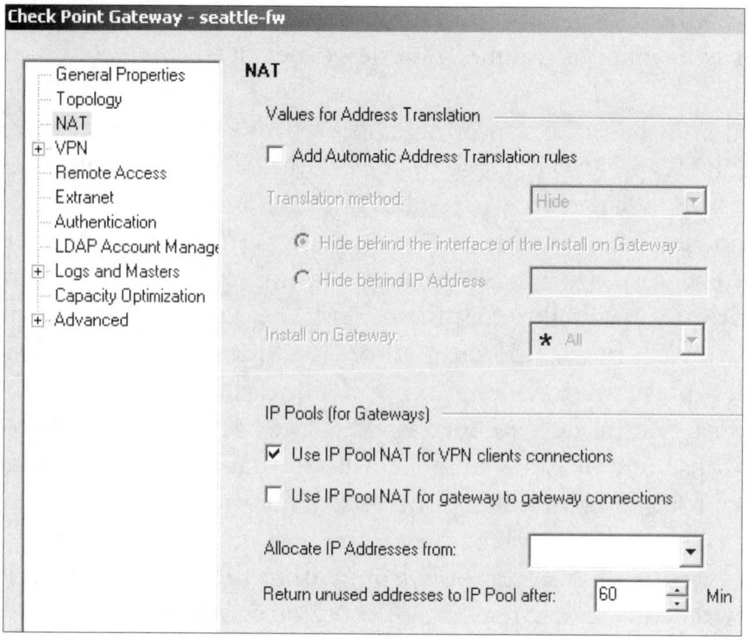

Figure 12.27   Gateway Object, NAT frame

Now edit the appropriate gateway object and go to the related NAT frame, as shown in Figure 12.27.

This frame shows the following options in the IP Pools section of the screen.

Use IP Pool NAT for VPN clients connections: This option enables the use of IP Pool NAT for SecuRemote users.

Use IP Pool NAT for gateway to gateway connections: This option enables the use of IP Pool NAT for site-to-site VPNs.

Allocate IP Addresses from: Here is where you specify what network(s) the firewall will choose to allocate IP addresses. Only groups and network objects are listed here. This address space should be within your encryption domain.

Return unused addresses to IP Pool after: An IP address is considered unused if the user originally allocated that IP address doesn't use it (i.e., doesn't connect through the firewall) for the specified period of time. Another user can then use that IP address.

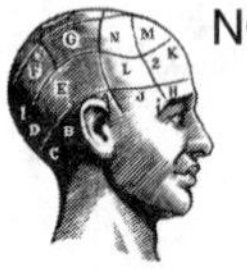

NOTE! In a Gateway Cluster configuration, you need to enable IP Pool NAT but configure the actual addresses in the member gateway objects. While you can specify the same set of addresses on all member gateways, this is not recommended.

Install the security policy, and have your SecuRemote clients update the site. The following caveats apply to Multiple Entry Point configurations:

- All gateways must belong to the same management console.
- Partial overlapping of encryption domains is not allowed.
- When a failover occurs, all existing connections will fail and need to be restarted.
- Each client must still have a unique nonroutable IP address.
- Gateway-to-gateway configurations are not supported—this feature was designed only for SecuRemote.

Microsoft Networking and SecureClient

A common configuration involving SecureClient includes the ability to access Microsoft Networking services, such as Network Neighborhood, and authenticate to a Windows domain. This section covers how to get this configuration working with SecureClient.

In the vast majority of situations, enabling two options solves almost all Microsoft Networking issues, including the ability to run domain logon scripts:

- Office Mode
- Secure Domain Logon (SDL)

Office Mode was discussed previously. SDL causes SecureClient to tie into the Microsoft GINA mechanism, which means that the Windows logon process will automatically invoke SecureClient upon logging into the system. Some additional registry settings are also tweaked (namely various delays) so that the VPN authentication process along with whatever is necessary to establish an Internet connection won't cause Windows to actually time out and allow the user to log in with cached credentials.

Unfortunately, Office Mode and SDL do not work together until the FireWall-1 NG FP3 client. Also, not everyone can pony up the money required to purchase the necessary licenses for Office Mode. The rest of this section explains how to make Microsoft Networking and SecureClient work together without Office Mode.

Forwarding DNS Requests inside the Encryption Domain

Prior to the introduction of Office Mode, SecuRemote could be configured to forward requests for certain "domains" to go to specific DNS servers inside the encryption domain. This would allow you to use your ISP's DNS servers for

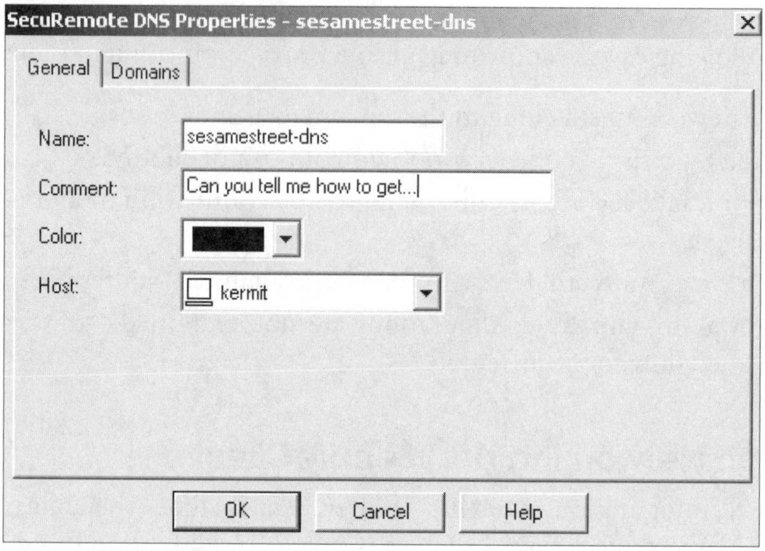

Figure 12.28   SecuRemote DNS Properties, General tab

Internet-based lookups but would forward all lookups for specific domains to DNS servers inside the encryption domain.

When users are logging onto a Windows 2000 Domain Controller, DNS is used for name resolution for various services. In this case, defining a SecuRemote DNS server and using SDL should be sufficient. To define a SecuRemote DNS server, go to the Servers section of the objects tree in SmartDashboard/ Policy Editor, right-click on SecuRemote DNS, and select New SecuRemote DNS. You may also choose Servers from the Manage menu, click on the New button, and select SecuRemote DNS. Either way, you should see a screen similar to Figure 12.28.

Specify the name of the object (it must be unique), a comment (if desired), a color (if desired), and the host object that represents the DNS server for the domains you care about. If more than one host contains these DNS entries, you can define another SecuRemote DNS object for each host. In this example, kermit is a host object that represents the DNS server.

In the Domains tab, shown in Figure 12.29, you can define which DNS domains this object represents. Check Point uses the term *label* to refer to the individual words in a domain name. For instance, phoneboy.com has two labels: phoneboy and com; support.checkpoint.com has three labels: support, checkpoint, and com.

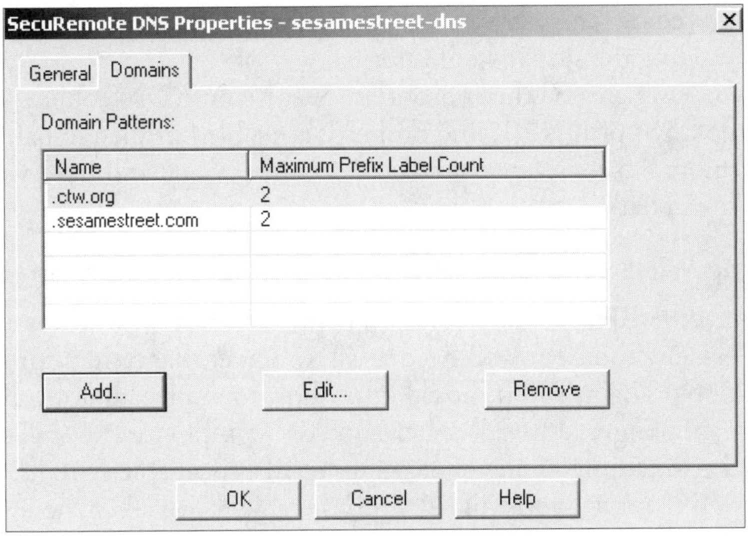

Figure 12.29 SecuRemote DNS Properties, Domains tab

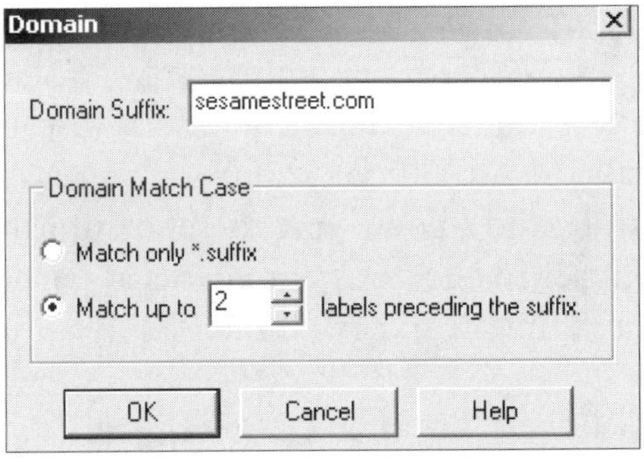

Figure 12.30 Adding a domain to a SecuRemote DNS object

Click on the Add button to add a domain. You will see a dialog like Figure 12.30.

Only certain DNS requests will be forwarded. Using this example, if you select "Match only *.suffix," it means that a DNS request for bigbird.sesamestreet.com would get forwarded inside the encryption domain, but alan.hoopers.sesamestreet.com would not get forwarded. If you select "Match up to N labels preceding the suffix," DNS requests for the specified domain that contain the specified number of labels would get forwarded. Using the pictured example, with the option set to match up to 2 labels before the suffix, snuffleupagus.sesamestreet.com (1 label preceding the suffix sesamestreet.com) would get forwarded and mrnoodle.elmosworld.sesamestreet.com would get forwarded

(2 labels preceding the suffix), but treelady.tv.elmosworld.sesamestreet.com (3 labels preceding the suffix) would not.

Once you have created the appropriate SecuRemote DNS object(s) and verified that the Encrypt DNS Traffic property is enabled in the Global Properties section, Remote Access frame, install the security policy and have your clients perform a site update.

Forwarding WINS Requests inside the Encryption Domain

To ensure that NetBIOS name resolution happens correctly, which is critical in a Windows NT environment, you need a WINS server that resides somewhere in the encryption domain, and it should know how to resolve all of your machines capable of speaking NetBIOS. Alternatively, you can use a well-populated lmhosts file containing names of all your NetBIOS-capable systems. However, without a WINS server, you will likely not be able to see all of these systems in Network Neighborhood.

If you have a WINS server, your SecuRemote client needs to be configured to use it. If the user accesses the encryption domain via a dial-up connection, configure it in the Dial-up Networking profile he or she uses to access the network. If the user uses a LAN card, configure the WINS server IPs on the LAN card profile. Information about lmhosts and WINS can be propagated with SecureClient. A file called $FWDIR/conf/dnsinfo.C is created. This file exists on your firewall module and allows you to send information about internal DNS and lmhosts entries to SecureClient clients as part of the network topology. The following is a sample dnsinfo.C file:

```
(
:LMdata (
    : (
            :ipaddr (10.10.1.10)
            :name (GORDON)
            :domain (SESAMESTREET)
    )
    : (
            :ipaddr (10.10.1.10)
            :name (GORDON)
    )
    : (
            :ipaddr (10.10.1.20)
            :name (MARIA)
            :domain (SESAMESTREET)
    )
  )
  )
```

WARNING! The `dnsinfo.C` file is extremely sensitive to spacing and capitalization. Use spaces where indicated in the sample shown here.

In this example, there are appropriate entries for 10.10.1.10 and 10.10.1.20. The second entry for GORDON is used explicitly for Windows 98, which requires it in order to browse the domain correctly.

Once you have created the `dnsinfo.C` file on your firewall modules and verified that the Encrypt DNS Traffic property is enabled in the Global Properties section, Remote Access frame, install the security policy and have your clients perform a site update.

Secure Domain Logon

SDL works for all Windows NT and 2000 platforms, although enabling the function requires local administrative privileges. It also works on Windows 9x platforms that connect to the Internet via a LAN adapter. SDL does not work for Windows 9x users who connect to the Internet via a dial-up adapter.

SecureClient Packaging Tool

Part of the problem with any sort of client-based VPN solution is getting the client installed and configured in the correct manner. Check Point makes this easier with the SecureClient Packaging Tool, which allows you to create your own preconfigured SecureClient installations. This makes the experience for the end user a much less confusing one. It's even possible to create totally "silent" installations, that is, ones that require no user prompts whatsoever and no dialog boxes.

When you start up the SecureClient Packaging Tool, you have to log in with a username and password similar to using SmartDashboard/Policy Editor, SmartView Tracker/Log Viewer, and other SMART Clients. In fact, none of these other GUIs can be active while the SecureClient Packaging Tool is connected to the management station.

The SecureClient Packaging Tool allows you to define a number of "profiles" that guide the SecureClient installation. By default, none are defined; you have to create one. Select New from the Profile menu or click on the New Profile button. You will be presented with a wizard dialog that will step you through the various options. Click on Next and you will see a dialog similar to Figure 12.31.

In this dialog, you specify a name and a comment for the profile. If you open an existing profile, this dialog will show the last date and time that profile was updated. Click Next. Figure 12.32 appears.

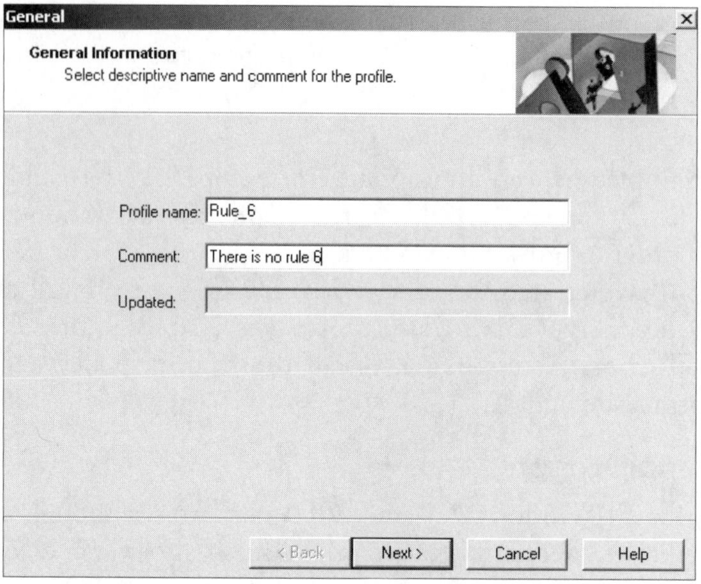

Figure 12.31 Naming the SecureClient profile

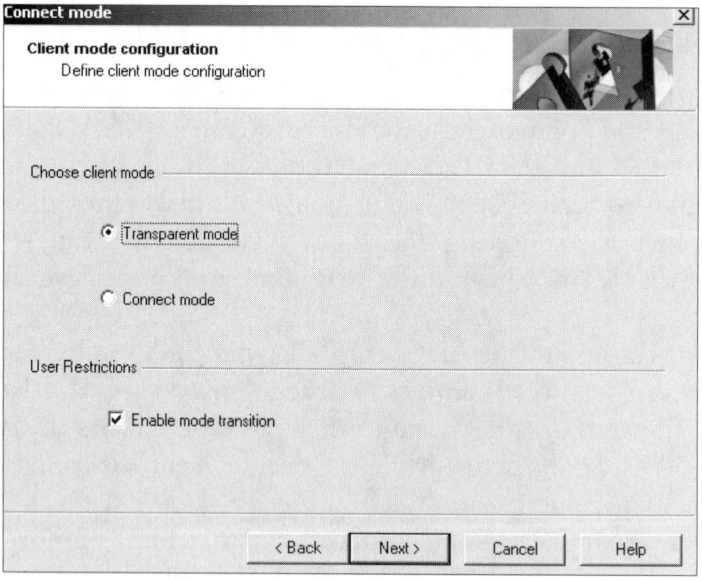

Figure 12.32 Choosing the default connection mode

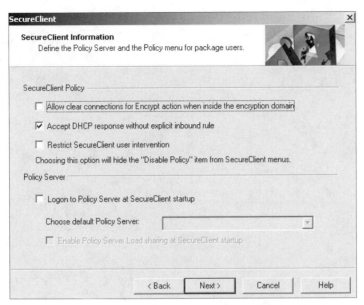

Figure 12.33   Choosing the security policy for clients

Here, you can choose which Connect Mode is the default and prevent an end user from being allowed to change that configuration (e.g., unchecking the "Enable mode transition"). Choose the options appropriate for your site and click Next. Figure 12.33 appears.

This screen presents the following options.

Allow clear connections for Encrypt action when inside the encryption domain: With this property enabled, any Desktop Security rules that have Encrypt as an action will also accept unencrypted traffic if the client has an IP address within the encryption domain.

Accept DHCP responses without explicit inbound rule: This permits inbound DHCP response packets without requiring a specific rule in the Desktop Security policy.

Restrict SecureClient user intervention: This prevents an end user from unloading the Desktop Security policy from his or her client. Specifically, it removes the entry from the menu that unloads the policy.

Logon to Policy Server at SecureClient startup: When SecureClient starts up, you can force a logon to the policy server. Choose the default policy server and (optionally) enable Policy Server Load Sharing. This option makes sense only in Transparent mode—Connect Mode always requires a logon to a policy server.

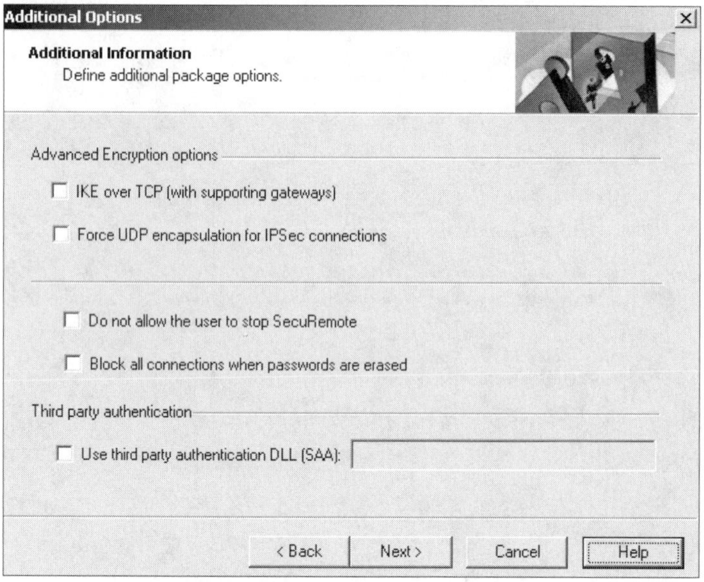

Figure 12.34 Selecting additional SecureClient options

After you have configured these options, click Next to move to the screen shown in Figure 12.34.

The options you can choose here are listed below.

IKE over TCP: Due to the fact that some home users' NAT routers do not deal with fragmented UDP packets very well and IKE Phase 1 packets can be fragmented, the option of doing IKE Phase 1 over TCP is supported. IKE Phase 2 is handled over UDP as usual.

Force UDP encapsulation for IPSec connections: By default, Secure-Client resorts to UDP encapsulation (see FAQ 12.1 for details) only when the client is subject to NAT. To force the client to use SecureClient even when it is not behind a NAT device, check this box.

Do not allow the user to stop SecuRemote: This removes the Stop VPN-1 SecureClient option from the menu, which should prevent an unprivileged user from stopping SecureClient.

Block all connections when passwords are erased: All encrypted connections will be blocked when the Erase All Passwords option is chosen in SecureClient. This should force the end user to reauthenticate before continuing.

Use third party authentication DLL: If you have a DLL that uses Secure Authentication, put the name of the file here. This file should then be copied

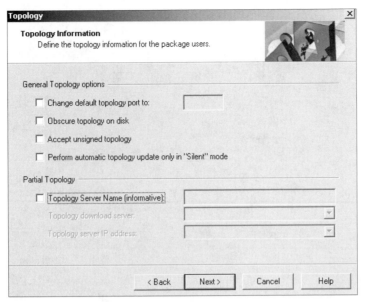

Figure 12.35   Setting SecureClient topology information

into your custom SecureClient installation package, described later in this chapter.

Choose the appropriate options and click on Next. A new screen appears (see Figure 12.35).

Here you can configure the following options.

Change default topology port to: If you wish to use a different port for allowing clients to download topology from TCP port 264, you can tell SecureClient which port to use. Note that you must make changes on your management station and firewall modules. See FAQ 12.7 later in this chapter for details.

Obscure topology on disk: Any topology information that exists in the userc.C file will be obscured (i.e., encrypted) so that it cannot be read by a human. However, SecureClient will be able to read it. Note that some parts of the file will remain unobscured (e.g., client options).

Accept unsigned topology: This allows the client to accept topology from any host without requiring any authentication. This is generally not recommended.

Perform automatic topology update only in "Silent" mode: When this box is checked, the client will request a site update at the time authentication

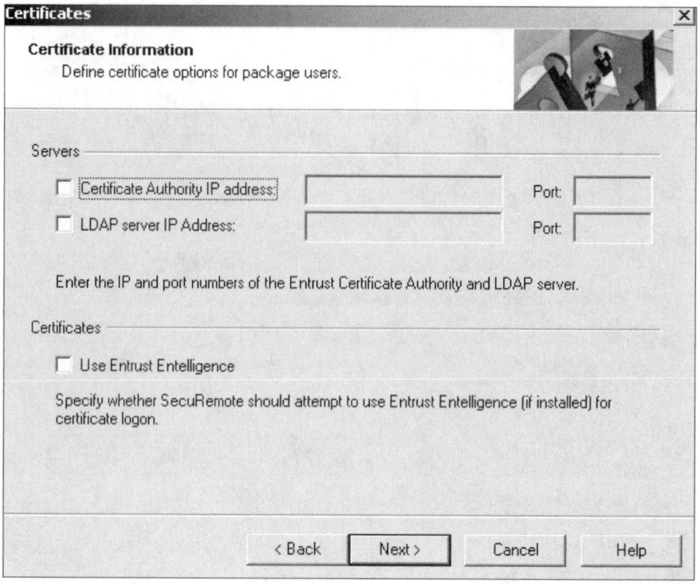

Figure 12.36 Defining certificate authority information

is requested. This makes the topology update process much more transparent to the end user.

Partial Topology: If you make your installation package generally available (say, on the Internet), you might not want to include a full site topology in order to avoid making available any sensitive information. An alternative is to include a partial topology, which consists of a "friendly name" (the topology server "informative" name), a network object (select a firewall or gateway cluster from the pull-down menu), and the IP address the client will use to obtain policy. The first time the client authenticates, a proper topology will be downloaded.

After selecting the appropriate options, click Next. Figure 12.36 appears. If you are using Entrust Certificates, you can configure a certificate authority, select an LDAP server to use to provide information about certificates, and indicate whether or not to use the Entrust Entelligence software.

If you aren't using Entrust Certificates, click Next to move to the next screen (see Figure 12.37).

On the Silent Installation screen, you can choose to make the installation silent or use prompts for certain user options. In a silent installation, all the defaults chosen in the packaging tool will be used. If the end users are prompted, they will be given some choices, with the default values being what the packaging tool specifies. You still end up having to make a manual change to the

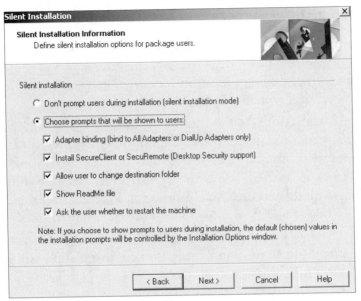

Figure 12.37   Configuring Silent Installation

`product.ini` file to prevent the display of the End User License Agreement (see the next subsection).

Once you have finished with the silent installation screen, click Next. Figure 12.38 shows the new screen.

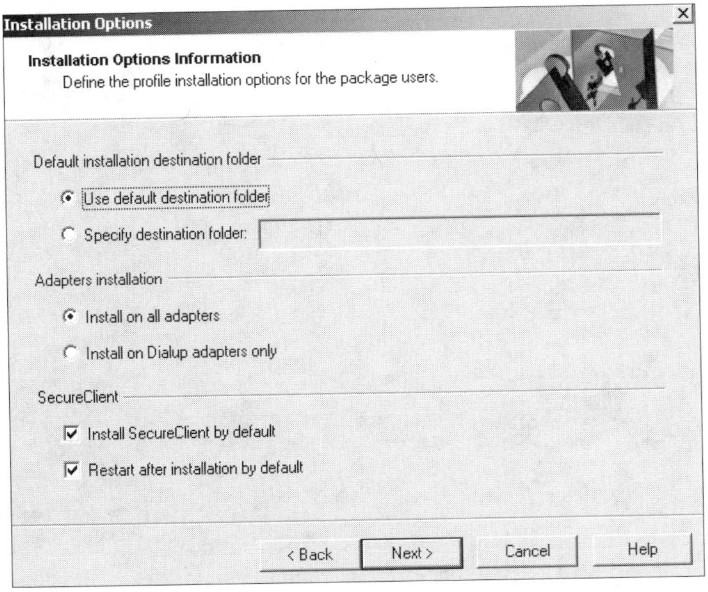

Figure 12.38   Setting installation options

You can set the following additional installation options.

Default installation destination folder: If you select the default location, the software will be installed in `C:\Program Files\CheckPoint\SecuRemote`. If a different location is desired, you can select "Specify destination folder" and type in the appropriate path.

Adapters installation: You can have SecureClient installed either on the dial-up adapters only or on every adapter. Since SecureClient can be used only on network interfaces to which it is bound, this choice affects how SecureClient can be used. While the option is not available at install time, it is possible to disable SecureClient on specific adapters after the fact. In Windows NT, 2000, and XP, administrator rights are required to do this.

Install SecureClient by default: Select this option to install SecureClient with Desktop Security options. If unchecked, installation will include only the basic VPN functionality.

Restart after installation by default: Once installation is completed, the client platform should be rebooted so the software can load. This option determines whether or not that should be the option by default.

Select the appropriate installation options and click Next. Set the logon options shown in Figure 12.39.

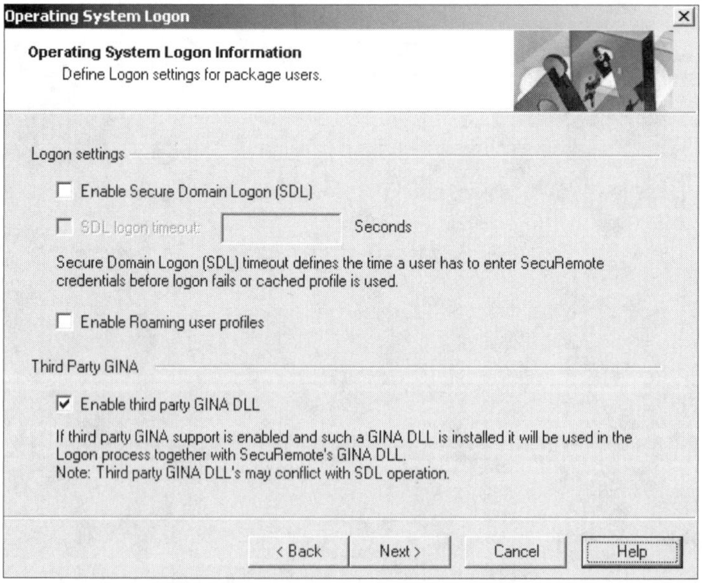

Figure 12.39 Defining the operating system logon

The options are described below.

Enable Secure Domain Logon (SDL): This option allows remote clients to establish a VPN connection before attempting to log into the domain. (See the Microsoft Networking and SecureClient section earlier in this chapter.)

SDL logon timeout: This option tells SecureClient how long it should wait for the client to enter authentication information before timing out and passing control back to the operating system, which will log you on with "cached credentials." This affects a parameter in the Windows registry that tells Windows how long to wait before giving up on attempts to talk to the domain controller.

Enable Roaming user profiles: In order for Roaming user profiles in Windows to work, SecureClient needs to keep the VPN connection operational for a period of time after the user logs off. Normally, the VPN connection is terminated once the client logs off. If this option is checked, the VPN will remain active for approximately 5 minutes after the user logs off.

Enable third party GINA DLL: If you are using other software that has its own GINA DLL file, you need to enable this option. This tells SecuRemote to try to cooperate with any GINA DLL file it finds and to attempt to "chain" to other GINA DLL files. However, this option doesn't always work, so you should test this carefully.

Once you have chosen the appropriate options, click on Next. The screen shown in Figure 12.40 appears.

If you have the appropriate version of SecureClient decompressed on your platform and you're ready to generate a package, select YES and click Next. If you haven't yet downloaded the Configurable versions of SecureClient and decompressed them for each platform type on which you wish to install Secure-Client, select NO and click Next. Figure 12.41 shows what happens if you select YES and click Next or if you select the profile and then select Generate from the Profile menu.

Select the appropriate location where the decompressed SecureClient installation is, specify where you want the generated executable file to reside, and click Next. This generates your installation file.

Manually Creating an Installation Image

Most of the options you can select in the SecureClient Packaging Tool can be specified in the `product.ini` file as well. If you change options in this file and use your own `userc.C` file instead of a custom one, you can make your own

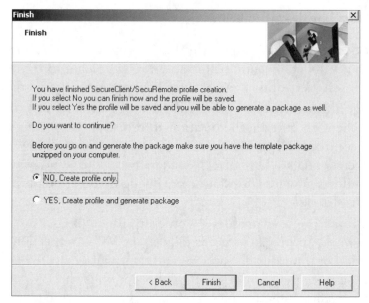

Figure 12.40   Almost finished with the SecureClient Packaging Tool

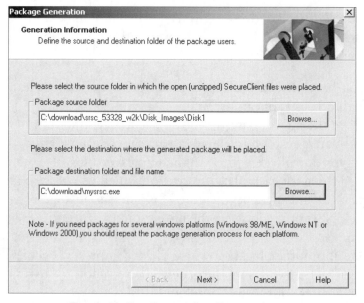

Figure 12.41   Generating the package

installation package. All you need is some method of generating a self-expanding archive and having it run `setup.exe`.

The following `product.ini` entries are relevant to FireWall-1 NG. Unless otherwise specified, you can also set these options in the SecureClient Packaging

Tool. Note that most of these options are binary, that is, they can be set with either a 1 or a 0. In most cases, the default values in the file are shown and the effect of changing from the default is described.

ShowWelcome=1: Suppresses the Welcome to Check Point SecureClient screen upon installation if set to 0.

ShowLic=1: Suppresses the display of the End User License Agreement if set to 0. This option cannot be set in the SecureClient Packaging Tool.

OverwriteConfiguration=0: Indicates that, when a previous version of SecureClient is detected, the default should be to upgrade the configuration if this option is set to 0. Overwrite will be the default if this option is set to 1.

ShowUpdateOverwrite=1: Does not present the end user with the choice of whether or not to overwrite the previous configuration if this option is set to 0. Instead, the client will use the default specified in the previous option.

PathAskUser=1: Asks the end user where the software should be installed if set to 1. If set to 0, the client will be installed in the default location, which is C:\Program Files\CheckPoint\SecuRemote.

DesktopSecurityDefault=1: Specifies whether this is a SecuRemote install (set to 0) or a SecureClient install (set to 1) by default, that is, whether or not to include the Desktop Security options.

DesktopSecurityAskUser=1: Does not prompt the user about Desktop Security if set to 0 and uses the previous option to determine whether to install SecuRemote or SecureClient.

InstallDialupOnly=0: Configures the usual default to install on all interfaces if set to 0. If set to 1, the default will be to install only on dial-up interfaces.

ShowNetworkBindings=1: Does not prompt the end user about whether to install on all interfaces or just dial-up ones if set to 0. Instead, the previous option will specify the installation on interfaces.

ShowReadmeFile=1: Suppresses the request to display the readme.txt file if set to 0.

EnableSDL=0: Enables Secure Domain Logon by default if set to 1.

SupportFWZ=0: Supports FWZ on the client if set to 1. Deprecated for NG FP2 and later.

OverwriteEntINI=0: Overwrites the entrust.ini file (if it exists) if this option is set to 1.

IncludeBrandingFiles=0: Includes a custom logo.bmp file, which replaces the Check Point logo everywhere, if set to 1.

Support3rdPartyGina=1: Attempts to chain with other GINA DLL files that might exist if set to 1. This is especially critical if you use Secure Domain Logon. If set to 0, no attempt to chain with other GINA DLL files will be made.

MajorVersion=5: Specifies the major version of SecureClient. NG is version 5.

MinorVersion=3: Specifies the minor version of SecureClient. For Feature Pack 3, it's 3. For NG AI, it's 4.

EnablePolicyView=1: Allows the end user to view the security policy pushed to their client if set to 1.

EnableLogView=1: Allows the end user to look at the local SecureClient logs if set to 1.

EnableDiagnosticsView=1: Allows the end user to view diagnostic information in SecureClient if set to 1.

EntrustSupport=1: Enables Entrust support if set to 1. Support is disabled if this option is set to 0.

ShowDriverSignatureWarning=1: Suppresses driver signature warnings (which might occur in Windows 2000 and XP during installation) if this option is set to 0.

MakeServiceNonInteractive=0: Allows the service to run in an unattended automated state (i.e., does not require a user to log on) if set to 1.

ShowRestart=1: Does not ask the end user to restart upon completion of installation if set to 0.

RestartAfterInstall=1: Specifies whether or not to default to a restart after installation. If the previous option is set to 0 and this option is set to 1, the end user's machine will be rebooted without prompting.

Frequently Asked Questions

This section answers some frequently asked questions about SecuRemote.

12.1: Can I Use SecuRemote if My Client Is Subject to NAT?

Unless you specifically disable UDP encapsulation, clients should work just fine if they are subject to NAT. However, clients behind some NAT routers or DSL connections may have issues. See FAQ 12.15 later in this chapter for troubleshooting hints.

If your firewall was upgraded from FireWall-1 4.1 or earlier and you did not enable SecuRemote clients to work over NAT, double-check that `userc_NAT` and `userc_IKE_NAT` are both set to `true` in `$FWDIR/conf/objects_5_0.C`.

If they are not, you should change these properties. See FAQ 4.2 for details on how to do this. The commands in **dbedit** to make these changes are:

```
dbedit> modify properties firewall_properties userc_NAT true
dbedit> modify properties firewall_properties userc_IKE_NAT true
dbedit> update properties firewall_properties
```

12.2: Can Multiple SecureClient Users behind the Same NAT Device Access the Same Firewall?

Generally speaking, yes. However, some routers (most notably ones by Nexland/ Symantec) attempt to track IKE negotiations. Instead of giving the outgoing IKE packet a different source port, the router will keep the packet at port 500. While this allows some IKE implementations to work, it can cause a problem with FireWall-1 NG when using UDP encapsulation and when multiple clients from behind the same NAT router talk to the firewall.

Use the **dbedit** utility to set the udp_encapsulation_by_qm_id property to false, as shown below. (You may also do this with the Database Tool, also called the GUIdbedit tool, or with manual editing as described in FAQ 4.2.)

```
dbedit> modify properties firewall_properties
               udp_encapsulation_by_qm_id false
dbedit> update properties firewall_properties
```

Open Smart Dashboard/Policy Editor and click Yes when asked to update your topology data due to inconsistencies. Install the security policy

12.3: How Do I Initiate an Encrypted Session to a SecuRemote Client?

SecuRemote was designed to handle encrypted connections initiated only from the client side. To handle the possibility of connections back to the client, FireWall-1 keeps track of IPs that are SecuRemote clients in a table called userc_rules. As long as the SecuRemote client has initiated a connection to the encryption domain within the previous 15 minutes, its IP address will be listed in this table. Any outgoing connection that is accepted by FireWall-1 is checked against this table. If the connection is going to an IP in this table, it is automatically encrypted. Note that this occurs despite the fact that the action of the rule is Accept versus Encrypt or Client Encrypt. If you want to allow certain services out, but only to those machines that have authenticated with SecuRemote (i.e., you wouldn't want to permit these services outbound in an unencrypted fashion), you can make this work.

In the case of using VPN Communities, you simply need to create the appropriate rule using your Remote Access community in the If Via column.

This will allow the service only if the destination currently has a VPN established with the firewall.

In a Traditional mode policy, you need to create the service srMyApp of type Other. Use 6 as the protocol number and have the following in the Match field (assuming for a moment that myApp is a TCP service on port 5555):

```
dport=5555,<dst,0>in userc_rules
```

Then simply put this service in an Accept rule. This rule matches only if it is going to the correct port and to an IP address that has recently initiated an encrypted session through the gateway.

Chapter 14 provides a more detailed explanation of what this code does.

12.4: What if My SecuRemote Client Must Pass through a FireWall-1 Gateway?

In some circumstances you may need to run SecuRemote to access an encryption domain where the client is behind a Check Point FireWall-1 gateway. Assuming that UDP encapsulation is enabled and you are not doing address translation (or can work around it, as explained in FAQ 12.1), part of what needs to be done depends on whether or not the remote FireWall-1 gateway is configured to use encapsulation for SecuRemote connections.

- TCP port 264 from client to firewall is needed only to fetch and update the site information.
- TCP port 18231 is used if SecureClient needs to authenticate with a policy server.
- UDP port 18234 is used for testing VPN tunnel availability in NG FP1 when Office Mode is enabled.
- UDP port 500 is needed to negotiate encryption keys when IKE is used.
- UDP port 2746 is needed when UDP encapsulation is used.
- IP protocol 50 is needed when IKE without UDP encapsulation is used.

Figure 12.42 shows a rule that permits all of these services.

SOURCE	DESTINATION	IF VIA	SERVICE	ACTION
✳ Any	🖪 firewall	✳ Any	ESP TCP FW1_pslogon_NG TCP FW1_topo IKE UDP VPN1_IPSEC_encapsulation UDP tunnel_test	🕀 accept

Figure 12.42   Rule permitting services necessary for SecureClient usage

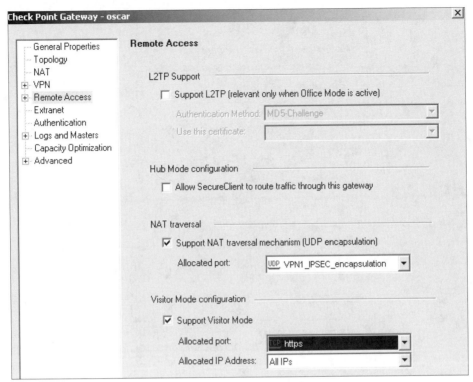

Figure 12.43 Gateway Properties, Remote Access frame

12.5: How Can I Use SecuRemote When I Am behind a Proxy?

Generally speaking, the protocols used by SecureClient do not work well through a proxy. However, NG AI supports Visitor Mode, which permits clients to connect using a standard HTTP proxy. This is configured in the gateway object in the Remote Access frame. Figure 12.43 shows the configuration options.

The administrator enables Visitor Mode support, selects the service on which the Visitor Mode service will run (the port for HTTPS is recommended), and sets the allocated IP address FireWall-1 will use to bind the special service that will listen on the specified service port. This is necessary only if another service running on the firewall platform must also bind to this same TCP port number.

Once these settings are changed, a policy installation is required for these changes to take effect.

In SecureClient NG AI, when needed, you will configure the client to use Visitor Mode. From the Tools menu, select Visitor Mode. You will see a screen similar to Figure 12.44.

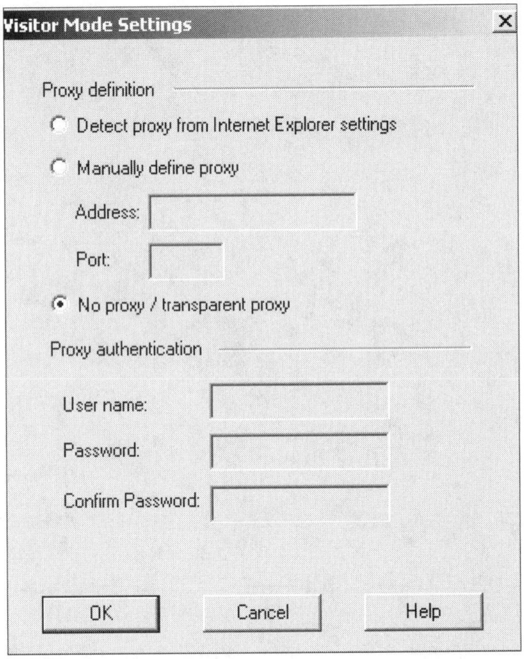

Figure 12.44   Configuring Visitor Mode in SecureClient NG AI

This screen includes the following options.

Detect proxy from Internet Explorer settings: Use the same proxy settings that Internet Explorer would use. Even if you use a proxy auto-configuration file, you may have to manually define a proxy server and port in Internet Explorer for this option to work.

Manually define proxy: If using a different browser (e.g., Mozilla) and an HTTP proxy server is needed, define the IP address and port of the proxy server to use.

No proxy/transparent proxy: Use this setting if either no proxy is needed or the proxy functions transparently (i.e., without requiring the end-user machine to terminate the HTTP connection on the outbound firewall).

Once the client and firewall have been configured accordingly, Visitor Mode will allow access through a standard HTTP proxy.

12.6: How Do I Disable SecuRemote at Startup?

On a Windows 9x/ME/NT platform, use **msconfig** to prevent `fwenc.exe` from running at startup. On Windows 2000/XP, you need to disable the Check Point SecuRemote service in Services.

12.7: How Do I Tell FireWall-1 to Use a Different Port for SecureClient Topology Requests?

On your firewall module, add the following line to `$FWDIR/conf/ports.conf`, which you may have to create if it doesn't exist:

```
fwd_gettopo = X
```

Replace X with the value for the port number you wish to use.

You also have to change two other things on your management station. Change the definition for the FW1_topo service to match the new port and edit `$FWDIR/lib/services.def`, changing the following line:

```
#define FWD_TOPO_PORT X
```

Perform a **cprestart** on the firewall module and reload the policy from the management station.

12.8: Can I Share an Internet Connection and Use SecuRemote?

It is common to want to run SecuRemote and some sort of NAT program on the same system, like SyGate, WinRoute, or Windows Internet Connection Sharing. This would theoretically allow your client to act as sort of a site-to-site VPN for machines behind the client. I have not seen or heard of any NAT solution that works with the NG version of SecureClient, particularly in Office Mode.

Standard proxy servers appear to work okay. For instance, I've used two different proxies from http://www.analogx.com as well as Squid (NT version available at http://www.serassio.it/SquidNT.htm), DeleGate (http://www.delegate.org), and Stone (http://www.gcd.org/sengoku/stone/).

> **WARNING!** Although there is nothing to prevent you from using a proxy server on a SecuRemote client, this configuration could potentially create a hole through which a hacker could access your internal network using a "trusted source" (i.e., the SecuRemote client).

A hardware solution to this problem would be to use a SofaWare-based platform as your home gateway. This can act like a SecuRemote client and allow all of your home machines to access the corporate network.

12.9: Can I Install SecureClient on the Same Machine with a VPN Client from Another Vendor?

Some people have successfully made this work, but this is generally not recommended or supported.

12.10: Can SecureClient be Controlled via the Command Line?

SecureClient NG FP3 and above contain a command-line interface (CLI). The scc binary in C:\Program Files\CheckPoint\SecuRemote\bin allows you to set authentication credentials, connect or disconnect from a site, check status, and more. When you switch into command-line mode with the command **scc setmode cli**, SecureClient will restart in a command-line mode. The Secure Client "envelope" will still be in the system tray and will still blink when talking to the encryption domain, but you will not be able to access any menus from the envelope. Table 12.1 documents the commands available from the CLI.

NOTE! The Linux version of SecuRemote uses these commands to control the client. As of this writing, no GUI is present for the Linux version of SecuRemote.

The only thing missing from the command-line mode is the ability to add or update site information. It also currently does not support automatic site updates. Other than these limitations, command-line mode works well enough.

On one of my systems, I have SecureClient set up with a batch job that I periodically run to refresh my VPN connection. The system is accessible via the Windows 2000 Telnet server, so I rarely need to see the screen on this particular platform. This script breaks the VPN connection, sets my credentials to the provided password (actually a SecurID passcode), connects to the site using the established VPN profile, checks to see that it actually did connect with an **ipconfig** just to make sure I got assigned, and finally erases the credentials. Erasing the credentials is necessary in my case because when the VPN requires reauthentication, my previously entered credentials will be used. Those credentials will be wrong since it's a SecurID passcode (it changes every 60 seconds) and it will eventually "lock" my SecurID card for too many failed attempts! Here's the code I use for the batch job:

```
scc disconnect
scc up dwelch %1%
scc connect "VPN Profile"
scc status
ipconfig
scc ep
```

NOTE! Technically, one-time password schemes are not supported when authenticating via SecuRemote's CLI. However, this scheme allows my one-time password to work well enough.

Table 12.1 Commands in the SecureClient Command-Line Interface

Command	Description
`scc connect profilename` `scc c profilename`	Establishes a connection to the specified profile. If the name has spaces in it, put the name in quotes (e.g., "Nokia Access Point"). Credentials should be specified prior to executing this command.

`scc connectnowait`
  `profilename`
`scc cn profilename`
	Establishes a connection asynchronously (i.e., the command prompt returns immediately versus waiting until authentication succeeds or fails). Credentials should be specified prior to executing this command.

`scc disconnect` `scc d`	Disconnects the currently active session.
`scc erasecreds` `scc ep`	Tells SecureClient to "forget" your supplied authentication requirements.
`scc status` `scc s`	Displays the current connection status.
`scc userpass userid password` `scc up userid password`	Sets the login credentials to the specified `userid` and `password`.
`scc passcert password file` `scc pc password file`	Tells SecureClient to use the certificate file specified by `file` (full path). The password is used to unlock the certificate.
`scc restartsc`	Stops and restarts the SecureClient service.
`scc setmode [cli|trans|con]`	Sets the mode of the client to either Transparent mode (`trans`), Connect Mode (`con`), or enable cli mode (`cli`). To disable cli mode, stop SecureClient and change `connect_api_support` to `false` in `C:\Program Files\CheckPoint\SecuRe-mote\database\userc.C`.
`scc setpolicy [on|off]` `scc sp [on|off]`	Tells SecureClient to enable or disable the default policy. If on or `off` is not specified, the status of the policy will be shown.
`scc startsc`	Starts the SecureClient service.
`scc stopsc`	Stops the SecureClient service.
`scc suppressdialogs [on|off]` `scc sd [on|off]`	Indicates whether to prevent pop-ups from Secure Client that ask for authentication. Useful in a totally command-line-driven setup.
`scc version` `scc ver`	Shows the version of SecureClient.

Troubleshooting

Troubleshooting SecuRemote can be somewhat tricky. Many problems with SecuRemote are a result of bad interactions with Windows, although there are also plenty of ways to misconfigure settings.

12.11: SecuRemote Communication Ports Are Blocked

See FAQ 12.4 for the list of ports and protocols that might need to be enabled.

12.12: ISP Uses a Custom Adapter to Connect

This situation applies to anyone who uses anything other than a standard Ethernet NIC or Microsoft's Dial-up Adapter to connect to the Internet.

It is becoming increasingly common, particularly with cable or DSL providers, to require PPP over Ethernet (PPPoE) to connect. PPPoE effectively treats your connection to the Internet like a dial-up connection. However, it adds additional protocols and virtual adapters to the TCP/IP stack, not to mention additional overhead due to the PPP encapsulation. This means that SecuRemote either will not bind to the PPPoE stack properly or will experience performance problems due to encapsulation (see FAQ 12.15).

The bindings for PPPoE and SecuRemote look something like this:

Ethernet adapter   →   PPPoE adapter   →   FW1 adapter   →   FW1 protocol   →   TCP/IP

You should not have TCP/IP bound to your Ethernet adapter or your PPPoE adapter.

12.13: Problems Adding the New Site

If you get the error message "Connection to site x.y.z.w has failed," ensure that your SecuRemote client can communicate to that IP via TCP port 264. A simple Telnet from a client without SecureClient installed should validate whether or not this is being blocked at the firewall.

When you create a new site, information about the encryption domain will be downloaded to the system and stored in a file called userc.C on the client. Check the userc.C file to ensure that your internal networks are listed. If they are not, the firewall administrator needs to make sure that the Exportable flag is checked in the firewall's network object under the Encryption tab. Once that change has been made and the security policy has been reinstalled, a site update should update userc.C with the correct information. You can update the site either by double-clicking the site icon in SecureClient or by removing and adding the site again in SecureClient.

12.14: Determining the IP Address When Using IP Pool NAT

You can't tell what your IP address is when using IP Pool NAT without the help of a Web server or some other server inside the network that can tell you what IP address you were assigned. For example, I have a simple CGI script that simply prints out the environment it is passed; one of those items is the remote IP address.

One advantage to Office Mode is that it gives you a virtual adapter on your PC, which you can query with the **ipconfig** command. This shows what address you were assigned.

12.15: Encapsulation, Packet Sizes, and Failing Applications

IPSec is an encapsulated protocol. However, encapsulation creates a problem with fragmentation. IPSec adds 100 bytes to the size of the packet. A packet with a size close to the TCP/IP stack's Maximum Transmit Unit/Maximum Receive Unit (MTU/MRU) becomes greater than the supported MTU/MRU once it is encapsulated in IPSec. Furthermore, some applications (most notably Microsoft Outlook and Lotus Notes) appear to send large packets with the Don't Fragment bit set. This isn't a problem per se, except that FireWall-1 copies this bit from the original packet into the encapsulated one. To resolve this problem, implement the suggestion in FAQ 11.20.

Another problem that comes up, particularly with some of the lower-end NAT routers, is with fragmented UDP packets. Some applications like to use large packets. They may or may not have the Don't Fragment bit set. Even if FireWall-1 or SecureClient doesn't end up copying this bit to the encrypted packet, there's still the business of passing a fragmented packet. Many low-end routers, particularly D-Link and SMC routers, do not appear to deal with fragmented UDP packets at all. Fragmented packets are considered a "bad thing" by these routers, and they refuse to pass these packets. You can troubleshoot this problem by using **ping** from your SecureClient machine.

In some cases, you may need to make an MTU adjustment on your client. This may be necessary if you are using PPPoE or having problems with fragmented packets. **ping** from the SecureClient machine can be used to troubleshoot this problem as well.

So how does **ping** help both these issues? With two specific flags in the Windows version: -l size, which simply refers to the size of the data portion of the packet, and -f, for setting the Don't Fragment bit. Simply specifying a size for the **ping** can test the fragmented UDP packets theory. In a standard Ethernet environment with a client-to-site VPN and SecureClient, fragmentation occurs with a packet larger than 1,400 bytes. Because the encryption and IP headers

Figure 12.45 MTU Adjuster

take a total of 128 bytes, this means the -1 parameter should be set to 1373 or higher (e.g., **ping -l 1373 host-in-encdomain**). You might have to gradually increase this number until you find the point at which this "breaks"; I found for my D-Link router that it took a slightly larger packet to cause a failure.

For MTU-related issues, it is vital that you set the Don't Fragment bit. This allows you to determine the largest possible MTU that can be used. Similar to the previous example, the largest nonfragmented packet you can send across the VPN is 1,400 bytes. This means that the command **ping -l 1373 -f host-in-encdomain** should fail, but **ping -l 1372 -f host-in-encdomain** should succeed. If neither command succeeds, try using lower and lower values for -1 until your command succeeds. Whatever value you find works for you, set the MTU to that value plus 128 bytes. For example, if you find that the largest **ping** that works is **ping -l 1364 -f**, set your MTU to 1,492 bytes.

How can you set the MTU? FireWall-1 NG FP3 and above comes with a utility called MTUAdjust in C:\Program Files\CheckPoint\SecuRemote\ bin. When you run this program, you will be able to adjust the MTU on all interfaces (see Figure 12.45).

12.16: Windows NT and File Permissions

As a nonprivileged user, you might receive the SecuRemote authentication dialog and the successful authentication message but then cannot connect to the internal network. No incoming packets from the SecuRemote client can be seen at the firewall. If you restart SecuRemote and authenticate again, everything works splendidly.

To resolve this issue, change the rights to the directory %SystemRoot%\ system32\drivers\etc to RWX:RWX. You can do this only if Windows is installed on an NTFS partition under Windows NT/2000.

12.17: Mixing NICs and Dial-up Adapters

If you have a NIC configured with an IP address inside the encryption domain, SecuRemote will not work correctly unless you use Office Mode. This happens most often with laptops used on the road as well as in the office. The following subsections contain a list of potential configurations, the problems associated with them, and workarounds.

NIC Uses Static IP and Has IP in the Encryption Domain

This particular problem occurs whether or not your NIC is using DHCP. If your NIC has an IP address in the encryption domain and you either dial up to the Internet or use the local LAN, SecuRemote will not attempt to talk to your internal network in an encrypted fashion because it will attempt to use the NIC directly. This is not a SecuRemote-specific issue.

You can remove the route associated with the network on which the NIC is configured. For instance, if your IP address is 172.17.55.10 and your netmask is 255.255.255.0, you can remove the route by typing the command `route delete 172.17.55.0 mask 255.255.255.0 172.17.55.10`. If SecuRemote is installed on all NICs and the NIC in question is not physically installed at the time, this command will fail. See the next subsection.

SecuRemote Is Bound to All Adapters

You need to bind SecuRemote to all adapters only in the following cases:

- When a NIC is used to access the Internet (e.g., for DSL and cable modems)
- If you use Windows NT (you do not have a choice)

Binding SecuRemote to all adapters can cause additional problems in the previously mentioned cases (e.g., the NIC has an IP address inside the encryption domain). If you bind SecuRemote to all adapters, it is advisable to keep your NIC cards plugged in at all times. Sometimes, removing and reinstalling a NIC will hose the TCP/IP stack entirely. A reboot is the only way to recover. For physically uninstalled but configured NICs (e.g., a laptop's unplugged PCMCIA card), the routing table shows the uninstalled NICs' routing information. Without SecuRemote installed on all interfaces, the information related to the removed NIC card will not be shown in the routing table (i.e., when you type `route print`).

12.18: NG FP1/FP2 System Status Viewer Shows No Response for Desktop Policy Server

If this problem occurs, the Desktop Policy Server DLLs did not get installed correctly. Execute the following commands on the firewall module to resolve this in NG FP2:

```
# cpstop
# amon_config cpstatdll add polsrv /opt/CPdtps-50-02/lib
  polsrvstatagent
# cpstart
```

In NG FP1, replace `CPdtps-50-02` with `CPdtps-50-01` in the appropriate command above.

Here's another approach that also solves this problem:

```
# cpstop
# cp /opt/CPdtps-50-02/lib/* $FWDIR/lib
# amon_config cpstatdll add polsrv $FWDIR/lib polsrvstatagent
# amon_config oidqfile add polsrv $FWDIR/conf dtps polsrv
# cpstart
```

Summary

The organizational security policy can be extended to remote desktops while enabling access to the organizational network thanks to SecureClient. It is an extension of site-to-site VPNs, but SecureClient has several unique issues to overcome, including having to potentially support the machines and networks of users at home. This chapter covered many of the major issues you are likely to face and provided strategies for dealing with them.

Sample Configurations

The three situations presented here are representative of situations I have encountered in the real world. Each is designed to demonstrate what people typically do with SecuRemote and SecureClient and how the situations are implemented on the chosen platform.

Creating a Simple Client-to-Site VPN

The Situation

You are the firewall administrator for a company that has one site and employs several telecommuters. The clients need to be able to fully access the internal network. The clients also require protection, so SecureClient will be used. Hybrid IKE will be used to authenticate the users. A Traditional mode security policy exists for outgoing traffic (listed in the Goals subsection). The management console and the firewall are on separate hosts (see Figure 12.46).

The Goals

- Allow SecuRemote clients to access all hosts on the internal network with any service.
- Internal hosts are allowed to access sites on the Internet via FTP, HTTP, or HTTPS.

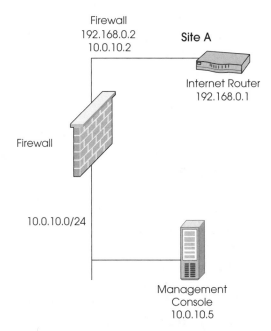

Figure 12.46 Sample client-to-site VPN network map

- SMTP can originate from predefined SMTP servers inside the network to the Internet. (They are in a group called SMTP-Servers.)
- SMTP can go to the external SMTP server from anywhere (external-smtp-server is already defined).
- SecureClient hosts are allowed to access both the Internet and the encryption domain.
- Only hosts in the encryption domain are allowed to access SecureClient hosts, no others.
- Deny all other traffic.

The Checklist

- Define the necessary users, put them into a group (if necessary), and install the user database.
- Define the encryption domains for the local site.
- Configure the firewall workstation objects for the correct encryption domain.
- Create the necessary encryption rules.
- Configure the rule to permit the FW1_Topo service to the management console.
- Configure the Desktop Security policy to permit outbound access to the Internet and the encryption domain.
- Configure the Desktop Security policy to allow encrypted access from the encryption domain to the SecureClient host, denying all other traffic.
- Install the security policy.

The Implementation

Ensure that your gateway object has the Policy Server package loaded and enabled. The gateway object should also have the SecureClient Policy Server option checked in the General Properties frame.

For this example, let's use the names beavis, butthead, stewart, and daria. Create these users and place them into a group called telecommuters. (See Chapter 8 for explanations of how to create users and groups.)

Hybrid Authentication will be used. This means each user's existing password as defined in the definition in the Password section will apply.

Next, you need to define the encryption domain. Generally speaking, if your topology is set up correctly and contains anti-spoofing, similar to what is shown in Figure 12.47, you need not explicitly define the encryption domain, though manually defining it makes it somewhat easier to use in a rulebase. To manually

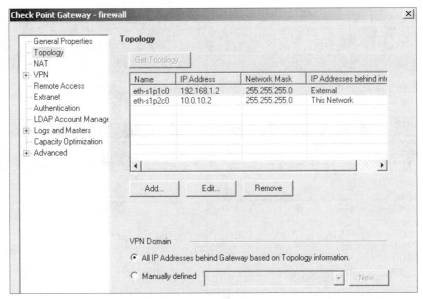

Figure 12.47 Gateway Object, Topology frame

define the encryption domain, create the appropriate network object(s), add them to a group, and then set the encryption domain for that group.

Your rulebase needs to look like the one shown in Figure 12.48. Rule 1 permits the telecommuters to access the internal network via SecuRemote. Rule 2 permits SecuRemote users to fetch the network topology, log into the Policy Server, and establish an encrypted session with the firewall. Without this rule, users cannot establish the site in the SecuRemote client. Rules 3 through 6 are necessary to establish the security policy defined in the Goals subsection above.

NO.	SOURCE	DESTINATION	SERVICE	ACTION	TRACK
1	telecommuters@Any	internal-network	✷ Any	Client Encrypt	Log
2	✷ Any	firewall	TCP FW1_pslogon_NG TCP FW1_topo IKE UDP VPN1_IPSEC_encapsulation ESP	accept	Log
3	internal-network	✷ Any	TCP ftp TCP http TCP https	accept	— None
4	SMTP-Servers	✷ Any	TCP smtp	accept	— None
5	✷ Any	external-smtp-server	TCP smtp	accept	Log
6	✷ Any	✷ Any	✷ Any	drop	Log

Figure 12.48 Sample rulebase

Inbound Rules

NO.	SOURCE	DESKTOP	SERVICE	ACTION	TRACK
1	🖳 internal-network	👤 All Users@Any	✳ Any	🔒 Encrypt	🗐 Log
2	✳ Any	👤 All Users@Any	✳ Any	⦿ Block	🗐 Log

Outbound Rules

NO.	DESKTOP	DESTINATION	SERVICE	ACTION	TRACK
3	👤 All Users@Any	🖳 internal-network	✳ Any	🔒 Encrypt	– None
4	👤 All Users@Any	✳ Any	✳ Any	🛡 Accept	– None

Figure 12.49 Sample Desktop Security policy

Because you also need to protect your SecureClient users, you need to create a Desktop Security policy. If you did not initially create a policy with a Desktop Security component, select New from the File menu, select the "Add policy to an existing package" option, and check the Desktop Security box.

Figure 12.49 shows how the final security policy looks. Install the security policy and test it.

Notes

This is a somewhat simplified example. Most sites have far more complex security policies. Just make sure your VPN rules are listed before any rules that allow outbound traffic to the Internet, that you have the necessary rules to permit IKE, and that the topology requests are listed before any firewall Stealth rules.

Using SecureClient with Gateway Clusters

The Situation

The previous firewall has been replaced with a pair of Nokia IP530s in an HA configuration using VRRP Monitored Circuits (see Figure 12.50). All other aspects of the network and the security policy are the same. Additional traffic must be permitted to the firewalls for management purposes. In addition, the company has decided to implement Office Mode.

The Goals

- Maintain the security policy as much as possible (from the previous configuration).
- Add rules to permit VRRP, if necessary.

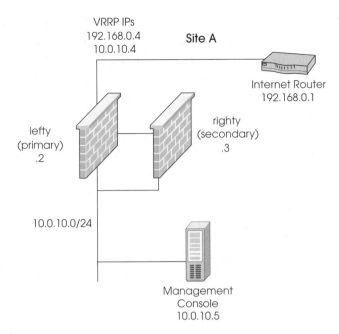

Figure 12.50 Sample configuration with VRRP pair

- Add rules to permit specific management clients the ability to use the SSH and HTTPS services to the firewalls to perform management functions.

The Checklist

- Define the gateway objects for each firewall.
- Define the gateway cluster object.
- Add the individual gateway objects to the gateway cluster object.
- Configure the gateway cluster object to use encryption.
- Configure the rulebase to allow the client management stations access to the firewalls.
- Install the security policy.
- SecureClient users must update the site definition.

The Implementation

First you need to create a gateway object for each firewall. Make sure the Interfaces tab for each gateway object has all of the physical interfaces properly defined. Next, create the gateway cluster object. In the General Properties frame, specify the VRRP IP address used in your Monitored Circuit configuration (use the external IP, of course). Define the synchronization network in the Synchronization frame.

The next step depends on which version of FireWall-1 you're using. In NG FP2, each VRRP IP address needs to be included in the Topology frame for the gateway objects that make up the gateway cluster. The interface names for these IPs is not important. In NG FP1, FP3, and above, define the VRRP IPs in the Topology frame using the corresponding physical interface names. Figure 12.51 shows this configuration.

Go to the VPN frame and click on the Traditional Mode Configuration button. Ensure that Exportable for SecuRemote/SecureClient is checked.

The next step is to configure the rulebase for VRRP. VRRP is a predefined service in NG (IP protocol 112). The rulebase and/or anti-spoofing must allow for the following actions.

- VRRP packets can originate from either firewall.
- VRRP packets can go to the VRRP Multicast Address (vrrp.mcast.net, 224.0.0.18) on any interface where VRRP is configured.
- VRRP packets can also go to a specific firewall interface for a triggered VRRP update.
- Each firewall must be allowed to originate IGMP traffic in order to join a multicast group. This is necessary on switches.

However, due to a bug in NG FP1 and NG FP2, FireWall-1 interprets VRRP packets as coming from the VRRP IP itself. This means you must also create host objects for each VRRP IP address. Put them into a group called firewalls. In addition, you need to create vrrp.mcast.net, which is a host object with the IP address 224.0.0.18 (as mentioned above).

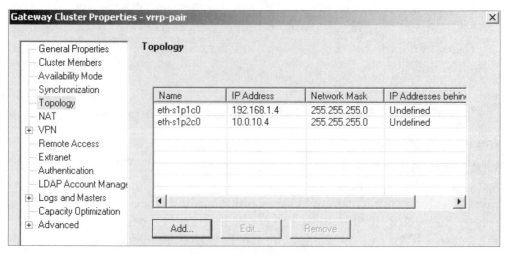

Figure 12.51   Gateway Cluster Properties, Topology frame

Next, create the rules to allow the workstations that manage the firewalls to access the firewalls via SSH and HTTPS. Create a group, add the various workstation objects to this group, and then use this group in a rule.

Other than these two rules, along with changing the rule permitting certain VPN traffic to the firewall so that it references the gateway cluster object, the rulebase shown in Figure 12.52 looks basically the same as it did in the previous configuration.

Once you install the security policy, users will have to update their sites to take full advantage of the Gateway Cluster configuration. The client's `userc.c` file will, after a site update, contain the IP addresses of the real firewalls and the virtual firewall's IP address.

Notes

This is an overly simplistic configuration, but it demonstrates how to use the Gateway Clusters feature. It also shows that, once implemented, the configuration does not change all that much.

In NG FP2 and before, you cannot use the gateway cluster object as part of a rule. In Rule 4, you would use a host object of the same IP as the external IP of the firewall instead.

IPSO 3.6 does not require a VRRP rule because this version of IPSO sends certain VRRP packets directly past FireWall-1. Refer to Resolution 14946 for details.

NO.	SOURCE	DESTINATION	SERVICE	ACTION	TRACK
1	firewalls	firewalls vrrp.mcast.net	vrrp igmp	accept	None
2	firewall-managers	firewalls	SSH https	accept	Log
3	telecommuters@Any	internal-network	Any	Client Encrypt	Log
4	Any	vrrp-pair	FW1_pslogon_NG FW1_topo IKE VPN1_IPSEC_encapsulation ESP	accept	Log
5	internal-network	Any	ftp http https	accept	None
6	SMTP-Servers	Any	smtp	accept	None
7	Any	external-smtp-server	smtp	accept	Log
8	Any	Any	Any	drop	Log

Figure 12.52 Sample rulebase with gateway cluster

Configuring Multiple Entry Point SecureClient

The Situation

The network used in the previous sample configurations has been merged into a larger network via a WAN link. Other parts of this WAN have their own Internet access protected by Check Point FireWall-1. It is desirable to use these other connections and firewalls as backup gateways for SecuRemote users. Because of this configuration, Office Mode will be used. Each firewall needs to be allocated a unique, nonroutable subnet so that incoming SecuRemote clients can be assigned an IP that routes to the specific firewall they enter. Also, the original site needs to be reorganized somewhat to account for the WAN link. A WAN router has been added between the Nokia IP440s and the internal network with a new subnet. This is to keep the routing configuration a bit simpler.

Note that most of your attention should be focused on the original site (Site A in Figure 12.53). I will discuss the changes that need to occur on Site B (they are similar) but will leave the actual steps as an exercise.

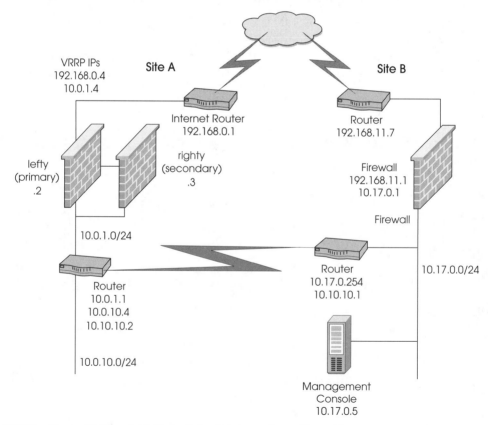

Figure 12.53 A Multiple Entry Point configuration with gateway clusters

The Goal

- Maintain the security policy as much as possible (from the previous configuration).

The Checklist

- Modify the encryption domains on all firewalls to include the same set of network objects, including all the firewalls.
- Configure the rulebase properties to enable backup gateways for SecuRemote clients and IP Pool NAT logging options.
- Choose appropriate address ranges for each gateway to use for IP Pool NAT.
- Configure each workstation and/or gateway cluster object so that the other firewalls are backup gateways.
- Configure each local gateway's workstation or gateway cluster object so that NAT is performed for SecuRemote connections.
- Install the security policy.

The Implementation

The other site (Site B in Figure 12.53) has an encryption domain of 10. 17.0.0/16. Both sites need to have an encryption domain that contains the following:

- All three firewalls at both sites
- 10.0.10.0/24
- 10.0.1.0/24
- 10.17.0.0/24

Create a group containing all of these objects. Edit the vrrp-pair object. In the Topology frame, specify the VPN domain as this group. A similar change will be made on maingw, the object for the firewall at Site B. In the VPN frame in the vrrp-pair object, check Enable Backup Gateways and specify maingw as your backup gateway. The analogous change should *not* be made on maingw.

Now go to the Cluster Members frame. Edit each member of the gateway cluster. Go to the VPN tab and set the Office Mode pool to the same network on both members of the cluster (see Figure 12.54).

After editing the cluster members, go to the Remote Access frame in the vrrp-pair object. Enable Office Mode for the telecommuters group and set the Office Mode method to Manual as shown in Figure 12.55.

Click on the Optional Parameters button and specify the DNS information as shown in Figure 12.56.

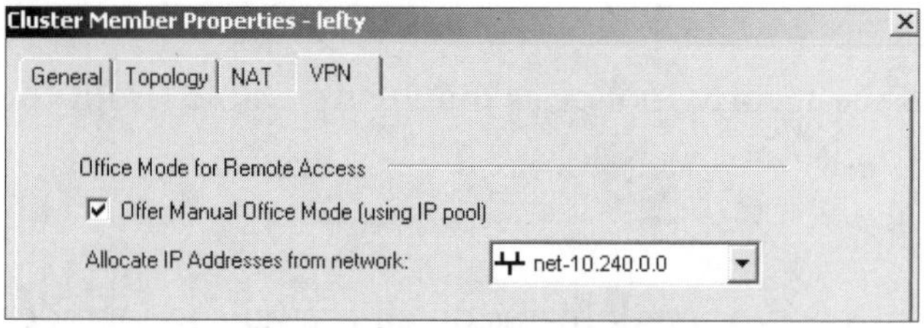

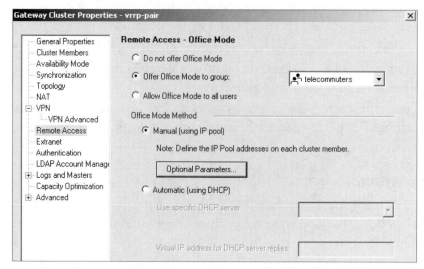

Figure 12.54   Cluster Member Properties, VPN tab

Figure 12.55   Gateway Cluster Properties, Remote Access frame

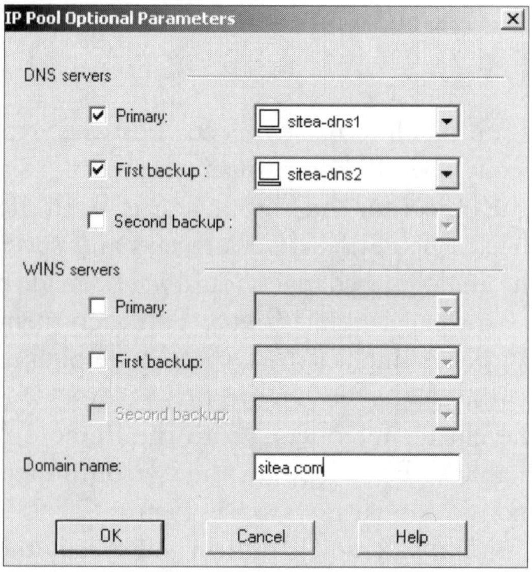

Figure 12.56   Optional Parameters for Office Mode

NO.	SOURCE	DESTINATION	SERVICE	ACTION	TRACK
1	firewalls	firewalls vrrp.mcast.net	vrrp igmp	accept	– None
2	firewall-managers	firewalls	TCP SSH TCP https	accept	Log
3	telecommuters@Any	encryption-domain	* Any	Client Encrypt	Log
4	* Any	vrrp-pair	TCP FW1_pslogon_NG TCP FW1_topo IKE UDP VPN1_IPSEC_encapsulation ESP	accept	Log
5	internal-network	* Any	TCP ftp TCP http TCP https	accept	– None
6	SMTP-Servers	* Any	TCP smtp	accept	– None
7	* Any	external-smtp-server	TCP smtp	accept	Log
8	* Any	* Any	* Any	drop	Log

Figure 12.57 Rulebase for Multiple Entry Point Configuration

To accommodate the new encryption domain, you have to change Rule 3 in your rulebase so that the rule includes encryption-domain instead of internal-network (see Figure 12.57). Other than that, the rulebase is identical to the one in the previous configuration.

Notes

Despite the fact that gateway clusters are being used, a failover of the primary firewall will cause any active connections to terminate. If both members of the cluster fail, only then will the backup gateway be used.

Chapter

13

High Availability

In today's business environment, downtime anywhere in the network is simply not an option. This includes your network security enforcement points. This chapter focuses on making firewalls highly available. I will touch on the issues that arise when you have more than one firewall in parallel and outline a strategy for load balancing traffic across multiple firewalls.

By the end of this chapter, you should be able to:

- Configure FireWall-1 State Synchronization
- Identify vendors that provide High-Availability and load-balancing solutions
- Understand asymmetric routing and why it is bad for firewalls
- Establish a method for load balancing across multiple firewalls

State Synchronization's Role in High Availability

An application is said to be highly available when you have taken steps to minimize single points of failure. In the mid-1990s, several companies introduced High-Availability (HA) software that provided an infrastructure allowing applications to be monitored on the primary system and "failed over" to a secondary system when a failure was detected. The applications were stored on a shared medium (usually a mirrored disk connected to both systems), and state for the applications had to be stored on the shared disk drive. This allowed the secondary system to pick up where the primary system left off. This setup is historically referred to as a *warm standby*.

Although this was a boon for many companies, it had some drawbacks.

- Only one system at a time was active. The secondary system was usually idle.
- Some state was always lost. Placing state on disk had its limits and was not possible with many applications, including FireWall-1.

A better way to handle High Availability is to have both systems active at the same time, actively sharing information. In FireWall-1, this can be done with a feature called *State Synchronization*.

State Synchronization is a mechanism in FireWall-1 that allows two firewalls to share information contained within their respective state tables. This allows a firewall to more readily take over in the event of a failure. This condition is referred to as a *hot standby*.

Although State Synchronization preserves most connections, any connections involving the Security Servers will not fail over properly. This is because all Security Server–related connections actually terminate at a single firewall. It is difficult to fail over connections that terminate at a specific firewall.

A Word about Licensing

There is no special license for High Availability, though each gateway must have its own unique firewall license, even in a hot-standby configuration. Check Point typically offers discounts to customers who purchase gateways that will be used in an HA configuration. Node-limited gateway licenses can be used in an HA configuration, though single-gateway products (i.e., firewall plus local management module licenses) cannot.

The notable exception to the "no extra licenses" rule is ClusterXL, which requires a separate license. This feature is discussed later in this chapter.

The State Synchronization Protocol

State Synchronization occurs via UDP port 8116, or at least that's the way sync *appears* to work. In reality, State Synchronization is a layer-2 multicast-type protocol that, in many protocol analyzers, looks an awful lot like UDP port 8116 traffic. Packets from the master host use one MAC address; packets from a slave host use a different MAC.

Within State Synchronization, there are two modes of operation: full sync and incremental sync. When firewalls begin synchronizing with each other for the first time (e.g., after a reboot or restart of FireWall-1) or after certain events (e.g., a policy install), a full sync is done. This means all tables marked as "sync" on these platforms are synchronized. Depending on how loaded the firewalls are, this can take a lot of communication, and thus time, to accomplish.

Once a full sync has been performed, every 100 milliseconds or so, the firewalls simply exchange the "changes" that have occurred since the last full sync. This is an incremental sync. In most cases, FireWall-1 operates in this mode.

Configuring State Synchronization

In FireWall-1 4.1 and earlier releases, synchronization was configured in $FWDIR/conf/sync.conf. This meant you could tie any two firewalls together, whether or not they ran the same security policy. In FireWall-1 NG, synchronization is now configured in a gateway cluster object. This makes sense because a gateway cluster is designed to treat two or more firewalls as if they were one. Ensuring all the cluster members have the same state information allows the cluster members to *act* as a single gateway.

You can create a gateway cluster object from the objects tree by clicking on the Network Objects icon, right-clicking New Check Point, and selecting Gateway Cluster. Alternatively, you can select Network Objects from the Manage menu, click on New, select Check Point, and then select Gateway Cluster. You will see a screen similar to Figure 13.1.

Configuring a gateway cluster object is similar to configuring a standard gateway object, so I cover only the differences in the procedures here. Options you might configure in this object apply to all members of the cluster.

For your gateway cluster object, you should use an IP address that addresses the "virtual" firewall. All of the supported HA schemes, including Check Point HA, Virtual Router Redundancy Protocol (VRRP), Nokia IP Clustering, Rainfinity, and Stonebeat have some sort of concept of a virtual IP address. The active firewall will respond to packets sent to this virtual IP address. In a load-balanced

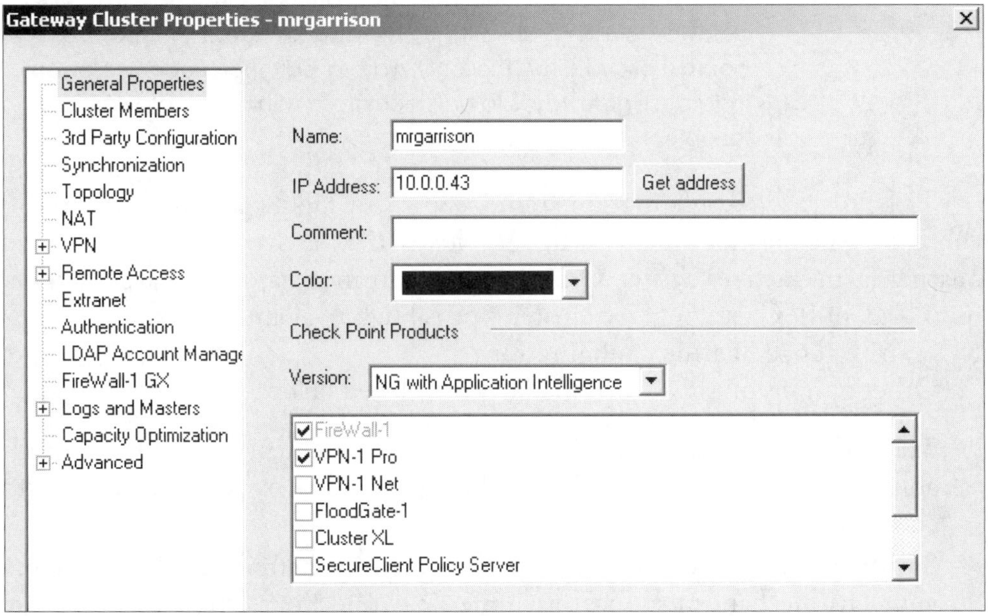

Figure 13.1   Gateway Cluster Properties, General Properties frame

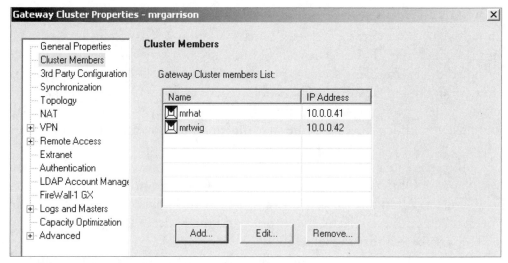

Figure 13.2 Gateway Cluster Properties, Cluster Members frame

configuration, multiple firewalls may be active at the same time, but only the appropriate firewall will respond. When a failover occurs, a different firewall will respond.

Figure 13.2 shows the Cluster Members frame, where you configure which gateways are part of your gateway cluster.

 WARNING! In FireWall-1 NG FP3, once you add an individual gateway to a gateway cluster, you will not be able to see it in SmartDashboard/Policy Editor. The only way to edit the properties of an individual gateway is to edit them from within the gateway cluster object.

The 3rd Party Configuration frame, shown in Figure 13.3, allows you to configure whether this cluster is an HA cluster (i.e., active-standby) or a Load Sharing (active-active) cluster. On a Nokia platform, regardless of whether you use VRRP or IP Clustering, the cluster type is High Availability. If you use ClusterXL, it is a Load Sharing configuration.

Other options on this screen include those listed below.

3rd Party Solution: Choose which "solution" will be providing High Availability. Unless High Availability is being provided by VRRP, you should choose OPSEC.

Support non-sticky connections: This might be better described as "Does your HA mechanism support asymmetric connections?" instead. The State Synchronization mechanism can account for connections that leave one fire-

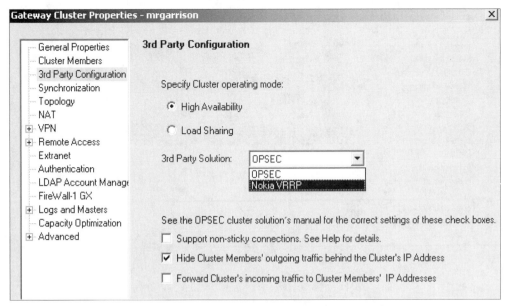

Figure 13.3   Gateway Cluster Properties, 3rd Party Configuration frame

wall and return through another. The checkbox controls whether or not FireWall-1 will do this. For Nokia IP Clustering, this option should be checked. For Nokia VRRP, uncheck this box. For other OPSEC-certified products, consult the appropriate documentation.

Hide Cluster Members' outgoing traffic behind the Cluster's IP Address: With this checkbox enabled, any traffic originating from any member of the cluster will be automatically translated to appear to come from the cluster IP address. Any NAT rules on the cluster or cluster members override this setting. I generally do not recommend enabling this option because it's quite likely to make troubleshooting packets originating from a specific gateway more difficult.

Forward Cluster's incoming traffic to Cluster Members' IP addresses: With this checkbox enabled, when a client establishes an incoming connection to the cluster IP address, it will be automatically translated to the physical IP address of one of the cluster members.

Figure 13.4 shows the Synchronization frame, where you configure which network will be used for State Synchronization. Add a network name (choose a name that doesn't match a network object name), an IP address, and a netmask. The chosen network should be a dedicated network segment, that is, one not used for other kinds of traffic (including traffic used by Nokia IP Clustering, which should be on its own dedicated segment).

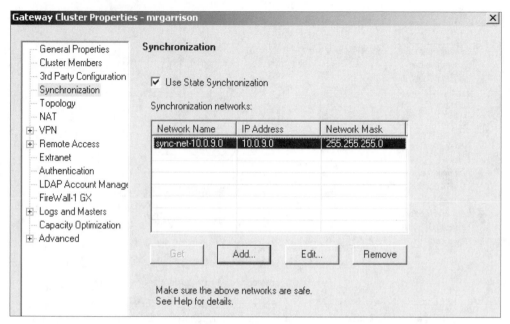

Figure 13.4 Gateway Cluster Properties, Synchronization frame

 WARNING! Under no circumstances should you provide a virtual IP address with VRRP, IP Clustering, or other HA mechanisms on the synchronization interface. This configuration has been shown to cause problems with State Synchronization.

What Are the Limitations of State Synchronization?

You should be aware that State Synchronization happens approximately every 100 milliseconds. All changes in the state table since the last sync interval are sent to the peer firewalls. It also takes roughly 55 milliseconds for these changes to be incorporated into the state tables. This means it takes a minimum of 155 milliseconds for the peer firewall to be updated. The actual amount of time varies based on system load.

What does this delay in synchronization mean? The long and the short of it is this: If one firewall receives a TCP SYN packet and the other firewall receives a corresponding TCP SYN/ACK packet before the synchronization actually occurs, you will end up dropping or severely delaying the establishment of the TCP connection. This is a condition known as *asymmetric routing*, which is discussed in its own subsection below.

Some other important restrictions concerning State Synchronization include those listed below.

- The firewalls must be running on the same type of platform. This means that two Nokia, two Windows, or two Solaris platforms may synchronize with one another, but a Nokia and a Windows platform cannot. This is due to differences in how each platform internally stores the tables.
- The firewalls must be running the same version of the software at the same service pack level.
- The firewalls must have the same security policy. By using a gateway cluster, this is enforced.
- With respect to NAT, careful consideration must be given to routing. Where routing is symmetric, it is usually only necessary to make the needed ARP and routing changes on both firewalls. Where routing is asymmetric, additional configuration of routers on either side may need to be done.
- No connections or information relating to Security Servers are synchronized because they rely on individual processes on the platforms in question and cannot be easily synchronized.
- If accounting logging is used, neither firewall will be able to provide accurate data on how much traffic was transferred because accounting data is not synchronized.
- State Synchronization starts becoming a huge burden when the rate of change in the connections table becomes too great. It is a difficult task to keep more than two firewalls synced, especially under these conditions. In some applications (particularly firewalls protecting HTTP farms), State Synchronization can be either eliminated or greatly reduced by disabling the Synchronize on Cluster option in some services, such as HTTP and DNS.

Implementing High Availability

State Synchronization is a very important component for implementing High Availability. Without it, other firewalls that may be called in to take over will not know the current status of connections and will cause a break in connectivity. However, State Synchronization is not the only piece to this equation. Another component must be involved to allow other routers or hosts around the firewall to know which firewall to use at the time. Dynamic routing protocols can certainly be used to achieve this, but this is not always practical and comes with its own problems—namely, these protocols can create asymmetric routing.

All HA solutions for FireWall-1 provide for some sort of virtual IP address, which is shared between the firewalls. The active firewall at any given time possesses a number of these virtual addresses, at least one on each physical interface except for the synchronization interface (exactly how and when are specific to each implementation). This provides a virtual firewall. Clients and routers can simply point to this virtual address where appropriate and can always be assured that a firewall will service that address.

Asymmetric Routing

In asymmetric routing, packets on a connection take different paths coming into and going out of a given network—namely, your own network. Anytime packets have multiple paths to take through a network, there is always a possibility they will take a different path. If you observe how the Internet as a whole works, it is quite customary for sent packets to take a slightly different path from packets that are received.

Asymmetric routing is not a problem if that's all that's occurring—that packets are being routed and connection state is being not tracked. If connection state must be tracked (for instance, when you are trying to perform network security functions), asymmetric routing causes problems. Any HA solution must ensure that asymmetric routing does not occur or must have some way to deal with it when it does occur.

Consider the network diagram in Figure 13.5.

For 10.0.10.0/24, there are two possible routes to the Internet: mrhat and mrtwig. There are also two possible routes back to 10.0.10.0/24 from the Internet: mrhat and mrtwig. This means that it is possible to have an asymmetrical routing situation. For illustrative purposes, let's assume that mrhat is the default route for clients on the 10.0.10.0/24 network and that the Internet router routes all packets destined for 10.0.10.0/24 to mrtwig. This means there is an asymmetric routing condition. Let's also assume that both firewalls in question are synchronizing their state tables via Check Point's State Synchronization mechanism.

Connections originating from 10.0.10.0/24 going to the Internet may actually work fairly well. It works better the longer the latency is between sending the first packet through mrhat and receiving its reply through mrtwig. Hosts out on the Internet can easily take more than 155 milliseconds to respond.

Connections originating from the Internet and destined for 10.0.10.0/24 will be slow in establishing (if they do at all) because the latency between the time the packet is initially received on mrtwig, responded to by the client, and then sent out via mrhat will likely be less than 155 milliseconds (in the preceding situation, it would be less than 10 milliseconds). This means State Synchronization will not have had an opportunity to do its job. If the packet received on mrtwig is a SYN packet and the packet received on mrhat is a SYN/ACK packet

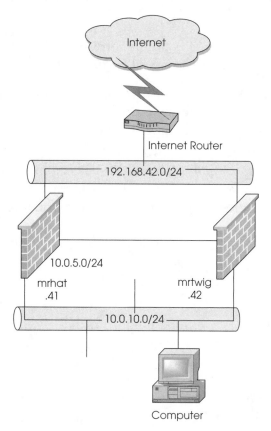

Figure 13.5 Sample network diagram with highly available firewalls

(i.e., packets that start a TCP session), mrhat will see that the packet is not part of an established connection and will drop the packet. About 3 seconds later,[1] the server on the 10.0.10.0/24 network, not having received an ACK packet to acknowledge the SYN/ACK packet, will resend the SYN/ACK packet. By that time, synchronization will have occurred, and the packet will be allowed through. Note that with UDP or any IP datagrams, retransmissions occur only if the application using the packets does it, so it is quite possible that these packets will simply be dropped.

The good news is that this problem has the potential to occur only within that 155 milliseconds or so right when the connection is being established. Once the connection is properly established and synchronized, an asymmetric condition is not a problem.

---

1. This time period for resending a SYN/ACK response actually depends on the TCP/IP implementation. However, most TCP/IP stacks are based on BSD's TCP/IP stack, which has a default of 3 seconds.

HA Solution Providers

You have several different choices of HA software and hardware products. The most common ones include those listed below.

- *Stonebeat's FullCluster for FireWall-1 (http://www.stonebeat.com):* This software product runs on the same platform as FireWall-1. It provides hot-standby failover as well as failover with load sharing.

- *Rainfinity High Availability Software for Check Point VPN-1/FireWall-1 (http://www.rainfinity.com):* Rainfinity delivers an accelerated HA platform for all gateway applications—from Internet connectivity to firewalls and content security—to ensure optimal performance across all network resources.

- *Check Point's ClusterXL (http://www.checkpoint.com):* This software product is integrated into FireWall-1, although it requires a separate license. It provides hot-standby failover and load sharing.

- *Nokia IP Security Platforms (http://www.nokia.com/securitysolutions/):* Nokia IP Security Platforms include support for VRRP, which provides failover capabilities to FireWall-1. Load balancing is not part of this solution but can easily be achieved with third-party hardware. Since IPSO 3.6, Nokia also provides patented IP Clustering technology, which adds the redundancy features of Dynamic Load Balancing and Active Session Failover for VPN traffic. Both of these features are included on the Nokia IP Security Platforms and do not require any extra Check Point licenses. Note that the IP30 and IP40 platforms also provide VRRP with the appropriate version of firmware (IP30 version 2.0 release and IP40 version 1.1, respectively).

- *Radware's Fireproof (http://www.radware.com):* This hardware product provides hot-standby failover as well as failover with load sharing.

- *F5 Networks BIG-IP FireGuard (http://www.f5.com):* This hardware product provides hot-standby failover as well as failover with load sharing.

From this list, you can see that there are two schools of thought: hardware-based solutions and software-based solutions. For High Availability, either solution works well, although software-based solutions do have somewhat of an edge because they can interact with FireWall-1 more directly. When load balancing is factored into the equation, hardware solutions quite simply scale better, although they tend to be somewhat more expensive. You can use both hardware and software HA systems together.

Any HA solution must address the problem of asymmetric routing. HA software vendors claim to be able to handle the asymmetric routing problem. However, I am skeptical of any software product's ability to handle this well. Assuming both firewalls are synchronized, there is simply no way to synchronize fast enough to be able to handle asymmetric connections in all situations. Packets can be held by some other process so that the synchronization process can catch up, or packets can be set up so that all firewalls hear the packets and only the right one responds, which seems to be a waste. Either latency or throughput is compromised in this situation. Specialized hardware can do this much faster than a general purpose platform can and is usually more scalable.

Load Balancing

When you have more than one firewall in parallel, the next logical question is, "How can I have each firewall take part in the overall network load to increase throughput?" Most people do not like the idea of purchasing extra equipment only to leave it sitting around unused most of the time.

Any effective load-balancing solution for FireWall-1 must handle packets for connections symmetrically (i.e., in and out through the same firewall), or at the very least, must be able to do this long enough for State Synchronization to catch up. The software approaches to load sharing exhibited by Stonesoft, Rainfinity, Check Point, and Nokia all share the same inherent design flaw: each firewall sees every packet destined for the cluster. Why is that? Because the virtual IP address used to represent the cluster is served via a multicast MAC address. Each cluster member will receive packets sent to this virtual MAC address and must do enough processing to determine whether or not the packet is one it needs to process.

What does this mean? It means that by adding a second firewall, you don't double your potential throughput. You do increase it, but only by about 50%. A third firewall might increase the throughput by about another 25%. In any case, the maximum available throughput will be the line speed by which a single firewall is connected (e.g., 100MB Ethernet).

The following subsections describe how Check Point and Nokia both implement their firewall and/or VPN load-balancing solutions. The subsections after those describe other load-balancing techniques you can employ.

ClusterXL

ClusterXL is Check Point's own method for providing load balancing. It is built into the core FireWall-1 product and uses the existing State Synchronization mechanism. In addition to being able to fail over all connections as in a standard HA configuration, ClusterXL also allows failover and load sharing of VPN connections. Up to five gateways are supported in a single cluster that uses ClusterXL.

ClusterXL is configured in SmartDashboard/Policy Editor. When a cluster is configured as having ClusterXL installed, a separate frame becomes available for ClusterXL-specific configuration options. In this frame you can configure exactly how the load will be shared with respect to VPN traffic.

ClusterXL is an extra-cost item, that is, it is not included in the base price of FireWall-1. It is available on all platforms on which FireWall-1 NG is available except for Nokia; however, ClusterXL for Nokia is planned for a future release.

Nokia IP Clustering

In 2000, Nokia acquired a company called Network Alchemy, which made VPN hardware that employed a clustering method able to scale extremely well. The products that originally employed this method are no longer being sold, but the clustering method has been integrated into the IPSO operating system since version 3.6.

As it is designed today, IP Clustering is designed primarily to load balance VPN connections. In the future, IP Clustering may load balance non-VPN connections as well. Up to four gateways can participate in an IP Cluster, with the most bang for the buck happening with three gateways.

IP Clustering is available as part of the IPSO operating system, that is, it is not necessary to purchase a license for it. IP Clustering is configured in the Voyager interface of IPSO. Check Point's State Synchronization mechanism is used in addition to IP Clustering's own synchronization protocol.

Static Load-Balancing Techniques

A cheap way to load balance is to logically group your hosts behind the firewall. This involves the following tasks.

- Hosts behind your gateway need to be configured with a static default route to the proper firewall for their group. Each group should be on different logical networks or at least be grouped on a reasonable subnet boundary.
- Border routers need to be configured with different routes to different firewalls.
- If VRRP (or something similar) is used, there must be multiple virtual IP addresses (one for each group) that can be failed over. This will provide resilience in case one of the firewalls fails.

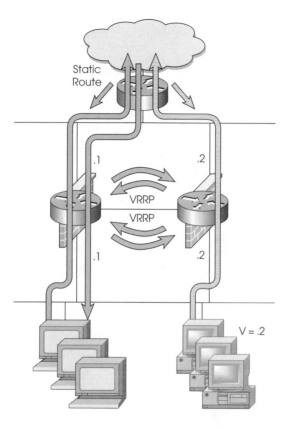

Static
Route

.1   .2

VRRP

VRRP

.1   .2

V = .2

Figure 13.6   Static load balancing

Figure 13.6 illustrates static load balancing in action.

In Figure 13.6, the hosts on the bottom left use the .1 firewall as their default route, the hosts on the bottom right use the .2 firewall, and the border router has static routes for both sets of hosts back to their respective firewalls.

You can also do something similar with multiple site-to-site VPNs, although it requires an internal router capable of doing policy routing based on source addresses to ensure that packets go to the proper firewall. Figure 13.7 illustrates static load balancing with policy routing.

The main issue with static load balancing is that load distribution is not automatic. If one part of your network starts consuming more bandwidth, you will have to manually adjust the load balancing. However, static load balancing is relatively inexpensive and straightforward to set up and maintain.

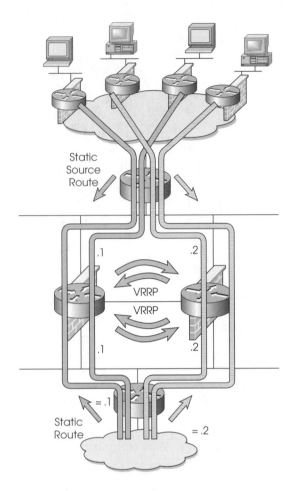

Figure 13.7   Static load balancing with VPN

Load Balancing with Switches

Thus far, I have assumed a single inbound and outbound connection. Although NIC cards and hubs/switches are generally pretty reliable, from time to time these components fail. To provide more throughput and greater resilience, you should double the number of connections and switches, as shown in Figure 13.8. Each interface must be associated with a logically different subnet, which gives you the ability to use multiple switches.

One advantage to this method is increased theoretical throughput. You now have two interfaces, which means you can potentially send twice as much data. Unfortunately, only the most powerful machines will be able to fully use both interfaces at maximum capacity. However, some modest performance gains can still be achieved, even without full utilization.

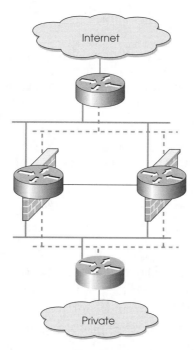

Figure 13.8   Load balancing with switches

Dynamic Load Balancing

Dynamic load balancing is generally preferable to static load balancing because it usually provides a better load balance and is more accommodating of changes that occur in your network. However, extra care must be taken to ensure symmetry. Most load-balancing techniques use some sort of hash function that is nondeterministic. This creates asymmetric routing. Deterministic forwarding on both sides of the firewall ensures that the same path is taken in both directions. This also provides a nice way to load balance.

Deterministic load balancing can also be done with a hash. Most load balancers perform an XOR of the source and destination IP addresses. This produces a symmetric result with packets going from host A to host B or host B to host A, as shown in Figure 13.9.

Assuming only two paths (i.e., two parallel firewalls), you simply look at the last bit in the XOR. A 0 means pass the packet to one firewall; a 1 means send it to the other firewall. Using hashing only, you are limited to the number of firewalls that are powers of 2 (2, 4, 8, 16, and so on). However, most systems enhance the hashing mechanism to support any number of firewalls and include methods that check the chosen path before using it and require their own sort of state synchronization.

```
Incoming
Source IP       172.16.64.1     10101100.00010000.01000000.00000001
Destination IP 192.168.30.65    11000000.10101000.00011110.01000001
XOR             108 184 94 64   01101100 10111000 01011110 01000000

Outgoing
Source IP       192.168.30.65    11000000.10101000.00011110.01000001
Destination IP 172.16.64.1       10101100.00010000.01000000.00000001
XOR             108 184 94 64    01101100 10111000 01011110 01000000
```

Figure 13.9   XOR of incoming and outgoing packets by IP

Because of these accessible techniques, you can now build a fully meshed solution with resilient load balancers and firewalls. Many different products can perform this function, including products from Nortel Networks, Cisco, Cabletron, F5, Foundry, Radware, and TopLayer. Once the connection is established and state synchronization takes place, a failure can occur in any component, and the connections will continue to flow (see Figure 13.10).

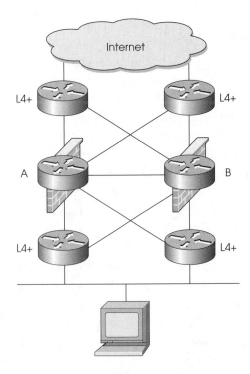

Figure 13.10   Dynamic load balancing

Network Address Translation

NAT makes load balancing much more complex, mainly because packets look different inside and outside the firewall. However, if only the source *or* destination IP address is subject to NAT, you can still use a hash function to accomplish load balancing by hashing against the IP address that does not change.

Consider Figure 13.11. The machine with IP address 192.168.32.2 is accessed via 128.0.0.24 on the Internet by means of NAT. If 192.168.32.2 initiates a connection to the Internet, the destination IP address will not change. Conversely, if something initiates a connection to 128.0.0.24, the source address will not change.

Therefore, on the outside routers, you can perform a hash based on the source IP address. On the inside routers, you can perform a hash based on the destination IP address. Both of these hashes should return the same value, thus allowing you to forward all traffic through a particular firewall. This technique will not work with dual NAT (i.e., where source and destination are both translated) or in a VPN. The next subsection discusses load balancing with VPNs.

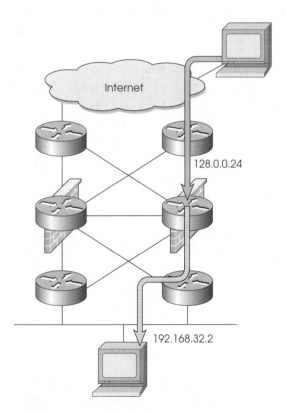

Figure 13.11   Dynamic load balancing with NAT

Site-to-Site VPNs

The problem you have with a VPN is that, from the outside world, the packets look like they are coming from host A and going to host B, even though inside the packet it may be host X going to host Y. This is because the packets are encapsulated and encrypted. Encrypted packets have zero correlation to their unencrypted counterparts, so none of the hashing techniques that have been discussed thus far will handle them.

A system that will map a particular application or connection to a next hop Ethernet address is required. This can be done with a fairly sophisticated hash table that stores where to forward a packet. An example of this might be:

```
(hash key: [srcIP: ingress if, ingress MAC],
           [dstIP: egress if, egress MAC])
```

When a packet arrives at the load balancer, a symmetric hash is performed, usually on layer 3 and 4 information. You then check to see if there is a match in the table based on the hash value and the source IP address. You check the hash for a match, and you check to see if either the source or destination IP address in the table entry matches the source address of the received packet. If there is a match, you forward it to the appropriate MAC address based on the source IP address of the packet and refresh the table entry. If there is no match, you figure out the ingress and egress interfaces and MAC address, create a new table entry, and forward accordingly. Figure 13.12 shows a flowchart of this process.

For example, assume you have a situation similar to the one shown in Figure 13.10 except you are using load balancers that implement the technique discussed in this section. Let's follow an IPSec-encrypted TCP SYN packet as it enters the network from the Internet and the SYN/ACK reply as it exits. Let's call the load balancers on the outside of the firewalls elb1 and elb2, the two firewalls A and B, the two firewalls' virtual IP address C (which is also the gateway cluster address), and the load balancers inside the firewalls ilb1 and ilb2.

The IPSec packet has a source IP address of F and a destination IP address of C. It is received at elb1 via interface elb1-1. The packet it hashed to value x and elb1 determines that no flow entry exists. The next hop for this packet is determined to be firewall A out interface elb1-3. An entry is added to the table that looks like this:

```
(hash x, F [elb1-1, upstream router MAC],
         C [elb1-3, firewall-A's external MAC])
```

Firewall A receives the packet, accepts the packet, decrypts it, and forwards it to ilb1. The packet now has a source IP address of P and a destination IP address of Q. ilb1 hashes the packet to value y and determines that no flow entry exists.

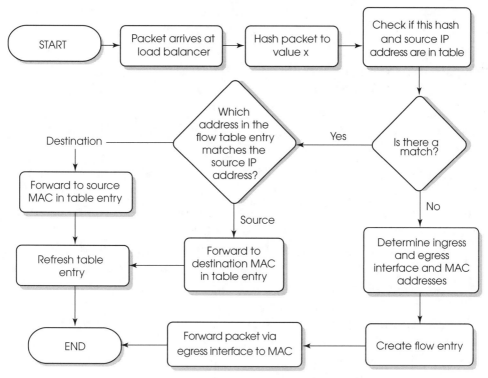

Figure 13.12 Flowchart of dynamic load balancing with VPNs

The next hop for this packet is determined to be an internal router out interface elb1-4. The packet was received on elb1-1. An entry is added to the table, which looks like this:

```
(hash y, P [elb1-1, Firewall-A's internal MAC],
        Q [elb1-4, downstream router MAC])
```

When the SYN/ACK packet comes back to elb1, it has a source IP of Q and a destination IP of P. ilb1 hashes the packet to value y (remember, the hash function is symmetric). An entry for this hash exists in the table. Because Q matches the "destination" IP address of this entry (it is a reply, so the source/destination are reversed), the packet is forwarded out interface elb1-1 to firewall A's internal MAC address. Firewall A receives the packet, accepts it, encrypts it, and forwards it out to elb1, where a similar process takes place.

This process is beneficial because it is interface independent. The forwarding is unit independent, thus NAT and VPNs will work. This approach is particularly clever because the forwarding technique is deterministic—it does not matter that the switch does not know of a flow. Obviously the hash table has to be aged. It can be viewed as a sophisticated ARP table.

Products by Foundry and F5 support load balancing as described in this section.

Frequently Asked Questions Regarding State Synchronization

The following section details various issues that come up when employing State Synchronization on your firewalls, regardless of the underlying HA mechanism.

13.1: How Do I Know State Synchronization Is Working?

FireWall-1 4.1 and earlier used a TCP connection to synchronize information about the connections table. This meant you could use **netstat** to determine whether or not synchronization was taking place. In FireWall-1 NG, the State Synchronization method cannot be tracked in this way. You could do a **snoop** or a **tcpdump** to witness the synchronization packets, but this doesn't necessarily mean State Synchronization is doing the job.

The "correct" way to check the status of synchronization is the command **cphaprob state**. However, executing the command **fw tab -t connections -s** on each firewall has proven to be more reliable. If State Synchronization is working, both firewalls will show a similar value for #VALS (i.e., the number of entries in the table). It's reasonable that these values won't be exactly the same, but they should be fairly close. For instance, if one firewall shows 25,000 entries and the other shows 24,500 entries, the firewalls are synced. If one firewall shows 25,000 and the other shows 50, the firewalls are quite likely not synced.

13.2: Can I Change the MAC Address Used by the State Synchronization Mechanism?

Because each cluster uses the same MAC addresses for active and standby modes, it would not be possible to connect more than one cluster's synchronization interface to the same switch, possibly even different VLANs on the same switch. In NG FP3 HFA-310 or above, you can perform the following steps to change the MAC address.

There are actually two MAC addresses, set by the kernel variables fwha_mac_magic and fwha_mac_forward_magic. This isn't actually the full MAC address, but rather the last octet of the MAC address. You can modify these MAC address by choosing any hexadecimal number between 0x1 and 0xfc—0xfe and 0xfd cannot be used. All members of the same cluster must have these changes made, though each cluster should use unique values with respect to other clusters. In the following examples, I have chosen 0x42 for one system and 0x69 for the other.

On Solaris machines, add the following line to the bottom of the `/etc/system` file, and then reboot:

```
set fw:fwha_mac_magic = 0x42
set fw:fwha_mac_forward_magic = 0x69
```

On Linux machines, edit `$FWDIR/boot/modules/fwkern.conf` and add the following lines, rebooting afterward:

```
fwha_mac_magic = 0x42
fwha_mac_forward_magic = 0x69
```

Check Point states that these variables cannot be changed on Nokia or Windows. However, the IPSO version of the FireWall-1 loadable kernel module does contain the appropriate values, and using the **modzap** utility from Nokia Resolution 1261 on these values appears to work. Here are the commands you must enter before rebooting:

```
nokia# modzap $FWDIR/boot/modules/fwmod.o _fwha_mac_magic 0x42
nokia# modzap $FWDIR/boot/modules/fwmod.o
       _fwha_mac_forward_magic 0x69
```

13.3: Can I Perform State Synchronization between Two Platforms of Differing Performance Characteristics?

Generally speaking, you can do this. However, the system with the better performance characteristics should be the master.

In one instance, an IP330 with 128MB of RAM was paired with an IP650 with 256MB of RAM. The IP330 was the master. In this configuration, the system frequently lost synchronization with the other members.

13.4: How Can I Prevent a Specific Service from Being Synchronized via State Synchronization?

In FireWall-1 NG FP2 and above, it is possible to configure a service so that it does not synchronize across a cluster by simply unchecking the Synchronize on Cluster checkbox in the appropriate service's Advanced section. In NG FP1 and prior, add the following line to `$FWDIR/lib/table.def` on the management station and reinstall the security policy:

```
non_sync_ports = { <80, 6>, <443, 6>, <53, 17> };
```

The format of each entry is `<port number, protocol number>`. In the above example we have HTTP (TCP port 80), HTTPS (TCP port 443), and DNS (UDP port 53).

Error Messages That Occur with ClusterXL or State Synchronization

A number of error messages show up when using ClusterXL or State Synchronization. The following subsections document some of the more common ones and what, if anything, you need to do about them.

13.5: Various Error Messages Occur during a Full Sync

During a full sync between firewalls running State Synchronization, a number of error messages might show up, particularly if the gateways are under load. One or more of the following messages might appear.

- "h_rename: entry not found"
- "h_slink: an attempt to link to a link"
- "kbuf id not found"
- "fw_conn_post_inspect: fwconn_init_links failed"

During full sync, an existing member sends its firewall tables to a new member while at the same time updating the tables with information from incoming packets. Updates are necessary when receiving packets because the firewall should not stop handling packets while a full sync is under way. Unfortunately, a full sync can be somewhat lengthy, and these errors will show up during that time. You can safely ignore these errors.

13.6: Error Changing Local Mode from <mode1> to <mode2> because of ID <machine_id>

You may see this error message when using ClusterXL if the working mode of the cluster members isn't in sync. For example, one member might be in HA mode, and another might be in Load Sharing mode. ClusterXL resolves this by reducing the working mode to the lowest common mode. This error is safe to ignore.

13.7: Inconsistencies Exist between Policies Installed on Cluster Members on My Console

This error may appear if the State Synchronization mechanism detects that cluster members have different policies. Such a condition may result from a **fw fetch** command executed on a cluster member after a policy on the management module was pushed but not successfully installed on any cluster member. This results in the two cluster members actually enforcing different policies, which is an unstable situation. To resolve it, reinstall the policy to the entire cluster.

13.8: CPHA: Received Confirmations from More Machines Than the Cluster Size

This message occurs during a policy installation on the cluster. It means that your cluster configuration is inconsistent or another cluster is using the same network for State Synchronization and you haven't configured the other cluster to use different MAC addresses as documented in FAQ 13.2.

13.9: FwHaTimeWorker: Wait Failed (Status N)

This error message occurs on a multiprocessor Windows platform. When this occurs, ClusterXL will not function at all. Check Point reports this is a failure within the operating system. Check Point does not provide a resolution to this problem.

13.10: fwha_reset_timer: Failed to Allocate Timer DPC or Timer Object

This error message, which occurs only on Windows, indicates FireWall-1 was unable to allocate either a timer DPC or a timer object. Either way, ClusterXL will not be able to function due to a failure in the underlying operating system. Check Point does not provide a resolution to this problem.

13.11: There Are More Than 4 IPs on Interface <interface name> Notifying Only the First Ones

This message means that some cluster members have more than three virtual IP addresses (in addition to the one real one) defined on the same interface. This is unsupported and will break ClusterXL functionality. However, this error message also shows up on IPSO when using State Synchronization with VRRP and not ClusterXL. In this instance, the error message is addressed in NG AI as well as in HFA-310 and above for NG FP3. Contact Check Point support to obtain HFA-310.

13.12: fwha_create_icmp_echo_request: Failed to Create Packet

This error occurs when system resources are very low, which means that ClusterXL is probably failing. Troubleshoot your system to ensure it has adequate resources.

13.13: fwha_receive_fwhap_msg: Received Incomplete HAP Packet (Read <number> Bytes)

Check Point claims this is a rare log message. You should contact Check Point Support if this error occurs because it likely points to ClusterXL not functioning correctly.

13.14: Inconsistencies Exist between Policies Installed on the Cluster Members

If the policy is different between two cluster members, you will see this error message. It will also occur if you install two cluster members on different operating systems (e.g., IPSO and Windows). This message does not appear in NG AI. In FP3 you can ignore it if policy installation succeeded on all members.

13.15: Sync Could Not Start Because There Is No Sync License

If you have a basic firewall license, even a node-limited license, you should be able to use sync. Notable exceptions are small-office licenses and single-gateway licenses (e.g., management and firewall on the same platform). Ensure your firewalls have the correct license.

13.16: fwldbcast_timer: Peer X Probably Stopped

This error shows up when the member that prints this message stops hearing particular messages from member X. Use the command **cphaprob state** to validate the state of all members. The command **fw ctl pstat** should also report that sync is configured correctly and working correctly on all members. Perhaps there was a temporary connectivity problem that was resolved (meanwhile, a few connections through the cluster might experience problems), or perhaps peer X is really down.

13.17: fwlddist_adjust_buf: Record Too Big for Sync

This error message indicates that the amount of information that needs to be synced between cluster members is larger than the buffers designed to hold that information. Things that can affect this buffer include the following.

- *Active connections view in SmartView Tracker/Log Viewer:* This uses the same infrastructure as the State Synchronization mechanism.
- *High rate of change of connections:* If a number of connections are being created, torn down, and then created again, likely due to heavy load, a lot of activity is going on in the state tables. This causes State Synchronization to work extra hard to keep the state tables in sync.

You can attempt to reduce the number of services being synchronized (see FAQ 13.4), or you can increase the size of the sync buffer, which can be anywhere from 8K (0x2000) to 64K (0x10000). You can do this in FireWall-1 NG FP3 HFA-308 or later. (You can obtain HFA-308 from Check Point Support.) The following examples set the sync buffer size to 64K.

On Solaris machines, add the following line to the bottom of the /etc/system file, and then reboot:

```
set fw: int fwlddist_buf_size = 0x10000
```

On Linux machines, edit `$FWDIR/boot/modules/fwkern.conf` and add the following lines, rebooting afterward:

```
fwlddist_buf_size= 0x10000
```

Check Point states that this variable cannot be changed on Nokia or Windows. However, the IPSO version of the FireWall-1 loadable kernel module does contain the appropriate values, and using the **modzap** utility from Nokia Resolution 1261 on these values appears to work. Here is the command you must enter before rebooting:

```
nokia# modzap $FWDIR/boot/modules/fwmod.o _fwlddist_buf_size
0x10000
```

13.18: fwha_pnote_register: Too Many Registering Members, Cannot Register

The Pnote mechanism can store only up to 16 different devices. Attempts to configure a seventeenth device, either by editing `$FWDIR/conf/cphaprob.conf` or by using the **cphaprob -d ... register** command, fail and generate this error message.

13.19: fwha_pnote_register: foo Already Registered (#5)

This message may occur when registering a new Pnote device. The example message used for this subheading means that the device foo is already registered as with Pnote number 5. Each Pnote device must have a unique name.

13.20: fwha_pnote_reg_query: Pnotes Not Relevant in Service Mode

This error shows up when third-party HA/Load Sharing solutions attempt to use a Pnote. These are supported only in ClusterXL.

13.21: fwldbcast_update_block_new_conns: Sync in Risk: Did Not Receive ack for the Last 410 Packets

Synchronization load is considered heavy when the synchronization transmit queue of a firewall starts to fill beyond the `fw_sync_buffer_threshold`, which is set by default to 80%. Increasing the sync buffer size as described in FAQ 13.17 will improve synchronization performance substantially and allow a larger `fw_sync_buffer_threshold` value.

When the `fw_sync_buffer_threshold` reaches over 80% of the sync buffer size, you might also see the following error messages on your console:

```
Jun 5 10:21:25 nokiafw2 [LOG_CRIT] kernel: FW-1: It is
recommended to set the global parameter fw_sync_block_
new_conns to 0.
FW-1: State synchronization is in risk. Please examine
your synchronization network to avoid further problems!
```

The kernel variable `fw_sync_block_new_conns` can be modified to allow FireWall-1 to detect heavy loads and start blocking new connections. The default behavior in NG AI, and the way things worked in previous releases, was to allow new connections into the connections table despite not being fully synchronized. This allows new connections at the expense of possibly not being able to recover if failover occurs. By default `fw_sync_block_new_conns` is set to -1 (load detection is disabled).

To enable load detection on sync and block new connections when the `fw_sync_buffer_threshold` is over 80%, you must first update your firewall cluster members to NG FP3 HFA-315 or higher, which includes NG AI. Contact Check Point or your support provider for the latest HFA for NG FP3.

On Solaris machines, add the following line to the bottom of the `/etc/system` file:

```
set fw:fw_sync_block_new_conns = 0
```

On Linux machines, edit `$FWDIR/boot/modules/fwkern.conf` and add the following lines, rebooting afterward:

```
fw_sync_block_new_conns=0
```

Check Point states that this variable cannot be changed on Nokia or Windows. However, the IPSO version of the FireWall-1 loadable kernel module does contain the appropriate values, and using the **modzap** utility from Nokia Resolution 1261 on these values appears to work. Here is the command you must enter before rebooting:

```
nokia# modzap $FWDIR/boot/modules/fwmod.o _fw_sync_block_new_cons 0
```

By default, if more than 410 consecutive packets are sent without getting an ACK on any one of them, new connections are dropped. When blocking starts, `fw_sync_block_new_conns` is automatically set to 1. When the situation stabilizes, the variable is set back to 0.

 WARNING!   Under no circumstances should you manually set `fw_sync_block_new_conns` to 0.

Apply the above changes to all members of the cluster. On Nokia platforms, you need to make some additional changes to your IPSO configuration. For VRRP configurations, you need to set the Coldstart Delay to an appropriate value to give the firewalls an adequate amount of time to synchronize prior to accepting any traffic. Here are some guidelines based on platform type.

- IP650: 180 seconds
- IP440: 240 seconds
- IP120/330: 300 seconds
- Other platforms: 120 seconds

Note that the most up-to-date recommendations regarding the settings for this situation are in Resolution 17111 in Nokia's Knowledge Base.

Once the **modzap** and VRRP Coldstart Delay changes are made, reboot each of the cluster members.

WARNING! Do not perform a reboot on any of the cluster members until they all have their `fw_sync_block_new_conns` values changed. Failure to do so will result in lost synchronization upon a reboot of any cluster member!

13.22: fwhandle_get: Table kbufs—Invalid Handle— Bad Entry in Pool 0

This error condition appears when the kbuf pointer stored in a connections table entry is incorrect. This may indicate that the kbuf was already freed or this pointer was overwritten. There were some issues in the base NG FP3 release that caused this problem, which can be fixed by a hotfix obtainable from Check Point Support. However, the most likely cause of this problem is a result of a software mismatch between the members of the gateway cluster.

All members of the same cluster need to have the same Check Point packages loaded on them, *even if they are deactivated*. For example, even if the Flood Gate package was installed on only one member of the cluster but never started, State Synchronization can become corrupted. The reason for this is that every Check Point package installation notifies the FireWall-1 product of its existence through the Check Point registry so that it can integrate with FireWall-1 when enabled. This registry is read at boot time.

Mismatched packages on cluster members can lead to several problems with firewall functionality including inaccurate sync of address translation information. This later leads to the inability to correctly free the NAT information, which is partially stored in the `fwx_alloc` table. If you look at the `fwx_alloc` table using the command `fw tab -t fwx_alloc`, and either the `#VALS` or `#PEAK` is close to 25,000 entries (the default limit for this table), it is likely the result of mismatched package installation in your cluster.

To resolve this issue, uninstall the Check Point packages not present on all cluster members, and reboot. Once the machine is rebooted, it will contain the same configuration as its cluster peer, the Check Point registry will be reread, and the firewall module will be updated. A full sync will be performed, synchronization should work correctly with the other cluster members, and the cluster should be intact after that.

Summary

This chapter touched on many of the issues that come up in High Availability. It is by no means a complete guide on the subject. The two important issues covered were how to implement State Synchronization in FireWall-1 and the dangers of asymmetric routing.

Chapter
14

INSPECT

INSPECT is a feature in Check Point FireWall-1 that is poorly documented but can be *very* useful if people become familiar with it. Certain people within Check Point claim INSPECT is poorly documented because the language itself has not stabilized. I've also heard from various sources that the next version of FireWall-1 will have better INSPECT documentation. However, none of these facts have changed in quite some time. In fact, almost all information about the INSPECT language has been removed from the FireWall-1 documentation.

This chapter offers a brief introduction to how INSPECT works. The information should be useful to those who are looking for a more detailed understanding of how FireWall-1 works and to those who want to permit more-advanced services through FireWall-1. This chapter is not meant to cover the INSPECT language comprehensively. However, several examples of INSPECT code are included.

By the end of this chapter, you should be able to:

- Understand what INSPECT is
- Determine what you can and cannot do with INSPECT
- Understand how FireWall-1 converts your rulebase into INSPECT
- Write your own INSPECT code

What Is INSPECT?

INSPECT is a programming language for Check Point's Stateful Inspection engine in FireWall-1. When you install your security policy generated in the Policy Editor, your rulebase is converted to an INSPECT script. Most people never need to look at INSPECT code, but if you need to make FireWall-1 support more than just simple services (e.g., where only one connection is opened from the client to the server), you will need to use INSPECT. You may not have to write a full INSPECT script, but you may have to use snippets of INSPECT to accomplish your goals.

The primary purpose of INSPECT is to analyze a packet from the network layer down to the application layer and make decisions based on what is found. INSPECT, although a very powerful language, has only a few basic functions:

- Makes comparisons based on any part of a packet
- Adds, modifies, or deletes entries from state tables
- Accepts, rejects, drops, or vanishes a packet
- Calls functions (such as log)

Basic INSPECT Syntax

This section, by presenting simple examples, provides a rudimentary description of how to read and understand INSPECT code.

INSPECT is a fairly simple script-like language that contains a series of statements designed to evaluate packets and make decisions about what to do with the packet. Although this is not a complete BNF[1] for the language, it should give you a rough idea of what to expect.

```
inspect script   ::= { <statement> }

statement        ::= <scope> <condition> { "," <condition> |
                     "and" <condition> | "xor" <condition> |
                     "or" <condition> }  ";"

scope            ::= <direction> "@" <host>

direction        ::= "<" | ">" | "<>" | "" | all | <interface name>

condition        ::= <short circuit> | <table command> |
                     <identifier> { <operand> <identifier> }  |
                     <function>

operand          ::= + | - | / | * | % | "|" | ^ | "==" | "!=" | ">" |
                     "<" | "<=" | ">="

short circuit    ::= accept | reject | drop | vanish

table command    ::= get <table entry> from <table name> |
                     delete <table entry> from <table name> |
                     modify <table entry> in <table name> |
```

---

1. BNF is an acronym for Backus Normal Form or Backus Naur Form. It is a standard format used to describe programming languages, first introduced in the Algol-60 report by John Backus and Peter Naur. Computer science luminary Donald Knuth recommended that Backus Normal Form should be renamed Backus *Naur* Form to honor the two authors of the Algol-60 report. Whatever it's called, I always thought it was a way to torture unsuspecting computer science students.

```
record <table entry> in <table name> |
get <table entry> to <register name> |
<table entry> in <table name>
```

Basically, statements are a series of conditions separated by ANDs (signified by a comma or the keyword `and`) and ORs (signified by the keyword `or`). There is very limited ability for indirection with functions. There are no loops or recursion in INSPECT. What you see is pretty much what you get with INSPECT.

Each statement is processed in order until the operation either reaches the end of the script (which means INSPECT will drop the packet) or hits a short circuit as defined earlier (`accept`, `reject`, `drop`, and `vanish`). Descriptions of these short circuits appear in Table 14.1.

The difference between `drop` and `vanish` involves how FireWall-1 handles packets received for established TCP packets (i.e., have the ACK flag set but not the SYN flag) for which FireWall-1 holds no state information. The `drop` action doesn't really "drop" the packet but mangles the packet and passes it through the firewall. All the data in the packet is removed, leaving only the IP and TCP headers. This effectively makes the packet harmless. The TCP sequence numbers of the packet are also changed. When the destination host receives the mangled packet, it should immediately respond due to the mangled sequence number. If the TCP connection is still valid, this response will be matched by the security policy and the connection will be re-recorded in the connections table. If the connection has become invalid, the host will send back a TCP RST packet. FireWall-1 notices that the host drops a reply to a mangled TCP packet and therefore does not mangle it again but rather drops it for good.

Prior to FireWall-1 4.1 SP2, you could send unsolicited ACK packets through FireWall-1 and cause a denial-of-service attack against hosts behind the firewall (the ACK DoS attack). This was because FireWall-1 used `drop` when process-

Table 14.1   Short circuits in INSPECT

Action	Description
`accept`	Accepts the packet (allows it to pass)
`reject`	Drops the packet loudly (i.e., sends a TCP RST or ICMP Unreachable message)
`drop`	Drops the packet silently
`vanish`	Drops the packet silently and leaves no trace

ing unestablished TCP packets. In FireWall-1 4.1 SP2 and later, `vanish` is used on these packets. This does not do the packet mangling that `drop` performs; it simply causes the packet to disappear without a trace. For earlier versions of FireWall-1, there is an ACK DoS fix you can apply that resolves this issue.

Consider the following statement (note that a and b are generic conditions):

```
a, b, accept;
```

This line tells FireWall-1 to accept the packet if conditions a and b are both true. You can also write the statement as:

```
accept a, b;
```

This means the same thing (accept if a and b are both true). Note that `drop`, `reject`, and `vanish` can also be used in this manner.

In both statements, if a is found to be false, b is never evaluated. This is a very important concept to understand, which also applies to `or` statements (e.g., in the statement a `or` b, if a proves to be true, b is never evaluated). In a long, complex statement, you can essentially "skip the rest" if part of the statement is false. For example, if a is false in the following statement, none of the other statements are evaluated:

```
a, b, c, d, e, f, accept;
```

You can also combine ANDs and ORs. The following statement:

```
a, b or c, d or e, f, accept;
```

is evaluated as if it were (logically, in pseudocode in C):

```
if ( a AND ( b OR c ) AND ( d OR e ) AND f ) { accept ; }
```

Note that you can force operator precedence with parentheses. You can also do something like this:

```
a, b or reject, accept;
```

This gives FireWall-1 the following instructions: If a and b are true, accept the packet (`reject` is skipped in this case). If a is false, simply go to the next statement. If a is true and b is false, reject the packet. Note that this is different than:

```
(a, b) or reject, accept;
```

which would reject the packet if either a or b were false.

Conditions

In the previous example, a single letter (e.g., a) was used to represent a generic condition. An actual condition looks more like this:

```
x = y
x != y
x > y
x < y
```

This script evaluates true if x equals y, if x does not equal y, if x is greater than y, or if x is less than y. You can also see if something is in a table (see the Manipulating Table Entries subsection):

```
<ip_src, ip_dst, sport> in http_table
```

Note that you can negate a particular statement by using not and parentheses. For example:

```
not (<ip_src, ip_dst, sport> in http_table)
```

You can also AND (&), OR (|), or XOR (^) two values together in a bitwise fashion to determine their value or use arithmetic functions (+, -, *, and /). In addition, you can bitshift values left and right with << or >>.

You can see some of the parts of a packet by looking at its predefined parts in $FWDIR/lib/tcpip.def, which includes information from IP, TCP, and UDP headers. INSPECT also defines several identifiers, which you can use as well. Table 14.2 documents some of these identifiers.

Table 14.2 Predefined identifiers

Identifier	Description
src	Source IP address
sport	Source TCP/UDP port
dst	Destination IP address
dport	Destination TCP/UDP port
ip_p	IP protocol number
tcp	True if current packet is TCP (same as ip_p = 6)
udp	True if current packet is UDP (same as ip_p = 17)
icmp	True if current packet is ICMP (same as ip_p = 1)
tod	Time of day (in 24-hour hh:mm:ss format)
date	Current system date (in dd mmm format)
day	Day of the week (using standard three-letter abbreviations)

You can also specify which parts of the packet you would like to look at in chunks of up to 4 bytes at a time. For example, if you would like to see if the 50th through 53rd bytes of the packet contain the command GET with a space character after it, you would do the comparison like this:

```
[50, b] = 0x47455420 // ASCII for "GET "
```

The ", b" portion of the line means to read the data in big-endian format and is generally needed if you want to look at TCP/IP packets more than 1 byte at a time. By default, 4 bytes are captured. If you want to look at only the 50th byte of the packet, you would use this:

```
[50:1, b] = 0x47 // ASCII for "G"
```

Constants

FireWall-1 interprets numbers in octal, hexadecimal, and decimal formats. A number beginning with a 0 is always evaluated as an octal value. Hexadecimal numbers begin with 0x. All other numbers are treated as decimals.

Time periods can be represented in hh:mm:ss format. For example, the format for 11:59 P.M. and 30 seconds is 23:59:30. Dates are represented in dd mmm format. For example, June 20 is represented as 20 Jun. Each of the standard three-letter abbreviations for days of the week (i.e., sun, mon, tue, wed, thu, fri, sat) is a constant that refers to the specific day of the week.

INSPECT also handles IP addresses entered in their dotted-quad notation (e.g., 192.168.42.69) as well as their physical interface name (e.g., eth-s1p1c0, le0, el59x1) and domain names (e.g., .phoneboy.com, .awl.com). Note the leading dot (.) on domain names.

Registers

Registers are the closest elements INSPECT has to variables. Check Point actually uses registers to modify certain internal functions, but you can use them for variables in your own code as well. They are of the format srN, where N is a number between 0 and 15. You set the value of a register as follows:

```
set sr1 15;
```

You can use the following code to accept a particular packet if the 60th byte is equal to 15:

```
accept sr1 = [60:1];
```

You can also use a register to specify an offset to a specific place in a packet. For example, you could do something like this:

```
sr1.[4:2, b]
```

which would give you bytes 19 and 20 in big-endian format (15 + 4 = 19).

Manipulating Table Entries

Tables allow FireWall-1 to remember various details about connections. Each entry in a table has the following format:

```
< KEY ; VALUE @ TIMEOUT >
```

where KEY and VALUE are one or more comma-separated items. TIMEOUT is an integer value that determines how long (in seconds) a particular entry will last in the table before expiring. For tables defined with the refresh tag (more on this in the next subsection), any read or write to a particular table entry resets this timeout. Note that only a KEY is required; the other parameters are optional. The TIMEOUT, if not specified, is taken from the default specified by the table. Consider this example:

```
<42,69;5@50>
```

The KEYs in this table are 42 and 69, the value is 5, and the entry has a timeout value of 50 seconds. If the entry is not accessed again during that time (if the table is defined with the refresh tag), the entry will expire and be removed from the table. If you want to add this entry to a table called foobar, you would use the following command:

```
record <42,69;5@50> in foobar;
```

If you want to verify whether <42,69> is in the table foobar, you would use this command:

```
<42,69> in foobar
```

which returns true if the entry is in the table, false if not. If you want to read the value stored in this table entry, you would use this command:

```
foobar [42,69]
```

You can also read the values into registers directly, which you must do if the value is a tuple. In this case, use the command get. For the following table entry in foobar:

```
<5,42,69;7,9,73>
```

use this command:

```
get <5,42,69> from foobar to sr1
```

This puts the values in successive registers (i.e., sr1 = 7, sr2 = 9, and sr3 = 73). Note that if this entry does not exist in foobar, the command returns false, and the registers maintain their previous values.

You can also simply verify that an entry exists in a table by checking to see if a particular key exists in the table. For instance:

```
<src,sport,dst,dport,ip_p> in connections
```

If the entry exists, the command returns `true`.

You can remove a particular entry from `foobar` by using the `delete` command:

```
delete <5,42,69> from foobar
```

You can also modify a particular table entry without resetting the timeout counter by using the `modify` command:

```
modify <5,42,69;5,20,71> in foobar
```

Creating Your Own Tables

Before you can start adding your own entries to tables, the tables must first be created. There are several predefined tables in `$FWDIR/lib/table.def`. Note that this technique does not define all the tables used in FireWall-1, but it does define tables that can be modified by the user's INSPECT code (such as the connections table).

There are actually two kinds of tables in FireWall-1: static and dynamic. Static tables are defined as follows:

```
name = static {} ;
```

In a static table, you can use your own name. This table, once defined, cannot be changed. A comma separates each entry in the table. For example:

```
authors = static { 10.0.0.1, 10.68.0.1, 10.31.0.1 } ;
```

If each entry in the table has more than one value, the group of entries is enclosed in angle brackets:

```
authors = static { <1, 10.0.0.1>, <2, 10.68.0.1>,
                    <3, 10.31.0.1> } ;
```

Dynamic tables are defined as follows:

```
name = dynamic {}  attributes;
```

The `name` variable represents the name of the table, `dynamic` tells FireWall-1 that this is a dynamic table, and `attributes` refers to one or more of the items listed in Table 14.3.

Table 14.3 Table attributes

Attribute	Description
`expires N`	When entries are added to the table without an explicit timeout, the entries are given a default timeout of N seconds.
`refresh`	This attribute resets the timeout value for an entry in the table when the entry is accessed.
`hashsize N`	This value should be set to a power of two roughly equal to the table size.
`keep`	All tables are flushed on a policy install except for those defined with a `keep` attribute.
`kbuf N`	The Nth argument in the value section is a pointer to an encryption key (used internally by FireWall-1 for encryption).
`implies table_name`	If an entry is removed from this table, also remove it from `table_name` if this attribute is used.
`limit N`	This attribute limits the number of entries in the table to N. The default is 25,000.
`sync`	When enabled, this attribute synchronizes the table with the State Synchronization mechanism.

 NOTE! People who have dabbled in INSPECT code in FireWall-1 4.1 and earlier should note the keyword `table` is no longer used when defining a table. Using this keyword in NG causes a compilation error.

How Your Rulebase Is Converted to INSPECT

Your security policy is stored as a `.W` file on the management console as well as inside the `rulebases_5_0.fws` file. Your rulebase file contains all of the rules you have defined in the Security Policy Editor referencing network objects. Your `objects_5_0.C` file contains the definitions for the network objects referenced in your rulebase file as well as properties that further define your rulebase (the *implicit rules*). When you load a policy, the `.W` file is put through a compiler that takes the `.W` file along with your `objects_5_0.C` file (and other files) and creates a `.pf` (packet filter) file. This `.pf` file contains INSPECT code that represents your security policy as well as some familiar-looking compiler directives: `#include` and `#define`. These directives work pretty much the same as they do in a normal C compiler.

NO.	SOURCE	DESTINATION	IF VIA	SERVICE	ACTION	TRACK
1	★ Any	broadcast-ones	★ Any	UDP dhcp-rep-localmodule UDP dhcp-req-localmodule	accept	– None
2	cablemodem	mcast-224.0.0.1	★ Any	?? igmp	accept	– None
3	All Users@Any	oscar-encdomain	RemoteAccess	★ Any	accept	Log
4	★ Any	media.altnet.com	★ Any	★ Any	reject	– None
5	net_10.0.0.0	★ Any	★ Any	★ Any	accept	– None
6	net_10.0.116.0	internal-networks	★ Any	★ Any	accept	Log
7	★ Any	oscar	★ Any	UDP L2TP	accept	Log
8	★ Any	★ Any	★ Any	★ Any	drop	Log

Figure 14.1 Sample rulebase

Each packet that enters the Stateful Inspection engine is processed according to your security policy as defined by the `.pf` file. The packet goes through, line by line, statement by statement, until it is accepted, rejected, dropped, or vanished. As an example, let's use the rulebase shown in Figure 14.1.

At the very top of the `.pf` file, you should see something like the following:

```
// INSPECT Security Policy Script Generated by
// dwelch@kermit at 16Mar2003 23:34:51
// from Rulebase pb-simple2.W by FireWall-1 NG
// Feature Pack 3 Code Generation
// Running under WindowsNT 5.0
```

This tells you who generated the INSPECT code on what platform.

The next section is denoted by the following:

```
/////////////////////////////
// Exported Rules Database //
/////////////////////////////
```

This shows you what the rulebase looks like. It looks very similar to what `rulebases_5_0.fws` would show you for this rulebase. Listed after the rulebase are some tables that get defined as a result of the rulebase and `objects_5_0.C`.

The next section is indicated by the following in the `.pf` file:

```
/////////////////////////////
// Beginning of Prologue //
/////////////////////////////
```

What follows is based on several things:

- Constants based on settings in the policy properties
- Defined services

- Various settings based on the global properties
- Definitions of any clusters and their IP addresses
- A list of services (TCP, UDP, and other) with various property definitions

Actual INSPECT code is not in this section.

The next section is denoted by the following in the .pf file:

```
///////////////////////////////////////
// Beginning of Security Policy Code //
///////////////////////////////////////
```

This section contains definitions for all of your network objects. For example:

```
ADDR_gateway(oscar, 192.168.5.2)
ADDR_host(broadcast-ones, 255.255.255.255)
ADDR_host(cablemodem, 192.168.100.1)
ADDR_host(mcast-224.0.0.1, 224.0.0.1)
ADDR_network(net_10.0.0.0, 10.0.0.0, 255.255.255.0)
ADDR_network(net_192.168.0.0, 192.168.0.0, 255.255.255.0)
ADDR_network(net_10.0.116.0, 10.0.116.0, 255.255.255.0)
ADDR_gateway(low, 3.3.3.1)
ADDR_gateway(medium, 3.3.3.2)
ADDR_gateway(high, 3.3.3.3)
ADDR_gateway(hi-med-low_profile, 3.3.3.4)
ADDR_gateway(bert, 10.0.0.41)
ADDR_gateway(ernie, 10.0.0.42)
ADDR_gateway_cluster(bernice, 10.0.0.43)
ADDR_host(kermit, 10.0.0.2)
```

The preceding list contains various network objects I had defined. After this, you will see your encryption domains, if appropriate. For example:

```
// VPN and SecuRemote encryption domain tables for gateway oscar
all@oscar sr_enc_domain = { <10.0.0.0, 10.0.0.255>,
                            <10.0.116.0, 10.0.116.255>,
                            <192.168.5.2, 192.168.5.2>,
                            <192.168.0.0, 192.168.0.255> };
all@oscar sr_enc_domain_valid = { <10.0.0.0, 10.0.0.255>,
                                  <10.0.116.0, 10.0.116.255>,
                                  <192.168.5.2, 192.168.5.2>,
                                  <192.168.0.0, 192.168.0.255> };
all@oscar vpn_enc_domain = { <10.0.0.0, 10.0.0.255>,
                             <10.0.116.0, 10.0.116.255>,
                             <192.168.5.2, 192.168.5.2>,
                             <192.168.0.0, 192.168.0.255> };
all@oscar vpn_enc_domain_valid = { <10.0.0.0, 10.0.0.255>,
                                   <10.0.116.0, 10.0.116.255>,
                                   <192.168.5.2, 192.168.5.2>,
                                   <192.168.0.0, 192.168.0.255> };
```

NO.	ORIGINAL PACKET			TRANSLATED PACKET		
	SOURCE	DESTINATION	SERVICE	SOURCE	DESTINATION	SERVICE
1	internal-networks	internal-networks	✳ Any	≡ Original	≡ Original	≡ Original
2	internal-networks	net_10.0.116.0	✳ Any	≡ Original	≡ Original	≡ Original
3	internal-networks	✳ Any	✳ Any	oscar	≡ Original	≡ Original
4	net_10.0.116.0	✳ Any	✳ Any	oscar	≡ Original	≡ Original

Figure 14.2 Sample NAT rulebase

You will also see a number of other VPN-related items, such as VPN Routing tables and interface resolving tables.

Next, you will see any NAT rules you have defined. Figure 14.2 shows the NAT rulebase I am using.

The corresponding INSPECT code looks like this:

```
// Address Translation Code
all@target_list22 xlate_rulebase = {
<0x80010001,
FWXT_SRC_STATIC_SRVSIDE, RANGE_NETWORK(net_10.0.0.0), net_10.0.0.0,  0,
FWXT_DST_STATIC_CLISIDE, RANGE_NETWORK(net_10.0.0.0), net_10.0.0.0,  0,
FWXT_EOX, FWXT_EOX, FWXT_EOX, FWXT_EOX, FWXT_EOX
>,
<0x80010002,
FWXT_SRC_STATIC_SRVSIDE, RANGE_NETWORK(net_10.0.0.0), net_10.0.0.0,  0,
FWXT_DST_STATIC_CLISIDE, RANGE_NETWORK(net_192.168.0.0),
net_192.168.0.0,  0,
FWXT_EOX, FWXT_EOX, FWXT_EOX, FWXT_EOX, FWXT_EOX
>,
<0x80010003,
FWXT_SRC_STATIC_SRVSIDE, RANGE_NETWORK(net_192.168.0.0),
net_192.168.0.0,  0,
FWXT_DST_STATIC_CLISIDE, RANGE_NETWORK(net_10.0.0.0),
net_10.0.0.0,  0,
FWXT_EOX, FWXT_EOX, FWXT_EOX, FWXT_EOX, FWXT_EOX
>,
<0x80010004,
FWXT_SRC_STATIC_SRVSIDE, RANGE_NETWORK(net_192.168.0.0),
net_192.168.0.0,  0,
FWXT_DST_STATIC_CLISIDE, RANGE_NETWORK(net_192.168.0.0),
net_192.168.0.0,  0,
FWXT_EOX, FWXT_EOX, FWXT_EOX, FWXT_EOX, FWXT_EOX
>,
<0x80020001,
```

```
FWXT_SRC_STATIC_SRVSIDE, RANGE_NETWORK(net_10.0.0.0),
net_10.0.0.0,  0,
FWXT_DST_STATIC_CLISIDE, RANGE_NETWORK(net_10.0.116.0),
net_10.0.116.0,  0,
FWXT_EOX, FWXT_EOX, FWXT_EOX, FWXT_EOX, FWXT_EOX
>,
<0x80020002,
FWXT_SRC_STATIC_SRVSIDE, RANGE_NETWORK(net_192.168.0.0),
net_192.168.0.0,  0,
FWXT_DST_STATIC_CLISIDE, RANGE_NETWORK(net_10.0.116.0),
net_10.0.116.0,  0,
FWXT_EOX, FWXT_EOX, FWXT_EOX, FWXT_EOX, FWXT_EOX
>,
<0x80030001,
FWXT_HIDE_SRVSIDE, RANGE_NETWORK(net_10.0.0.0), oscar,  0,
FWXT_EOX, FWXT_EOX, FWXT_EOX, FWXT_EOX, FWXT_EOX, FWXT_EOX, FWXT_EOX,
FWXT_EOX, FWXT_EOX, FWXT_EOX
>,
<0x80030002,
FWXT_HIDE_SRVSIDE, RANGE_NETWORK(net_192.168.0.0), oscar,  0,
FWXT_EOX, FWXT_EOX, FWXT_EOX, FWXT_EOX, FWXT_EOX, FWXT_EOX, FWXT_EOX,
FWXT_EOX, FWXT_EOX, FWXT_EOX
>,
<0x80040001,
FWXT_HIDE_SRVSIDE, RANGE_NETWORK(net_10.0.116.0), oscar,  0,
FWXT_EOX, FWXT_EOX, FWXT_EOX, FWXT_EOX, FWXT_EOX, FWXT_EOX, FWXT_EOX,
FWXT_EOX, FWXT_EOX, FWXT_EOX
>
};
```

The group internal-networks contains two networks: 10.0.0.0/24 and 192. 168.0.0/24. The NAT rule that used this group generated four "internal" rules:

1. No translation between 10.0.0.0/24 and 10.0.0.0/24 (Rule 0x80010001)
2. No translation between 10.0.0.0/24 and 192.168.0.0/24 (Rule 0x80010002)
3. No translation between 192.168.0.0/24 and 10.0.0.0/24 (Rule 0x80010003)
4. No translation between 192.168.0.0/24 and 192.168.0.0/24 (Rule 0x80010004)

A group of three objects would generate nine rules, a group of four objects would generate sixteen rules, and so on.

 WARNING! The way FireWall-1 translates NAT rules with groups can lead to a situation where performance degrades due to the number of NAT rules. When designing your rulebase, keep in mind how and where you are using groups in the rules. Use them sparingly in your NAT rulebase.

Further down the .pf file, you will see your NAT rules shown again. Note that these are for display purposes; this set of rules shows when the module is queried for its current rulebase.

Next, you will see what defines the valid addresses for your gateway. For instance:

```
// Interfaces valid addresses tables
all@oscar valid_addrs_list1 = { <0.0.0.0, 9.255.255.255>,
<10.0.1.0, 10.0.115.255>, <10.0.117.0, 126.255.255.255>,
<128.0.0.0, 192.167.255.255>, <192.168.1.0, 192.168.5.1>,
<192.168.5.3, 223.255.255.255>, <240.0.0.0, 255.255.255.254> };
all@oscar valid_addrs_list2 = { <10.0.0.2, 10.0.0.254>,
<192.168.0.0, 192.168.0.255> };
all@oscar valid_addrs_list3 = { <10.0.116.1, 10.0.116.254> };
```

In many of the tables given in the preceding examples, you will see things listed as a range. For example, valid_addrs_list1 shows:

```
<10.0.117.0, 126.255.255.255>
```

This includes all IP addresses from 10.0.117.0 through 126.255.255.255, including the endpoints.

Next are your address translation rules. The format should look very similar to the rules shown in the Security Policy Editor.

The next interesting section is denoted by the following in the .pf file:

```
// User defined init code and global init code
```

In this section, various parts of FireWall-1's lib directory are included as well as your user-defined file, user.def. A call to include the file code.def is listed below this line. The main purpose of this file is to accept established connections and make sure the IPs that are trying to access the system are not blocked by Suspicious Activity Monitoring (SAM). This section would also include any anti-spoofing checking defined in the firewall's network object.

You then have the following section:

```
// Rule-Base And Before-Last Properties Code
```

In this section, you start getting into the real security policy. For the rulebase shown in Figure 14.1, the first rule is represented by the following INSPECT code:

```
all@oscar
 accept      eitherbound, start_rule_code(1),
             (udp, dhcp-rep-localmodule or dhcp-req-localmodule),
             (ip_dst in ip_list12),
             RECORD_CONN(1), ALLOW_TEMPLATE_ACCELERATION;
```

This code is translated into English line-by-line as follows.

> If the packet is being inspected inbound from any interface on oscar,
>
> Accept the packet if all of the following conditions are true:
>> The packet is eitherbound, which means it will be inspected both entering and leaving the gateway.
>>
>> start_rule_code is true (this always returns true).
>>
>> The service is UDP.
>>
>> One of the INSPECT functions dhcp-rep-localmodule or dhcp-req-localmodule returns true.
>>
>> The destination IP is in ip_list12, which is a list that contains 255.255.255.255.
>>
>> The connection is recorded under Rule 1 (this always returns true).
>>
>> The packet is allowed to be accelerated by SecureXL or Flows as necessary.

If you want to put a rule in that generates a log entry, you might use the following rule:

```
all@oscar
 accept    eitherbound, start_rule_code(7),
     (udp, l2tp),
     (ip_dst in ip_list19),
     RECORD_CONN(7),
     LOG(long, LOG_NOALERT, 7), ALLOW_TEMPLATE_ACCELERATION;
```

A translation of the preceding code into English follows.

> If the packet is being inspected inbound from any interface on oscar,
>
> Accept the packet if all of the following conditions are true:
>> The packet is eitherbound, which means the packet will be inspected both entering and leaving the gateway.
>>
>> start_rule_code is true (this always returns true).
>>
>> The service is UDP.
>>
>> The service is L2TP.
>>
>> The destination IP is in ip_list19, which in this case is a list of IPs for the firewall.

The connection is recorded under Rule 7 (this always returns `true`).

The packet is allowed to be accelerated by SecureXL or Flows as necessary.

Note that in either of these examples, if one of the statements after `accept` returns `false`, the rest of the statement is not evaluated. So, for example, if the packet were of type TCP, both of these rules would be bypassed before the destination port was evaluated.

Services of Type Other

A service of type Other contains two parts that must be defined: the protocol number and the Match field. The protocol number depends on the protocol in question. For example, TCP is always 6, ICMP is 1, and UDP is protocol 17. The Match field should contain INSPECT code that matches the service. For example, if you want the code to match HTTP, the protocol number would be 6, and the Match field would contain `dport=80`. You could also reference your own INSPECT code in this field.

Sample INSPECT Code

Now that I have talked about how INSPECT works and how your rulebase translates to INSPECT code, I can show you some sample INSPECT code.

 WARNING!   Exercise appropriate caution before implementing any of this code in a production network. This includes testing in a nonproduction environment to ensure the code does what you expect.

Check Point allows you to place custom INSPECT scripts in `$FWDIR/lib/user.def`. Check Point does not overwrite this file during an upgrade; therefore, it is the recommended location for any custom INSPECT code. All INSPECT changes should be done on the management console. A policy reinstall is required after any of these types of changes in order for them to take effect.

Allowing Outbound Connections to SecuRemote Clients

Allowing outbound connections to SecuRemote clients was mentioned in Chapter 12, but it is worth bringing up again simply because it can be used as an example of INSPECT code. Recall that the quandary was how to allow a connection on port TCP 5555 to a particular machine only if it were an authenticated SecuRemote client. Whenever a SecuRemote client successfully authenticates to FireWall-1, an entry is created in the table `userc_rules: <ip, 0>`. This is so FireWall-1 knows to encrypt all traffic to this IP address. You can also use this table entry as a basis for allowing a service. Create a service of type Other. The protocol number will be 6 (for TCP). The following will be in the Match field:

```
dport=5555,<dst,0> in userc_rules
```

This service will accept the packet if it is of type TCP. Its destination port (service) is 5555, and the entry `<dst,0>` appears in the table `userc_rules`. As you will recall from Table 14.2, `dst` means the destination IP address of the current packet.

Point-to-Point Tunneling Protocol

Another example of INSPECT code is useful for the service Point-to-Point Tunneling Protocol (PPTP), which is defined in RFC2637, only because it uses a variation of the GRE protocol. Normally, to allow GRE through FireWall-1, you need to create two services:

1. TCP port 1723 for a control session
2. A variation of the GRE protocol (IP protocol 47) for data

Create the latter service as a service of type Other. Use 47 for the protocol number. For the Match field, enter:

```
[22:2,b] = 0x880B
```

This code indicates that you are using PPTP embedded in GRE (you look at the 22nd and 23rd bytes together to see if they equal 880B).

> **NOTE!** PPTP is not supported with hide NAT, only static NAT. This is due to the fact that the transport mechanism used does not lend itself to many-to-one IP address translations.

Allowing a Connection Based on a Previous Connection

There is a particular application available that uses UDP destination port 3000 for both packets originating from the client as well as replies coming from the server. If the application were normal, the client would send packets to the server on UDP port 3000, but the reply packets coming from the server would have a UDP source port of 3000. FireWall-1 doesn't normally handle services that communicate in this manner. In order to allow this service, you need to generate custom INSPECT code.

Because you need to write code to catch certain types of reply packets, you need to add some code to `$FWDIR/lib/user.def`. You want to accept the packet if and only if the first packet is accepted. You can create an entry in a table for that specific kind of packet and look for entries in that table later.

First, create a service of type Other. Since this is UDP, the protocol number will be 17. You do not need to check Accept Replies because you are going to do that in your own code. In the Match field for this service of type Other, you need the following:

```
dport=3000, record <src,0,dst,3000,ip_p> in accepted_udp
```

Now you need some code to catch the reply packets. In `$FWDIR/lib/user.def`, add the following lines between the `#ifdef` and the `#endif` in the file:

```
all@oscar
    accept udp, dport=3000, <dst,src,dport,ip_p> in accepted_udp;
```

Finally, you need to create the table `accepted_udp`. It cannot be done in `user.def` because the actual service appears in the INSPECT script before the `user.def` file is referenced. In FireWall-1 4.1 and earlier, services of type Other had a mechanism called Prologue, which allowed you to define tables and such prior to the service definition. Unfortunately, this means modifying a file that will get changed on an upgrade. `$FWDIR/lib/table.def` seems the most appropriate choice for this purpose. Here is the code to add to that file, prior to the ending `#endif`:

```
accepted_udp = table {} sync keep;
```

Now you can use this new rule in a rulebase and install the security policy.

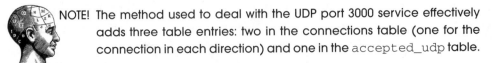 NOTE! The method used to deal with the UDP port 3000 service effectively adds three table entries: two in the connections table (one for the connection in each direction) and one in the `accepted_udp` table.

Different Rules for Different Interfaces

SmartDashboard/Policy Editor does not allow different rules for different interfaces, but INSPECT does. You could take an existing `.pf` file and simply change the rules to apply only to a specific interface. The following example was used previously. The only change made below is that `all@oscar` becomes `eth-s2p1c0@oscar`. This means that the rule applies only on interface eth-s2p1c0.

```
eth-s2p1c0@oscar
  accept     eitherbound, start_rule_code(7),
      (udp, l2tp),
      (ip_dst in ip_list19),
```

```
RECORD_CONN(7),
LOG(long, LOG_NOALERT, 7), ALLOW_TEMPLATE_ACCELERATION
```

NOTE! FireWall-1 Virtual System Extension (VSX) implements something similar to this within the VSX version of SmartDashboard/Policy Editor. Each virtual system is made up of specific interfaces. Internally, FireWall-1 compiles these rules in terms of the specific interfaces that make up that virtual system. Thus, a single copy of FireWall-1 can effectively serve multiple virtual systems concurrently.

Changing Your Default Filter

The default filter is the security policy that loads when FireWall-1 starts up before it attempts to load a policy from the management console. If FireWall-1 fails to load a policy, the default filter remains active until a new policy is manually loaded. FireWall-1 comes with several such policies:

- `defaultfilter.boot`, installed by default, allows all outgoing as well as incoming communications on ports that had previous outgoing communications. ICMP and broadcast packets are also allowed.
- `defaultfilter.drop` drops all communication into the gateway except for established connections.
- `defaultfilter.ipso` allows SSH (port 22) and HTTPS (port 443) to the gateway, dropping everything else.
- `defaultfilter.ipso_ssh` allows SSH to the gateway, dropping everything else.
- `defaultfilter.ipso_ssl` allows HTTPS to the gateway, dropping everything else.

FireWall-1 4.1 and earlier gave you the ability to switch default filters in **fwconfig** or **cpconfig**. You can switch to a particular default filter manually by executing the following commands (in the following example, `defaultfilter.ipso` is used):

```
# rm $FWDIR/state/default.bin
# cp $FWDIR/lib/defaultfilter.ipso $FWDIR/conf/defaultfilter.pf
# fw defaultgen
# cp $FWDIR/state/default.bin $FWDIR/conf/default.bin
```

On a Windows platform, the commands below are used:

```
C:> del %FWDIR%\state\default.bin
C:> copy %FWDIR%\lib\defaultfilter.ipso %FWDIR%\conf\
        defaultfilter.pf
```

```
C:> fw defaultgen
C:> copy %FWDIR%\state\default.bin %FWDIR%\conf\default.bin
```

> **NOTE!** Users of Nokia Horizon Manager will have the default filter changed to `defaultfilter.ipso` during the initial install/upgrade of a Nokia platform. This allows Nokia Horizon Manager to manage the platform despite FireWall-1 not being fully configured.

The next obvious question might be, "Can I write my own default filter?" Certainly, if you know how to write INSPECT code. The following caveats apply: The INSPECT script in question must not include any of the default `.def` files from `$FWDIR/lib`. You must define everything you need to use as part of the script. When you are ready to compile the script, it needs to be placed in `$FWDIR/conf/defaultfilter.pf`, which is where **fw defaultgen** expects to find the script.

Keep in mind that this policy is a fail-safe policy, not a policy that will generally be used. IP Forwarding will typically be disabled, so the firewall will not be able to forward packets unless you tell FireWall-1 to not control IP Forwarding (which is not recommended). As a result, this policy is relevant only to packets originating from or going to the firewall.

Appendix F provides a sample default filter policy that accepts packets coming to port 22 (SSH) or port 256 (FireWall-1 management protocol), which permits you to load a policy to the firewall or SSH to the firewall for further management. Remember that IP Forwarding should be disabled on the platform, so even if a packet destined for another host is permitted by this policy, it will not be forwarded past the firewall.

fw monitor

fw monitor is similar to a packet sniffer and is built into FireWall-1. Secure Client NG FP3 also includes this functionality as **srfw monitor**. It shows you how packets are entering and exiting the FireWall-1 kernel module. Because FireWall-1 resides just above the MAC layer, **fw monitor** cannot be used to see layer 2 traffic, but it can still be useful as a packet sniffer for layer 3 and above, and it can also be used to monitor multiple interfaces simultaneously.

> **NOTE!** On IPSO 3.3 and later, when Flows is enabled in the IPSO kernel (it is by default), **fw monitor** shows only the initial packet exchange for TCP and UDP. This is because the IPSO kernel handles the inspection and forwarding of packets that have been flowed directly in the kernel, which increases performance and throughput. FireWall-1 never sees the flowed packets.

This command is documented in this chapter instead of Chapter 10 on NAT, where it might also be appropriate, because INSPECT is necessary to make use of **fw monitor**. Usage for this command is as follows:

```
fw monitor [-d] [-D] -e inspect-filter -f filter-file
           [-l len] [-m mask] [-x offset[,len]] [-o file]
```

There are four inspection points as packets pass through FireWall-1. You choose where you want to see packets with the -m option:

- Before FireWall-1 processes the packet in the inbound direction (i or PREIN)
- After FireWall-1 processes the packet in the inbound direction (I or POSTIN)
- Before FireWall-1 processes the packet in the outbound direction (o or PREOUT)
- After FireWall-1 processes the packet in the outbound direction (O or POSTOUT)

Because there can be lots of packets, you need some way to determine which packets you are interested in seeing. You do this by means of an INSPECT filter, which can be typed in directly on the command line or provided via an INSPECT filter file. One of the options -f or -e is required; these are described in Table 14.4.

Table 14.4   Command-line options for fw monitor

Flag	Description
-d	Turns on debugging
-D	Turns on debugging
-e script	Specifies an INSPECT script via the command line
-f filename	Specifies an INSPECT script contained in filename
-l numbytes	Specifies the number of bytes to capture in each packet
-m mask	Specifies inspection points mask (any one or more of i, I, o, or O as explained in the text)
-o outfile	Specifies an output file in Solaris **snoop** format
-x offset,len	Performs a hex dump of received data, starting at specified offset, showing len bytes

Once you execute this command, FireWall-1 compiles the specified INSPECT script (either on the command line or in a file), loads it into the kernel module, and displays the packets in the terminal window or prints them to an output file, which is a Solaris **snoop** format. FireWall-1 continues to do this until an interrupt signal is sent to the program (Ctrl-C) or another security policy is loaded, after which it will unload the filter and exit.

The INSPECT script should return an `accept` in order for packets to be displayed. Any other return code causes packets to not be displayed. If you want to catch packets only on a certain interface, do not use `le0@all` (for example), but instead use `direction=x, ifid=y` (where x is 0 for inbound and 1 for outbound, and y is an interface number returned by the **fw ctl iflist** command). Do not use table names that are used by the security policy.

Table 14.4 lists the command-line options for **fw monitor**.

Examples

The following code line displays all TCP packets entering and leaving FireWall-1.

```
fw monitor -e '[9:1]=6, accept;' -l 100 -m iO -x 20
```

Although 100 bytes of data are captured for each packet, up to 80 bytes of TCP header and data will be displayed starting at offset 20 (assuming no IP options are used).

The following code line displays all packets entering and exiting FireWall-1 in the inbound direction (i.e., before the operating system routes the packet).

```
fw monitor -e 'accept;' -m iI
```

The following code line displays all packets entering interface ID 0 that are coming from or going to 10.0.0.1. The value used for `ifid` corresponds to a number given to an interface by FireWall-1. You can determine which interface has which number by using the command **fw ctl iflist**.

```
fw monitor -e 'accept ifid=0,src=10.0.0.1 or dst=10.0.0.1;'
```

The following code line does the same thing as the previous command except that it looks for packets of IP protocol 47 only.

```
fw monitor -e 'accept ifid=0,src=10.0.0.1 or dst=10.0.0.1,ip_p=47;'
```

The following code line displays all TCP packets going to or coming from 10.0.0.1 with either a source port of 80 or a destination port of 80.

```
fw monitor -e 'accept tcp,dport=80 or sport=80,src=10.0.0.1
              or dst=10.0.0.1;'
```

Warnings

Here are some important notes about using **fw monitor**.

- Do not alter tables used in the security policy; unexpected behavior (including a system crash) may result if you do.
- Packets are defragmented as the packets leave FireWall-1 in both the inbound and outbound directions.
- Anything that causes a fetch, load, or unload of your security policy will cause **fw monitor** to terminate.
- All INSPECT code used in **srfw monitor** (for Secure Client) should be in RAW format, which means no macros from `tcpip.def` or other places. If you don't feel like figuring this out yourself, try using Joost De Cock's ginspect tool, available at http://www.bdc-networks.be/joost/ginspect.php.

Summary

This chapter presented an overview of the INSPECT language in a format very different than Check Point's documentation. Several working and documented examples of INSPECT code were provided so you could see for yourself how it works. INSPECT is a very powerful language designed to give you maximum control over your security policy. It is a pity that Check Point does not make more information about this language available to customers.

Appendix

Securing Your Bastion Host

The following sections assume the host in question either is not connected to a network or is connected to an isolated network; this is the best way to make sure no one compromises your system before you have had a chance to secure it. This appendix covers Solaris 2.8, Windows NT 4.0, Windows 2000, and Linux.

Securing Solaris

Installing only the Core packages in Solaris is recommended because minimizing the amount of software on the system minimizes the potential security holes. If you require a GUI on your Solaris platform, need additional functionality, or are new to Solaris, you might consider the End User installation, though it adds over 100 additional packages—exposing your system to far greater risk. I strongly discourage you from using anything but Core.

Partitioning Your Drive

During the initial installation, you will be asked to partition the hard drive. Here's a recommended approach:

- `/` (root filesystem): everything else not listed below
- `swap`: the greater of 256 or double the amount of RAM
- `/var`: 400MB
- `/var/opt/CPfw1-50`: 15GB or a different drive entirely
- `/usr`: 500MB (optional, if you want a separate read-only partition)

The `/var/opt/CPfw1-50` partition is where FireWall-1 log files are typically stored. Thus you should put this on a separate partition or on a rather large partition on the disk.

Patching Your Installation

Once the system has rebooted after the installation, be sure to install the Recommended Patch Cluster from Sun. Also, FireWall-1 NG requires two additional patches that are not part of the cluster, specifically 108434-02 and 108435-02. You can download patches from http://sunsolve.sun.com.

Minimal Packages for SPARC Solaris 2.8

A core installation on Solaris 2.8 installs the following packages.

```
system   SUNWadmr     System & Network Administration Root
system   SUNWatfsr    AutoFS, (Root)
system   SUNWatfsu    AutoFS, (Usr)
system   SUNWauda     Audio Applications
system   SUNWaudd     Audio Drivers
system   SUNWauddx    Audio Drivers (64-bit)
system   SUNWcar      Core Architecture, (Root)
system   SUNWcarx     Core Architecture, (Root) (64-bit)
system   SUNWcg6      GX (cg6) Device Driver
system   SUNWcg6x     GX (cg6) Device Driver (64-bit)
system   SUNWcsd      Core Solaris Devices
system   SUNWcsl      Core Solaris, (Shared Libs)
system   SUNWcslx     Core Solaris Libraries (64-bit)
system   SUNWcsr      Core Solaris, (Root)
system   SUNWcsu      Core Solaris, (Usr)
system   SUNWcsxu     Core Solaris (Usr) (64-bit)
system   SUNWdfb      Dumb Frame Buffer Device Drivers
system   SUNWdtcor    Solaris Desktop /usr/dt filesystem anchor
system   SUNWeridx    Sun RIO 10/100 Mb Ethernet Drivers (64-bit)
system   SUNWesu      Extended System Utilities
system   SUNWfcip     Sun FCIP IP/ARP over FibreChannel Device
                      Driver
system   SUNWfcipx    Sun FCIP IP/ARP over FibreChannel Dev Drvr
                      (64-bit)
system   SUNWfcp      Sun FCP SCSI Device Driver
system   SUNWfcpx     Sun FCP SCSI Device Driver (64-bit)
system   SUNWfctl     Sun Fibre Channel Transport layer
system   SUNWfctlx    Sun Fibre Channel Transport layer (64-bit)
system   SUNWftpr     FTP Server, (Root)
system   SUNWftpu     FTP Server, (Usr)
system   SUNWged      Sun Gigabit Ethernet Adapter Driver
system   SUNWhmd      SunSwift SBus Adapter Drivers
system   SUNWhmdx     SunSwift SBus Adapter Drivers (64-bit)
system   SUNWi15cs    X11 ISO8859-15 Codeset Support
system   SUNWi1cs     X11 ISO8859-1 Codeset Support
system   SUNWkey      Keyboard configuration tables
system   SUNWkvm      Core Architecture, (Kvm)
system   SUNWkvmx     Core Architecture (Kvm) (64-bit)
```

```
system    SUNWlibms    Sun WorkShop Bundled shared libm
system    SUNWlmsx     Sun WorkShop Bundled 64-bit shared libm
system    SUNWloc      System Localization
system    SUNWlocx     System Localization (64-bit)
system    SUNWluxdx    Sun Enterprise Network Array sf Device Drvr
                       (64-bit)
system    SUNWluxop    Sun Enterprise Network Array firmware and
                       utilities
system    SUNWluxox    Sun Enterprise Network Array libraries
                       (64-bit)
system    SUNWm64      M64 Graphics System Software/Device Driver
system    SUNWm64x     M64 Graphics System Software/Device Driver
                       (64-bit)
system    SUNWmdi      Sun Multipath I/O Drivers
system    SUNWmdix     Sun Multipath I/O Drivers (64-bit)
system    SUNWnamos    Northern America OS Support
system    SUNWnamow    Northern America OW Support
system    SUNWnisr     Network Information System, (Root)
system    SUNWnisu     Network Information System, (Usr)
system    SUNWpcelx    3COM EtherLink III PCMCIA Ethernet Driver
system    SUNWpcmci    PCMCIA Card Services, (Root)
system    SUNWpcmcu    PCMCIA Card Services, (Usr)
system    SUNWpcmcx    PCMCIA Card Services (64-bit)
system    SUNWpcmem    PCMCIA memory card driver
system    SUNWpcser    PCMCIA serial card driver
system    SUNWpd       PCI Drivers
system    SUNWpdx      PCI Drivers (64-bit)
system    SUNWpl5u     Perl 5.005_03
system    SUNWpsdpr    PCMCIA ATA card driver
system    SUNWqfed     Sun Quad FastEthernet Adapter Driver
system    SUNWqfedx    Sun Quad FastEthernet Adapter Driver (64-bit)
system    SUNWrmodu    Realmode Modules, (Usr)
system    SUNWses      SCSI Enclosure Services Device Driver
system    SUNWsesx     SCSI Enclosure Services Device Driver (64-bit)
system    SUNWsndmr    Sendmail root
system    SUNWsndmu    Sendmail user
system    SUNWsolnm    Solaris Naming Enabler
system    SUNWssad     SPARCstorage Array Drivers
system    SUNWssadx    SPARCstorage Array Drivers (64-bit)
system    SUNWswmt     Install and Patch Utilities
system    SUNWtleux    Thai Language Environment user files (64-bit)
system    SUNWudf      Universal Disk Format 1.50, (Usr)
system    SUNWudfr     Universal Disk Format 1.50
system    SUNWudfrx    Universal Disk Format 1.50 (64-bit)
system    SUNWusb      USB Device Drivers
system    SUNWusbx     USB Device Drivers (64-bit)
system    SUNWwsr2     Solaris Product Registry & Web Start runtime
                       support
```

```
system   SUNWxwdv    X Windows System Window Drivers
system   SUNWxwdvx   X Windows System Window Drivers (64-bit)
system   SUNWxwmod   OpenWindows kernel modules
system   SUNWxwmox   X Window System kernel modules (64-bit)
```

Of these 83 packages, the following 58 are not needed for FireWall-1 and can be removed using the command **pkgrm**. Don't worry about errors on dependencies because you are also removing the dependencies. Note that on Sun Blade 100 and Sun Blade 1000 platforms, you should not remove the two USB-related devices.

```
system   SUNWadmr    System & Network Administration Root
system   SUNWatfsr   AutoFS, (Root)
system   SUNWatfsu   AutoFS, (Usr)
system   SUNWauda    Audio Applications
system   SUNWaudd    Audio Drivers
system   SUNWauddx   Audio Drivers (64-bit)
system   SUNWcg6     GX (cg6) Device Driver
system   SUNWcg6x    GX (cg6) Device Driver (64-bit)
system   SUNWdfb     Dumb Frame Buffer Device Drivers
system   SUNWdtcor   Solaris Desktop /usr/dt filesystem anchor
system   SUNWfcip    Sun FCIP IP/ARP over FibreChannel Device
                     Driver
system   SUNWfcipx   Sun FCIP IP/ARP over FibreChannel Dev Drvr
                     (64-bit)
system   SUNWfcp     Sun FCP SCSI Device Driver
system   SUNWfcpx    Sun FCP SCSI Device Driver (64-bit)
system   SUNWfctl    Sun Fibre Channel Transport layer
system   SUNWfctlx   Sun Fibre Channel Transport layer (64-bit)
system   SUNWftpr    FTP Server, (Root)
system   SUNWftpu    FTP Server, (Usr)
system   SUNWi15cs   X11 ISO8859-15 Codeset Support
system   SUNWi1cs    X11 ISO8859-1 Codeset Support
system   SUNWkey     Keyboard configuration tables
system   SUNWluxdx   Sun Enterprise Network Array sf Device Drvr
                     (64-bit)
system   SUNWluxop   Sun Enterprise Network Array firmware and
                     utilities
system   SUNWluxox   Sun Enterprise Network Array libraries
                     (64-bit)
system   SUNWm64     M64 Graphics System Software/Device Driver
system   SUNWm64x    M64 Graphics System Software/Device Driver
                     (64-bit)
system   SUNWmdi     Sun Multipath I/O Drivers
system   SUNWmdix    Sun Multipath I/O Drivers (64-bit)
system   SUNWnamos   Northern America OS Support
system   SUNWnisr    Network Information System, (Root)
system   SUNWnisu    Network Information System, (Usr)
```

```
system    SUNWpcelx    3COM EtherLink III PCMCIA Ethernet Driver
system    SUNWpcmci    PCMCIA Card Services, (Root)
system    SUNWpcmcu    PCMCIA Card Services, (Usr)
system    SUNWpcmcx    PCMCIA Card Services (64-bit)
system    SUNWpcmem    PCMCIA memory card driver
system    SUNWpcser    PCMCIA serial card driver
system    SUNWpl5u     Perl 5.005_03
system    SUNWpsdpr    PCMCIA ATA card driver
system    SUNWrmodu    Realmode Modules, (Usr)
system    SUNWses      SCSI Enclosure Services Device Driver
system    SUNWsesx     SCSI Enclosure Services Device Driver (64-bit)
system    SUNWsndmr    Sendmail root
system    SUNWsndmu    Sendmail user
system    SUNWsolnm    Solaris Naming Enabler
system    SUNWssad     SPARCstorage Array Drivers
system    SUNWssadx    SPARCstorage Array Drivers (64-bit)
system    SUNWtleux    Thai Language Environment user files (64-bit)
system    SUNWudf      Universal Disk Format 1.50, (Usr)
system    SUNWudfr     Universal Disk Format 1.50
system    SUNWudfrx    Universal Disk Format 1.50 (64-bit)
system    SUNWusb      USB Device Drivers
system    SUNWusbx     USB Device Drivers (64-bit)
system    SUNWwsr2     Solaris Product Registry & Web Start runtime
                       support
system    SUNWxwdv     X Windows System Window Drivers
system    SUNWxwdvx    X Windows System Window Drivers (64-bit)
system    SUNWxwmod    OpenWindows kernel modules
system    SUNWxwmox    X Window System kernel modules (64-bit)
```

FireWall-1 NG needs the following 5 packages if you install a Core installation. You may have others you want or need to add based on your requirements. At a minimum, add these 5 packages.

```
system    SUNWlibC     Sun Workshop Compilers Bundled libC
system    SUNWlibCx    Sun WorkShop Bundled 64-bit libC
system    SUNWter      Terminal Information
system    SUNWadmc     System administration core libraries
system    SUNWadmfw    System & Network Administration Framework
```

The following are some optional packages you can install if desired. Keep in mind that extra software may introduce extra vulnerabilities that can be exploited.

```
system    SUNWbash     GNU Bourne-Again shell (bash)
system    SUNWbzip     The bzip compression utility
system    SUNWbzipx    The bzip compression library (64-bit)
system    SUNWgzip     The GNU Zip (gzip) compression utility
system    SUNWzip      The Info-Zip (zip) compression utility
system    SUNWdoc      Documentation Tools
```

```
system   SUNWman     On-Line Manual Pages
system   SUNWadmc    System administration core libraries
system   SUNWadmfw   System & Network Administration Framework
system   SUNWntpu    NTP, (Usr)
system   SUNWntpr    NTP, (Root)

# Truss and other troubleshooting tools
system   SUNWtoo     Programming Tools
system   SUNWtoox    Programming Tools (64-bit)

# Snoop sniffing utility (Snort is an optional sniffing utility
# included with the Sun Companion CDROM.)
system   SUNWfns     Federated Naming System
system   SUNWfnsx    Federated Naming System (64-bit)

# To support Secure Shell X Tunneling
system   SUNWxcu4    XCU4 Utilities
system   SUNWxcu4x   XCU4 Utilities (64-bit)
system   SUNWxwplt   X Window System platform software
system   SUNWxwplx   X Window System library software (64-bit)
system   SUNWxwrtl   X Window System & Graphics Runtime Library
Links
system   SUNWxwrtx   X Window System Runtime Compat. Package
                     (64-bit)

# To support compiling (not recommended)
system   SUNWsprot   Solaris Bundled tools
system   SUNWhea     SunOS Header Files
system   SUNWtoo     Programming Tools
system   SUNWtoox    Programming Tools (64-bit)
system   SUNWarc     Archive Libraries
system   SUNWarcx    Archive Libraries (64-bit)
system   SUNWbtool   CCS tools bundled with SunOS
system   SFWaconf    autoconf - GNU autoconf
system   SFWamake    automake - GNU automake
system   SFWgcc      gcc - GNU Compiler Collection
```

Removing Unnecessary Services

Many unnecessary services originate from `inetd`, which is configured with the file `/etc/inetd.conf`. You should comment out (i.e., add a comment character, #, at the beginning of the line) every service in this file except for the two lines for Telnet and FTP. If you install SSH on your firewall, you can probably eliminate these two as well.

Next, look at `/etc/rc2.d` and `/etc/rc3.d`, which also contain many unneeded services. Table A.1 lists the services that can be disabled. You can simply disable these services by renaming the file from `S<whatever>` to `s<whatever>`.

Table A.1 Startup files you can disable in Solaris

Startup File	Description
/etc/rc2.d/S73nfs.client	Used for NFS mounting a system.
/etc/rc2.d/S74autofs	Used for automounting.
/etc/rc2.d/S80lp	Used for printing.
/etc/rc2.d/S88sendmail	Used for listening for incoming mail. You can still send mail without running this.
/etc/rc2.d/S71rpc	Used for RPC Portmapper, which is highly insecure but required if CDE is running.
/etc/rc2.d/S99dtlogin	Used to start CDE.
/etc/rc3.d/S15nfs.server	Used if you want to be an NFS server.
/etc/rc3.d/S76snmpdx	SNMP daemon, not usually necessary.

This keeps the file in the directory in case you want to run it in the future but prevents Solaris from starting the file.

Logging and Tweaking

Once you have eliminated as many services as possible, you should enable some logging. Most system logging occurs in /var/adm. You should add two additional log files to that directory: sulog and loginlog. The file /var/adm/sulog logs all **su** attempts, both successful and failed. This allows you to monitor anyone who attempts to gain root access on your system. The file /var/adm/loginlog logs consecutive failed login attempts. When a user attempts to log in five times, and all five attempts fail, it is logged. To enable this, use the following commands:

```
# touch /var/adm/loginlog /var/adm/sulog
# chmod 640 /var/adm/loginlog /var/adm/sulog
```

Tweaking involves some file administration. You first want to create the file /etc/issue. This file is an ASCII text banner that appears for all Telnet logins. You also want to create the file /etc/ftpusers. This file simply contains names of accounts that cannot FTP to the system. It is meant to restrict root and other common system accounts from using FTP.

Ensure that root cannot Telnet to the system. This forces users to log in to the system as themselves and then **su** to root. This is a system default, but always confirm this in the file `/etc/default/login`, where `console` is left uncommented.

In addition, eliminate the Telnet OS banner, and create a separate banner for FTP. (It is usually not wise to advertise the operating system.) For Telnet, you can do this by creating the file `/etc/default/telnetd` and adding the statement:

```
BANNER=""    # Eliminates the "SunOS 5.x" banner for Telnet
```

For FTP, you can do this by creating the file `/etc/default/ftpd` and adding the statement:

```
BANNER="WARNING: Authorized use only"    # Warning banner for ftp
```

To protect the operating system itself when FireWall-1 is not running, it is recommended that you install and use TCP Wrappers. TCP Wrappers, although they do not encrypt, do log and control who can access your system. It is a binary that wraps itself around `inetd` services, such as Telnet or FTP. With TCP Wrappers, the system launches the wrapper for `inetd` connections, logs all attempts, and then verifies the attempt against an access control list. If the connection is permitted, TCP Wrappers hands the connection to the proper binary, such as Telnet. If the connection is rejected by the access control list, the connection is dropped. For more information on TCP Wrappers, visit ftp://ftp.porcupine.org/pub/security/index.html.

Securing Windows NT

Windows NT, by default, runs many services that are potential security risks. The following subsections contain some tips for setting up your Windows NT box to make it more secure. Note that the system should be physically disconnected from your network until you have made all of these changes. This minimizes the possibility that your firewall system will be compromised before you even get started.

You might wonder why I am bothering to include this despite the fact that Microsoft will no longer support Windows NT after the end of 2003. The fact is that Windows NT is well understood by many organizations and will likely still be in use long after Microsoft stops supporting it. Almost all security issues that may be present in Windows NT can be mitigated by proper configuration of the platform.

Network Protocols

When setting up Windows NT for FireWall-1, only TCP/IP is needed. Use a static IP address.

Machine Name and Domain

Choose a machine name (firewall seems like a good choice, though do not choose fw, fw-1, firewall-1, or similar), and choose a domain/workgroup that is unreachable. Disable Microsoft Networking services as well.

Services

By default, Windows NT installs the following services:

- Computer Browser
- NetBIOS Interface
- RPC Configuration
- Server
- Workstation

None of these services are needed by FireWall-1. Remove NetBIOS, RPC, and Server. The others will be disabled subsequently. You also need to install the SNMP service at this time (FireWall-1 uses this service). Install SNMP before installing FireWall-1 or any service packs.

You may wonder why Workstation remains. The AT utility requires the Workstation service, which is useful. Computer Browser remains because Workstation has a dependency on it. It will be disabled.

IP Routing

In the Network Control Panel applet, click Protocols, and then double-click TCP/IP. Make sure that IP Routing is enabled in the TCP/IP Properties under the Routing tab. Also ensure that only your external interface has a default route defined (the other interfaces should not).

WINS TCP/IP

In the Network Control Panel applet, click Bindings. From the pull-down menu next to Show Bindings For, select All Protocols. Select WINS TCP/IP, and click Disable.

WINS Client

If you are installing Windows NT from scratch, you will not be able to disable WINS Client on install. After a reboot, you will experience a hang of up to two minutes. This is perfectly normal and should not occur after disabling the WINS Client.

Go to Devices in Control Panel; scroll down, and find WINS Client (TCP/IP). Click Startup, and change it to Manual.

Services to Disable after Installation

Go to Services in Control Panel. For each of the following services, select the service, click Startup, and change it to Manual. When you reboot, these services will be disabled:

- Computer Browser
- TCP/IP NetBIOS Helper
- Net Logon
- Workstation
- Server (if present)
- Network DDE
- Network DDE NSDM
- Messenger

Local Hosts File

Although not necessarily a security recommendation, it is highly advisable that you make sure that your hostname is resolvable to an IP address. In fact, FireWall-1 4.1 and above automatically add an appropriate entry. Go to the local host file (`%SystemRoot%\System32\drivers\etc\hosts`), and make sure your firewall's hostname has an entry in the hosts file (it probably won't). Make it resolve to your external IP address.

Registry Hacks

Some registry hacks help protect against people physically coming up to the machine and logging on to it.

- To disable the display of the last userid in the logon window:
  Set `DontDisplayLastUsername` to 1
  `HKEY_LOCAL_MACHINE\SOFTWARE\Microsoft\Windows NT\`
  `Current Version\Winlogon` (REG_SZ)

- To display a warning message when logging on to the server:
  Set `LegalNoticeCaption` to Notice
  `HKEY_LOCAL_MACHINE\SOFTWARE\Microsoft\Windows NT\`
  `Current Version\Winlogon (REG_SZ)`
  Set `LegalNoticeText` to Authorized Users Only
  `HKEY_LOCAL_MACHINE\SOFTWARE\Microsoft\Windows NT\`
  `Current Version\Wilogon` (REG_SZ)

- To disable caching of logon credentials:

  Set `CachedLogonsCount` to 0

  `HKEY_LOCAL_MACHINE\SOFTWARE\Microsoft\Windows NT\`
  `Current Version\Winlogon` (REG_SZ)

- To restrict anonymous connections to list account names:

  Set `RestrictAnonymous` to 1

  `HKEY_LOCAL_MACHINE\SYSTEM\CurrentControlSet\Control\Lsa`
  (REG_SZ)

- To restrict network access to the Registry, create the following Registry key:

  `HKEY_LOCAL_MACHINE\SYSTEM\CurrentcontrolSet\Control\`
  `SecurePipeServers\win reg`

Account Names Policies

It is important that you change the name of the Administrator account. Everyone knows that on a Windows NT platform, it is called Administrator. Changing this name to something else adds another level of security. Have all Admin users log on with their own respective accounts, and do not give them the password for the Admin account. This allows you to track who is doing what. Another idea is to create a new fictitious Administrator account that has no privileges and track to see if anyone attempts to log on with that account.

Next, you want to control who has access to what on the system. No more than two groups should have access to the firewall: Administrators (for full access) and Power Users or Users (depending on what access they need). If access can be limited to only members of the Administrators group, that is even better. Regardless, the actual number of people who have authorized access should be no more than two to four people.

The next step is to focus on and modify the system policies, specifically the Account Policies:

- User Rights and Audit Policies are found under User Manager and control how user passwords and logon accounts are used. Two changes are recommended to these policies:
  - Set Minimum Password Length to eight characters.
  - Set Account Lockout to lock out users after three bad logon attempts and reset the counter after 30 minutes.
- User Rights controls who can access what, such as Log On Locally and Manage Auditing and Security Log. Limiting access to the two Windows

NT groups discussed earlier (Administrators and Power Users or Users) is recommended. Be sure to eliminate the group Everyone from all access.

- Audit Policy determines which events are logged. Because this is your firewall, you want to log a variety of events you may not normally care to log. You should log the following events:
  - Logon and logoff (both success and failure)
  - Security policy changes (both success and failure)
  - Restart, shutdown, and system (both success and failure)

Whenever users are done using the system for a particular session, they should *always* log out using Ctrl-Alt-Del. In case users forget to do this, ensure that you have a password-protected screen saver that kicks in within five minutes of inactivity.

Service Packs and Critical Updates

Make sure the latest service pack and critical updates are installed on your platform. You can downloaded them from http://www.microsoft.com/ntserver/nts/downloads/default.asp.

Securing Windows 2000

Note that there are a *ton* of different opinions on what services need to be enabled or disabled on a server. The truth is this: It depends on how paranoid you are and what you're trying to accomplish. If you follow these steps, you will have a fairly braindead system for much of anything else *except* running FireWall-1. That's good, because it's what we are trying to accomplish.

Initial Installation

Hardening an OS installation begins during the initial installation. The first choice is how to install the server—as a standalone server or as a domain controller. A standalone server should be chosen. Your firewall should not be a domain controller, for that goes against the idea that a firewall should be nothing but a firewall. Additionally, the firewall should not be a member of a domain.

When presented with the Windows Components Wizard dialog, ensure that all components *except* for SNMP are unchecked because none of the other components will be necessary. FireWall-1 does make use of SNMP, however.

Network Protocols and Services

When setting up Windows 2000 for FireWall-1, only TCP/IP is needed. Use a static IP address. The non-IP protocols are undesirable (FireWall-1 cannot filter these protocols). Also, the Client for Microsoft Networks service and the File and Print Sharing service are not necessary and may create a potential security risk.

Machine Name and Domain

Choose a machine name (firewall seems like a good choice, though do not choose fw, fw-1, firewall-1, or similar), and choose a domain/workgroup that is unreachable.

Hotfixes

After installing the operating system, make sure you install any service packs and critical security hotfixes, which are available at http://www.microsoft.com/windows2000/downloads/default.asp.

Services to Disable after Installation

After you have installed these fixes, services should be disabled. Windows 2000 has quite a number of services—most of them are unnecessary on a firewall. Below I describe the various services you might want to keep **enabled**. Other services not in this list should be stopped and marked as **disabled**. For a more complete listing of the services and what they do, review the Glossary of Windows 2000 Services at Microsoft's site, available at http://www.microsoft.com/windows2000/techinfo/howitworks/management/w2kservices.asp.

- *COM+ Event System:* The main reason to keep this service enabled is to track logons and logoffs by local users.
- *DHCP Client:* You should leave this enabled only if you plan to get IP addresses via DHCP; otherwise, disable this service.
- *Event Log:* This service provides the interface for reading/writing the Windows 2000 Event logs.
- *Logical Disk Manager:* This service allows you to manage locally attached disks. Set this service to manual startup instead of automatic.
- *Network Connections:* This service allows you to modify your network connection properties.
- *Plug and Play:* This service provides hardware device installation and configuration.
- *Remote Procedure Call:* This service allows a program on one system to execute a program on another remote system. Note that we are going to remove the listeners for this service later to ensure this service cannot be used to compromise the platform.

- *RunAs Service:* If you want to be able to use the RunAs functionality where one user can run commands as a user with elevated privileges like the UNIX **su** command, keep this service enabled.
- *Security Accounts Manager:* If you want to be able to manage local user accounts, this service needs to be enabled.
- *Task Scheduler:* If you want to be able to use the **at** command to run scheduled jobs, this service needs to be enabled.
- *Windows Management Instrumentation:* If you want to use the Microsoft Management Console on the platform, leave this service enabled.
- *Windows Management Instrumentation Driver Extensions:* If you want to use the Microsoft Management Console on the platform, leave this service enabled too.

IP Routing

In order to route packets, IP Routing must be enabled. This requires editing the following registry key using **regedit**:

Set `EnableIPRouter` to 1
`HKEY_LOCAL_MACHINE\System\CurrentControlSet\Services\TCPIP\`
`Parameters` (REG_DWORD)

DNS Registration

The next step is to disable DNS Registration. In the TCP/IP configuration screen for each interface, select Advanced, then the DNS tab. Ensure that the "Register this connection's address in DNS" checkbox is unchecked. This prevents the firewall from attempting to register with a Windows 2000 DNS server, which is not necessary for a firewall to do.

NetBIOS over TCP

The next step is to disable NetBIOS over TCP. This is done in the Device Manager, which you can access by right-clicking on My Computer, selecting Properties, then clicking on the Hardware tab and clicking on the Device Manager button. Then from the View menu, select Show Hidden Devices. Under the Non Plug and Play section, you will see "NetBIOS over tcpip." Right-click on this service, and select Disable.

Preventing RPC Locator from Listening

Finally, you will want to prevent the RPC Portmapper from listening on Windows 2000. To do this, remove the following two registry entries:

```
HKLM\Software\Microsoft\RPC\ClientProtocols\ncacn_ip_tcp
HKLM\Software\Microsoft\RPC\ClientProtocols\ncacn_ip_udp
```

You will also need to edit the registry key `HKLM\Software\Microsoft\RPC\DCOM Protocols` so that it no longer includes `ncacn_ip_tcp`.

After you reboot, you can verify this change took effect by using the **netstat** command to validate that nothing is listening on TCP port 135.

Securing Linux

This discussion of securing Linux assumes Red Hat 7.3, which is the latest version officially supported by Check Point. It should be similar for other versions of Red Hat.

Make sure you have the latest security fixes applied. The latest ones for Red Hat are available at http://www.redhat.com/apps/support/errata/.

Partitioning Your Hard Drive

A recommended partitioning scheme includes the following:

- `/boot`: 256MB (should be first partition)
- `/` (root filesystem): everything else
- `/var`: 400MB (for logging)
- `swap`: larger of 256MB or twice the physical RAM
- `/var/opt`: 15GB or a separate drive (FireWall-1 logs and configuration files)

Choosing the Packages to Install

Using the graphics-based or text-based installer, choose which grouping of packages to install. Choose Custom, then choose the package groups Network and Router/Firewall. Also select Choose Packages to Install.

In the graphical installer, there is a flat view that shows all the packages to load outside of their normal grouping. Ensure only the following packages are selected (you will have to disable a few):

```
bind-utils
ftp
gmp
gnupg
libcap
libpcap
lsof
lynx
m4
```

```
make
minicom
mtr
ncftp
nmap
ntp
perl
rdate
rmt
sash
statserial
strace
stunnel
sudo
sysinit
tcp_wrappers
tcpdump
telnet
traceroute
tripwire
unzip
vlock
wget
whois
xinetd
zip
```
`zebra` (if you need dynamic routing)

Eliminating Services

If you follow my package recommendations above, there should be almost no unnecessary services. However, sendmail gets installed by default and there is no way to prevent it from installing by default. The command **rpm -e sendmail** should remove the package.

Logging and Tweaking

Tweaking involves some file administration. You should first secure your `/etc/passwd` file (this is the database file that holds your user accounts and passwords). Ensure that your system is using `/etc/shadow`, which securely stores all passwords as hashes in a file that only root can access. This protects your passwords from being easily accessed and cracked (one of the first exploits for which a hacker searches). The use of shadow passwords is the default as of Red Hat 6.0; however, it never hurts to be sure. All you have to do is type **pwconv** as root. This automatically converts your passwords to the `/etc/shadow` file.

Next, remove most of the default system accounts in /etc/passwd. Linux provides these accounts for various system activities that you may not need. If you do not need the accounts, remove them. The more accounts you have, the easier it is to access your system. An example is the "news" account. If you are not running NNTP, a newsgroup server, you do not need the account (be sure to update /etc/cron.hourly because this looks for the user "news"). Also, make sure you remove the "FTP" account because this is the account used for anonymous FTP.

Create the file /etc/issue. This file is an ASCII text banner that appears for all Telnet logins.

It is recommended that you use TCP Wrappers. TCP Wrappers, although it does not encrypt, does log and control who can access your system. It is a binary that wraps itself around inetd services, such as Telnet or FTP. With TCP Wrappers, the system launches the wrapper for inetd connections, logs all attempts, and then verifies the attempt against an access control list. If the connection is permitted, TCP Wrappers hands the connection to the proper binary, such as Telnet. If the connection is rejected by the access control list, the connection is dropped.

Fortunately for Linux users, TCP Wrappers is already installed; you only need to edit the /etc/hosts.allow and /etc/hosts.deny files. The syntax is relatively simple. Put the IP addresses or networks in the file /etc/hosts.allow that you want to permit connections from. Put IP addresses or networks in the file /etc/hosts.deny that you do not want to permit access from. By default, Linux allows connections from everyone, so you need to modify these files.

The following sample /etc/hosts.allow file allows a few services from specific hosts.

```
# Allow a few things
sshd:ALL
ALL:10.0.0.0/255.255.255.0
ALL:10.0.1.0/255.255.255.0
ALL:10.0.10.0/255.255.255.0
ALL:10.0.43.0/255.255.255.0
ALL:10.0.69.0/255.255.255.0
ALL:192.168.43.40/255.255.255.248
ALL:127.0.0.1/255.0.0.0
```

This /etc/hosts.deny file denies everything not allowed by /etc/hosts.allow.

```
ALL:ALL:DENY
```

Appendix

B

Sample Acceptable Usage Policy

The following is a sample Acceptable Usage Policy.

Company X Information Security Policy
Section 003: Internet Access and Usage

SUMMARY

While Company X wants to maintain our culture of trust, openness, and integrity, we must also protect employees, partners, and the company itself from illegal or damaging actions by individuals, either knowingly or unknowingly. This document describes Company X's official policy regarding Internet security and access.

Internet/intranet/extranet-related systems, including but not limited to computer equipment, software, operating systems, storage media, network accounts providing electronic mail, WWW browsing, and FTP, are the property of Company X. These systems are to be used for business purposes, supporting the needs of the company and clients thereof.

Each person who deals with information and/or information systems plays a role in an effective security process. All computer users are responsible for knowing these guidelines and must conduct themselves accordingly.

I. INTERNET DOWNLOADS

A. Downloads: All nontext files (databases, software object code, spreadsheets, formatted word processing package files, and so on) downloaded from non–Company X sources via the Internet must be screened with virus detection software prior to being installed or executed. Whenever an external provider of the software is not trusted, downloaded software should be tested on a standalone nonproduction machine that has been recently backed up. If this software contains a virus, worm, or Trojan horse, damage will be restricted to the involved machine only.

II. INFORMATION CONFIDENTIALITY

A. Information Exchange: Company X's software, documentation, and all other types of internal information must not be sold or otherwise transferred to any non–Company X party for any purposes other than business purposes expressly authorized by management. Exchanges of software and/or data between Company X and any third party may not proceed unless a written agreement has first been signed. Such an agreement must specify the terms of the exchange as well as the ways in which the software and/or data are to be handled and protected. Regular business practices, such as shipment of a product in response to a customer purchase order, need not involve such a specific agreement because the terms are implied.

B. Message Interception: Wiretapping and other types of message interception are straightforward and frequently encountered on the Internet. Accordingly, Company X's secret, proprietary, or private information must not be sent over the Internet unless it has first been encrypted by approved methods described in Section 005 of the Information Security Policy. Unless specifically known to be in the public domain, source code must always be encrypted before being sent over the Internet.

C. Security Parameters: Credit card numbers, telephone calling card numbers, fixed login passwords, and other security parameters that can be used to gain access to goods or services must not be sent over the Internet in readable form. The use of 128-bit or greater encryption is an acceptable Internet encryption standard for the protection of security parameters. The Security Council must approve other encryption processes or standards.

III. ACCESS CONTROL

A. User Authentication: All users wishing to establish a real-time connection with Company X's internal computers via the Internet must authenticate themselves at a firewall before gaining access to Company X's internal network. This authentication process must be achieved via a dynamic password system approved by the Chief Security Officer. Examples of approved technology include handheld smart cards with dynamic passwords and user-transparent challenge/response systems. These systems will prevent intruders from guessing fixed passwords or from replaying a fixed password captured via a "sniffer attack" (wiretap). Designated "public" systems (anonymous FTP, Web surfing, and so on) do not need user authentication processes because anonymous interactions are expected.

B. Internet Service Providers: With the exception of telecommuters and mobile computer users, workers must not employ Internet Service Provider (ISP) accounts and dial-up lines to access the Internet with Company X's computers. Instead, all Internet activity must pass through Company X's firewalls so that access controls and related security mechanisms can be applied.

C. Vendors, Partners, and Suppliers: Any external party connecting to any part of Company X's information network must abide by Company X's security policies. No connection is permitted until approved in writing by the Security Council. The outside party must fully understand and agree to all security terms and conditions. Any and all such connections must be limited to only what the clients need, and no more. An example would include having an isolated, protected network for vendor or partner connections.

IV. PRIVACY EXPECTATIONS

A. No Default Protection: Workers using Company X's information systems and/or the Internet should realize that their communications are not automatically protected from being viewed by third parties. Unless encryption is used, workers should not send information over the Internet if they consider it to be confidential or private.

B. Management Review: At any time and without prior notice, Company X's management reserves the right to examine electronic mail messages, files on personal computers, Web browser cache files, Web browser bookmarks, and other information stored on or passing through Company X's computers. Such management access assures compliance with internal policies, assists with internal investigations, and assists with the management of Company X's information systems.

C. Logging: Company X routinely logs Web sites visited, files downloaded, time spent on the Internet, and related information. Department managers may receive reports of such information and use it to determine what types of Internet usage are appropriate for the business activities of their departments.

Appendix
C

firewall-1.conf File for Use with OpenLDAP v1

To use OpenLDAP v1 with FireWall-1, add the following line to your `slapd.conf` file:

```
include          /etc/openldap/firewall-1.conf
```

The contents of `firewall-1.conf` follow.

```
attribute        fw1auth-method                          ces
attribute        fw1auth-server                          ces
attribute        fw1pwdlastmod                           ces
attribute        fw1skey-number                          ces
attribute        fw1skey-seed                            ces
attribute        fw1skey-passwd                          ces
attribute        fw1skey-mdm                             ces
attribute        fw1expiration-date                      ces
attribute        fw1hour-range-from                      ces
attribute        fw1hour-range-to                        ces
attribute        fw1day                                  ces
attribute        fw1allowed-src                          ces
attribute        fw1allowed-dst                          ces
attribute        fw1allowed-vlan                         ces
attribute        fw1SR-keym                              ces
attribute        fw1SR-datam                             ces
attribute        fw1SR-mdm                               ces
attribute        fw1enc-fwz-expiration                   ces
attribute        fw1sr-auth-track                        ces
attribute        fw1grouptemplate                        ces
attribute        fw1ISAKMP-EncMethod                     ces
attribute        fw1ISAKMP-AuthMethods                   ces
attribute        fw1ISAKMP-HashMethods                   ces
```

```
attribute          fw1ISAKMP-Transfork                      ces
attribute          fw1ISAKMP-DataIntegrityMethod            ces
attribute          fw1ISAKMP-SharedSecret                   ces
attribute          fw1ISAKMP-DataEncMethod                  ces
attribute          fw1enc-methods                           ces


objectclass fw1template
        requires
                objectClass,
                cn
        allows
                member,
                description,
                fw1auth-method,
                fw1auth-server,
                fw1pwdlastmod,
                fw1skey-number,
                fw1skey-seed,
                fw1skey-passwd,
                fw1skey-mdm,
                fw1expiration-date,
                fw1hour-range-from,
                fw1hour-range-to,
                fw1day,
                fw1allowed-src,
                fw1allowed-dst,
                fw1allowed-vlan,
                fw1SR-keym,
                fw1SR-datam,
                fw1SR-mdm,
                fw1enc-fwz-expiration,
                fw1sr-auth-track,
                fw1grouptemplate,
                fw1ISAKMP-EncMethod,
                fw1ISAKMP-AuthMethods,
                fw1ISAKMP-HashMethods,
                fw1ISAKMP-Transform,
                fw1ISAKMP-DataIntegrityMethod,
                fw1ISAKMP-SharedSecret,
                fw1ISAKMP-DataEncMethod,
                fw1enc-methods
objectclass fw1person
        requires
                objectClass,
                cn
        allows
                description,
                fw1auth-method,
```

```
fw1auth-server,
fw1pwdlastmod,
fw1skey-number,
fw1skey-seed,
fw1skey-passwd,
fw1skey-mdm,
fw1expiration-date,
fw1hour-range-from,
fw1hour-range-to,
fw1day,
fw1allowed-src,
fw1allowed-dst,
fw1allowed-vlan,
fw1SR-keym,
fw1SR-datam,
fw1SR-mdm,
fw1enc-fwz-expiration,
fw1sr-auth-track,
fw1grouptemplate,
fw1ISAKMP-EncMethod,
fw1ISAKMP-AuthMethods,
fw1ISAKMP-HashMethods,
fw1ISAKMP-Transform,
fw1ISAKMP-DataIntegrityMethod,
fw1ISAKMP-SharedSecret,
fw1ISAKMP-DataEncMethod,
fw1enc-methods
```

firewall-1.schema File for Use with OpenLDAP v2

To use the firewall1.schema file, add the following lines to your slapd.conf file. These lines assume the core, cosine, and inetorgperson schemas are stored in /etc/openldap/schema.

```
include     /etc/openldap/schema/core.schema
include     /etc/openldap/schema/cosine.schema
include     /etc/openldap/schema/inetorgperson.schema
include     /etc/openldap/schema/firewall1.schema
```

The firewall1.schema file looks like this.

```
attributeType ( 1.3.114.7.4.2.0.1
    NAME 'fw1auth-method'
    SYNTAX 1.3.6.1.4.1.1466.115.121.1.26 )
attributeType ( 1.3.114.7.4.2.0.2
    NAME 'fw1auth-server'
    SYNTAX 1.3.6.1.4.1.1466.115.121.1.26 )
attributeType ( 1.3.114.7.4.2.0.3
    NAME 'fw1pwdlastmod'
    SYNTAX 1.3.6.1.4.1.1466.115.121.1.26 )
attributeType ( 1.3.114.7.4.2.0.4
    NAME 'fw1skey-number'
    SYNTAX 1.3.6.1.4.1.1466.115.121.1.26 )
attributeType ( 1.3.114.7.4.2.0.5
    NAME 'fw1skey-seed'
    SYNTAX 1.3.6.1.4.1.1466.115.121.1.26 )
attributeType ( 1.3.114.7.4.2.0.6
    NAME 'fw1skey-passwd'
    SYNTAX 1.3.6.1.4.1.1466.115.121.1.26 )
attributeType ( 1.3.114.7.4.2.0.7
```

```
          NAME 'fw1skey-mdm'
          SYNTAX 1.3.6.1.4.1.1466.115.121.1.26 )
attributeType ( 1.3.114.7.4.2.0.8
          NAME 'fw1expiration-date'
          SYNTAX 1.3.6.1.4.1.1466.115.121.1.26 )
attributeType ( 1.3.114.7.4.2.0.9
          NAME 'fw1hour-range-from'
          SYNTAX 1.3.6.1.4.1.1466.115.121.1.26 )
attributeType ( 1.3.114.7.4.2.0.10
          NAME 'fw1hour-range-to'
          SYNTAX 1.3.6.1.4.1.1466.115.121.1.26 )
attributeType ( 1.3.114.7.4.2.0.11
          NAME 'fw1day'
          SYNTAX 1.3.6.1.4.1.1466.115.121.1.26 )
attributeType ( 1.3.114.7.4.2.0.12
          NAME 'fw1allowed-src'
          SYNTAX 1.3.6.1.4.1.1466.115.121.1.26 )
attributeType ( 1.3.114.7.4.2.0.13
          NAME 'fw1allowed-dst'
          SYNTAX 1.3.6.1.4.1.1466.115.121.1.26 )
attributeType ( 1.3.114.7.4.2.0.14
          NAME 'fw1allowed-vlan'
          SYNTAX 1.3.6.1.4.1.1466.115.121.1.26 )
attributeType ( 1.3.114.7.4.2.0.15
          NAME 'fw1SR-keym'
          SYNTAX 1.3.6.1.4.1.1466.115.121.1.26 )
attributeType ( 1.3.114.7.4.2.0.16
          NAME 'fw1SR-datam'
          SYNTAX 1.3.6.1.4.1.1466.115.121.1.26 )
attributeType ( 1.3.114.7.4.2.0.17
          NAME 'fw1SR-mdm'
          SYNTAX 1.3.6.1.4.1.1466.115.121.1.26 )
attributeType ( 1.3.114.7.4.2.0.18
          NAME 'fw1enc-fwz-expiration'
          SYNTAX 1.3.6.1.4.1.1466.115.121.1.26 )
attributeType ( 1.3.114.7.4.2.0.19
          NAME 'fw1sr-auth-track'
          SYNTAX 1.3.6.1.4.1.1466.115.121.1.26 )
attributeType ( 1.3.114.7.4.2.0.20
          NAME 'fw1grouptemplate'
          SYNTAX 1.3.6.1.4.1.1466.115.121.1.26 )
attributeType ( 1.3.114.7.4.2.0.21
          NAME 'fw1ISAKMP-EncMethod'
          SYNTAX 1.3.6.1.4.1.1466.115.121.1.26 )
attributeType ( 1.3.114.7.4.2.0.22
          NAME 'fw1ISAKMP-AuthMethods'
          SYNTAX 1.3.6.1.4.1.1466.115.121.1.26 )
```

```
attributeType ( 1.3.114.7.4.2.0.23
    NAME 'fw1ISAKMP-HashMethods'
    SYNTAX 1.3.6.1.4.1.1466.115.121.1.26 )
attributeType ( 1.3.114.7.4.2.0.24
    NAME 'fw1ISAKMP-Transform'
    SYNTAX 1.3.6.1.4.1.1466.115.121.1.26 )
attributeType ( 1.3.114.7.4.2.0.25
    NAME 'fw1ISAKMP-DataIntegrityMethod'
    SYNTAX 1.3.6.1.4.1.1466.115.121.1.26 )
attributeType ( 1.3.114.7.4.2.0.26
    NAME 'fw1ISAKMP-SharedSecret'
    SYNTAX 1.3.6.1.4.1.1466.115.121.1.26 )
attributeType ( 1.3.114.7.4.2.0.27
    NAME 'fw1ISAKMP-DataEncMethod'
    SYNTAX 1.3.6.1.4.1.1466.115.121.1.26 )
attributeType ( 1.3.114.7.4.2.0.28
    NAME 'fw1enc-methods'
    SYNTAX 1.3.6.1.4.1.1466.115.121.1.26 )
objectClass ( 1.3.114.7.3.2.0.1
    NAME 'fw1template'
    SUP top STRUCTURAL
    MUST ( objectclass $ cn )
    MAY ( member $ description $ fw1auth-method $ fw1auth-server $
fw1pwdlastmod $ fw1skey-number $ fw1skey-seed $ fw1skey-passwd $
fw1skey-mdm $ fw1expiration-date $ fw1hour-range-from $ fw1hour-
range-to $ fw1day $ fw1allowed-src $ fw1allowed-dst $ fw1allowed-
vlan $ fw1SR-keym $ fw1SR-datam $ fw1SR-mdm $ fw1enc-fwz-
expiration $ fw1sr-auth-track $ fw1grouptemplate $ fw1ISAKMP-
EncMethod $ fw1ISAKMP-AuthMethods $ fw1ISAKMP-HashMethods $
fw1ISAKMP-Transform $ fw1ISAKMP-DataIntegrityMethod $ fw1ISAKMP-
SharedSecret $ fw1ISAKMP-DataEncMethod $ fw1enc-methods )
    )
objectClass ( 1.3.114.7.3.2.0.2
    NAME 'fw1person'
    SUP top AUXILIARY
    MUST ( cn )
    MAY ( description $ fw1auth-method $ fw1auth-server $
fw1pwdlastmod $ fw1skey-number $ fw1skey-seed $ fw1skey-passwd $
fw1skey-mdm $ fw1expiration-date $ fw1hour-range-from $ fw1hour-
range-to $ fw1day $ fw1allowed-src $ fw1allowed-dst $ fw1allowed-
vlan $ fw1SR-keym $ fw1SR-datam $ fw1SR-mdm $ fw1enc-fwz-
expiration $ fw1sr-auth-track $ fw1grouptemplate $ fw1ISAKMP-
EncMethod $ fw1ISAKMP-AuthMethods $ fw1ISAKMP-HashMethods $
fw1ISAKMP-Transform $ fw1ISAKMP-DataIntegrityMethod $ fw1ISAKMP-
SharedSecret $ fw1ISAKMP-DataEncMethod $ fw1enc-methods )
    )
```

Appendix
E

Performance Tuning

This appendix discusses how to tune FireWall-1 and the operating system of the three major platforms for FireWall-1: Solaris, Windows NT, and IPSO.

Number of Entries Permitted in Tables

FireWall-1 keeps track of all connections in state tables that are maintained in the kernel. By default, most of the tables are limited to 25,000 entries. The connections table often needs to be increased.

In NG FP2 and beyond, memory management for state tables and the number of connections are controlled in the GUI in the gateway or gateway cluster object, Advanced frame. The memory management can be automatic (the default) or manual. In either case, you must still specify the number of connections permitted.

In FireWall-1 NG FP3 and above, perform the following steps in Smart-Dashboard.

1. Edit the Check Point object for the Firewall module.
2. Select the Capacity Optimization frame.
3. Modify the maximum number of concurrent connections (the default is 25,000).
4. Install the security policy.

In FireWall-1 NG FP2, perform the following steps in the Policy Editor.

1. Edit the Check Point object for the Firewall module.
2. Select the Advanced frame, then Capacity Planning.
3. Modify the maximum number of concurrent connections (the default is 25,000).
4. Install the security policy.

In FireWall-1 NG FP1 and prior NG releases, use the **dbedit** utility to make the change. Issue the following commands in **dbedit**. (Note that you can specify any value; 50,000 is an example.)

```
dbedit> modify properties firewall_properties connections_limit
          50000
dbedit> update properties firewall_properties
```

If you decide to manually tweak the parameters, you should know how the hashsize parameter works. The hashsize parameter must be a power of 2 and should be the next highest power of 2 based on the number of connections you want to support. The hashsize is therefore 2^n where:

$$2^{n-1} < \texttt{connections\_limit} < 2^n$$

So for 50,000 connections, the hashsize should be 65,536:

$$2^{15} = 32{,}768 < 50{,}000 < 2^{16} = 65{,}536$$

Reinstall the security policy after making these changes.

Memory Used for State Tables

If you are manually tweaking the configuration or want to know how much memory to have available in your firewall system, it would be useful to know how much memory each connection takes. The memory requirements for various types of connections are outlined in Table E.1.

Assuming the worst-case scenario (NAT), you would need to allocate at least 57.7MB to handle 100,000 connections.

Table E.1 Approximate memory requirements for specific connections

Connection Type	Memory Requirement
Simple (e.g., accept, no NAT)	325 bytes
NAT (e.g., a standard connection with NAT)	542 bytes
Resources (authentication, content security, and so on)	401 bytes
Encrypted connections	399 bytes
General overhead (not per-connection)	6MB

Tweaks for Specific Operating Systems

The following subsections discuss how to tweak IPSO's TCP/IP stack, Solaris, and Windows NT, as well as provide some changes to help the Security Servers function better.

IPSO-Specific Changes

Each of the following changes should be added to `/var/etc/rc.local` so they will be active across reboots. Most of these changes increase the performance of the Security Servers (which benefit from increased packet sizes) and also help general TCP/IP traffic.

```
ipsctl -w net:ip:tcp:sendspace 65535 # TCP/IP specific changes
ipsctl -w net:ip:tcp:recvspace 65535
ipsctl -w net:ip:tcp:default_mss 1460 # Should be MTU minus 40 bytes
```

Solaris-Specific Changes

All **ndd** commands listed in this section should be added to an `rc` startup script. My suggestion is to create a new one, such as `/etc/rc2.d/S99nddcmds`.

The following commands force 100MB full duplex on hme-type interfaces and will disable autonegotiation. You can also do this on qfe-type interfaces as well by replacing `/dev/hme` with `/dev/qfe` in the following commands:

```
ndd -set /dev/hme adv_autoneg_cap 0
ndd -set /dev/hme adv_100fdx_cap 1
```

The following commands tune the TCP stack with optimal settings:

```
ndd -set /dev/tcp tcp_xmit_hiwat 65535
ndd -set /dev/tcp tcp_recv_hiwat 65535
ndd -set /dev/tcp tcp_cwnd_max 65535
ndd -set /dev/tcp tcp_slow_start_initial 2
ndd -set /dev/tcp tcp_conn_req_max_q 1024
ndd -set /dev/tcp tcp_conn_req_max_q0 4096
ndd -set /dev/tcp tcp_close_wait_interval 60000
```

Additionally, you should add the following to `/etc/system` and reboot:

```
set tcp:tcp_conn_hash_size = 16384
```

Windows NT-Specific Changes

All of the following changes apply to Windows NT Server 4.0, not Windows 2000.

1. Set the Windows NT memory strategy to Maximize Throughput for Network Applications. By default it is set to Maximize Throughput for File

Sharing, which allocates all available Windows NT memory to file caching. To change this setting, go to Control Panel, select Network, and then select Server.

2. Next, disable all unnecessary services and drivers. If you followed the suggestions for securing a Windows NT box in Appendix A, you have done most of this already.

3. If you are using the Security Servers, you should disable performance boost for foreground applications. Go to Control Panel, select System, and then select Performance. Move the Application Performance slider to None.

4. The Page file (i.e., `swap`) should be a fixed size at least twice the size of physical RAM and should exist on another (preferably dedicated) drive.

5. TCP/IP should be tuned for maximum performance. You need to employ **regedt32** to make the following changes.

```
KEY_LOCAL_MACHINE\System\CurrentControlSet\Services\Tcpip\
Parameters\ForwardBufferMemory = 296960
```

This REG_DWORD must be a multiple of 256 and be set to a default of `74240`. This is the size of the buffer the IP stack allocates to store packet data in the router queue. The default value is enough for 50 1,480-byte packets.

```
HKEY_LOCAL_MACHINE\System\CurrentControlSet\Services\Tcpip\
Parameters\NumForwardPackets = 200
```

This REG_DWORD has a default of `50`. This corresponds to the number of IP headers allocated for router queue. It should be at least as large as the ForwardBufferMemory/IP data size of the network. Increasing these two parameters can have a significant effect on throughput, especially with slow policies.

```
HKEY_LOCAL_MACHINE\System\CurrentControlSet\Services\Tcpip\
Parameters\TcpWindowSize
```

This REG_DWORD has a default of `8760` for Ethernet. A larger TCP receive window size improves performance over high-speed networks. For highest efficiency, the TCP window size should be an even multiple of TCP Maximum Segment Size (MSS), which is usually `1460` for Ethernet.

```
HKEY_LOCAL_MACHINE\System\CurrentControlSet\Services\Tcpip\
Parameters\MaxFreeTcbs = 4000
```

This REG_DWORD has a default of `2000` and corresponds to the TCP TIME_WAIT table size.

```
HKEY_LOCAL_MACHINE\system\CurrentControlSet\Services\Tcpip\
Parameters\MaxHashTableSize = 65536
```

This REG_DWORD should be a power of 2 and corresponds to the hash value for the TCP TIME_WAIT table size.

```
HKEY_LOCAL_MACHINE\System\CurrentControlSet\Services\Tcpip\
Parameters\MaxUserPort = 65534
```

This REG_DWORD with a default value of 5000 increases the number of TCP user ports available to applications, which prevents the Security Servers from running out of ports to use.

6. Improve the CPU servicing of interrupts generated by network interface cards (NICs). Change the Processor Affinity Mask using **regedt32**:

```
HKEY_LOCAL_MACHINE\System\CurrentControlSet\Services\NDIS\
Parameters\ProcessorAffinityMask = 0
```

7. Tune the specific vendor NIC's parameters for maximum performance. Note that not all vendors allow you to tune these variables, or the variables may have slightly different names. Go to Control Panel, select Network, select Adapter Properties, and then select Advanced. The actual performance gain will vary depending on the types of traffic. You may want to adjust these parameters for maximum performance gain; otherwise, use these suggestions:

> Receive Buffers = 256
> Transmit Control Blocks = 64
> Coalesce Buffers = 16

8. If you are using encryption, make the following registry changes with **regedt32**:

```
HKEY_LOCAL_MACHINE\System\CurrentControlSet\Services\
FW1\ Parameters\PacketPoolSize = 3000 (default of 1000)

HKEY_LOCAL_MACHINE\System\Current\ControlSet\Services\
FW1 \parameters\BufferPoolSize = 6000
                    (default of 2000, should be
2xPacketPoolSize)
```

Appendix

F

Sample defaultfilter.pf File

The following is a sample default filter INSPECT script.

```
// IP source and destination
#define src [12,b]
#define dst [16,b]

// TCP or UDP source and destination ports
#define sport [20:2,b]
#define dport [22:2,b]

// IP protocol
#define ip_p [9:1]

// Table for recording outgoing sessions. Incoming packets are
// matched against this table.

connections = dynamic refresh expires 300;

// The following two rules deal with outgoing and incoming
// packets in which the IP source and destination are the same as
// well as connections originating from the firewall going to tcp
// port 256 (e.g., for fetching the security policy from the
// management console) or to tcp port 22 (for ssh access). The
// first rule accepts and records such outgoing packets. The
// second rule accepts such packets if a matching packet was
// previously recorded.

<= all@all
   accept (
      (src = dst,
       record <0,src,ip_p,sport,dport> in connections)
         or
      (ip_p = 6, dport = 256 or dport = 22,
```

```
            record <src,dst,ip_p,sport,dport> in connections)
        );
=> all@all
    accept (
        (src = dst,
        <0,src,ip_p,sport,dport> in connections)
            or
        (ip_p = 6, sport = 256 or sport = 22,
        <dst,src,ip_p,dport,sport> in connections)
    );

// The next rule just drops everything else.
drop;
```

Appendix

Other Resources

The URLs provided in this appendix were valid as of October 2003. The most up-to-date version of this list is available on http://www.phoneboy.com.

Internet Resources

@stake Advisories: http://www.atstake.com/research/advisories/index.html

CERT Advisories: http://www.cert.org/advisories/

Check Point's Knowledge Base: http://support.checkpoint.com/

Check Point's News Server: news://nntp.checkpoint.com

Common Vulnerabilities and Exposures Database: http://cve.mitre.org/

DNS Resource Directory: http://www.dns.net/dnsrd/

Firewall Wizards Mailing List: http://honor.trusecure.com/mailman/listinfo/firewall-wizards (not specific to FireWall-1)

FireWall-1 FAQ Page: http://www.phoneboy.com

FireWall-1 Mailing List: http://www.checkpoint.com/services/mailing.html (searchable indexes at http://msgs.securepoint.com/fw1/)

FireWall-1 Gurus Mailing List: http://www.phoneboy.com/gurus

Firewalls Mailing list: http://www.isc.org/services/public/lists/firewalls.html (not specific to FireWall-1)

Internet Firewalls FAQ: http://www.ranum.com/pubs/fwfaq/

Internet Security Servers Security Center: http://xforce.iss.net

Lance Spitzner's Publications: http://www.spitzner.net/ (contains various topics, including using **snoop**, configuring your NICs, hardening Solaris, and stuff on Honeypots)

NTBugtraq: http://www.ntbugtraq.com/ (Windows Security site)

ntsecurity.nu: http://www.ntsecurity.nu/ (Windows NT and 2000 Security site)

SANS Institute: http://www.sans.org/ (security education, research, and training)

Software

Analyzer: http://netgroup-serv.polito.it/analyzer/ (a public-domain protocol analyzer for Windows 95/ 98/NT)

cron: http://www.kalab.com/freeware/cron/cron.htm (a Windows port of the UNIX utility)

GNU Utilities for Win32: http://www.weihenstephan.de/~syring/win32/ UnxUtils.html (ports of various GNU utilities for Win32 that run natively without an emulation layer; covers `tar`, `gzip`, and `md5sum`)

MinGW: http://www.mingw.org/ (minimalist GNU for Windows, which provides a `gcc` that produces Windows-native binaries)

Nessus: http://www.nessus.org/ (an open-source security scanner)

Netcat: http://www.atstake.com/research/tools/network_utilities/ (the TCP/IP Swiss Army Knife)

NMAP: http://www.insecure.org/nmap/ (the Network Mapper)

Osiris: http://osiris.shmoo.com/ (a tripwire-like program for Windows NT)

Perl for Windows: http://aspn.activestate.com/ASPN/Downloads/ActivePerl/ index/

SniffIt: http://reptile.rug.ac.be/~coder/sniffit/sniffit.html (a packet sniffer for LINUX, SunOS, Solaris, FreeBSD and IRIX)

The Laughing Bit: http://www.tlb.ch/ (some useful FireWall-1 scripts and programs)

Zebra: http://www.zebra.org/ (a multipurpose routing daemon available under the GNU license)

Third-Party Log Analysis Tools

fwgold: http://www.rotoni.com/FwGold/

fwlogsum: http://fwlogsum.sourceforge.net

logrep: http://logrep.sourceforge.net

NetIQ's Webtrends suite: http://www.netiq.com/webtrends/default.asp

Netspective Webreporter: http://www.getnetspective.com/

PATROL for Check Point FireWall-1 from BMC Software: http://www. bmc.com/products/proddocview/0,,19052_0_0_7072,00.html

Peter Sundstrom's fwlogsum: http://www.ginini.com/software/fwlogsum/

Rajeev Kumar's fwlogstat: http://www.rajeevnet.com/fw1/fwlogstat/v1.0/

S/Key Generators

Archive of OTP clients: http://www.tifosi.com/OTP/

Opie: http://www.inner.net/pub/opie/ (One-Time Passwords in Everything)

optgen: http://www.phoneboy.com/files/otpgen.zip

Appendix

H

Further Reading

The following books are recommended for further reading.

Brenton, Chris, with Cameron Hunt. 2001. *Active Defense: A Comprehensive Guide to Network Security*. San Francisco: Sybex. ISBN 0-7821-2916-1.

Cheswick, William R., Steven M. Bellovin, and Aviel D. Rubin. 2003. *Firewalls and Internet Security: Repelling the Wily Hacker. 2nd ed.* Boston, MA: Addison-Wesley. ISBN 0-201-63466-X.

Garfinkel, Simson, and Gene Spafford. 1995. *Practical UNIX and Internet Security*. Sebastopol, CA: O'Reilly & Associates. ISBN 1-565-92148-8.

McClure, Stuart, Saumil Shah, and Shreeraj Shah. 2003. *Web Hacking*. Boston, MA: Addison-Wesley. ISBN 0-201-76176-9.

McClure, Stuart, Joel Scambray, and George Kurtz. 2003. *Hacking Exposed: Network Security Secrets and Solutions*. 4th ed. Berkeley, CA: Osborne/McGraw Hill. ISBN 0-07-222742-7.

Miller, Philip, and Michael Cummins. 2000. *LAN Technologies Explained*. Boston, MA: Digital Press. ISBN 1-555-58234-6.

Norberg, Stefan. 2000. *Securing Windows NT/2000 Servers for the Internet*. Sebastopol, CA: O'Reilly & Associates. ISBN 1-565-92768-0.

Rubin, Aviel D. 2001. *White-Hat Security Arsenal*. Boston, MA: Addison-Wesley. ISBN 0-201-71114-1.

Schneier, Bruce. 2000. *Secrets & Lies*. New York: Wiley. ISBN 0-471-25311-1.

———. 1996. *Applied Cryptography: Protocols, Algorithms, and Source Code in C*. 2nd ed. New York: Wiley. ISBN 0-471-11709-9.

Sonnenreich, Wes, and Tom Yates. 1999. *Building Linux and OpenBSD Firewalls*. New York: Wiley. ISBN 0-471-35366-3.

Spitzner, Lance. 2003. *Honeypots.* Boston, MA: Addison-Wesley. ISBN 0-321-10895-7.

Steudler, Oliver. 2000. *Managing Cisco Network Security: Building Rock-Solid Networks.* Rockland, MA: Syngress Publishing. ISBN 1-928-99417-2.

Stevens, W. Richard, and Gary R. Wright. 1993–95. *TCP/IP Illustrated.* Vols. 1, 2, and 3. Boston, MA: Addison-Wesley. ISBN 0-201-63346-9 (Vol. 1, 1993); ISBN 0-201-63354-X (Vol. 2, 1994); ISBN 0-201-63495-3 (Vol. 3, 1995).

Zwicky, Elizabeth D., Simon Cooper, and D. Brent Chapman. 2000. *Building Internet Firewalls.* 2nd ed. Sebastopol, CA: O'Reilly & Associates. ISBN 1-565-92871-7.

Index

Note: Page numbers followed by *f* and *t* indicate figures and tables, respectively.

A

abandon_time setting, for SMTP Security Server, 303
Accept action, in rules, 86
accept short circuit, in INSPECT, 523*t*
account names, in Windows NT, 555–556
account policies, in Windows NT, 555–556
Action, in rules, 86
action properties
    for Client Authentication, 227–229, 228*f*, 266*f*, 267*f*
    for encryption, in VPN, 396–397, 396*f*
    for Session Authentication, 225–226, 226*f*, 264*f*
    for URI resource, 275–276, 276*f*
    for User Authentication, 222–223, 222*f*, 262, 262*f*
address range objects, about, 73
address space. *See also* IP address
    adding, for firewalls, 15
    breakdown of, 337*t*
    sharing, in VPN, 405–406
address translation, introduction to, 335–338
address translation policy. *See* NAT rules
address translation tables, remote viewing of, 167
Administrative notifications, 134
administrative user
    adding, in management console installation, 45, 46*f*
    creating, 210
    logging actions of, 122
Administrator account, in Windows NT, 555
administrators, in operating system selection, 27, 29–30
aggressive mode, for IKE, 392

AIX
    FireWall-1 on, 30
    packet sniffer in, 355
alerts
    about, 133–136
    on Client Authentication, 229
    defining, 115–116, 116*f*
    by e-mail, 136
aliases, in SIC policy, 187, 188
anti-spoofing
    defining, 80–81, 81*f*
    in INSPECT, 534
    local interface, error on, 145
    for NAT, 350, 350*t*
        in double-blind network, 376
        in network migration, 372
        in simple network, 367, 367*t*
    in Office Mode, 445
    packet checked against, 342
AOL Instant Messenger, blocking, 149, 150*t*
application(s), Check Point
    alerts defined for, 115
    queried with `cpstat`, 119*t*–121*f*
    states of, 114, 114*t*–115*t*
application(s), in OS security, 37, 38
application layer gateways. *See* application proxies
application proxies
    authenticated requests forwarded to, 249
    filtering traffic through, error on, 257
    in FireWall-1, 8–9
    FireWall-1 as, 250
    vs. NAT, 336
    overview of, 4–5
    Passive FTP handled by, 6
    Stateful Inspection and, 5

application proxies (*cont.*)
    traceroute handled by, 8
    URI resource applied with, 273
<apply-to>, in SIC policy rules, 187
ARPs, for NAT
    in double-blind network, 375, 375*f*
    in network migration, 370–371
    setting up, 345–347
    in simple network, 366
    troubleshooting, 356–357
assets, in security policy, 16
asymmetric connections, gateway cluster options
    for, 496–497
asymmetric encryption, definition of, 381
asymmetric routing
    dynamic load balancing and, 507
    in High Availability, 500–501
    Office Mode and, 444
    in State Synchronization, 498–499, 500–501
    VPN and, 443
attributes, of dynamic tables, 528, 529*t*
authentication
    certificates for, 163
    configuring, for management users, 62–63, 62*f*
    custom message on, 249
    DLL for, SecureClient and, 460–461
    expiration of, 229
    failure of, settings for, 221, 223, 242
    gateway support for, error on, 255
    Global Properties for, 220–221, 220*f*
    in OS security, 39
    prompt for, absence of, 257
    purpose of, 193
    rule processing and, 90
    in SecureClient, 439–441, 440*f*, 441*f*
    in SecuRemote
        timeout on, 433
        in user creation, 429
    settings for, for user, 212–218, 213*f*–216*f*
    setting up, 208–221
    troubleshooting, 255–259
    in VPN, 379
    of VPN, changing FQDN and, 175
Authentication Header, in IPSec, 385
authentication servers
    firewall and, 37–38
    integrating, 230–243
    users in, FireWall-1 use of, 247

authentication services. *See also specific services*
    unavailable, 256
Automatic ARP Configuration, 341–342

B

Backward Compatibility package, installation of,
    42–43, 43*f*
banner, removal of, 250
buffer, HTTP, increasing size of, 293–294
buffer, log, full, 148
buffer, sync, error on, 516, 517–519

C

caching proxy server, requests forwarded to, 286
central gateway, in Star Community, 398
central license, 24
certificate(s)
    for authentication, 163–164
    configuring, for management users, 62–63,
        63*f*
    defining, for SecuRemote user, 430–431, 430*f*
    expiration of, 220
    generating, for user, 217–218, 217*f*
    in L2TP, 447
    on management station, deletion and, 175
    vs. pre-shared secrets, 387
    reserved, 430–431, 431*f*
    in Windows, 447–449
certificate authority. *See also* ICA
    definition of, 383
    SecureClient options for, 462, 462*f*
certificate authority keys
    exchanging, 392, 393*f*
    in VPN, 387
certificate key, for licenses, 24
Certificate Revocation List (CRL), in LDAP, 236
characters, in naming, illegal, 104, 105*t*
Check Point applications
    alerts defined for, 115
    queried with `cpstat`, 119*t*–121*f*
    states of, 114, 114*t*–115*t*
Check Point banner, removal of, 250
Check Point Express, license for, 23
Check Point gateway object
    about, 67–69, 67*f*
    configuring, for High Availability management
        modules, 180–181, 181*f*
    defining, 92, 94, 94*f*

externally managed, about, 70
log forwarding with, 138–139, 138*f*
log rotation with, 137–138, 137*f*
SecuRemote behind, 470, 470*f*
for VPN, 394, 394*f,* 417
Check Point host object
for remote management, with NAT, 165
for secondary management module, 178–179,
178*f*
Check Point licenses. *See* license(s)
Check Point Management Interface (CPMI),
190–191
Check Point modules
connections between, 162, 162*f*
states of, 114, 114*t*
Check Point node objects, about, 69
Check Point objects, 70–73, 92. *See also* Check
Point gateway object
checksum, from hash functions, 382
Cisco PIX, VPN issues with, 409
Class E addresses, 335–336
Cleanup rule, 88, 88*f,* 99
CLI. *See* command-line interface
Client Authentication
in cleartext, 256
explanation of, 202–205
over HTTP
custom pages for, 254–255
debugging, 320*t*
limitations of, 207
redirect on, 257
rule for, 227, 227*f*
error on, 256
sample configuration for, 265
security policy installation and, 257
setting up, 227–230
over Telnet, 202, 203–204
debugging, 320*t*
option for, 228
usage guidelines for, 207*t*
Client Encrypt action, for SecuRemote, 432,
432*f*
Clientless VPN
enabling, 243–244
in FireWall-1, 243–247
issues with, 246–247
client/server model, application proxies in, 4
clients file, for RADIUS, adding firewall to, 231

ClusterXL
error messages with, 514–520
license for, 494
load balancing with, 503–504
command line
blocking connections from, 129–131,
129*t*–130*t*
firewall configuration from, 190–191
fw monitor options from, 541*t*
license update from, 169–171
logs accessed from, 124–126
object created with, 143–145
for policy control, remote, 166
state tables viewed from, remotely, 167–169
system status accessed from, 116–118
command-line interface (CLI)
in AIX, 30
in IPSO, 31, 32
for SecureClient, 474–475, 474*t*–475*t*
in SPARC Solaris, 29
in Windows NT/2000, 29
Comment, in rules, 87
compiler, for INSPECT, 529–531
compressed connection, for SmartDashboard/
Policy Editor, 108
compression method, for VPN, selecting, 397
conditions, in INSPECT, 524–526
connection
accepting based on previous connection,
INSPECT for, 537–538
blocking
from command line, 129–131,
129*t*–130*t*
with fw sam, 143
passwords erased and, 460
in SmartView Tracker, 128–129
sync buffer and, 518
disconnecting, at specific time, 143
firewall bypassed by, NAT and, 352–355
hiding, IP address for, 340
to HTTP Security Server, number of, 293
for L2TP, creating, 449–450
outbound, for SecuRemote, 536–537
to Security Servers, origin of, 318
to SMTP Security Server, number of, 305
successful, packet sniffer output for, 356
unidirectional, 152–153
connection mode, for SecureClient, 458*f,* 459

connections table
    creating, with INSPECT, 528
    of firewall module, remote viewing of, 167–169
    kbuf pointer in, incorrect, 519–520
    manipulating, in INSPECT, 527–528
Connect Mode, for SecureClient, 443
constants, in INSPECT, 526
content, CVP for scanning, 270, 282–284
Content Security
    e-mail error messages for, 305
    for FTP, 299–302
    for HTTP, 271–298
    with Session Authentication, 256, 319
    for SMTP, 302–316, 303*f*
        sample configuration for, 322–326
    for TCP, 316–318
    third-party software for, 269
    with User Authentication, 319
Content Vectoring Pool. *See* CVP
`cpconfig`, user configuration with, 58
`cpd`, 183
CPMI (Check Point Management Interface),
    190–191
CPRID connections, accepting, 83, 96, 97*f*
`cprlic`, 170–171
`cpstat`, 118, 118*t*–121*t*
CPVP-VSC, license for, 426
CPVP-VSR, license for, 426
critical updates
    for Windows 2000, 557
    for Windows NT, 556
CRL (Certificate Revocation List), in LDAP, 236
cryptography, definition of, 380
CVP (Content Vectoring Protocol)
    about, 270
    with FTP Security Server, 300, 300*f,* 316–317,
        317*f*
        sample configuration for, 328–329, 328*f*
    with HTTP Content Security, 282–284
        sample configuration for, 330, 333*f*
    with SMTP Security Server, 312, 325, 325*f*
    in URI resource, 276–277, 277*f*

D

data, protection of, in security policy, 16–17
data integrity methods, for VPN
    selecting, 397
    settings for, 390

`dbedit`
    documentation of, 190
    object creation with, 143–145
    rulebase edited with, 103
defaultfilter.pf, sample of, 581–582
Defender, about, 196–197
Defender users, FireWall-1 use of, 247
defragmentation, virtual, error on, 146
delivery failure, e-mail stuck on, 313
demilitarized zone (DMZ)
    group for, 93, 93*f*
    need for, 14
denial-of-service (DoS) attacks
    ACK packets in, vanish action for, 523
    traceroute packets in, 8
Desktop Policy Server
    installation of, on IPSO, 40
    no response for, 480
Desktop Security
    policy for
        for client-to-site VPN, 484, 484*f*
        defining, 436–438, 436*f,* 437*f*
    for SecuRemote, setting up, 434–438
destination, in rules, 86
destination port static NAT, 340
destination static NAT, 340
detailed_av_err_mail setting, for SMTP Security
    Server, 305
detailed_rb_err_mail setting, for SMTP Security
    Server, 305
detailed_smtp_err_mail setting, for SMTP
    Security Server, 305
DHCP server
    link-local addresses and, 339
    for Office Mode, 445
DHCP traffic, accepting, 83, 98
DH (Diffie-Hellman) keys, definition of,
    383
dial-up adapters
    installing SecureClient on, 439, 464
    mixing with NICs, SecuRemote and, 479
dial-up networking
    VPN integrated with, 443
    WINS server and, 456
Diffie-Hellman (DH) keys, definition of,
    383
DLL, for authentication, SecureClient and,
    460–461

DMZ (demilitarized zone)
    group for, 93, 93*f*
    need for, 14
DNS, split-horizon, 159
DNS domain, defining, for Office Mode, 445
DNS lookup
    domains and, 71
    enabling, 106
    HTTP Security Server and, 297–298
    service connection slowed by, 158
DNS registration, disabling, in Windows 2000, 558
DNS server, defining, for Office Mode, 445
DNS traffic, encrypting
    Global Properties for, 456
    in SecureClient, 434
domain. *See* Windows NT domain
domain name
    for external user group, 211
    in INSPECT, 526
domain objects, about, 71
DoS (denial-of-service) attacks
    ACK packets in, vanish action for, 523
    traceroute packets in, 8
downloads
    policy on, 563–564
    preventing, 287–288
Drop action, in rules, 86
drop short circuit, in INSPECT, 523, 523*t*
Dst, in rule enforcement, 87
dual NAT, 353–354, 353*f*
dynamic load balancing, 507–508, 508*f*
    with NAT, 509, 509*f*
dynamic object
    resolution failure for, log/alert on, 135
    on ROBO Gateway, 190
dynamic tables, creating, with INSPECT, 528

E
Early Version Compatibility, for SecureClient, 438, 438*f*
education, in network security, 18
ELA (Event Log API), 270
e-mail
    alerts by, 136
    in SMTP Security Server, 305
        settings for, 303, 306
        size of, 312
        stuck, 313–316

e-mail headers, rewriting, 308–309
e-mail recipients, number of, under SMTP
    Security Server, 313–316
embedded device objects, about, 70
Encapsulating Security Payload (ESP)
    in IPSec, 385
    rules for, 407, 407*f*
Encrypt/Client Encrypt action, in rules, 86
Encrypt DNS Traffic, in Global Properties, 456
encryption
    asymmetric, definition of, 381
    concepts in, 380–383
    definition of, 380
    for LDAP server, 239–240, 239*f*
    licensing for, 383–384, 384*t*, 426
    NAT and, 405
    of Session Authentication, 256
    symmetric, definition of, 381
    User Authentication with, 406
    in user properties, 218, 218*f*
    in VPN, 379
        configuring, 386–402
        load balancing and, 510
    VPN rules for, 396, 396*f*
        for SecuRemote access, 431–432
encryption algorithm, for VPN, selecting, 397
encryption domain
    address space shared in, 405–406
    for client-to-site VPN, 482–483, 483*f*
    compiled, in INSPECT, 531
    definition of, 383
        issues with, 410
    determining, 387
        for simplified mode, 397
        for traditional mode, 389, 390*f*
    disconnection from, issues with, 443
    DNS requests forwarded inside, in Microsoft
        Networking, 453–456
    downloading to SecuRemote client, 427
    incorrect, 407–408
    limiting access to, 403
    multiple entry points to, 450–453
    NIC IP address in, 479
    SecuRemote used within, 443
    selecting, 394, 395*f*
    for site addition, 417
    for three-site VPN, 413–414
    unencrypted traffic in, 459

encryption keys, definition of, 380
encryption schemes, defining, for SecuRemote user, 428–430, 428f, 429f
End User License Agreement, IP address limits in, 22
end-user support, for SecuRemote, 426
entropy, in pseudo-random number generators, 380–381
entry points
    to encryption domain, multiple, 450–453
    SecureClient with multiple, 488–491, 488f
    in security, 14
error messages
    via e-mail, 305
    from security policy installation, 100–101, 101f
    in system log, 145–148
ESP (Encapsulating Security Payload)
    in IPSec, 385
    rules for, 407, 407f
evaluation licenses
    about, 24–25
    installation of, 45
    removal of, 170–171
Event Log API (ELA), 270
excessive log grace period, 135
exclusion, grouping by, 72, 73f
expiration date
    for management users, 62
    for users, 212
externally managed gateway objects, about, 70
externally managed node objects, about, 70
external user profile, 210, 211f

F
file descriptors, adjusting, for HTTP Security Server, 295–296
file downloads
    policy on, 563–564
    preventing, 287–288
filter, default
    changing, 539–540
    sample of, 581–582
fingerprints
    in encryption, 382
    validating, in SecureClient, 441, 441f
FIN packets, out of sequence, 157

firewall. See also FireWall-1; firewall module
    access to, by SecureClient with NAT, 469
    adding to RADIUS, 231
    authentication enabled on, 218–219, 219f
    authentication servers and, logon with, 37–38
    connections bypassing, NAT and, 352–355
    definition of, 1–2
    in encryption domains, 383
    gateway cluster and, switching to, 419–422, 420f
    limitations of, 2–3
    as MX, 310
    network logon to, 37–38
    number of, issues with, 189
    Passive FTP handled by, 5–6
    without security policy, 18
    security policy enforced with, 16
    Telnet to, error on, 258
    traceroute handled by, 6–8
    virtual, gateway clusters as, 401–402
FireWall-1
    alerts defined for, 116, 116f
    Clientless VPN in, 243–247
    components of, 161–163, 162f
    configuration of, common questions about, 141–145
    flexibility of, 10–11
    installation of, 39–52
        directory for, 43, 43f
        planning, 13–26
    integration with Windows NT domain, 247–248
    interoperability with, of third-party VPN products, 403
    kernel variables in, modifying, 141–142
    L2TP clients and, 446–450
    large-scale use of, management issues with, 188–191
    NAT in, 336, 339–343
    need for, 9–11
    operating system for
        installing, 34–39
        securing, 37–39, 545–561
        selecting, 27–34
    order of operations in, 341–343
    packet sniffer in, 355
    as proxy, 250

as reverse proxy, 250
technologies in, 8–9
upgrading, 52–53
firewall-1.conf, 567–569
FireWall-1 control connections, accepting, 83, 96, 96*f*
FireWall-1 host, license for, 22
FireWall-1 Password
about, 194
enabling, on firewall, 219
settings for, for user, 215, 215*f*
firewall-1.schema, 571–573
firewall Internet gateway. *See* single-gateway products
firewall module
dynamic addressing used by, SIC and, 184
in FireWall-1, 161
installation of, 49–52
license for, 20–26
updating remotely, 169–171
logging on, local, 164–165
one-time password for, 163–164, 164*f*
security policy on, remotely controlling, 166–167
state tables of, remote viewing of, 167–169
synching clock of, to management station, 184
firewall object
for NAT implementation, 350, 351*t*
in double-blind network, 376, 376*t*
in network migration, 372, 373*t*
in simple network, 367, 368*t*
for SecuRemote, configuring, 427
floating evals, 24–25
FQDN (fully qualified domain name), changing, 48, 48*f*
FTP commands, FTP Security Server and, 300–301
FTP connections
with random source port, 157
over SSL, 157–158, 158*t*
FTP proxy, FireWall-1 as, 250
FTP resource, for Content Security, 299–300, 299*f*, 300*f*
sample configuration for, 327–329, 327*f*, 328*f*, 329*f*
FTP Security Server
about, 299–302
debugging, 320*t*

sample configuration for, 326–329
site access through, 301–302
FTP service
Client Authentication over, 228
ident required by, 157
ports for, problems with, 157
problems with, 156–158
User Authentication for, 198–201
rule order and, 224
FTP traffic, Content Security for, 299–302
sample configuration for, 326–329
full sync
definition of, 494
error on, 514
fully qualified domain name (FQDN), changing, 48, 48*f*, 175
fw, *vs.* fwm, 167
fw fetch, 167
fw log, 124–126, 126*t*
fw logswitch, 136–137
fwm
vs. fw, 167
user configuration with, 58–59, 59*t*
fwm load, 166
fw monitor
example code for, 542
guidelines for use of, 543
INSPECT used with, 540–542, 541*t*
NAT issues and, 355
fwm unload, 167
fw parameter, of cpstat, application flavors for, 120*t*
fw putkey, 163
fw sam, 129–131, 129*t*–130*t*
connection blocking with, 143
FWZ, about, 384–385

G
gateway
IP addresses for, in INSPECT, 534
management module moved from, 176–178
management of, with ROBO Gateway Profile, 189–190
packets from, accepting, 83, 97, 97*f*
rule enforcement by, specifying, 87
in VPN Communities, 401, 407

gateway cluster
    creating, 421, 421*f*
    firewall switching to, 419–422, 420*f*
    for High Availability VPNs, 401–402
    IP address for, 495–496
    IP Pool NAT in, 452
    policies installed in, inconsistencies in,
        514–515, 516
    SecureClient with, sample configuration for,
        484–487, 485*f*
    SecuRemote failover with, 450
        sample configuration for, 488–491, 490*f*
    software mismatch within, 519–520
    for State Synchronization
        configuration of, 495–497, 495*f*, 496*f*,
            497*f*
        working mode of, error on, 514
    third-party, interoperability with, 403
gateway cluster objects
    about, 70
    configuring, 495–497, 495*f*, 496*f*, 497*f*
Gateway Components, installation of, 40
gateway object. *See also* Check Point gateway
       object
    for gateway cluster creation, 419–420, 485
    IP Pool NAT settings for, 452, 452*f*
    Office Mode configured on, 444–446, 444*f*
    for SecuRemote, configuring, 427–428
    User Authentication configured on, 223
GINA DLL, enabling, for SecureClient, 465
Global Properties
    for authentication, 220–221, 220*f*
    for High Availability management modules,
        179–180
    IP Pool NAT in, 451, 451*f*
    for LDAP, 235–236, 235*f*
    for rulebase
        about, 82–85, 82*f*, 84*f*, 85*f*
        alerts settings in, 133–136, 133*f*, 134*f*
        application of, 106
        tweaking, 96–98
    for SecuRemote, 432–434, 433*f*
        encryption in, 429–430, 429*f*
    VPN modes in, 388–389, 388*f*
Gnutella, blocking, 288–289
group, user. *See* user groups
group objects
    about, 72, 72*f*

configuring, for management users, 62, 62*f*
creating, with `dbedit`, 144
defining, 92, 93, 93*f*
for DMZ, 93, 93*f*
for VPN domain, 390
GUIdbedit tool, rulebase edited with, 103,
    103*f*

H

HA. *See* High Availability
hackers, firewall design and, 3
hard drive partitioning
    for Linux, 559
    for SPARC Solaris, 545
hardware support, in SPARC Solaris, 29
hardware token
    in Defender, 196–197
    in SecurID, 196, 196*f*
hash functions
    for dynamic load balancing, 507, 508*f*, 509
        with VPN, 510
    in encryption, 382
High Availability (HA), 270
    asymmetric routing in, 500–501
    hardware-based solutions for, 502
    implementation of, 499–512
    licensing for, 494
    load balancing in, 503–512
    SecuRemote in, 450–453
    S/Key and, 196
    software-based solutions for, 502
    solution providers for, 502–503
    State Synchronization in, 493–499
High Availability management modules. *See also*
       secondary management module
    about, 178–183
    certificate authority errors in, 184–185
    failover in, 182–183, 182*f*
    synchronizing, 179, 179*f*
High Availability VPNs, gateway clusters for,
    401–402
host
    grouping, for load balancing, 504
    for Management GUIs
        configuring, 63–64
        fetching, 108
    number of, error on, 146–147
    specification of, in rules, 86

hostid, license based on, 24
host objects. *See also* node host objects
    creating, with `dbedit`, 144
hosts file, in Windows NT, 554
hotfix accumulators, about, 145
hotfixes, for Windows 2000, 557
hot standby, definition of, 494
HTML, weeding, 276
HTTP buffer, increasing size of, 293–294
HTTP connection
    authenticated, logging on, 135
    file descriptors for, 295–296
    tunneled, blocking, 288–289
HTTP proxy, FireWall-1 as, 250
HTTP Security Server
    about, 271–298
    CVP with, 282–284
    debugging, 319–320, 320*t*
    enabling, 271–272
    error messages in, 292–293
    instances of, increasing, 294
    memory for, 295, 298
    performance tuning, 293–296
    port for, 297–298
    requests forwarded by, to caching proxy
        server, 286
    sample configuration for, 330–333
    schemes permitted by, 291–292
    troubleshooting, 297–298
    UFP with, 278–282
    Web site access through
        issues with, 290, 290*t*–291*t*
        troubleshooting, 298
HTTP server, user authentication properties
    for, 223
HTTP service
    authenticating over different ports, 251
    authentication with, on remote site, 253
    Client Authentication over, 202, 204, 204*f*,
        228
        custom pages for, 254–255
        debugging, 320*t*
    for Clientless VPN, 244–246, 245*f*, 246*t*
    connections dropped with, 258
    User Authentication for, 198–199, 199*f*
        rule order and, 224
HTTPS server, internal, authenticating access to,
    251–252, 253*f*

HTTPS service
    Client Authentication over, 202
    User Authentication for, 198–199
HTTPS traffic, outbound
    authenticating, 251
    Content Security for, 288
HTTP traffic
    Content Security for, 271–298
        sample configuration for, 330–333
    filtering, 272–278
        on other ports, 285–286
        UFP for, 271, 278–282
hub-and-spoke model, for VPN, 404–405

I

IANA (Internet Assigned Numbers Authority),
    335
ICA (Internal Certificate Authority)
    in High Availability management configura-
        tion, 184–185
    random number generator for, 47, 47*f*
    SIC for, 163
ICA certificates
    exporting, 392
    on management station, deletion and, 175
    revoking, 185–186
ICANN (Internet Corporation for Assigned
        Names and Numbers), 335
ICMP packets
    blocking, 150
    NAT support for, 352
ICMP Redirect, dual NAT and, 353–354, 354*f*
ICMP requests, accepting, 83, 98, 98*f*
ICMP service object, about, 77
ICMP traceroute, firewall handling of, 7–8
identifiers, in INSPECT, 525, 525*t*
ident packets
    accepting, 99–100, 99*f*
    rejecting, 158–159
    required by FTP, 157
If Via, in rules, 86
IGMP packets, accepting, 99, 99*f*
IKE
    about, 386
    aggressive mode for, 392
    debugging with, 408
    maximum concurrent connections for, 408
    rules for, 407, 407*f*

IKE (*cont.*)
over TCP, SecureClient options for, 460
in traditional mode, settings for, 390–392, 391*f*
IKE pre-shared secrets
encryption key for, 242
with L2TP, 447
simplified mode and, 388
for VPN gateways, 401
IKE rekey, VPN failure after, 409–410
incremental sync, definition of, 494
individuals, in security policy, 17
information confidentiality, policy on, 564
INSPECT
definition of, 521
documentation of, 521
purpose of, 522
rulebase converted to, 529–536, 530*f*
sample of, 536–543
syntax for, 522–529
installation image, for SecureClient, 465–468
Install On
in rules, 87
in S/Key, 214
Insufficient Information problem, 223–225
interface
definition of, 143
different rules for, INSPECT for, 538–539
fetching, 108
support for, 143
Internal Certificate Authority. *See* ICA
Internet, DNS definitions for, 159
Internet Assigned Numbers Authority (IANA), 335
Internet connection, sharing, SecuRemote and, 473
Internet Corporation for Assigned Names and Numbers (ICANN), 335
Internet Explorer, HTTP Security Server and, 298
Internet Relay Chat (IRC), ident used by, 100
Internet Service Providers, policy on, 565
interoperable device objects, about, 72
Intranet, DNS definitions for, 159
IP address
for connection hiding, 340
determining, with IP Pool NAT, 477

in domain objects, 71
for gateway cluster, 402, 402*f*
more than four, 515
in State Synchronization configuration, 495–496
in INSPECT, 526
Internet, in internal network, 443
license based on, 24–25
for Management GUIs, configuring, 63–64
for management station, moving management module and, 174–176
for MX records, in SMTP Security Server, 306, 308
for NAT
binding to loopback interface, 354–355
determining, 345
in double-blind network, 375
in network migration, 370
in simple network, 366
of NIC, in encryption domain, 479
in node-limited license, 21–22, 147
for remote management, installation of, 46, 46*f*
virtual, for High Availability, 499–500
for VPN clients
assigned in Office Mode, 443–444, 445
conflicting, 442
IP Options
dropping, logging on, 134
enabling, 84
packet checked against, 342
IP Pool NAT
allocating to Office Mode clients, 446
asymmetric routing and, 443
determining IP address with, 477
for SecuRemote connections, 451, 451*f*
in VPN, 397
IP routing, enabling
in Windows 2000, 558
in Windows NT, 553
IPSec
about, 385–386
starting, for L2TP, 449
UDP encapsulation for
fragmentation with, 477–478
SecureClient option for, 460
IPSec rekey, IKE rekeys and, 409–410

IPSO
   FireWall-1 on, 31–32
      installation of, 40
   firewall module on, installation of, 49–52
   packet sniffer in, 355
   preinstallation of, 35–36
   proxy ARP on, 347
   static routes on, 348–349
   tweaking, 577
IPv4 address space, 335–336
IPv6 address space, 336
IPxxx. *See* IPSO
IRC (Internet Relay Chat), ident used by, 100
ISPs (Internet Service Providers), policy on, 565

J
JAVA code, blocking, 276

K
KaZaA, blocking, 288–289
kernel URL logging, HTTP Security Server and,
   295
kernel variables, modifying, 141–142
KEY, in connections table, 527
key exchange, for VPN, settings for, 390

L
L2TP clients, configuring for, 446–450
label, in domain names, 454–456
lab network, for testing OS configuration, 36
Large Scale Manager
   gateway management with, 189
   purpose of, 56
LDAP (Lightweight Directory Access Protocol)
   about, 197–198
   Global Properties for, 235–236, 235*f*
   integrating, 234–243
   license for, 24
LDAP account unit
   authentication properties for, 241–242,
      241*f*
   properties of, 236–237, 237*f*
   server added to, 237–238, 237*f*
LDAP group
   properties for, 242–243, 242*f*
   rule for, 243
   in user creation, setting for, 210

LDAP server
   adding to account unit, 237–238, 237*f*
   branches of, specifying, 240, 240*f*
   encryption properties for, 239–240, 239*f*
   properties of, 238–239, 238*f*
   schema checking for, 234–235
   SecureClient options for, 462
LDAP users, FireWall-1 use of, 247
LEA (Log Export API), 270
license(s)
   adding, 171
   for evaluation, 24–25
   for firewall module, installation of, 50–51
   for High Availability, 494
   for High Availability management modules,
      178
   installation of, 171
   issues with, 24–25, 109
   for management console, installation of, 45, 45*f*
   obtaining, 24–26
   for planning and installation, 20–26
   for State Synchronization, error on, 516
   third-party software and, 269
   updating, remotely, 169–171
license key, for licenses, 24
Lightweight Directory Access Protocol. *See* LDAP
link-local addresses, 339
Linux
   FireWall-1 on, 32–34
   packet sniffer in, 355
   securing, 559–561
   tweaking, 560–561
load balancing
   dynamic, 507–508, 508*f*
      with NAT, 509, 509*f*
   in High Availability, 503–512
   static, 504–505, 505*f*
   with switches, 506, 507*f*
localhost, connection to Management GUIs, 64
local interface anti-spoofing, error on, 145
local license, 24
location, in user properties, 216, 216*f*
log
   on Client Authentication, 229
   grace period in, 135
   for High Availability management modules,
      181, 181*f*

log (*cont.*)
    location of, 139–140, 139*f*
    maintenance of, 136–140
    number of, issues with, 190
    rule viewed from, 126–127
log, system, error messages in, 145–148
log buffer, full, 148
Log Export API (LEA), 270
logging
    enabling
        for Linux, 560–561
        in SPARC Solaris, 551
    on firewall module, local, 164–165
    guidelines for, 123–124
    of implied rules, 84, 98
    in OS security, 38–39
    in rules, 86–87
    to syslog, 142–143
    in usage policy, 565
login accounts, generic, issues with, 39
login name, for management users, 61
Log Manager. *See* SmartView Tracker
logon, SecureClient options for, 464–465, 464*f*
Log Viewer. *See* SmartView Tracker
Lumeta, for network topology, 14

M
MAC address
    for ARP
        determining, 345–347
        in double-blind network, 375
        in network migration, 370–371
        in simple network, 366
        verifying, 357–359
    for State Synchronization, changing,
        512–513
machine name
    for Windows 2000, 557
    for Windows NT, 553
mail alerts, 136
management (organizational), security policy
        supported by, 16, 18
management console. *See also* management
        station; SmartConsole
    installation of, 40–49
    license for, 22
    purpose of, 20–21
    in single-gateway products, 22

Management GUI applications. *See also specific
        applications*
    about, 55–66
    administrator accounts for, 39
    backward compatibility of, 106
    demonstration mode of, 66
    hosts for, configuring, 63–64
    installation of, 44, 44*f*
    license for, 23
        error on, 109
    purpose of, 21
    reliance on, issues with, 190–191
    over slow connections, 107–108
    status of, 113, 113*f*
    users for, configuring, 58
management module
    in FireWall-1, 162
    highly available (*See* High Availability
        management modules)
    moving, 172–178
        from standalone gateway, 176–178
    NAT on, remote management from, 165
    one-time password for, 163–164, 164*f*
    testing, after migration, 176
management object
    deleting, after moving, 175
    IP address of, moving management module
        and, 174–176
    log rotation with, 137
management station. *See also* management
        console
    fingerprint of, 48, 48*f*
    installation of, 40–49
    limitations on moving, 176
    synching clock of, to firewall module, 184
management users
    configuring
        in Policy Editor, 60–63, 60*f,* 61*f,* 62*f,* 63*f*
        in SmartDashboard, 58
manual rules, for NAT, 339
max_conns_per_site setting, for SMTP Secu-
        rity Server, 305
max_conns setting, for SMTP Security Server,
        305
max_ips_per_mx_node setting, for SMTP Secu-
        rity Server, 306
max_mail_size setting, for SMTP Security Server,
        305

max_mails_per_conn setting, for SMTP Security
Server, 305
max_mx_node_per_mail setting, for SMTP
Security Server, 305
maxrecipients setting, for SMTP Security Server,
306
MD5 Challenge, authentication with, 447
memory
for HTTP Security Server, 295, 298
used for state tables, 576, 576*f*
Meshed Community, creating, 397–401, 398*f*,
399*f*, 400*f*
<methods>, in SIC policy rules, 188
Microsoft Internet Explorer, HTTP Security
Server and, 298
Microsoft Networking, SecureClient and, 453–457
Microsoft Visio, for network topology, 14
MIME type, filtering on, 309–310
modules. *See also specific modules*
connections between, 162, 162*f*
states of, 114, 114*t*
Motif GUI, license for, 23
MTA, connection failure at, 312
MTU Adjuster, 478, 478*f*
multicast addresses, 335–336
MX records, under SMTP Security Server
firewall as, 310
IP address of, 306, 308
number of, 305–306
subject of, 310

N
NAT (Network Address Translation)
disadvantages of, 337–338
for double-blind network, 374–377, 374*f*
dual, 353–354, 353*f*
dynamic load balancing with, 509, 509*f*
encryption and, 405
in FireWall-1, 336, 339–343
firewall bypassed and, 352–355
for firewalls, 15
implementation of, 343–351, 344*f*
samples of, 365–377
IP addresses for
binding to loopback interface, 354–355
determining, 345
L2TP and, 450
limitations of, 351–355

network migration with, 369–373, 369*f*
network objects for, 349, 349*t*
proxy ARPs for, setting up, 345–347
purpose of, 336
remote management with, 165
SecureClient with, firewall access by, 469
SecuRemote with, 468–469
simple network with, sample of, 365–369, 365*f*
State Synchronization and, 499
static host routes for, setting up, 348–349
troubleshooting, with packet sniffer, 355–364
types of, 339–340
with VPN, 405–406
IP conflicts with, 442
in VPN Community, disabling, 400–401
NAT rules
compiled, in INSPECT, 532–534, 532*f*
creating, 350–351, 351*f*
in double-blind network, 377, 377*f*
dual, 353–354, 353*f*
encryption and, 405, 405*f*
manual, 339
in network migration, 373, 373*f*
packet checked against, 342
in simple network, 368, 368*f*
NetBIOS
name resolution in, SecuRemote and, 456–457
over TCP, disabling, in Windows 2000, 558
network
double-blind, NAT for, 374–377, 374*f*
Internet IP addresses routed through, 443
migrating, with NAT, 369–373, 369*f*
size of, security needs and, 9–11
unsecured operating systems on, 36
Network Address Translation. *See* NAT
network objects
about, 70–71, 70*f*
compiled, in INSPECT, 531
creating, with dbedit, 144–145
defining, 92, 93*f*
for encryption domain, 389
for site addition, 417
for three-site VPN, 413–414
for NAT implementation, 349, 349*t*
in double-blind network, 376, 376*t*
in network migration, 371, 371*t*–372*t*
in simple network, 367, 367*t*
number of, issues with, 188

network topology
    anti-spoofing settings in, 80–81, 81*f*
    for Check Point gateway, 68–69, 69*f*
    creating, 91
    defining, error on, 148
    in firewall planning, 13–15
    for gateway cluster, 486, 486*f*
    in rulebase creation, 91–92, 92*f*
    SecureClient options for, 461, 461*f*
    SecureClient request for, port for, 473
    as VPN domain, 389, 390*f*
network traffic, order of operations in, 341–343
newline characters, FTP problems with, 156–157
NIC, mixing with dial-up adapters, SecuRemote
    and, 479
node gateway objects, about, 70
node host objects, about, 70
node-limited firewalls
    in HA configuration, 494
    host number error in, 146–147
    license for, 21–22
    in single-gateway products, 22
node objects (workstation objects)
    about, 70–73
    defining, 92, 94*f*
    externally managed, about, 70
    in FireWall-1 upgrade, 52–53
    for RADIUS server, creating, 232–233
    for TACACS, 233, 233*f*
Nokia Crypto Cluster, VPN issues with, 409
Nokia IP Clustering, load balancing in, 504
Nokia IP Security Platform. *See* IPSO
NT domain. *See* Windows NT domain
numbers, in INSPECT, 526

O
objects
    creation of, from command line, 143–145
    defining, 92–94
    naming, 104, 105*t*–106*t*
    types of, 66–73
    viewing, in SmartDashboard, 57
objects_5_0.C
    corruption of, 147–148
    editing, 102–103
    in rulebase compiling, 529–530
objects list, in SmartDashboard, 57
objects tree, in SmartDashboard, 57

OBSEC Management Interface (OMI), 270
Office Mode, for SecureClient, 442–446
    anti-spoofing in, 445
    configuring, 444–446, 444*f*
    connections in, 446
    issues resolved by, 442–444
    limitations of, 446
    Microsoft Networking and, 453
    with multiple interfaces, 445
OMI (OBSEC Management Interface), 270
one-request method, for UFP caching, 294–295
one-time password (OTP)
    for firewall module, 163–164, 164*f*
    for management module, 163–164, 164*f*
    vs. static password, 194
OpenLDAP v1, file for, 567–569
OpenLDAP v2, file for, 571–573
Open Platform for Security (OPSEC), about, 270
operating system. *See* OS
OPSEC (Open Platform for Security), about, 270
OPSEC application
    for CVP server, 283, 283*f*
    for UFP server, 279–280, 279*f*, 281*f*
organization, security needs of, 9–11
OS (operating system)
    for FireWall-1
        configuration of, 36
        installing, 34–39
        securing, 37–39, 545–561
        selecting, 27–34
    firewall limitations and, 2–3
    of management module, moving module and,
        172–173
    patches for, 38
OSE device objects, about, 71
os parameter, of `cpstat`, application flavors for,
    119*t*
OS password
    about, 194
    enabling, on firewall, 219
Other type services, INSPECT for, 536
OTP. *See* one-time password
ownership, in security policy, 17

P
packages
    for Linux, 559–560
    for SPARC Solaris, 546–550

packet
  accepting based on previous packet, INSPECT for, 537–538
  fragmentation of, in VPN, 411
  inspection of, with `fw monitor`, 541
  processing of, in FireWall-1, 342
  virtual defragmentation of, error on, 146
packet filters
  overview of, 3–4
  Passive FTP handled by, 6
  Stateful Inspection and, 5
  traceroute handled by, 7–8
packet integrity check, in VPN, 379
packet sniffer
  for NAT troubleshooting, 355–364
  password discovered with, 194
Passive FTP, firewall handling of, 5–6
password(s)
  about, 193–198
  erased, SecureClient and, 460
  for management users, 59
  in S/Key, 214
    resetting, 253–254
  user, changing, 253
password, one-time. *See* one-time password (OTP)
password number, in S/Key, 195
<peers>, in SIC policy rules, 187
permissions, defining, for management users, 61, 61*f*
.pf file, in rulebase compiling, 529–531
`ping`, fragmented packet troubleshooting with, 477–478
PKI (Public Key Infrastructure), 270
Pnote devices, errors on, 517
Point-to-Point Tunneling Protocol (PPTP), INSPECT for, 537
Policy Editor. *See also* SmartDashboard
  about, 56–58, 57*f*
  crashing of, 108–109
  demonstration mode of, 66
  NAT rules in, 339
  purpose of, 55
  restrictions on, 65, 65*f*
  on SPARC Solaris, 30
  troubleshooting, 107
policy names, in FireWall-1 upgrade, 53
policy routing, load balancing with, 505, 506*f*

policy server, SecureClient and, 434
  logon to, 459
<ports>, in SIC policy rules, 187
postmaster, e-mail address for, 306
postmaster setting, for SMTP Security Server, 306
PPPoE, SecuRemote and, 476
PPTP (Point-to-Point Tunneling Protocol), INSPECT for, 537
pre-shared secrets
  vs. certificates, 387
  for IKE
    encryption key for, 242
    simplified mode and, 388
    for VPN gateways, 401
privacy, in usage policy, 565
private key, in public-key cryptography, 381
protocol(s). *See also specific protocols*
  NAT incompatibility with, 351–352
  for State Synchronization, 494
  for Windows 2000, 556–557
  for Windows NT, 552
proxied conns, entries in, increasing, 293
proxies. *See* application proxies
proxy ARPs. *See also* ARPs
  setting up, for NAT implementation, 345–347
pseudo-random number generator, in encryption, 380–381
public key
  certification of, 383
  in public-key cryptography, 381
public-key cryptography, asymmetric encryption in, 381
Public Key Infrastructure (PKI), 270

R
RADIUS (Remote Access Dial-In User Service)
  about, 197
  integrating, 231–233
  settings for, for User Authentication, 215, 215*f*
RADIUS server, on NT domain, 248
RADIUS server object, creating, 232–233, 232*f*
RADIUS service, creating, 232
RADIUS users, FireWall-1 use of, 247
random keystrokes
  in firewall installation, 51
  in management console installation, 47, 47*f*
random number generator, seeding, 47, 47*f*
registers, in INSPECT, 526

registry, hacking, in securing Windows NT, 554–555

Reject action, in rules, 86

reject short circuit, in INSPECT, 523t

Remote Access, SCV for, 435–436, 435f

Remote Access community, gateway object for, for SecuRemote, 427

Remote Access Dial-In User Service. *See* RADIUS

remote administration
    IP address for, installation of, 46, 46f
    in Windows NT/2000, 28–29

remote management
    capabilities of, 165–171
    with NAT, 165
    troubleshooting, 183–188

Remote Procedure Call (RPC), support for, 149

Reporting Tool, purpose of, 56

resend_period setting, for SMTP Security Server, 303

resources, definition of, 271, 271t. *See also specific types*

reverse proxy, FireWall-1 as, 250

revision control, for security policy, setting for, 85

RFC1918 addresses, 338

RIP, accepting, 97, 97f

rlogin Security Server, debugging, 320t

rlogin service
    Client Authentication over, 228
    User Authentication for, 198–199
        rule order and, 224

Roaming user profiles, with SecureClient, 465

ROBO Gateway Profile, 189–190

routers
    firewalls compared to, 1–2
    packet filtering in, 3

routing
    asymmetric
        Office Mode and, 444
        VPN and, 443
    in firewall OS, 39
    for Office Mode network, 446

RPC (Remote Procedure Call), support for, 149

RPC locator, Windows 2000 and, 558–559

RPC service object, about, 77, 77f

RST packets
    dropping, 155
    SYN packets followed by, in NAT trouble-shooting, 359–361

rule(s). *See also* NAT rules; VPN rules
    changing, responsibility for, 17
    for Client Authentication, 227, 227f, 266f
        error on, 256
    for Clientless VPN, 244, 244f
    for client-to-site VPN, 483, 483f
    conflicting, 101, 101f
    defining, 94–95
    for Desktop Security, 436–438, 436f, 437f
    for FTP Content Security, 300, 300f, 329f
    for groups, 218
    hierarchical management of, 189
    for HTTP Content Security, 278, 278f
        with CVP, 284, 285f
        with UFP, 282, 282f
    implied, logging, 84, 98
    for interfaces, 106–107
    for LDAP group, 243
    for multiple-entry point SecureClient, 491, 491f
    for NAT implementation, 350, 350f
    necessary, 99–100
    number of, issues with, 188
    order of, 88–90, 89f
        guidelines for, 90
        Security Servers and, 319
        setting, 82
        in User Authentication, 223–225
    parts of, 85–87
    sample, 87–88, 88f
    for SecureClient with gateway cluster, 486–487, 487f
    for Session Authentication, 225, 225f
    in SIC policy, 187
    for SMTP Content Security, 310f, 326f, 329f
    for TCP Content Security, 317, 317f
    for User Authentication, 221–223, 222f
    for users, 218

rulebase
    about, 85–90
    components of, 66–85
    converted to INSPECT, 529–536, 530f
    creating, 90–101
        network topology in, 91–92, 92f
        objects in, defining, 92–94
    disappearance of, 107
    e-mail directed through, 308
    e-mail not allowed by, notification on, 305

importing, 107
for multiple-entry point SecureClient, 491, 491*f*
for NAT implementation, 350, 350*f*
  in double-blind network, 377, 377*f*
  in network migration, 373, 373*f*
  in simple network, 368, 368*f*
number of, issues with, 188–189
order of operations in, 88–90, 89*f*
packet checked against, 342
sample of, 95*f*
for SecureClient with gateway cluster, 486–487, 487*f*
for SecuRemote, 431–432, 432*f*
for Session Authentication, 264*f*
for User Authentication, 262, 262*f*
rulebasese.fws, editing, 102–103
rundir setting, for SMTP Security Server, 304

S
SA (Security Associations)
  about, 386
  simplification of subnets in, 410
SAA (Secure Authentication API), 270
Safe@ products, license for, 23
SAM. *See* SmartDefense
SAMP (Suspicious Activity Monitoring Protocol), 270
SANS Institute, security policy documents of, 20
satellite gateway, in Star Community, 398
scan_period setting, for SMTP Security Server, 303
scheduled event object, 78, 79*f*
schema checking, for LDAP server, 234–235
script, as alert action, 135–136
SCV (Secure Configuration Verification), for Remote Access, 435–436, 435*f*
SDL. *See* Secure Domain Logon
secondary management module
  failover to, 182–183, 182*f*
  installing, 178–179, 178*f*
secret key, in S/Key, 195
  settings for, 214
Secure Authentication API (SAA), 270
SecureClient
  adding site to, 441–442, 441*f*
  anti-spoofing in, 445
  certificate obtained with, 430–431

command line interface for, 474–475, 474*t*–475*t*
configuring, 439, 440*f*
connection mode for, 458*f*, 459
custom prepackaged version of, 442, 457–468
DNS traffic encrypted for, 434
with gateway clusters, sample configuration for, 484–487, 485*f*
installation of, 438–442
  image for, 465–468, 466*f*
  options for, 463–464, 463*f*
  profiles for, 457, 458*f*
introduction to, 425–426
license for, 24, 426
Microsoft Networking and, 453–457
with multiple entry points, sample configuration for, 488–491, 488*f*
with NAT, firewall access by, 469
Office Mode for, 442–446
options for, 459–462, 460*f*
policy server and, 434
profiles for installation of, 457, 458*f*
sample configurations for, 481–491
vs. SecuRemote, 425–426
third-party VPN and, 473
topology request by, port for, 473
traceroute with, 411
SecureClient Packaging Tool, 56, 457–468
Secure Configuration Verification (SCV), for Remote Access, 435–436, 435*f*
Secure Domain Logon (SDL)
  platforms compatible with, 457
  for SecureClient
    Microsoft Networking and, 453
    options for, 465
Secure Internal Communication. *See* SIC
SecuRemote. *See also* SecureClient
  binding to all adapters, 479
  behind Check Point gateway, 470, 470*f*
  communication ports blocked in, 476
  configuring, 426–442
  custom adapters and, 476
  disabling at startup, 472
  encrypted session to, initiating, 469–470
  failover of, gateway cluster for, 450, 488–491, 490*f*
  interface bound to, 439

SecuRemote (*cont.*)
 introduction to, 425–426
 IP Pool NAT for, 451, 451*f*
 license for, 24, 426
 with NAT, 468–469
 NetBIOS name resolution and, 456–457
 NT file permissions and, 478
 outbound connections allowed to, code for, 536–537
 behind proxy, 471–472, 471*f*, 472*f*
 sample configurations for, 481–491
 vs. SecureClient, 425–426
 site added to, 476
 troubleshooting, 476–480
 user creation for, 428–431, 428*f*
SecuRemote DNS server, 454, 454*f*, 455*f*
Secure Platform (SPLAT), for Linux installation, 32–34
secure server, license for, 22
Secure Sockets Layer. *See* SSL
SecureUpdate. *See* SmartUpdate
SecurID
 about, 196, 196*f*
 authentication failure with, 258–259
 integrating, 230–231
 settings for, 216
SecurID users, FireWall-1 use of, 247
Security Associations (SA)
 about, 386
 simplification of subnets in, 410
Security Focus, 38
security policy
 configuring, frequently asked questions about, 101–107
 default filter and
  changing, 539–540
  sample of, 581–582
 developing, 15–20
 enforcement of, 16
 example of, 19–20
 files in, 102
 firewall implementation and, 18
 firewall limitations in, 2
 guidelines for, 16–18
 in INSPECT, 534–536
 installation of, 100–101, 100*f*
  Client Authentication and, 257
  errors on, 147–148

 on gateway cluster, inconsistencies in, 514–515, 516
 setting for, 85
 large-scale environment, 188
 management support for, 16
 reinstallation of, 104
 remotely controlling, on firewall module, 166–167
 responsibility for, 17, 19–20
 revision control for, 85
 in rule generation, 94–95
 specifics in, 17–18
Security Servers. *See also specific servers*
 connections to
  failover of, 494
  origin of, 318
 debugging, 319–321, 320*t*
 enabling, 221
 issues with, 318–319
 rule order and, 319
 State Synchronization and, 499
seed value, in S/Key, 195
 settings for, 212
selection criteria, in SmartView Tracker, 123–124
server object
 for LDAP account unit, 236
 for RADIUS, 232–233, 232*f*
 for TACACS, 233, 233*f*
service(s)
 "any," 104, 104*t*
 Client Authentication for, 202
 common questions about, 148–150
 disabling
  in SPARC Solaris, 550–551, 551*t*
  in Windows 2000, 557–558
  in Windows NT, 554
 excepting from State Synchronization, 513
 in FireWall-1 upgrade, 53
 not running, RST packets from, 360–361
 in OS security, 38
 of Other type, INSPECT for, 536
 removing, from Linux, 560
 Session Authentication for, 201
 slow, 158
 User Authentication for, 198
 through VPN, not encrypting, 399–400
 in Windows 2000, 556–557
 in Windows NT, 553

Service, in rules, 86
Service Level Agreement (SLA), violation of,
    log/alert on, 134
service objects
    about, 73–77
    creating, 73
service packs
    for Windows 2000, 557
    for Windows NT, 556
service port, error message about, 145–146
<services>, in SIC policy rules, 187
Session Authentication
    in cleartext, 256
    for Client Authentication, 202, 228
    with Content Security, 256, 319
    encryption for, 256
    error on, 255
    explanation of, 201, 201f, 202f
    limitations of, 207–208
    rule for, 225, 225f
    sample configuration for, 263–264
    setting up, 225–227
    SSL for, 226
    usage guidelines for, 207t
short circuit, in INSPECT, 523, 523t
SIC (Secure Internal Communication)
    about, 163–164
    debugging, 186–188
    dynamic addressing and, 184
    failure of, in remote management, 183–184
    general failure of, 184
    one-time password for, establishing, 51–52
    for OPSEC application, 280
    random number generator for, 47, 47f
    resetting, 185–186
    with secondary management station, 179
SIC certificates, clock sync and, 184
SIC key, copying, to destination management
    module, 173–174
SIC name, in moving management module,
    175
SIC policy, debugging, 187–188
Sign On Method, for Client Authentication,
    228–229, 228f
silent installation, for SecureClient, 462–463,
    463f
Simple Object Access Protocol (SOAP), for URI
    resource, 278, 278f

single-gateway products
    about, 22
    in HA configuration, 494
S/Key
    about, 195–196
    enabling, on firewall, 219
    resetting passwords for, 253–254
    settings for, 212–215, 213f
S/Key generator, 195, 195f
SLA (Service Level Agreement), violation of,
    log/alert on, 134
small-office environments, Check Point Express
    for, 23
SmartCenter. *See* SmartConsole
SmartClients
    backward compatibility of, 106
    installation of, directory for, 44, 44f
    license for, 22–23
SmartConsole. *See also* management console
    files modified by, 65
    in FireWall-1, 162
    license for, 22–23
    reliance on, 190–191
SmartDashboard. *See also* Policy Editor
    about, 56–58, 57f
    authentication configured in, 163–164
    crashing of, 108–109
    purpose of, 55
    reliance on, 190–191
    restrictions on, 65, 65f
    rules viewed in, 126–127
    troubleshooting, 107
    users created in, 208
SmartDefense (SAM)
    FTP commands enabled in, 301, 301f
    log/alert settings for, 134
SmartDirectory, license for, 24
SmartMap, crashing of, 108–109
"smart" SMTP server, 311, 311f
SmartUpdate (SecureUpdate)
    license update with, 169, 171, 172f
    purpose of, 56
SmartView Monitor, purpose of, 56
SmartView Status. *See also* Status Manager
    about, 111–118, 112f
    purpose of, 56
SmartView Tracker (Log Viewer)
    about, 121–131, 121f

SmartView Tracker (*cont.*)
  active mode in, 127–131, 127*f,* 127*t*–128*t*
  audit mode in, 131, 132*f,* 132*t*
  bottleneck in, 190
  demonstration mode of, 66
  fields in, 122*t*–123*t*
  IP resolution timeout for, 135
  purpose of, 56
SMTP resources, for Content Security, 306–310,
    307*f,* 308*f,* 309*f*
  sample configuration for, 323–326, 324*f,*
    325*f,* 326*f*
SMTP Security Server
  about, 302–316, 303*f*
  CVP with, 312, 325, 325*f*
  debugging, 320*t*
  mail stuck in, 313–316
  MX records used by, issues with, 311
  parameters for, 302–306, 304*f*
  sample configuration for, 322–326
  spam and, 311–312
  troubleshooting, 312–316
SMTP server, "smart," 311, 311*f*
SMTP traffic
  Content Security for, 302–316, 303*f*
    sample configuration for, 322–326
  ident used by, 100
snoop
  expressions for, 364, 364*t*
  flags for, 363, 363*t*
  for NAT troubleshooting, 355–361
SOAP (Simple Object Access Protocol), for URI
    resource, 278, 278*f*
social engineering, 2
SOCKS, ICMP proxied by, 8
software, uninstalling, for security, 37
Solaris x86, FireWall-1 on, 29. *See also* SPARC
    Solaris
Sonicwall, VPN issues with, 409–410
source, in rules, 86
source hide NAT, 340
source static NAT, 339–340
spam, SMTP Security Server and, 311–312
SPARC Solaris
  FireWall-1 on, 29–30
  packet sniffer in, 355
  patching, 546

securing, 545–552
tweaking, 551–552, 577
specific sign-on, for Client Authentication,
    202–205, 206*f,* 227
SPLAT (Secure Platform), for Linux installation,
    32–34
split-horizon DNS, 159
  NAT and, 352–353
spool files, in SMTP Security Server,
    313–316
spool_limit_scan_period setting, for SMTP
    Security Server, 304
spool_limit setting, for SMTP Security Server,
    304
Src, in rule enforcement, 87
SSH, for Management GUI access, 64
SSL (Secure Sockets Layer)
  FTP over, 157–158, 158*t*
  for LDAP server, 239–240, 239*f*
  for Session Authentication, 226
  in SIC, 163
standard sign-on, for Client Authentication,
    202–205, 205*f,* 227
Star Community, 398, 404–405, 404*f*
Stateful ICMP replies, accepting, 98
Stateful Inspection
  in FireWall-1, 8–9
  overview of, 5
  Passive FTP handled by, 6
  of TCP connections, problems with,
    150–156
  traceroute handled by, 8
statements, in INSPECT, 524
State Synchronization
  asymmetric routing and, 500–501
  checking, 512
  configuration of, 495–497
  definition of, 494
  error messages with, 514–520
  frequently asked questions about, 512–513
  in High Availability, 493–499
  limitations of, 498–499
  MAC address used by, changing, 512–513
  network used for, 497, 498*f*
  platform interoperability in, 513
  protocol for, 494
  service not synchronized with, 513

state tables. *See also* address translation tables; connections table
  of firewall module, remote viewing of, 167–169
  memory used for, 576, 576*f*
  number of entries in, 575–576
static host routes
  for load balancing, 504
  for NAT implementation, 348
    in double-blind network, 375, 375*f*
    in network migration, 371
    in simple network, 367
static load balancing, 504–505, 505*f*
static password, problems with, 194
static tables, creating, with INSPECT, 528
status information, interval for fetching, 135
Status Manager, 135. *See also* SmartView Status
Stealth rule, 99, 99*f*
streaming media, preventing access to, 287–288
subnet
  firewall and, 15
  simplification of, in IPSec SAs, 410
support, end-user, for SecuRemote, 426
Suspicious Activity Monitoring Protocol (SAMP), 270
SVN Foundation
  alerts defined for, 115–116, 115*f*
  status of, 113, 113*f*
switches, load balancing with, 506, 507*f*
symmetric encryption, definition of, 381
SYN-ACK packets, unexpected, 155
sync buffer, error on, 516, 517–519
SYN packets
  dropping, 155
  in NAT troubleshooting, 357–359
    followed by RST, 359–361
syslog, logging to, 142–143
system log, error messages in, 145–148

T
table, for SecuRemote clients, 469–470
TACACS/TACACS+ (Terminal Access Controller Access Control System)
  about, 197
  integrating, 233–234
  settings for, for user, 216, 216*f*
TACACS users, FireWall-1 use of, 247
TCP ACK packet, Stateful Inspection of, 151

TCP connection
  bidirectional, 153–154
  conflicting, 154–155
  Stateful Inspection of, problems with, 150–156
  timeout on
    adjusting, 156
    disabling, 156
    issues with, 154–155
  unidirectional, 153
tcpdump
  expressions for, 362, 362*t*
  flags for, 361, 361*t*
  for NAT troubleshooting, 355–361
TCP/IP stack, SecuRemote bound to, 426
TCP packet
  NAT support for, 352
  out of state, 151–152
TCP port, of management module, 162
TCP resource, for Content Security, 316–318, 317*f*
TCP Security Server
  about, 316–318
  with CVP, 316–317, 317*f*
  debugging, 320*t*
  with UFP, 318
TCP Sequence Verifier, 154, 155
TCP service
  DNS over, accepting, 83, 98, 98*f*
  IKE over, SecureClient options for, 460
  NetBIOS over, disabling, in Windows 2000, 558
TCP service object, about, 73–75, 74*f*, 75*f*
TCP traffic, Content Security for, 316–318
Telnet Security Server, debugging, 320*t*
Telnet service
  Client Authentication over, 202, 203–204, 228
    debugging, 320*t*
  User Authentication for, 198–199
    error on, 258
    rule order and, 224
Terminal Access Controller Access Control System. *See* TACACS/TACACS+
third-party software
  for AIX, 30
  for Content Security, 269
  for High Availability, 502–503
  for IPSO, 32

third-party software (*cont.*)
  for SPARC Solaris, 29
  for Windows NT/2000, 28
time, in user properties, 217, 217*f*
time objects
  about, 77–78, 78*f*, 79*f*
  in rules, 87
timeout
  for Client Authentication, 229, 229*f*
  on SecuRemote authentication, 433
  on TCP
    adjusting, 156
    disabling, 156
    issues with, 154–155
  on UDP, adjusting, 156
  for User Authentication, 223, 262, 263*f*
TIMEOUT, in connections table, 527
timeout setting, for SMTP Security Server, 303
token, hardware
  in Defender, 196–197
  in SecurID, 196, 196*f*
topology. *See* network topology
traceroute
  firewall handling of, 6–8
  through VPN, 410–411
  in Windows, problem with, 148–149
Track, in rules, 86–87
Traffic Monitoring, purpose of, 56
training
  for AIX, 30
  for SPARC Solaris, 29–30
Translate Destination on Client Side option,
    342–343
transparent connection, URI resource applied
    with, 273
trust, levels of, in firewall usage, 1
trust, zones of. *See* zones of trust
tunnel connection
  over HTTP, blocking, 288–289
  URI resource applied with, 273
two-request method, for UFP caching, 294–295

U
UAA (User Authority API), 270
UAM (User-to-Address Mapping), 270
UDP connection
  timeout on, adjusting, 156
  unidirectional, 153

UDP packets
  fragmentation of, troubleshooting, 477–478
  NAT support for, 352
UDP service
  DNS over, accepting, 83, 97–98, 97*f*
  State Synchronization and, 494
UDP service object, about, 76, 76*f*
UDP traceroute, firewall handling of, 7–8
UFP (URL Filtering Protocol)
  about, 270
  caching, 294–295
  OPSEC application for, 279–280, 279*f*, 281*f*
UNIX. *See also* Linux
  command-line mail in, 136
  proxy ARP on, 347
  static routes on, 348
Upgrade Verification Utilities, 53
URI resources, for Content Security, 272–278,
    273*f*, 274*f*, 275*f*
  with CVP, 283–284, 284*f*, 285*f*
  rule for, 278, 278*f*
  sample configuration for, 330–333, 331*f*, 332*f*
  with UFP, 280–282, 281*f*
URI specification file, 275
URL, filtering by. *See also* UFP; URI resources
  specifying match for, 274
URL Filtering Protocol. *See* UFP
usage policy
  redirection to, 286–287
  sample of, 563–565
user
  access permissions of, in Windows NT, 555
  adding to RADIUS, 231–232
  in authentication server, FireWall-1 use of,
    247
  authentication settings for, 212–218,
    213*f*–216*f*
  creation of, 208–218, 208*f*–212*f*
  Office Mode allowed for, 445
  for SecuRemote, creation of, 428–431, 428*f*,
    482
  for VPN, creation of, 417–418
  Windows usernames for, access based on, 248
user access, to operating system, securing, 39
User Authentication
  in cleartext, 256
  for Client Authentication, 202, 228
  with Content Security, 319

on each URL, 256
with encryption, 406
in SecuRemote, 426
explanation of, 198–201
failure of, settings for, 221, 223
file downloads allowed with, 287–288, 287*f*
prompt for, absence of, 257
rule for, 221–223, 222*f*
rule order in, 223–225
sample configuration for, 260–262
setup for, 221–225
usage guidelines for, 207*t*
in usage policy, 564
User Authority API (UAA), 270
UserAuthority server, for Session Authentication, 226
User/Client/Session Auth action, in rules, 86
user database
import/export of, 248–249, 248*t,* 249*t*
in User Authentication, 222
user groups
adding users to, 212, 213*f*
creation of, 210, 218, 219*f*
Office Mode allowed for, 445
for policy server, for Desktop Security, 434, 434*f*
User Monitor, purpose of, 56
user password, changing, 253
users file, for RADIUS, adding users to, 231–232
user template, 209, 210
with LDAP server, 241
User-to-Address Mapping (UAM), 270

V
VALUE, in connections table, 527
vanish short circuit, in INSPECT, 523, 523*t*
variables, in INSPECT, 526
virtual defragmentation, error on, 146
virtual IP addresses, for High Availability, 499–500
virtual LANs (VLANs), zones of trust in, 15
Virtual Link, statistics for, logging, 135
virtual memory, for HTTP Security Server, 295
Virtual Private Network. *See* VPN
Virtual Router Redundancy Protocol (VRRP)
configuring, 419
for SecureClient with gateway clusters, 484–487
Visitor Mode, 471–472, 471*f,* 472*f*

Visual Policy Editor (VPE)
crashing of, 108–109
in SmartDashboard, 57
VLANs (virtual LANs), zones of trust in, 15
VPE. *See* Visual Policy Editor
VPN (Virtual Private Network). *See also* Secure-Client; SecuRemote
adding site to, 415–418, 416*f*
asymmetric routing and, 443
authentication of, changing FQDN and, 175
blocked communication in, 408
certificate criteria for, 394–395, 395*f*
client software for (*See* SecureClient; SecuRemote)
client-to-site, sample configuration for, 481–484, 481*f*
configuration error on, log/alert on, 134
with dial-up networking, 443
encryption in, configuring, 386–402
failover of, with ClusterXL, 504
frequently asked questions about, 403–407
interoperability issues with, 409
introduction to, 379–383
IP addresses for, at different sites, 403–404
key exchange for, log/alert on, 133, 134
license for, 24, 383–384
limiting access to, 403
load sharing in, 511*f*
with ClusterXL, 504
dynamic, 510–512, 511*f*
with policy routing, 505, 506*f*
with NAT, 405–406
packet fragmentation in, 411
packet handling errors in, log/alert on, 134
planning for, 386–387, 387*f*
sample configurations for, 412–422
sharing address space in, 405–406
simplified mode for
configuring, 397–401
Remote Access community rules for, 431, 432*f*
SecuRemote configuration in, 427
vs. traditional mode, 388–389
status of, 113, 113*f*
third-party products for
interoperability with, 403
SecureClient and, 473
three-site, configuration for, 412–415, 413*f*

VPN (Virtual Private Network) (*cont.*)
    traceroute through, 410–411
    traditional mode for
        configuring, 389–397
        SecuRemote configuration in, 427, 427*f*
        vs. simplified mode, 388–389
VPN-1
    alerts defined for, 116, 116*f*
    Pro *vs.* Net, 384
VPN-1 control connections, accepting, 83, 96, 96*f*
VPN-1 Embedded NG, license for, 23
VPN Community
    creating, 397–401
    gateway in multiple, 407
    logging traffic on, 135
    NAT disabled in, 400–401
    in simplified mode, 388
    for site addition, 417
    specification of, in rules, 86
    for three-site VPN, 414, 414*f*
vpn parameter, of cpstat, application flavors for,
    120*t*–121*t*
VPN Routing, 404–405
VPN rules
    for client-to-site VPN, 483, 483*f*
    for encryption, 396, 396*f*
        for SecuRemote access, 431–432
    in FireWall-1, 379
    for multiple-entry point SecureClient, 491, 491*f*
    for SecureClient with gateway cluster,
        486–487, 487*f*
    in simplified mode, 401, 401*f*
    for site addition, 417, 417*f*, 418, 418*f*
    for three-site VPN, 415, 415*f*
VRRP (Virtual Router Redundancy Protocol)
    configuring, 419
    for SecureClient with gateway clusters, 484–487
VRRP packets, accepting, 99, 99*f*

W
wait mode, for Client Authentication, 230
warm standby, definition of, 493
Web sites, access to, through HTTP Security
    Server, 298
.W file, 529–530
wildcards, definition of, 271, 271*t*
Windows
    ClusterXL failure on, 515

VPN client software for (*See* SecureClient;
    SecuRemote)
Windows 9x/ME, Office Mode and, 446
Windows 2000
    command-line mail in, 136
    FireWall-1 on, about, 28–29
    management console on, installation of, 40–49
    packet sniffer in, 355
    proxy ARP on, 347
    securing, 556–559
    static routes on, 348
    traceroute in, problem with, 148–149
Windows NT
    command-line mail in, 136
    file permissions in, SecuRemote issues with,
        478
    FireWall-1 on, about, 28–29
    management console on, installation of, 40–49
    packet sniffer in, 355
    proxy ARP on, 347
    securing, 552–556
    static routes on, 348
    traceroute in, problem with, 148–149
    tweaking, 577–579
Windows NT domain
    FireWall-1 integration with, 247–248
    in securing Windows 2000, 557
    in securing Windows NT, 553
Windows NT domain users, FireWall-1 use of, 247
Windows user names, access based on, 248
WINS client, disabling, in Windows NT, 553
WINS requests, forwarding in encryption
    domain, 456–457
WINS server, defining, for Office Mode, 445
WINS TCP/IP, disabling, in Windows NT, 553
wizards, enabling, 84
words, in naming, reserved, 104, 105*t*–106*t*
workstation objects. *See* node objects
wrapper, for FireWall-1 installation, 40

Y
Yahoo Messenger, blocking or enabling, 150, 150*t*

Z
ZeBeDee, for Management GUI access, 64
zones of trust
    determining, 14–15
    in VLANs, 15

informIT